D0559994

Dictionary of Latin and Greek Origins

A Comprehensive Guide to the Classical Origins of English Words

Bob Moore and Maxine Moore

This edition published by Barnes & Noble, Inc.,
by arrangement with NTC/Contemporary Publishing Group

2000 Barnes & Noble Books

ISBN 0-7607-2082-7

Printed and bound in the United States of America

02 03 MC 9 8 7 6 5 4 3

CONTENTS

Introduction

The English Language has an enormous number of words—no matter what method you use to count them. Many of the words in English are based on Latin and Greek roots. A great deal of the terminology of science and medicine, and indeed much of the vocabulary of higher education, is based on Latin and Greek roots worldwide. These roots are dependable and unchanging and serve as the key to understanding the vocabulary of English and many of the modern European Languages. An understanding of the core meaning of each root will provide a tool for unlocking the meanings of thousands of Latin and Greek based words in many languages. Mastering the knowledge of these roots will open doors to new knowledge and provide the reader with a more powerful and useful vocabulary.

This collection of Latin and Greek roots presents the English words built on each root in a readable and informative way that will sustain the interest of the reader, browser, and serious student alike. Example sentences show the roots in action and an index is provided to help the reader locate the story of a particular English word.

Preface

"The difference between the right word and the almost right word," Mark Twain once observed, "is the difference between lightning and the lightning bug." It can also be the difference between a letter of acceptance by a college and one beginning, "We are sorry to . . . ." Current college entrance examinations stress not only being able to identify synonyms, to supply the most appropriate words in sentence completions, and to recognize the clearest analogies, but, as well, to master the reading comprehension problems.

The shelves of bookstores and libraries are heavy with vocabulary texts of varying descriptions, many newspapers and magazines carry columns that feature interesting and unusual words, and page-a-day calendars entreat their users to learn 313 words a year (most have only one page for the weekend) plus a bonus word every fourth year.

In this book the key words are grouped according to the root family from which they have sprung. The thousands of words that the reader will find here stem from several hundred primarily Latin roots, all of them having made contributions to the eclectic language that we call English. As many as half the words in our dictionaries stem from Latin.

The process of assimilating Latin words began long ago. In A.D. 43 Roman legions under Emperor Claudius crossed what we call the English Channel. They stayed around for about 350 years, founding the city of London on the Thames River, setting up army posts, building walls to keep the natives at bay, and bathing in the warm springs in what is now the city of Bath. In A.D. 410, however, the news from Rome was not at all good, and it was decreed that they had better pull out and return home to help save the tottering Roman Empire. They left behind a few native Britons who had adopted a new religion called Christianity, numerous buildings, and miles of walls, along with a smattering of Latin words such as *camp, colony, mountain, port, street,* and *village.*

By the end of the fifth century, members of three Germanic tribes, the Angles, Saxons, and Jutes, had crossed the North Sea in sufficient numbers to fill the vacuum that the Romans had left. Eventually one of them, the Angles, gave their new turf the name *Engla-land* and to their utterances and people the adjective and noun *Englisc.*

And then in 597 a second Latin wave washed upon England and its language. This was when Ethelbert, the Saxon king of Kent, was baptized by St. Augustine, a missionary sent to convert the Anglo-Saxons to Christianity. The establishing of a Roman Catholic seat at Canterbury brought to the island a considerably larger number of Latin words, not only such clerical ones as *altar, angel, apostle, bishop, church, deacon, devil, hymn, mass, minister, minster, monk, priest, temple,* and *wine,* but also everyday household words like *cook, cup, kitchen, noon, pear, pepper, pillow, pound,* and *sock.*

However, the most far-reaching impact upon English life and its language occurred in 1066 when the Normans came calling, uninvited, from Normandy. Under the leadership of William the Conquerer, they defeated the English forces at the Battle of Hastings and marched on to London, where William, on Christmas Day, was crowned king of England. He and his followers spoke French, a language descended from Latin.

These newcomers were a highly civilized people who brought with them the language and knowledge of architecture, government, law, and the military, and a way of life far different from that known to the natives, a relatively uneducated and unsophisticated people of the soil.

Thus the Anglo-Saxon *pig* of the field became the *pork* of the table, and, likewise, *calf* became *veal; deer, venison; ox, beef;* and *sheep, mutton.* The islanders soon became acquainted with a wide range of strange words that affected citizens in all walks of life: *army, captain, castle, court, dinner, feast, govern, honor, judge, jury, justice, mayor, navy, officer, peace, people, state, supper,* and *tower.*

Greek words entered our language from a different direction. Some words came via Latin and French, while others were borrowed directly, especially those in the fields of science and technology, and are seen in such compound words as *telephone, photography,* and *microscope.*

One of the extraordinary byproducts of this melting pot of languages is the richness that it has bequeathed to our speech. It is said that no other language offers so many choices. In the following list the first word is of Germanic origin, from the Anglo-Saxons and the Danes; the second from Latin-French: *bloom/flower; buy/purchase; forefather/ancestor; foretell/predict; fire/conflagration; friendly/amiable; height/altitude; lowly/humble; luck/fortune; name/appellation; offspring/descendant; outclass/surpass; outfit/equip; outlaw/criminal; scare/terrify; teach/instruct; unfriendly/hostile; unwilling/reluctant; walk/perambulate; wish/desire; withdraw/remove; work/labor.*

Bob Moore
Maxine Moore

Sample Entry

VARIUS, bent, changeable, crooked, diverse, manifold, speckled: VARI ← (3)

As is obvious, this Latin root has **VARIous** meanings. But whether that results in a great **VARIety** of words is open to question. Back in the Middle Ages, in the lands and times dominated by dukes and duchesses and kings and queens, spotted animal fur was the trim of choice on the elaborate ceremonial robes of the royals. The fur came from ermines or weasels and was called **MINIVER,** literally, "small fur." The pattern of spots on such animals usually **VARIes** from one to another. That's just the way they develop their coats, i.e., **VARIable,** unpredictable, inconstant, and **VARYING.** ← (6)

(4) → **VARIcolored** or **VARIegated** houseplants are the ones that are higher priced because their leaves have streaks or specks of white or yellow on them. They are **VARIants,** deviations from the normal, **UNVARYING,** usual, and ordinary all-green leaves.

A **VARIation** is a change, modification, departure, innovation, or metamorphosis. ☞ *The poor chap needs a bit of variation from the dull routine of his life.* **VARIance** is used to express the degree of difference.
(5) → ☞ *In this experiment we found a daily variance of ten degrees centigrade.* It also refers to an official permit to do something usually forbidden. ☞ *We got a variance from city hall to put up a larger sign.* To be **AT VARIANCE** is to be in disagreement. ☞ *Everything we did was at variance with the rules.*

(7) → **Additional English words related to the root:** invariable, prevaricate.

(8) → **But not:** *varicose* [*varix,* swollen vein], swollen, as a vein.

(9) → **Combining forms:** *-gate,* to do; *mini-,* small; *ver,* fur, from *varius,* speckled, partly colored.

(10) → **Antonyms:** *variable*—fixed, predictable, immutable, rigid; *variance*—similarity, correspondence, accord, unison, agreement; *variation*—uniformity, permanence, sameness; *variegated*—monotone, monochromatic; *variety*—homogeneity, uniformity, conformity; *various*—identical, alike, same.

Key

① Latin or Greek Root.

② Core Meaning.

③ Common Base Form of Root.

④ Each word from the root is set in bold type the first time it appears.

⑤ This mark ☞ indicates that an example sentence follows.

⑥ Derived word(s) from Root.

⑦ Additional English Word(s) related to Root.

⑧ "But not" words are similar in spelling or sound, but do not derive from this root.

⑨ Prefixes and other combining forms are defined.

⑩ Antonyms are valuable as vocabulary learning tools.

Abbreviations

AR–Arabic
AS–Anglo-Saxon
D–Dutch
F–French
G–German
Gk–Greek
Heb–Hebrew
Icel–Icelandic
Inupiaq–Eskimo Indian
Ir–Irish
L–Latin
ME–Middle English
OE–Old English
OF–Old French
ON–Old Norse
Pg–Portuguese
Scand–Scandinavian
Skt–Sanskrit
Sp–Spanish
[?]–unknown or obscure origin
esp.–especially
imit.–imitative
orig.–originally
per.–perhaps
usu.–usually
var.–variation

A

AEDES, a building, temple: EDIF

The original meaning of *aedes* was "building a hearth," the fire in the hearth being the center of the home in early times, furnishing both heat and light. For centuries poets, among others, have spoken of the joys of family and hearth. Over time, its meaning expanded from the hearth itself to the home and building that enclosed it.

It is from this root that our **EDIFICE** derives, usually used in reference to a large and imposing building, often a temple. ☞ *The Greeks worshiped their gods in imposing edifices.*

Eventually **EDIFY** came to mean instruct, educate, and enlighten, especially morally or spiritually. ☞ *The sight of Michelangelo's painting on the ceiling of the Sistine Chapel in Rome edified all of us. We had never experienced such an edifying moment.* Thus **EDIFICATION** is enlightenment, education, instruction, guidance, improvement, and schooling. ☞ *For my edification, would you kindly tell me how this fender bender came about?* The Apostle Paul wrote in Corinthians, "Knowledge puffeth up, but charity **EDIFIETH.**"

An AEDILE (also EDILE) in ancient Rome was an official in charge of buildings, sports, roads, sanitation services, and other public projects.

Combining forms: *-fication,* a making; *-fy,* to make.

AEVUM, age: EV

The word PRIMEVAL (also PRIMAEVAL) refers to the first age or ages of the world, hence the words primitive, antediluvian, ancient, primordial, embryonic, and prehistoric. ☞ *As we wandered through the forest, we felt as though we were in a primeval wilderness.*

The Middle Ages, the name given to the period in European history from about A.D. 500 to 1500 is synonymous with MEDIEVAL (also MEDIAEVAL), meaning literally "middle [*medi-*] age [*aev*]." Medieval is also used informally to mean extremely old-fashioned, archaic, passé, and behind the times. ☞ *When Jill was eighteen, she thought of her parents as being hopelessly medieval, out of touch with reality; five years later she was amazed at how sensible their ideas had become.* **CoEVAL** means belonging to the same age and time as another, i.e., contemporary, coexistent, modern, and up-to-date.

LONGEVITY refers to long length of life. ☞ *Longevity is a characteristic of our family line.* It is also a synonym for the word seniority, as in one's length of employment; having seniority is often considered a plus, especially when promotions are based on length of service.

An additional English word related to the root: eternity.
Combining forms: *co-,* together; *long-,* long; *medi-,* middle; *prime-,* young.
Antonyms: *primeval*—recent, current, modern, advanced.

AGER, field: GRI

The **PEREGRINE** falcon is the bird most used in falconry or hawking, the ancient sport of hunting with the aid of a bird of prey. Peregrine means foreign, roaming, and migrating, and it is to that wanderlust that the bird owes its name, for it is at home over most of the globe. The lofty nest of a bird of prey such as an eagle, falcon, or hawk is called an **AERIE**; this has also become the name of a home or fortress located high on a hill or mountain.

To **PEREGRINATE** is to travel abroad, away from one's land, one's field, and, in earlier times, on foot. Thus one's **PEREGRINATIONS** are the journeys, odysseys, and voyages that we all undertake.

Traditionally, **PILGRIMS** walked no matter the terrain, the weather, or the thinness of their soles. The object of a **PILGRIMAGE** was most often a religious shrine, as it was in Geoffrey Chaucer's *Canterbury Tales,* the story of an April pilgrimage to Saint Thomas á Becket's shrine at Canterbury, then England's religious center.

The **AIR** that means "appearance" comes from *ager.* ☞ *There's a certain air about that fellow that I can't stand.* So does the air that means "to circulate or publicize." ☞ *We must air that topic at the meeting this evening.* But not the air that we breathe, even though clean air and fruitful fields would seem to go together; it comes from the Greek *aer,* "breath, atmosphere."

AGRARIAN, relating to land and farming, is another member of the family. ☞ *Our schools' long summer vacations reflect the agrarian nature of our nation's early days when children were expected to work in the fields.* The word **AGRICULTURE** refers to the science of the cultivation of fields and the raising of crops and livestock. ☞ *New methods of agriculture are needed in the production of crops.*

> **But not:** *grievous* [*gravis,* heavy], tragic, serious, outrageous; *integrity* [*integer,* whole, perfect], honesty, virtue.
> **Combining forms:** *-culture,* to till; *per-,* away, beyond.

AGERE, to act, do, drive: ACT

An **ACT** refers to a deed, feat, achievement, or accomplishment. ☞ *Oh, no! That act was not of* my *doing!* It is an edict, decree, statute, law, or order. ☞ *It'll take an act of Congress to get him turned around.* It is a pose, posture, attitude, stance, or affectation. ☞ *Can you believe the act she put on?* It is also a routine, division or segment of a play, or a performance. ☞ *That juggler's act is the best yet.* As a verb, it means to perform, mimic, mime, portray, represent, and impersonate. ☞ *That's one play she's never acted in.* It is to feign, pretend, simulate, fake, and counterfeit. ☞ *Please, John, act pleased when Mother arrives.* It is also to work, operate, function, behave, and execute. ☞ *You must act now to take advantage of this special low price!*

Besides being an art, pastime, and profession, **ACTING** is an adjective that means temporary, substitute, surrogate, and interim. ☞ *And just who will be acting chair until the election?* **ACTORS** are both men and women who act in stage plays, movies, television broadcasts, etc.; an actor is also anyone who is a participant, doer, worker, or agent in a project. ☞ *We'll need a lot of actors to make this charitable campaign a success.* However, many women who are professionals in the dramatic arts prefer to be known as **ACTRESSES. ACTORISH** and **ACTRESSY** refer to exaggerated and affected acting. ☞ *If the director could wipe out the actorish and actressy stage bits, it could become a good play.*

An **ACTIVIST** is a doer, enthusiast, partisan, or advocate, i.e., a person who may be involved in protests, confrontations, causes, and commitments. **ACTIVISM** frequently demands a measured amount of ardor, fervor, and zeal.

ACTUAL occurrences are real, factual, and authentic. **ACTUALITY** is reality, fact, certainty, and existence. **ACTUALLY** means really, truly, literally, and indeed. ☞ *Okay, so my selfless deed didn't actually happen like that.*

Many thesauruses list **ACTIVATE** and **ACTUATE** as synonyms. However, they have their differences. The former word means start, move, push, turn on, and put into action; its antonyms include stop, turn off, check, cease, and halt. ☞ *Push the green button to activate the display; the red button will deactivate it.* Synonyms of actuate are drive, arouse, motivate, prompt, and inspire. ☞ *It was the love of money that actuated every move that Jane made.*

The meanings of most of the words in this root family are determined by the affixing of a combining form. For example, a military unit can be **DEACTIVATED**, **INACTIVATED**, and **REACTIVATED**.

To **COUNTERACT** is to act in an opposite way, to thwart, or neutralize. ☞ *We got a prescription to counteract the baby's fever.* The literal meaning of **ENACT** is "to make or put into an act," hence to legislate, pass into law, decree, institute, and authorize. ☞ *The legislature enacted two new tax laws.* It then becomes an **ENACTMENT**. To enact is also to act out, as on a stage. ☞ *It's preposterous for you to even consider enacting Lady Macbeth, Harold.* To act something out again is to **REENACT** it. ☞ *The clerk reenacted the robbery. The reenactment was shown on the evening news.*

An **EXACT** measurement is explicit, precise, accurate, and specific. ☞ *Mom had to know the exact moment and exactly who did what to whom.* An **EXACTING** teacher is demanding, punctilious, meticulous, and hardnosed; an exacting course is tough, difficult, rigorous, and trying. ☞ *Your assignments in this course will require exactness and exactitude on every single problem.*

INEXACT work is careless, vague, imprecise, and slipshod. ☞ *Students who have a tendency to tolerate inexactness are requested to forgo registering.* **ACTION** refers to an act, deed, feat, or process; **ACTIVE** means busy, vigorous, and zealous.

How one responds to a situation is how one **REACTS**. ☞ *The quickness of one's reactions may determine whether one gets the job or not.* A **REACTOR** can be one who reacts, but it most commonly names an apparatus in which some kind of chemical or nuclear reaction takes place. A **REACTIONARY** is a political conservative; whether or not he or she is a die-hard, rightwinger, or traditionalist may depend upon the perspective of the accuser. To **REDACT** is to edit. ☞ *The initial project will be to redact a technical manuscript for publication.* A **REDACT** is one who selects or adapts works for publication and is, thus, an editor.

A pay raise that is **RETROACTIVE** is one that is effective as of a past day or period of time.

To TRANSACT business, negotiations, or activities is to carry them on or conduct them to a settlement or conclusion; a TRANSACTION is a business agreement, deal, contract, exchange, or arrangement.

The job of an ACTUARY is to mathematically compute insurance rates and premiums; in earlier times, he was a clerk who recorded deeds and documents.

But not: *didactic* [Gk *didaktikos,* instructive], instructive, preachy; *olfactory* [*olere,* to smell + *facere,* to make, do], pertaining to one's sense of smell; *practical* [Gk *praktikos,* to practice], pragmatic, useful.
Combining forms: *counter-,* against; *de-,* reversal; *en-, in-,* to make; *ex-,* out; *in-,* not; *re-,* again, back; *retro-,* backward; *trans-,* across.
Antonyms: *act*—procrastinate, put off, stop; *action*—rest, complacency, inaction; *activate*—deaden, paralyze; *active*—lethargic, sedentary, inoperative; *activist*—neutral, fence-sitter, spectator; *actual*—fictional, fictitious, theoretical, probable; *actuate*—deter, dampen, inhibit, hinder; *exacting*—easygoing, lax, lenient, permissive; *inexact*—accurate, precise, meticulous; *reactionary*—liberal, progressive, radical, revolutionary.

AGERE: GATE

To CASTIGATE is to criticize, rebuke, and reprimand severely. ☞ *The coach castigated the defiant football players by suspending them for the rest of the season.*

To DIVAGATE is to wander from place to place or to digress in speech. ☞ *The speaker divagated from one topic to another.*

To EXPURGATE is to censor a written work by removing words or passages that are considered objectionable; it is to excise, purge, cleanse, and abridge. ☞ *The committee voted to have the unabridged and unexpurgated dictionary removed from the school library.*

To FUMIGATE is to exterminate pests, such as insects by the use of smoke or fumes. ☞ *We had to fumigate the kitchen three times before all the roaches were gone.*

FUSTIGATE means to beat with a club or stick or to castigate severely. ☞ *The man fustigated the dog when it attacked the child.*

To LEVIGATE is to grind a substance into a powder. ☞ *The chef levigated the dried herb leaves.*

To LITIGATE is to engage in legal proceedings, to bring before a court of law. ☞ *The order in question is now being litigated in district court.* A LITIGANT is a person participating in a lawsuit; LITIGATION is the process. ☞ *The suit is in litigation at the present time.*

To MITIGATE is to make something, such as pain or punishment, milder and less severe; to alleviate, ameliorate, mollify, and appease. ☞ *The principal decided to mitigate the students' punishment.*

To NAVIGATE is to direct a ship or airplane or to find one's way home. ☞ *The route was shorter by way of the park, but we found it much more difficult to navigate in the dark.* A NAVIGABLE waterway is deep and wide enough for passage; NAVIGATION is the art or science of directing aircraft, missiles, and ships.

To OBJURGATE is to denounce harshly or rebuke sharply. ☞ *The mayor lashed out at his detractors, objurgating them with some pretty racy language.*

To VARIEGATE is to give something a varied appearance by adding different colors, especially in the form of spots and streaks. It is also to give variety to, to diversify. ☞ *The clusters of yellow blossoms variegated the mass of green houseplants.*

But not: *billingsgate* [from the name of a seventeenth century London fish market where foul language was common], vulgar talk; *congregate* [*con-*, together + *greg,* herd], to assemble; *instigate* [*in-*, against + *stig,* to goad], to incite, goad; *obligate* [*ob-*, towards + *ligare,* to bind], to oblige; *surrogate* [*sur-*, in place of + *rogare,* to ask], a substitute.

Combining forms: *casti-*, pure; *di-*, about; *ex-*, thoroughly; *fumi-*, smoke; *fusti-*, club; *jur-*, law; *levi-*, smooth; *lit-*, lawsuit; *miti-*, mild; *navi-*, a ship; *ob-*, against; *pur-*, clean; *vag-*, to wander; *vari-*, various.

Antonyms: *castigate*—pardon, absolve, excuse; *mitigate*—magnify, intensify, increase, expand.

AGERE: GEN

A COGENT statement or argument is a potent, convincing, and compelling one, and COGENCY refers to power, force, or strength. ☞ *The cogency of the attorney's closing argument was lost, for he phrased his most cogent points in legal jargon that few of the jurors understood.*

An AGENDUM is, strictly speaking, one item on a list of items that make up an AGENDA, which, strictly speaking, is a plural form but is usually used as singular with the plural being AGENDAS. It is a program, docket, order of business, schedule, or timetable. ☞ *So what's on the agenda for today?*

A travel AGENT works in an AGENCY that sometimes deals with urgent, critical, or EXIGENT matters, such as missed train connections. Such EXIGENCIES are predicaments or dilemmas that demand immediate attention. ☞ *When Sallie lost her purse, the exigent nature of the exigency prompted a collect call home.*

An INTRANSIGENT person is unwilling to compromise, remaining stubborn, resolute, and hardnosed. ☞ *The ballplayer and his agent remained intransigent, insisting that neither could face his family again for less than $5,000,000 a year.*

But not: *emergency* [*e-*, out + *mergere,* to sink], crisis; *intelligent,* [*legere,* to gather], smart; *urgent* [*urgere,* to push], very important.
Combining forms: *co-,* together; *ex-,* out; *in-,* not.
Antonyms: *cogent*—ineffective, irrelevant, unconvincing; *cogency*—impotence, infirmity, weakness; *exigent*—unimportant, frivolous, insignificant; *intransigent*—flexible, compromising, reasonable.

AGERE: GI, GU

All humans are capable of COGITATION, i.e., consideration, contemplation, or deliberation. When we COGITATE, we ponder, meditate, think, deliberate, and speculate; and most likely when we do that, we use words.

AGILITY comes in two different packages. A physically AGILE person is nimble, spry, supple, and lithe. ☞ *That's agile? Bosh! You should see* my *daughter on the parallel bars!* One who is mentally agile is alert, bright, quick, clever, and incisive.

To AGITATE a substance is to shake, jiggle, and disturb it. ☞ *The strong gusts of wind agitated the surface of the pond.* AGITATORS try to excite and stir up people, to arouse and provoke them to action. ☞ *Those speakers certainly got to Mother; when she got home she was in a state of real aGItation.*

AMBIGUITIES are equivocal and unclear words or expressions. Few of us have the gall of this Lewis Carroll character in *Through the Looking-Glass:* " 'When I use a word,' Humpty Dumpty said in rather a scornful tone, 'it means just what I choose it to mean—neither more nor less.' " Nothing AMBIGUOUS about that! It's clear, straight-forward, and precise, UNAMBIGUOUS—and downright illogical.

Blood and pudding COAGULATE; without one, we bleed to death; without the other, we have nothing to pour the milk on or eat cookies with. A COAGULANT is a substance that produces or aids the process, a COAGULUM is the clot or mass that is produced.

Something that is EXIGUOUS is meager, paltry, small, and scanty. ☞ *Despite their exiguous income, the elderly couple was too proud to accept anyone's help.*

> **Additional English words related to the root:** assay, cache, essay, exam, prodigal, purge, squat.
> **But not:** *virgule* [*virgula,* little rod] diagonal mark (/) used to separate words and/or lines of poetry, also called diagonal, separatrix, shilling mark, slant, slash, and solidus.
> **Combining forms:** *ambi-,* around; *co-,* together; *ex-,* out.
> **Antonyms:** *agile*—clumsy, ponderous, plodding, oafish, klutzy; *agility*—languor, lethargy; *agitate*—soothe, allay, pacify; *coagulate*—liquefy, flow, thin out, bleed; *cogitate*—ignore, disregard, neglect, overlook; *exiguous*—abundant, generous, plentiful, copious.

AGORA, marketplace: GOR

The AGORA was the chief marketplace and public square of Athens in ancient Greece, as well as the center of the city's civic and commercial life; what existed in the country's principal city was typical of almost all of the smaller towns. Times change; today all we have left of the word is AGORAPHOBIA, which refers to an abnormal dread and fear of open areas, crowds, and public places. ☞ *Ms. Smith's agoraphobia keeps her a prisoner behind the drawn drapes of her home.*

CATEGORY originally meant "to speak before the Agora, usually to make an accusation against someone"; it was Aristotle who took the word and applied it to the listing of all classes of things that can be named. Thus, CATEGORIZE has come to mean classify, designate, describe, catalog, pigeonhole, group, rank, organize, and brand, among others.

CATEGORICAL means absolute, unequivocal, positive, and unmistakable. ☞ *The officer issued a categorical denial of the bribery charges.* When one CATEGORICALLY denies ever having made a southbound turn onto a northbound one-way street, he or she does so absolutely, unequivocally, and unconditionally, with no ifs, ands, or buts.

We are also indebted to that ancient marketplace for PANEGYRIC, a eulogy or statement of lofty praise in honor of someone or something; we witness panegyrics every four years during the national political conventions when dozens of speechmakers line up in front of the TV cameras to nominate their candidates.

But not: *Angora cat/goat/rabbit* [*Ankara,* capital of Turkey], soft wool of its coat.
Combining forms: *cate-,* against; *-phobia,* abnormal fear or hate; *pan-,* all.
Antonyms: *categorical*—conditional, ambiguous, vague, dubious, indefinite.

AKADEMIA, park near Athens: ACADEM

The park in the Athens of ancient Greece was named in honor of Akademos, a hero of Greek mythology. The offshoots of the park's name have survived, because it was there in the groves of **ACADEM**E that the renowned philosopher Plato established his school in 387 B.C. Literature, music, and philosophy were taught there, with some accounts having Plato sitting on the ground, resting against the trunk of an olive tree.

Today **ACADEM**IES abound as private secondary schools; as United States military institutions; as art, literary, and scientific societies; and, in the entertainment world, such as the Academy of Motion Picture Arts and Sciences.

It is in some of these that **ACADEM**ESE is written or spoken, a specialized language that is often denounced as gobbledygook, double-speak, or gibberish: The absence of priorities had the result of the preclusion of the superintendent's determinations as to the effectiveness and efficacy of the. . . . Members of some academies are called **ACADEM**ICIANS, who often hold rigorously to the traditional ways and means in their teachings. ☞*Several curriculum changes were made over the protests of the academicians.*

One who enjoys the **ACADEM**IC life is partial to its scholarly, collegiate, educational, and professional aspects. An academic mind is one that is usually bookish, erudite, and learned. An academic curriculum in a school places emphasis upon the liberal arts, college-preparatory, and nontechnical studies. But an academic question or discussion is one that is conjectural, hypothetical, and abstract. ☞ *How you would have steered the* Titanic *past the iceberg, Archibald, is purely academic.*

The plural form **ACADEM**ICS refers to the scholarly activities of a school or college. ☞ *The parents' group charged the administration with placing more emphasis upon athletics than academics.* NON**ACADEM**IC courses and schools are generally of a professional, technical, or vocational nature. A PSEUDO**ACADEM**IC is someone whose claims to sound scholarship are false, inflated, or pretentious.

> **Combining forms:** *non-,* not; *pseudo-,* false.
> **Antonyms:** *academese*—sense, logic, reason; *academic*—nonscholarly, uneducated; *academician*—reformer, progressive, innovator.

AKROS, a point, topmost, at the tip: ACRO

One of the features of many of the cities of ancient Greece was their **ACRO**POLIS, a fort or fortified place built on a high area. The most famous of these is the Acropolis of Athens, which is also the site of the Parthenon, a temple built in the fifth century B.C.

An **ACRO**BAT is said to walk on tiptoe when performing **ACRO**BATIC feats. Also, a skilled acrobat does not have **ACRO**PHOBIA, a fear of heights. Not all acrobats are gymnasts, however. ☞ *The senator is a regular acrobat the way he changes opinions and viewpoints.* **ACRO**BATICS are what an acrobat does or performs; gymnastics is a synonym.

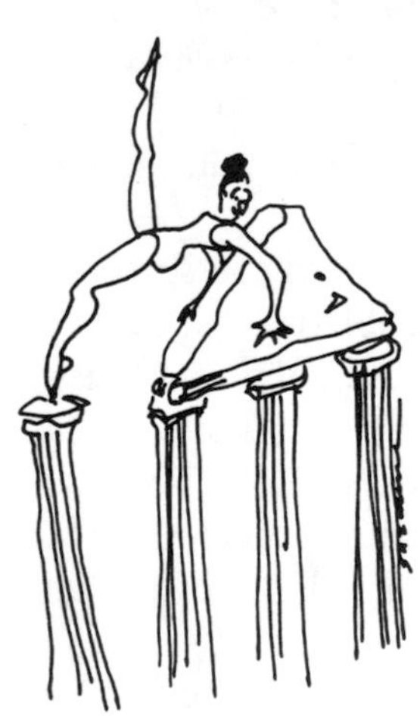

Acrobat

ACROMEGALY is a disease that causes the enlargement of one's hands or feet, i.e., the extremities or tips of one's body.

ACRONYMS are formed from the initial—or tip—letters of several words, often to save space and time. People who operate computers are familiar with WYSIWYG, ***w**hat **y**ou **s**ee **i**s **w**hat **y**ou **g**et*; military personnel know the meaning of AWOL, ***a**bsent **w**ith**o**ut **l**eave*, and SNAFU, ***s**ituation **n**ormal, **a**ll **f**ouled **u**p*; editors often consult the OED, ***O**xford **E**nglish **D**ictionary*; a business may be run according to its SOP, ***s**tandard **o**perating **p**rocedure*, and its highest officials may be referred to as its CEO, ***c**hief **e**xecutive **o**fficer*, and its COO, its ***c**hief **o**perating **o**fficer*; sitcom fans are familiar with M*A*S*H, the initials of ***m**obile **a**rmy **s**urgical **h**ospital*; and everyone may from time to time be tempted to use KISS, ***k**eep **i**t **s**imple, **s**tupid*.

One form of an **ACROstic** is a poem in which the first letters of each line often spell out a name. The following words are the first of each of the sixteen lines in a poem written by Lewis Carroll, the author of *The Adventures of Alice in Wonderland:* **L**ittle, **O**n, **R**eading, **I**ts, **N**ever, **A**re; **A**nd, **L**essons, **I**f, **C**hildren, **E**ach; **E**ach, **D**aily, **I**n, **T**hen, **H**ave. The first letters spell out the names of the three Liddell sisters, one of whom became the model of his most famous books. Lorina was thirteen, Alice ten, and Edith eight.

Additional English words related to the root: acme, acne.
But not: *across* [OF a *croix*], from one side of a thing to the other.
Combining forms: *-bat,* to go, walk; *-megaly,* abnormal enlargement; *-onym,* name; *-phobia,* fear; *-stic,* line of verse.

ALBUS, white: ALB

One of the poems we all hear or read or open our books to in school is Samuel Taylor Coleridge's *The Rime of the Ancient Mariner,* and among its most famous passages is "God save thee, ancient Mariner! / From the fiends that plague thee thus! Why look'st thou so?—With my crossbow / I shot the **ALBatross.**" Believing that the live bird was an omen of good luck, the mariner's shipmates hung the dead bird around his neck. Today, therefore, an albatross (besides being a large, mostly white, seabird) is a burden that is difficult to get rid of. ☞ *B.J.'s feeling of guilt for his part in the disastrous fraternity prank was an albatross that plagued him the rest of his life.*

An **ALB** is a long, traditionally white robe worn by a priest. **ALBumen** is the white of an egg. An **ALBum** was originally a book of blank pages for holding photographs and later a holder for phonograph records. **Auburn** comes from *albus,* but as its spelling gradually changed, so did its meaning, from white to reddish-brown or golden-brown.

ALBinism is the absence of certain pigments in humans and other animals; the term "white elephant," an unwanted possession that is difficult to dispose of, possibly came from the King of Siam's (now Thailand) awarding of a white elephant—**ALBino** elephants were usually natives of that country—to someone he didn't like, knowing that the cost of keeping the animal would ruin the new owner.

ALBion is a literary name for Britain, possibly inspired by the chalk cliffs along the English Channel. "Perfidious Albion" ("deceitful England") is a phrase that Napoleon turned into a double buzzword during the French Revolution.

Although **ALBedo** is not likely to achieve widespread usage, the word means the ratio of the light reflected by Mars, or any other planet or satellite, to that received by it. It is also the name of the white, inner rind of a citrus fruit.

An **aubade** is a song or poem deemed suitable for greeting the dawn. Its evening counterpart is a nocturne, that piece of dreamy music for a quiet evening.

A verb form of *albus* once meant "to whiten or plaster"; from that we got **daub.** To daub a coat of plaster on a wall is not a chore requiring great skill; the object is to cover, not to create a work of art. Among its synonyms are smear, smudge, splash, and splatter. To **bedaub** is to smear with paint or mud.

> **But not:** *albacore* [Ar *al-bakrah, al,* the + *bakr,* young camel], a kind of tuna; *albeit* [ME *al,* completely + *be,* + *it,* al(though) it be], although, even if, though.
> **Combining form:** *be-,* prefix once used in English to form verbs.

ALERE, to feed, nourish, grow: AL

Keeping fueled up throughout the **adolescent** years is not always an easy task. Sufficient sustenance and support must be provided by the food and nourishment that is properly known as **ALiment.** When these are processed in the **ALimentary** canal of the digestive system, energy is produced, and with continued **ALimentation** or nourishment one is enabled to not only endure **adolescence,** but be adequately fueled to make a successful transition into **adulthood** as well.

The difficulty of the growing years can be attested to by the size of the **coALition,** partnership, or union of family, teachers, friends, or counselors who nourish one along a road littered with intimidating detours. But somehow, and in time, the rough edges get smoothed out, and one **coALesces** or grows into an adult, all this long before such words as divorce and **ALimony,** literally the supplying of sustenance and support for one's former spouse, have entered one's working vocabulary.

The difficult part about graduating from a school, college, or university is not all the years and sweat that it takes to get there nor even the requests for money that inevitably follow; it is instead figuring out which category you will someday fit into: **ALumna** (one female), **ALumnae** (plural), **ALumnus** (one male), or **ALumni** (plural).

Some schools refer to their graduates as alumni and alumnae (men and women) and preface their solicitation letters to couples on their lists as Dear Alumnus and Alumna (Mr. and Mrs.). **ALum** (accent on the second syllable) is the informal word of choice for some grads, but others find it confusing—see "alum" (accent on the first syllable) below.

But not: *alum* [*alumen*], an astringent.
Combining form: *co-,* together.
Antonyms: *adolescent*—full-grown, developed, tired, experienced, sophisticated; *coalition*—schism, split, severance, disagreement.

ALLOS, other: ALLE

When Mrs. Malaprop says of another woman in Richard Sheridan's 1775 play *The Rivals,* "She's as headstrong as an **ALLEgory** on the banks of the Nile," she means, of course, an alligator. Allegories are fables, parables, or stories with a message and are quite harmless.

George Orwell's 1945 **ALLEgorical** novel *Animal Farm* is a satire about the communism of the then Union of Soviet Socialist Republics (U.S.S.R.); one of its most famous lines is "All animals are equal but some animals are more equal than others." As an **ALLEgorist**, Orwell created **parALLEls** between his animals and human beings: Napoleon, the head pig, represents the Russian dictator Joseph Stalin; Snowball, his enemy, is Stalin's bitter rival Leon Trotsky; and Boxer, the horse, stands for the ordinary person.

Dust, grass, and pollens are **ALLErgens,** common substances that can produce an **ALLErgy,** which, if seriously distressing, may have to be treated by an **ALLErgist,** a physician specializing in its diagnosis and treatment. However, some allergies do not need medical treatment; many people have strong aversions or dislikes toward certain activities or people. ☞ *Drabble claimed he was not allergic to the work itself; it was the wood in the handle of the shovel.*

But not: *allegation* [*legare,* to bind], assertion made without proof; *alleviate* [*levare,* to lighten], ease, mitigate.
Combining forms: *-ergy,* work; *-gory,* speak in public; *para-,* beside.
Antonyms: *allegory*—facts, history, true story.

AMARE, to love: AMA, AMO

An **AMA**TEUR is one who plays for the love of the game rather than for money. When something is said to be **AMA**TEURISH, however, it is considered not only unprofessional but inept, inexpert, and inadequate as well. ☞ *For an acting group that boasts about its professional standards, that certainly was a very amateurish and disappointing performance.*

An **AMO**ROUS person is one who tends to fall in love; amorous or **AMA**TORY literature is concerned with love. An **AMO**UR is a love affair; to be EN**AMO**RED is to be inflamed with love. ☞ *We were enamored of the colorful countryside.* An **AMO**RETTO is a cherub or cupid. An IN**AMO**RATA is a female lover; an IN**AMO**RATO is a male; if it is an illicit affair, he or she is a PAR**AMO**UR.

But not: *amorphous* [Gk *a-*, without + *morphe,* form], vague, shapeless.
Combining forms: *en-*, in; *in-*, into; *para-*, with.
Antonyms: *amateur*—professional, expert, polished, skilled; *amorous*—indifferent.

AMICUS, friend: AMI

We all know that an ENEMY is not a friend; what we may not know is that the literal meaning of the word is "not (a) friend"; *en-*, not + *emy,* friend. Among its synonyms are foe, opponent, adversary, and antagonist.

So it is with INIMICAL, its literal meaning being "not friendly," hence harmful and unfavorable. ☞ *Bea found the climate to be inimical to her lungs.* It also means hostile and unfriendly. ☞ *There was an inimical atmosphere about the castle, the source of which I could never pinpoint.*

At the other end of the field are the friendly folk. An **AMI**ABLE chap is genial, warm, kind, and sociable. ☞ *Helen's such a wonderful neighbor, so amiable and gracious.*

AMICABLE has the same general meaning, but some usage texts argue that it makes a better fit when used to describe actions, such as the relations between groups, parties, companies, governments, and countries. Its most common synonyms are peaceable, harmonious, civil, and benevolent. ☞ *The company and the union have reached an amicable settlement. Our two countries have enjoyed an amicable relationship for generations.* That is generally true of **AMI**TY as well, i.e., cooperation, friendship, good will, understanding, or brotherhood. ☞ *The Secretary General said he hoped the accord between the two governments would result in lasting amity.*

Some usage books also make the claim that in Spanish only a male friend is an **AMI**GO and a female is an **AMI**GA, but recent studies reveal that the vast majority of senoritas have no objection to being called an amigo. The same is rumored to be true in France, although the rules state that it's **AMI** for a male friend and **AMI**E for a female.

In court an **AMI**CUS brief may be filed by a person or party not involved in the case who wants to offer relevant advice; it is called "Friend of the Court" or, officially, *amicus curiae.*

But not: *Amish* [G *amisch,* after Jakob Ammann, seventeenth-century Swiss Mennonite bishop], Mennonite religious groups found primarily in Indiana, Ohio, and Pennsylvania.
Combining form: *curiae,* meeting place, court.
Antonyms: *amiable*—hostile, sullen, surly, cold; *amicable*—quarrelsome, antagonistic, belligerent; *amity*—enmity, animosity, discord.

AMPLUS, large, wide: AMPL

An **AMPL**IFIER, an electronic component contained in certain household instruments such as television sets, radios, and telephones, **AMPL**IFIES or increases the volume of sound, often at the twist of a knob.

When listeners in an audience do not understand a statement made by a public official, they often ask the speaker to **AMPL**IFY, enlarge, elaborate, expand, or complete it. Synonyms of **AMPL**IFICATION are enlargement, expansion, or elaboration. ☞ *The chief's amplification on the reasons for closing down the carnival did not satisfy us.*

AMPLITUDE means size, scope, magnitude, or abundance. ☞ *The amplitude of the Milky Way is too vast for me to even think about.* Something that is **AMPL**E is sufficient, enough, and adequate. ☞ *We had ample room on the bus. A football field wouldn't have been ample enough to hold that crowd.* **AMPL**Y is an adverb meaning sufficiently, completely, and generously. ☞ *We were more than amply supplied with homework last weekend.*

But not: *example* [*ex-,* out + *emere,* to buy], model, specimen.
Combining forms: *-fication, -fier, -fies, -fy,* variations of "to make."
Antonyms: *ample*—meager, scant, sparse; *amplification*—reduction, simplification, contraction; *amplify*—reduce, pare

down, abbreviate; *amplitude*—limitation, narrowness, circumspection; *amply*—insufficiently, meagerly, inadequate.

ANGELOS, messenger: ANGEL

Someone who is truly **ANGEL**IC is supposed to be saintly, pure, perfect, ideal, heavenly, and beautiful.

To some people an **ANGEL** is a messenger of God, a heavenly spirit, an ARCH**ANGEL**, or a cherub. The angel next door is a dear, a dream, a saint, or a doll. In the business district an angel is a financial backer, patron, sponsor, underwriter, or investor.

An EV**ANGEL**IST is a preacher, one who may travel from revival to revival EV**ANGEL**IZING night after night. TELEV**ANGEL**ISTS stay close to home, spreading their message electronically from their own EV**ANGEL**ICAL temples. The original EV**ANGEL**IZERS were Matthew, Mark, Luke, and John of the New Testament. The EV**ANGEL** is the gospel; an evangel is also an evangelist.

An **ANGEL**ENO is a native or inhabitant of Los Angeles, the City of Angels.

Combining forms: *arch-,* chief; *ev-* (from *eu-*), good.
Antonyms: *angelic*—fiendish, diabolic, demonic, repulsive, impish, mischievous.

ANIMUS, mind, soul: ANIM

The most obvious word that stems from this root is, of course, **ANIM**AL. Among its synonyms are creature, beast, brute, mammal, pet, living thing, and nonhuman. One dictionary defines animal as "any living being other than a human; any living being distinguished from a plant." The lists of adjectives are not exactly complimentary: brutal, beastly, **ANIM**ALISTIC, ruthless, savage, crude, and subhuman. In *Following the Equator,* Mark Twain states: "Man is the only animal that blushes—or needs to."

Yet children who are filled with animal spirits are vivacious, good-humored, and irrepressible. As they grow into adulthood, many of them trade their exuberance for EQU**ANIM**ITY, i.e., serenity, composure, and poise. The transition, however, is not a UN**ANIM**OUS (solid, unchallenged, and like-minded) one, and that may be just as well, for UN**ANIM**ITY, i.e., accord, conformity, agreement, and solidarity might make us all perfect and thus boringly alike.

ANIMism is the belief that natural objects possess souls, but **ANIMalism** is the theory that human beings lack a spiritual nature. An **ANIMalist** is motivated by animal desires and acts in an animalistic or beast-like fashion. To **ANIMalize** is to reduce people to the level of subhuman creatures. ☞ *The soldiers were animalized by the long and brutal war.* It is also to give savage features to a human figure in a drawing. ☞ *The artist animalized the dictator by portraying him with horns on his head.*

ANIMa means life, soul, and spirit, and the literal meaning of magn**ANIMous** is "great-souled"; such a person is big-hearted, forgiving, generous, and unselfish. ☞ *Only a saint as magnanimous as Lil could have forgiven such a vulgarity.* **MagnANIMity** refers to selflessness, nobility, highmindedness, or greatness.

To **ANIMate** something is to give life and spirit to it. ☞ *Milly's arrival really animated the party.* An **ANIMated** debate is lively and spirited. **ANIMators** put life into cartoons that would otherwise be in**ANIMate**, i.e., lifeless, unconscious, immobile, and cold drawings. **ANIMation** is vivacity, energy, buoyance, and spirit. An ex**ANIMate** object is inanimate, lifeless, and spiritless. ☞ *". . . Frome's saw-mill . . . looked exanimate enough, with its idle wheel,"* Ethan Frome, *Edith Wharton.*

ANIMosity is hostility, hatred, ill will, dislike, and **ANIMus**. ☞ *The animosity between the two brothers gradually abated.* To **ANIMadvert** is to make critical, cutting, carping, and censorious comments. ☞ *Jorge animadverted at length, calling his opponent pusillanimous, but we all knew she was neither cowardly nor timid.* An **ANIMadversion** is an unfavorable, negative, or derogatory comment about someone. ☞ *The campaign now consists of candidates shouting animadversions at each other.*

ANIMacules are microscopic beings invisible or barely visible to the naked eye.

> **Combining forms:** *-advert,* to turn; *equ-,* even; *ex-,* out of; *in-,* not; *magn-,* great; *pusill-,* tiny; *un-,* one.
> **Antonyms:** *animadversion*—praise, commendation, approval; *animadvert*—acclaim, applaud, extol; *animalistic*—civilized, refined, cultured; *animate*—dampen, discourage, dishearten; *animated*—lethargic, sluggish, torpid, boring; *animation*—apathy, lethargy, passivity; *animosity, animus*—harmony, amity, good will; *equanimity*—hysteria, panic, agitation; *magnanimity*—pettiness, meanness; *magnanimous*—base, grudging, hateful, resentful; *pusillanimous*—brave, courageous, heroic; *unanimity*—discord, disagreement, divisiveness; *unanimous*—discordant, dissenting, differing.

ANNUS, year: ANNI, ANNU, ENNI

An ANNUAL event happens once a year, a SEMIANNUAL report is published twice a year; a BIENNIAL plant such as parsley lives for two years, and a biennial meeting is scheduled to be held every second year. Anything that is PERENNIAL is supposed to be everlasting, continuous, ongoing, and enduring.

A BIANNUAL event occurs twice a year (or SEMIANNUALLY) or every two years BIENNIALLY), depending on who makes up the schedule.

An ANNIVERSARY is the annual return of the date of an event. A cent is a 100th part of a dollar; hence a CENTENNIAL is a 100th anniversary.

Although a SEMICENTENNIAL is a 50th anniversary, a BICENTENNIAL occurs every two hundred years. The combining form *sesqui* means one and a half; therefore, a SESQUICENTENNIAL is a 150th anniversary. The Columbus QUINCENTENNIAL was celebrated in 1992: 500 years had passed.

As a mill is a 1,000th part of a dollar, so a MILLENNIUM is a period of one thousand years, although the word is often used to mean any lengthy period of time. ☞ *Your long absence has seemed like a millennium to me.* An ANNUITY is an annual payment, often made following one's retirement. ANNALS are yearly records kept by an ANNALIST or historian. A.D. stands for ANNO DOMINI, meaning "in the year of our Lord," and referring to all years since the birth of Jesus Christ.

But not: *annul* [*an-,* to + *nullus,* none], to cancel or nullify.
Combining forms: *bi-,* two; *cent,* 100; *mill,* 1,000; *per-,* through; *quin-,* five; *semi-,* half; *sesqui-,* one and a half; *super-,* above; *-versary,* to turn.
Antonyms: *perennial*—ephemeral, sporadic, transient.

ANTHOS, a flower

The roots of ANTHOLOGY can be traced back to *anthos,* which means "the part of a plant that grows above the ground." And what a curious path for a word to take, from there to: the gathering of flowers in ancient Greece to, a compilation of short poems to, our contemporary collections of stories, poems, songs, paintings, sculpture, or excerpts. It also refers to a collection of practically anything. ☞ *The current comic at the Bijou offers an anthology of hilarity, from jokes to juggling.*

An ANTHOLOGIST or ANTHOLOGIZER is the person who does the ANTHOLOGIZING, or the gathering, collecting, amassing, compiling, and accumulating.

Students of botany know the ANTHER, the pollen-bearing part of a flower's organ, as well as the ANTHESIS, the period when the flower expands.

Combining form: *-logy,* to pick up, collect. (Note: see *logos* for other words ending in *-logy,* beginning on page 174.

ANTIQUUS, ancient: ANTIQU

Old paintings, relics, and odd trinkets are often found in an **ANTIQU**E shop.

Yet not all antiques are suitable for the marketplace. In "Ozymandias" poet Percy Bysshe Shelley says, "I met a traveller from an antique land." And myriad teenagers feel thwarted by their parents' antique or old-fashioned ideas.

To **ANTIQU**ATE something is to make it obsolete. ☞ *The camcorder has antiquated the home movie camera.* An **ANTIQU**ITY is something ancient. ☞ *We found several tools of great antiquity.* And the word **ANTIQU**ATED means obsolete, old-fashioned, and passé.

An **ANTIQU**ARY is a dealer in antiques; an **ANTIQU**ER may collect and deal, too, or may be one who takes a manufactured article and makes it look as if it were a true antique; an **ANTIQU**ARIAN is a collector, often specializing in rare books, but he or she may also be a person quaintly attached to the opinions and practices of ages past.

As an adjective ANTIC means funny and ludicrous; an amusing book of parodies of American writers is entitled *The Antic Muse.* As a noun it is a playful trick, caper, prank, or practical joke. ☞ *Such antics have no place in this school!*

Antonyms: *antic*—serious, solemn, dignified; *antiquated*—modern, current, stylish, fashionable; *antique*—modern, new, recent; *antiquity*—modernity, modern times.

ARISTOS, best

ARISTOCRATS are members of the nobility in countries that still have noblemen and noblewomen; they are blue bloods, Brahmins, lords, or ladies. Because they are ARISTOCRATIC, they do not often hobnob with peasants, commoners, plebeians, or just plain ordinary folks, for they are (or make an effort to be) regal and courtly.

An ARISTOCRACY is a government or state ruled by the elite or upper crust; those they rule are the common people, i.e., the populace, citizenry, or common folk.

Combining forms: *-cracy,* government, rule; *-crat,* ruler.

ARKHEIN, to rule, begin: ARCH

It was shortly after noon in Washington, D.C., on January 20, 1961, when Robert Frost, then eighty-six years old, tried to read a poem he had written for the inauguration of John F. Kennedy as president of the United States. But the bright sunlight on the new-fallen snow blinded him, and he had to give it up. So he then recited a poem he had written some years before entitled "The Gift Outright": "The land was ours before we were the land's" he began, ". . . but we were England's, still colonials, possessing what we still were unpossessed by. . . ."

England's ruler in the time of which he spoke was the monARCH George III. But, there was to be, in his new land no monARCHy or autARCHy with a built-in autocratic, despotic ruler; no oligARCHy, a government controlled by a few; no anARCHy, a state without government or law. Those were, the Founding Fathers felt, ARCHaic forms, long out-of-date, obsolete, and antiquated. We would become, instead, a representative democracy, an ARCHetype, i.e., model, prototype, original, or exemplar for the world to look up to.

Among humankind's earliest social groups were those based upon families, clans, or tribes. PatriARCHies were headed by the father or patriARCH, matriARCHies by the mother or matriARCH. Throughout the centuries that the human species has lived with social organizations, many positions of leadership have been so identified. A high priest or hierARCH is at the top of the hierARCHy, the ladder of rank and importance. An ARCHbishop presides over an ARCHbishopric or ARCHdiocese and is followed by an ARCHdeacon and then an ARCHpriest. A chief angel is an ARCHangel, as is a Russian port city north of Moscow named long ago for the archangel Michael and known to the Russians as Arkhangelsk.

ARCHitects were originally thought of as the chief workers or builders or carpenters or artisans, none of which describes their tasks these days. An ARCHipelago, a group or chain of islands, got its name from the Aegean Sea, which was sometimes called "The Chief Sea." Important documents and records are kept in ARCHives, a word stemming from *archeion,*

Archfiend

Greek for "public office"; the person in charge is an **ARCH**IVIST. **ARCH**AEOLOGY (also **ARCH**EOLOGY) is the study of antiquity, of times long since past.

In yesterday's world there were great numbers of **ARCH**DUCHESSES and **ARCH**DUKES, the people in charge of the **ARCH**DUCAL matters of their **ARCH**DUCHIES or **ARCH**DUKEDOMS.

An **ARCH**CONSERVATIVE is someone who is extremely conservative, often biased, bigoted, and prejudiced against every racial, religious, and political group other than his own. **ARCH**ENEMY, **ARCH**FIEND, and **ARCH**RIVAL qualify as one or more of the following: adversary, nemesis, scoundrel, antagonist, or devil. An **ARCH** smile is one that is playfully crafty, mischievous, or shy.

But not: *arch* [*arcus,* bowl], part of the foot.
Combining forms: *an-,* without; *arch-,* chief, principal; *-diocese,* district; *hier-,* sacred; *matri-,* mother; *mon-,* one; *olig-,* few; *patri-,* father; *-pelago,* sea; *-tect,* artisan.
Antonyms: *anarchy*—order, control, regimentation; *archaic*—current, modern, trendy.

ASTRON, star: ASTER, ASTRO

The setting is Rome, the year is 44 B.C. Crowds of Romans have gathered to honor Julius Caesar, their victorious general. Standing nearby, Brutus and Cassius, according to Shakespeare's play, hear the shouts of jubilation. "I do believe," Brutus says, "that these applauses are/For some new honours that are heap'd on Caesar." To which Cassius replies, "Men at some time are masters of their fates:/The fault, dear Brutus, is not in our stars,/But in ourselves, that we are underlings."

Men and women who hold with **ASTRO**LOGY might not agree with Cassius, for it is their belief that the position of the stars and planets at the exact moment of one's birth has a powerful ASTRAL influence on one's life, today, tomorrow, and beyond. The words DIS**ASTER** and DIS**ASTRO**US reflect that belief in the influence of heavenly bodies on our lives. In *King Lear* Shakespeare wrote, "We make guilty of our disasters the sun, the moon, and the stars." Instead of, as Cassius said, taking the blame ourselves.

Departments of science in many universities offer courses in **ASTRONOMY**, some even have access to observatories where aspiring **ASTRONOMERS** can learn to track the stars and planets for scientific purposes.

The flower we call an **ASTER** is shaped like a star, as is the **ASTERISK** (*). An **ASTERISM** is a constellation or group of stars, and thousands of **ASTEROIDS**, minor planets, form a belt between Mars and Jupiter. An **ASTEROIDEAN** is a starfish. The Houston **ASTROS**, so named because of the city's Johnson Space Center, play on **ASTROTURF** in the **ASTRODOME**. **ASTRONAUTICS** is the science of space travel, the occupation of American **ASTRONAUTS** and Russian cosmonauts. **ASTRONOMICAL** means extremely large, exceedingly great, enormous, and humongous.

But not: *astern* [Icel *stjorn,* helm], in a position behind a ship.
Combining forms: *dis-,* in a pejorative or sinister sense; *-isk,* small; *-logy,* the study of; *-naut,* sailor; *-nomy,* law; *-oid,* similar.
Antonyms: *astronomical*—miniscule, Lilliputian, diminutive, minute; *disastrous*—advantageous, providential, beneficial.

ATHLON, a prize: ATHL

The most common synonyms for **ATHLETIC** are strong, husky, brawny, and muscular, but the world of **ATHLETICS** is wide and varied, and the physical attributes that benefit a weightlifter, shotputter, or football lineman would be disastrous to a gymnast, polevaulter, swimmer, or soccer forward.

An **ATHLETE** competes for a prize. Among the most demanding competitions are the **DECATHLON**, a contest comprising ten track and field events; the modern **PENTATHLON**, one featuring swimming, running, horseback riding, fencing, and target shooting; and the **TRIATHLON**, the men's consisting of three consecutive races—swimming, bicycling, and running—the women's of a 100-meter run, the shotput, and the high jump. A **HEPTATHLON** consists of seven track and field contests; it is an Olympic event for women.

Not all decathlons, however, are athletic competitions. The National Academic Decathlon is held each year for high school teams that have won their state contests. These **DECATHLETES** must write essays and answer questions on ten subjects including economics, fine arts, literature and language, math, science, and social studies.

Combining forms: *deca-,* ten; *hepta-,* seven; *penta-,* five; *tri-,* three.
Antonyms: *athletic*—frail, weak, sedentary.

B

BALLEIN, to throw, BLEM, BOL, PARL

An emBLEM is a symbol, insignia, or badge; organizations, athletic teams, schools, and manufactured products can usually be identified by their emblems. ☞ *That car has sported the same emblem for more than sixty years.* Something that is emBLEMatic is representative, relates to, or serves as an emblem. ☞ *Eleanor Roosevelt was emblematic of the political wives of a new generation; they were peers with their husbands.*

A symBOL is, literally, something "thrown together"; the standard dictionary meaning is "something that stands for something else." Algebra and chemistry have many symbols, and so does literature. The horse in Robert Frost's poem "Stopping By Woods on a Snowy Evening" stands for the being or animal that is unable to appreciate beauty, whether it is the woods filling up with snow or a sunset or a smile. To symBOLize is, then, to stand for, represent, emBLEMize, and personify. ☞ *My wedding ring symbolizes unending love.* Because symbols stand for something else, a poem, for example, that is said to be symBOLic may also be described as figurative, allegorical, and metaphorical. Writers who are classified as symBOLists feel that because their emotions and ideas cannot be expressed in realistic terms, they must use symBOLism, some of which is often private. Parables are fables, morals, lessons, allegories, or stories that commonly use symbolic language.

Examples of hyperBOLas and paraBOLas can be found in geometry texts, just as the glossaries of literature textbooks may define hyperBOLic as exaggerated, puffed up, and overstated and paraBOLic as pertaining to or involving parables. HyperBOLe is obvious exaggeration, i.e., an assertion that cannot be taken literally. Medical students learn about metaBOLism, the process by which food is built up and used in our bodies, as well as of the dangers of emBOLism, the obstruction of an artery or vein by an emBOLus (pl. emBOLi), an air bubble, clot of blood, etc. AnaBOLic steroids have been used by athletes to temporarily increase the size of their muscles. ☞ *Charges of anabolic cheating rocked the Olympic Village yesterday.*

Physics texts devote space to ballistics, the study of missiles and projectiles. To go ballistic is to become agitated, irrational, or unhinged. ☞ *Coach Kling went ballistic when she learned that three starters on the Wings had been declared ineligible.*

PARLance is speech, talk, lingo, jargon, diction, or idiom. ☞ *The school's course in vocabulary had to be called "Language Arts" to fit in with the acceptable educational parlance.* A PALAVER and a PARLey have much in common; they are both names of a discussion, conference, or confabulation and as verbs they both mean to talk, speak, and confer. One who palavers, however, tends to talk profusely, often about trivial, idle matters. Such talks could take place in a PARLor or in a PARLiament, although the proBLEMs discussed might well be far different. PARLiamentarians are experts in legislative procedures, rules, or debates. The word proBLEMatic refers to debatable, questionable, chancy, dubious, and moot.

The literal meaning of DEVIL is "to throw across" that is, to assault one's character, to slander another in a DEVILISH, satanic, fiendish, hellish, wicked, and evil way. ☞ *That's the most devilish gang in the city.* It also means mischievous, crazy, impish, madcap, and extreme. ☞ *We decided not to go along with McGoo's devilish plan for stealing the cheesecake. You seem to be in a devilish hurry.*

The devil is the supreme spirit of evil, a fiend in human form, as well as Satan, Mephistopheles, Lucifer, Old Nick, Beelzebub, or the Prince of Darkness. It's *diable* in French, *diavolo* in Italian, *teufel* in German, *duivel* in Dutch, *djavol* in Russian, and it's always a monster, ogre, demon, villain, hellion, or terror.

A DAREDEVIL is a thrill-seeker, show-off, exhibitionist, madcap, or hotshot. A DEVIL'S ADVOCATE is a person who takes the opposite side in a debate to draw the others out or merely for the sake of argument.

DEVILMENT and DEVILTRY (also DEVILRY) are mischief, mischievous pranks, shenanigans, tomfoolery, or horseplay. ☞ *Jinny's latest bit of deviltry is hiding her father's slippers.* It also means cruelty, harm, injury, hurt, or trouble. ☞ *Hans' reputation for deviltry kept him out of the club.* A DEVIL-MAY-CARE ATTITUDE is a reckless, careless, cheerful, and rollicking one; a DEVILKIN is an imp; and DEVILED EGGS are usually prepared with a hot or savory sauce.

Ballein also gives us diaBOLic and diaBOLical, both meaning evil, demonic, cruel, malevolent, and monstrous. ☞ *Expert police work unearthed the diabolic/diabolical plot to blow up the nursing home.* DiaBOLism is witchcraft, sorcery, voodoo, wizardry, or shamanism and a belief in devils. DiaBOLo, also known as a devil on two sticks, is an instrument of amusement and skill in which a top-like object is balanced and tossed and caught on a string stretched between the ends of two sticks.

But not: *abolish* [*abolere,* destroy], do away with; *blemish* [ME *blemisshen,* to make pale], flaw; *parlay* [*par,* equal], increase, multiply.

Combining forms: *dia-,* across; *em-,* in; *hyper-,* over; *meta-,* beyond; *para-,* beside; *pro-,* forward; *sym-,* together.
Antonyms: *devil*—paragon, saint, angel, ideal; *devilish*—obedient, respectful, easy, boring; *devil-may-care*—prudent, cautious, wary, provident; *devilment, devilry, deviltry*—benefit, improvement, help, advantage; *diabolic*—virtuous, good, benevolent, saintly; *hyperbole*—litotes, understatement, depreciation; *problem*—answer, solution, simple, normal, manageable, perfect; *problematic*—sure, settled, certain, undisputed, unquestionable.

BASSUS, low, short: BASE, BASS

In Sergei Prokofiev's symphonic children's tale *Peter and the Wolf,* the characters are represented by musical instruments: the duck by an oboe, the bird by a flute, the cat by a clarinet in a low register, and Grandfather by a **BASS**OON, an instrument that is deep and low in sound. This is most appropriate, for it matches Grand-father's **BASS** voice, one so deep and low that as a singer he would be class-ified as a **BASS**O PROFUNDO. After all, a deep voice is necessary to properly match Grandfather's fearful warning to Peter, who has wandered off from the house; "The meadow is a dangerous place," he says. "What if a wolf should come out of the forest. What would you do *then?*"

Something that is **BASE** is evil, wicked, sinister, contemptible, or despicable. It also has the meaning of menial, servile, inferior, or wretched. ☞ *"I have always heard, Sancho, that doing good to base fellows is like throwing water into the sea," Miguel de Cervantes,* Don Quixote.

To A**BASE** someone is to lower in esteem, prestige, and rank, hence to humiliate, belittle, and demean. ☞ *"Whosoever exalteth himself shall be abased," Luke 14:11.* A person who has been A**BASE**D has been humbled, brought down, and degraded. An A**BASE**MENT is the act of being abased. ☞ *Every appearance before the board of directors was one more abasement for poor Rafael.* The definitions of abase and DE**BASE** are quite similar in meaning—both mean to lower in rank, dignity, or importance. ☞ *Inflation is bound to debase the nation's currency.* However, synonyms of the latter have a sharper, harsher, and more drastic edge when referring to human beings: cheapen, adulterate, desecrate, dishonor, and disgrace. ☞ *Dr. Bey spoke of the cruel debasing of human values by the Nazis.*

A **BASS**ET hound is low to the ground; a BAS-RELIEF is a form of sculpture in which the figures project only slightly from the background

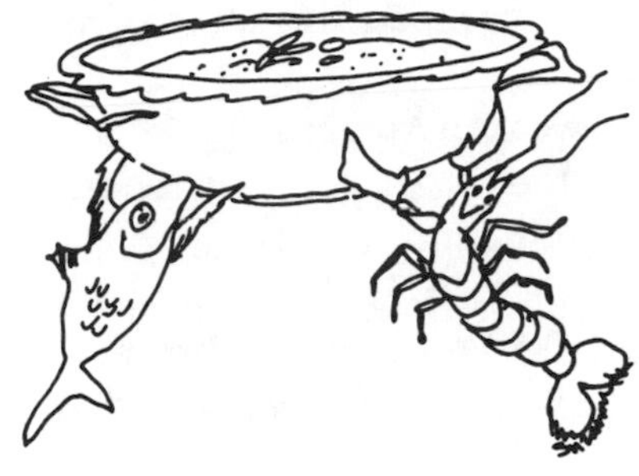
Bouillabaisse

(it is also called low relief); and BOUILLABAISSE is a soup or stew made with several kinds of fish along with tomatoes and olive oil; cooking directions are built into the word: its literal meaning is "boil it, then lower the heat."

But not: *base* [Gk *bainein,* to go], foundation, bottom, support; *bass* [ME *bas*], a fish.

Combining forms: *a-,* to; *bouilla-,* to boil; *de-,* down; *profundo,* deep; *relief,* projection in a sculpture.
Antonyms: *abase*—dignify, extol, laud; *abased*—honored, enhanced, praised; *base*—noble, exalted, superior; *debase*—consecrate, hallow, exalt.

BATTUERE, to beat: BAT

The sense of "to beat" is built into many words common to the realms of baseball, law, and the military. In baseball, the catcher and the pitcher form a **BAT**TERY. At least three **BAT**TERS step into the batter's box in the top or bottom half of every inning trying to beat the ball to a place where no opposing player is waiting for it. In law, an attack with an actual touching or other violence upon someone is known as ASSAULT AND **BAT**TERY. An artillery unit in the army or on a **BAT**TLESHIP is a battery; artillery fire **BAT**TERS a target; a **BAT**TALION is an army unit; a **BAT**TLEMENT is a wall set up upon a roof or another wall as a protection from enemy fire.

But there are other more tranquil domains. The naming of the device we use to crank the motor of our car or light our way on a dark and stormy night was most likely inspired by the concept of the discharge of electricity. A ballerina's beating together of her calves and feet during a leap is called a **BAT**TERIE, as is the rapid succession of a tap dancer's movements that make a sound like machine-gun fire.

The game we call badminton originated in the Orient in ancient times where it was called **BAT**TLEDORE AND SHUTTLECOCK, the former being the paddle the player used. Our name for it derives from that of the country estate where it was first played in England.

Athletic contests are a form of COM**BAT**; the protective armor worn in football and hockey brings up images of the COM**BAT**ANTS of old, as does the COMBATIVE, i.e., bellicose, aggressive, and competitive nature of many of the rivalries.

To ABATE is to lessen, diminish, and weaken something. ☞ *It was hoped that the entertainment would abate the passengers' anxieties.* An ABATEMENT is a lessening, moderating, or reduction. ☞ *Ms. Fay pleaded for the abatement of the pollution from the factory.* To BATE is to moderate or lessen the force of something; hence BATED BREATH is breath held back. ☞ *I await your answer with bated breath!, our heroine cried.* And an ABATTOIR is a slaughterhouse.

In schools and colleges a DEBATE is a formal argument. ☞ *The debate will begin in Jones Hall at 2:00 P.M.* It also refers to consideration, deliberation, or reflection. ☞ *After much debate, I decided to refuse the offer.* To debate is to argue, dispute, and deliberate. ☞ *Council members debated the point far into the night.* A point or matter that is capable of being discussed or argued is DEBATABLE, i.e., dubious, questionable, problematical, and uncertain. ☞ *It's debatable whether the school will join the conference.*

A REBATE is a deduction from an amount that is to be paid. ☞ *We had hoped for a hearty rebate from our taxes, but we were called in for an audit instead.*

BATTING is the material made of cotton or other fibers that is used in quilts, bedspreads, and in the tops of pill bottles. A RABBET is a groove made in wood in order to make a firm joint with another piece.

> **But not:** *bat* [Scand or ME *bakke*], nocturnal flying mammal; *batten* [F *baton*], to close the hatches or shipboard; small strips of wood to cover joints; *batty* [*bakke*], crazy.
> **Combining forms:** *a-*, to; *com-*, with; *de-*, down; *re-*, back.
> **Antonyms:** *abate*—grow, intensify, increase; *abatement*—excess, intemperance, expansion; *combat*—detente, harmony, peace; *combative*—pacific, cooperative, retiring; *debatable*—definite, irrefutable, decided, unquestionable.

BELLUM, war: BELL

"What is a REBEL?" asks Albert Camus, the 1957 Nobel prize for literature laureate, in his novel *The Plague;* his answer: "A man who says No." On one level, that may be adequate. But in the court of public opinion, saying "No" is not specific enough; we may want to know if this rebel is dangerous (a traitor, heretic, mutineer, insurrectionist, deserter, or turncoat; bearable (a nonconformist, dissenter, maverick, or loner); or eccentric (a crackpot, screw ball, weirdo, freak, or character). To **REBEL** is to resist, defy, disobey, flinch, and quail. ☞ *Parker rebelled at the very thought of having to face thirty children hour after hour, day after day.*

REBELLION refers to disobedience, resistance, insubordination, and defiance to revolution, insurrection, or coup d'etat. In a letter to James Madison in 1787 Thomas Jefferson wrote, "A little rebellion now and then is a good thing, as necessary in the political world as storms in the physical."

Mobs seeking the overthrow of a despotic government are considered **REBELLIOUS**, but the condition is not unknown among children, beginning quite early in life. Rebellious young ones are often intractable, uncontrollable, defiant, difficult, and unbearably stubborn.

Oddly enough, *bellum* also gives us the word **REVEL**, which means delight, relish, enjoy, savor, and gloat. ☞ *We secretly reveled when George lost the election.* **REVEL** also means to carouse, celebrate, romp, and have a ball. ☞ *The hometown fans reveled all night long.* As a noun, it is a festival, gala, fete, fiesta, jamboree, or bash. ☞ *The revels included games, dancing, and magic.* **REVELRY** is rejoicing, merriment, boisterousness, or feasting. ☞ *The revelry could be heard for blocks.*

BELLICOSE and **BELLIGERENT** are twins with these synonyms in common: aggressive, argumentative, cantankerous, and quarrelsome. Their noun forms, **BELLICOSITY**, **BELLICOSENESS**, **BELLIGERENCE**, and **BELLIGERENCY**, are interchangeable, too: aggressiveness, animosity, antagonism, combativeness, and hostility.

ANTEBELLUM means "before the war" and **POSTBELLUM** means "after the war." These words most frequently refer to the American Civil War. Thus, *status quo antebellum* means, roughly, the conditions that existed before the Civil War. A **CASUS BELLI**, is an event or spark that brings about a declaration of war. ☞ *The casus belli that set off World War I occurred on June 28, 1914, when the Austrian Crown Prince Franz Ferdinand was assassinated in the city of Sarajevo, Bosnia.*

War is in the heavens, too. In the constellation Orion, named for a mighty hunter and warrior, the third brightest point of light is a giant blue-white star called **BELLATRIX**, a female warrior. The woman goddess of war was **BELLONA**. Her name was originally "Duellona," for at one time *bellum* was *duellum,* and it was from that form that we got **DUEL**, a friendly contest or hostile combat between two parties.

America's most famous **DUELISTS** are Aaron Burr, Jefferson's vice-president, and Alexander Hamilton, the first Secretary of the Treasury; the duel took place in 1804, resulting in the latter's death. **DUELLO** is the code of rules for the sport, whether friendly or otherwise.

But not: *bellwether* [ME *wether,* flock-leading male sheep wearing a bell], guide, ringleader.
Combining forms: *ante-,* before; *-gerere,* to bear, carry; *post-,* after; *re-,* again.
Antonyms: *belligerence*—friendliness, peacefulness; *bellicose, belligerent*—easygoing, amicable, accommodating; *rebel*—conformist, loyalist, obey, submit; *rebellion*—obedience, submission, conciliation; *rebellious*—agreeable, submissive, manageable.

BENE, good, well; MALUS, bad, evil: BENE, BENI, MAL, MALE, MALI

A language reflects the nature of those who speak it. Consider, then, how balanced the English language seems to be between good (*bene*) and evil (*malus*).

BENEDICTIONS and **BENI**SONS are blessings. ☞ *Reverend Hugh will now give the benediction.* **MALE**DICTIONS and **MALI**SONS are curses. A **BENE**FACTOR is one who gives aid, and the deed itself is a **BENE**FACTION. A **MALE**FACTOR is one who does ill or breaks the law, and the act is a **MALE**FACTION.

BENEFIC and **BENE**FICENT acts are kindly ones, while **MALE**FIC and **MALE**FICENT acts are harmful. **BENE**VOLENT people desire to do good to others. They are filled with good will, charitableness, and **BENE**VOLENCE, and are amicable, compassionate, and merciful. But **MALE**VOLENT people wish evil or harm to others. They are filled with ill will, hatred, and **MALE**VOLENCE and are spiteful, vicious, and pernicious.

A **BENI**GN climate is pleasant, a benign grandfather is kindhearted, and a benign tumor is harmless. A long siege of gloomy weather can have a **MALI**GN influence on people, giving them a malign disposition; but the word is more frequently used as a verb meaning to speak ill of, slander, and vilify. ☞ *The two candidates maligned each other throughout the entire campaign.* When tumors are toxic, cancerous, and inoperable, they are **MALI**GNANT. Such abnormal growths are called **MALI**GNANCIES.

But not: *benefict* [alteration of *Benedick,* a bachelor in Shakespeare's *Much Ado about Nothing*], a long-time bachelor who is newly married; *malamute* [Inupiaq *malimiut,* name for Native Americans who bred sled dogs], Alaskan sled dog; *malleable* [*malleus,* hammer], adaptable.

Combining forms: *-diction,* to say; *-factor,* one who does; *-fic,* to do; *-volent,* to wish.
Antonyms: *benediction*—curse, calumniation; *benevolence*—animosity, malice, heartlessness; *benevolent*—cold, hostile, nasty; *benign*—mean, violent, unhealthy; *malevolent*—cordial, kind, compassionate; *malignant*—amicable, amiable, efficacious.

BIBERE, to drink: BIB

To IM**BIB**E is to drink. ☞ *By the time the game ended, we'd imbibed a dozen cans of soda.* It also means to absorb moisture. ☞ *The plants imbibed the moisture from the soil.* It is also to take in, as into the mind. ☞ *They had crossed the Atlantic to imbibe European culture.* To some, it means consuming alcoholic drinks. ☞ *Just a soft drink for me, thank you; I don't imbibe.* A **BIB**ULOUS person is fond of or addicted to drink and may be described as being alcoholic, intemperate, tipping, and guzzling. A BEVERAGE is any drinking liquid other than water.

The now-archaic verb **BIB** meant "to drink, tipple, and imbibe." It is most likely that we got the name for a cloth used as a protection for a child's chest while eating or drinking from that word.

Some etymologists trace BEER back to this root, along with BEVY, meaning a group, as of quail or larks, or of people. ☞ *A bevy of noisy sailors boarded the ship.*

To IMBRUE (also EMBRUE) is to stain, defile, and dirty. ☞ *I refuse to imbrue myself with one more lie or falsehood.*

But not: *bible* [from *Byblos,* a Phoenician city from which papyrus (material on which to write) was exported], handbook, scripture.
Combining forms: *-em,* in; *-im,* in.
Antonyms: *bibulous*—moderate, sober, temperate.

BIBLION, book, papyrus, scroll: BIBLI, BIBLIO

The combining form *biblio-* refers to books. Hence a **BIBLIO**CLAST destroys books, a **BIBLIO**KLEPT steals them, and **BIBLIO**LATRY is an unusual dependence upon or reverence for books particularly the BIBLE. **BIBLIO**MANIA is an excessive and abnormal fondness for acquiring and possessing books. A **BIBLIO**PHAGE is an ardent reader. A **BIBLIO**PHILE loves and collects books, especially fine bindings and print work, and a **BIBLIOphobe** distrusts, fears, or hates books. A **BIBLIOpole** is a bookseller, usually of fine or rare editions, a **BIBLIOtaph** accumulates or hoards books, and a **BIBLIOgraphy** is a list of articles or books on a particular subject or by a certain author.

Most large private or public collections of books in this country are called libraries, but some have ATHENAEUM or **BIBLIOtheca** engraved above their entrances or designating special reading rooms. In France, it's **BIBLIOtheque**; in Italy, Portugal, Romania, and Spain it's **BIBLIOteca**; in German, **BIBLIOthek**; in Denmark, Norway, and Sweden, **BIBLIOtek**; and in Russia it's **BIBLIatyeka.**

Papyrus was the material that the ancient Egyptians, Greeks, and Romans used for writing. The source of much of the Greeks' papyrus was shipped from the Phoenician port of Byblos, and it is quite likely that from the name of the port came *biblion,* and from that came the English word Bible. We capitalize the word when it refers to the sacred writings of the Christian religion. ☞ *Dr. Foss will head the Bible school this fall.* It is not capitalized when it names an authoritative book or reference. ☞ *The football coach referred to his play book as his bible.* The poet Dylan Thomas used the word in an adjectival sense in his play *Under Milk Wood,* "It is spring, moonless night in a small town, starless and bible-black. . . . ."

BIBLIcism is the literal interpretation of the Bible, and a person who so interprets it is a **BIBLIcist** or **BIBLIst.**

Combining forms: *-clast,* to break; *-graphy,* writing; *-klept,* thief; *-mania,* extreme enthusiasm; *-phage,* devourer; *-phile,* lover; *-phobe,* one who fears or hates; *-pole,* to sell; *-taph,* tomb; *-theca,* place.

BOMBOS, a booming, humming sound

In November of 1932, thirteen years before the first atomic **bomb** was exploded, Stanley Baldwin, a British statesman, in a speech said, "I think it is well . . . to realize that there is no power on earth that can protect [the man in the street] from being bombed . . . The **bomber** will always get through."

A **bombardier** is a member of the crew of a **bombing plane** who operates the **bombsight** and the **bomb-release** mechanism during a **bombardment.**

To bomb also means to fail, flop, blunder, and stumble. ☞ *The play bombed on Broadway.* To be bombed is to be drunk or high on drugs. ☞ *They were bombed out of their minds.* A bomb is a dud, failure, or bust.

☞ *That movie's a real bomb.* It also refers to a long completed pass in football, an insecticide can, an old car, or a lousy TV show.

To **BOMBARD** is to attack someone in a most peaceful way, as with questions or pamphlets. ☞ *Sen. Porque was bombarded with questions after the hearing.* A **BOMBSHELL** is something that has a sensational effect. ☞ *News of her resignation was a bombshell to all of us.* Noise that **BOMBINATES** buzzes, drones, and hums. ☞ *The idle gossip of chattering small-talkers bombinated throughout the room.*

Bomb

To **BOUND** is to leap forward or upward, jump, bounce, and vault. ☞ *Fido and Rover bounded over the fence.* It is also a noun. ☞ *Business is growing by leaps and bounds.* Bound is also used as an adjective. ☞ *The poet described the swell of the waves on the high seas as the bounding main.*

A **REBOUND** is a comeback, recovery, bounce, ricochet, or return. ☞ *We were sure that she had married him on the rebound. Our team didn't grab one rebound in the second half.* As a verb rebound means to perk up, rally, and recover. ☞ *Our sales rebounded after two flat months. The line drive rebounded off the right field wall.*

Combining form: *re-*, back.
Antonyms: *bomb*—success, hit, smash, triumph; *rebound*—worsen, weaken, fail.

C

CABALLUS, horse: CAVAL

In the English Civil War that broke out in 1642, those who supported Charles I in his battle against Parliament chose to call themselves **CAVAL**IERS and their opponents Roundheads. As it turned out, the principal head that was round enough to roll belonged to Charles; it was chopped off.

Today people who are CAVALIER are arrogant, haughty, and curt, just as if they were looking down from the horses their namesakes always rode. ☞ *No matter what you say, Smidgen'll cavalierly tell you you're wrong.* Cavalier also means offhand, unceremonious, and thoughtless. ☞ *To me the ceremony was touching and heartrending, and I thought Blankman's cavalier attitude was inexcusably offensive.*

A **CAVAL**CADE used to be a ceremonial parade of horsemen, but today it's more likely to be a pageant of sorts, just as the **CAVAL**RY charge of old is now one of motor-powered armored vehicles.

> **Antonyms:** *cavalier*—courteous, attentive, considerate, thoughtful, humble.

CADERE, to fall: CAD, CAS, CID

An AC**CID**ENT is often a misfortune, mishap, blunder, or calamity. ☞ *Police cars, ambulances, and tow trucks rushed to the scene of the accident.* It can also be fortuity, fate, luck, fortune, or act of God. ☞ *It was by pure accident that Susan got her first job.*

An AC**CID**ENTAL occurrence is unanticipated, unintended, and uncalculated. ☞ *The insurance policy pays double in the event of accidental death.* Something that happens AC**CID**ENTALLY happens unintentionally, randomly, and inadvertently. ☞ *America was discovered accidentally by Christopher Columbus.* Historical accidents are somewhat CHANCY. That means risky, hazardous, dangerous, precarious, and uncertain. ☞ *Crossing that bridge at night is chancy at best.* Chancy also means haphazard, random, dubious, and speculative. ☞ *All lotteries are chancy; look at the odds.*

CHANCE is luck, providence, or happenstance. ☞ *We met by chance.* It is also probability, possibility, or likelihood. ☞ *There is a slight chance of showers today.* As a verb it has two meanings. One meaning is gamble, speculate, dare, risk, and venture. ☞ *It's risky; I'm not going to chance it.* The second meaning of chance as a verb is to happen, occur, and take place. ☞ *It chanced that a doctor was right there.* And as an adjective, chance refers to unforeseen, unpremeditated, lucky, and casual. ☞ *A chance meeting brought mother and daughter together.*

A **CAD**AVER is a dead body; someone who looks **CAD**AVEROUS resembles a corpse by being ashen, deathly pale, or gaunt. A **CAS**UALTY is a victim, sufferer, or fatality; in fact, it is anyone or anything injured or lost by accident or disaster. ☞ *Our only casualty was Junior's hamster.*

A **CAS**UAL encounter is unplanned or unexpected. A casual attitude is vague, offhand, and halfhearted. ☞ *I haven't even a casual interest in fishing.* It is also nonchalant, cool, and indifferent. ☞ *Pam won the election on the strength of her casual outlook.* Casual attire is informal, sporty, relaxed, and comfortable.

CASUISTRY is reasoning that is faulty, deceptive, and tricky. ☞ *No casuistry will ever convince us that the war was a victory for humanity.*

A **CAS**E is an instance, sample, or illustration. ☞ *I admit it was a case of poor judgment.* It can be a situation, circumstance, or position. ☞ *Hers is a hardship case.* It can also be an affliction, illness, or problem. ☞ *He has a bad case of chicken pox.* Finally, a case is a lawsuit, dispute, hearing, or argument. ☞ *The case will go before the jury tomorrow.*

A **CAS**CADE is a waterfall or something that resembles a rush of falling water. ☞ *Bright flowers cascaded over the wall.* A **CAD**ENZA is a flourish near the end of a piece of music; and **CAD**ENCE is the beat, rhythm, tempo, or measure of sounds. **CAD**UCITY means senility, frailty, and the infirmity of old age. ☞ *Rev. Willet spoke of the caducity of life.* And **CAD**UCOUS means transitory, perishable, and falling, as the leaves of such DE**CID**UOUS trees as elms, maples, and oaks.

ESCHEAT, to fall due, is the taking of one's property by a king or other government upon one's death. From the word escheat we get CHEAT, to defraud, swindle, and bilk. Hence, to cheat on a test is to break the rules, act unfairly, and practice trickery. To try to cheat overpowering forces such as fate, death, or the law is to try to evade, outwit, and thwart. ☞ *Marley tried in vain to cheat fate; finally he cheated the law by committing suicide.*

A CHUTE, whether natural or man-made, is a trough, incline, or trench. When supplies are chuted down to a marooned group of adventurers, they are dropped by means of a PARACHUTE. A GOLDEN PARACHUTE is a contract by which a key officer is guaranteed pay and other benefits in the case of job loss through company sale or merger.

To **coinCIDe** is to meet, come together, and occur simultaneously. ☞ *Unfortunately, our vacations never seem to coincide.* Coincide also means to concur, conform, and agree. ☞ *The two witnesses' testimony did not coincide.* A **coinCIDence** is a chance, accident, and a bit of luck. ☞ *Seeing the actress come out of the theater was pure coincidence.* It also refers to simultaneous concurrence. ☞ *The coincidence of smoking and lung cancer convinces me that there's a connection.*

DeCADence is degeneration, decay, decline, or corruption. ☞ *It was decadence that brought about the end of the Roman Empire.* When an individual or society becomes **deCADent,** it becomes immoral, corrupted, debauched, and degenerate. When something **decays** it may atrophy, sicken, weaken, wane, decompose, and die.

A sociologist who speaks of the high **inCIDence** of crime in the city is referring to the frequency, occurrence, or rate of the criminal acts.

An **inCIDent** is an act, affair, event, or episode. ☞ *That incident will not be forgotten for a long time.* As an adjective incident means apt or likely to happen, arising from, and connected with. ☞ *Ian's chances incident to making it to the major leagues are zilch and less.* **InCIDental** costs are those that are secondary, accessory, and subordinate. ☞ *The tuition at State was high enough, but it was really the incidental expenses that forced me to drop out.* **InCIDentals** are minor items, extras, or accessories. ☞ *Take sufficient cash to cover the incidentals that always crop up.* **InCIDentally** is an alternate word for such phrases as by the way, speaking of that, by the bye, and while we're on the subject. ☞ *Incidentally, watch your pronunciation of the word; there is no* incidently.

An **ocCASion** is any important event, occurrence, or incident. ☞ *Her eighteenth birthday was a big occasion.* It is an important, suitable, or special opportunity or time. ☞ *I want to take this occasion to thank everyone who helped.* It is also a reason, cause, or motive. ☞ *Hey! What's the occasion for all the racket?* **OcCASional** doings are infrequent, unscheduled, and sporadic. ☞ *Kay says her headaches are only occasional now. Occasional showers are forecast for the late afternoon and evening.* Things that occur only **ocCASionally,** happen now and then, from time to time, sometimes, and intermittently. ☞ *We see the Pattersons only occasionally these days.* The phrase **on occasion** has the same meaning. ☞ *We still play tennis on occasion.*

The **OcCIDent** comprises Europe and the Americas; generally speaking, it means "the West"; the word comes from the fall or setting of the sun. The Orient is the East, mostly the countries of Asia; the word comes from the rising of the sun, [*oriri,* to rise].

ReCIDivism, a tendency to relapse into crime, literally means to "fall back." ☞ *Recidivism has increased dramatically in recent years according to figures released by probation officers.* To **reCIDivate** is to return to criminal habits; a **reCIDivist** is one who relapses.

But not: *cad* [short for *caddie,* an errand boy], a vulgar person; *caduceus* [Gk *karykion,* herald's staff], emblem of the medical profession; *case* [*capere,* to take], a container, to examine; *decade* [Gk *deka,* ten], period of ten years; *lucidity* [*lucere,* to shine], clarity, rationality.
Combining forms: *ac-,* upon; *co-,* together; *de-,* down; *es-,* to; *in-,* upon; *oc-,* towards; *para-,* protection against; *re-,* back.
Antonyms: *accident*—purpose, plan, intent, design, calculation; *accidental*—foreseen, expected, intended; *cadaverous*—hardy, robust, lively; *cascade*—trickle, drip; *casual*—predetermined, premeditated, calculated, planned; *chance*—intention, certainty, impossibility, plan; *chancy*—certain, inevitable, fixed, sure; *coincide*—disagree, differ, diverge, conflict, counter, contradict; *decadence*—flowering, blossoming, vigor; *decadent*—young, vigorous, hearty; *decay*—flourish, expand, increase, strengthen; *incidental*—crucial, basic, fundamental, essential; *occasional*—regular, habitual, routine; *occasionally*—constantly, continuously, habitually.

CALERE, to be warm, hot: CAL, CHA

Recipes for chowder vary, but many cookbooks suggest that one put lots of onions, garlic, celery, and tomatoes in water in a **CALdron/cauldron** and simmer until tender; add plenty of shrimp, clams, crab, fish. When done, pour into a **CHAfing** dish to keep it warm (but not **sCALding**).

NonCHAlant literally means "*not* to get hot under the collar." **CHAlant** comes from French and means "be concerned," hence the word's synonyms are casual, cool, detached, uninterested, indifferent, and apathetic. **NonCHAlance** refers to one's composure, cool, calm, insouciance, or sang-froid. ☞ *TV's* Columbo *fans have long enjoyed the detective's nonchalance.*

To **CHA**FE is to warm by rubbing, as on a cold day one rubs one's hands together. Sometimes the rubbing is uncomfortable, as when the new shoes chafe the toes or heels. It also means to annoy, harass, irritate, and irk someone. To **CHA**FF means to tease, kid, mock, and ridicule, usually in a lighthearted manner.

A **CAUDLE** is a warm drink for the sick or bedridden, made with ale or wine mixed with eggs, bread, sugar, and spices and drunk from a **CAUDLE CUP**, one having two handles and a cover. **CAL**ENTURE is a violent fever with delirium that affects people in the tropics.

A **CAL**ORIC food is high in **CAL**ORIES.

> **But not:** *chaff* [OE *ceaf*], grain husks, trivial matter.
> **Combining forms:** *-fe,* to do, make; *non-,* not.
> **Antonyms:** *nonchalance*—concern, involvement, anxiety, excitement; *nonchalant*—disturbed, concerned, involved, impassioned.

CALVI, to deceive: CAL, CHAL

In Shakespeare's *Hamlet,* the Prince of Denmark urges Ophelia, the woman he loves, to "get thee to a nunnery." Pretending madness, he denies that he loves her, and says that if she does marry, ". . . be thou as chaste as ice, as pure as snow, thou shalt not escape **CAL**UMNY." Calumny refers to slander, libel, slur, or hate. Unfortunately, attacks of that kind are often difficult to defend against. As Ben Jonson, a Shakespeare contemporary, said in his play *Volpone,* "**CAL**UMNIES are answered best with silence." It is not always easy to keep one's cool when **CAL**UMNIOUS, slanderous, malicious, and libelous barbs are being hurled your way.

In his inaugural address John F. Kennedy said, "The New Frontier of which I speak is not a set of promises—it is a set of **CHAL**LENGES." Promises are vows, pledges, or bonds; challenges are dares, spurs, stimuli, provocations, or lures. ☞ *I challenge you to a duel.* Leaders must often be **CHAL**LENGERS, people who prod, goad, provoke, or stimulate. Being a leader is **CHAL**LENGING, i.e., intriguing, stirring, exciting, and inspiring.

> **But not:** *calumet* [*calamus,* a reed], a ceremonial peace pipe used by Native Americans; *chalupa* [Sp boat, launch], fried tortilla topped with meat, lettuce, tomato, and hot sauce.
> **Antonyms:** *caluminous*—eulogistic, laudatory, commendatory; *calumny*—eulogy, praise, approval; *challenge*—accept, concede, agree with, acquiesce.

CANERE, to sing: CANT, CHANT

The crowd at a sporting event often monotonously **CHANTs**—or sings—a phrase in support of its team. ☞ *We chanted over and over, "Beat the Falcons, beat the Falcons, beat 'em, beat 'em."* A **CHANTey** (also **CHANTy**, shantey, or shanty) is a sailor's song sung as he works. A **CHANTeuse** is a female singer in a nightclub or cabaret; her male counterpart is a **CHANTeur.** In medieval times **CHANTicleer,** literally, "to sing clear," was a proper name given to a rooster in fables. Geoffrey Chaucer's Chauntecleer matched wits with Reynard the Fox in *The Canterbury Tales.* A **CHANTry** is money donated to cover the costs of the singing of masses for someone's soul.

A **CANTata** is a musical composition for singers; a **CANTor** is the chief singer or **CHANTer** in a synagogue; and a **CANTicle** is a hymn, poem, or song of praise. In music, something that is **CANTabile** is songlike and flowing in style; and a **CANTo** is one of the main divisions of a long poem.

An in**CANTation** is the chanting of words in order to cast a magical spell; this is what the three witches do in Shakespeare's *Macbeth* when they chant, "Fair is foul, and foul is fair; / Hover through the fog and filthy air."

The literal meaning of re**CANT** is to "sing back, to sing again"; what it means today is to take back, withdraw, retract, recall, and abjure. ☞ *The losing candidate recanted all the charges he had made during the campaign.* One of the early meanings of **CANT** was the language of thieves, a special vocabulary that could not be understood by outsiders; it is known today as argot, jargon, lingo, slang, or vernacular. ☞ *The cant of the computer world was completely foreign to me.* It also means hypocrisy, humbug, pretense, sham, or insincerity. ☞ *The advertisement's claim that the ring was solid gold was just a lot of cant.* **DesCANT** is both a noun (song) and a verb (to sing). ☞ *The birds' descants filled the air. The troubadour's descanting delighted the audience.*

To accent is to stress or emphasize, as a syllable or a word. ☞ *The British accent the second syllable of the word laBORatory.* As a noun, accent refers to pronunciation or inflection. ☞ *Ivan has never lost his Russian accent.* To accentuate is to accent, stress, and dwell on. ☞ *The speaker urged us to accentuate the positive and eliminate the negative.*

To some a charm is a lucky piece, amulet, or talisman. ☞ *Grandpa wore a ring made of a horseshoe nail as a charm to ward off rheumatism.* To others, charm means magnetism, attraction, or fascination. ☞ *The new talk show host radiated enough charm to lure most of the viewers.* To charm people is to delight, allure, bewitch, or fascinate them. ☞ *Our granddaughter charms everyone who sees her.* Charming manners, people, personalities, and smiles are engaging, bewitching, irresistible, charismatic, and **enCHANTing.**

To **enCHANT** is to charm and mesmerize, captivate, and cast a spell over. **EnCHANTment** is magic or witchcraft, as well as anything that is charming or captivating. New Mexico's motto is "The Land of Enchantment." An **enCHANTress** is a temptress, femme fatale, vamp, or siren; an **enCHANTer** is a magician or sorcerer. To **disenCHANT** is to disillusion or discourage. ☞ *Pop's first day out disenchanted him about his ever getting a decent job.* To be **disenCHANTed** is to be cynical, disheartened, and frustrated.

An **incentive** is something that stimulates one into action, that, in a sense, sings your tune; synonyms are motive, provocation, incitement, or inducement. ☞ *Pat's telling me that I lack ambition was all the incentive I needed.* A **disincentive** is something that discourages or dissuades. ☞ *The Senate hearings have resulted in a disincentive for qualified people to serve in government.*

But not: *cant* [*canthus,* iron tire], a slope, incline; *canter* [short for *canterbury,* the supposed gait of horses ridden by pilgrims to Canterbury in England], an easy gallop; *decanter* [*canthus*], a container for liquid, such as wine; *shanty* [perh. from Ir *sean tig,* old house], a dilapidated house.
Combining forms: *ac-,* to; *dis-,* not; *en-,* in; *in-,* in; *re-,* back.
Antonyms: *accent*—downplay, understate, minimize; *cant*—formal speech, educated speech; *charm*—irritate, offend; *disenchanted*—naive, gullible, trusting; *enchant*—repulse, repel, disgust; *incentive*—deterrent, dissuasion.

CAPERE, to seize, lay hold of, contain: CAP

A **CAPable** person is able, competent, qualified, and suitable. ☞ *Barker often wondered if he was really capable of filling his predecessor's shoes.* One's **CAPability** is his or her ability, competence, or skill. ☞ *Your test scores indicate that you have the capability to do well in college.* One sense of **CAPacity** is aptitude, ability, intellect, or talent. ☞ *Theoretical physicist Stephen Hawking is a man of extraordinary capacity.* Another sense means size, volume, scope, compass, or extent. ☞ *The gas tank on this subcompact has a seven-gallon capacity.* And a third sense refers to function, position, office, or role. ☞ *In my capacity as mayor, I will enlarge our park system.* INCAPACITY and INCAPABILITY mean lack of ability, qualification, or strength.

A **CAP**SULE holds something; it is a container. As an adjective it means small or concise. ☞ *Capsule biographies are found in the appendix.* To EN**CAP**SULATE is to summarize, condense, and abridge. ☞ *The secretary encapsulated the lengthy report.* It also means to enclose and surround. ☞ *As a child, Judi was encapsulated in affection.*

CAPACITATE means to enable, qualify, prepare, and equip. To IN**CAP**ACITATE is to disable, make one unfit, or IN**CAP**ABLE. ☞ *His lack of a high school diploma incapacitated him for the job he sought.* A person who is disabled, crippled, handicapped, and debilitated is said to be IN**CAP**ACITATED.

On board a ship a **CAP**STAN is used to wind up ropes or cables; in a tape recorder, it is a revolving spindle around which the tape passes. A **CAP**ACITATOR is an element in an electric circuit; it was formerly called a condensor.

> **But not:** *caper* [*capra,* a she-goat], skip, dance about; *capillary* [*capillus,* hair], one of the tiny blood vessels that connect our arteries and veins.
> **Combining forms:** *en-,* to confine in; *in-,* not.
> **Antonyms:** *capability*—incompetence, ineptitude, inability; *capable*—inept, clumsy, inexpert, unskilled; *incapable*—competent, efficient, qualified.

CAPERE: CAPT

A **CAPT**IVE is a prisoner, hostage, convict, or jailbird; but the word also has its less physical senses. ☞ *When the bus ran out of gas, the preacher found that he had a captive audience. The candidate was a captive of business interests. Ray was a captive of Margaret's charms.* Animals in zoos are held in **CAPT**IVITY; their **CAPT**ORS **CAPT**URED them in the wilds. As people grow older, they may try to RE**CAPT**URE some past incident or encounter, to re-experience or recollect pleasant memories.

To **CAPT**IVATE is to charm, fascinate, and enchant others. A **CAPT**IVATING person is bewitching, seductive, attractive, and irresistible.

A **CAPT**ION is a title, heading, or explanation of a picture in a newspaper or magazine; it is also the titles or headings of books, chapters of books, and of stories on film.

A **CAPTious** remark or attitude is critical, faultfinding, carping, and biting. ☞ *The boss never gave out any praise without tacking on a captious remark.*

But not: *captain* [*caput,* head], leader.
Combining form: *re-,* again.
Antonyms: *captious*—flattering, uncritical, approving, appreciative; *captivate*—repulse, repel, offend, alienate, antagonize; *captivating*—offensive, unpleasant, repellant, repugnant; *captive*—free person, unconfined, liberated; *capture*—release, liberation, escape.

CAPERE: CAS, CHAS

A **CASe** is a box, container, or carton, or other piece of hand luggage. To case is to examine, survey, and check into. ☞ *In the movie the guys cased the joint for weeks before moving in.* A **CASement** is a frame of a window. The outer covering of some sausages and salamis are **CASings** that must be peeled off; it is a wrapping, jacket, sheath, or cover. The tapes one plays come in **CASsettes.** To **enCASe** is to enclose, wrap, box, and put into a case. ☞ *The librarian encased the rare book in glass to preserve it.*

It is from **CAShier,** the handler of money in a bank or a store, that we get the word **CASh.** Synonyms of cash are legal tender, coin of the realm, bread, and dough. It is what one often uses when making a **purCHASe.** A purchase is also the grip, grasp, hold, or leverage one uses when trying to open a jar, for instance. ☞ *My hands were too greasy to get a purchase on the lid.*

Large **CASkets** were formerly called coffins, sarcophagi, or boxes; they hold bodies. Small caskets are chests or boxes for holding jewelry. Some etymologists claim that **CASk** comes from casket, others credit the Spanish *casco,* meaning "a skull, the coat of an onion"; whatever its parentage, it remains a barrel, keg, hogshead, or firkin.

To **CHASe** is to pursue, hunt, follow, and trail. To chase away, off, or out is to repulse, evict, repel, or disperse. A chase is a quest, pursuit, and search, as well as the object such as the game, prey, victim, or quarry. Printers work with an iron frame known as a chase. Engravers chase or **enCHASe** designs or letters on metal; the resultant design is called a **CHASing.**

The **CHASsis** is the frame of an automobile, the landing gear of an aircraft, and a frame for the components of a radio or television set.

But not: *case* [*cadere,* to fall], instance, situation; *cashew* [Pg *caju*], edible nut; *cashier* [*cassus,* null, void], dismiss; *chaste* [*castus,* pure, clean], celibate, abstinent, simple.
Combining form: *en-,* in.

CAPERE: CEIT, CEIV

When President Lincoln gave his address at Gettysburg in 1863, he spoke of America as being "conCEIVed in liberty, and dedicated to the proposition that all men are created equal." He had a wide choice of synonyms at his disposal, among them, formed, begun, started, and created. The idea of such a nation was hardly conCEIVable before the American Revolution, not believable, tenable, thinkable, and imaginable. Absolute monarchies, and similar forms of government, had been the way of the world for thousands of years, making certain that thoughts, ideas, or notions of liberty and equality were inconCEIVable, i.e., unthinkable, unheard-of, and improbable.

Occasionally, as we read books from an earlier age, we come across conCEIT as a notion, thought, or idea. ☞ *Sir Olinger jotted down the conceits of his leisure hours.* A conceit also refers to an elaborate, far-fetched metaphor in poetry. But today, the word is largely synonymous with egotism, vanity, arrogance, or narcissism. ☞ *Jock's conceit about his athletic prowess is unbearable.* ConCEITed people are vain, cocky, smug, and haughty.

To deCEIVe others is to mislead, trick, delude, and cheat them; hence, to be deCEIVed is to be taken in. ☞ *Don't be deceived by her innocent looks.* A deCEITful person is dishonest, two-faced, dissembling, wily, and dishonest. DeCEIT is fraud, hypocrisy, duplicity, or dishonesty. ☞ *The attorney charged that the sales department was guilty of fraud and deceit.*

To perCEIVe the taste and aroma of sage in breakfast sausage is to notice, recognize, and distinguish, just as it is when an artist perceives certain subtle shades of color. To perceive the sarcasm in someone's voice is to comprehend, grasp, and understand. Both the sage and the sarcasm can be perCEIVable. In *Nicomachean Ethics* Aristotle said, "To be conscious that we are perCEIVing or thinking is to be conscious of our own existence."

The Bible says, "It is more blessed to give than to reCEIVe," thus to take, acquire, accept, and collect. To receive friends is to welcome, greet, and admit them. To receive a degree or other honor is to have it bestowed and conferred upon one. It also means to suffer, endure, experience, and put up with. ☞ *No customer, however rude or demanding, is to receive discourteous treatment.* A book that is well received by the reviewers is approved and accepted; if it isn't, it is likely to become a dusty dud.

A **reCEIVer** is a part of a radio, telephone, or television set, a catcher on a baseball team, the target of a pass in football, one who accepts stolen goods, or a person who is appointed to take charge of a bankrupt business, such as one in **reCEIVership.** The adjective **reCEIVed** means standard, conventional, and generally accepted; in England the generally agreed upon pronunciation of British English is called "Received Pronunciation" and the dialect spoken by educated people is called "Received Standard English."

Parties and ceremonies often have **reCEIVing** lines, babies have receiving blankets, the business world has accounts **reCEIVable,** and we all collect and save **receipts** from time to time, for the rent, the car payment, and at the supermarket checkout line. The receipts are the profits, income, or proceeds. ☞ *Our opening-day receipts were above expectations.* In some parts of the country a receipt is a recipe. ☞ *Abby's receipt for pecan pie is a well-kept secret.*

Combining forms: *con-,* together; *de-,* from; *in-,* not; *per-,* thoroughly; *re-,* back.
Antonyms: *conceit*—humility, modesty; *conceited*—humble, meek, modest; *conceivable*—questionable, doubtful, unbelievable; *deceit*—honesty, sincerity, candor; *deceitful*—candid, honest, forthright; *inconceivable*—credible, likely; *perceivable*—unrecognizable, indistinguishable; *receive*—refuse, reject; *received*—non-standard, irregular, unconventional.

CAPERE: CEPT

Comedian Groucho Marx wrote in his autobiography, "I sent the club a wire stating, 'Please **acCEPT** my resignation. I don't want to belong to any club that will *accept* me as a member.' " On March 31, 1968, President Lyndon Johnson told the nation, "I shall not seek, nor will I *accept* the nomination of my party for another term as your President." All three uses of the word accept mean receive willingly, agree to, allow, acknowledge, and assent to. It also means to assume, undertake, admit, and bear. ☞ *I don't like the plan, but I guess I'll have to accept it.*

AcCEPTance is approval, consent, recognition, or agreement. ☞ *It took the Gardleys months to win the town's acceptance.* It also means taking, receiving, and getting. ☞ *It was his acceptance of bribes that finally led to his arrest.* An acCEPTed standard or method or theory, etc., is one that is generally approved. ☞ *Walking shorts are now accepted attire at our school.* Something that is acCEPTable is agreeable, satisfactory, and suitable. ☞ *The union members found the contract acceptable.* But acceptable is not always satisfactory; in some cases, it is considered fair, passable, adequate, and tolerable. ☞ *The counselor said my grades were barely acceptable.* Contracts or grades that are unacCEPTable are unsatisfactory, improper, unsuitable, and unseemly. ☞ *I agree; Susan's behavior has been totally unacceptable.*

A conCEPT is a human being's ideas, thoughts, views, or theories. To conCEPTualize is to form a concept, idea, notion, and hypothesis; one who thinks in conCEPTual terms postulates, theorizes, or hypothesizes about things ideal, abstract, pure, and mental. ☞ *Not everyone is capable of conceptual, abstract thinking.* The conCEPTion of something is its imagining, creating, birth, or genesis. It is an image, idea, or notion. ☞ *The architect's conception of the house was miles apart from ours. I don't suppose you have any conception of the sorrow I feel.* It is also becoming pregnant, the beginning of pregnancy, or fertilization. ☞ *Conception took place in the west, but our baby was born in New England.* To contraCEPT is to prevent conception; contraCEPTion is birth control; and a contraCEPTive is a device to prevent impregnation.

DeCEPTions come in two different wrappings. If it is done to swindle, cheat, or deceive people, it is fraudulence, duplicity, dishonesty, or deceit. English author John Ruskin nailed it down when he said in *Modern Painters,* "The essence of lying is in deception, not in words"; it's not the *what* one says so much as it is the *why* and *how* of it. On the other hand, if the purpose of the deception is to entertain, as, say, by a magician, it is artifice, illusion, prestidigitation, or sleight-of-hand.

Something that is deCEPTive may be misleading, dishonest, deceitful, and fraudulent. ☞ *That magazine is filled with deceptive advertising.* Deceptive may also mean disingenuous, deluding, beguiling, and foxy. ☞ *I found his appearance to be quite deceptive; he certainly didn't* look *like a movie star.*

An exCEPTional accomplishment is remarkable, extraordinary, and phenomenal. ☞ *I found it a good read, but nothing exceptional.* An exceptional occurrence is unusual, singular, rare, and abnormal. ☞ *High temperatures so early in the spring are really exceptional in this area.*

When critics label a movie unexCEPTional, they may well mean banal, humdrum, stereotyped, and pedestrian.

An EXCEPTION is something that doesn't conform to the general rule. ☞ *Everyone in the class wore something red with the exception of Johnny Greene.* An exception also means an objection. ☞ *I took exception to what the coach said about my sister.*

When EXCEPT is used as a verb, it means to exclude, leave out, and omit. ☞ *No one is excepted from taking the final exam in this course.* As a preposition it has the meaning of save, but, excluding, other than, and besides. ☞ *Put everything on the top shelf except the clock.*

At Cambridge University in England the act of graduating, especially with a master's or doctor's degree, is not, as it is with us, called a "commencement"; it is, instead, an INCEPTION. Obviously, both of the words mean beginning, initiation, inauguration, or debut. ☞ *Labor Day used to mark the inception/commencement of the school year.*

In football an INTERCEPTOR is a player who catches a forward pass intended for someone on the opposing team; in the military, it is a fighter plane that hinders or prevents enemy aircraft from completing its mission. Both of these acts are INTERCEPTIONS; so is the monitoring of enemy radio transmission to gain information. Hence, to INTERCEPT is to stop, check, interfere, obstruct, and detain an action. ☞ *We tried to intercept the letter before it got to our friend.*

PERCEPTION is one's awareness, understanding, insight, or grasp. PERCEPTIBLE objects are noticeable, discernible, and palpable. ☞ *The lights were barely perceptible in the fog. The perceptible change in Junior's behavior is most welcome.* An IMPERCEPTIBLE object is undetectable, insignificant, and minute.

A person who is PERCEPTIVE is insightful, astute, understanding, and intelligent. ☞ *Ms. Thorsen was the most perceptive teacher we had; she knew we could do better.* PERCEPTIVENESS refers to astuteness, acumen, or intelligence.

APPERCEPTION is the process of understanding a new experience by integrating it into one's previous experiences and knowledge. ☞ *When Juanita finally realized that all her life she'd been searching for a father figure, it came about through apperception.*

A PRECEPT is a principle, commandment, axiom, or rule. ☞ *My uncle lived by his precepts and influenced others by his example.* Instructors in some schools, particularly in the medical field, are known as PRECEPTORS; their classes are called PRECEPTORIALS.

A RECEPTACLE is a vessel, container, bin, or basket. A RECEPTION is an affair, party, or gathering. ☞ *Many voters showed up at the reception for the candidates.* It is also a greeting, recognition, response, or reaction.

☞ *The superintendent's cool reception upset Jo's parents.* A **reCEPTionist** is employed to greet callers and clients. A **reCEPTive** audience or listener is one that is accessible, interested, approachable, and open-minded. ☞ *We were fearful that the boss wouldn't be receptive to our suggestions.*

Persons who are **susCEPTible** to certain diseases are unresistant, liable, vulnerable, and prone. A ruling, principle, law, or remark can be susceptible to differing interpretations. If by nature we are emotional, tender, soft-hearted, and responsive, we will tend to be susceptible to another's tears, pleas, condition, etc. One's **susCEPTibilities** are one's feelings and sensitivities.

Combining forms: *ac-*, to; *ap-*, to; *con-*, together; *contra-*, against; *de-*, from; *ex-*, out; *im-*, not; *in-*, in; *inter-*, between; *per-*, thoroughly; *pre-*, before; *re-*, back; *sus-*, under.
Antonyms: *conception*—finish, ending, termination, completion, outcome; *deception*—truth, fact, actuality; *deceptive*—genuine, real, true; *except*—include, count, including; *exception*—inclusion, conformity, regularity; *exceptional*—ordinary, customary, common, average; *imperceptible*—obvious, clear, distinct; *inception*—end, close, finish; *intercept*—expedite, permit, transmit; *perceptible*—hidden, obscure, concealed; *receptive*—intolerant, closed, narrow-minded; *susceptible*—resistant, hardened, immune; *unexceptional*—outstanding, noteworthy, significant.

CAPERE: CIP, CUP

The prefix *anti-* of **antiCIPate** does not mean "against," as in antibiotic and antifreeze; it is a variant form of *ante-*, before, as in antedate (to come before in time) and antepenultimate (to come before the next to the last). Hence the literal meaning of the word is "to take before," a cumbersome way of saying expect, foresee, and await. ☞ *We did not anticipate such a large crowd.* It also means precede, prefigure, and foreshadow. ☞ *Quite a few modern inventions were anticipated in the drawings of Leonardo da Vinci.* Anticipate also means prevent, preclude, and nip in the bud. ☞ *We anticipated the high water by stocking up on sandbags.* **AntiCIPation** is expectation, hope, or premonition. ☞ *We were filled with anticipation as the big event approached.*

The word EMANCIPATE is an excellent example of the power of a prefix. The Latin *manceps* is a combination of the words hand and take, meaning literally, "he who takes by the hand," hence a slave. But when the prefix *e-*, out, is affixed, we get "freeing of slaves."

Because President Lincoln issued the EMANCIPATION Proclamation on January 1, 1863, freeing the slaves in the territories still at war with the Union, he earned the epithet, "The Great EMANCIPATOR." One can, of course, be EMANCIPATED from other forms of restraint, such as customs, traditions, prejudices, and fears.

Anything that is in its INCIPIENT stages is beginning, commencing, embryonic, and initial. ☞ *It takes nothing more than an incipient head cold to keep Barfield from work.*

A MANCIPLE is an officer in a monastery or college authorized to purchase provisions; the original meaning of the word was "slave."

In Roman times a MUNICIPIUM was a town whose people enjoyed Roman citizenship but were governed by their own leaders and laws. Today a MUNICIPALITY is a self-governing city, district, parish, town, or village. MUNICIPAL pertains to such a place and its local government. ☞ *In our state all municipal elections are held on Saturdays.*

The literal meaning of PARTICIPATE is to "take a part," hence engage in, enter into, and partake. A PARTICIPANT is a partner, one who takes part, a partaker, PARTICIPATOR, member, party, or actor. ☞ *No professionals can be participants in our amateur tournament.* PARTICIPATION refers to sharing, partaking, or involvement.

A PARTICIPLE is a verbal form used as an adjective. Peggie was devoted (verb) to her devoted (participle) grandparents. PARTICIPIALS beginning with participles, (Listening intently, I heard every creaking board) are intelligible so long as they tie in with the word they modify; in the example above, "listening intently" modifies "I." It is when they dangle, which means "do not so modify," that they cause problems. Note these sentences: A. Reaching the top of the hill, our house could be seen. B. After years of lying on the attic floor, Elinor finally found the family picture album. C. Coming around the bend in the river, the church tower came into view. A PERCIPIENT student, one who is astute, sagacious, sharp, or clever will quickly spot the problems: A. Is this the Case of the Hill-climbing House? B. Didn't Elinor ever come downstairs for meals? Or was she just too dusty? C. Was the tower floating along or stuck in the muddy river?

PRINCIPALS that are adjectives are main, paramount, essential, and fundamental. ☞ *The folks at the head table are the town's principal political figures.* When principals are nouns they are headliners, leads, actors, or protagonists. ☞ *You never get the principals in the touring companies.* Principals are also school heads, preceptors, deans, directors, or chief authorities. ☞ *Biggly spent more time in the principal's office than he did in the classroom.* **PrinCIPally** means mainly, mostly, chiefly, and primarily. ☞ *We sell principally to hardware stores.* A **prinCIPality** is a small state ruled by a **prince.**

Principal's homonym, **prinCIPle,** is a rule, law, theorem, or axiom. ☞ *Ms. Slocum is a whiz when it comes to the principles of physics.* It is also a belief, doctrine, creed, or attitude. ☞ *His principles keep him from working on Sunday.* A **prinCIPled** person is one with high morals, ethics, and standards. One who is **unprinCIPled** is unscrupulous, corrupt, and immoral.

A **reCIPient** is one who receives. ☞ *Three of our saleswomen were recipients of top awards this year.* **ReCIPes** are not confined to the kitchen; they are also procedures, scenarios, schemes, or designs. ☞ *Gomer, what's the recipe for your great success?*

One who lives in an apartment or house is an **ocCUPant,** a resident, householder, tenant, or inhabitant. **OcCUPancy** is use, lodgment, or tenancy. ☞ *The present hotel rate is $49.95 per night, double occupancy.* To **ocCUPy** is to invade, seize, conquer, and capture, or garrison territory in warfare. ☞ *Rebel troops now occupy over half the country.* Occupy also means to fill, take up, use, hold, and utilize. ☞ *The President occupies the White House.* **OcCUPation** is military control, subjugation, conquest, or possession. However, in more peaceful times it is one's job, profession, vocation, calling, or career. ☞ *The witness gave his occupation as office manager.* An **ocCUPational** hazard is a danger that occurs while on the job, such as silicosis for coal miners.

To be **preocCUPied** means for something to be occupied earlier or prior to. ☞ *This apartment is brand new, never preoccupied.* But far more commonly, preoccupied means to be engrossed, absorbed, and immersed. ☞ *Kerri was so preoccupied that she rode right past her bus stop.* **PreocCUPation** may be a matter of concern for renters, but for the most of us it is to be lost in thought.

As it is with all of the large root families, *capere* boasts of a few shirt-tail relatives. A prince and **princess,** as heads of a principality, are members of royalty, but the words are also used to describe those not so high-born. ☞ *He's a prince of a fellow.* **Princely** means noble, magnificent, and grand. ☞ *We thanked them for the princely gift.*

Cable was originally very strong rope; then it became woven metal wire, but today it is a household word for the coaxial cable used for the transmission of television signals.

In earlier times and books a CAITIFF was a despicable person; Oliver Wendell Holmes wrote of one in "Non-Resistance" (1861): "Wisdom has taught us to be calm and meek / To take one blow and turn the other cheek; / It is not written what a man shall do / If the rude caitiff smite the other too!"

Additional English words related to the root: catch, cater, partake, sash.
But not: *disciple* [*discere,* to learn], follower; *hiccup* [imit., earlier *hicket*], sudden breath stoppage and coughing sound; *precipice* [*caput,* head], steep cliff; *reciprocal* [*reciprocus, re-,* back + *pro-,* forth], mutual, sharing.
Combining forms: *anti-,* before; *e-,* out; *in-,* in; *man-,* hand; *muni-,* official duties; *oc-,* against; *parti-,* a part; *per-,* thoroughly; *pre-,* before; *re-,* back; *un-,* not.
Antonyms: *emancipate*—oppress, subjugate, dominate; *incipient*—finished, realized, accomplished; *occupancy*—vacancy, eviction, evacuation; *occupy*—liberate, evacuate, withdraw, abandon; *preoccupied*—attentive, curious, alert; *princely*—vulgar, lowly, base; *principal*—secondary, lesser, peripheral; *unprincipled*—reputable, ethical, conscientious.

CARUS, dear: CHERI, CHARI

Many of the words that derive from *carus* are found in dictionaries of quotations.

"Take a perfect circle, CARESS it and you'll have a vicious circle," Eugene Ionesco, *The Bald Soprano.* To caress is to cuddle, embrace, pat, hug, kiss, and stroke.

"Let us . . . **CHERI**SH, the means of knowledge. Let us dare to read, think, speak, write," John Adams, *A Dissertation on the Canon and Feudal Law.* To cherish is to hold dear, care for, value, prize, and appreciate.

"Romeo: 'I would I were thy bird.' Juliet: 'Sweet, so would I;/Yet I should kill thee with much **CHERI**SHING,' " William Shakespeare, *Romeo and Juliet.* Cherishing is loving, idolizing, nurturing, treasuring, and venerating.

CHARITY is benevolence, humanity, good will, and generosity. "The happiness of life is made up of minute fractions—the little soon forgotten **CHARI**TIES of a kiss or smile, a kind look, a heartfelt compliment. . . ," Samuel Taylor Coleridge, *The Friend. The Improvisatore.* Charities are favors, gifts, and kindnesses.

"I bequeath my soul to God. . . ./For my name and memory, I leave it to men's **CHARITABLE** speeches. . . ," Francis Bacon, from his will.

"But how shall we expect charity towards others when we are **UNCHARITABLE** to ourselves?" Sir Thomas Browne, *Religio Medici.* Uncharitable means unkind, harsh, mean, unforgiving, and not generous.

"From all blindness of heart, from pride, vainglory, and hypocrisy; from envy, hatred, and malice, and all **UNCHARITABLENESS,** Good Lord, deliver us," *The Book of Common Prayer.* Uncharitableness is unkindness, harshness, mercilessness, or hatred.

> **But not:** *charisma* [Gk *charizesthai,* to favor], special magnetic charm or appeal.
> **Combining form:** *un-,* not.
> **Antonyms:** *charitable*—mean, stingy, miserly, cruel, malevolent; *cherish*—despise, neglect, abandon.

CENSERE, to assess, judge: CEN

When the **CENSUS** was taken in ancient Rome, all citizens had to register themselves and their property for purposes of taxation. Today there are people who feel that the census takers seek more information than the government has a right to know about them. It is a battle that flares up every ten years.

CENSURE is the blaming or criticizing of someone. In a legislative body it is an official reprimand. ☞ *There is a resolution on the floor to censure Rep. Smith.* Outside those hallowed halls, however, we may censure anyone we wish to—or not. ☞ *Bull Feathers, our 0 and 9 football coach, is more to be pitied than censured.*

A **RECENSION** is the editing and revision of a literary work; it is also the product of that revising. ☞ *The recension of Orbakov's manuscript improved it immensely.*

An **EXCISE** tax is an internal duty on certain commodities such as tobacco and alcoholic beverages within a country. ☞ *"Excise, a hateful tax levied upon commodities," wrote Samuel Johnson in his 1755 English dictionary.* **EXCISABLE** articles are those subject to excise taxes.

CENSORS are people who attempt to delete or ban articles, books, movies, art works, or anything else they consider objectionable. In attempting to expurgate, suppress, or bury whatever they do not approve of, they often carry out their mission with **CENSORIOUS** attitudes. These attitudes are abusive, carping, faultfinding, and condemnatory.

But not: *censer* [*cendere,* to set on fire], container for burning incense; *recent* [*recens,* fresh] current.
Combining forms: *ex-,* to; *re-,* thoroughly.
Antonyms: *censorious*—endorsing, uncritical, encouraging; *censure*—approval, encouragement, compliment.

CHRONOS, time: CHRON

An ANACHRONISM occurs when a person or event is placed in the wrong time period. In Shakespeare's *Julius Caesar,* Cassius says, "The clock has striken three." But striking clocks were centuries into the future; the first may have sounded at St. Paul's Cathedral in London in 1286. His *Anthony and Cleopatra* includes a reference to the game of billiards, but the two lovers died about 1,500 years before the game is believed to have originated in France. The legend about young George Washington throwing a silver dollar across the Potomac River is also ANACHRONISTIC; our first silver dollars were not issued until 1794, when he was sixty-two years old.

A **CHRON**IC complainer is a person for whom faultfinding is continual, habitual, and persistent. ☞ *Don't look for Mary to be on time; she's a chronically late starter.*

A **CHRON**ICLER of events has to list them in their proper **CHRON**OLOGICAL order. For instance, if the **CHRON**ICLE reports that the *Lusitania* was sunk by a German U-boat before the *Titanic* hit an iceberg, an error in **CHRON**OLOGY has been made. Just as it would if you listed two of the books of the Old Testament by placing 2 **CHRON**ICLES before 1.

SYN**CHRON**OUS events or movements occur simultaneously. Thus, the members of a SYN**CHRON**IZED swimming team perform certain movements at the same time and in the same way. Officials who time sporting events have to make sure their watches—which are most likely highly accurate **CHRON**OMETERS—are synchronized. They are then said to be in SYNC (or SYNCH). When the lips of the movie actors do not move in harmony with the spoken words, the picture and the soundtrack are out of sync. ☞ *The rock group was censured for lip-syncing the songs on their recording.* Relationships between people can be in or out of sync, too. ☞ *Dad and Mom were completely out of sync on where we should spend our vacation.*

A **CHRON**OGRAM is a complicated word game that involves hiding Roman numerals in a phrase or sentence and having them add up to a certain date. Upon the death of Queen Elizabeth I someone supposedly wrote, *My Day Closed Is In Immortality*. Note that the initial letters of each word are, in order, MDCIII, which in Roman numerals, is 1603, the year she died. Beginners, however, would be best advised to stick with simpler forms such as XL, which translates to the number forty and sounds like the word excel.

Another related word is **CRONYISM**, i.e., the practice of appointing one's close friends to important positions. Originally **CHRONY**, a slang word popular at Cambridge University, meant a close and longtime companion.

Combining forms: *ana-*, against; *-gram*, something written; *-meter*, a measuring device; *-ology*, writings; *syn-*, together.
Antonyms: *chronic*—fleeting, temporary; *synchronous*—different, staggered.

CIVIS, citizen: CIT, CIV

To **CIVILIZE** someone is to educate, cultivate, enlighten, and refine that person. That may be what the Romans did to the barbarians way back when, and the barbarians may well have benefited from it. But Huck Finn didn't want any of it. On the first page of Mark Twain's classic, *Huckleberry Finn*, Huck says, "The Widow Douglas she took me for her son, and allowed she would sivilize me; but it was rough living in the house all the time, considering how dismal regular and decent the widow was in all her ways; and so when I couldn't stand it no longer I lit out. I got into my old rags . . . and was free and satisfied." **CIVILIZATION** was hardly Huck's cup of tea; for one thing, it tolerated slavery, and Huck's companion on the raft was Jim, the runaway slave.

An **UNCIVILIZED** person is barbarous and uncouth. Someone who is **CIVIL** is always respectful of his or her elders. **INCIVILITY**, or discourteous behavior is not tolerated.

Someone who is **CITIFIED** enjoys living in a **CITY**. A good **CITIZEN** exchanges **CIVILITIES** with his neighbors and does his **CIVIC** duty when called upon. One doesn't have to take a course in **CIVICS** to appreciate the privileges, rights, and responsibilities of **CITIZENSHIP**.

Additional English words related to the root: citadel, civvies.
But not: *citation* [*ciere*, to move], award, summons.
Combining forms: *in-*, not; *un-*, not.
Antonyms: *citified*—countrified, rustic, rural, pastoral; *citizen*—alien, foreigner, transient, immigrant; *civil*—boorish,

churlish, hostile, rude; *civility*—insolence, rudeness, hostility; *civilization*—savagery, backwardness, barbarousness.

CLAMERE, to call out, shout: CLAIM, CLAM

William Safire, the author of the "On Language" feature in the *New York Times,* says that "The exCLAMation point can be properly used at the end of quoted sentences along with *he shouted* or *she screamed* or *it roared,* but in narrative prose it is used to excess."

In comic strips, "punctuation mark excess" is a daily reality. Seven days a week one can find doubles: "Dang it all, Snuffy!! I fergit!!"; triples: "Well, hi, Andy!!!"; and variety packs: "What are you doing, Beetle?!!"

To exCLAIM is to cry out, blurt, bellow, and howl. ☞ *"You lie!" she exclaimed.* An exCLAMatory sentence is one that shows emotion and rightfully deserves more than a mere period. ☞ *"Wow! Quintuplets!"*

One who deCLAIMs may speak loudly, too, but the turned-up volume may not necessarily reflect strong emotions; the speaker is more likely addressing a group of people in the manner of orating, lecturing, preaching, and pontificating. In Shakespeare's play, *Julius Caesar,* when Mark Antony stands over the body of Julius Caesar and says, "Friends, Romans, countrymen, lend me your ears; I come to bury Caesar, not to praise him," his words qualify as a deCLAMation, an oration, discourse, eulogy, and panegyric. Those who characterize such a speech as deCLAMatory may mean that it is eloquent, fluent, articulate, and expressive, or they may react differently, charging it with being bombastic, pompous, flowery, and pretentious.

To proCLAIM is to declare, announce, broadcast, and report. Proclaiming is often carried out in an official or formal manner. ☞ *At dawn today the government proclaimed a state of war.* As such, it is classified as a public proCLAMation. But it may also be a simple announcement or statement. ☞ *The saleswoman proclaimed that her product was the best on the market.*

To acCLAIM is to shout with joy, call out, praise, and cheer. ☞ *The faculty acclaimed the members of the academic decathlon team.* As a noun it means applause, great praise, enthusiasm, or ovation. ☞ *The drama group's production of* Death of a Salesman *was greeted with acclaim.* acCLAMation is loud shouts of approval, cheers, hurrahs, or hosannas; when a candidate is elected by acclamation, it is by shouts and handclapping rather than by a formal ballot. ☞ *I move that Ophelia be elected chairperson by acclamation.*

To DISCLAIM is to deny, renounce, decline, and reject. ☞ *The suspect disclaimed any responsibility or involvement in the bank heist.* A DISCLAIMER may be either the person who denies any involvement or a statement announcing that denial. ☞ *Parke's disclaimer of authorship of the threatening letter did not sway the jury.*

CLAIM as a verb means to demand, request, and insist on. ☞ *Winnie claimed the house because of her father's will.* It also means to hold, believe, maintain, and think. ☞ *The boys still claim their bikes were stolen, not lost.* As a noun it means a requirement, call, demand, request, or right. ☞ *The parents made unreasonable claims on the coaches' time.* It also means a declaration, statement, assertion, or plea. ☞ *All of us on the jury believed Bill's claim of innocence.* The person who makes a claim is a **CLAIMANT.**

The adjective **CLAMANT** means noisy. ☞ *We were distracted by the clamant cries of the street vendors.* It also means urgent. ☞ *The candidate spoke of the clamant need for reform.*

To RECLAIM is to restore, regain, and get back. ☞ *They were able to reclaim this vast wasteland by irrigation.* The process is called RECLAMATION. ☞ *That couple devoted their lives to the reclamation of our urban homeless.* Unfortunately, some land and some human beings are considered to be IRRECLAIMABLE, i.e., incapable of regeneration, restoration, or rehabilitation. **RECLAME,** a French word that has been taken up by writers of English, means public attention, a talent for getting publicity, and self-advertisement.

In "The Poets" Henry Wadsworth Longfellow claimed that triumph and defeat are found in ourselves and "Not in the **CLAMOR** of the crowded street,/Not in the shouts and plaudits of the throng." Synonyms are racket, din, uproar, tumult, or chaos. As a verb clamor means to shout, cry out, bluster, make a racket, vociferate, and yell. ☞ *The crowd clamored for the actors to come on stage.* **CLAMOROUS** means tumultuous, turbulent, boisterous, and noisy. ☞ *The team returned home to a clamorous welcome.*

But not: *clam* [*clam,* a clamp, from the clamp-like action of the shell], a bivalve mollusk; *clammy* [ME *clammen,* to stick, smear], uncomfortably damp and cold.

Combining forms: *ac-,* to; *de-,* completely; *dis-,* away; *ex-,* out; *pro-,* forward; *re-,* again, back.

Antonyms: *acclaim*—denounce, condemn, criticize; *acclamation*—disapproval, censure, denunciation; *exclaim*—deny, reject, refuse; *clamor*—quiet, calm, tranquility;

clamorous—peaceful, reposed, tranquil, serene; *disclaim*—accept, affirm, consent, approve, acknowledge; *exclamation*—statement, question, mutter, murmur; *proclaim*—retract, recant, recall; *reclaim*—abandon, neglect, waste, reject.

CLAUDERE, to shut, close: CLOS, CLUDE, CLUS

To conCLUDE is to close, end, and terminate. ☞ *I'll conclude my program with a selection from Mozart.* It also means to decide, deduce, infer, and surmise. ☞ *When eight-thirty came around, we concluded that the game had been called off.* A conCLUSion is a close, end, or windup. ☞ *The lawyer finally brought his argument to a conclusion.* A conclusion also refers to a judgment, finding, or decision. ☞ *My conclusion is that you were not at fault.* ConCLUSive evidence is final, decisive, and undeniable. ☞ *Her fingerprint on the knife was the conclusive evidence.*

The original meaning of disCLOSe was to "unopen"; today it means to reveal, make known, and uncover. ☞ *The governor will disclose the details of his plan today.* A disCLOSure is an announcement, declaration, and revelation. ☞ *The disclosure of their relationship caused a scandal.*

To enCLOSe (also inCLOSe) is to close in, surround, and fence. ☞ *When they got their dog, they enclosed the yard.* It is also to insert, contain, and add. ☞ *I am enclosing my check for $7.95.* An enCLOSure is a pen, yard, sty, and corral. ☞ *For an enclosure of this size we need a whole roll of fencing. The envelope contained several enclosures.*

To exCLUDE is to shut out, keep out, and bar. ☞ *The club no longer excludes women.* Exclude also means rule out, omit, leave out, and eliminate. ☞ *Doc excluded food poisoning as the cause of my illness.* An exCLUSion is rejection, barring, or denial. ☞ *The exclusion of non-residents was discussed and voted down.* Something exCLUSive is select, closed, private, and restricted. ☞ *They go to only the most exclusive restaurants.* It also means sole, unshared, and single. ☞ *Tim won't handle a real estate deal unless he is given an exclusive.*

To foreCLOSe on a loan that has not been repaid is to take possession of the property. ☞ *The villain fingered his handlebar moustache as he foreclosed on the poor aged widow's farm.*

To inCLUDE is to contain, have, and hold. ☞ *This package includes everything you will need for the job.* InCLUSive means comprehensive and full. ☞ *Ms. Barky worked here from 1991 to 1996 inclusive.*

To ocCLUDE is to close, shut, or stop up. ☞ *The protesters brought in cars and buses to occlude access to the capitol.* Weather forecasters speak of ocCLUDEd fronts that are formed when a cold front overtakes a warm front and forces it up; to dentists an ocCLUSion is the fitting together of the teeth of the upper jaw with those of the lower jaw when the jaws are closed.

To preCLUDE is to shut off something ahead of time. ☞ *My failure to get a diploma precluded my getting the job I really wanted.*

A reCLUSe is a hermit, loner, or monk. ☞ *I enjoy living in reclusion.* A reCLUSive existence refers to a lifestyle of solitude and privacy.

To seCLUDE is to shut off, keep apart, and isolate. ☞ *Whitley, a very seclusive individual, has again secluded himself in his house.* A seCLUDEd place is isolated, remote, and cloistered. ☞ *I often longed to find a secluded island far away from this troubled world.* SeCLUSion is solitude, privacy, or sequestration. ☞ *Ms. Ima went into seclusion to avoid the press.*

A cloister is a courtyard with open walkways, often in a religious or educational institution; it can also be any quiet, secluded place. ☞ *The closure of the cloister to outsiders took away our place for meditation.* A claustrophobe is a person who has an abnormal fear of enclosed places, such as an elevator or a CLOSet. Cloture is a legislative method of closing debate on an issue and causing an immediate vote to be taken.

A simple sentence is a clause; a subordinate clause contains a subject and predicate but cannot stand alone. A clause is also a provision, proviso, or stipulation. ☞ *Unfortunately, I didn't read all the clauses that were in small print; as a result the dealer repossessed my car.*

But not: *cluster* [AS *clyster,* a bunch], a number of things of the same kind.

Combining forms: *con-,* together; *dis-,* apart; *en-,* in; *ex-,* out; *fore-,* out; *in-,* in; *oc-,* against; *pre-,* before; *re-,* back, away; *se-,* apart.

Antonyms: *conclusive*—doubtful, questionable, tentative; *exclusion*—acceptance, admittance, access; *exclusive*—open, shared, unrestricted; *inclusive*—apart, discrete, unconnected; *reclusive*—monastic, isolated, cloistered; *secluded*—open, public, social; *seclusion*—accessibility, participation, openness.

COLARE, to strain, filter

A coulee is a deep gulch, canyon, or gorge, originally formed by running water. One of these on the Columbia River in central Washington is the site of the Grand Coulee Dam, begun in 1934 and finished in 1942.

To PERCOLATE a liquid is to pass it through a filter. When coffee is brewed in a PERCOLATOR, the liquid is forced up a hollow tube and into a small, usually glass-topped, dome. The liquid gets bubbly and lively as it PERKS.

The process of PERCOLATION is familiar to pharmacists who know of its being used in the extraction of certain drugs, and to geologists who know of it as the movement of water through pores in the soil.

A COLANDER (also CULLENDER) is a perforated kitchen utensil used for draining and straining foods. ☞ *After I wash these vegetables, I'll put them in the colander and let the water drain off into the sink.*

A PORTCULLIS is a heavy protective gate that can be seen guarding the entrance of medieval castles. This gate is made of a large grating of iron or heavy timbers that can be suspended by chains over the opening and let down when intruders approach.

Combining forms: *per-,* through; *port-,* gate.
Antonyms: *percolate*—be lifeless, enervated.

COQUERE, to cook: COC, COT

A PRECOCIOUS child is one who is smart, bright, quick, and clever.

The literal meaning of precocious is "early ripened and cooked beforehand." In other words, precocious children are supposed to be super smart before they are supposed to be.

And that's how the APRICOT got its name, too: it was originally thought of as an early-ripening, sun-cooked peach.

The dry, crisp, toast-like cracker or bread that we call zwieback is twice-cooked; in German "zwie" means twice, and "back" means to bake. And that's the way it is with the BISCUITS we eat. In earlier times they were a seaman's bread, and back then some foods that went to sea on long journeys had to be cooked ahead of time to reduce the chance of spoilage. Before the biscuits were served in the messroom, they were heated once again by the COOK, who was known to the sailors on shipboard as the COOKY.

It is in KITCHENS that tasty treats are CONCOCTED, cooked up, invented, and prepared. Such CONCOCTIONS are the products of men and women who are skilled in the CULINARY arts, those that pertain to COOKING.

A style or quality of COOKERY is called a CUISINE. Many recipes in the Italian cuisine, for instance, call for generous amounts of RICOTTA, a food similar to cottage cheese; it is a RECOOKED cheese used in sandwiches, salads, and desserts.

A KILN is an oven used for firing pottery, baking bricks, and drying lumber.

Combining forms: *apri-*, beforehand; *bis-*, twice; *con-*, together; *pre-*, before; *ri-*, again.
Antonyms: *precocious*—backward, immature, undeveloped.

CREDERE, to believe, trust: CRED

A person who is owed money is a **CRED**ITOR; the one who owes is a debtor. To **CRED**IT means to recognize, honor, attribute, and ascribe. ☞ *The mayor was credited with stopping the riot.* It also means to believe, trust, or accept. ☞ *If we can credit their story, then everything's on the up-and-up.*

As a noun credit is praise for something done. ☞ *You deserve a lot of credit for what you did.* It is a sourse of pride. ☞ *Sal is a credit to the school.* Credit also refers to approval of one's ability to pay on time. ☞ *Your credit is always good at McGafferty's.* In schools, a credit is the unit used to measure a student's progress toward fulfilling requirements for a degree. ☞ *Six more credits and I'm outta here.*

Something that is **CRED**ITABLE is admirable, laudable, commendable, exemplary, or deserving. ☞ *Given the material she had this year, I think Coach Haffley did a creditable job.*

A **CRED**IBLE story is believable, reasonable, and plausible. ☞ *I certainly didn't think their story was credible.* An IN**CRED**IBLE tale is one that is absurd, preposterous, farfetched, and nonsensical. A **CRED**ULOUS person is gullible, overly trustful, and naive. ☞ *Don't let Aunt Emma loose among all those salespersons; she's so credulous she'll buy everything in the store.* An IN**CRED**ULOUS person refers to someone who is skeptical, doubting, distrustful, suspicious, and dubious. ☞ *We were incredulous when Whitney told us the story of his bizarre adventure.* **CRED**ULITY is the willingness to believe, often to the point of trusting too readily.

CREDENCE is belief, acceptance, trust, or confidence. ☞ *Surely you don't give credence to that old wives' tale.* **CRED**ENTIALS are certificates, official testimonials, references, or recommendations. ☞ *With her credentials, she's bound to get the job.*

A **CRED**ENZA is a table, shelf, sideboard, or cabinet used in a church, office, or home. It owes its name to its former use as a place for holding a lord's food for a servant to taste to make sure there was no poison in it.

To ACCREDIT is to assign, attribute, and credit. ☞ *The invention of the sewing machine should be accredited to Elias Howe, not Isaac Singer.* An ACCREDITED school is one that is certified, official, licensed, and recognized; ambassadors and other diplomatic representatives must be accredited by their governments. ACCREDITATION is the act or process of being licensed or officially recognized. ☞ *Several unaccredited schools have recently applied for accreditation.*

To DISCREDIT is to disparage, degrade, defame, and slander. ☞ *The candidate's entire campaign was based on discrediting his opponent.* It also means to disbelieve and to give no credence to. ☞ *We had plenty of reasons to discredit the testimony of the witness.* A DISCREDITABLE act is disgraceful, shameful, and reprehensible. ☞ *Voters finally brought an end to his discreditable career.*

A CREED is usually a statement of a religious belief, doctrine, or dogma. ☞ *Dr. Fields explained the church's creed to the visitors.* Both the Apostles' Creed and the Nicene Creed of the Christian church begin with "I believe," the words that are the literal meaning of both creed and CREDO, its synonym.

To GRANT is to allow, give, permit, and consent. ☞ *The principal granted the club permission to hold a cake sale.* Grant also means to concede, accede, yield, and acknowledge. ☞ *She's too stubborn to grant that I'm always right.* To take for GRANTED, is a phrase meaning to accept without question and to assume. ☞ *We must never take our freedoms for granted.* Grants are gifts, donations, awards, and bequests. ☞ *A foundation made a grant to our school for this project.* GRANTSMANSHIP is the skill in securing grants from government agencies, foundations, or corporations for research and other special projects.

A MISCREANT was originally an infidel, heretic, pagan, or heathen. Its literal meaning being "wrong belief." Today's miscreant is more likely to be a villain, evildoer, scoundrel, or wretch. As an adjective it means villainous, wicked, fiendish, vile, and diabolical. A RECREANT is a coward or quitter, one who is fainthearted, dastardly, or yellow.

But not: *sacred* [*sacer,* holy], hallowed, inviolable.
Combining forms: *ac-,* to; *dis-,* apart; *in-,* not; *mis-,* wrong; *re-,* back.
Antonyms: *accredited*—unofficial, unlicensed, unauthorized, illicit; *credence*—doubt, incredulity, distrust, mistrust, disbelief; *credible*—unbelievable, dubious, unlikely; *credit*—blame, disgrace, disapproval, mistrust; *creditable*—unworthy,

undeserving, disreputable, dishonorable; *credulity*—uncertainty, distrust, suspicion; *credulous*—unbelieving, suspicious, suspecting, wary; *discredit*—praise, laud, support; *discreditable*—admirable, worthy, honorable; *grant*—refuse, withhold, deny, withdraw; *incredible*—believable, unremarkable, ordinary, conventional; *incredulous*—trustful, unsuspecting, naive, gullible; *miscreant*—virtuous, ethical, moral, righteous; *recreant*—valiant, stouthearted, bold, brave.

D

DARE, to give, DAT, DIT

CAPE CANAVERAL, Fla., May 5, was the **DATELINE** on a 1961 news dispatch concerning a Navy test pilot that rocketed 115 miles into space. The pilot, as most Americans know, was Comdr. Alan B. Shepard Jr. Even though datelines still appear in newspaper stories, its namesake, the **DATE**, is usually omitted.

The majority of the articles in a daily paper published several decades ago are of limited interest and are considered **DATED** or OUT-OF-DATE. But stories as historic as the one above are **DATELESS**, meaning timeless, limitless, and endless; some current events are of as much permanent interest to us as, for example, the signing of the Declaration of Independence in 1776.

DATIVE is the name of the grammatical case showing the indirect object, such as the word Ron, in the following sentence: Bill loaned Ron his shotgun.

Strictly speaking, **DATUM** means a piece of information; its plural is **DATA**, meaning facts, information, statistics, or details. In most cases today, however, data is considered correct in both singular and plural senses. ☞ *These data are questionable. Not much data is available at this time.*

An ADDENDUM is something added, such as an appendix found in the back of a book; as it is with the words datum and data, its plural form, unchanged from the original Latin, is ADDENDA. ☞ *The addenda in the back of the book is more than fifty pages long!*

To ADD is to join, sum up, and continue. An ADDITION is both a joining, combining, or summing up, and an addendum, appendage, or annex. ☞ *We'll use this money to pay for an addition to the garage.* As a preposition, it is used in the phrase "in addition to." ☞ *The store now sells videos in addition to books.* Something that is ADDITIONAL is extra or supplementary, whereas an ADDITIVE is combined with or added to something else, such as thinner to paint or coloring to food.

A DIE is one of a pair of DICE; it is a stamping device for the impressing of designs on coins and other metal items; and it is the part of the wall of a building that is different from the upper part, as well as the part of a pedestal between the base and the cap.

To **EDIT** written material is to change, revise, and alter it. ☞ *Marcy is editing her mother's collected letters.* An **EDITOR** prepares and organizes copy for publication. To **EDIT OUT** parts of writing is to expunge, censor, delete, and blue-pencil. An **EDITION** of a book or newspaper is one of a series of printings that are made over a period of time. ☞ *The library has a valuable collection of first editions.* An **EDITORIAL** is a statement of policy or opinion written or spoken by an owner, publisher, or editor of a publication or broadcasting station. To inject one's opinion in what is supposed to be a factual account is called **EDITORIALIZING**; it is often called interpretation or opinion.

A **TRADITION** is a belief, custom, or ritual that is given or handed down from one generation to another. Something **TRADITIONAL** is customary, habitual, routine, and conventional. ☞ *Coach Martin spoke at the traditional homecoming banquet.* **TRADITIONALISM** is the adherence or clinging to tradition; people who revere the past or stick to its beliefs, customs, or habits are called **TRADITIONALISTS.**

A **TRAITOR** gives something across, as to an enemy, and thus **BETRAYS** his or her country. According to some dictionaries, when the betrayer is a woman, she is a **TRAITRESS** or **TRAITORESS.** One infamous example is Mata Hari, the French dancer who spied for the Germans in World War I and was dispatched to **PERDITION,** ruin, damnation, hell, or doom by a firing squad.

If such a **TRAITOROUS, TREASONABLE,** or **TREASONOUS** action is a betrayal of one's country or sovereign, the act is usually regarded as high **TREASON;** petty or petit treason is the murder of a husband by his wife or a master by his servant. A **TRADITOR** was a Christian who betrayed other Christians in early Rome.

To **RENDER** as in the Biblical admonition, "Render therefore unto Caesar the things which are Caesar's" is to **SURRENDER,** yield, hand over, and give up. It also means to play, execute, perform, and do. ☞ *The piano concerto was rendered beautifully.*

To **RENT** is to lease, let, and hire; one's rent is the dues, fee, and payment for the use of something; **RENTAL** agencies may provide **RENT-A-CARS,** housing, or even home maintenance equipment. A **RENTER** is one who has the use of such items in return for payment; if it is housing, he or she is also a tenant, leaseholder, and inhabitant.

RENDEZVOUS was borrowed from the French; its literal meaning meant "present yourself"; synonyms are meeting, appointment, assignation, or date. Thus when Alan Seeger, an American poet who had enlisted in the French Foreign Legion in World War I, wrote a poem entitled "I Have a Rendezvous with Death," he was, as it turned out, predicting his own fate; he was killed shortly thereafter.

To VENDEE is to offer merchandise for sale; its most common synonyms are peddle, hawk, and barter. The seller is a VENDOR and the buyer is a VENDEE. A VENDUE is a public auction at which, usually, VENDIBLE or salable commodities are offered, usually items that are not available through coin-operated VENDING machines.

But not: *date* [Gk *daktylos,* finger], a fruit.
Combining forms: *ad-,* to; *be-,* over; *e-,* out; *per-,* away; *re-, ren-,* back; *sur-,* over; *tra-,* across; *ven-,* sale; *-vous,* you.
Antonyms: *add*—deduct, eliminate, reduce; *addition*—subtraction, decrease, deduction; *dated*—new, fashionable, current; *out-of-date*—stylish, popular, up-to-date; *perdition*—ecstasy, heaven, bliss; *render*—keep, retain, withhold; *surrender*—withstand, oppose, resist; *tradition*—novelty, innovation; *traditional*—unusual, uncommon, unconventional; *traitor*—patriot, loyalist; *traitorous*—true, loyal, steadfast, patriotic; *treason*—loyalty, patriotism; *treasonous*—loyal, faithful, resolute.

DECEM, DEKA, ten: DEC

In the calendars of ancient Rome, back when March opened the new year, the tenth month was **DEC**EMBER. A **DEC**ADE is a period of ten years. A group of ten leading officials of that time was known as **DEC**EMVIRS, literally "ten men." As a method of keeping their soldiers in order, from time to time commanders would select every tenth man for punishment; it was called **DEC**IMATING. Today, however, the tenth part has lost its force so that a newspaper headline saying "Tornado Decimates Forest" means great numbers, rather than ten percent.

Decimating

A **DEC**ATHLETE is a person who participates in a **DEC**ATHLON, a track-and-field contest consisting of ten events. A DOZEN is twelve; it grew from *duodecim* (two + ten) in Latin, to *douzaine* in French, and then to *dozeine* in the fourteenth century English of Geoffrey Chaucer. The Ten Commandments of the Christian religion are also known as the **DEC**ALOGUE.

The DEANS in secondary schools and colleges owe their titles to a Latin word meaning "a person heading a group of ten," and some students owe their scholarships and their parents' good graces to being on the Dean's List or honor roll. Dean and DOYEN are cognate words, both coming from the Latin *decanus*, meaning "chief of ten" in matters of age and experience. ☞ *Mr. Rand and Mrs. Gray, the doyen and doyenne, respectively, for our tour of the museum, were articulate and scholarly guides.*

Just as a quinquennial is a fifth anniversary and a quinquennium is a period of five years, a **DEC**ENNIAL is a tenth anniversary and a **DEC**ENNIUM lasts ten years or a decade. And just as to quadruple one's efforts means to multiply them by four, to **DEC**UPLE is to go at it ten times as hard. ☞ *The counselor said that just doubling my efforts wouldn't make it; she said I'd have to decuple them!*

There are two versions of the history of the word DIXIE, a name given to the Confederate states and popularized by Southern soldiers during the Civil War in the song of that name. One theory is that the word is a spin-off from the Mason-DIXon line. The other view has it coming from *dix*, the French word for "ten," which was the name given to $10 notes issued by a New Orleans bank. ☞ *I crammed my pocket with dixies.*

To DICKER, means to bargain. ☞ *We dickered for hours over the contract.* This word has also traveled a rather twisting road. This is the most likely story: in ancient Rome animal hides were sold in lots of ten; these sets were called *dicuria*. Over the centuries both the bargaining and its word evolved through a number of changes, as has the attitude of many people toward the use of animal furs.

> **But not:** *decant* [Gk *kanthos,* corner of the eye], to pour a liquid from one container into another; *decay* [*cadere,* to fall], to rot; *decease* [*cedere,* to go], to die; *decisive* [*caedere,* to cut], firm.

DERMA, skin: DERM

Oftentimes words that we might think are applicable only to non-human beings hop over into more familiar territories. Consider, please, the PACHY**DERM**. Elephants, rhinoceroses, and pigs are classified as pachyderms; they all have thick skins. But when one person calls another a pachyderm, the meaning is not that he or she loves wallowing in muddy sloughs, but, instead, is thick-skinned to the point of being insensitive to criticism, ridicule, or slander. The same holds true for the adjective PACHY**DERM**ATOUS, which means callous, obtuse, dense, and stupid.

☞ *Good grief, Charlie, your pachydermatous lack of sensitivity to those horrific insults is totally unreal.*

When we run afoul of a slender piece of wood known as a sliver, it goes through the EPI**DERM**IS without any feeling, on its part or ours; however, when it penetrates the **DERM**IS, the nerve network lets us know that we have met with an intruder.

DERMATOLOGY is the branch of science dealing with the skin, and it is our friendly **DERM**ATOLOGIST who is best able to treat **DERM**ATITIS, an inflammation of the skin, or **DERM**ATOSIS, a skin disease.

> **Combining forms:** *epi-*, outer; *-osis*, disorder; *pachy-*, thick.
> **Antonyms:** *pachydermatous*—perceptive, responsive, sharp, alert, keen.

DEXTER, on the right, skillful: DEXT

DEXTERITY is agility, aptitude, skill, adroitness, or expertise. The word works in two ways. First, it is skill in using one's hands, in having good physical coordination. ☞ *Jane used her crutches with great dexterity.* Second, one can have mental dexterity as well. ☞ *It was Kelly's dexterity that won the debate for us.*

The same is true for **DEXT**EROUS (also **DEXT**ROUS); such people may be agile, skillful, adroit, and proficient in the use of their hands. ☞ *That piano number was perfect for showing off her dexterous playing.* On the mental side, the Irish statesman Edmund Burke observed in a 1775 speech that "the study [of law] renders men acute, inquisitive, dexterous, prompt in attack, ready in defense. . . ."

An AMBI**DEXT**ROUS baseball pitcher or tennis player, of which there are few, can throw or serve with either hand. ☞ *We know you're ambidextrous, Jen, but, please, just one hand at a time when eating.* Ambidextrous writers and artists are able to express themselves competently in more than one form, genre, or media. But there is a darker, third side here: an ambidextrous person may be a double-dealer, cheat, deceiver, Judas, and rat.

DEXTER means on the right, as on the right-hand side. And that means favorable, auspicious, fortunate, and of good omen. A person who is **DEXT**ROSINISTRAL is left-handed (sinistral) but has trained the right hand (dextro) for writing.

DEXTROSE, a shortening of **DEXT**ROGLUCOSE, is used in foods and beverages, in making caramel, and in intravenous feedings; it is also called corn sugar and grape sugar.

Combining forms: *ambi-,* both; *dextro-,* chemical term meaning "turning clock-wise."
Antonyms: *ambidextrous, dexterous*—clumsy, inept, bungling, awkward, gauche, unskilled; *dexterity*—maladroitness, ineptitude, awkwardness, languor, sluggishness.

DICARE, to tell, DICERE, to say: DIC

On December 11, 1936, King Edward VIII ABDICATED the throne of the United Kingdom. After renouncing, waiving, relinquishing, and abandoning the kingship, he explained his ABDICATION in a radio broadcast, saying that he could not serve as "I would wish to do without the help and support of the woman I love." When he married Mrs. Wallis Simpson, he gained a new title, that of BENEDICT, a word that comes from a character named BENEDICK, a confirmed bachelor in Shakespeare's *Much Ado About Nothing* who courts and finally marries Beatrice. The word's literal meaning is to "speak well," as it is with BENEDICTION and BENISON, expressions of good wishes, blessing, thanksgiving, or praise. ☞ *The priest gave the benediction at the end of the service.* MALEDICTION and MALISON are the opposite, meaning a curse, anathema, or evil spell. ☞ *The witches chanted a malediction against the king.*

The word ADDICT is frequently used in relation to drugs, and so we have dopefiend, junkie, pothead, or user, but ADDICTIONS are everywhere. Baseball, rock music, the Civil War, and rich, gooey, chocolate desserts are ADDICTIVE to some people. Most of the latter group prefer such synonyms as admirers, devotees, followers, fans, enthusiasts, or buffs.

As a noun CONDITION has three meanings. First, it means state, status, standing, or aspect. ☞ *My car and bank balance are both in lousy condition.* Second, it refers to demand, requirement, proviso, or stipulation. ☞ *My mom says we can get the car repaired if my grades meet her conditions.* Finally, condition as a noun means health, trim, fitness, or problem. ☞ *Meanwhile, working after school will get me in great condition.* As a verb it means prepare, ready, equip, and train. ☞ *Jogging to work will condition me for track.* It also means accustom, habituate, and acclimate. ☞ *Coach has tried to condition us team members to all kinds of football fans.* The word CONDITIONAL means qualified, tentative, or provisional.

President Abraham Lincoln's address at Gettysburg was less than three minutes long and was composed of ten sentences. The occasion was the

DEDICATION, meaning the sanctification, consecration, or hallowing of the national cemetery that was the final resting place of the more than 43,000 soldiers who had given their lives in the three-day battle. Lincoln used the word DEDICATE six times; he also used the synonyms consecrate and hallow in what has become the most famous speech in American history. A DEDICATED person is one who is wholly committed to something such as an ideal or political cause, hence steadfast, committed, faithful, and constant. ☞ *Fran is a dedicated teacher.*

The verb **DICTATE** means to command, order, rule, and direct. ☞ *Hitler dictated what his followers could say and do.* It also means to compose, communicate, say, and speak. ☞ *Ms. Royal dictated those letters yesterday.* As a noun, it is a decree, law, order, ordinance, fiat, or demand. ☞ *I'm glad he finally listened to the dictates of his conscience.* A **DICTATORIAL** attitude or manner is despotic, overbearing, bossy, imperious, and arrogant. ☞ *The new department head is much too dictatorial to suit me.* The noun **DICTATOR** refers to someone who is a tyrant, a despot, or an autocrat.

DICTION refers to one's style of speaking or writing, choice of words, usage, language, or phrasing. ☞ *I done told teach that I ain't got real good diction.* It also means one's speaking effectiveness based on enunciation, pronunciation, articulation, or elocution. A **CONTRADICTION** is a refutation, denial, rebuttal, or negation. ☞ *Your statement is a direct contradiction of the truth.* To **CONTRADICT** is to deny, refute, and counter. ☞ *Do I contradict myself?* The adjective **CONTRADICTORY** means conflicting, opposing, paradoxical, and incongruous. ☞ *The two witnesses gave contradictory statements to the officers.*

We often hear someone say, "That's what the **DICTIONARY** says." *The* dictionary? *A* dictionary would be accurate, for there are many, and no two are alike, and no one dictionary says it all. Some have etymologies, some don't; some report what is considered correct English, but some creators of dictionaries (usually called lexicographers) feel that usage should find a home elsewhere.

A **DICTUM** is a commandment, **EDICT**, fiat, or order. ☞ *The office manager issued a revised dictum this morning.* It is also a saying, adage, axiom, or proverb: A stitch in times saves nine. An **OBITER DICTUM** is an incidental or passing remark or an unofficial opinion. ☞ *The judge insisted that his obiter dictum had no bearing on his decision in the case.*

A DITTY is a short, simple song or poem intended to be sung. **DITTO** marks (" ") placed beneath a word, phrase, or other symbol **INDICATE** that the above is repeated or, more literally, "that which has been said."

The forefinger or INDEX finger is often used as a pointing device, that is, as an **INDICATOR** quite similar in function to the pointer on the dial of a mechanical or electronic instrument. Indexes or INDICES are guides, directories, or listings. ☞ *When I examine reference books, I look first for their indexes.* An index can be a mark, sign, indicator, or guide. ☞ *The pitch of Sister Clara's voice is an index of her mood.*

To indicate is to point out, call attention to, and show. ☞ *Indicate on the map where your land is located.* It is to hint, suggest, imply, make known, and disclose. ☞ *Maude's tone of voice indicated her impatience.* It is also to measure, make known, record, and register. ☞ *These barometer readings indicate the approach of a storm.* An INDICATION is both a sign, signal, hint, or clue. ☞ *The condition of Sue's office was an indication of foul play.* It is also an omen, foreboding, premonition, or portent. ☞ *The look on the principal's face was an indication of an impending outburst.* Something INDICATIVE is suggestive, typical, INDICATORY, symbolic, and characteristic. ☞ *Doc said outright that Bob's behavior could be indicative of mental problems.*

A person who is INDICTED is charged with a crime or other offense, thus accused of, blamed for, and arraigned for. ☞ *The grand jury indicted her for fraud.* It is also used to mean criticize, castigate, censure, and blame. ☞ *Barney indicted all his pals for plotting against him.* An INDICTMENT is an accusation, allegation, implication, or charge. INDICTABLE persons are subject to being indicted.

To INTERDICT is to prohibit or forbid. ☞ *Such actions were interdicted by the church.* As a military term it means to impede or stop an enemy by steady bombing. ☞ *Our constant bombing interdicted their advance; our interdiction saved the city.*

To INDITE is to compose, pen, and write, as a poem or a speech.

JUDGE comes to us from *dicare* (with the help of *jus,* law); a judge is an arbitrator, moderator, ADJUDICATOR, or JUDICATOR. ☞ *Why'd they ask Fred to be a judge at the quilting contest?* It is also to be a critic, evaluator, appraiser, or assessor. ☞ *You voted for me? Hey, you're a good judge of character.* To judge is to give a hearing to, try a case, and sit in judgment, often in a court of law, but perhaps more frequently on the outside. ☞ *"Judge not, that ye be not judged," Matthew 7:1.* It is also to consider, guess, suppose, suspect, and believe. ☞ *The archaeologist judged the shards to be at least 20,000 years old.* A JUDGMENT is a verdict, opinion, finding, or decision. ☞ *The jury's judgment is that she is guilty.* It is also discretion, sense, or acumen.

To ADJUDGE is to assign, award, or decide JUDICIALLY or legally. ☞ *The prize was adjudged to Fred. The defendant was adjudged guilty.* To ADJUDICATE is to settle or judge judicially. ☞ *The faculty committee asked the provost to adjudicate the dispute.* ADJUDICATION is a JUDICIAL, legal, or official decision or sentence; a judicial manner is judgelike, magisterial, and distinguished; it may also be critical, discerning, and careful. The JUDICIARY is the judicial branch of the government. A JUDICIOUS act, decision, or person is sensible, intelligent, and perceptive. ☞ *Many members of the club suspected that the treasurer had not made judicious use of their dues, but only George dared accuse him of being injudicious.*

JURIDICAL pertains to the administration of justice; juridical days are those on which the court can lawfully sit. JURISDICTION is the power, authority, and judicial right, as well as the scope, range, and bailiwick of law enforcement agencies. ☞ *They live outside the jurisdiction of the city police.*

A PREDICAMENT is a dilemma, plight, or quandary, or, on another level, a jam, mess, pickle, or fix. Predicaments are those difficult situations that novelists put their heroes in so that they have to work their way out.

Students of English know that a PREDICATE is usually the tail end part of a sentence, the occupant of the space that follows the subject, and the home of the verb. But when predicate is used as a verb, it is less familiar; it means to proclaim, assert, affirm, and declare. ☞ *Toni's selfless action predicated her basic generosity.* It also means to found, base, or establish. ☞ *The couple's values were predicated on their faith in humanity.*

To PREDICT is to prophesy, prognosticate, and divine, as well as forecast, foresee, and foretell. A PREDICTION is a prophecy, prognosis, or omen. PREDICTORS, i.e., prognosticators, prophets, oracles, or sages claim to have PREDICTIVE powers.

"PREJUDICES," wrote Charlotte Bronte in *Jane Eyre* ". . . are most difficult to eradicate from the heart whose soil has never been loosened or fertilized by education; they grow there, firm as weeds among stones." A PREJUDICED person is biased, opinionated, predisposed, and partisan. ☞ *Moriarty's testimony was stricken on the grounds that he was a prejudiced witness.* In more extreme cases, a prejudiced person might be bigoted, intolerant, racist, sexist, chauvinist, and xenophobic. As a verb, prejudice means to indoctrinate, brainwash, bias, and poison. ☞ *The rabblerouser attempted to prejudice the crowd against us.* It also means to harm, damage, undermine, and injure. ☞ *Van's open hostility prejudiced his chances for parole.* Finally, the word prejudice can be used to mean affect, influence, sway, and slant. ☞ *Her modesty prejudiced us in her favor.*

Something that is PREJUDICIAL is damaging, detrimental, and harmful. ☞ *Don't make any statements that might be prejudicial to our case.* The literal meaning of prejudice is "to PREJUDGE," which, in turn, means to pass judgment prematurely. However, it is also used in the sense of a preliminary judging as in a contest in which PREJUDGING is an early round of evaluating the entrants.

AVENGE and REVENGE are somewhat like fraternal twins; as verbs they are closely related but do not necessarily resemble each other. The word avenge suggests an act of deserved retribution, usually for wrongs done to others; whereas the word revenge suggests malice rather than justice, like getting back at one's enemy by inflicting pain, hitting back, and getting even. Most thesauruses list VENGEANCE, VINDICTIVENESS, reprisal, compensation, and satisfaction among the synonyms of both words. Revenge is also a noun. ☞ *I'll get my revenge!* Both AVENGEFUL and REVENGEFUL persons tend to be VENGEFUL, resentful, spiteful, and unforgiving.

To VINDICATE someone or something is to clear, exonerate, excuse, and pardon; VINDICATION is justification, defense, apology, or exoneration. ☞ *The psychiatrist wrote that Tim's oppressive childhood was a vindication for his antisocial behavior.* A VINDICABLE act is justifiable, defensible, proper, and fitting. ☞ *Did that mean, we wondered, that what Pat did was entirely vindicable?* A VINDICTIVE person is revengeful, pitiless, and bitter. ☞ *Although he seemed to take his dismissal in stride, he later became vindictive, spreading vicious rumors about the company.*

The VALEDICTORIAN of one's high school class is usually the student with the highest academic ranking. The VALEDICTION is the bidding of farewell to the school on behalf of the graduating students. A VALEDICTORY is any farewell address.

Additional English words related to the root: digit, preach.

But not: *dichotomy* [Gk *dichotomia,* in two parts], division into two parts; *mendicant* [*mendicus,* needy], beggar; *modicum* [*modicus,* moderate], minimum; *syndicate* [Gk *sun,* with + *dike,* judgment], alliance.

Combining forms: *a-,* to; *ab-,* away, from; *ad-,* to; *bene-,* well; *con-,* together; *contra-,* against; *de-,* down; *e-,* out; *in-,* in, not, to, upon; *inter-,* between; *ju-, juri-, juris-,* law; *mal-,* bad; *pre-,* before; *re-,* again; *vale-,* farewell; *ver-,* true.

Antonyms: *addict*—withdraw, give up; *adjudge*—adjudicate, decide, pronounce; *avenge, revenge*—forgive, excuse, pardon; *benediction*—curse, malediction; *condition*—incapacitate, disqualify, unaccustom; *conditional*—absolute, unlimited, unrestricted; *contradict*—confirm, endorse, agree; *contradiction*—corroboration, affirmation, agreement; *contradictory*—consistent, compatible; *dedicate*—desecrate, violate, taint; *dedicated*—distant, detached, unconcerned; *dedication*—aloofness, apathy, detachment; *dictatorial*—democratic, liberal, open-minded; *interdict*—allow, permit, legalize; *judgment*—indiscrimination, imprudence, foolishness; *judicial*—hasty, imprecise, uncritical; *judicious*—tactless, imprudent, silly, foolish; *prejudiced*—objective, unbiased, tolerant, fair; *prejudicial*—helpful, understanding, charitable; *vengeance*—mercy, pity, tolerance; *vindicate*—accuse, blame, punish, convict.

DIDONAI, to give: DOS, DOT

The original meaning of ANEC**DOT**E was "unpublished," in the sense of giving out little known facts—frequently secrets—of biography or history. Today, an anecdote is usually an entertaining account of an amusing or personal happening. An ANEC**DOT**AL history is one that features such accounts, often informal and based on the ANEC**DOT**IST's observations or experiences.

British prime minister Benjamin Disraeli, a punster, once said of the elderly in *Lothair* (1870), "When a man fell into his ANEC**DOT**AGE, it was time for him to retire"; the pun was based on an aged man's living with his anecdotes from his past and thus being in his dotage or senility.

An ANTI**DOT**E is a remedy given to counteract something that is poisonous or injurious. ☞ *The good doctor happened to have on hand an antidote for snake bites. More education and jobs are two antidotes for teenage crime.*

A **DOS**E is a portion, amount, or measure. ☞ *A dose of this medicine should soothe her nerves for a while.* It also refers to a disagreeable substance or situation. ☞ *Being turned down by the police academy was a hard dose to swallow.*

To OVER**DOS**E means to take so much of a drug that serious illness or death results. It can also mean to experience or take an excessive degree or **DOS**AGE of something less lethal. ☞ *Henny's problem was that he'd overdosed on French novels, Italian art, and Greek sculpture.*

But not: *dote* [ME *dotein,* to be foolish], fuss over.
Combining forms: *anti-,* against; *anec-,* out.

DISCERE, to learn: DISCI

DISCIPLINE has three distinct meanings. First, it is a field, subject, branch, area, or curriculum. ☞ *Economics is one discipline that I know I could never fathom.* It is also a drill, exercise, training, indoctrination, or enforcement of rules. Finally, discipline means to check, curb, regulate, manage, train, and control. ☞ *Let the word go forth from this time and place . . . that the torch has been passed to a new generation of Americans, born in this century, tempered by war, disciplined by a hard and bitter peace. . . ," John F. Kennedy, Inaugural Address.*

To discipline is to instruct, train, educate, and prepare. ☞ *Her parents disciplined her in both manners and mathematics.* It also refers to punish, reprimand, chastise, and castigate. ☞ *It's no wonder Budd's the way he is; no one ever disciplined him.*

DISCIPLINARY committees are those that enforce or administer discipline. A **DISCIPLINARIAN** is an authoritarian, taskmaster, autocrat, or dictator. ☞ *Is there a drill sergeant alive who is not a strict disciplinarian?* A **SELF-DISCIPLINED** person is self-controlled, independent, stable, and self-possessed; an **UNDISCIPLINED** person isn't.

St. Matthew, one of the twelve Apostles of the New Testament of the Bible and a **DISCIPLE** of Jesus said, "The disciple is not above his master, nor the servant above his lord." A disciple is a follower, adherent, devotee, supporter, student, or pupil. The Irish wit George Bernard Shaw spoofed himself in *The Doctor's Dilemma,* one of his own plays, having a character say, "I don't believe in morality. I am a disciple of Bernard Shaw." And Oscar Wilde, his countryman, said in *Intentions* (1891) that "Every great man nowadays has his disciples, and it is always Judas who writes the biography."

Combining forms: *self-,* by oneself; *un-,* not.
Antonyms: *disciple*—master, guru, leader, teacher, dissenter, critic; *discipline*—weakness, instability, irresponsibility; *undisciplined*—thoughtful, steady, wise, constant, trained, schooled.

DOCERE, to teach: DOC

The original meaning of **DOCTOR** was "teacher," and today most of the professors in our universities have a Ph.D., a Doctor of Philosophy degree. A few of the other earned **DOCTORATE** degrees are D.D.S., Doctor of Dental Science (or Surgery); D.V.M., Doctor of Veterinary Medicine; Ed.D., Doctor of Education; M.D., Doctor of Medicine; S.Sc.D., Doctor of Social Science; and Th.D., Doctor of Theology. While they were in graduate school, they were **DOCtoral** candidates. D.D., Doctor of Divinity, and Litt.D., Doctor of Literature are honorary degrees.

To doctor a cold, aching back, or bruise is one thing, but to doctor a birth certificate, driver's license, or passport is quite another; among its synonyms are adulterate, alter, fabricate, and falsify.

A **DOCument** was once a lesson; later it came to mean written instruction; today it is an official paper, instrument, or legal form. ☞ *The current exhibit features several documents signed by President Cleveland.* A motion picture or television film that is classified as a **DOCumentary** is supposed to be factual; a **DOCudrama,** on the other hand, is a fictionalized account that is based on actual happenings, and a **DOCutainment** is a documentary that is intended to entertain. **DOCumentation** is the presentation of data, evidence, facts, or statistics to back up an assertion or claim. ☞ *What I have said is true, and I have plenty of documentation to prove it.*

A **DOCtrine** is a belief, dogma, philosophy, principle, or tenet relating to a specific subject. ☞ *Their church teaches the doctrine of free will.* A person who is **DOCtrinaire** is dogmatic, rigid, inflexible, or opinionated. A doctrinaire idea is impractical and theoretical. ☞ *We found it impossible to even consider his doctrinaire arguments.* A **DOCtrinal** dispute is often a debate or argument over the fine points of a political, governmental, or religious doctrine. The verb **inDOCtrinate** has two dissimilar meanings. The first meaning is to teach, school, educate, instruct, and inspire. ☞ *Ms. Wilte indoctrinated us with the idea that we could make something of our lives.* The second meaning refers to brainwash, convert, drill, propagandize, train, and proselytize. ☞ *That whole generation was indoctrinated to believe that they were special.*

A **DOCile** child is teachable, manageable, tractable, and amenable, whereas an **inDOCile** one is restive, rebellious, defiant, and disobedient.

A **DOCent** is a guide in an art gallery, museum, zoo, etc., and most often a learned volunteer.

> **But not:** *docket* [orig. obscure], list of cases in court for trial.
> **Combining forms:** *-tainment,* entertainment; *-in,* in, not.
> **Antonyms:** *doctrinaire*—realistic, reasonable, practical, sensible.

DOKEIN, to seem, think: DOX

A DOGMA is a set or system of beliefs, opinions, principles, or tenets, as of a church or a political party. ☞ *I'll never be able to accept the dogmas of that political movement.*

From the word dogma came DOGMATIC, opinionated, intolerant, and doctrinaire. DOGMATISM refers to positiveness, arrogance, and intolerance.

The literal meaning of ORTHODOX is "of the right opinion." Thus, orthodox beliefs are traditional, approved, established, and conventional. ☞ *The older we get the tighter we cling to the orthodox ways of thinking.* It also has the connotation of dogmatic, rigid, strict, conformist, and narrow. ☞ *We'll never hit upon any new ideas if we insist on looking at the problem in the same old orthodox fashion.* A DOXY is a doctrine or opinion; an ORTHODOXY is an orthodox belief.

The literal meaning of HETERODOX is "of strange opinion." Thus, heterodox beliefs or opinions are dissident, iconoclastic, heretical, UNORTHODOX, and radical. ☞ *There is no room in this organization for persons of such heterodox opinions as you have voiced.*

A PARADOX is a seeming contradiction; i.e., it is a statement that at first sight seems to be absurd, but on second sight is proved to be true (or at least not absurd). Consider the opening words of Charles Dickens' *A Tale of Two Cities:* "It was the best of times, it was the worst of times, it was the age of wisdom, it was the age of foolishness. . . ."

A DOXOLOGY is a hymn that contains a statement of praise to God.

> **Combining forms:** *hetero-,* other; *-logy,* ending for names referring to writing, etc.; *ortho-,* correct, right, straight; *para-,* beside; *un-,* not.
> **Antonyms:** *dogmatic*—indecisive, equivocal, ambiguous, uncertain; *heterodox, unorthodox*—approved, devout, pious, conventional, fundamentalist; *orthodox*—peculiar, eccentric, erratic, heretical, offbeat.

DOLERE, to feel pain, grieve, suffer: DOL

To CONDOLE is to sympathize, commiserate, and empathize. ☞ *We condoled with our classmate who had been declared ineligible to play.* CONDOLENCE is sympathy, comfort, consolation, or pity. ☞ *We sent a card of condolence to the child in the hospital. The family received many condolences.* People who are compassionate, sympathetic, kindhearted, and humane are CONDOLENT.

A **DOL**EFUL person is gloomy, sad, dismal, and sorrowful. ☞ *Our speaker related the story of the "Knight of the Doleful Countenance" in Cervantes' novel* Don Quixote. A **DOL**OROUS occasion or event is grievous, wretched, pitiable, and lamentable.

IN**DOL**ENT people are lazy, slothful, languid, lethargic, and sluggish. ☞ *The indolent fellow ordered me to fetch him a couple of cookies and a glass of milk.* But the llama is, too; here's English poet Hilaire Belloc on the subject in *More Beasts for Worse Children* (1897): ☞ *"The Llama is a wooly sort of fleecy hairy goat, / With an indolent expression and an undulating throat. . ."* IN**DOL**ENCE is sloth, laziness, inertia, lethargy, or torpidity. ☞ *It's not illness that keeps Ziggy from working, it's his indolence.*

DOLOR is sorrow and grief; **DOL**ORES is a female name meaning sorrows. CON **DOL**ORE and **DOL**OROSO are directions in music meaning sorrowfully.

> **But not:** *dole* [AS *gedal,* sharing], allotment, portion.
> **Combining forms:** *con-,* together; *in-,* not.
> **Antonyms:** *condolence*—ill will, malice, spite; *doleful, dolorous*—cheerful, happy, bright, lighthearted; *indolence*—industriousness, diligence, exertion; *indolent*—bustling, industrious, energetic, diligent.

DOMINUS, master: DOMIN

Although today the principal synonyms of the word master are chief, leader, boss, principal, and employer, along with those reflecting unusual skills and abilities such as expert, virtuoso, ace, and professional, the word often struck terror into the hearts of the common people back in the days when Lords and Ladies **DOMIN**ATED, controlled, subjugated, **DOMIN**EERED, and tyrannized their lives. Any misstep and they might be tossed into a DUNGEON and their lives ENDANGERED, for the power of the **DOMIN**ANT, controlling, governing, and PRE**DOMIN**ANT rulers spread over their entire DOMAIN, i.e., realm, property, land, estate, or **DOMIN**ION. The chance of DANGER multiplied when the rulers were **DOMIN**EERING, dictatorial, despotic, tyrannical, and oppressive.

Interesting, too, is the number of feminine words in European languages that stem from *dominus:* DAM, DAMA, DAME, DAMSEL, DONA, DONNA, DUENNA, MADAM, MADAME, MADONNA, and MADEMOISELLE. Once an everyday word, today dame is generally reserved for use as a title, e.g., actress

Dame Judith Anderson and ballerina Dame Margot Fonteyn. The corresponding male title, as with actor Sir Alec Guinness and mountain climber Sir Edmund Hillary, is short for sire and comes from the Latin *senex,* "old," while **DON** is a title for a gentleman in Spanish-speaking countries, for a priest in Italy, for a head, tutor, or fellow in England's Cambridge and Oxford universities, and the head of a family in the Mafia.

The mask worn by guests at a masquerade party is called a **DOMINO,** and from that, some speculate, came the name of the game. But an offshoot of that, the placing of great numbers of the tiles upright in rows, just far enough apart so that when the first one is pushed over, a chain reaction results, gave birth to the domino theory that **PREDOMINATED** political thinking during the days of the Vietnam War.

A Scottish schoolmaster is often called a **DOMINE.** Among the given names that mean "of the lord" are **DOMINGO, DOMINIC,** and **DOMINICK** for boys and **DOMINICA, DOMINIQUE,** and **DONNA** for girls. The era since the birth of Jesus is called **ANNO DOMINI** (A.D.), which means "in the year of the Lord."

A **CONDOMINIUM** (**CONDO,** for short) is a large multiple-unit complex in which each component is individually owned.

> **Combining forms:** *anno,* year; *con-,* together; *en-,* to cause to be in; *ma-,* my; *pre-,* before.
> **Antonyms:** *danger*—safety, protection, security; *dominant, predominant*—secondary, minor, lesser, inferior, subordinate; *domineering*—docile, subservient, servile, tractable, timid.

DONARE, to give: DON

One of the fourteenth century characters making the annual April pilgrimage to Becket's shrine at Canterbury in Geoffrey Chaucer's *The Canterbury Tales* is a **PARDONER,** a hypocrite who tries to sell worthless holy relics, a truly **UNPARDONABLE,** inexcusable, and outrageous scheme.

A **PARDON** refers to forgiveness, excuse, release, or absolution. To pardon is to forgive, **CONDONE,** absolve, and exonerate. ☞ *The priest pardoned the man on his deathbed.* A **PARDONABLE** offense is one that can be forgiven, that is **CONDONABLE.**

A **DONATION** is a gift, grant, present, or gratuity. ☞ *Small donations came from former students of the university.* Land given by the government to encourage settlement is known as **DONATION LAND. DONABLE** items are available from government surpluses. ☞ *Our school is eligible* *for donable foods.* A giver is a **DONOR** or **DONATOR**, a recipient is a **DONATEE** or **DONEE**.

But not: Donald [Celtic, world, power], male given name.
Combining forms: *con-*, wholly; *par-*, fully.
Antonyms: *condone, pardon*—condemn, punish, accuse.

DROMEIN, to run: DROME

If during World War I you had been an English Royal Air Force pilot revving up a Sopworth Camel to engage a German Fokker Eindecker in aerial combat, chances are it would have been at an **AERODROME.** That is the British version of our **AIRDROME,** a word that has been largely superseded by landing field and, now, airport.

There are a few **HIPPODROMEs** scattered about today, usually arenas where horse shows are held. A racetrack in ancient Greece was called a **DROMOS.** The one humped camel, native to Arabia and northern Africa and known as a **DROMEDARY,** was once bred for riding and racing.

PRODROME comes to us from medicine and means a sign or symptom of an oncoming disease; a **SYNDROME** is a group of symptoms that are characteristic of a specific disease or disorder.

The **PALINDROME**—a word, phrase, or sentence that reads the same forward and backward—is about four hundred years old, a pretty long run for a word game, although the anagram (rearrange the letter in "post" and you get "pots," "tops," etc.) has a longer history.

"Did," "mam," and "noon" are **PALINDROMIC** starters. A step gets you "live-evil," "Madam, I'm Adam," and "Poor Dan is in a droop." Napoleon's lament regarding his exile to the island of Elba is the subject of this one: "Able was I ere I saw Elba," and the last is in tribute to C. W. Goethals, the engineer of the Panama Canal: "A man, a plan, a canal—Panama."

Combining forms: *hippo-*, horse; *palin-*, again; *pro-*, before; *pseudo-*, false; *syn-*, together.

DUNAMIS, force, power, strength: DYNA

In 1866 when thirty-three-year-old Alfred Nobel, a Swedish chemist, invented a safe form of nitroglycerin, which he called **DYNAMITE,** he took the first step toward the establishment of the world's most prestigious awards. Each year on the anniversary of Nobel's death, prizes are given in the fields of chemistry, economics, literature, medicine, peace, and physics.

Today the word dynamite has also branched out; as an adjective it means wonderful, fabulous, terrific, and awesome. ☞ *That is one dynamite idea!*

A **DYNAmo** is an electric generator; it is short for **DYNAmoelectric,** an adjective pertaining to the conversion of mechanical energy into electric energy (or vice versa). In the workaday world a dynamo is a person who is vigorous, spirited, forceful, aggressive, and hardworking.

In physics, **DYNAmic** pertains to force or power; related words are kinetic, active, and propulsive. A dynamic person is energetic, vigorous, magnetic, charismatic, and intense. Its antonym is static.

DYNAmics is a branch of physics that deals with matter in motion; in the nonscientific world it describes the driving forces in any complex matter. ☞ *Simon is the one candidate who understands the dynamics of congressional politics.*

DYNAmism refers to great force, energy, power, or vigor. ☞ *The dynamism of our new charter has excited the townsfolk.* In philosophy it is a theory or system that explains the workings of nature by the action of force.

To **DYNAmize** something is to activate, energize, mobilize, and animate. ☞ *We all agreed that something must be done to dynamize our local economy.*

A **DYNAst** is a person in power, ruler, or sovereign, especially one who is hereditary. A **DYNAsty** is a sequence of rulers from the same line, family, heritage, or house. ☞ *The Ming dynasty ruled China from 1356 to 1644.* It also may refer to a line of family members who are extremely wealthy and/or powerful. ☞ *The Bayne dynasty has ruled this town since Elmer Bayne founded it a century ago.*

BioDYNAmics is a branch of biology dealing with the activity of living organisms; those who farm **bioDYNAmically,** for example, use only organic fertilizers, etc.

> **Combining form:** *bio-,* life.
> **Antonyms:** *dynamic*—fixed, stable, inert, passive; *dynamite, dynamo*—bore, commonplace, triviality, trifle.

DUO, two: DOU, DUB, DUO, DUP

To be in **DOUbt** about something is to be of two minds, filled, perhaps, with questions, misgivings, **DUBiety,** uncertainty, and apprehension. As a verb it means to question, suspect, dispute, and have misgivings. ☞ *They doubted my ability to get the job done.* **DOUbters** are skeptics, iconoclasts, or disbelievers. The **DOUbting Thomas** of the Bible (John 20: 24–

29) refused to believe in the resurrection of Jesus until he saw Jesus with his own eyes.

Something **DOUBTFUL** is questionable, unconfirmed, speculative, and **DUBIOUS.** ☞ *Her reappointment is rather doubtful at this time.* When people are doubtful, i.e., hesitating between two alternatives, they may be skeptical, distrustful, suspicious, and indecisive. ☞ *I'm doubtful whether this old bus will get us home.*

DOUBTLESS is an adverb meaning absolutely, **INDUBITABLY,** positively, and certainly. ☞ *You doubtless remember last year's 72 to 14 shellacking.* It also has a less positive meaning: probably, most likely, seemingly, ostensibly, and presumably. ☞ *That film will doubtless win an Oscar.* The word **UNDOUBTEDLY** is intended to leave no doubts; among its synonyms are beyond a shadow of a doubt, undeniably, obviously, and incontrovertibly. ☞ *That was undoubtedly the most inane speech I have ever had to listen to.* A **REDOUBTABLE** force is awesome, formidable, commanding, indomitable, and **REDOUBTED.** ☞ *Early in WWII the German army was considered to be redoubtable.*

Dozens (**DUO**, two + *decem,* ten) of **DOUBLES** populate our dictionaries, from double agents (spies in the service of two countries), double negatives (such as, "He didn't never like me"), and double-U, the twenty-third letter of our alphabet.

To **REDOUBLE** is to make twice as great. ☞ *We must redouble our efforts to find that document.*

In the study of languages a **DOUBLET** is one of two words that came into English from the same source, but then followed a different route. For example, the words frail and fragile stem from the Latin root *frangere,* "to break." But frail came into English via the French language, while fragile was borrowed directly from Latin.

To replace the foreign language sound track of a movie with English is to **DUB** it in; the word is short for double. A century or so ago Lewis Carroll, the author of *Alice's Adventures in Wonderland,* invented a game he called **DOUBLETS.** The object is to turn one word into another in a series of steps by changing one letter at a time. (Here's how to change the word pig into the word sty in five steps: *pig* to *wig* to *wag* to *way* to *say* to *sty.*)

Duo + *plicare,* to fold, gives us **DUPLICATE,** an exact copy of something, especially written material, although one can duplicate another's actions or voice. ☞ *Junior often duplicates his father's gestures.* Approximately thirty years ago the office machine that we now refer to as a "Xerox" or "copier" was often referred to as a **DUPLICATOR,** Ditto, or mimeograph.

DUPLICITY is not an admirable characteristic in a person: it means deception, deceitfulness, hypocrisy, or insincerity. A **DUP**LICITOUS person is dishonest, tricky, double-dealing, and untrustworthy.

A **DUP**LEX apartment is one with rooms on two connected floors, whereas a duplex house is a two-family dwelling connected side by side.

Both the **DUB**LOON, an old Spanish coin and the Dutch **DUB**BELTJE were so named because they had twice or double the value of the next smaller piece.

DUAL controls are necessary on cars used in driver education courses; DUALISM refers to something consisting of two parts, such as the belief that humans consist of two parts, body and soul; DUALITY means doubleness and dichotomy, as in the duality of one's citizenship or the duality of truth and fiction.

A DUEL is a contest or combat between two DUELISTS and often carried on according to the official rules of DUELLO. A DUET is a musical composition for two voices or instruments; if the music has two beats to the measure it is called **DUP**LE time.

A playing card with two spots or pips is called the DEUCE; the same is true for dice. Deuce in tennis occurs when the score is 40–40 in a game or 5–5 in a match; two successive points are then needed to win the game or two games to win the set. Deuce is also used as a mild oath. ☞ *Where the deuce is my pen?*

But not: *arduous* [*arduus,* steep], difficult; *redoubt* [*re-,* back + *ducere,* to lead], a small fortification; *redound* [*red-,* back + *unda,* wave], result in, lead to.
Combining forms: *in-,* not; *-logue,* talk; *re-,* back; *un-,* not.
Antonyms: *deuce*—angel, saint, paragon; *doubt*—believe, trust, certainty, belief; *doubtful*—decisive, determined, likely; *doubtless*—arguably, questionably, unlikely; *dubious*—positive, certain, sure; *duplicate*—original, archetype, prototype; *duplicitous*—scrupulous, upright, virtuous; *duplicity*—candor, honesty, veracity.

DURARE, hard, to continue in existence: DUR

In his speech accepting the Nobel Prize for Literature in Oslo, Norway, on December 10, 1950, William Faulkner said, "I believe man will not merely EN**DUR**E, he will prevail. He is immortal . . . because he has a soul, a spirit capable of compassion and sacrifice and ENDURANCE." To endure in that sense is to continue, remain, persist, PERDURE, survive, live on; it also means to suffer, tolerate, bear up, withstand, and sustain. ☞ *"People wish to be liked, not to be endured with patient resignation," wrote Bertrand Russell, British philosopher, in* The Conquest of Happiness (1930).

Endurance is stamina, strength, **DURABILITY**, fortitude, or persistence. An ENDURANCE RACE is designed to test the staying power of both a racing car and its driver; it is also called an **ENDURO.**

ENDURABLE working conditions are bearable, tolerable, and acceptable. If they are **UNENDURABLE,** they are unbearable or intolerable. Something that is **ENDURING** is long-lasting, permanent, continuing, and steadfast. ☞ *It was their enduring faith that enabled them to survive.* **DURABLE** is similar in meaning, especially in the sense of "lasting," but it is most commonly used to mean strong, sturdy, and tough. ☞ *Our products are so durable we guarantee them for life.*

The **DURATION** of something is its term, extent, period, or stretch. ☞ *When I enlisted, I knew I was in for the duration, however long it was to be.* The preposition **DURING** means throughout the duration or continuance of. ☞ *We lived in town during the winter.* It also refers to some time or point in the course of. ☞ *A raccoon got into our garbage can during the night.* **DURESS** is force, constraint, pressure, coercion, threat, or intimidation. ☞ *He claimed that he confessed only because he was under duress.*

INDURATE means to harden. ☞ *A freeze last night indurated the soil in our garden.* As an adjective it means callous, hardened, and unfeeling. ☞ *Despite his own life of suffering, he remained indurate regarding the plight of the orphans.* To be **OBDURATE** is to be stubborn, pitiless, obstinate, and unmoved by persuasion or pity. ☞ *She remained an obdurate sinner for the rest of her life.* It also means to be merciless, cruel, hardhearted, and pitiless. ☞ *The teacher was obdurate in refusing to raise my vocabulary grade.*

Something **PERDURABLE** is permanent, imperishable, and extremely durable; in theology it means eternal and everlasting. ☞ *Rev. Glossip spoke of the perdurable values of a truly religious life.*

> **But not:** *corduroy* [F *cord du roy,* the king's cords], a fabric; *durned* [form of darn, mild curse word]; *verdure* [OF *verd,* green], the green of fresh vegetation.
> **Combining forms:** *en-,* in; *in-,* in; *ob-,* near; *per-,* very; *un-,* not.

Antonyms: *durable*—perishable, cheap, shoddy; *endurance*—frailty, weakness, debility; *endure*—collapse, fall, fail, perish, wither away; *endurable*—insufferable, unbearable, oppressive, overpowering; *enduring*—fleeting, transient, transitory, ephemeral; *obdurate*—flexible, tractable, amenable, compliant, obedient, compassionate, softhearted; *perdurable*—perishable, short-lived, mortal, momentary, transient, limited.

E

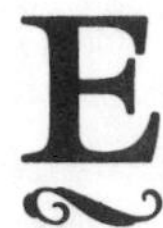

EGO, I: EGO

While some dictionaries and thesauruses lump the **EGOISTS** and the **EGOTISTS** in the same bracket, others draw a thin line between the two, defining an egoist as being self-centered, narcissistic, selfish, arrogant, or conceited, one who believes that every person's actions are motivated by self-interest. ☞ *Sprigley's running for Congress? What we don't need is another egoist in the House!* An egotist, on the other hand, is defined as a braggart, boaster, blowhard, windbag, and show-off.

EGOISM is seeing all things in terms of one's personal interest; it is the opposite of altruism, meaning generosity, good will, humanity, or benevolence. Members of that group are considered **EGOISTIC** or **EGOISTICAL**, i.e., selfish, vain, self-centered, narcissistic, and arrogant.

EGOTISM is boastfulness or conceit, usually accompanied by the excessive use of the "Big I" in conversation and writing; this person is egoistic or **EGOTISTIC**, i.e., boastful, bragging, and conceited.

As is obvious, the line is thin. Members of both classes may well qualify for inclusion in the **EGOCENTRIC** circle, regarding the self as the center of all things. **EGOMANIA** is extreme, abnormal, and excessive self-love, **EGOCENTRICISM**, and **EGOCENTRICITY**. ☞ *Several former party members described the leader as a dangerous egomaniac.*

One's **ALTER EGO** may be one's "second self," such as a deputy or substitute. ☞ *When Al's traveling, Cal, his alter ego, runs the business.* It can also be another aspect of one's self as well as an inseparable friend.

An **EGO TRIP** is a slang expression that describes an act or series of acts that are done to satisfy one's vanity. ☞ *Their heading up that charity drive is one big ego trip, believe me.*

> **Combining forms:** *alter-*, another; *-centric*, centered upon; *-mania*, extreme enthusiasm.
> **Antonyms:** *egoism*—modesty, humility, shyness; *egotism*—bashfulness, self-criticism, self-abnegation; *egotistic*—modest, humble, reserved, unselfish, unpretentious.

EIDOS, form, shape: IDO

An **IDOL** is a hero, inspiration, favorite, god, darling, celebrity, or role model. ☞ *Out of all the good guys in football, why'd you have to pick that fool for an idol?* Back in the days of Nebuchadnezzar, about 2,500 years ago, the people were **IDOLATERS**, worshippers of lifeless golden idols, statues, icons, graven images, symbols, or fetishes. ☞ *The Oscar that Jeffrey won was the golden idol that destroyed his acting career.* But an immoderate or excessive adoration or affection for other kinds of objects also allows one to qualify. ☞ *Young Simson is an idolater of anything on wheels.*

An **IDOLATROUS** person is blindly adoring, worshipful, reverent, pious, and devout. ☞ *The speaker said that too many of us have an idolatrous worship of the past. He repeated advice from Lord Chesterfield's* Letters to His Son *(1774): "Speak of the moderns without contempt, and of the ancients without **IDOLATRY**."*

To **IDOLIZE** is to adore, venerate, revere, glorify, and worship. ☞ *Cartson remarked that he, too, had once passed through the age when youth idolizes military and sports heroes.*

An **IDYLL** is a poem or prose piece describing a picturesque episode or scene of bucolic, pastoral, or rustic life. The mood of such writing is usually one of contentment and peace and is, for the most part, brief. But there are exceptions such as Alfred Lord Tennyson's lengthy *Idylls of the King.* Idyll also denotes a brief and not very serious romantic affair. ☞ *We talked as though we were to be together for life, but it turned out to be but an idyll.* **IDYLLIC** means peaceful, rustic, sylvan, charmingly simple, unspoiled, and romantic. ☞ *Once out of the city we feasted our eyes on the idyllic countryside.*

An **EIDOLON** is an apparition, ghost, spirit, or phantom.

A **KALEIDOSCOPE** is an optical instrument that creates ever-changing patterns and designs; from there, the word spreads out to mean any constantly changing scene or pattern. ☞ *The pageant was a kaleidoscope of elaborate costumes and dances.* The adjective **KALEIDOSCOPIC** pertains to such changes. ☞ *The kaleidoscopic political events confused even the veteran observer.*

EIDETIC pertains to mental images that are so clear, vivid, and lifelike that they appear to be almost actual and physical. ☞ *Our guide at the art museum explained that artists have greater eidetic powers than most people.*

The suffix *-oid* means like and resembling; hence an ANDROID has human features, an ANTHROPOID ape resembles a human being, and ASTEROIDS and PLANETOIDS look like planets or stars in the sky.

Combining form: *kal-,* beautiful.
Antonyms: *idolize*—scorn, despise, loathe; *idolatrous*—impious, blasphemous, irreverent; *idyllic*—homely, familiar, commonplace.

EIKON, image, likeness: ICON

An **ICON** (also IKON) is an image, often of a Christian saint, Jesus, or Mary. On a computer monitor it is a picture or symbol that may be selected by the cursor to exercise the option it represents. ☞ *You need to get the cursor exactly on the icon.* **ICON**IC refers to something that resembles or has the nature of an icon.

Originally an **ICON**OCLAST was a person who had a habit of bashing and smashing religious images and statues, but over the years the meaning has broadened to take in anyone who uses words when trying to batter and shatter another's cherished beliefs and attitudes. ☞ *The instructor's iconoclastic article attacking the fraternity-sorority system is the talk of the campus.* **ICON**OCLASM is the action or the spirit of those who attack traditions or beliefs that they think are based on error or superstition.

ICONOLATRY is the worship of icons; **ICON**OLOGY is the study and analysis of icons, images, and symbols; and an **ICON**OGRAPHY is, among other things, a book of illustrations.

Combining forms: *-clast,* to break; *-graphy,* drawing, writing; *-olatry,* worship; *-ology,* body of knowledge.
Antonyms: *iconoclast*—conformist, assenter, believer, follower, adherent.

ERGON, work: ERG, URG

An **ERG** is a unit of work or energy. Hence, **ERG**OPHOBIA is an aversion to or a fear of work. ☞ *Hey, it's past get-up time; are you an ergophobe or something?* **ERG**OMANIA is a compulsive and excessive addiction to work, often as a symptom of a mental disorder.

There is another out to a person-to-work confrontation, and that is to have an ALL**ERG**Y to physical exertion, to claim to be ALL**ERG**IC to any kind of labor or toil, a condition that an **ALLERGIST** would in ordinary circumstances not be equipped to cope with. However, if the nature of the work involves one or more of such common **ALLERGENS** as dust, pollen, grasses, and certain medications, the doctor may be able to help the patient.

The **ENERGY** that many human beings exult in goes by such names as vigor, verve, vim, vivacity, pep, or power. ☞ *Jog? Now? At this hour? Where in blazes do you get the energy?* **ENERGETIC** people are active, vigorous, animated, spirited, and robust. Technically, to **ENERGIZE** is to supply electrical current, but it is also used in the people sense of vitalize, strengthen, activate, motivate, animate, and stimulate. ☞ *All it took was Tammy's enthusiasm to energize the whole crew.* At the pharmacy an **ENERGIZER** is an antidepressant.

LITURGY is a form of public worship, i.e., religious ceremony, rite, ritual, or mass.

METALURGY is the study of metals and their ores as well as heating, working, and shaping them.

The word **SURGERY** comes from the Greek *kheirourgos,* meaning "working by hand." A good **SURGEON** treats injury and disease by instrumental and manual means. A surgeon works in a **SURGICAL** laboratory or operating room.

> **But not:** *ergo* [L], therefore, consequently; *surge* [*surgere,* to rise], wave, flood; *urgency* [*urgere,* press, push], insistence, importance.
> **Combining forms:** *all-,* different, other; *en-,* in; *lit-,* public; *metal-,* a mine.
> **Antonyms:** *energetic*—lethargic, listless, torpid, lackadaisical; *energy*—inertia, lassitude, listlessness, sluggishness.

ERRARE, to wander: ERR

To **ERR** is to wander, stray, and deviate, often from the straight and narrow path of truth and righteousness; that means to sin, transgress, do wrong, trespass, and misbehave. ☞ *Our pastor admitted to having erred.* It also means to misjudge, miscalculate, misconstrue, and make a mistake. ☞ *The umpire denied that he had erred in calling the runner safe.*

"To err is human" is a centuries-old proverb. "To err is human, to forgive, divine," was written by Alexander Pope almost three hundred years ago. Today's version, credited to the 1978 *Farmer's Almanac,* is "To err is human but to really foul things up requires a computer."

An **ERRor** can be a blunder, oversight, misunderstanding, mistake, or solecism. An error also refers to a fallacy, delusion, offense, transgression, or sin. ☞ *If Frita doesn't see the error of her ways pretty soon, she's going to end up in the slammer.* Something **ERRoneous** is fallacious, mistaken, untrue, spurious, and counterfeit. ☞ *Your data is on the mark, but your conclusions are erroneous.*

An **ERRatum** is an error in printing or writing; it is also called a corrigendum. ☞ *The worst erratum in my article is the misspelling of my own name.* The plural form of erratum is **ERRata** (also corrigenda), but it is often used as a singular noun, especially when it refers to a list of errors. ☞ *The book's errata is listed on page 187.*

Something that is **ERRatic** is odd, peculiar, eccentric, abnormal, deviant, ab**ERRant**, and peculiar. ☞ *Has it occurred to you that Uncle Joe's behavior has been a bit erratic lately? The hike has been postponed because of the erratic weather.*

In medieval times knights used to aimlessly rove the land in search of damsels in distress and other adventures. The most famous of these was Cervantes' Don Quixote, to whom we owe quixotic, meaning absurdly romantic, whimsical, dreamy, madcap, preposterous. It was he who fancied that the windmills he saw were giants and charged them with his lance. Such quixotic dragon-slayers came to be known as knights-**ERRant** and their actions, behavior, and characteristics as knight-**ERRantry**.

Knight-Errantry

An ab**ERRation** is two-sided. First, it is an act of departing from the normal, right, or usual course; synonyms are deviation, oddity, nonconformity, or irregularity. ☞ *The chief warned that there must be no aberrations from the master plan.* Second, aberration is an eccentricity, abnormality, delusion, hallucination, or mental lapse. ☞ *When Grandfather complained about his inability to remember things, Doc assured him it was but a normal aberration.*

But not: *errand* [AS *aerende*], mission; *interrogate* [*inter-,* + *rogare,* to ask], to question.
Combining form: *ab-,* from.
Antonyms: *aberration*—conformity, regularity, standard, sanity; *erratic*—predictable, steady, normal, dependable,

customary, unvariable; *erroneous*—correct, true, factual, valid, sound, right; *error*—accuracy, correctness, flawlessness.

ESSE, to be, exist: SEN, SENT

Irish playwright Brendan Behan had a character in his play entitled *The Hostage* give the word **abSENce** a clever twist: "When I came back to Dublin, I was court-martialled in my absence and sentenced to death in my absence, so I said they could shoot me in my absence."

But there are few if any clever twists when a person serving in the military is AWOL (**abSENT** without leave) from one's base and charged with being a deserter. To be an **abSENTee** from school makes one a truant, from work a shirker or malingerer, and from home a runaway. A citizen expecting to be away from home when the polls are open may vote absentee. However, **abSENTeeism**, frequent or habitual absence from school or work, often becomes a serious problem. However, a person can be sentenced or given an award while **in abSENTia.** ☞ *Because the legislature was in session, Sen. McNeil was awarded her degree* in absentia. An **abSENT-minded** person is one who might turn the cat off and put the TV out for the night.

The **esSENce** of something is its soul, heart, core, or basic quality. The ancient saying, "Time is of the essence" means that it is critical, crucial, imperative, or requisite. But as near perfection as that would seem to be, there is yet another up-step, for the **quintesSENce** of something is even more pure and vital. German philosopher Arthur Schopenhauer urged in *Counsels and Maxims* that we "not shorten the morning by getting up late, [but to] look upon it as the quintessence of life." How did we get the word quintessence? In the philosophy of ancient Greece there were four elements of essences—air, earth, fire, and water. The philosopher Aristotle felt that a fifth essence existed, ether, the substance of which he believed the heavenly bodies were composed. Something that is fundamental, **esSENTial**, or the purest and best of its kind can be labeled **quintesSENTial.**

An **entity** is an object, thing, being, or individual. ☞ *The tribal group has been struggling to retain its entity. Neptune is an entity that we know little about.* A **nonentity** has a much narrower scope, its usual meaning being a person or thing of no importance. ☞ *His problem is that he thinks he's a nobody, a nonentity.* It also refers to a person or thing that exists only in the imagination. ☞ *Little Pam's constant companion is a nonentity, her own creation.*

INESSENTIAL, NONESSENTIAL, and UNESSENTIAL items are unnecessary, superfluous, needless, redundant, and extrinsic. ☞ *These books are nonessential expenditures.* As nouns the words mean excess, superfluity, and extravagance. ☞ *Hey! How come the new unabridged dictionary is listed as a nonessential?*

The word INTEREST means to catch, attract, kindle, arouse, and engage one's attention. A matter of interest is one of concern, significance, importance, note, and consequence. ☞ *I really don't find that idea of any interest at all.* It is attention, reward, curiosity, notice, and scrutiny. ☞ *Fran's new plan has drawn a lot of interest.* It is also a share, portion, percentage, and stake. ☞ *He used to have a substantial interest in that supermarket.* Interest also refers to yield, dividend, profit, gain, and bonus. ☞ *We'd hoped to get a loan at less than 9 percent interest.*

INTERESTS has two meanings. When one's principal interests are reading and gardening they may also be described as hobbies, pastimes, pursuits, or avocations. But at other times one's interests may be affairs, businesses, properties, concerns, or occupations.

To BE INTERESTED (or interested *in*) is to be fascinated or attracted (by), drawn (to), curious (about), and involved (in). ☞ *We talked about the change, and they seemed interested. We're very interested in helping out.* It also means to be involved, concerned, biased, partial, and nonobjective. ☞ *Don't ask Henry about its worth; as an owner, he's an interested party.* A DISINTERESTED person is impartial, objective, neutral, and unbiased. ☞ *Hey! Isn't the judge supposed to be a disinterested party?* An UNINTERESTED person, on the other hand, would be indifferent, uncaring, unconcerned, and bored. A book that one find INTERESTING may be pleasing, entertaining, rewarding, absorbing, and provocative; an UNINTERESTING one is most likely boring, monotonous, tedious, unsatisfying, and trite.

PRESENCE has numerous meanings. One meaning refers to attendance. ☞ *Your presence is requested.* Another meaning is proximity or vicinity. ☞ *It happened in the presence of witnesses.* Presence also means charisma or poise. ☞ *Vivian has remarkable stage presence for a girl her age.*

PRESENT as a noun refers to at the moment or right now. ☞ *At present I am not ready to announce for office.* Present also means now or the time being. ☞ *My accident has taught me to live for the present.* In Lewis Carroll's *Through the Looking-Glass,* Alice and Humpty Dumpty discuss the importance of birthdays: the latter has just celebrated the receiving of an "un-birthday present." "What *is* an un-birthday present?" Alice asks. "A present given when it isn't your birthday, of course," the good old egg answers, and then explains that every year has 364 un-birthdays.

As a verb, present means give, donate, award, and contribute. It also means introduce or bring forward. ☞ *I now wish to present Dr. Lois Gillings.*

And as an adjective, present refers to current and existing. ☞ *Our present governor is up in the polls.* It also means nearby and here. ☞ *Everyone present heard him shouting.*

The adverb PRESENTLY means shortly, pretty soon, and forthwith. ☞ *The film will begin presently.* It also means at present, now, currently, at the moment, and at this time. ☞ *We're presently working on a model of the Globe Theatre.*

A PRESENTATION is an exhibition, production, performance, or proposal. ☞ *This year's presentation was not up to par.* It is a donation, award, contribution, or endowment. ☞ *The award presentation will follow the invocation.* Presentation is also an introduction, ceremony, debut, or unveiling. ☞ *We hope you will attend the presentation of our latest model.* At conventions and conferences, persons heading up small meetings are often called PRESENTERS. One who receives an award may be recognized as the PRESENTEE. At formal ceremonies, participants are expected to be PRESENTABLY attired, meaning suitably, acceptably, neatly, satisfactorily, and appropriately, and the award itself should not be an UNPRESENTABLE object.

To REPRESENT has three meanings. The first is to symbolize, exemplify, epitomize, and stand for. ☞ *Sarah represents all the goodness of our people.* The second meaning is to portray, present, describe, depict, and picture. ☞ *Farnley was represented to us as an industrious worker.* And the third meaning is to stand in for, substitute for, replace, and act for. ☞ *I asked Gene to represent me at the meeting.*

A REPRESENTATION is a likeness, portrait, reproduction, or image. ☞ *This is an accurate representation of what our barn looked like before the fire.* It is also a statement, presentation, position, or assertion. ☞ *A number of representations have been made concerning falsified expense accounts by three employees.* Finally, it is the act of standing in for, substituting for, or acting for. ☞ *One of the cries of our founding fathers was, "Taxation without representation is tyranny!"*

The adjective REPRESENTATIVE means characteristic, typical, symbolic, and exemplary. ☞ *Are these drawings representative of her best work?* It also refers to chosen, elected, democratic, and REPRESENTATIONAL. ☞ *Ours is a representative form of government.* As a noun it is a delegate, emissary, legislator, advocate, or envoy. ☞ *We send our representatives to Congress to act on our behalf.* It is also a salesperson, agent, or worker. ☞ *From now on you're our representative—or rep—in New England.*

Additional English words related to the root: future, improve, pride.
But not: *entitle* [*titulus,* writing on a tomb], authorize; *presentiment* [*sentire,* to feel], a foreboding; *resent* [*sentire*], feel bitter about; *sentient* [*sentire*], conscious, discerning.
Combining forms: *ab-,* away; *dis-,* apart; *im-,* to; *in-,* in, not; *inter-,* between; *non-,* not; *re-,* again; *un-,* not.
Antonyms: *absence*—existence, appearance, attendance; *absent*—available, at home; *absent-minded*—alert, observant, attentive, perceptive; *disinterested*—biased, prejudiced, partial, unfair, inequitable, concerned; *essence*—shell, periphery, adjunct, nonessential; *interest*—indifference, unconcern, apathy; *interested*—bored, wearied, detached; *quintessence*—nonessential, appendage, auxiliary; *representative*—odd, atypical, abnormal, aberrant; *uninterested*—involved, alert, curious, concerned; *uninteresting*—humdrum, trite, insipid, monotonous; *unpresentable*—stylish, proper, tasteful, respectable.

EUS, good, well: EU

EUPHEMISMS are words that sound better, not to the ear, but to one's sensibilities. Because people are sometimes embarrassed by references to body parts, they put a drumstick (but not a leg) on Sissy's plate and some white meat (but not from the breast) on Grandma's. Ladies excuse themselves to go to the powder room, males look for the sign Gentlemen on the door, and when traveling with the kids, parents are ever alert for signs reading Rest Stop or Comfort Station.

EUPHORIA is a feeling of relaxation and well-being, or, as Robert Browning put it in "Pippa Passes," "God's in his heaven, / All's right with the world." **EU**PHONIOUS sounds are sweet and mellow, like church bells in the distance and the cooing of a mourning dove. A **EU**PHONIA is a small tanager with yellow and black feathers and a pleasing song, and a **EU**PHONIUM is a musical instrument similar to the tuba but with a more mellow tone. **EU**PHONY means agreeable sound.

EULOGIES are standard fare at funerals, ceremonies at which we can indulge in high praise without being contradicted or questioned. To **EU**LOGIZE someone on less solemn occasions often seems awkward. Language that is **EU**PHUISTIC is affected and ornate.

EUGENICS is the controversial science of improving the health and strength of human beings through heredity and breeding; Adolf Hitler, the dictator of Nazi Germany, considered it his mission to help perpetuate a master race through eugenics and selective breeding. **EUTHENICS** is the science of bettering the human condition through the improvement of the environment.

The **EUCHARIST** is the sacrament of Holy Communion in the Christian church. **EUTHANASIA** refers to mercy killing or painless death, but it is often pronounced as though it referred to the young people of our planet's largest continent.

EUNICE, a girl's name, means "good victory," and **EUGENE**, a boy's name, means "wellborn."

But not: *eunuch* [Gk *eune,* bed + *echein,* to guard], castrated man; *eureka* [Gk *heureka,* "I have found (it)!"], expression of triumph at a discovery.
Combining forms: *-charist,* to show favor; *-genics,* born; *-log,* to speak; *-phemism,* to speak; *-phony,* sound; *-phoria,* to bear; *-thanasia,* death; *-thenics,* to thrive.
Antonyms: *eulogize*—criticize, condemn; *euphonious*—cacophonous, raucous, harsh; *euphony*—cacophony, harshness, distortion, noise.

F

FACERE, to make, do: FAC, FACE

"There will be time to/Prepare a **FACE** to meet the faces that you meet" is a line in T.S. Eliot's poem entitled "The Love Song of J. Alfred Prufrock." The poet's face is one's visage, countenance, and physiognomy. It is also the look, appearance, or **FACIAL** expression that we prepare to fit the occasion. It can be a mask, facade, or veneer. ☞ *She put on a bold face to hide the hurt that she felt.* An attempt to save face is to protect one's dignity, image, self-respect, name, or reputation. ☞ *Of course he lied; he had to save face, didn't he?* As a verb, it means to confront, meet, encounter, and brave. ☞ *I didn't have the nerve to face Carol after I backed into her car.* And, one might add, especially **FACE TO FACE**, i.e., eye to eye, head to head, and tête-à-tête.

Face

To **deFACE** the **surFACE** of an object is to disfigure or mar it. To **efFACE** an unhappy memory is to eradicate or obliterate it. However, that can be accomplished only if the image is **efFACEable**; like some kinds of graffiti, some haunting memories are **inefFACEable** and indelible. An ombudsman in government, corporations, or universities serves as an intermediary or **interFACE**. ☞ *Troutsen will attempt to interface between the union and management.* **FACing** is decorative trim on such as clothing or walls.

The **FACulty** of an educational institution is its teaching and administrative staff, but it is also a special skill, capacity, knack, or talent that one possesses. ☞ *Natalie has a faculty for management along with putting visitors at ease.* It also refers to one's functions and powers. ☞ *Fortunately, the stroke did not affect his faculty of speech.* One's **FACulties** are one's wits, mental powers, reason, or abilities. ☞ *Even at her advanced age Aunt Nell is still in possession of all her faculties.*

A **FACade** is a front, pretense, veneer, or mask. ☞ *Jeremy always puts up a facade of innocence when confronted.* A **FACsimile** is something made similar, such as a copy, reproduction, photostat, duplicate, replica, and likeness. From facsimile comes FAX, a way of transmitting copies of documents electronically.

Someone who is **FACile** might be skillful or fluent. ☞ *The artisan is extremely facile with his hands.* Facile also means superficial and shallow. ☞ *He answered my serious question in a facile manner.*

The **FACEts** (little faces) of a diamond are the small cut surfaces. A facet of one's character, personality, or philosophy can be a part, side, angle, or perspective. ☞ *Ann's upbeat attitude is one of the finer facets of her character.*

FACility refers to dexterity, fluency, skill, or expertise. ☞ *Tonya speaks French with enough facility to get around in Europe.* It also means ease, effortlessness, or practicability. ☞ *These machines will provide us with far greater facility in our packaging procedure.* To **FACilitate** is to speed up, ease, expedite, and accelerate. ☞ *This computer will vastly facilitate our entire operation.*

> **But not:** *facetious* [*facetia,* humorous, witty], humorous; *preface* [*pre-,* before + *fari,* to speak], introductory statement.
> **Combining forms:** *de-,* undoing; *ef-,* out; *inter-,* between; *-simile,* similar.
> **Antonyms:** *face*—back off, avoid; *facile*—arduous, complex; *facilitate*—complicate, hinder; *facility*—ineptness, rigidity, difficulty; *facsimile*—original; *faculty*—inability, incapacity.

FACERE: FACT

A **FACT** is a reality, truth, deed, or occurrence. ☞ *What are the facts in this case?* **FACTual** accounts are authentic, actual, and unembroidered. A **FACTitious** action or object is the opposite: artificial, contrived, and unnatural. ☞ *Mr. Blasingame's factitious sympathy annoyed us.* ☞ *Jean detests factitious floral decorations; for one thing, she says they cheat her* ol**FACTory** *senses, being without fragrance.* A **FACToid** is a false or made-up statement presented as a fact, often to gain publicity. ☞ *The press agent's factoids didn't fool the newspaper reporters.*

A **FACTion** is a group, sect, or bloc, often one that splinters or breaks off from the larger body, sometimes in conflict and disagreement. Those who break away are charged with being **FACTious,** i.e., divisive, contentious, rebellious, and promoting **FACTionalism** and selfish interests.

A **FACTor** is a consideration or an element. ☞ *Many factors led to Janine's leaving home.* In math it is a divisor. In business it may be a person who acts for another as an agent. ☞ *Uncle Bert is a factor for a company* *that manufactures lawn mowers; he is their leading agent and yet has never visited the factory.* ☞ *He recently dropped his* **UNSATISFACTORY** *line of coffee mugs, key chains, and other such* **ARTIFACTS**. Lawn mowers and coffee mugs are **MANUFACTURED**; excuses and apologies and explanations and alibis also may be **SATISFACTORILY** fabricated, invented, and concocted.

BENEFACTORS and **MALEFACTORS** are opposites. The former is a helper, patron, donor, or supporter, one who provides financial backing. The latter is an offender, lawbreaker, felon, or scoundrel. **FACTOTUMS** are most likely neither; they are usually solid, conscientious folk who, as jacks-of-all-trades, go about the business of tending to their many responsibilities.

An **EX POST FACTO** law is one in which a person is punished for having done something that was not punishable by law at the time. ☞ *My cousin was charged ex post facto with having smuggled a tropical plant into the country; she was finally able to prove that it happened before the plant was banned.*

Combining forms: *arti-*, art; *bene-*, good, well; *male-*, bad, evil; *ol(ere)-*, give off a smell of.
Antonyms: *fact*—fiction, invention, fancy; *factious*—neutral, independent, objective; *factitious*—natural, genuine, artless, real; *factual*—illusory, false, fictitious, imaginary.

FACERE: FEAS, FEAT

One's **FEATURES** are one's qualities or characteristics. ☞ *He has that rare feature of being a good listener.* Features are also the elements of one's face. ☞ *The huge brim on her hat obscured her fine features.* A **FEATURE** story in a magazine or newspaper is one that is given a prominent position; the **FEATURED** speaker at the luncheon is the main one on the program; the featured act at the circus is the special attraction, drawing card, and highlight. As a verb, it means to display prominently. ☞ *The next act features Zelda Zoe.* It also means envision and imagine. ☞ *Well, can you feature* that! To **DISFEATURE** something is to deface, mar, and scar it.

A **DEFEATIST** is a pessimist, sourpuss, quitter, or spoilsport. For such a person life is one **DEFEAT** after another, and he or she is likely to feel thwarted, frustrated, vanquished, and **DEFEATED**.

Although **FEASANCE**, meaning the performing of one's duty, is now obsolete, several descendants survive in the field of law. **DEFEASANCE** is the voiding of a contract or deed. **MISFEASANCE** occurs when a lawful act is carried out in an unlawful manner. ☞ *The judge ruled misfeasance, saying the officer should not have arrested for speeding a man with whom* *he had hitchhiked a ride.* **MALFEASANCE** is malpractice, misbehavior, or misconduct, especially by a public official. **NONFEASANCE** means not doing what one is obligated to do, i.e., failing to act when one's responsibility is to act. ☞ *Our landlord was charged with nonfeasance when he refused to repair our roof.*

A **FEASIBLE** idea or plan is one that is workable, practicable, possible, and reasonable. ☞ *Expecting everyone to contribute one hundred dollars is not a feasible idea.*

> **But not:** *feast* [*festur,* joyous], elaborate meal; *feather* [OE *fether*], type, kind, as in "two birds of a feather."
> **Combining forms:** *de-,* not; *dis-,* away; *mal-,* bad, evil; *mis-,* wrong.
> **Antonyms:** *defeat*—victory, triumph, success; *defeated*—triumphant, successful, victorious; *defeatist*—optimist, achiever; *feasible*—impractical, impossible, unworkable.

FACERE: FECT

AFFECT is a verb with several different meanings. The first meaning is to change. ☞ *Is the rain going to affect our plans?* The second meaning is to move. ☞ *His sad plight affected all of us.* And the third meaning is to fake and feign. ☞ *Two days in London and Martha affects a British accent! Now that's what I call an affectation.*

EFFECT is both a noun and a verb. As a noun it means outcome or result. ☞ *The town felt the effect of the flood for months.* It is force or clout. ☞ *My pleading to use the car had no effect on Mom.* It is operation or action. ☞ *The new rules go into effect immediately.* It also means possessions. ☞ *The court ordered all his personal effects confiscated.* As a verb it means to bring about. ☞ *Her rabbi's lecture effected a complete change in Kathi's attitude.*

The adjective **AFFECTED** means touched and moved. ☞ *Eve was deeply affected by her friend's generosity.* It also means conceited and phony. ☞ *Those two are so affected you can't even talk to them.* An **UNAFFECTED** person is sincere, genuine, and without affectations. **AFFECTING** means heartrending and poignant. ☞ *It was a surprisingly affecting movie; four out of five on the Kleenex scale.* An **AFFECTIONATE** person is filled with love and **AFFECTION**. Oddly enough, the latter also means sickness or disease. ☞ *The heavy smoker suffered from a pulmonary affection.* Its plural form means feelings or emotions. ☞ *She was simply toying with his affections.*

A CONFECTION is a sweet preserve or candy sold by a CONFECTIONER in an immaculate little CONFECTIONERY in a corner of the mall.

To DISAFFECT others is to alienate them. ☞ *The new office manager lost no time in disaffecting all of us.* The DISAFFECTED are alienated and discontented. ☞ *There was no way the governor would get the support of that large bloc of disaffected voters.*

One who DEFECTS is a DEFECTOR, a deserter from the ranks, and DEFECTIONS are not usually taken lightly. A DEFECT is a fault, blemish, failing, or peccadillo, and DEFECTIVE products are not reliable or worth one's while.

EFFECTIVE and EFFECTUAL are generally interchangeable, both meaning adequate, useful, and forceful. ☞ *"Learning, I knew, would be the most effective weapon against the coming years," Gordon Parks,* A Choice of Weapons. Both become negatives when the prefix *in-* is affixed: INEFFECTIVE and INEFFECTUAL. EFFECTUATE means to bring about.

INFECT, INFECTION, and INFECTIOUS are generally negative terms. The flu bug contaminates its prey, as our bad moods or angry words tend to infect or leave a mark on those around us. Infections and infectious ailments are bad news; we try to avoid them. There is, however, a shaft of light here: laughter can be infectious, too, as it catches others in its rays.

PERFECTION may be the ideal state, but that does not mean it is always easy to live with. In the movie *The Odd Couple* there is a PERFECT contrast between roommates Felix, the PERFECTIONIST, and Oscar, the PERFECTLY dreadful slob who would sooner flick the ashes from his PERFECTO onto the rug than into a handy ashtray. Eventually they split; Oscar was totally IMPERFECTIBLE, and his IMPERFECTIONS were far too numerous for Felix to bear. Oscar the Oaf and Felix the Finicky made for an IMPERFECT union.

In English grammar, the past perfect tense of a verb is also called the PLUPERFECT tense; it is the *had* in "She had left by the time I got home." But it also has a broader meaning: more than perfect. ☞ *Carol figure skated with pluperfect precision.*

The dining hall in some colleges and monasteries is called a REFECTORY. It is a place where REFECTIONS are served; they are usually light refreshments, with perhaps a confection for dessert.

If the refectory is in a Jesuit college, the dean or PREFECT might be at the table. In France and Japan a prefect may be a chief civil officer of a PREFECTURE, which is a department or district. In this country some private secondary schools refer to their student leaders as prefects.

Combining forms: *af-*, to; *con-*, together; *de-*, not; *dis-*, away; *ef-*, out; *im-*, not; *in-*, not; *per-*, thoroughly; *plu-*, plus; *pre-*, before; *re-*, again; *un-*, not.
Antonyms: *affectation*—sincerity, simplicity, honesty; *affected*—natural, sincere, apathetic, unmoved; *affection*—coolness, antipathy, detachment; *affectionate*—uncaring, distant, cold, unfeeling; *defective*—intact, functional, whole, normal; *effective*—weak, negligible, inconsequential; *imperfect*—flawless, ideal, absolute; *ineffective*—capable, effectual, productive; *perfect*—flawed, inept, inaccurate, defective.

FACERE: FEIT, FIT

A COMFIT is a confection, usually a candy containing a nut or a piece of fruit. But to DISCOMFIT others is to confuse, embarrass, frustrate, and upset them. ☞ *When I was overweight, I was often discomfited by remarks about the importance of being fit and trim.* DISCOMFITURE is confusion or embarrassment. ☞ *Sensing her discomfiture, we dropped the subject.* It is also defeat or frustration. ☞ *The candidate's hopes resulted in her obvious discomfiture.*

To PROFIT is to gain, BENEFIT, and reap. ☞ *We had hoped Tom would profit from the experience.* A profit is a return, benefit, yield, and harvest. ☞ *Even one year of college will be to your profit.* Something PROFITABLE is gainful, worthwhile, beneficial, or useful, while UNPROFITABLE ventures are useless, harmful, and damaging. Organizations engaged in civic or charitable endeavors are usually classified as NONPROFIT or not for profit; in other words, they were not established for the purpose of making a profit. A PROFITEER is someone who seeks to gain excessive or exorbitant profits, often from the sales of goods that are scarce or rationed.

COUNTERFEIT greenbacks are fake, bogus, phony, and illegal, as all COUNTERFEITERS know. To counterfeit is usually to copy, forge, fake, and falsify. ☞ *The painting they counterfeited wouldn't fool a schoolchild.* It also means to feign, pretend, and deceive. ☞ *Their expressions of sympathy were counterfeited; their tears were as phony as a three-dollar bill.* In Shakespeare's day a counterfeit was a portrait; he mentions "Fair Portia's counterfeit" in *The Merchant of Venice.*

To FORFEIT something is to yield, surrender, waste, and miss. ☞ *We had to forfeit the game because we had an ineligible player.* A forfeit or

FORFEITURE is a penalty, fine, loss, payment, and assessment. ☞ *If I don't get there on time, I'll have to pay a forfeit.*

A SURFEIT is an excess, surplus, or overabundance. ☞ *I thought the store would have a surfeit of those dolls, but they're sold out!* As a verb it means to overeat, stuff, and cram, but it also means to be overloaded, stuffed, and cloyed. ☞ *We were soon surfeited with speeches and ready to go home.*

But not: *fit* [AS *fitt,* struggle], spasm, tantrum; *fit* [ME *fitten*], appropriate, healthy.
Combining forms: *bene-,* good, well; *com-,* together; *counter-,* against; *dis-,* apart, away; *for-,* outside; *non-,* not; *pro-,* forward; *sur-,* above.
Antonyms: *benefit*—loss, detriment; *counterfeit*—genuine, authentic, honest; *discomfit*—support, expedite, encourage; *profit*—drawback, disadvantage, handicap; *surfeit*—dearth, fast.

FACERE; FIC, FICE

An enthusiastic fan of bullfighting in Spanish-speaking countries is called an AFICIONADO; over the years the word's use has broadened, and it now means any enthusiast. ☞ *James is an aficionado of murder mysteries.* An ARTIFICE is a trick or deception. ☞ *It's not really magic; palming that card was a clever artifice.* ARTIFICIAL objects are human-made, synthetic, and spurious, and an artificial smile is forced, feigned, and insincere.

BENEFICENCE is goodness, virtue, or love. ☞ *Marge radiates beneficence.* Something BENEFICIAL is helpful, advantageous, or valuable. A BENEFICIARY of an insurance policy is an heir, inheritor, or receiver, but one can also be the beneficiary of less material things. ☞ *I've long been grateful that I was one of the many beneficiaries of your teaching.*

CERTIFICATES are documents, permits, credentials, diplomas, or written evidence regarding the truth of something. ☞ *We can't complete this sale until I locate my certificate of ownership.*

A DEFICIT is a shortage; DEFICIENT means lacking something. ☞ *His work record proves that he is not deficient in stamina;* a DEFICIENCY is a flaw or an inadequacy. ☞ *Your deficiency in history has now been made up.* A DIFFICULT reading assignment can be arduous and demanding; a difficult math problem can be perplexing, enigmatic, and intricate; a difficult new kid on the block can be ill-behaved, intractable, and obstinate. A DIFFICULTY is a problem, obstacle, tribulation, or hardship.

An EFFICIENT person is capable, competent, and productive. ☞ *What you need is an efficient secretary-wife.* An EFFICIENCY is a small apartment. ☞ *They lived in an efficiency until the baby came.* It is also a measure of the effectiveness of an operation. ☞ *Plan A proceeded with speed and efficiency.* Something that is EFFICACIOUS is efficient, effective, and useful.

An EDIFICE is a large structure or building; it is sometimes a complex argument or idea somewhat similar to an architectural structure. ☞ *His entire career was built on that philosophy, and then one day the entire edifice collapsed.* EDIFICATION is enlightenment, education, improvement, or guidance. ☞ *For your edification, young man, I suggest that you listen to my sermon this morning.*

MAGNIFICENCE is elegance, style, splendor, and grandeur. ☞ *I really didn't appreciate the magnificence of the prairie until I moved to the city.* Something MAGNIFICENT is impressive, imposing, and spectacular. ☞ *The view from her office is—there is no other word to describe it—magnificent.* MUNIFICENCE is generosity, benevolence, largesse, or philanthropy. ☞ *Our symphony owes its success to the munificence of our patrons.* A MUNIFICENT gift or contribution is extremely generous, bountiful, and lavish. ☞ *Without their munificent gifts, this project would be history.*

An OFFICE is a duty, role, position, or post. ☞ *Ted was elected to the office of corporation vice president.* OFFICEs means help, assistance, or favor. ☞ *I landed the job through the offices of a friend.* An OFFICIAL is an executive, director, functionary, or OFFICER; as an adjective it means sanctioned, authorized, certified, authentic, and formal. ☞ *An official investigation will be undertaken.* An OFFICIOUS person is obtrusive, meddling, interfering, and domineering. ☞ *Did you ever know of an office manager who* wasn't *officious?* An UNOFFICIAL action may be informal, private, and unauthorized, not sanctioned or recognized. An ORIFICE is an opening, aperture, vent, pore, or hole.

One who PONTIFICATES, sermonizes, lectures, and harangues. ☞ *Hoo boy! Here comes an hour of pontificating on account of I parked in the wrong space this morning.* A member of the clergy may don PONTIFICAL robes, but when others, such as members of the laity, *become* pontifical, they are pompous, pretentious, overbearing, and patronizing.

A PROFICIENT teacher, businessperson, or worker is adept, expert, competent, and skillful, while one who displays PROFICIENCY is blessed with skill, facility, competence, and expertise.

A SACRIFICE is the offering of an animal, plant, or material possession to a deity. ☞ *The natives sacrificed a lamb to their gods. A priest led the sacrificial lamb to the slaughter.* It is the giving up of one thing for the sake of something else of greater value. ☞ *Our parents made plenty of sacrifices in helping us get through school.* In baseball it is a bunt or fly ball made to advance a runner to another base.

A SIGNIFICANT event is important, meaningful, and indicative. ☞ *My decision to go on to college was a significant turning point in my life.* SIGNIFICANCE is importance, meaning, consequence, or relevance. ☞ *He refused to consider the significance of the doctors' findings.*

Something SPECIFIC is precise, exact, definite, or unequivocal. ☞ *We have to determine the specific time that you left the store.* It also means especial, peculiar, unique, or singular. ☞ *Alf's specific talents are what helped him get a promotion.* SPECIFICALLY means especially, notably, and particularly. ☞ *Meg objected specifically to the clause in fine print.* SPECIFICATIONS (often SPECS) are details, conditions, features, requirements, or stipulations. ☞ *That's a good point, but we need to get down to the specifications of the case.*

To SUFFICE is to serve, satisfy, and measure up. ☞ *Just a simple "thank you" will suffice.* A SUFFICIENT amount of food is enough, adequate, and satisfactory; not enough is an INSUFFICIENCY. A SUPERFICIAL understanding of a subject is fragmentary, shallow, incomplete, and INSUFFICIENT; a superficial wound or mar or cut is skin-deep, surface, and outer; a superficial person is empty-headed, mindless, and frivolous.

The *-fic* endings on the following words come from *facere:* BEATIFIC, meaning blissful, elated, and ecstatic; FELICIFIC, meaning making or tending to make happy; HONORIFIC, meaning implying respect and a title given out of appreciation; PACIFIC, meaning peaceable and calm; PROLIFIC, meaning fertile, fruitful, and productive; and SOPORIFIC, meaning drowsy, causing sleep.

Additional English words related to the root: affair, artifact, chafe, confetti, fashion, feckless, fetish, hacienda, laissez faire, pontiff, and most words ending in *-fy.*

But not: *fictitious* [*fingere,* to touch], imaginary, fanciful; *traffic* [*trans-,* across + *figere,* to fasten], commerce, trade, movement of vehicles.

Combining forms: *a-,* to: *arti-,* art; *bene-,* good, well; *certi-,* sure; *de-,* away; *dif-,* not; *edi-,* building; *ef-,* out; *felici-,* happy; *honori-,* honor; *in-,* not; *magni-,* great; *muni-,* gift; *of-*, work; *ori-*, mouth; *ponti-*, bridge; *pro-*, forward; *proli-*, offspring; *sacri-*, holy; *signi-*, a sign; *speci-*, look; *suf-*, under; *super-*, over; *un-*, not.

Antonyms: *artifice*—honesty, candor; *deficient*—enough, plentiful, normal; *deficiency*—excess, glut, plethora; *deficit*—surplus; *difficult*—docile, obvious, tractable; *difficulty*—ease, pleasure; *efficacious*—impotent, useless; *efficiency*—incompetency; *efficient*—unproductive, slipshod; *insufficient*—ample, adequate; *magnificent*—unassuming, humble, modest; *munificent*—stingy, penurious, parsimonious; *officious*—aloof, indifferent; *proficient*—clumsy, inept; *prolific*—barren, sterile; *significance*—irrelevance, triviality, frivolity; *significant*—meaningless, ambiguous, trifling; *specific*—vague, abstract, general; *soporific*—exciting, stimulating; *suffice*—disappoint, fall short; *sufficient*—meager, scanty; *superficial*—complex, authentic, thoughtful.

FALLERE, to deceive: FAL, FAIL, FAUL

In Shakespeare's *Hamlet,* Polonius gives the following advice to his son, Laertes: "This above all: to thine own self be true, / And it must follow, as the night the day, / Thou canst not then be **FAL**SE to any man." The "false" Polonius is referring to is untrue, inaccurate, wrong, dishonest, and deceitful. In another sense the word means FAUX, artificial, synthetic, ersatz, and fake. ☞ *His words seemed sincere, but the tears were certainly false.* A **FAL**SEHOOD is a lie, prevarication, deception, **FAL**SITY, fabrication, or **FAL**SIFICATION. ☞ *"Do not veil the truth with falsehood, nor conceal the truth knowingly," The Koran 2:42.* A FALSE STEP is a FAUX PAS, blunder, or error, and to **FAL**SIFY is to fake, distort, pervert, disguise, and adulterate. ☞ *It was obvious that Mike had falsified a number of items on his tax return.* A **FAL**SETTO is an unnaturally high-pitched voice, usually in a man.

A **FAL**LACY is an error, mistake, misconception, or false notion. ☞ *It's a common fallacy that everyone needs eight hours' sleep each night.* It is also a flaw, inconsistentcy, non sequitur, or sophism. ☞ *The fallacy in your argument is too obvious to even discuss.* Hence we have **FAL**LACIOUS or false reasoning, **FAL**LIBLE information (false or inaccurate), and fallible human beings (liable to make mistakes). **INFAL**LIBLE refers to sure, trustworthy, free from error, and irrefutable.

As **F** is for false, it is also for **FAIL**, a word most of us are well acquainted with. A **FAIL**ING is a shortcoming, foible, imperfection, weakness, or defect. ☞ *My inability to take tests has been a serious failing.* As a preposition it also means in the absence of, lacking, and without. ☞ *Failing a written excuse, we had to expel him.* A **FAIL**URE can be anything from a collapse, fiasco, or debacle to bankruptcy, insolvency, or ruin. A **FAIL**-SAFE device is one that insures a sound, protected condition in the event of a breakdown or other failure of equipment.

A **FAUL**T is a flaw, failing, an error, or blunder; it is also a break in the layers of rock, usually caused by the movement of the earth's crust. The phrase TO A FAULT means to an extreme degree. ☞ *Mom's generous to a fault.* To FIND FAULT is to seek out flaws. Something **FAUL**TLESS is assumed to be perfect, flawless, immaculate, and impeccable. **FAUL**TY is its opposite, even to the extreme of corrupt, culpable, defective, bad, and inferior. To DE**FAUL**T is to fail to appear, show up, or pay; as a noun it means inaction, neglect, or absence. ☞ *The car was repossessed when the buyer defaulted on his car payment. When Toni failed to show up, Marianne won the title by default.* In computer language, a default is a selection automatically used by a program in the absence of a choice made by the operator.

An additional English word related to the root: faucet.
But not: *falter* [ME *falteren*], hesitate.
Combining forms: *de-*, down; *in-*, not.
Antonyms: *default*—fulfill, satisfy, comply with, appear; *fail*—succeed, thrive, flourish, prosper; *failing*—steadiness, strength, integrity; *failure*—triumph, victory, conquest, luck, winner, achiever; *fallacious*—true, exact, real, factual; *fallacy*—fact, truism, certainty, truth, soundness; *fallible*—perfect, divine, superhuman, infallible; *false*—true, honest, straightforward, genuine; *falsehood*—truth, reality, fact, honesty, honor; *falsity*—truth, candor, authenticity, reality; *fault*—merit, virtue, sufficiency, praise; *faultless*—flawed, defective, incomplete, imperfect, erroneous; *faulty*—sound, blameless, correct, perfect, accurate; *infallible*—errant, errable, mortal, unreliable, dubious, questionable, refutable, untrustworthy.

FELIX, happy, lucky: FELI

Before Walt Disney breathed life into Mickey Mouse, there was **FELIx** the Cat, who, we gather from the name, must have been a happy—or perhaps lucky—feline. Parents who name their daughters **FELIce**, **FELIcia**, **FELIcita**, or **FELIcity** or one of their sons Felix may well have such synonyms as happiness, bliss, joy, ecstasy, or contentment in mind, just as the three Roman Catholic popes who took that name for themselves may have had centuries ago. Or they may have had in mind the alternate meaning of skill, aptness, fitness, or ingenuity. ☞ *Your poems are written with unusual and refreshing felicity.* **InFELIcity** is unhappiness, misfortune, inappropriateness, or inaptness. ☞ *Archie never let us forget what he called the infelicity of his early years. The senator's off-the-cuff remarks were marred by his usual infelicity.*

A **FELIcitous** occasion is enjoyable and happy; it is also one that is appropriate, apt, and suitable. In Marianne Moore's poem entitle "O to be a dragon" she envies that creature because it can be "of silkworm size or immense" or even invisible. The poem ends with "Felicitous phenomenon!" a phrase that demonstrates both meanings of felicitous: the phenomenon is a *happy* one, and the words are most *appropriate.* Certainly, at any rate, not **inFELIcitous** at all.

To a child a kitten or puppy may be **FELIcific** little creatures that bring or create happiness. To **FELIcitate** is to congratulate or compliment on a happy event, just as one can substitute "**FELIcitations!**" for "Congratulations!"

> **But not:** *felicide* [*felis,* cat + *cide,* kill], the killing of a cat.
> **Combining form:** *in-,* not.
> **Antonyms:** *felicitous*—solemn, unhappy, irrelevant, clumsy, inept, awkward; *felicity*—misery, sorrow, clumsiness.

FEMINA, woman: FEMIN

Synonyms listed in many thesauruses for **FEMINine**, an adjective pertaining to a female, girl, or woman, are womanly, girlish, ladylike, dainty, docile, but no **FEMINists**, women who believe in and seek equal rights, would agree with most of them. Certainly not Mary Wollstonecraft, the author of the first feminist manifesto in 1792, nor any of those who attended the first Women's Rights Convention in Seneca Falls, New York, in 1848. **FEMINism** is the doctrine of the movement that advocates social, political, professional, and other rights equal to those of men.

Feminine is also used in a derogatory sense when describing some males, along with EFFEMINATE, meaning womanish, unmanly, weak, and soft. ☞ *After our visitor left, there was a good deal of talk about his effeminate manners and behavior.*

Synonyms listed for **FEMIN**INITY are femaleness, womanliness, girlishness, softness, and gentleness, as the qualities of being feminine. ☞ *Amy is a tough-minded executive and boss, but she's never lost her femininity; no one can say she is unfeminine.*

Book shelves are filled with stories of irresistibly attractive women who, in an aura of charm and mystery, lead men into a trap; such a woman is a FEMME FATALE. Synonyms for the word femme are siren, seductress, or temptress; the fatale situations that men are led into are dangerous, difficult, or disastrous. One of history's most notorious femmes fatales was Mata Hari, a Dutch dancer who assumed that name when she became a German spy during World War I. Today the name is a synonym for a femme fatale or seductive female secret agent. ☞ *Hey, guess who I just saw Ivan with, a regular Mata Hari, I'll bet.* Another femme fatale was the irresistible Cleopatra of Egypt, and two are FEMMES FATALES.

Combining forms: *ef-*, thoroughly; *un-*, not.
Antonyms: *feminine*—masculine, manly, virile, rough, tough, mannish; *femininity*—masculinity, virility, toughness, manliness.

FENDERE, to ward off, strike: FEN

In his poem entitled "Mending Wall," Robert Frost says, "Before I built a wall I'd ask to know/What I was walling in or walling out,/And to whom I was like to give OFFENSE." His sense of offense is insult, disrespect, rudeness, harm, outrage, or impudence. Other meanings of offense are crime, misdemeanor, felony, infraction, or transgression. ☞ *Is that the only offense he was arrested for?* It also refers to attack, aggression, charge, or assault. ☞ *Coach says the Sharks have the best offense in the league.*

OFFENSIVE is an adjective meaning insulting, disagreeable, obnoxious, abusive, and insufferable. ☞ *I refuse to put up with your offensive remarks about our gerbil.* It also means attacking, assaulting, assailing, bombarding, and charging. ☞ *The offensive unit dominated play in the first half.* As a noun it means an attack, onslaught, or aggression. ☞ *Don't try to discuss the crime bill with him; he's always on the offensive.* Someone or something that is INOFFENSIVE is harmless, innocuous, unobtrusive, UNOFFENDING, and tolerable. ☞ *I sensed that you were hurt, but I think she meant it as an innocent and inoffensive remark.*

To OFFEND is to anger, outrage, provoke, and antagonize. ☞ *I had to apologize; after all, I had offended her.* It is also to sin, transgress, and err. ☞ *Her common prayer was that she would never offend.* An OFFENDER is a perpetrator, wrongdoer, culprit, or miscreant.

To DEFEND is to protect, preserve, safeguard, fortify, and secure. ☞ *That's our land, and we intend to defend it.* Defend also means to support, uphold, champion, justify, and stand by. ☞ *I will defend your honor at all costs.* A DEFENDANT is a person against whom a charge is brought in a court, a person accused or sued. ☞ *No, your honor, I happen to be the plaintiff; Mr. Jones is the defendant.*

DEFENSE is protection, support, justification, or vindication; something DEFENSIBLE means being capable of being defended in argument or from assault; anything INDEFENSIBLE, then, is inexcusable, unforgivable, unpardonable, and unspeakable. Which leads us to a remark made by author George Orwell in "Politics and the English Language": "In our time, political speech and writing are largely the defence [British spelling] of the indefensible." In other words, the support of the inexcusable, and that adds up to a DEFENSELESS, weak, and powerless argument.

FENCING is the art or sport in which a FENCER uses a foil or saber to defend and attack her or his opponent. To FEND for oneself is to provide for oneself; to find off blows is to parry, ward off, and resist them. The FENDER on a vehicle protects the rider from splashed-up mud or water, and the one on the front of a fireplace defends the wood floor, rug, or entranced onlookers from hot coals.

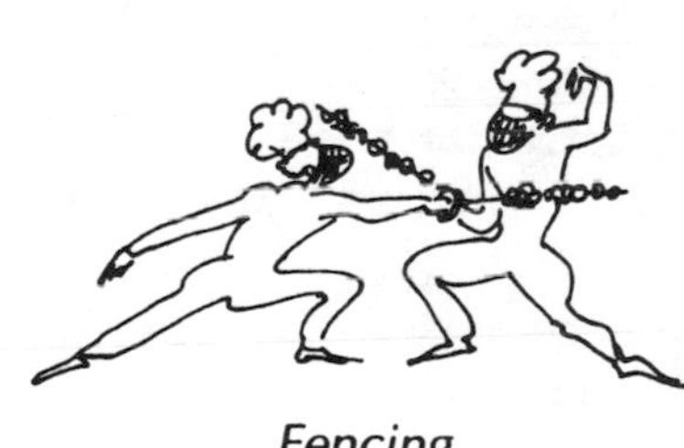

Fencing

But not: *defenestration* [*fenestria,* window], the act of throwing something out of a window; *fen* [AS], a marsh or bog; *fennel* [*faeniculum*], an herb of the parsley family.
Combining forms: *in-,* not; *un-,* not.
Antonyms: *defend*—destroy, attack, undermine; *defense*—offense, prosecution; *defensible*—unsound, implausible, unwarranted; *indefensible*—sound, reasonable; *offend*—please, captivate, charm, beguile; *offense*—innocence, honor, pleasure, satisfaction; *offensive*—agreeable, amiable, polite, respectful, conciliatory, meek.

FERRE, to bear, bring, carry: FER

An **aquiFER** is an underground rock formation that supplies wells, springs, and other sources of our tap water.

To **conFER** is to bestow, consult, grant, and advise. ☞ *Not this evening, Chauncy; we'll confer in the morning.* A **ConFERee** is one who attends a **conFERence** or on whom honors have been **conFERred.** ☞ *Mother Teresa of Calcutta was the conferee of the Nobel Peace Prize in 1979.* A **coniFERous** tree is conebearing; a deciduous tree bears leaves. **CircumFERence** refers to boundary, perimeter, or distance around. ☞ *All the leaves from that oak will fall within the circumference of our yard!*

DeFER means to delay or postpone. ☞ *May we defer payment until next week?* **DeFERence** is respect, esteem, or consideration. ☞ *Everyone stood out of deference to the woman's age and accomplishments.*

DifFER refers to disagree and take issue. **DifFERence** is a disagreement and distinction; **difFERent** is extraordinary, dissimilar, *sui generis.* Thus to be **indifFERent** is to be impartial, uninterested, mediocre, and insignificant. To **difFERentiate** is to understand the differences among those preceding adjectives. The **difFERential** gear in a car enables one wheel to turn at a different rate from the other. The difference between the cost of two comparable products is the differential. ☞ *I don't buy that brand; the price differential between it and this house brand is too great.*

FERtile means creative, productive, and abundant. ☞ *Years of abuse had turned the once-fertile valley into a wasteland. Connat's fertile mind will come up with a new idea before long.* **FERtility** is fruitfulness. ☞ *Our constant composting of kitchen wastes and shredded leaves helps us maintain our garden's fertility.*

InFER means to deduce, conclude, and suppose; obviously, an **inFERence** is a deduction, conclusion, or supposition. Infer is often confused with the word imply. When Frank says, "Hey, I saw you look over at my test paper," he is quite likely implying, hinting, and insinuating that you were cheating. The key point here is that we imply when we speak (or write); we infer from what someone else says (or writes or does).

As a noun **ofFER** is a proposal or bid. As a verb it is to put forward, tender, suggest, and volunteer. ☞ *We made an offer for the car. I offered to help at the library's book sale.* An **ofFERtory** is a collection at a religious service. **OfFERing** has that meaning, too, but it is also any contribution, donation, or gift.

PreFER means to select, like, opt for, and single out. ☞ *I prefer to eat white meat rather than dark meat.*

ProliFERate refers to multiply, increase, and overproduce. ☞ *Those who introduced the rabbit into Australia apparently had no idea how rapidly they would proliferate.*

ReFER means to turn to, pass on, associate with, attribute, and cite. ☞ *Kindly refer to my last letter. Dr. Key referred me to several books in the reference room.* A **reFERent** is that which is referred to. ☞ *When she said, "I love him," her referent, unfortunately, was Sam, not me.* A **reFERral** is an instance of referring as well as a word for a person who has been recommended for something. ☞ *Jon's referral as a transfer patient has finally been approved. Ninety percent of the referrals to this office have found employment.* A **reFERendum** is a popular vote on a measure such as a state lottery; if the results are so close that they are disputed, a **reFERee** may have to be brought in to make the call.

To **sufFER** is to ache, despair, put up with, and endure. Conditions that are **sufFERable** are tolerable, bearable, and endurable. But those conditions that are not are **insufFERable.**

Note how in this passage from Shakespeare's *Measure for Measure* one can substitute the word endurance for **sufFERance** without any great loss: "The poor beetle, that we tread upon,/In corporal sufferance finds a pang as great/As when a giant dies."

TransFER means to sign over, consign, and deed, as well as the word for a ticket used in changing from one public vehicle to another. ☞ *The folks hope to transfer the title to the new owners tomorrow.*

VociFERate means to shout or speak out loudly. Only a noisy and boisterous person could rightly be called **vociFERous,** and only such a person would ever vociferate.

An additional English word related to the root: infertile.
But not: *ferocious* [*ferox,* fierce], savage; *fervor* [*fervere,* to boil], zeal.
Combining forms: *aqui-,* water; *circum-,* around; *con-,* together; *coni-,* cone; *de-,* away; *dif-,* apart; *in-,* in, not; *of-,* to; *pre-,* before; *proli-,* offspring; *re-,* back; *suf-,* up from under; *trans-,* across; *voci-,* voice.
Antonyms: *defer*—advance, expedite, speed up; *differ*—correspond, cooperate; *difference*—similarity, accord, peace; *different*—unvaried, uniform; *differentiate*—homogenize, mix; *fertile*—sterile, impoverished; *indifferent*—concerned, avid, partisan, exceptional; *offer*—refusal, refuse; *prefer*—reject, demote, dislike; *suffer*—repudiate, eliminate, banish, oppose; *sufferance*—intolerance; *vociferous*—muted, silent, taciturn.

FERVERE, to boil, be hot: FERV

Something **FERVENT** or **FERVID**, such as an admirer or plea, is earnest, passionate, fiery, **PERFERVID**, and intense. ☞ *Fervent crowds greeted the president at every stop. "The effectual fervent prayers of a righteous man availeth much," James 5:16.* **FERVOR** is ardor, enthusiasm, excitement, **FERVENCY**, or warmth. ☞ *Bette always greets each new school year with fervor.*

FERMENT is agitation, unrest, turbulence, or uproar. ☞ *The ferment resulting from the robbery went on for several days.* It is also a verb meaning to stir up, provoke, and foment. ☞ *The incident helped to ferment a riot.* **FERMENTATION** is a chemical change caused by a substance such as yeast that produces heat, as when sugar is converted into alcohol.

This process involves **EFFERVESCENCE**, the giving off of small bubbles of gas. An **EFFERVESCENT** person is lively, bubbling, merry, and animated. ☞ *Si's effervescent personality brightens our day.* One's effervescence is one's vivacity, spirit, buoyancy, or ebullience. ☞ *The elderly actress's effervescence saved the play.*

COMFREY is an herb that is sometimes cooked like spinach, planted for its blue or pink blossoms, and used to make tea to cure broken bones—it was once called "knitbone." The word's literal meaning is "boil together."

> **Combining forms:** *com-*, together; *ef-*, out; *per-*, very.
> **Antonyms:** *effervescence*—lethargy, seriousness, sedateness, despondency; *effervescent*—flat, sedate, sober, subdued; *fervent*—apathetic, impassive, dispassionate, detached; *fervor*—apathy, boredom, coolness, detachment.

FIDERE, to trust, FID

According to three handy dictionaries, the verb **AFFIANCE** means to pledge by promise of marriage; to betroth, which means to promise to give in marriage, which means to engage to be married. The man engaged to be married, that is, the man to whom a woman is engaged, is known as the **FIANCE**; the woman engaged to be married, that is, the woman to whom a man is engaged, is known as the **FIANCEE**. Both words are pronounced exactly the same, with the accent on either the second syllable or the third but never the first.

To **CONFIDE** in someone is to reveal, impart, divulge, and confess, usually secrets or inside information passed on in a whisper. ☞ *Jerry* *confides in no one but his wife.* A conFIDant is a close friend or associate to whom secrets are confided.

ConFIDence refers to self-assurance, self-possession, and self-reliance, along with, at times surely, a touch of boldness, daring, nerve, and spunk. Confidence is also certainty, assurance, conviction, or trust in someone or something. ☞*I have absolute confidence in our new treasurer.* ConFIDences are secrets, intimacies, tips, or bits of inside information that one shares with another.

To defy a force is to dare, challenge, confront, flout, and stand up to. ☞*I defy you to prove those charges.* It is also to thwart, resist, baffle, defeat, and repulse. ☞*The airplane defies the laws of gravity. That magician's tricks defy the imagination.* A defiant person is rebellious, fractious, stubborn, and recalcitrant. ☞*Your defiant attitude is going to get you nothing but trouble.* Defiance is rebellion, hostility, contempt, or opposition. ☞*"In war: resolution. In defeat: defiance. In victory: magnanimity. In peace: goodwill,"* wrote Great Britain's Winston Churchill in *The Second World War (1948–54).*

In John Bunyan's *The Pilgrim's Progress,* Giant Despair has a wife, and her name is DifFIDence; because the names of the characters reflect their qualities, she is timid, shy, unsure, self-effacing, and difFIDent.

In "Young Goodman Brown," an allegorical short story by Nathaniel Hawthorne, the hero keeps company with the devil only to lose Faith, his wife, as well as the faith, belief, religion, and trust that he had known all his life. He becomes, in short, a faithless person, i.e., doubting, disbelieving, skeptical, false, and, in more than one way, unfaithful. To be faithful is to be conscientious, scrupulous, and thorough. ☞*We honor you today for your faithful service to this company.* It is to be exact, accurate, precise, literal, and true. ☞*Park's translation is the most faithful to the original Russian story.* It is also to be loyal, devoted, firm, staunch, and reliable.

FIDelity is a favorite name for commercial institutions, for it means loyalty, dependability, integrity, or fealty. ☞*Let's call the folks at the Fidelity Bus Company; they'll get us there on time.* A FIDuciary is a person to whom property is placed in trust for the benefit of another. This person might also be required to sign an afFIDavit, a written declaration made under oath.

InFIDelity is heresy, adultery, unfaithfulness, or falseness. ☞*Infidelity is a frequent cause of divorce.* An inFIDel is an unbeliever, heathen, heretic, pagan, agnostic, or atheist. ☞*In the play now being performed at the village green, St. George slays the infidel knight.* PerFIDy is faithlessness, treachery, betrayal, deceit, or duplicity; the word Judas has come to have a meaning similar to perfidy. Some historians claim that in 1803 Napoleon Bonaparte of France referred to England as "PERFIDIOUS Albion," using the literary name for Britain; it became a popular term in France during the French Revolution. Calling a neighboring country shifty, treacherous, traitorous, and Janus-faced does not make for healthy international relations.

Combining forms: *af-*, to; *con-*, together; *de-*, apart; *dif-*, apart; *in-*, not; *per-*, away; *un-*, not.
Antonyms: *confidant*—stranger, outsider, interloper; *confide*—deny, repudiate; *confidence*—distrust, suspicion, doubt; *defiance*—good will, benevolence, warmth; *defiant*—docile, dutiful, compliant; *defy*—yield, comply, agree, obey; *faith*—mistrust, incredulity, disbelief; *faithful*—deceitful, untrustworthy, imprecise; *faithless*—unwavering, steadfast, true; *fidelity*—unreliability, apostasy, perfidy, falseness; *infidel*—believer, conformist, pietist, religionist; *infidelity*—faith, allegiance, loyalty; *perfidious*—upright, dependable, loyal, reliable; *unfaithful*—chaste, accurate, scrupulous.

FIGERE, to fasten: FIX

FIX is a word of many uses. Who's fixing dinner? Flats fixed here. Let's fix on a time to meet. How are we fixed for cash? I'm fixing to call them right now. This traffic ticket will fix his wagon.

We have light **FIX**TURES in our houses, permanently attached; and at times even real, live people are looked upon as being kind of permanent. ☞ *Fred and Ginger Koss are regular fixtures at our high school games.* The seating in our boardrooms or classrooms is in a **FIX**ED order; it seldom changes. **FIX**INGS (or **FIX**IN'S) are the ingredients or extra dishes at mealtime. ☞ *Grandma'll have turkey and all the fixings.* A **FIX**ATIVE or **FIX**ER is a substance or chemical used in the development of photographs and in the preserving of certain materials for study under a microscope. **FIX**-IT shops are usually run by people who are good **FIX**ER-UPPERS.

As a verb, AF**FIX** means to attach or append. ☞ *The current inspection sticker has now been affixed to the windshield.* As a noun it means something attached or joined; hence a PRE**FIX** (*un*kind, *re*tire) is an affix placed before the base word and a SUF**FIX** is one at the end (kind*ly*, retir*ing*). Titles such as Sergeant, Professor, and Mayor are also prefixes. To IN**FIX** is to implant or fix in the mind. ☞ *The coaches tried to infix the concept of fair play in the athletes' minds.*

When we are TRANSFIXED, we are frozen with amazement or awe. ☞ *We were transfixed by the daring spectacle of the tightrope walker.* A hunter using a bow and arrow, on the other hand, hopes to transfix his prey, i.e., spike, skewer, and impale it.

A **FIXATION** is an idea that gets fixed in one's mind. Many people refer to it as a **FIXED IDEA**, but those who find foreign languages more impressive often prefer the French **IDEE FIX**. Fixation also means obsession, neurosis, quirk, or fetish. ☞ *I'm afraid Aunt Mary will never get over the fixation she has about snakes.*

A **CRUCIFIX** is a cross, with or without the figure of Jesus on it; it is also the name given to a gymnastics stunt. The **CRUCIFIXION** refers to that of Jesus or a picture of it; with the capital letter C it means persecution. ☞ *Life was constant crucifixion for those poor souls.* The literal meaning of **CRUCIFY** is "to put to death on a cross." Its more general meaning is to persecute and torment, or just annoy, tease, and harass someone. ☞ *I hear Rex got crucified for blowing the whistle on the kids who cheated.*

The eave of a building is the overhanging edge of its roof; the board nailed to the underside of the eave is called a **SOFFIT**, meaning, literally, "to fasten underneath."

> **Combining forms:** *af-*, to; *cruci-*, cross; *in-*, in; *pre-*, before; *sof-*, *suf-*, under; *trans-*, through.
> **Antonyms:** *affix*—detach, remove, unfasten; *crucify*—soothe, console, assuage; *fix*—loosen, undo, break, damage; *fixed*—mobile, wavering, pliant.

FLUERE, to flow: FLU

People who are **AFFLUENT** are wealthy, moneyed, rich, and opulent. Money flows to them. **AFFLUENCE** is wealth, riches, means, prosperity, or opulence; it may be in the form of money, property, or other material goods.

A **CONFLUENCE** of people is the flowing together of a crowd, throng, group, or gathering. A confluence is also a flowing together of two or more rivers or streams. ☞ *The confluence of the two longest rivers in the United States, the Mississippi and the Missouri, is just north of St. Louis; that is where the two flow together.*

Sewage and other liquid wastes that flow out of industrial plants and from heavily fertilized farmlands are called **EFFLUENTS**. They often poison the waters of many of the world's great rivers; meantime, aboveground, there is the pollution of the air we breathe by barely visible gases and vapors that we call **EFFLUVIA**.

FLUORESCENT lamps are commonplace in our lives, as are the fluorescent colors that make some children's toys glow so vividly. **FLU**ORIDATION is the addition of sodium **FLU**ORIDE to drinking water to prevent tooth decay. A **FLU**OROSCOPE is a device used to view the internal structure of various objects. ☞ *When Aunt Eva was a child, the shoe stores had fluoroscopes so customers could see how their feet fit into the shoes they were trying on.*

As all poker players know, a **FLU**SH is a hand with all cards of one suit. A player with only four cards of one suit has a FOUR **FLU**SH. Should that player try to bluff the others, he or she FOUR-**FLU**SHES. In poker that's all part of the game, but in the outside world, a FOUR-**FLU**SHER, a person who hopes to deceive others, is not treated so kindly.

The literal meaning of IN**FLU**ENCE is "a flowing in." Its noun synonyms are power, importance, control, domination, prestige, and clout. As a verb it means to sway, bend, induce, motivate, and persuade. A common belief of ancient times was that the power that controlled our destinies flowed in from the stars above.

From influence came the word IN**FLU**ENZA, the name of a disease that killed more than twenty million people worldwide in 1918, for when it first struck the people of Italy during the Middle Ages it was assumed that heavenly bodies were responsible for the epidemic. It is also called **FLU**, grip, or grippe.

A sound that is sweet, musical, and melodious is said to be MELLI**FLU**OUS. ☞ *The place was so quiet that only the mellifluous songs of birds could be heard.* Something that is considered extra, excessive, redundant, and needless is SUPER**FLU**OUS. ☞ *As editor you must blue-pencil all superfluous words.* A SUPER**FLU**ITY is an amount far beyond what is considered necessary or adequate. ☞ *One more word and our speaker will qualify for the Superfluity-of-the-Year Award.*

Additional English words related to the root: fluctuate, fluent, fluid, flux.

But not: *flumadiddle* [*flum(mery),* nonsense + *diddle,* to waste time], utter nonsense; *flurry* [blend of *flutter* and *hurry*], brief bit of activity or excitement; a light snowfall, to confuse; *flush* [ME *flusshen*], to drive birds from cover.

Combining forms: *af-,* to; *con-,* together; *ef-,* out; *in-,* in; *melli-,* honey; *re-,* back; *-scope,* instrument for viewing; *super-,* over.

Antonyms: *affluence*—need, poverty, insolvency; *affluent*—indigent, insolvent, broke; *influence*—ineffectiveness, debility; *mellifluous*—harsh, rough, cacophonous; *superfluity*—dearth, lack, shortage; *superfluous*—essential, vital, indispensable.

FORMA, shape: FORM

ConFORMity, wrote Ralph Waldo Emerson in "Self-Reliance," is "the virtue in most request. Self-reliance is its aversion." That's one side of the coin: submission, obedience, **conFORMance**, subservience, and docility. On the other side it means harmony, accord, affinity, and congruity. ☞ *In this business we must live in conformity with each other as well as with the rules.*

Emerson went on to say, "Whoso would be a man must be a **nonconFORMist**," that is, an individualist, free spirit, rebel, **reFORMer**, or maverick. A nonconformist is also negatively referred to as a kook, oddball, crackpot, or weirdo.

That makes a **conFORMist** a yes-man, standpatter, conventionalist, or **FORMalist**, and makes **nonconFORMity** a rebellion, heresy, defiance, or disobedience.

One meaning of **conFORMation** is compliance, agreement, adaptation, and the act of conforming, but more commonly it has to do with the shape, figure, **FORMation**, structure, or arrangement of something; historian Thomas Macaulay used the word in describing Horace Walpole's mind in *Essays Contributed to the Edinburgh Review* (1843): its "conformation . . . was such that whatever was little seemed to him great, and whatever was great seemed to him little."

To **deFORM** is to distort, mar, disfigure, warp, and misshape. ☞ *That logging operation will inevitably deform that primitive wilderness.* A **deFORMity** is an irregularity, **deFORMation**, **malFORMation**, or disfigurement. Someone or something that is **deFORMed** is abnormal, misshapened, awry, lame, and unnatural. Quasimodo was the deformed hero of Victor Hugo's *The Hunchback of Notre Dame,* and Somerset Maugham gave his semi-autobiographical Philip Carey a clubfoot in his novel *Of Human Bondage* in place of his own severe stammer.

FORM has numerous meanings. As a noun it refers to a body, figure, build, physique, or anatomy. ☞ *He has the form of a weight lifter.* It also means a species, genus, type, genre, or breed. ☞ *A zillion forms of life can be found in that pond.* Another definition of the word form is blank, model, application, or questionnaire. ☞ *I had to fill in a dozen forms at the employment office.* And it could also refer to a mold, pattern, cast, matrix, or outline. ☞ *Remove the form as soon as the wax cools.* Something that is **FORM**LESS is shapeless and UN**FORM**ED.

As a verb form means to devise, develop, fashion, and create. ☞ *Have you formed an overall plan for the exhibit yet?* It also means to fabricate, shape, make, construct, and mold. ☞ *The first step is to form the clay with your hands.*

FORMAL occasions are often proper, legal, ceremonial, and boring, while formal dress and manners are prim, uncomfortable, and pretentious. A **FORM**ALITY is holding firmly to established rules and procedures, sometimes just because that's the way it has always been done. ☞ *After the meeting we all signed the agreement, but that was a mere formality.* An IN**FORM**AL occasion is one in which dress and manners are casual and unpretentious. An IN**FORM**ALITY is ease, laxity, simplicity, and spontaneity. To **FORM**ALIZE something is to make it proper, legal, or formal, in order to give it official acceptance. ☞ *Maybe we should formalize this agreement by drawing up a legal contract.*

A **FORM**AT is a plan, arrangement, blueprint, or proposal. ☞ *The format of this program needs a real overhaul.* To format a computer disk is to prepare it for reading and writing; an UN**FORM**ATTED disk is one that has not been prepared.

A **FORM**ULA is a recipe, prescription, modus operandi, technique, or pattern. ☞ *What I wouldn't give to know her formula for success.* To **FORM**ULATE something is to define or analyze it, to express as a formula; in T. S. Eliot's "The Love Song of J. Alfred Prufrock," the protagonist says, "I have known the eyes already . . . The eyes that fix you in a formulated phrase," that, in other words, reduce you to a meaningless impersonal formula. A **FORM**ATION is a grouping or arrangement, as, for example, in the military. One's **FORM**ATIVE, impressionable years are those in which much molding, shaping, fashioning, and forming occurs.

In the 1935 classic movie *The* ***In*****FORM*****er,*** the actor Victor McLaglen IN**FORM**S, rats, snitches, and squeals on his buddy for a reward; an informer is a stool pigeon, sneak, or IN**FORM**ANT. But an IN**FORM**ED person is one who is knowledgeable, intelligent, and up-to-date. An IN**FORM**ATIVE article is revealing, communicative, edifying, and educational. An IN**FORM**ERCIAL (sometimes INFOMERCIAL) is a radio or television commercial that is intended to inform or instruct as well as to sell you a bottle of Better Breath mouthwash or a box of Oatzie-Branzie cereal.

"Knowledge," in *The Life of Samuel Johnson* by James Boswell, "is of two kinds. We know a subject ourselves, or we know where we can find IN**FORM**ATION about it"; the latter means data, facts, accounts, reports, or intelligence. **DisinFORMation** refers to **misinFORMation**, lies, fabrications, misrepresentations, or prevarications. To **disinFORM** is to **misinFORM**, deceive, delude, and bamboozle. And there are always the **uninFORMed**, the ignorant, illiterate, uneducated, or unenlightened.

"Let us **reFORM** our schools, and we shall find little reform needed in our prisons," John Ruskin wrote in *Unto This Last* in 1862. Along with, he might have added, our **reFORMatories** or the so-called reform schools we have for young offenders.

Protestantism grew out of the **ReFORMation** led by John Calvin and Martin Luther in the 16th century. This is the act of **reFORMing**, altering, or improving. People who have succeeded in wiping out all their faults, blemishes, peccadilloes, and other evil ways and habits are declared to be **reFORMed.** Those who perfect such skills, are then free to become **reFORMists** and to then start working on their neighbors' shortcomings.

TransFORM means to change, modify, alter, and convert. But unlike reform, there is no promise of improvement. Hard work may transform an old house into a showplace, but a tornado might transform it into rubble. A **transFORMation** is a change, conversion, alteration, metamorphosis, or modification. ☞ *Dr. Locke's lecture today is on the transformation of America from a rural to an urban economy.* A **transFORMer** is a device used to alter the voltage in an electric circuit.

Objects that are **uniFORM** are alike, homogenous, and **conFORMable.** ☞ *The homeowners were uniform in their attitude toward the amendment.* The uniforms that members of organizations or professions wear are generally similar. **UniFORMity** refers to regularity, symmetry, conformity, and agreement. ☞ *The uniformity of the countryside began to get on their nerves.*

Pro FORMa means according to form, for the sake of form, perfunctory, and superficial. ☞ *The fact that there was but one candidate on the ballot make it a pro forma election.*

But not: *former* [AS *forma,* first], previous; *formicary* [*formica,* ant], an ant colony; *formidable* [*formidare,* to fear], awesome.

Combining forms: *e-,* together; *de-,* away; *dis-,* away; *in-,* in, not; *mal-,* bad; *mis-,* wrongly; *non-,* not; *pro-,* for the sake of; *re-,* again; *un-,* not; *uni-,* one; *trans-,* across.

Antonyms: *conformable*—dissonant, incongruous; *conformation*—opposition, resistance, dissent; *conformist*—rebel, heretic, dissenter; *conformity*—discord, disagreement, rebellion; *deformed*—natural, sound, normal; *formal*—

unconventional, irregular, casual; *formality*—eccentricity, spontaneity, nonconformism; *formula*—invention, improvisation, impromptu; *informality*—constraint, stiffness, ritualism; *informative*—obfuscatory, muddying, confusing; *nonconformist*—loyalist, yes-man, company man; *reform*—worsen, deteriorate, degeneration, corruption; *uniform*—uneven, irregular, inconsistent, civvies, mufti; *uninformed*—knowledgeable, conversant, erudite.

FORTIS, strong: FORCE, FORT

Originally, the word COMFORT meant to "give strength to," as in the phrase "to give aid and comfort to the enemy." Today it is contentment, solace, consolation, and reassurance. And, as a verb it means to console, quiet, assuage, gladden, and cheer. Henry David Thoreau wrote in *Walden* that "many of the so-called comforts of life are . . . but positive hindrances to the elevation of mankind." Nevertheless, he did appreciate a few of those basics called CREATURE COMFORTS: a warm winter's fire, a handy supply of water, and a COMFORTABLE bed, along with, we assume, a minimum of DISCOMFORTS, i.e., pain, hardships, distress, or trouble.

COLD COMFORT are words that convey extremely limited assurance or encouragement. ☞ *I told Coach Johnson that even though they didn't finish the race, there was always next year, but I knew that it was cold comfort.* Such cheery words often make people UNCOMFORTABLE.

COMFORTING words are soothing, reassuring, supportive, and consoling. One who offers solace is a COMFORTER, as is a quilt and one of those long knitted woolen scarves that make one feel comfy when the windchill factor hovers around zero degrees. A comfort station is a euphemism for a toilet, similar to powder room, rest room, and bathroom.

To make an EFFORT is to try, attempt, and endeavor. ☞ *The club made an effort to clean up the old headquarters.* Effort is work, power, exertion, or struggle. ☞ *Just a little bit of effort will get that job done.* It is also achievement, accomplishment, feat, or attainment. ☞ *Our membership drive was a worthwhile effort.* Someone who makes a great achievement look EFFORTLESS makes it look easy, casual, graceful, and painless. ☞ *Baseball great Willie Mays always made that kind of up-against-the-wall catch look effortless.*

FORCE refers to power, might, strength, potency, or vigor. But one's personality can have force, too: attraction, magnetism, charisma, or charm. The force of one's words is their effectiveness, efficacy, cogency, weight, persuasiveness. A force may also be a legion, army, battalion, corps, or squadron. When a law or rule is IN FORCE, it is in effect, in operation, valid, binding, or current. ☞ *That old regulation is no longer in force here.*

To force people to do something is to compel, coerce, intimidate, pressure, and make them do it. ☞ *The entire class was forced to apologize.* To force something using pressure is to push, drive, thrust, and wrench. ☞ *They had to force the door open.* **FORCE**D labor is compulsory, mandatory, and obligatory; a forced smile is unnatural, strained, and affected. **FORCE**FUL actions may be drastic, powerful, dynamic, and emphatic.

To DE**FORCE** is to keep property from its rightful owner; it is also to evict a tenant from housing by force. To EN**FORCE** is to implement, insist upon, impose, and coerce. ☞ *The police will enforce the new curfew tonight.* Law EN**FORCE**MENT is its execution, compulsion, obligation, or coercion. ☞ *The attorney claimed that the enforcement of the truancy law was misguided.* In professional ice hockey an EN**FORCE**R is a willingly belligerent player who goes after the rough one on the opposing team.

In 1945 President Harry S. Truman and the prime ministers of Britain and Canada, in signing the Declaration of Atomic Energy, agreed that there must be "effective, reciprocal, and EN**FORCE**ABLE safeguards acceptable to all nations." An UNEN**FORCE**ABLE ruling or law is one that cannot be implemented effectively. To REIN**FORCE** (also REEN**FORCE**) is to strengthen, invigorate, intensify, and augment. ☞ *We need to reinforce this part of the fence.* A REIN**FORCE**MENT is a strengthening, shoring up, or bracing of something; REIN**FORCE**MENTS are those troops, forces, or reserves that arrive at the **FORT** or at the front just in the nick of time. A FORCIBLE entry or seizure may be legal or illegal, depending on when and why who is doing what to whom.

A **FORT**RESS is a large **FORT**IFICATION that is sometimes called a citadel and often includes a town. To **FORT**IFY is to arm, barricade, guard, and defend. ☞ *Folks, looks like we're going to have to fortify city hall tonight.* It also means to strengthen, reinforce, toughen, and brace. ☞ *If you intend to go the distance, you'd better fortify yourself with a big breakfast.*

In one of her last poems, "Elysium is as far to" (1882), Emily Dickinson, referring to one's afterlife in heaven, wrote "What **FORT**ITUDE the Soul contains,/That it can so endure/The accent of a coming Foot—/The opening of a Door." Fortitude means grit, courage, bravery, and strength. A **FORT**E is one's strong point, specialty, skill, gift, or talent. ☞ *It is apparent that courtesy is not her forte.* In music forte means loud or loudly, and piano means soft or softly; consequently the direction **FORT**EPIANO means loud, and then soft, and a PIANO**FORT**E (or fortepiano) is an instrument that has a range extending from loud to soft. **FORT**ISSIMO is a musical direction meaning very loud.

But not: *forceps* [*capere,* to take], tongs; *fortnight* [AS *feowertene niht*], fourteen days; *fortuitous* [*fortuna,* fortune], lucky.
Combining forms: *de-,* away; *dis-,* apart; *ef-,* out; *en-,* put in; *in-,* put in; *re-,* again; *un-,* not.
Antonyms: *comfort*—misery, hurt, trouble, bother; *comfortable*—unsatisfactory, uncongenial, nervous, tense; *effort*—leisure, play, rest, defeat, debacle; *effortless*—painstaking, tough, complicated; *enforce*—ignore, disregard, waive; *force*—impotence, infirmity, weakness, frailty; *forced*—natural, sincere, spontaneous; *forceful*—insipid, impotent, powerless; *forcible*—amicable, noncoercive, peaceable; *forte*—weakness, foible, deficiency; *fortify*—sap, weaken, disable; *fortitude*—cowardice, weakness, timidity, panic.

FORTUNA, luck: FORT

FORTUNA was the ancient Roman goddess of **FORT**UNE, that aspect of life that we have little or no control over. A **FORT**UNATE person is successful, happy, and prosperous. A fortune is also wealth, riches, capital, income, or circumstances. ☞ *There certainly are not so many men of large fortune in the world, as there are pretty women to deserve them," Jane Austen,* Mansfield Park.

FORTUITOUS meetings or events are accidental, unintentional, unexpected, and unforeseen. ☞ *My running into Uncle Rich after all these years was entirely fortuitous.* A **FORT**UITY is an accidental occurrence, but it is most often one on which Lady Luck or Dame Fortune has smiled.

The opposite of fortune is MIS**FORT**UNE, i.e., sorrow, trouble, and adversity, often resulting from an injury or accident or calamity. The victims then join the ranks of the UN**FORT**UNATE.

But not: *forte* [*fortis,* strong], one's strong point; *fortnight* [ME *fourtene niht*], two weeks.
Combining forms: *mis-,* bad; *un-,* not.
Antonyms: *fortuitous*—planned, deliberate, expected; *fortunate*—cursed, hapless, ill-fated; *fortune*—poverty, destitution, purpose, intent; *misfortune*—prosperity, godsend.

G

GAMOS, marriage: GAM, GAMY

A BIGAMIST is a person who marries while having a living spouse; BIGAMY is a crime according to law and a sin in the eyes of most religions. After the death of or divorce from one's mate, one is free to marry again; such a union is called DEUTEROGAMY and DIGAMY.

MONOGAMY is marriage with only one person at a time or marrying only once during a lifetime. In the bird world the blue jay, loon, and tufted titmouse, among others, are MONOGAMOUS. POLYGAMY is the practice of having more than one spouse at a time. House wrens, indigo buntings, and red-winged blackbirds are POLYGAMOUS.

In botany ALLOGAMY is cross-fertilization, the fertilizing of the flower of one plant with a reproductive cell of a closely related flower; AUTOGAMY is self-fertilization. CRYPTOGAMS are plants such as algae, ferns, fungi, and mosses that have no true flowers or seeds and reproduce by spores.

> **Combining forms:** *allo-*, other; *auto-*, self; *bi-*, two; *crypto-*, hidden; *deutero-*, second; *di-*, twice, two; *mono-*, one; *poly-*, many.

GENUS, race, kind: GEN

To GENERALIZE is to make a large, sweeping, inexact, vague, and unsubstantiated statement based upon a few facts. For example: I drove past the high school today, and I can tell you that today's young people have no sense of decency at all. In this case a thirty-second drive past *one* school results in a generalization about *all* of today's youth. GENERALITIES are abstract, vague, and sweeping statements or opinions whether they are about the youth of today or those of years past.

Another sense of GENERALITY means majority, preponderance, or lion's share, as in this statement written by John Stuart Mill in 1869 in *The Subjection of Women:* "The generality of the male sex cannot yet tolerate living with [a wife who is] an equal."

Something that is GENERAL is widespread, broad, and extensive. ☞ *"Snow was general all over Ireland . . . falling on every part of the dark central plain, on the treeless hills . . . falling, too, upon every part of the lonely churchyard... where Michael Furey lay buried," James Joyce, "The Dead."* It may also be vague, unspecific, inexact, and imprecise. ☞ *Me, a techie? I haven't even a general idea of how a telephone works!* And general also refers to ordinary, usual, customary, and current.

A **GENERATION** is the entire group of beings born and living at about the same time; for *human* beings it is a period of about thirty years, which is the average length of time between the birth of parents and the birth of their offspring. ☞ *"Let the word go forth . . . that the torch has been passed to a new generation of Americans. . . ," President John F. Kennedy said at his inauguration.* A lack of communication between parents and their children is known as a **GENERATION GAP.**

To **GENERATE** is to produce, **ENGENDER,** fabricate, and contrive. ☞ *The boss was unable to generate much enthusiasm for her idea.* It is also to spawn, procreate, breed, and propagate. ☞ *The preacher said that the human race was generated by Adam.* A human **GENERATOR** is one who produces an idea, concept, solution, or theory; as a machine it is an apparatus or device that converts one form of energy into another; in a computer it is a program that produces a particular kind of output on demand.

A **DEGENERATE** is a reprobate, scoundrel, or pervert. ☞ *Only a degenerate could have committed such a crime.* As an adjective it means dissolute, decadent, and depraved. ☞ *Following their divorce, Anne sank into a degenerate condition.* As a verb it means to deteriorate, disintegrate, and regress. ☞ *Buy why do men degenerate ever? What makes families run out?," Henry David Thoreau asks in* Walden. **DEGENERACY** is depravity, corruption, evil, and immorality.

To **REGENERATE** is to rejuvenate, reform, and rehabilitate. ☞ *Many in the congregation were regenerated by the new evangelist.* It is to recreate or replace a lost body part, such as a lost claw on a lobster or tail on a lizard. **REGENERATION** is spiritual rebirth; it is a physical renewal, such as the growing of a plant from a cutting and a feedback process in electronics. An **UNREGENERATE** is one who is not reborn or reformed and is, thus wicked, immoral, or unrepentant.

GENEROUS people are magnanimous, benevolent, and charitable. In *Roving Commission: My Early Life* (1930), British prime minister Winston Churchill gave this advice to youth, "You will make all kinds of mistakes; but as long as you are generous and true, and also fierce, you cannot hurt the world." A generous amount is abundant, bounteous, and copious; a generous spirit is humane, unselfish, noble, and high-minded. **GENEROSITY** is kindliness, large-heartedness, and liberality, as well as a gift, present, and donation. To give **GENerously** is to give freely, abundantly, and liberally. An **unGENerous** person is stingy, greedy, and avaricious.

GENeric products are sold without brand names. ☞ *Our pharmacy stocks the generic equivalent of many medicines.* Generic also means general, common, and universal, i.e., belonging to, relating to, and pertaining to. ☞ *The science teacher listed some of the generic differences between birds and reptiles.*

A **GENre** is a class, type, sort, or category; Shakespeare's play *Macbeth* is an example of the tragic genre of drama. A **GENus** is a family or group of animals or plants that have common characteristics and usually consists of more than one species. ☞ *The roadrunner is a large terrestrial cuckoo of the genus geococcyx.*

In English grammar the **GENder** of certain nouns is indicated by the choice of the pronoun that is used to replace it: masculine, man, he; feminine, woman, she; neuter, house, it.

MisceGENation is the interbreeding of persons of different racial types, a practice that was prohibited in a number of states until a Supreme Court decision in 1967 ruled such laws illegal.

> **But not:** *exigent* [*agere,* to drive], pressing; *genuflect* [*genu,* knee + *flectere,* to bend], to bend one knee to the ground in reverence; *regent* [*regere,* to rule], a ruler.
> **Combining forms:** *de-,* down; *en-,* in; *misce-,* to mix; *re-,* again; *un-,* not.
> **Antonyms:** *degeneracy*—morality, decency, goodness; *degenerate*—flourish, improve, wholesome, healthy, sound; *general*—local, restricted, uncommon, extraordinary, unparalleled; *generality*—detail, specific; *generate*—end, terminate, annihilate; *generic*—particular, distinctive, explicit; *generosity*—meagerness, greediness, meanness; *generous*—stingy, miserly, scanty, small, mean, ignoble; *regenerate*—corrupt, deprave, demolish, unreconstructed; *ungenerous*—plentiful, bountiful, charitable, liberal.

GIGNOSKEIN, to know: GNOS

GNOSis means secret knowledge of spiritual matters. In the second to sixth centuries **GNOSticism** was a religious system of heretical Christians who called themselves **GNOStics** and held that matter is evil, spirit is good, and salvation comes from the acquisition of secret, esoteric knowledge, or gnosis.

In 1869 the British biologist Thomas Henry Huxley coined the word **aGNOSticism**, the prefix *a-* meaning "not," thus "not knowing." Over a half century later, in Dayton, Tennessee, attorney Clarence Darrow said in a speech at the world famous "monkey" trial of John Thomas Scopes, "I do not consider it an insult, but rather a compliment to be called an **aGNOStic**. I do not pretend to know where many ignorant men are sure—that is all that agnosticism means."

A medical doctor's **proGNOSis** is the prediction of the course and outcome of a disease, a sports reporter's of an athletic contest, an economist's of a boom or bust, or a political analyst's of an upcoming election. Skeptics are convinced that many alleged **proGNOStic** powers depend on which side of the flipped coin lands face up. **ProGNOSticate** means to forecast, foretell, predict, and prophesy. A **proGNOSticator** is a forecaster, foreseer, foreteller, predictor, seer, or sybil.

One's **physiognomy** is one's face. Even though one of Shakespeare's characters long ago proclaimed that there is no way one can read another's mind or character by checking out his or her expressions (says King Duncan about the treasonous Thane of Cawdor: "There's no art / To find the mind's construction in the face. / He was a gentleman on whom I built / An absolute trust"), the habit lives on: "You sure can tell ol' Slim's got no character. Look at that weak chin of his. Know what I mean?"

To **diaGNOSe** or **diaGNOSticate** or analyze a situation, whether one is a medical or automotive **diaGNOStician**, requires knowledge and skill in the practice of **diaGNOStics**, and the resulting **diaGNOSis** will usually reflect that.

Combining forms: *a-*, not; *dia-*, between; *physio-*, nature; *pro-*, before.

GLOSSA, tongue: GLOSS

The **GLOSSary** that we often find in the back pages of a professional or scientific text is a collection of **GLOSSes**, explanatory notes regarding an unusual or difficult word or expression. Sometimes a gloss also serves as an annotation, note, commentary, addendum, or interpretation and may be placed in the margin or the foot of the page or in between the lines of print.

As a verb, **GLOSS** means to explain away something, such as a difficult or sticky problem. ☞ *The manufacturer's representative tried to gloss away the erroneous and dangerously misleading instructions in the owner's manual.*

A POLYGLOT is a person who is multilingual. An ISOGLOSS is a boundary line made on a map to mark the areas where certain dialects are spoken. GLOSSOLALIA is unintelligible speech, sometimes the product of one's inventiveness, as with a child, and sometimes the involuntary "speaking in tongues" that a person in a religious trance or state of ecstasy exhibits; it is also known as "gift of tongues." GLOSSAL pertains to the tongue; the GLOTTIS is the opening between the vocal cords at the upper part of the larynx.

But not: *gloss, glossy* [Scand], sheen, luster.
Combining forms: *iso-,* equal; *-lalia,* babble; *poly-,* many.

GNOSCERE, to get to know: COGN, GNOR, NOTI

A **COGN**ITIVE experience is one of learning, of gaining knowledge. ☞ *Elinor's parents made the effort to oversee her cognitive as well as her emotional development.* In doing so, Elinor's parents took **COGN**IZANCE of the many forces that influence a child's growth and maturation.

PRE**COGN**ITION is foreknowledge, clairvoyance, prescience, and telepathy; PRE**COGN**ITIVE abilities, then, are clairvoyant, prescient, and telepathic. ☞ *Okay, so our candidate lost; I never claimed I had precognitive powers, did I?*

To RE**COGN**IZE someone or something is to identify, perceive, or acknowledge. ☞ *The chair recognized the delegate from Elkton.* To be **COGN**IZANT is to be aware. ☞ *None of us was cognizant of the danger we were in.* RE**COGN**ITION is a synonym of recollection, remembrance, attention, and appreciation. ☞ *Kim was given an alarm clock in recognition of her chronic tardiness.* A personal RE**COGN**IZANCE bond in a legal proceeding binds a person to a particular act, such as appearing in court. ☞ *Don was released early this morning on a personal recognizance bond, according to court records.*

A **COGN**OSCENTE is a person who has or claims to have top-drawer knowledge in a field, especially in literature, the fine arts, or fashion; if there are two or more of them, they're **COGN**OSCENTI. They also like to be called connoisseurs, experts, authorities, and, when dining, epicures or gourmets.

On a negative note, we have I**GNOR**ANCE, illiteracy, backwardness, or lack of education. I**GNOR**ANT refers to unlearned, naive, and uninformed; and I**GNOR**AMUS, a word originally meaning "we do not know," and used in court by a jury in rejecting an indictment on those grounds; today it describes an extremely ignorant person. To **iGNORe** is to overlook, eschew, and disregard. ☞ *The voters did not ignore Pat's many accomplishments.*

A **NOBLE** act is praiseworthy, excellent, and admirable; add the same prefix and we get **IGNOBLE** and its synonyms contemptible, despicable, and vulgar. ☞ *The assassination of the president was one of the most ignoble deeds of all time.* **NOTORIETY** qualifies for membership in this company with such synonyms as infamy, dishonor, disrepute, and ignominy. **NOTORIOUS,** its adjective form, means infamous, shameless, disreputable, and ignominious; writers and speakers who use it in an affirmative, favorable sense are misguided. ☞ *Abraham Lincoln is well-known and famous; John Wilkes Booth is well-known and notorious.*

An **ACQUAINTANCE** is a person one knows but who is not a close friend. To have an acquaintance with a subject, however, means to have knowledge, experience, and familiarity with it. ☞ *Since you have a good acquaintance with this area, can you show me the best route?* To **ACQUAINT** is to make familiar, thus to familiarize, enlighten, inform, and reveal. ☞ *Let me try to acquaint you with how this plan works; as a long-time employee, I am well acquainted with it.* Something that is **QUAINT** is charming, picturesque, and old-fashioned. ☞ *That village is filled with quaint old houses.* It also has the meaning of strange, bizarre, unusual, and singular.

When and Bill and Jill receive an invitation to a costume party, the message is "Come **INCOG.**" They will, therefore, wear masks to hid their identity. They will both consider themselves to be **inCOGNito,** i.e., unidentified, unknown, and nameless. An **INCOGITANT** act or remark is a thoughtless or inconsiderate one. An **inCOGNizant** person is unaware or lacking in knowledge.

NOTIce as a noun means heed, observation, glance, and **COGNizance.** ☞ *Sallie's new book is certainly worthy of notice.* Notice also means mention, information, and knowledge. ☞ *We never got a notice regarding the auction.* As a verb, notice means to see, observe, and recognize. ☞ *Did you notice Betty's engagement ring?* It also refers to mention, comment on, call attention to, and allude to. ☞ *You never even noticed my engagement ring," Betty said.*

To **NOTIfy** is to inform, advise, serve notice, and apprise. ☞ *I was never notified that the bill was past due.* When something is **NOTIceable,** it is clear, plain, distinct, and perceptible. ☞ *The therapy has resulted in a noticeable improvement in Beth's disposition.*

A **NOTIon** is a thought, opinion, concept, or suspicion. ☞ *I have absolutely no notion of where Tom went.* It is also a whim, fancy, inclination, and penchant. ☞ *When Tracey gets a notion in her head to do something like that, she just does it.*

To RECONNOITER is primarily a military term meaning to inspect or survey an area; today this is done with RECONNAISSANCE satellites. When one is well acquainted with the target layout, such missions are necessary.

Combining forms: *ac-,* to; *co-,* together; *-fy,* to make; *i-,* not; *in-,* not; *pre-,* before; *re-,* again.

GRADI, to go, step, walk: GRAD, GRESS

In New York City in 1841 a man named Phineas T. Barnum opened a museum that he had stocked with hundreds of curiosities, dead and alive, real and phony. It was a great success and during the next twenty-five years more than eighty million customers crowded into the building, so many at times that hundreds had to wait outside.

One day when he saw that all those outside were growing impatient to be inside, Barnum racked his brain for a way to get the ins out and the outs in. What he did was simple; he posted a large sign that was similar to the ones that pointed to other exhibits. TO THE EGRESS was all it said. When the insiders rushed to see the new "exhibit," they found themselves outside. An e**GRESS,** they suddenly learned, is an exit. And thus the insiders were e**GRESS**ed and the outsiders were in**GRESS**ed. Barnam, it is said, was satisfied with both the e**GRESS**ion and in**GRESS**ion.

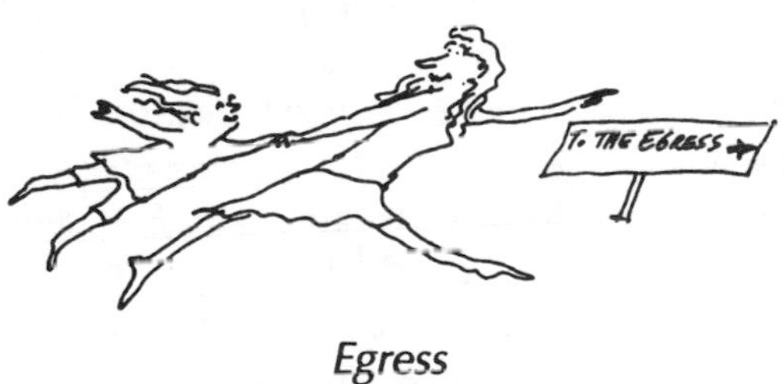

Egress

Had the inside-outers known that the prefix *e-* means out, and that *gress* means to go, step, and walk, they would not have been fooled. And as it is with egress, so it is with a number of other words that stem from *gradi.*

As a verb, con**GRESS** means to step together, but we use it primarily as a noun meaning an assembly or legislative body. ☞ *When May ran for Congress, she promised to work together harmoniously with her new congressional colleagues.*

To di**GRESS** is to go away or around. ☞ *"Let me digress for a moment," the candidate said, "to relate this story." The digression went on for fifteen minutes, crammed full of pointless, digressive remarks.*

To INGRESS is to go in. It is also a noun. ☞ *We were denied ingress to the bank.*

To PROGRESS is to go forward. ☞ *His academic progress is satisfactory, but he is not progressing in other areas. The chart outlined the company's yearly progression. She ran for reelection on her progressive record.*

REGRESS and RETROGRESS mean to go back or backward. ☞ *His health has regressed over the past few months. The foreign ship was given ingress and regress rights.* A REGRESSION is a relapse, backsliding, or retreat; REGRESSIVE means backward, retrograde, debilitating, and declining.

To TRANSGRESS is to step over or across. ☞ *Their conduct transgressed every code including that of common sense.* TRANSGRESSIONS are sins, trespasses, offenses, or lapses.

GRESSORIAL means adapted for walking, as with the feet of some birds.

The prefix *ag-* means "to or toward," hence AGGRESSION is assault, offense, encroachment or hostility. ☞ *The rebels' aggression must be stopped.* An AGGRESSIVE person is hostile, belligerent, forceful, and competitive. ☞ *We need more aggressive salespeople in this firm.* An AGGRESSOR is an assailant, attacker, or challenger. ☞ *It was obvious who the aggressor was in that relationship.*

A GRADE is a mark or rank. ☞ *My grade in the course was third from the top.* It is also an incline or slope. ☞ *Count me out; that's too steep a grade for me to climb.* As a verb it means to rank and classify. ☞ *Joan said grading papers was not quite like grading eggs.* A GRADUATE is a person who receives a diploma or a degree, and it is also a beaker in a chem lab. To graduate is to finish school; it is also to measure out, as INGREDIENTS when cooking, as you check the GRADATIONS or DEGREES on the cup.

A GRADIENT is a slope, tilt, or incline that may be GRADUAL, very steep, or in-between. ☞ *I wouldn't attempt that gradient without four-wheel drive.* GRADUALISM is the policy of moving very slowly or GRADUALLY toward a goal.

A corporal who loses a stripe and becomes a private has technically been DEGRADED, that is, lowered in rank; it also means shamed, dishonored, and humbled. Suffering from DEGRADATION, humiliation, or disgrace can be a DEGRADING experience.

DEGRADABLE materials can be broken down by chemicals; those that are BIODEGRADABLE can be broken down or decayed by living organisms. ☞ *It is said that disposable diapers are biodegradable—it takes only about one hundred years.*

Combining forms: *ag-,* to; *bio-,* life; *con-,* together; *de-,* down; *di-,* away; *e-,* out; *in-,* in; *pro-,* forward; *re-,* back; *retro-,* back, backward; *trans-,* across.
Antonyms: *aggressive*—peaceful, apathetic, timid, lethargic; *degrading*—dignified, worthy, uplifting; *gradual*—sudden, hasty, intermittent, precipitate; *progress*—retreat, loss, decline.

GRANUM, grain, seed: GRAN

The words of an old English folksong go like this, "Some talk of Alexander, and some of Hercules, of Hector and Lysander, and such great names as these; but of all the world's great heroes there's none that can compare, with . . . the British **GRENADIERS.**" About four hundred years ago, they were soldiers who, as it says in the second verse, threw "hand **GRENADES** . . . about the enemies' ears." A grenade is filled with explosives much as a **POMEGRANATE** is with seeds; hence the name comes to us through the Spanish *granado,* "full of seeds" and the French *grenade,* "a *pomegranet,* a ball of wild-fire." The **GARNET**, a gem used in jewelry, got its name from its resemblance to the color of the pomegranate seeds, and **GRENADINE** is a syrup made from the fruit.

Meanwhile, back at the farm or **GRANGE,** as it is sometimes called, the **GRAIN** is ready to be harvested. The **GRANGER** and his family will be out in the field **GARNERING** it so they can store it in the **GRANARY** until the time comes to take it to the mill to be ground into flour. If a coarsely ground product is desired, it will be **GRANULATED**, resulting in a **GRANULAR** or **GRAINY** texture. Some of the **GRANULES** will be put aside to be used in the making of whole or cracked grain breads or rolled to be put in **GRANOLA** or other cereals. **GRAVY** sometimes has grains in it, and **GRANITE,** a rock used in building and road paving, is **COARSE-GRAINED.** An idea or attitude that is **INGRAINED** is deep-seated and fixed. ☞ *Pat has an ingrained fear of heights.*

But not: *aggrandize* [*ag-,* to + *grandir,* grow larger], enlarge, exaggerate; *grant* [*credere,* to trust], to consider, give.
Combining forms: *in-,* in; *pome-,* apple.
Antonyms: *grainy*—creamy, unctuous; *granular*—smooth, homogenized; *ingrained*—superficial, external, surface, learned.

GRATUS, beloved, dear, pleasing: GRAC, GRAT, GREE

In 1893 on a visit to Pikes Peak Katherine Lee Bates, an educator and poet, wrote a poem that she entitled, "America the Beautiful." After she set it to a piece of music written by Samuel Ward, it became very popular. "American! America! God shed His **GRAC**e on thee/And crown thy good with brotherhood / From sea to shining sea."

That grace means virtue, piety, love, or goodness. The grace that an aspiring actress must walk with is elegance, **GRAC**efulness, or ease. The principal's grace that allows an unruly student to have a second chance is pardon, forgiveness, or clemency. The grace of a host or hostess is skill, charm, polish, or tact. The grace that is said before a meal is a prayer, blessing, or benediction. The grace period that follows the due date for a bill to be paid is exemption, reprieve, indulgence, and charity.

As a verb, grace means to adorn, embellish, beautify, and enhance. ☞ *Fresh flowers graced every table.* It also means to dignify, honor, favor, and endow. ☞ *The Governor and the First Lady graced the affair with their presence.* Something that is **GRAC**eful is pleasing, elegant, charming, and tasteful.

A dis**GRAC**e is shame, dishonor, odium, or ignominy. ☞ *That vacant lot turned junkyard is a disgrace.* As a verb it means to tarnish, discredit, humiliate, and degrade. A dis**GRAC**eful act is shameful, outrageous, degrading, and contemptible. ☞ *All it took was one disgraceful act to destroy his career.* A **GRAC**eless person or object lacks beauty, charm, refinement, and class. A remark may be graceless and cruel; a graceless person may be considered uncouth, awkward, loutish, and clumsy or even shameless, evil, and depraved.

A **GRAC**ious person is kind, courteous, warm, and humane. ☞ *What a gracious note of thanks from Zelda!* Gracious living is characterized by elegance, refinement, and luxury. Somewhere along the line the word grace slipped over into the interjection category. "Gracious!" and various combinations are used as exclamations of surprise. ☞ *Gracious, I haven't seen you for ages!*

A **GRAT**eful person is appreciative, beholden, and indebted; one who is un**GRAT**eful is thankless, unthankful, and unappreciative. ☞ *John has an ungrateful attitude.*

GRATitude is appreciation, thankfulness, **GRAT**efulness, or acknowledgement, while in**GRAT**itude is thanklessness or unappreciativeness. To **GRAT**ify is to please, delight, satisfy, and gladden.

In a letter to the Young People's Society in Brooklyn (1901), Mark Twain offered this advice: "Always do right. This will gratify some people, and astonish the rest." The adjective **GRATIFYING** means delightful, rewarding, and pleasant. **GRATIFICATION** is satisfaction, enjoyment, or fulfillment. ☞ *She volunteers at that hospital just for the gratification she gets from helping the helpless.*

GRATUITOUS is one of those words whose meaning can be determined only by the phrasing that surrounds it. On the one hand it means free, **GRATIS**, complimentary, and spontaneous. ☞ *Your gratuitous help saved more than one person's life, and we shall never forget it.* On the other hand it means unjustified, uncalled for, and impertinent. ☞ *Your gratuitous insults and lies damaged more than one person's reputation, and we shall never forget it.*

A **GRATUITY** is a tip, gift, honorarium, bonus, or present.

To **CONGRATULATE** is to compliment, salute, and offer your best wishes. "**CONGRATULATIONS!**" is synonymous with "Best wishes!," "Well done!," "Felicitations!," or "Nice going!"

People who try to **INGRATIATE** themselves with others flatter, cajole, and fawn on; when they do so, thus becoming **INGRATIATING**, they are thought to be servile, fawning, smarmy, and obsequious. ☞ *His phony, ingratiating manner didn't fool the boss for a minute.* There is, however, an opposite meaning. One's ingratiating manner can be winning, charming, engaging, magnetic, and personable.

An **INGRATE** is an ungrateful person. ☞ *I've given you the best years of my life, and you turn out to be nothing but an ingrate!*

A character in *Lothair* (1870) by Benjamin Disraeli says, "My idea of an **AGREEABLE** person is someone who **AGREES** with me." His reference to agreeable means pleasing, enjoyable, and gratifying. His reference to agree means to consent, assent, be of one mind, and go along with. Agreeable also means complying, in accord, and concurring. ☞ *Assuming everyone is agreeable, we will meet again tomorrow morning.* Other meanings of the word agree are to conform, coincide, and reconcile. ☞ *The bank statement and my checkbook never agree.* And also to concur, endorse, sanction, and support. ☞ *The disciplinary committee has agreed that Leslie should be given one more chance.* An **AGREEMENT** is an understanding, meeting of minds, contract, or treaty. ☞ *The goal of life is in living in agreement with nature," Zeno the Stoic, 300 B.C.*

To **DISAGREE** is to differ, dissent, contend, and oppose. ☞ *I disagree with most of your political beliefs.* A **DISAGREEMENT** is a quarrel, conflict, dissension, unlikeness, or incompatibility. ☞ *The disagreement led to the* *resignation of the company's vice-president.* **DISAGREEABLE** weather and medicines are nasty, unpleasant, and obnoxious, but disagreeable people are ill-tempered, churlish, grouchy, petulant, and brusque. ☞ *"Yet everybody says I'm such a disagreeable man! / And I can't think why!" from a character in Gilbert and Sullivan's operetta* Princess Ida.

But not: *gracile* [*gracilis,* thin], slender; *grate* [*cratis,* lattice], metal frame work; *degree* [*gradus,* a step], rank, step.

Combining forms: *a-,* according to; *con-,* together; *dis-,* not; *in-,* in, not; *un-,* not.

Antonyms: *agreeable*—unlikable, offensive, inappropriate; *agreement*—discord, dissension; *congratulate*—rebuke, censure, condemn; *disagree*—concur, subscribe, reconcile; *disagreeable*—pleasant, propitious, inviting; *disagreement*—unity, similarity; *disgrace*—honor, credit; *disgraceful*—honorable, worthy; *grace*—clumsiness, gawkiness, dishonor, shame; *graceful*—awkward, clumsy, ugly, ponderous; *graceless*—blessed, pure, well-bred, comely; *gracious*—harsh, rough, boorish, surly, sullen; *grateful*—unappreciative, disobliged, heedless, irksome; *gratification*—disappointment, sorrow, discipline, denial; *gratify*—disappoint, dissatisfy, curb, restrict; *gratitude*—thanklessness, ungratefulness; *gratuitous*—justified, warranted, compulsory, involuntary; *ingratiating*—overbearing, brash, unlovable, austere; *ingratitude*—thanks, acknowledgement, appreciation; *ungrateful*—appreciative, mindful, thankful.

GRAVIS, heavy, serious, weighty: GRAV, GRIEV

The first kind of **GRAVITY** that most of us learn about in school is the law of **GRAVITATION** that Sir Isaac Newton formulated one day in 1655 when he saw an apple fall in his garden. T.S. Eliot described it—and cats—humorously in his "Macavity: The Mystery Cat." "Macavity, Macavity, there's no one like Macavity,/He's broken every human law, he breaks the law of gravity."

Today gravitation is used to express a movement, force, attraction, bent, or proclivity. ☞ *Mass gravity toward the suburbs seems to be slowing down.* The verb to **GRAVITATE** means to move toward, be attracted, and converge. ☞ *As usual at these gatherings, the Ph.D.'s soon gravitated toward one another.*

Another meaning of gravity is importance, seriousness, or magnitude, as well as dignity or composure. A **GRAVE** person tends to be earnest, gloomy, and sedate. ☞ *When I saw the grave look on the doctor's face, I knew what she was going to say.* A grave situation is critical, crucial, and urgent. ☞ *The national deficit is a matter of grave concern to him.*

To AG**GRAV**ATE is to worsen, exacerbate, and intensify. ☞ *You're going to aggravate that insect bite if you keep scratching it.* It also means to annoy, provoke, pester, and exasperate. ☞ *The lead editorial in this week's paper really aggravated me.* Things or people that are AG**GRAV**ATING are troublesome, pesty, and annoying, take the case of Rebecca, a youngster found in Hilaire Belloc's *Cautionary Tales* who "was not really bad at heart,/But only rather rude and wild:/She was an aggravating child."

A **GRIEV**ANCE is a hardship, injustice, or injury. Our First Amendment states that "Congress shall make no law . . . abridging . . . the right of the people . . . to petition the government for a redress of grievances." To redress means to set right and rectify. To **GRIEVE** is to mourn, lament, and regret. ☞ *"Who made him dead to rapture and despair, / A thing that grieves not and that never hopes, / Stolid and stunned, a brother to the ox," Edwin Markham, "The Man with the Hoe."* Grieve also means sadden, hurt, and wound. ☞ *The grieving child buried the puppy in the backyard.*

A **GRIEV**OUS happening is tragic, sorrowful, and agonizing. ☞ *In 1968 the assassinations of Robert F. Kennedy and Martin Luther King, Jr. were grievous losses to our country.* It also means heinous, dreadful, and monstrous. ☞ *We felt it would be a grievous mistake to bring up that matter in her time of tragedy.* To AG**GRIEVE** is to injure by injustice, wrong **GRIEV**OUSLY, distress, and afflict. ☞ *We were aggrieved to learn that her name had been left off the list of honorees.* The adjective AG**GRIEV**ED means **GRIEV**ING, troubled, sorrowful, and offended. ☞ *The jury awarded the aggrieved party adequate compensation.*

GRIEF is heartbreak, misery, desolation, or agony. ☞ *Their grief was such that no one dared try to console them.* It also refers to trouble, grievance, burden, or anxiety. ☞ *This neighborhood has been nothing but grief since the day that family moved in.* A GRIEF-STRICKEN person is inconsolable, heartsick, heartbroken, ravaged, and devastated.

But not: *grave* [AS *grafan*], to carve, engrave; *grave* [AS *graef*], burial place; *gravy* [*granum,* grain], sauce.
Combining form: *ag-,* to.
Antonyms: *aggrieved*—happy, joyous, blissful; *aggravate*—soothe, please, calm, ease; *grave*—trivial, inconsequential, merry, boisterous, flippant; *gravitate*—retreat, diverge;

gravitation—repulsion, deviation, disinclination; *gravity*—unimportance, insignificance, casualness, frivolity, facetiousness; *grief*—comfort, consolation, bliss, happiness; *grievance*—boon, benefit, privilege, compliment; *grieve*—console, solace, revel, celebrate; *grievous*—pleasurable, delightful, comforting, light, facetious, frivolous.

GREGARE, to herd: GREG

A **GREGARIOUS** person is affable, outgoing, and sociable, one who loves to be with people. ☞ *Good-time Charley says he's not really the gregarious type, he just likes the free food he gets at parties.* Animals that **CONGREGATE** in flocks or herds are also gregarious. **CONGREGANTS** are members of **CONGREGATIONS,** which are usually assemblies or groups or gatherings of like-minded religious worshippers. The Pilgrims who sailed on the *Mayflower* and landed at Plymouth Colony in 1620 were **CONGREGATIONALISTS.**

To **SEGREGATE** a group means to separate it from the flock. ☞ *In an experiment the teachers segregated the right-handed children from the left-handed ones.* **SEGREGATION** is the process of isolating a group, whether it is the shelving of books in a library, the seating of children in a school, or the cells of violent criminals in a prison. On May 17, 1954, the United States Supreme Court unanimously declared in *Brown v. Board of Education of Topeka* that **SEGREGATED** schools were unconstitutional. One year later the court ordered the **DESEGREGATION** of public schools.

An **AGGREGATION** is a collection or gathering of people or things. ☞ *An aggregation of rare animals toured the small towns.* As an adjective **AGGREGATE** means amassed, combined, and cumulative. ☞ *The aggregate amount raised in the fund drive was disappointing.* As a noun it means a sum total. ☞ *The aggregate of all his debts was overwhelming.* As a verb it means to bring together, amount to, and gather into one mass. ☞ *All the crowds on the tour will aggregate nearly a million people.*

Many years ago when someone was referred to as **EGREGIOUS,** it was considered a compliment; it meant that the person was distinguished, eminent, illustrious, and outstanding. Today it still means outstanding, but now it means outstandingly bad, monstrous, gross, and glaring, such as an egregious error, or mistake. ☞ *Getting the speaker's name wrong when I introduced her was an egregious mistake.* Where the word took a turn for the worse is not recorded.

Combining forms: *ag-*, to; *con-*, together; *e-*, out; *se-*, apart.
Antonyms: *aggregate*—individual, separate, discrete; *congregate*—disperse, scatter; *egregious*—minor, unnoticeable, tolerable; *gregarious*—standoffish, introverted; *segregate*—unify, integrate.

GUSTUS, a tasting: GUST

The adjective **GUSTATORY** pertains to our sense of taste. ☞ *What? You don't like my dish? Something wrong with your gustatory senses?* **GUSTATION** is the act of tasting as well as the faculty or sense of taste. **GUSTABLE** and **GUSTFUL** both mean appetizing. ☞ *Ah, such gustable and gustful morsels these be.*

GUSTO is enjoyment, enthusiasm, appetite, relish, or vigor. ☞ *We were so hungry we could have eaten most anything with gusto.* **RAGOUT** (ra GOO), a word that came to us from Latin by way of France, is a highly seasoned stew of fish or meat and, usually, vegetables.

Then there's the other side of this coin. The literal meaning of **DISGUST** is "not to one's taste." Hence, when one is **DISGUSTED**, he or she may feel nauseous, sickened, queasy, and fed up. ☞ *I am so disgusted by this show that I feel sick. I* have *to leave.* Of course one can feel disgust and not be nauseated; even those with strong stomachs can still be displeased, irritated, appalled, and offended. **DISGUSTING** refers to something that is offensive, odious, and hateful.

How strong is the feeling that disgust can have in men? In the "Heart of Darkness" (1902) Joseph Conrad addressed that when he weighed the power of hunger, he who had seen starving men eat what would normally sicken them: "No fear can stand up to hunger, no patience can wear it out, disgust simply does not exist where hunger is."

But not: *gust* [ON *gustr*], a sudden rush of wind.
Combining forms: *ra-*, again, back; *dis-*, not.
Antonyms: *disgust*—please, delight, fondness, satisfaction; *disgusting*—attractive, delightful; *gusto*—nausea, revulsion, loathing.

H

HELIOS, SOL, sun: HELIO, SOL

Helios was the Greek sun god; hence **HELIOcentric** describes our solar system: the sun is at the center. **HELIOtherapy** is the use of the sun's rays for medical treatment, and the glass-enclosed rooms at some hospitals and convalescent homes are used for that purpose; they are frequently called **SOLariums**, a word-gift from Latin that also fits sunny rooms for houseplants. A **HELIOgraph** is a signaling device using sunlight reflected by a mirror, and helium, an element present in the sun's atmosphere and in natural gas, is a non-explosive fuel used in dirigible balloons.

The Latin sun god was Sol, and from it have come a larger number of words in everyday use. People build **SOLarized** houses that utilize **SOLar** energy. Colorful para**SOL**s appear on hot days, particularly at fashionable gatherings. On June 22 and again on December 22 ("the darkest evening of the year," as Robert Frost says in his poem, "Stopping by Woods on a Snowy Evening"), a **SOLstice** occurs.

The bleaching or drying of an object in the sun is called in**SOLating**. To expose an object to the sun is to in**SOLate** it; the process of sun-drying is called in**SOLation**. ☞ *The Scout troop is learning to insolate certain fruits such as apples, currants, and bananas.*

The Latin gira**SOL** and the Greek **HELIOtrope** refer to a plant that turns toward the sun; that is what sunflowers do, and the girasol is a sunflower. The tubers of the girasol plant, lightly sauteed in margarine or cooking oil or mashed like a potato, are recommended by nutritionists. A fire opal, which reflects sunlight in a bright, luminous glow, is also known as a girasol.

> **But not:** *insole* [*solea,* sandal], the inner sole of a shoe; *insolent* [*solere,* to be accustomed], rude, impertinent; *resolute* [*solvere,* to loosen], firm; *solo* [*solus,* alone], unassisted; *solon* [after Solon, 639–558 B.C., Athenian statesman and wise lawgiver], member of a legislative body.
> **Combining forms:** *-arium,* a place; *-centric,* centered around; *gira-,* to turn; *-graph,* writing; *in-,* in; *-ize,* to convert; *para-,* to shield; *-stice,* stopping; *-therapy,* treatment; *-trope,* to turn.

HEPTA, seven: HEPTA

For thousands of years the number seven has been considered a mystic or sacred number. There are seven days in the Biblical creation, seven days in the week, seven divisions in the Lord's Prayer, the seventh son of a seventh son was long held to be notable, and the first seven books of the Bible are called the **HEPTA**TEUCH.

A **HEPTA**GON is a polygon of seven angles and seven sides, a **HEPTA**HEDRON is a solid seven-sided figure, and a **HEPTA**THLON is an athletic contest, usually for women, consisting of seven events.

A few hundred years before the Normans crossed the English Channel under William the Conqueror, Anglo-Saxon England was divided into seven kingdoms known as the **HEPTA**RCHY; a line of verse consisting of seven metrical feet or *stresses* is a **HEPTA**METER. ☞ *"So Agamemnon did sustain the torment of his wound," the* Iliad *as translated by George Chapman.* A **HEPTA**D is a group of seven. ☞ *The closing number was a heptad of early hymns.*

But not: *hepatitus* [Gk *hepathepar,* the liver], inflammation of the liver.

Combining forms: *-ad,* group of a certain number; *-archy,* rule; *-athlon,* prize; *-gon,* angled; *-hedron,* face; *-meter,* measure; *-teuch,* book.

HERES, an heir: HEIR, HERI

An **HEIR** is a beneficiary, one who IN**HERI**TS, receives, and acquires a bequeathed property, money, legacy, or birthright. ☞ *"Blessed are the meek: for they shall inherit the earth," Matthew 5:3. Pity poor Paul; he didn't inherit even one thin dime.*

A woman who inherits is an IN**HERI**TRESS or IN**HERI**TRIX. **HEIR**ESS is often used to refer to (and generally limited to) a woman who has inherited a vast fortune.

An HEIR APPARENT is someone who seems certain to inherit a position. ☞ *I Sir, am the heir apparent to Daddy's position and salary as president of this corporation.* An HEIR PRESUMPTIVE is someone whose inheritance is based on presumption or likelihood.

HEREDITY is the transmission of mental or physical characteristics from one's parents or ancestors. One's **HERI**TAGE is a birthright, endowment, legacy, tradition, or family possession. ("Guided by my heritage of a love of beauty and a respect for strength—in search of my mother's garden, I found my own," author Alice Walker, from *In Search of Our Mothers' Gardens* [1974]). Something **HEREDITARY** is **INHERITED**, **INHERITABLE**, **HERITABLE**, inbred, congenital, or genetic. ☞ *I know that her red hair is hereditary.* It is also inherited, handed down, traditional, or bequeathed. An **INHERITANCE** is like one's heritage; if it is money or other kinds of property, the cynical advice of Johann Kaspar Lavater, a Swiss poet, in *Aphorisms on Man* (1788) may well apply: "Say not you know another entirely, till you have divided an inheritance with him."

To **DISINHERIT** is to exclude someone from an inheritance, such as an heir or next of kin; it is also to deprive a people from the rights, heritage, and privileges of a group, city, tribe, nation, or race. "Private beneficence is totally inadequate to deal with the vast numbers of the city's **DISINHERITED**," wrote Jane Addams, social worker and Nobel Peace Prize winner in *Twenty Years at Hull House* (1910).

> **Combining forms:** *dis-*, not; *in-*, in.
> **Antonyms:** *hereditary*—acquired, earned, saved; *disinherited*—advantaged, privileged, favored.

HODOS, way, journey: OD

How did we get the word **PERIOD** from *hodos*? In just two steps, that's how. The prefix *peri-*, "around," was added to the root to result in *perihodos*. Then at some point on its considerable journey from then to now three letters were excised. Today the word covers a superabundance of ground. There's the dot that marks, as the British put it, the "full stop" at the end of a sentence. A period is an interval of time, ranging from an age, eon, epoch, and era, through the hour or so that students spend in and between classes, to the stopwatch-measured minutes and seconds that a game may be divided into. It can also refer to a particular or special spell or stage in one's life. ☞ *It was during that difficult period that I decided I had to go back to school.*

A **PERIODIC** sentence is one that creates a certain amount of suspense by saving the completion of the main clause until the end. ☞ *Yesterday, just as I was leaving the classroom—that would be Ms. King's in 204—at the end of what I think must have been third period—no, come to think of it, it was second period—I felt faint.* Periodic happenings are frequent, repeated, regular, and seasonal. ☞ *We charted the periodic phases of the moon. As she matured, her periodic tantrums became less frequent.*

And then there are the PERIODICALS, magazines, journals, papers, annuals, or newsletters, we subscribe to that are published PERIODICALLY, regularly, at fixed intervals, and from time to time.

An EPISODE is an incident or a happening; a TV soap opera is EPISODIC.

A METHOD is a system, procedure, plan, or design. A person who is METHODIC or METHODICAL is well-organized, businesslike, systematic, and deliberate. METHODOLOGY is a system of procedures and rules in, for example, schools of education. ☞ *Lily said she had four years of educational methodology, all about the "how-to" but hardly anything about the subject matter she was supposed to teach.*

The METHODIST church was founded by John and Charles Wesley, who lived "by rule and method" while students at England's Oxford University in 1729. A SYNOD is a council of churches or church officials. EXODUS is the title of the second book of the Bible and means the departure of a large group of people.

Additional English words related to the root: cathode, odometer.
But not: *modus,* manner, measure, method, usually with *operandi,* method of operating or working, or *vivendi,* manner of living; *OD,* overdose, esp. a fatal one; officer of the day, Old Dutch, olive drab, overdrawn; *ode* [Gk *aeidein,* to sing], long lyric poem.
Combining forms: *epis-,* into; *ex-,* out; *met-,* after; *peri-,* around; *syn-,* together.

HORRERE, to bristle, dread, shudder: HORR

In 1741 Jonathan Edwards, one of the great preachers of our country's Puritan Age, delivered a sermon entitled "Sinners in the Hands of an Angry God." According to one witness, "There was such a breathing of distress and weeping, that the preacher was obliged to speak to the people and desire silence, that he might be heard." The following are a few words from one sentence delivered about mid-stream: "The God that holds you over the pit of hell, much as one holds a . . . loathsome insect over the fire, ABHORS you, and is dreadfully provoked; his wrath towards you burns like fire . . . you are ten thousand times so abominable in his eyes, as the most hateful and venomous serpent is in ours." To abhor someone, then, is to detest, abominate, disdain, and despise, and an ABHORRENT being or thing is detestable, despicable, contemptible, and offensive. ☞ *The very idea of war was quite abhorrent to our visitors from outer space.*

HORRendous happenings, stories, or things are appalling, **HORRifying**, awful, **HORRific**, gory, and frightful. ☞ *Mary's handwriting and spelling are horrendous. Sgt. Sprigs used the word horrendous in describing the crime scene.* **HORRible** fits into the same category: gruesome, vile, obnoxious, and unbearable. ☞ *"I feel that life is—is divided up into the horrible and the miserable,"* Annie Hall, *film by Woody Allen.* To **HORRify** is to shock, sicken, disgust, dismay, and terrify. ☞ *That is the kind of story that will horrify the children.* To be **HORRified** is to be scared, shocked, outraged, **HORRor-struck**, and frightened. ☞ *I was horrified to learn that the two Rottweilers were on the school grounds.*

HORRor is fear, terror, dread, panic, or alarm. ☞ *"You gain strength . . . by every experience in which you really stop to look fear in the face [and] say to yourself, 'I lived through this horror. I can take the next thing that comes along.' " from* You Learn by Living, *Eleanor Roosevelt.* As an interjection **HORRors** is a mild expression of dismay or upset. ☞ *Horrors! I left our tickets on the kitchen counter!* As a noun, it refers to suffering, cruelty, inhumanity, misery, and anguish. ☞ *It was the horrors of his war experiences that finally drove him over the edge.*

HORRid means frightful, shocking, abominable, and grisly. ☞ *Being lost in the cave was the most horrid night of my life.* But the word does have its less dreadful side. Horrid weather can be merely unpleasant, disagreeable, annoying, and upsetting; perhaps it was along those lines that Henry Wadsworth Longfellow was thinking when he wrote with his baby daughter in mind, "There was a little girl/Who had a little curl/Right in the middle of her forehead;/And when she was good/She was very, very good,/But when she was bad she was horrid."

Additional English word related to the root: ordure.
Combining forms: *ab-,* from; *-fic,* making; *-fy,* to do, make.
Antonyms: *abhorrent*—likable, congenial, admirable, pleasing; *horrendous*—fascinating, enchanting, agreeable, idyllic; *horrible*—delightful, delectable, fetching, lovely; *horrify*—soothe, calm, reassure, cheer; *horror*—liking, pleasure, gratification, joy, reward, benefit.

HOSTIS, enemy, stranger, HOSTIL

In a letter written in 1800 to Dr. Benjamin Rush, a fellow signer of the *Declaration of Independence,* Thomas Jefferson said, "I have sworn upon the altar of God eternal **HOSTILity** against every form of tyranny over the mind of man." In doing so Jefferson was swearing, as well, against animosity, enmity, antagonism, bitterness, and hatred.

Elizabeth Bowen, an Irish novelist and short story writer, observed in *The Death of the Heart* (1938) how "some people are moulded by their admirations, others by their **HOSTIL**ITIES." In the sense that Ms. Bowen used the word, its synonyms are enmities and hatreds, but it is more commonly seen as meaning conflict or fighting, ranging from a scuffle or fracas to an act or state of war. ☞ *Hostilities between France and Germany broke out on September 3, 1939.*

John Haynes Holmes, in his book entitled *The Sensible Man's View of the Universe,* wrote, "The universe is not **HOSTIL**E, nor is it friendly. It is simply indifferent," i.e., neither angry, contentious, and malacious, nor congenial, sociable, or neighborly.

One afternoon in 1807 the British poet William Wordsworth "wandered lonely as a cloud [when] all at once [he] saw a crowd,/A HOST, of golden daffodils." It was a sight that raised his spirits, but it then began to rain, and he hurried home where, one story goes, he sat down and wrote the poem entitled, "I Wandered Lonely As a Cloud" that was to become world-famous. In the poem, the word host refers to a great number or multitude.

> **But not:** *host* [*hospes,* guest], one who extends hospitality; *hostage* [*obsidere,* to stay], pledge, pawn.
> **Antonyms:** *host*—sprinkling, handful, remnant; *hostile*—friendly, amiable, congenial; *hostilities*—peace, truce; *hostility*—agreement, sympathy, affability, good will.

I

INSULA, island: SOLA, SULA

As we look at the words ISLET, ISLE, and island, our first guess is that they came from the same root. But only the first two did; the latter is from the Middle English word "iland." ("No man is an iland, entire of itself," John Donne, 1624). Somehow over the years, no doubt because of its similarity to the word isle, the "s" wormed its way into the word. The relationship of the three is somewhat similar to that of the three bears of childhood: tiny, medium, and large.

An islet is a very small tract of land surrounded by water; an isle is a larger piece of land, such as the Isle of Man (221 square miles); and an island can be as big as Greenland (840,000 square miles) but smaller than Australia, a continent of approximately 3,000,000 square miles.

A penin**SULA** is a land mass that is *almost* completely surrounded by water. Which is exactly what the parts of the word add up to: *pen-*, almost + *insula,* island.

Insula also gives us several words that have to do with a different kind of separation. Just as an island is separated from land, so we in**SULA**te our buildings to separate the inside from the heat or cold that is outside. In**SULA**tion is wrapped around electrical wires to spare us from the current that goes through them, and the insulation in cars is intended to filter the loudest of the road noises.

When a German doctor named Paul Langerhans discovered some islets of cells in the pancreas, a gland located near our stomachs, the hormone that they normally produce was given the name INSULIN; it is a substance used in the treatment of diabetes. The cells are called the islet (or island) of Langerhans.

A person who lives on an island is said to be i**SOLA**ted, standing alone, in**SULA**r. The latter word has also come to mean narrow-minded, provincial, intolerant, bigoted, and limited. ☞ *When Slim finally came out of the backwoods where he was born, he had an insular approach to everyday life.* An i**SOLA**tos is a hermit or recluse who is out of sync with the physical or spiritual world in which he or she lives.

An i**SOLA**tion ward in a hospital is used to separate patients with contagious or infectious diseases from others. **ISOLA**tionism is a governmental policy of refusing to have alliances or agreements with other nations.

But not: *insolate* [*in-*, in + *sol,* sun], to dry or bleach in the sun.
Antonyms: *insular*—urbane, tolerant, worldly, experienced.

IRE, to go: IT

Terry's high school counselor tells her that because she has the AMBITION, goal, or objective of becoming an elementary school teacher and has shown herself as being a sufficiently AMBITIOUS, aspiring, persevering, and determined student, she will get into the college of her dreams and do well.

Now let's slip back to Rome in 44 B.C. and listen in as Mark Antony speaks of Julius Caesar as he stands over his corpse in Shakespeare's play: "Brutus says he was ambitious . . . When the poor have cried, Caesar hath wept . . . I thrice presented him a kingly crown, which he did thrice refuse: was this ambition?"

How different was Brutus' meaning of the word ambitious from that of Terry's counselor: avaricious, audacious, covetous, and greedy. Two different viewpoints, two different interpretations. Both valid.

The literal meaning of ambition is "a going about," that of AMBIENCE (also AMBIANCE) is "a going around," in the sense of "things going on around it." Its meaning is atmosphere, surroundings, vibrations, and spirit. ☞ *The ambience of the stately old mansion was that of a half-dozen elderly, whispering aunts.* AMBIENT means surrounding. ☞ *Milton cherishes the ambient quiet of the countryside.*

An ARRANT snob is an unmitigated and notorious elitist. An ERRANT breeze is an aimless one. In medieval times KNIGHTS-ERRANT rode about in search of adventure, particularly that of rescuing damsels in distress; they are the foolish adventurers whom Cervantes satirized in his novel *Don Quixote.*

An electrical CIRCUIT goes around unless the breaker trips; circuit courts and judges move from place to place; and in days of yore circuit riders were preachers who rode horseback from pulpit to pulpit. A CIRCUITOUS argument or path goes round and round.

A COMMENCEMENT ceremony is often thought of as being the end of a segment of one's formal education, but its literal meaning is "to begin together." To COMMENCE is to start, inaugurate, INITIATE, and launch. ☞ *Tomorrow we commence our yearly fund drive.* To initiate is also to admit, accept, introduce, and usher in. ☞ *We expect to initiate six new members.* It also means to teach, drill, instruct, and coach. ☞ *We must initiate these children about water safety and pool behavior.*

An initiate is a beginner, novice, novitiate, proselyte, or rookie. ☞ *Most initiates seem lost for the first few days of the training course.* A person's INITIAL public performance is the first, primal, original, and INITIATORY one. The INITIATION of the baseball season is its opening, commencement, and debut. An initiation or induction ceremony is one held for new members.

INITIALISMS are acronyms such as NIMBY (*N*ot *I*n *M*y *B*ack *Y*ard) or KISS (*K*eep *I*t *S*imple, *S*tupid). INITIATIVE is enterprise, leadership, AMBITIOUSNESS, or resourcefulness, along with first step, lead, or opening move. ☞ *I took the initiative of telling him to buzz off.*

To EXIT is, literally, to "go out."

An assembly in ancient Rome was known as a COMITIA, meaning "to go together." At that time an advisor and companion to the emperor was called a COMES. In astronomy when two stars are seen as one, the fainter one is a comes or companion star; in anatomy a comes is a blood vessel that accompanies another one.

Something that is CONCOMITANT is attendant, concurrent, or connected to something else. ☞ *The salesperson's extraordinary gift of gab was a concomitant reason for her success.*

There is an abundance of ISSUES: children are the issue of their parents; the issue in a discussion is the topic, subject, question, or point; the issue of a newspaper or magazine is the edition, version, number, or printing; the issue that comes at the completion of a dispute, discussion, or meeting is the outcome, culmination, result, or consummation; when something is at issue, it is in dispute, in contention, or to be decided; and to take issue with another is to disagree, contend, oppose, and argue.

The post office issues (publishes) stamps; lava issues (spews forth) from volcanoes; public officials issue (announce) proclamations; and one's feelings of inferiority may issue (emerge from) an insecure childhood.

ITINERANTS are wayfarers, vagabonds, nomads, or TRANSIENTS. As an adjective it means nomadic, roaming, migratory, and wandering. ☞ *Itinerant minstrels used to stroll throughout the countryside.* An ITINERARY is a plan of one's trip; to ITINERATE is to go from place to place on a circuit; and ITINERACY is the act of moving from place to place, as a judge or preacher. An ITINERARIUM is a prayer in the breviary of the Roman Catholic religion that is used for a person who is about to travel; an INTROIT is the beginning part or song of a church service.

An OBIT or OBITUARY is the notice of the death of a person; its literal meaning is "gone away." Having PERISHED, that person has literally "gone completely." PERISHABLE objects are decomposable, biodegradable, short-lived, TRANSITORY, and ephemeral. ☞ *Please bring two items of nonper-*

ishable food to the meeting. The latter and IMPERISHABLE objects are stable, long-lasting, durable, and indestructible.

SEDITION is mutiny, defiance, insurrection, or rebellion. ☞ *Because it was wartime, he was accused of sedition.* A SEDITIOUS act is subversive, disloyal, treasonable, revolutionary, and insurgent. ☞ *In Boston the seditious colonists dumped tea into the harbor.*

SUDDEN means quick, abrupt, brisk, and brief. Ira Gershwin's lyrics for brother George's "A Foggy Day" sing out that "the age of miracles hadn't passed,/For SUDDENLY, I saw you there/And through foggy London town the sun was shining everywhere." Suddenly refers to hastily, sharply, swiftly, and abruptly. SUBITO is a musical direction meaning suddenly or abruptly.

TRANSIENT means temporary, passing, momentary, and impermanent. In Robert Frost's poem "Nothing Gold Can Stay" reminds us that all beauty is transient, brief, and TRANSITORY. "Nature's . . . early leaf's a flower;/But only so an hour." A TRANSITION is a change, passage, movement, or modification. ☞ *We all suffer through the transition from adolescence to adulthood.* A TRANSIT is a surveyor's instrument; it is the process of conveying people or goods from one place to another. ☞ *The package must have been lost in transit.*

A TRANSITIVE verb has an object: Sandy flew her plane home. An INTRANSITIVE verb has none: The bird flew away. A TRANCE is a daze, dream, reverie, or stupor. ☞ *Sometimes she writes as though she's in a trance.*

Additional English words related to the root: constable, county.
But not: *ire* [*ira-*, anger, wrath].
Combining forms: *amb-*, around; *cir-*, around; *com-*, thoroughly; *ex-*, out; *im-*, not; *in-*, not; *non-*, not; *ob-*, down; *per-*, away; *sed-*, apart; *sud-*, secretly; *trans-*, across.
Antonyms: *ambition*—apathy, lethargy, laziness; *ambitious*—idle, aimless, undemanding, easy; *circuitous*—straightforward, direct; *commence*—terminate, cease; *itinerant*—settled, fixed, established; *perish*—survive, endure, remain; *sedition*—loyalty, obedience; *seditious*—faithful, loyal; *sudden*—prolonged, protracted, cautious, prudent; *suddenly*—leisurely, hesitantly; *transient*—constant, lasting, permanent; *transitory*—eternal, permanent, perpetual.

J

JACERE, to lie, throw: EAS, JAC, JECT, JET

Often on cold winter mornings we can trace the TRAJECTORY of a **JET** by its contrail, that white skein of vapor etched against the blue sky.

Meanwhile, down below, clusters of flotsam and **JET**SAM or unwanted cargo **JET**TISONED, thrown overboard, and dumped by a ship far out at sea, along with a waterlogged house JOIST or beam that the tide is returning to the shore bob up and down in the **EAS**Y undulations of the water along the huge rocks of a **JET**TY.

In an AD**JAC**ENT, adjoining, and near by area a falconer, a seldom-seen hunter who uses hawks as his weapon, holds his bird with his JESS, a strap that keeps the falcon on a short leash. Sightseers have gathered, some CON**JECT**URING that the bird is in fact an electronic toy to be controlled from the ground, others wondering about the OB**JECT** of such a hunt, and a few finding it OB**JECT**IONABLE or offensive on the assumption that the falcon is being mistreated.

Gulls hover over an incoming fishing trawler, their OB**JECT**IVE, goal, or target being the RE**JECT**S that the crew throw into the water. The **EAS**E of the birds' flight awes the tourists in a passing pleasure boat.

A statement that is objective is impartial, candid, and open-minded. ☞ *I want to keep my remarks as objective as I can.* OB**JECT**IVITY refers to fairness, neutrality, or impartiality. A statement that is SUB**JECT**IVE is biased, emotional, personal, and prejudiced. ☞ *Let's hope that Uncle will not try to saddle Jimmy with all his subjective likes and dislikes.* In the introduction to his novel *Native Son,* Richard Wright discusses a writer's difficulties in converting subjective and private experiences into objective, concrete, detached, disinterested, and unbiased forms.

A SUB**JECT** is a topic, issue, text, or theme. ☞ *That is one subject that I hope will not come up in the meeting.* It is a citizen, native, or countryman. ☞ *I know that she has always been a loyal subject of this country.* It is also a field, branch of knowledge, course of study, or discipline. ☞ *"Any subject can be taught effectively in some intellectually honest form to any child at any stage of development," Jerome Bruner,* The Process of Education. As a verb it means to expose to, experience, endure, and suffer. ☞ *How could anyone subject a friend to such ridicule?* As a modifying word it is usually "subject to" and means bound by, dependent upon, or at the mercy of. ☞ *All of us are subject to this law. Our plans are subject to the weather. He is subject to asthma attacks.*

Subjects and objects are integral parts of most sentences. **AdJECTives** are our primary modifying words, and an **interJECTion** is a word or phrase that expresses emotion: Hey! Good grief! Holy cow! Ouch! Such expressions are often **interJECTed** into a conversation.

AbJECT means miserable and hopeless. ☞ *They rose out of abject poverty.* It also refers to contemptible and despicable. ☞ *The braggart turned out to be an abject coward.*

DeJECT means depress. ☞ *The news from the war zone always dejects them.* **DeJECTed** means depressed, disheartened, forlorn, and sad. ☞ *Their dejected looks told us the story of the game.*

To **eJECT** someone or something is to throw out, expel, get rid of, and oust. ☞ *Six of us were ejected from the council meeting.* **EJECTa** is matter thrown out. ☞ *The farm buildings were covered by the ejecta from the volcano.* **EJECTion** is expulsion, banishment, ouster, or dismissal. ☞ *Your ejection by the mortgage company was completely illegal.*

ProJECT is to throw forward, propel, shoot, and cast. ☞ *You must try to project your voice to the back row.* Project refers to extend, protrude, overhang, and jut out. ☞ *I want the ledge to project two feet in the front of the building.* Project also means to forecast, compute, estimate, and predict. ☞ *I see that the experts are again projecting an economic upturn.* As a noun it is a venture, undertaking, plan, or program. ☞ *My next major project is to clean out my closet.* A **proJECTion** is a prediction, estimate, computation, or calculation. ☞ *Their projection is that our population will double in the next decade.* It is also an overhang, ledge, protrusion, or extension. ☞ *Crawl along* that *projection? Not me! No way!* A **proJECTile** is a missile, bullet, or arrow, and a **proJECTor** is one who plans or schemes as well as a device for throwing an image on a screen.

ReJECT means to turn down, veto, expel, and cast off. ☞ *The board rejected every idea we submitted.* A reject is a loser, castoff, or pariah. ☞ *Those are human beings whom society looks upon as rejects.* A **reJECTion** is a refusal, dismissal, or rebuff. ☞ *The party's rejection of his offer to serve caused him to run as an independent candidate.*

Something **circumJACent** lies around or surrounds an object, (circumjacent mountains); if it is **interJACent,** it lies between or among other objects, (interjacent remarks); **subJACent** entities are below and **superJACent** above (subjacent patio; superjacent balcony).

Malaise means vague discomfort, discontent, **unEASiness,** and angst. **EASement** is a legal right to use another's land for a limited purpose, such as a kind of right of passage. ☞ *Now that our neighbors have given us the easement, we're able to get in and out of our property more easily.*

Additional English words related to the root: ejaculate, gist.

But not: *easel* [D *ezel,* ass, easel], display, stand; *jet* [Gk *gagates,* from Gagai, a mining town], a black coal used in making jewelry.

Combining forms: *ab-,* from; *ad-,* to; *con-,* together; *de-,* down; *dis-,* away; *e-,* out; *inter-,* between; *mal-,* ill; *ob-,* against; *pro-,* forward; *re-,* back; *sub-,* below; *tra-,* across.

Antonyms: *adjacent*—distant, remote, removed; *dejected*—cheerful, lighthearted, carefree; *easy*—difficult, harsh, stern; *malaise*—complacency, contentment, serenity; *object*—approve, support, void, illusion; *objectionable*—pleasing, agreeable, acceptable; *objective*—mental, subjective, intellectual, prejudiced; *reject*—keep, accept, save; *subject*—privileged, exempt, superior, ruler; *subjective*—impartial, objective, concrete, tangible.

JUGUM, yoke: JUG

The CONJUGATION of a verb is the listing of its forms in a particular tense; for example, the present tense of the verb *be:* I *am,* you *are,* it/he/she *is,* we *are,* you *are,* they *are.* To CONJUGATE also means to unite and join together, especially as a couple in marriage. To SUBJUGATE a people is to conquer, control, and enslave them. ☞ *The German forces under Hitler in World War II subjugated the citizens of six countries.* One can also attempt to subjugate or control one's own emotions, an unruly student, or a wild horse. Orator and statesman Daniel Webster in an 1834 speech spoke of how the colonies "raised their flag against a power, to which, for purposes of foreign conquest and SUBJUGATION, Rome, in the height of her glory, is not to be compared."

In anatomy, JUGULAR pertains to the throat or neck, but the word takes on additional meanings in the phrase "Go for the jugular." ☞ *The candidate went right for the jugular in his attempt to destroy his opponent's credibility.*

But not: *conjugal* [*jungere,* to join], pertaining to marriage; *jug* [from Jug, pet form of Joan or Judith], tall, rounded container for liquids; *juggernaut* [Skt *aganatha,* "Lord of the world"], an overwhelming force; *juggle* [*joculare,* to joke], manipulate.

Combining forms: *con-,* together; *sub-,* under.
Antonyms: *subjugate*—free, liberate, release.

JUNGERE, to join: JOIN, JUNCT

"I died for Beauty," Emily Dickinson wrote in about 1862,"—but was scarce/Adjusted in the Tomb/When One who died for Truth, was lain/ In an **ADJOINING** room." Her room was **JOINED** to, connected, next-door, and tangent; **ADJOIN** also has the broader meaning of to border, neighbor, bound, and rim. ☞ *The east end of our property adjoins the lake.*

An **ADJUNCT** is a supplement, auxiliary, appendix, or addendum. ☞ *An outgoing personality is a necessary adjunct for a salesperson.* In grammar it is a word or phrase that helps complete the meanings of other words; in the sentence "Few students volunteered willingly," "few" is an adjunct to the subject and "willingly" to the verb.

To **CONJOIN** is to connect, combine, consolidate, and incorporate. ☞ *The only chance we had was to conjoin our political parties; conjoined, we won the election.*

CONJUGAL pertains to marriage; its synonyms are matrimonial, marital, spousal, and wedded. ☞ *Those two exemplify conjugal faithfulness.*

Things that are **CONJUNCT** are bound closely together; in grammar they are the conjoining of, say, "we" and "have" to form the contraction "we've" and "will" and "not" to make "won't." Coordinating **CONJUNCTIONS** are words such as and, but, and or; subordinating conjunctions include because, while, and although. They are called **CONJUNCTIVE** words because they are connective, combined, **JOINING**, **CONJOINED**, and conjunct. In the world outside the grammar book, a conjunction has a similar meaning: union, combination, alliance, and league. ☞ *The mayor, in conjunction with several council members, got the meeting postponed.*

To **ENJOIN** is to command, order, and direct. ☞ *The police enjoined the crowd to disperse.* It is also to forbid, prohibit, and bar. ☞ *The judge enjoined the group from blocking access to the clinic.* An **INJUNCTION** is a command, **ENJOINDER**, regulation, or ordinance. ☞ *The recent injunction halted the picketing.* It is also a warning, instruction, or admonition. ☞ *Mother's daily injunction is for me to stop saying "you know."*

To **JOIN** is to connect, merge, and unite with; to DIS**JOIN** is to separate, divide, and isolate. A **JOIN**ER is a carpenter who specializes in woodworking; it is also a person who belongs to many clubs, societies, or associations. ☞ *Ted lost out because he simply isn't the joiner type.*

A **JOIN**T is a place where two things are joined or united; it is also a cut of meat; a saloon, restaurant, or nightclub that is thought of as a dive or dump; a marijuana cigarette. Something DIS**JOIN**TED is DIS**JOIN**ED, separated, dismembered, and disconnected. ☞ *The design of the building seemed disjointed to me.* It also means loose, illogical, and DIS**JUNCT**. ☞ *The play was so disjointed I couldn't make head nor tail of the plot.* To DIS**JOIN**T a chicken is to separate the parts for cooking.

When a task is undertaken **JOIN**TLY, it is done together, CON**JOIN**TLY, in conjunction, and unitedly. ☞ *We're more likely to make a go of this project if we work at it jointly.* A **JUNCT**ION is a union, fusion, merger, or intersection. ☞ *That's the most dangerous junction in the county.* A DIS**JUNCT**ION is a separation or an act of disjoining. ☞ *I admitted to a disjunction between what I thought and what I did.*

A **JUNCT**URE is a junction as well as a seam, joint, connection, nexus, or suture; it is also a point of time, moment, occasion, or crisis. ☞ *At this juncture, I urge that we take a brief recess.*

To RE**JOIN** is to reunite. ☞ *The title of her sermon was "Let's rejoin the human race.* It also means to answer, respond, or retort. A RE**JOIN**DER is a response, reply, or comeback. ☞ *"No way!" was the man's rejoinder.*

To SUB**JOIN** is to append or add on to the end of a piece of writing; when added it becomes a SUB**JOIN**DER, an appendix, or a post script. In grammar a SUB**JUNCT**IVE verb is one that is used to express doubtful, hypothetical, or subjective statements such as "If I were you. I wish I were rich. So be it. Be that as it may."

A JUNTA (sometimes JUNTO) is a clique, cabal, or faction. ☞ *A military junta assumed power after the overthrow of the prince.*

Combining forms: *ad-,* to; *con-,* together; *dis-,* apart; *en-,* in; *in-,* in; *re-,* again; *sub-,* under.
Antonyms: *adjoining*—separated, disconnected, individual, discrete; *conjoin*—separate, disband; *conjugal*—single, unmarried; *conjunctive*—disparate, separate, discrete; *disjoint*—connect, fasten; *disjointed*—coherent, logical, rational, consistent; *join*—sever, detach, diverge; *joint*—disconnect, part, divide.

JURARE, to swear: JUR, JUS

In 1616 Galileo Galilei was called to Rome and forced to **ABJURE** the doctrine set forth by Nicolas Copernicus of Poland that the earth revolves around the sun: to abjure is to recant, renounce, and repudiate.

In 1692 at the Salem witchcraft trial a judge **ADJURED** 12-year-old Anne Putnam to tell the truth about the "witch" that had put a curse upon her; to adjure is to entreat (as if under oath or penalty), beg, implore, or solemnly command.

Many of those present at the trial believed that Goody Brown had **CONJURED** up the image she swore she'd seen; to conjure is to make appear, call forth, and command; it also means to bewitch, cast a spell, charm, and practice magic. ☞ *Oh, yes! I've seen her conjure up a rabbit right out of a hat and then make that rabbit believe it was a chicken!* A **CONJURER** is a magician, wizard, juggler, sleight-of-hand artist, or one who practices voodoo. A **CONJURATION** is an incantation, spell, mumbo jumbo, abracadabra, hocus-pocus, or legerdemain. ☞ *"Double, double toil and trouble,/Fire burn and cauldron bubble," from the witches' conjuration in Shakespeare's* Macbeth.

To **INJURE** is to damage, hurt, offend, and wound. ☞ *My dear sir, I did not intend to injure your reputation.* An **INJURY** is a hurt, wound, or violation of another's rights under the law. Something **INJURIOUS** is abusive, defamatory, insulting, and offensive. ☞ *Patty filed a suit against Britt for his injurious personal attacks.* It can also be detrimental, deleterious, pernicious, and abusive. ☞ *Do you really believe that chewing tobacco is not injurious to your health?*

To **OBJURGATE** is to renounce, rebuke, and upbraid someone harshly or vehemently. ☞ *The nominee objurgated his opponent for injecting racism into the campaign.*

To **PERJURE** is to lie under oath. ☞ *Janice perjured herself when she denied ever meeting with Brad.* **PERJURY** is the willful giving of **PERJURED**, false, or dishonest testimony.

JURIDICAL pertains to the administration of justice as well as to law or **JURISPRUDENCE**, which is the philosophy of law; synonyms are legal, judicial, and forensic. ☞ *The quandary of whether this or that system was juridical was one of the factors that led Thorpe to his study of jurisprudence.* **JURISDICTION** is the right to interpret and apply the law as well as the territorial limits of that right. ☞ *Attley strongly objected to the judge's ruling that the local police had jurisdiction over the two soldiers.*

A **JURist** is a person versed in the law, as a judge, lawyer, or scholar. ☞ *Prof. Ferrer called Chief Justice Warren the most outstanding jurist of our times.* A **JURor** is a member of a **JURy**, a word that came into English as *juree* and then *jurie* before settling into its present form. But perhaps not exactly into its present position of respect; here is Dr. Samuel Johnson's question, as recorded by James Boswell, his biographer: "Consider, Sir, how should you like, though conscious of your innocence, to be tried before a jury for a capital crime, once a week?"

To be **JUSt** is to be virtuous, decent, and impartial. ☞ *They tried to teach their children to be just. The court handed down what was generally regarded as a just ruling.* As an adverb it means exactly, precisely, perfectly, only, and positively. ☞ *That is just what we've been looking for. His honor was just an average student. The girls were just radiant.* **JUStly** is an adverb meaning fairly and honestly. ☞ *There's a passage in the Bible that asks, "What does the Lord require of thee, but to do justly, and to love mercy, and to walk humbly with thy God?"* An **unJUSt** act is wrongful, inequitable, and **unJUStified.** ☞ *I felt the punishment was quite unjust.*

To **JUStify** one's actions is to legitimize them, as well as to vindicate, verify, excuse, and exonerate them. The **JUStification** of an action is a reason, circumstance, or explanation that defends or justifies it. ☞ *When asked what justification Betsy had for hitting Midge, she said, "Well, she hit me first."* Something that is **JUStifiable** is defensible, legitimate, right, proper, and fitting. ☞ *The court ruled that it was justifiable homicide.* An **unJUStifiable** act is inexcusable, indefensible, unpardonable, and intolerable. ☞ *Two senators today called the court's ruling "completely unjustifiable."*

JUS is a legal term meaning law; a legal power, principle, or right. **InJUStice** is inequity, unfairness, bias, or prejudice. **JUStice** is integrity, virtue, truth, or honesty.

Living a satisfactory life is often a matter of **adJUSting, readJUSting,** correcting, and compromising. In his poem "The Star-Splitter," Robert Frost speaks of the man who burned his farmhouse down to get enough money to buy—of all things—a telescope. His neighbors got a bit riled up about it, but soon they realized that if they cut off everyone who had sinned, there wouldn't be anyone left they could jaw with over a cup of coffee. "For to be social is to be forgiving," the poet concluded. So there you have it: **adJUStments** and **readJUStments.**

> **But not:** *jury-rig* [?], to improvise a repair; *jus* [F], juice, gravy, usu. *au jus,* served with its own juices.

Combining forms: *ab-,* away; *ad-,* to; *con-,* together; *-diction,* to say; *-fi, -fic, -fy,* to make, do; *-gate,* to drive, do; *in-,* not; *ob-,* against; *per-,* thoroughly; *-prudence,* knowledge; *re-,* again; *un-,* not.
Antonyms: *abjure*—uphold, embrace, swear by; *injure*—soothe, benefit, help; *injurious*—advantageous, salutary, beneficial; *injury*—blessing, favor, boon; *injustice*—equity, fairness, evenhandedness; *just*—bad, base, prejudiced, unreasonable, undeserved, illegitimate; *justice*—favoritism, inequity, illegality, bias, perfidy; *justifiable*—unwarranted, implausible, indefensible; *objurgate*—approve, extol, praise; *perjury*—verity, truth, fact.

JUVENIS, young, JUV

In Shakespeare's time a JUVENAL was a youth. In the bird world the first feathers of the young is its JUVENAL PLUMAGE.

Juvenal Plumage

Today's JUVENILES are youngsters, minors, teenagers, or kids, and their adjectives remain most unflattering: immature, childlike, pubescent, infantile, and sophomoric. Oh, that sophomore year; the word stems from the Greek *sophos,* wise + *moros,* dull, foolish, stupid! And so on to the junior year: inferior, lesser, minor, subordinate, and secondary. Oh, to be a senior, hence mature, advanced, superior, and veteran.

But then, years later, comes the yearning for REJUVENATION, a return to the past that one could hardly wait to grow out of, and dreaming of JUVENESCENCE, of being youthful in appearance and spirit, of appearing to be JUVENESCENT and youthful.

True, one can REJUVENATE an old piano, a badly-worn shoe, or a neglected garden, and sometimes a nap, a shower, or a vacation can rejuvenate one's energy and vitality, for among its synonyms are revive, restore, and revitalize. But the garden of youth? Alas, it is gone and can be captured again only by reading one's JUVENILIA, the writings of those years long past.

Combining form: *re-,* again, back.

K

KAIEIN, to burn: CAU

A **CAU**stic substance is capable of burning, corroding, and destroying living tissue; a caustic remark is capable of searing, burning, mortifying, outraging, and antagonizing the feelings of a living being. To **CAU**terize a wound is to burn or sear any abnormal or infected tissue.

A holo**CAU**st is any mass slaughter or destruction of life or any total devastation, especially by fire. ☞ *All the town's books and documents were destroyed when the holocaust wiped out the Square. The* Holocaust was the attempt by the rulers of Nazi Germany before and during World War II to destroy the Jewish people. By the end of the war six million of the eight million Jews in the countries occupied by the Nazis had been murdered.

Calm comes to us from *kaiein* by way of the Latin *cauma,* "heat of the day." Hence it meant a rest or resting place at about high noon, a spot, preferably, that is placid and peaceful, cool and collected, or sedate and serene. The verb becalm means that the sailor will have no wind to fill the sails and move the boat. ☞ *The girls were late for their appointment when their sailboat was becalmed for more than three hours.* A calmative is a sedative or a tranquilizer.

But not: *cause* [*causa,* reason], motive; *cautious* [*cavere,* to heed], wary.
Combining forms: *be-,* verb forming; *holo-,* whole, entire.

KAMARA, vault: CAM, CHAM

In Shakespeare's time a cumrade was a **CHAM**ber-fellow, a person with whom one shared a room, barracks, or lodging, most often in the military. Today it is comrade in English, **CAM**arade in French, Kamerad in German, **CAM**arada in Spanish and is an associate, companion, partner, colleague, or co-worker in any field of endeavor. In 1755, Dr. Samuel Johnson's dictionary defined a chum as a chamberfellow, a term used in the universities. **CAM**araderie, a word that means comradeship and good fellowship, also comes to us from that sharing of quarters.

A legislative hall is known as a **CHAMber**, as is the legislature itself. ☞ *Both chambers passed the resolution unanimously.* **CAMeral** pertains to a judicial or legislative chamber. ☞ *We learned that Nebraska is the only state with a unicameral legislature, and all the other states are bicameral.*

The predecessor of the **CAMera** that we take pictures with was originally a dark chamber or box called the **camera obscura**, which means "dark box." That name persisted until L.J.M. Daguerre developed the first photographic camera. The **CAMcorder** is a television camera with an incorporated VCR [*cam(era) + (re)corder*]. **On camera** refers to being filmed. ☞ *Please refrain from scratching when on camera.*

A judge's private office is called a camera, hence the phrase **in camera**, meaning "in the privacy of a judge's **CHAMbers**." ☞ *The judge called the attorneys to a meeting in camera.*

A restaurant or cafe that offers music, a dance floor, and entertainment is often called a **cabaret**. The literal meaning of the word is "small chamber."

A **CHAMberlain** used to be the manager of a royal household; today he or she is more likely to be a receiver of rents and revenues in a municipal government, a treasurer. It was **CHAMbermaids** who were employed to do the actual work of keeping those enormous households neat, tidy, and fit for a king.

Combining forms: *bi-*, two; *uni-*, one.

KOSMOS, order, the world or universe: COSM

A **COSMopolis** is a large, internationally important city inhabited by a melting pot of people from all over the world. It is sometimes described as a capital city or a world capital, its residents being **COSMopolitan**, i.e., sophisticated, broad-minded, worldly, and urbane. What they are *not* is insular, provincial, narrow-minded, parochial, and local. Socrates said it ages ago in *Plutarch:* "I am not an Athenian nor a Greek, but a citizen of the world."

That is not to say that true **COSMopolites** turn their backs on their own cities or countries. English poet laureate Alfred Lord Tennyson said in "Hands All Round" (1885), "That man's the best Cosmopolite/Who loves his native country best."

A **COSMic** event, matter, or happening is vast, immense, infinite, and stupendous. ☞ *Our American history teacher said that the Civil War was a cosmic battle between powerful people and enormous principles.*

Cosmic dust consists of fine particles of matter in space; **cosmic noise** is radio frequency sound that comes from outside the earth's atmosphere; and a **cosmic ray shower** is composed mainly of atomic nuclei that originate in space and reach the earth from all directions.

A **COSModrome** is a launching site for spacecraft and **COSMonauts** in countries of the former USSR. **COSMogony** is a story or theory of the origin and growth of the universe, solar system, etc., **COSMography** is the mapping of—or a kind of geography of—the universe, and **COSMology** is the branch of philosophy that deals with the study of the evolution and structure of the universe.

A **macroCOSM** is the universe considered as a whole; it is also the total or entire structure of something. ☞ *The speaker referred to the macrocosm of war.* A **microCOSM** is the opposite; it is a world in miniature, a little world. ☞ *The science teacher said that the cup of water that we got from the pond contained a microcosm of marine life.*

A **COSMetic** is a beauty preparation, most often applied to the face. It is also any alteration or change made for the sake of appearance. ☞ *The changes made at the concert hall were entirely cosmetic; it looks better, but the acoustics are still dreadful.* **COSMetology** is the art of applying cosmetics and a **COSMetician** applies, manufactures, or sells cosmetics. **Cosmetic surgery** is often called a face-lift. It can be done to eliminate wrinkles and other signs of aging from one's skin or evidence of deterioration from a structure or other manmade object.

> **Combining forms:** *-drome,* referring to a large structure; *-graphy,* form of drawing; *-ician,* denoting an occupation; *-agony,* origination; *-ology,* study of; *-polis,* city; *-polite,* citizen.
> **Antonyms:** *cosmic*—small, tiny, minute; *cosmopolis*—village, hamlet, town.

KRINEIN, to distinguish, separate: CRIT

A **crisis** is an emergency, dilemma, predicament, or quandary. ☞ *I've got a real crisis in my life; I finally got a date with Cathy and I'm flat broke.* If you have two of these, you have **crises.**

A **CRITerion** is a yardstick when it is used in the sense of a standard, guideline, measure, or parameter, by which to judge something. ☞ *The criterion Professor Sills uses in her writing class is this book of essays by E.B. White.* No "s" here to form a plural either. ☞ *What are the criteria for judging the outstanding photographs at the exhibit?*

A **CRITic** is a judge, reviewer, expert, or authority. **CRITicism** has three distinct meanings. First, it is often negative, i.e., sarcastic, panning, and censuring (Your poem has no redeeming features; I suggest you take up another occupation). Second, when it is constructive, it is a horse of a different feather (While I think your theme is rather badly organized, you have some cogent points here, and if you will follow my suggestions, you can turn this into a fine paper). And third, it is often neutral, such as in a factual or objective review of a book or play (This is a factual account of the rise and fall of a family business). In this sense it is also an evaluation, review, comment, analysis, or **CRITique.**

Synonyms of **CRITicize** are generally divided into two camps: judge, evaluate, and analyze. ☞ *Lynn frequently criticizes books for the university quarterly.* And condemn, ridicule, blame, and denounce. ☞ *Have you noticed how they both constantly criticize each other?*

A person who is **CRITical** of another may be faultfinding, carping, picky, and disparaging. If someone announces that this is a critical time in our lives, it is grave, serious, crucial, and perilous. When hospitalized patients' vital signs are abnormal and unstable, their condition is grave, serious, and critical. A critical measurement must be exact, precise, and true.

William Hazlitt, a nineteenth-century English writer, said that the only vice that cannot be forgiven is **hypocrisy,** i.e., fakery, deceit, duplicity, and pretense. The culprit who rates such low praise is a **hypoCRITe,** one who pretends to be what he is not; instead he or she is a fake, imposter, charlatan, or deceiver, all of which add up to one who is insincere, false, two-faced, dissembling, and phony. In short, **hypoCRITical.**

But not: *critter* [var. of *creature*], animal, bug, or little kid.
Combining form: *hypo-,* under.
Antonyms: *critic*—advocate, supporter; *critical*—supportive, helpful, safe, sound, loose, lax; *criticism*—approval, acclaim, praise; *criticize*—laud, commend, applaud; *hypocrisy*—sincerity, honesty, integrity; *hypocritical*—genuine, heartfelt, true.

KYKLOS, cycle, wheel: CYCL

The most popular form of transportation in the world today is the **biCYCLe,** a person-powered, two-wheeled **CYCLing** vehicle originally called a velocipede [*veloci-* speed + *-pede,* foot] and today generally referred to as a **bike,** a shortened, alternative form. One of the earliest models was the "Dandy Horse," a two-wheeler propelled by pushing one's feet against the ground, a kind of child's scooter with a seat. One of the first pedal-powered bikes had tires of iron; it was known by its riders as "the boneshaker." This was *not* the bike that **CYCList** Jose Meiffret was pedaling in Freiburg, Germany, in 1962 when his **CYCLometer** peaked at a record 127.243 miles per hour!

Today we have **triCYCLes** for tots and the physically impaired, **uniCYCLes** for entertainers, **motorbikes** or motor scooters for faster transportation, **motorCYCLes** for sport, speed, and maneuverability, **CYCLeries** for their rent, sale, and repair, and **CYCLe-clips** for the rider who is forgetful enough to wear long pants.

A **biker** is anyone who rides in competition or as a hobby, as well as those who are members of organized motorcycle gangs or groups. A bicycle path is one that runs alongside a roadway; other names are bike path and **bikeway.** Some roadways are **CYCLable,** while others are more suitable for the heavy-duty bikes that are built to compete in **CYCLocross** races over rough terrain.

CYCLes are periods of time or series of occurrences, ages, eons, eras, or epochs that repeat themselves. We experience and speak of life cycles, business cycles, weather cycles, and we are ever aware of the some twenty-nine and a half days that constitute the lunar cycle from full moon to full moon. **CYCLic** and **CYCLical** are its adjective forms. ☞ *So much of our retail business is cyclic/cyclical: Valentine's Day, Easter, graduations, all the way to Christmas.* To **reCYCLe** something is to put it to new use such as processing waste materials or adapting an object to a new use; synonyms are alter, reuse, restore, and rehabilitate. ☞ *Those two stand-up comics make their living recycling old jokes.* Fortunately for us, not all jokes are **reCYCLable.**

Cyclops

The winds of a **CYCLone** swirl in circles, counterclockwise in the Northern Hemisphere, clockwise down South. **CYCLonic** winds have been clocked at up to 120 miles per hour. A **CYCLorama** is a pictorial display of an epic event such as the Civil War painted on the interior walls of a cylindrical room. In psychiatry a **CYCLoid** personality is characterized by cyclic variations in the patient's moods. The **CYCLamen,** a houseplant, is so-called because of its rounded bulbs and, perhaps, its circular leaves. **CYCLops,** a giant of Greek mythology, had one large round eye in the middle of his forehead; its adjective

CYCLOPEAN means huge, gigantic, humungous, and vast.

An **enCYCLopedia** (also **enCYCLopaedia, CYCLopedia**) is a book or set of books that includes information about all branches of knowledge that lie within the circle of education. Someone with an **enCYCLopedic** memory has one that is comprehensive, omniscient, and erudite. An **enCYCLical** in the Roman Catholic Church is a letter from the pope addressed to the bishops; elsewhere it is a letter or article intended for wide and general circulation.

But not: *cylinder* [Gk *kylindros,* roller], object with straight sides and circular ends.

Combining forms: *bi-,* two; *-cross,* as in cross-country; *en-,* in, within; *-meter,* measure; *-pedia,* education; *-rama,* view; *re-,* again; *tri-,* three; *uni-,* one.

Antonyms: *cyclopean*—miniature, Lilliputian, microscopic, dwarfish; *encyclopedic*—illiterate, shallow, uninformed, ignorant, unlettered.

L

LABOR, exertion, labor, toil: LABOR

At the Democratic party's convention in Chicago in 1896 William Jennings Bryan, a magnetic orator, concluded his speech for the presidential nomination with this sentence: "We will answer their demand for a gold standard by saying to them: You shall not press down upon the brow of **LABOR** this crown of thorns, you shall not crucify mankind upon a cross of gold." His speech assured his nomination but not his election: he lost to William McKinley, the Republican candidate.

When Shakespeare's Macbeth describes the sleep that he fears he may never have again, he calls it "sore labor's bath," the labor that is exertion, effort, drudgery, or toil. In childbirth labor is known as birth pangs, birth throes, or parturition. To labor is to strive, strain, plod, and struggle. It is also to suffer, agonize, and be troubled by. ☞ *Poor Henry labored under the delusion that he was president.*

A **LABOR**ER is a workman, worker, wage earner, or hired hand. Both labor and BE**LABOR** are verbs meaning to carry on about something for too long a time. ☞ *I suggest we end the discussion; all we're doing is laboring/belaboring the obvious.*

A piece of writing that is strained, forced, unnatural, and contrived is said to be **LABOR**ED. ☞ *Macall's speech was praised, but I found it much too labored.* When people are so described, they may be awkward, clumsy, wooden, and halting. ☞ *Brit's walk has been somewhat labored ever since the accident.* **LABOR**IOUS activities are tiresome, arduous, and strenuous. ☞ *The higher we climbed, the more laborious our breathing became.*

LABORING means working, toiling, and struggling. A **LABOR**ATORY is a workshop, workroom, lab, or atelier, any place where observation, investigation, experimentation, is or can be done. ☞ *"We're all of us guinea pigs in the laboratory of God," Tennessee Williams,* Camino Real.

To COL**LABOR**ATE is to team up, cooperate, create together, and coauthor. ☞ *Rodgers and Hammerstein collaborated on the movie* The Sound of Music. But since the days of Hitler's Germany and Mussolini's Italy, COL**LABOR**ATOR and COL**LABOR**ORATIONIST have often been used to indicate a traitor, puppet, turncoat, or renegade. ☞ *Many collaborators/collaborationists were executed following the liberation of Paris in August, 1944.* COL**LABOR**ATION is also two-sided; if it's undercover, as with the enemy, it's bad; if it's with a friend and on the up and up, then it's cooperation, partnership, affiliation, or teamwork.

To **eLABORate** on a point is to enlarge, expand, clarify, and amplify. ☞ *Several reporters asked the senator to elaborate on his statement.* As an adjective it means complex, involved, and complicated. ☞ *The lighting system was much too elaborate and expensive for our little theater.* It also means ornate, showy, fancy, and ostentatious. ☞ *Everyone in the pageant wore an elaborate costume.*

> **Combining forms:** *be-*, verb forming; *col-*, together; *e-*, out.
> **Antonyms:** *elaborate*—plain, simple, natural, basic; *labor*—rest, leisure, loaf, shirk; *labored*—effortless, facile, easy, offhand, light; *laborious*—simple, facile, natural, easy.

LATUS, carried, borne: LAT

When a missile, rocket, or spacecraft reenters through the atmosphere, the nose cone or protective surface is **abLATed** by the intense heat. Its literal meaning is "carried and borne away," or, in this case, burned, heated, and melted. ☞ *A glacier's ice, the guide explained, is ablated by melting or evaporation.*

When the pages of a manuscript are put into their proper sequence or order they are **colLATed**, i.e., carried or put together. ☞ *The graduate student collated the pages of Dr. Fern's latest textbook.* This also occurs when two or more sets of data are merged or carried together by a computer operator. The act of doing this is called a **colLATion**, which is also the name of a light meal or snack, as well as the practice in a monastery of reading Scripture at the close of day.

Something that is **colLATeral** is secondary, subordinate, and ancillary. ☞ *These stories are merely collateral to Hemner's major literary goals.* The word also means confirming, supportive, substantiating, and additional. ☞ *The new witness's collateral evidence influenced the jury.* As a noun it means security, guarantee, bond, or surety. ☞ *Carlos had to give his watch as collateral for the money he borrowed.*

When two or more things correspond, relate, and connect, they **correLATe**. ☞ *The attorney attempted to correlate the seemingly unconnected testimony of the various witnesses.* Hence **correLATion** is the mutual relationship of two or more items or things; synonyms are interdependence, correspondence, reciprocity, or give-and-take. ☞ *The CEO says there must be a positive correlation between the employees'* *performance and their pay.* Words that correspond to each other are said to be **correLATive**; examples are *either . . . or, former . . . later,* and *not only . . . but also.*

Medicines can be used to **diLATe** one's blood vessels and prevent clotting; thus the vessels are expanded, enlarged, and widened. When one comments at length on a topic, he or she can be said to dilate on it. ☞ *Superintendent Oswell dilated on the importance of the honor code.* To be **diLATory** is to be slow, tardy, delaying, and procrastinating. ☞ *The chess player's dilatory tactics infuriated his opponent.*

To **eLATe** others is to make them happy or proud. ☞ *This good news will elate your mom.* People who are **eLATed** are joyful, exultant, exhilarated, and jubilant, and one can hope that their **eLATion**, their exaltation, delight, and rapture will be lasting.

An **obLATe** object is flattened at the poles; an American football is an oblate spheroid. In the Roman Catholic church an oblate is a lay person who performs special religious duties. An **obLATion** is a religious offering or something carried toward. ☞ *"Bring no more vain oblations; incense is an abomination unto me." Isaiah 1:13.* A **preLATe** is a high ranking member of the clergy, one ranking before (or above) others.

To **reLATe** a story is to narrate, tell, recount, and convey it. ☞ *Despite painful memories, Belle tried to relate the story of that terrifying hour.* To relate, say, Belle's story to another's life is to connect, join, link, and correlate the two. ☞ *I could not help relating Belle's experience to my own.* Two beings or objects that are **reLATed** are joined, linked, and united; when two ideas or occurrences are related, they are relevant, connected, and affiliated. ☞ *Why Kyle felt that his unhappy childhood was related to his D- in computer science was beyond me.*

A **reLATion** or **reLATionship** is a connection, coupling, bond, or liaison. ☞ *There is no relation between our store and the national chain of the same name.* A relation is a kin. ☞ *I think she's a very distant relation of mine.* It is a reference, application, regard, or bearing. ☞ *Your comments have absolutely no relation to the book we were discussing.* It is a telling, narration, report, or description. ☞ *Kim's relation of Mom's reaction to the new styles at the fashion show was hilarious.* Relations are also connections between peoples and countries. ☞ *She's a strong candidate for Secretary of State; her expertise is in foreign relations.*

A **reLATive** is a kin. As an adjective, it means relevant, pertinent, apropos, and germane. ☞ *Your work record was not relative to the demands of the position.* It also means comparable and comparative. ☞ *Relative to the other apartments we've looked at, this is a real bargain.*

There are those who claim that Albert Einstein's theory of **reLATivity** is beyond understanding to all but a chosen few; but he himself described it differently in the *News Chronicle* (1949): "When a man sits with a pretty girl for an hour, it seems like a minute. But let him sit on a hot stove for a minute—and it's longer than any hour. That's relativity."

SuperLATive is an adjective meaning peerless, supreme, nonpareil, and matchless. ☞ *Uncle Emmett's a superlative performer.* As a noun it can refer to a person or thing of the highest degree, as well as to exaggerated expressions of praise. ☞ *"I appreciated all those superlatives," the speaker said following his introduction, "and agree with everyone of them."*

To **transLATe** a foreign language into one's own is to convert or render it, i.e., to carry [the words] across into a second language. Sometimes we wish that the technical expert would translate his or her jargon into more common terms. One can also wish to translate one's wishes into deeds. Many of the classics that we read are **transLATions** from other languages.

When the football quarterback throws a **LATeral** pass, he tosses it sideways or to the side. When an employee is moved to a new position, it can be a demotion, a promotion, or a lateral move. ☞ *Barney was disappointed that his move was lateral rather than the upgrade he had hoped for.*

We learn about the lines marking the **LATitudes** (north and south) and longitudes (east and west) from maps and globes. **LATitude** is also used in the sense of having freedom from narrow restrictions; it means having leeway, liberty, indulgence, or elbowroom. ☞ *The students at Oxham Academy have more than the usual amount of academic and social latitude.* A **LATitudinarian**, therefore, is one whose conduct, ideas, interests, and opinions are not restricted and confined; such a person is said to have a **LATitudinous** outlook.

(Note: for **legisLATor** and related words also stemming in part from *latus* see *lex,* law, page 168.)

> **But not:** *latent* [*latere,* to be hidden], dormant, potential.
> **Combining forms:** *ab-,* away; *col-, cor-,* together; *di-,* apart; *e-,* out; *ob-,* toward; *pre-,* before; *re-,* back; *super-,* above; *trans-,* across.
> **Antonyms:** *correlate*—contradict, oppose; *dilate*—shrink, wane, reduce; *dilatory*—active, quick, diligent, prompt; *elated*—gloomy, mournful, dejected; *elation*—melancholy, misery, sadness; *relate*—separate, dissociate, be irrelevant; *related*—independent, isolated; *relation*—isolation, disconnection, separateness; *relative*—autonomous, unique, inappropriate, irrelevant.

LAUDARE, to praise: LAUD

To **LAUD** is to praise and extol; it is also a hymn of praise and, as **LAUDs**, a morning prayer. A **LAUDatory** speech is one that is filled with praise. ☞ *Burkly was embarrassed by the laudatory remarks the governor made about him.* Something that is **LAUDable** is deserving of praise. ☞ *It was, Robin felt, a laudable idea, but she wasn't sure that the town was quite prepared for it.* A **LAUDation** is an act of **LAUDing**, of praising; it is an eulogy, tribute, or testimonial.

College seniors who can boast of high grade-point averages often keep one eye on the standings of their peers. They would like to hit the top, **summa cum LAUDe**, graduating with highest distinction, or the next notch, **magna cum LAUDe**, graduating with great distinction, or, at the very least, **cum LAUDe**, graduating with distinction.

But not: *applaud* [*plaudere,* to clap hands], to show approval by clapping.
Combining forms: *cum,* with; *magna,* great; *summa,* highest.
Antonyms: *laudable*—contemptible, ignoble, execrable, reprehensible; *laudatory*—belittling, abusive, scornful.

LEGARE, to bind, choose, send: LEGA, LEGE, LEGI

An **alLEGEd** embezzler is one who someone has accused of having stolen money but who has not been convicted of the crime; in other words, the accused is said, supposed, purported, and claimed to have done wrong. **AlLEGEdly** means supposedly, presumably, possibly, and hypothetically. **AlLEGAtions** are charges, claims, accusations, or assertions. **AlLEGEs** refers to asserts, states, charges, and declares.

Professors in a **colLEGE** (or any other business or profession) are **colleagues,** persons with whom one has chosen to work. A workplace that has a **colLEGIal** atmosphere is one in which a group of colleagues share responsibilities. A **colLEGIan** is a student in a college, one who may or may not choose to wear **colLEGIate** apparel or to be active in either **intracolLEGIate** or **intercolLEGIate** activities.

A **LEGAte** is an envoy, emissary, agent, or delegate; in the Roman Catholic church he is a member of the clergy **deLEGAted** and appointed by the pope. A **LEGAtion** is a **deLEGAtion,** that is, a diplomatic minister and his or her staff, as well as serving as the name of its official headquarters.

A **LEGAcy** is anything handed down from the past. ☞ *Quincy had hoped for a large inheritance, but his grandfather's principal legacy to him was his uncommon integrity.*

Additional English word related to the root: relegate.
But not: *allegiance* [OF *liege,* vassal], loyalty; *legend* [*legere,* to read], myth.
Combining forms: *al-,* to; *col-,* together; *de-,* from; *intra-,* within; *inter-,* between; *re-,* away.

LEGEIN, to gather, speak: LEXI, LOG, LOGUE

A **LEXIcographer** is a writer of dictionaries; he or she is involved in the gathering of the words of a language, a process known as **LEXIcography**. Gathered with the words in their creating of a **LEXIcon** are their definitions and, often, their etymologies. The emphasis of such a book is **LEXIcal**, that is, it is concerned with the words of the language rather than the grammar.

A person suffering from **aLEXIa** is word-blind and unable to read. **DysLEXIa** is an impairment of the ability to read, but it can be overcome or compensated for. Leonardo da Vinci and Albert Einstein, two of the world's greatest geniuses, were **dysLEXIc**.

A **cataLOG** (also **cataLOGUE**) is a listing of items available for sale or use. An **eclectic** catalog (or anthology, philosophy, or course of study) is diverse, broad, catholic, comprehensive, and wide-ranging. ☞ *This year's catalog is an eclectic one, featuring a vast range of artists. Rose's taste in music is eclectic.*

A **dialect** is a variety of language that is set apart by geography or social differences. ☞ *I asked the man for a bottle of soda, but he didn't understand my dialect; he asked me if I meant "tonic," "pop," "a soft drink," or "sody water."* **Dialectics** is the practice of examining statements by question and answer.

A **diaLOGUE** (**diaLOG**) is a conversation, chat, or interview, whereas a **monoLOGUE** (**monoLOG**) is a one-person show, soliloquy, lecture, or tirade.

The **DecaLOGUE** is the Ten Commandments; its literal meaning is "ten words" or "ten sentences." An **anaLOGUE** (**anaLOG**) is something similar, like, or akin to something else. Shakespeare based many of the plots of his plays on actual events, and the accounts and books that he found these in are called analogues. For example, there are several analogues for the story of *The Tempest,* Shakespeare's last play, and from these he borrowed both ideas and details.

A PROLOGUE (PROLOG) is an introduction or preface to a literary work; in the theater it is delivered before a performance. An introductory essay to a book is sometimes called a PROLEGOMENON. An EPILOGUE (EPILOG) comes at the end as a supplement or postscript of sorts. A TRAVELOGUE (TRAVELOG) is a talk or visual presentation of someone's travels.

Combining forms: *a-,* without; *ana-,* upon; *cata-,* thoroughly; *deca-,* ten; *dia-,* between; *dys-,* bad; *ec-,* out; *epi-,* in addition; *-grapher,* writer; *-graphy,* writing; *mono-,* one; *pro-,* before.
Antonyms: *eclectic*—narrow, limited, specialized; *epilogue*—prologue, preface; *monologue*—colloquy, give-and-take; *prologue*—epilogue, postlude, sequel, aftermath.

LEVARE, to lighten, lift, raise: LEV

The Tuesday before Lent is known as Mardi Gras (literally "fat Tuesday"). In New Orleans and Paris it is the last day of the Lenten CARNIVAL, (literally the "lifting of flesh or meat") as well as the last day that a Roman Catholic is permitted to eat meat. A carnival is also a traveling circus or amusement park often setting up in a small town, or any festival, jamboree, festivity, celebration, or merrymaking.

One of the features of many such fiestas is an entertainer who is an expert in LEGERDEMAIN, pulling rabbits out of hats, long skeins of different-colored pieces of cloth from a small purse, or bright coins from a child's ear. It is known also as sleight of hand, magic, hocus-pocus, or prestidigitation. ☞ *The prime minister's triumph was a clever piece of legerdemain.* LEGERITY is physical or mental agility, quickness, or nimbleness. ☞ *Percy's unusual legerity won him a spot on a TV game show.*

When our pains, hurts, or worries are lightened, they are ALLEVIATED, lessened, mitigated, allayed, and lifted. To ELEVATE is to boost, uplift, exhilarate, and elate. ☞ *The good news elevated our spirits.* It is to raise, promote, advance, honor, and improve. ☞ *I had hoped to be elevated to assistant floor manager.* It is also, of course, to physically hoist, upraise, heighten, lift up, and boost. Our ELEVATOR is a "lift" in London.

The adjective ELEVATED means raised. ☞ *It was her first ride on an elevated railroad.* It refers to cheerful, elated, and animated. ☞ *Their elevated spirits won our hearts.* It also means noble, lofty, and exalted. ☞ *The speaker left us with elevated thoughts.* The ELEVATION, altitude, or height of Santa Fe, New Mexico, is 6,950 feet above sea level; New

Orleans is five feet. It is also a promotion, advancement, boost, or improvement. ☞ *Lynn's elevation to the presidency of the club was a surprise.*

Yeast is a LEAVEN or LEAVENING that makes bread dough rise. But leaven is an agent that works to alter or transform substances other than flour. ☞ *Annie's story would be too dreary to read were it not leavened by her unusually bright wit.* A **LEVER** is a simple tool such as a crowbar or pry used to lift a heavy object. **LEVERAGE** is the action of the lever; it also means influence, clout, or power. ☞ *As the town's former mayor, Millie can exert a lot of leverage in the negotiations.* A **LEVEE** is both an embankment intended to prevent river flooding and a party or reception, usually in someone's honor. ☞ *Herman claimed he attended a presidential levee at the White House.* The lands bordering the eastern shores of the Mediterranean Sea are known as the **LEVANT**; a **LEVANTINE** is a native of the area.

LEVITY is lightness, humor, horseplay, or fun. To **LEVITATE** is to rise or float in the air by supernatural means in defiance of gravity. The narrator of J. D. Salinger's short story entitled "For Esme—with Love and Squalor" is a lonely American soldier stationed in England in 1944. On the rainy afternoon before D-day he stops in at a church and sits in on a rehearsal of a children's choir. He finds the music so pure and melodious that the thought of experiencing **LEVITATION**—a supernatural rising of his body into the air—passes through his mind.

A **LEVY** is the assessment, collection, or imposition of a tax, fee, duty, or excise. ☞ *The legislature okayed the levy of a tax on cigarette sales.* It is also conscription, a military draft, the calling up of troops, or a draft. ☞ *Several Congressional leaders called for a levy of troops to meet the threat.* As a verb it means to impose, collect, demand, and charge. ☞ *The vote to levy a "sin" tax lost once again.* It also means to make war. ☞ *No one voted to levy war against the tiny country.*

To **LEVIGATE** is to grind something into a fine powder. ☞ *The pumice stone must be levigated before it can be used to polish the trophy.*

When something is re**LEVANT**, it is pertinent, apropos, germane, and to the point. ☞ *We liked the book because it was so relevant to what we had been studying in class.* Re**LEVANCE** and re**LEVANCY** are pertinence, aptness, relatedness, or appropriateness. ☞ *I was unable to see the relevance of the moderator's comment to the matter at hand.* An irre**LEVANCE** or irre**LEVANCY** is inappropriateness, unsuitability, or inapplicability. ☞ *The remark's irrelevance didn't escape the members of the jury—thanks to the defense attorney.* An irre**LEVANT** remark is unrelated, immaterial, impertinent, and inconsequent. ☞ *However interesting your point was, it was completely irrelevant.* But according to essayist Charles Lamb in *Last Essays of Elia* (1833), that can also apply to people: "A poor relation is the irrelevant thing in nature."

To RELIEVE pain or tension is to assuage, lighten, alleviate, and allay. ☞ *Ben's levity relieved the tension that had been building up.* It means comfort, cheer, encourage, and refresh. ☞ *The girls were relieved when their parents finally arrived.* It means remove, take out, replace, and substitute for. ☞ *The lieutenant was relieved of his command.* It also means rescue, liberate, and unburden. ☞ *Your timely check relieved me of my immediate worries.*

RELIEF is peace of mind, encouragement, release from anxiety, or rest. It is also welfare, dole, or public assistance.

> **But not:** *level* [*libra,* balance], flat; *leviathan* [Heb *liwyathan*], sea monster; anything of immense size.
> **Combining forms:** *al-,* to; *e-,* out; *-gate,* to drive; *ir-,* not; *re-,* again.
> **Antonyms:** *elevate*—degrade, belittle, lower, impair; *elevated*—mundane, pedestrian, mediocre, trivial; *leverage*—impotence, futility, frailty, weakness; *levity*—gravity, sobriety, seriousness, dignity; *legerity*—apathy, lethargy, lassitude, malaise; *relief*—relapse, discomfort, distress; *relieve*—hamper, irritate, undermine, abuse.

LEX, law: LEG

Something that is **LEG**ITIMATE is **LEG**AL, lawful, valid, and **LEG**IT. ☞ *I am the legitimate owner of that car. The court ruled that the teachers' demands were legitimate.* An IL**LEG**ITIMATE act is IL**LEG**AL, unlawful, unsanctioned, and improper. ☞ *The county commissioners were charged with making illegitimate use of public funds.* Transactions that are **LEG**ITIMIZED, are **LEG**ALIZED, authorized, and justified. An illegitimate child is born outside of a legal marriage. A PARA**LEG**AL is an attorney's assistant but not licensed to practice law.

The **LEG**ISLATIVE body of Nebraska is unicameral (having but one chamber or house); all the other state **LEG**ISLATURES or General Assemblies or General Courts consist of two houses. In most cases the **LEG**ISLATORS will be senators or representatives, although in some states they are called delegates. Unabridged dictionaries identify a woman member as a **LEG**ISLATRIX or **LEG**ISLATRESS, with plurals of **LEG**ISLATRIXES, **LEG**ISLATRICES, and **LEG**ISLATRESSES.

Voting is a PRIVI**LEG**E that all citizens of the United States should take advantage of. People who live in countries with democratic governments are the PRIVI**LEG**ED ones.

A friend who is LOYAL is true, devoted, trustworthy, and conscientious, whereas one who is DISLOYAL is false, unfaithful, and perfidious. Synonyms of LOYALTY are allegiance, fidelity, obedience, or devotion.

> **But not:** *delegate* [*legare,* to appoint], deputy; *legible* [*legere,* to read], readable.
> **Combining forms:** *dis-,* not; *il-,* not; *-late,* to propose; *para-,* lesser, subordinate; *privi-,* one's own.
> **Antonyms:** *disloyal*—steadfast, scrupulous, resolute; *illegal*—permissible, rightful, juristic; *illegitimate*—warranted, constitutional, reliable; *legal*—prohibited, banned, outlawed, unlicensed; *legitimate*—illicit, unprecedented, unfathered; *loyal*—treacherous, two-faced, apostate; *loyalty*—perfidy, treachery; *privileged*—disadvantaged, downtrodden, deprived.

LIBER, free: LIB

On July 4, 1776, Thomas Jefferson declared that all men "are endowed by their creator with certain unalienable rights; that among these are life, **LIB**ERTY, and the pursuit of happiness." In 1934, the Italian dictator Benito Mussolini held a funeral for liberty in a speech, saying, "We have buried [liberty's] putrid corpse." Liberty means freedom, independence, or self-determination.

To **LIB**ERATE is to set free from bondage, ignorance, poverty, prejudice, unfairness, or discrimination. The women's movement or Women's **LIB**ERATION is dedicated to securing full economic, educational, legal, social, and vocational rights for women.

On June 6, 1944 (known thereafter as D-Day), Dwight D. Eisenhower, commander in chief of Allied forces in Western Europe, DELIVERED a message by radio: "A landing was made this morning on the coast of France . . . This landing is part of the . . . plan for the liberation of Europe." Some months later a G.I. is reported to have said as he stood in the ruins of a French village, "We sure **LIB**ERATED the hell out of this place." Such is war. And such was the DELIVERANCE, salvation, liberation, and freeing of Europe.

When we see or hear the word **LIB**ERAL in today's news, it is usually in reference to someone's political persuasion. **LIB**ERAL refers to generous, tolerant, lenient, and charitable.

An IL**LIB**ERAL attitude tends to be narrow, bigoted, and intolerant. ☞ *In the hall outside the courtroom one of the attorneys said that the* *judge's ruling was nearsighted and smacked of illiberalism.* To **LIB**ERALIZE a company policy or a city ordinance is to loosen or broaden it.

A **LIB**ERTARIAN believes in the doctrine of free will and advocates complete liberty of conduct and thought. A **LIB**ERTINE, however, can be any one of the following: a person who is morally or sexually unrestrained, a profligate, or a fake; a freethinker in religious matters; or a person freed from slavery in ancient Rome.

The obstetrician DELIVERS or frees a baby from its mother's womb. Postal carriers deliver the mail, and boxers deliver a punch to their opponents. A baseball pitcher's DELIVERY may be what gets him into the major leagues, and a manufacturer hopes that this year a record profit will be DELIVERABLE.

LIVERY is a uniform worn by servants, the distinctive dress of members of certain companies and groups, the care and feeding of horses for pay, as well as the name of businesses that rent out carriages, cars, and boats.

Combining forms: *de-*, down, away; *il-*, not.
Antonyms: *liberal*—puritan, reactionary, conservative, biased, literal; *liberalize*—tighten, constrict; *liberate*—capture, imprison; *libertine*—puritan, ascetic, celibate, abstainer; *liberty*—oppression, denial, ban, proscription, discretion, timidity.

LINGUA, tongue, language: LINGU

Just as speakers of English may say, "What's Lee's native tongue?" meaning LANGUAGE, speakers of Latin used *lingua* in the same figurative way. A **LINGU**IST, then, is a person who speaks several languages fluently and is also known as a polyglot, literally, "many tongues." Having passed the BI**LINGU**AL square, such a person has gone on to being TRI**LINGU**AL or perhaps MULTI**LINGU**AL.

Language refers to diction, wording, idiom, phrasing, and vocabulary, as well as slang, jargon, and dialect.

Language also means expression, manner of speaking or writing, rhetoric, verbiage, and prose.

LINGUISTICS is the science of language, the study of nature and structure of human speech. **LINGU**A franca is any language that is used to communicate among speakers of other tongues. It is also the name given to one formerly spoken in Mediterranean ports and consisting primarily of Italian with elements of Arabic, French, Greek, Spanish, and Turkish.

LINGUINI or **LINGUINE** is a pasta shaped in flat, long, thin strands; the name comes from the Italian for "small tongue."

Combining forms: *bi-,* two; *franca,* Frankish tongue; *multi-,* many; *tri-,* three.

LIQUERE, to flow, to be liquid: LIQU

A **LIQUID** is something fluid, wet, moist, or watery. ☞ *If we don't get home soon, this ice cream is going to be liquid.* As an adjective it means shining, brilliant, clear, and bright. ☞ *The sunshine on the lake was like liquid gold.* It also means flowing, smooth, mellifluous, and sweet. ☞ *Their voices were like liquid in the evening air.*

Liquid assets are those easily converted into cash or are already in the form of cash; not so with **ILLIQUID** assets. ☞ *Lil has plenty of assets, but her house, car, and farm are not exactly liquid in this economy.* Assets that can be so converted are said to have **LIQUIDITY.** To **LIQUIDATE** is to pay a debt, turn assets into cash, or get rid of. ☞ *"I have not become the King's First Minister in order to preside over the liquidation of the British Empire," remarked Winston Churchill in a speech in London in 1942.* To **LIQUIFY** something is to transform or melt it into a liquid.

Something **LIQUESCENT** is becoming or tending to become liquid. **DELIQUESCENCE** is the process of becoming liquid by absorbing moisture from the air, as happens with salt and certain fungi. Digital watches and portable computers and calculators have LCDs, **LIQUID-CRYSTAL** displays.

LIQUOR is an alcoholic beverage, spirits, drink, or intoxicant. ☞ *"The lips that touch liquor must never touch mine," G. W. Young (1870).* It is also the broth, drippings, juice, or liquid from cooked meats or vegetables. ☞ *I mixed corn starch with the liquor from the roast to make the gravy.* A **LIQUEUR** is a sweet, alcoholic, usually after-dinner drink; it is also called a cordial.

Someone who is PROLIX is wordy, verbose, garrulous, and loquacious. ☞ *I am quite aware that I sometimes become prolix in my informal lectures.* PROLIXITY is wordiness, verbosity, verbiage, and bombast. ☞ *Yes, I think you might have enjoyed the talk this morning; I mean if you enjoy prolixity.*

But not: *liquorice* (var. spelling of licorice [Gk *glucus,* sweet + *rhiza,* root], herb used in making a candy.
Combining forms: *de-,* removal; *-fy,* to make; *il-,* not; *pro-,* forth.

Antonyms: *liquid*—solid, gaseous, hard, condensed, dry, ragged; *liquify*—solidify, freeze, congeal; *prolix*—concise, terse, succinct; *prolixity*—brevity, shortness, simplicity, conciseness.

LITHOS, stone: LITH

The Stone Age of humankind's history began about 2.5 million years ago with the development of **PALEOLITHIC** man, such as the Cro-Magnon, and the use of stone tools and paintings on the walls of caves. The **MESOLITHIC** period marked the development of the bow and arrow and the domestication of the dog. The wheel, linen weaving, agriculture, and settled village life came about in the **NEOLITHIC** period.

Paleolithic, Mesolithic, Neolithic

A **MONOLITH** is a statue or column made of one stone; Cleopatra's Needle is an example. If the monolith is large enough, it qualifies as a **MEGALITH.** ☞ *"I saw the horses: / Huge in the dense grey—ten together— / Megalith—still . . . / Grey silent fragments / Of a grey silent world," from Ted Hughes' poem, "The Horses" (1957).*

The printing process known at **LITHOGRAPHY** uses a large flat stone for the making of ink impressions. The finished product is a **LITHOGRAPH** and the operator is a **LITHOGRAPHER.**

The solid part of the earth and its rocky crust are the **LITHOSPHERE**; **LITHOLOGY** has to do with the study and classification of rock; **LITHIUM** is a metallic element processed into a lubricant for home and garage use. A **LITHOPHYTE** is a plant that grows in the cracks of rocks and concrete and is nourished chiefly from the atmosphere; coral, with its stony structure, also qualifies.

But not: *lithe* [AS *lithe*], easily bent, supple.
Combining forms: *-graph, -y,* written; *mega-,* large; *meso-,* middle; *mono-,* one; *-neo,* new; *-ology,* study of; *paleo-,* ancient, old; *-phyte,* plant; *-sphere,* planet.

LITTERA, letter of the alphabet: LITER

ILLITERACY is a greater problem in America today, studies show, than it was fifty to seventy-five years ago. While our language has increased in its size and complexity—*The Random House Dictionary, Second Edition, Unabridged* includes "over 50,000 new words and 75,000 new meanings"—the electronic media have captured the attention of millions who might otherwise be reading books, magazines, and newspapers.

A functional ILLITERATE is one who reads at approximately the fourth-grade level. That means that he or she LITERALLY cannot read a help wanted newspaper ad, the caution labels on a car battery, or the weather warnings that run silently across the bottom of the TV picture.

There are many degrees of LITERACY. People who can read the three samples referred to above are LITERATE, but if that is a measure of their skill, they are on the bottom rung of the ladder. On the next step up is one who can read with some proficiency the newsmagazines and the editorial and opinion pages of the daily paper. Above that is the person who is well read.

And on the top step is he or she who can be called LETTERED, meaning learned, highly educated, and qualified to stand among the LITERATI, the intelligentsia, the intellectuals, the academic class, or the thinkers. They are LITERARY folk, those who not only can and do read the classics, but often teach and write about them as well. Their classics are the works of lasting value that are often the subjects of the lectures delivered in a World LITERATURE class.

The LITERAL meaning of OBLITERATE is "to blot out or efface LETTERS," not the LETTER-PERFECT ones written on LETTERHEADS and then folded into envelopes, but those of the alphabet. Today it means to destroy, eradicate, extirpate, or deracinate.

ALLITERATION is the repetition of the initial letters of several words: You should hear silly Sally Sessions say "She sells sea shells by the seashore."

But not: *liter* [Gk *litra,* pound], liquid metric measure.
Combining forms: *al-,* to; *-head,* upper part; *il-,* not; *ob-,* away; *-perfect,* flawless.
Antonyms: *illiterate*—taught, educated, schooled, knowledgeable; *letter-perfect*—garbled, inexact, distorted, misquoted; *literal*—incorrect, erroneous, poetic, romantic, figurative; *literally*—vaguely, figuratively; *literary*—uneducated, untutored, unenlightened; *literate*—ignorant, uniformed, unschooled; *obliterate*—make, create, build, preserve, restore.

LOCARE, to place: LOCA

As an adjective, **LOCAL** means near or close. ☞*The whole family's gone to the local schools.* It also refers to townsperson or native. ☞*Most of the locals pronounce it that way.* Sometimes, however, it is used to mean limited, narrow, small-town, parochial, and provincial. ☞*Mac? Make it big time? No way. He's just a local, you know.*

A **LOCALISM** is a custom, a word or phrase, a pronunciation, or a manner of speaking that is generally limited to a particular place or area. Drivers in one rural area may greet oncoming neighbors with a thumbs-up sign from a hand on the steering wheel, while in another they may raise a couple of fingers or wave the whole hand.

To **LOCATE** is to settle, situate, pinpoint, and track down. To **ALLOCATE** is to set aside, apportion, and earmark. ☞*One hundred percent of the money collected will be allocated to the homeless families.* One's **ALLOCATION** is one's share.

To **COLLOCATE** is to arrange in proper order. ☞*When we put all the papers together, we had to collocate the numbered pages. The coaches will collocate the Field Day events.* To **DISLOCATE** is to put out of joint, as one's shoulder and to upset or throw out of order.

LOCOMOTION is the act or power of moving from one place to another.

A **LOCUS** is old hat to geometry students; it is a place, **LOCATION**, spot, or area, and its plural is **LOCI**. To **LOCALIZE** is to position, place, locate, and establish. ☞*The seismologists localized the quake as occurring along the San Andreas fault.*

> **Additional English words related to the root:** lieu, locale, locality, milieu.
> **Combining forms:** *al-*, to; *col-*, before; *dis-*, apart.
> **Antonyms:** *local*—broad, worldly, cosmopolitan, urbane; *localize*—broaden, amplify, widen, expand; *locate*—lose, conceal, abandon, vacate; *locomotion*—immobility, inactivity, inertia, stasis.

LOGOS, word: LOG, LOGY

When we talk **LOGIC**, we talk words. That is, logic has to do with reasoning, and we reason with words. A **LOGICAL** statement is reasonable, rational, coherent, and cogent. An **ILLOGICAL** assertion is fallacious, wrong, invalid, and implausible, perhaps not at first sight, but certainly after an objective examination. "If everyone would get out and vote, I know our party would win the election," is an obviously unreasonable, irrational, and illogical argument, and one does not have to be a trained **LOGICIAN** to see the fallacy.

The form of reasoning known as a SYL**LOG**ISM [Gk *syl-,* together] can be reduced from words to letters or other symbols. If A is B and C is A, then C is B. That's logical: All cats (A) are mammals (B). Trixie (C) is a cat (A). Therefore, Trixie (C) is a mammal (B).

The **LOG**ISTICS of an enterprise, military or otherwise, is the planning, the organizing, and the working out of a project or operation. ☞ *Once we got the logistics of the trip straightened out, we had smooth sailing.*

A company's **LOG**OTYPE or **LOG**O is its symbol or trademark used in advertising and on the product itself; tests show that many long-standing logos are now recognized even with the product name omitted. LOGO is a programming language used to teach children how to use computers (it is not an acronym despite its appearance).

A **LOG**OGRAM [Gk *gramma,* something written] is an abbreviated symbol for a frequently-used word or phrase: the ampersand (&) stands for the word and; other symbols appear above the numerals on the top line of the so-called "qwerty" keyboard.

A logogram is also a simple form of the word game we call an anagram [Gk *ana-,* back]. Other names for word games are **LOG**OGRIPH [Gk *griphos,* riddle] and **LOG**OMACHY [Gk *machia,* battle]; the latter also means a dispute about words.

A **LOG**ODAEDALIST [Gk *daidalos,* skillful] is a person skilled in the use of words, and **LOG**ODAEDALY is skill in the use of words, particularly in the game of coining or inventing words. The words blizzard, flumadiddle, and rowdy are notable examples of this skill.

"Shakespeare used 17,677 words in his writings," Bill Bryson says in his book *The Mother Tongue,* "of which at least one tenth had never been used before. Imagine if every tenth word you wrote were original." Here's a baker's dozen of Shakespeare's coinings: barefaced, countless, dwindle, excellent, frugal, gust, hint, hurry, leapfrog, majestic, monumental, obscene, and summit.

The wings of a bird and those of an airplane are ANA**LOG**OUS, i.e., similar, akin, alike, parallel, and HOMO**LOG**OUS [Gk *homo-,* same]. An APO**LOG**ETIC person is full of regret and remorse; he or she may also be, often needlessly, on the defensive. ☞ *There's no reason for you to be apologetic; you gave it one hundred percent.* To APO**LOG**IZE is to retract, confess, and repent one's act or statement. An APO**LOG**IA is usually a written work explaining, defending, or justifying one's motives or actions.

☞ *The former Gestapo functionary's book is a whining, self-serving apologia that will convince no one.* To EULOGIZE is to praise someone to the skies.

The key words immediately above lead to two large groups of words ending in *-logy*. For example, the words analogous, apologia, and eulogize have *-logy* forms and are members of a group that have a general reference to speech or writing or collections of related items, matters, or works. Here are a few other examples:

ANTHOLOGY [Gk *anthos,* flowers], collection of selected writings, such as essays, poems, short stories, by one or more authors.

ETYMOLOGY [Gk *etymos,* true, real], derivation of a word; account of the history of a certain word.

HAGIOLOGY [Gk *hagios,* holy, sacred], branch of literature dealing with saints, especially the biographies of saints.

LEXICOLOGY [Gk *lexikos,* words], study of the formation, meaning, and use of words and idioms.

MYTHOLOGY [Gk *mythos,* story], study or collection of the myths of a particular group of people.

NEOLOGY [Gk *neos,* new], neologism (a new word) or an example of it.

PHRASEOLOGY [Gk *phrasis,* style], manner or style of an expression, e.g., legal phraseology.

TAUTOLOGY [Gk *tauto,* the same], needless repetition of words, redundancy, verbiage, e.g., widow woman, hot water heater, my own personal opinion, to continue on, consensus of opinion, and future plans.

A second and larger group of words that employ *-logy* are names of bodies of knowledge and science. Here are a few examples:

ARCHEOLOGY [Gk *archaios,* ancient], scientific study of the cultures of historic and prehistoric peoples by analysis of their artifacts and other remains.

ASTROLOGY [Gk *astron,* star], study that deals with supposed influences of celestial bodies on the lives of human beings.

BIOLOGY [Gk *bios,* life], science of life and life processes.

CARDIOLOGY [Gk *kardio,* heart], study of the heart and its function.

DERMATOLOGY [Gk *dermato,* the skin], medical science dealing with diseases of the skin.

ECOLOGY [Gk *oikos,* house], science that deals with the relationships between organisms and their environments.

GENEALOGY [Gk *genea,* race], study of ancestry and pedigree.

HEMATOLOGY [Gk *haimat,* blood], study of blood, its nature and diseases.

IchthyoLOGY [Gk *ichthys,* fish], branch of zoology dealing with fishes.

MeteoroLOGY [Gk *meteoron,* a thing in the air], study of the atmosphere and the weather.

NumeroLOGY [Gk *numerus,* number], study of the occult meanings of numbers, as with the numbers of the year of one's birth, and their influence on one's life and future.

OphthalmoLOGY [Gk *opthalmos,* eye], medical science that deals with the functions and diseases of the eye.

PaleontoLOGY [Gk *palaios,* ancient], study of ancient forms and fossils.

RadioLOGY [Gk *radius,* beam], science dealing with x-rays and nuclear radiation for medical purposes.

SeismoLOGY [Gk *seismos,* quake], study of earthquakes and their phenomena.

TechnoLOGY [Gk *techne,* art, skill], application of technical improvements in industry, commerce, etc.

ZooLOGY [Gk *zoion,* animal, living being], study of the origin, evolution, structure, and classification of animals.

But not: *catalog* [*legein,* to gather, speak], a list of items.

LONGUS, long: LONG

LONGevity is the length of duration of life. On April 3, 1968, Martin Luther King, Jr. said in a speech in Memphis, "Like anybody, I would like to have a long life. Longevity has its place. But I'm not concerned about that now. I just want to do God's will." He was assassinated the following evening. Longevity also means seniority or length of service. ☞ *All promotions in the company were based on longevity.*

LONGitude is the distance east or west, measured in degrees, from the line that runs from pole to pole and passes through Greenwich, England. Latitude is the distance measured north or south from the equator. **LONGitudinal** means lengthwise.

To **proLONG** is to lengthen, extend, stretch, and **eLONGate.** ☞ *The arrival of the newcomers prolonged the meeting. "Gladness of the heart is the life of a man, and the joyfulness of a man prolongeth his days," Ecclesiastes 30:22.* Something **eLONGated** is slender, stretched, distended, **proLONGed**, and **proLONGated.** An **obLONG** is a figure such as a rectangle having an elongated shape.

To PURLOIN is to steal, pilfer, thieve, and grab. ☞ *Edgar Allan Poe's story "The Purloined Letter" is an early example of the detective who triumphs using logical reasoning.* To LUNGE is to make a sudden foreward movement. A **LONG**UEUR is a boring, dull, tedious passage in a book, musical composition, or dramatic production. ☞ *The longueurs in act one put us to sleep in no time.* **LONG**ANIMITY is forebearance, resignation, self-restraint, or endurance. ☞ *We were awed by the family's longanimity during those tragic days.*

But not: *long* [AS *lang*], having great length; *long* [AS *langian*], desire, yearn.
Combining forms: *-ev,* age; *-animity,* mind, reason, soul; *e-,* out; *ob-,* rather; *pro-,* forward; *pur-,* forward.
Antonyms: *elongate, prolong*—shorten, abbreviate, abridge, reduce, curtail, diminish.

LOQUI, to speak: LOCU, LOQU

"Who ya voting for?" Ardley asked his friend Zacharia. "Me, I like the way Lomow talks—ya know, everyday, common, ordinary. Like me and you."

"Ah, yes," Zacharia declared. "COL**LOQU**IAL, idiomatic, unsophisticated, vernacular."

"Whatever," Ardley said. "He don't throw around no college words and says what he's gotta say and that's it."

"I know precisely what you mean," Zacharia stated. "No ostentatious, showy, pretentious GRANDI**LOQU**ENCE, no high-flown or pompous language, and none of the **LOQU**ACIOUS, garrulous, and verbose speaking, replete with CIRCUM**LOCU**TIONS, or the wordy gobbledygook that characterize the speech of so many who mount the stump."

"Ya took the words right out of me mouth," Ardley said. "Some of them guys talk like they got this wooden dummy on their laps, ya know, going on like one of them Shakespeare guys talking all alone without nobody listening, like maybe they're talking in their sleep."

"Exactly!" Zacharia exclaimed. "Your analogy is *most* apt. Just like a VENTRI**LOQU**IST talking out of his stomach, so to speak, his "ventricle." And seemingly unaware that he is *not* alone, his SOLI**LOQU**Y is like a monologue, a steady stream of words, rather than a COL**LOQU**Y, a conversation or dialogue. And, yes, quite analogous to a SOMNI**LOQU**Y, the speech of a sleepwalker."

"Yeah, ya got it!" Ardley said. "That ain't Lomow, for sure. Like I says, he's down-to-earth, just like me and you."

"Well put. He has the gift of ELOQUENCE, the fluency, oratory, persuasion, and rhetoric," Zacharia opined. "Yet his ELOQUENT, articulate, and cogent message and style is not that of one schooled in a half dozen stuffy college courses in formal ELOCUTION, oratory, or enunciation. His speech is stirring, moving, striking, and forceful." Zacharia paused, and then, slowly, he began to shake his head. "Yet, oddly enough, I have concluded that his opponent, Oscar Hugo Himow, is more believable. I fear that I must cast my vote for him."

"Yeah, me, too," Ardley said. "Well, man, gotta go. Sure enjoyed the COLLOQUIUM. A conference like this here one is always enlightening. Especially with an INTERLOCUTOR like you being me conversational partner. Ya know, yer LOCUTION is first-rate, all of it, yer pronunciation or phrasing, the whole shebang. And, too, I really appreciate yer not engaging in OBLOQUY, not one word of slander, rebuke, or calumny did I hear ya utter. All of it on a high level. I mean, ya done *real* good. Well, see ya around. Don't take no wooden nickels."

But not: *locus* [*locus,* place], a locality; math term.
Combining forms: *circum-,* around; *col-,* together; *e-,* out; *grandi-,* great; *inter-,* between; *ob-,* against; *soli-,* alone; *somni-,* sleep; *ventri-,* belly.
Antonyms: *eloquent*—inarticulate, hesitant, vapid, enigmatic; *loquacious*—tactiturn, reticent, terse, quiet; *obloquy*—praise, respect, eulogy, panegyric.

LUCERE, to shine; LUMEN, light: LUC, LUM

Most of us who read more than we watch welcome writing that is LUMINOUS. ☞ *You have written a clear, concise, luminous report.* LUCID means precise, direct, and accurate. ☞ *I appreciate your lucid explanation; it is both comprehensible and rational.*

When we ELUCIDATE something, we throw light upon it, make it lucid, or just plain clear things up. ☞ *I believe my explanation has elucidated my reasons for forgetting our anniversary.*

People who claim that they possess special intellectual or spiritual enlightenment are said to be members of the ILLUMINATI or intelligentsia.

To LUCUBRATE is to study hard, especially at night; thus LUCUBRATION is laborious, overtime homework. It is likely that during such periods—one hopes with sufficient ILLUMINATION—there will be some who try to ELUCUBRATE, that is, produce something, such as a book or symphony, by long and intensive effort. If they do, and if it sells well, they will be hailed as LUMINOSITIES, i.e., intellectually brilliant, enlightened, and inspired.

Meanwhile, up in the heavens there's Sirius the Dog Star, the sixth nearest to us and the brightest in the skies, with a LUMINOSITY twenty-three times that of our sun. That would be a bit too bright to read by, just as our moon is a bit too faint. But, then, whoever wanted to *read* by the light of that big old LUCENT harvest moon, anyway?

Additional English words related to the root: Lucifer, pelucid, translucent.
But not: *lucre* [*lucrum,* profit], money; *lucrative* [*lucrum*], moneymaking; *lumbago* [*lumbus,* loin], a pain in the lower back.
Combining forms: *e-,* out; *il-,* thoroughly.
Antonyms: *elucidate*—confuse, perplex, obfuscate; *lucent*—dim, murky, dull, dense; *lucid*—unintelligible, vague, enigmatic, irrational, muddled; *luminous*—abstruse, cloudy, subdued, dull.

LUNA, SELENE, the moon: LUNA

We must suppose that the moon shone as brightly on ancient Greece as it did on Rome, but their word-legacies are strikingly different. From Selene, the Greek goddess of the moon, we get technical terms such as SELENOGRAPHY, the study of the moon's surface, SELENOLOGY, the branch of astronomy that deals with the moon, and a cluster of words that are largely confined to chemistry labs.

Across the waters of the Ionian and Adriatic seas, however, the words trickling down from Luna, the Roman moon goddess, were generally more people-oriented. Folks who supposedly lived on the moon were called LUNARIANS, and the minds of some people were thought to be affected by the phases of the moon, resulting in LUNES, fits of madness. Everytime there was a full moon, a bunch of LUNATICS were believed to come out of the LUNATIC closet. The INTERLUNAR period, the time between the full and new moons, were relatively pleasant and safe, the lunatics either back in the closet or reverting to their more normal phase. Those words are no longer used to denote insanity or dementia; we now tend to employ them in a lighter and less technical sense. ☞ *"The world," said David Lloyd George, in the* Observer *(1933), "is becoming like a lunatic asylum run by lunatics.*

LUNAcy has been spared, however. ☞ *That's sheer lunacy, quitting his job six weeks before Christmas!* **Lunatic fringe** refers to members of a group that hold extreme or fanatical views.

SubLUNAry denotes the vast area below the moon, pertaining to the earth, terrestrial affairs; thus, it sometimes means mundane, worldly, or mortal. ☞ *The guru prided himself on his avoidance of sublunary appetites.* **Demilune** refers to the half moon and, therefore, to a crescent or anything crescent shaped. We speak of the **LUNAr** month and lunar module as well as the Rover, the vehicle the Apollo astronauts used in exploring the moon's surface, of **LUNAte** or crescent-shaped bones or designs, and of **LUNAtion**, a period of approximately 29 1/2 days between returns of the new moon.

Combining forms: *demi-,* half; *-graphy,* a description; *inter-,* between; *-logy,* the study of; *sub-,* below.
Antonyms: *lunacy*—sanity, rationality, lucidity, common sense; *lunatic*—sane, rational, reasonable, sound.

M

MAGISTER, a master: MAS, MIS

As an adjective **MAS**TER means chief, head, foremost, and primary. ☞ *Their master bedroom is on the ground floor.* It also means expert, authoritative, professional, and accomplished. ☞ *As a cabinet maker, Art is the town's master craftsman.*

As a verb master means to conquer, triumph over, manage, and dominate. ☞ *If Robin ever masters putting, she'll really go places on the golf circuit.* It also refers to grasp, be adept in, excel at, get the hang of, or be skilled at. ☞ *From my first day in class I was convinced that I would never master algebra.*

As a noun master means owner, ruler, manager, head, sahib, employer, or head honcho. ☞ *Loy claims he's the master of all he surveys.* A master is an expert, past master, virtuoso, wizard, ace, or maestro. ☞ *Marie is a master at both chess and the piano.* Master also refers to a noun of address for a boy or young man. ☞ *I believe, your highness, that Master Kensington is on the tennis court.* And, master means original, source, prototype, key, or basis. ☞ *I hope this tape is the master and not a copy.*

A **MAS**TERFUL person is accomplished, skillful, **MAS**TERLY, and wise. A **MAS**TERMIND is a genius, wizard, prodigy, pundit, or sage. ☞ *Only a mastermind will be able to solve this one.* To mastermind something is to direct, supervise, lead, and manage. ☞ *Who in the world masterminded this fiendish crossword puzzle?* A **MAS**TERPIECE is a classic, old master, prize, treasure, **MAS**TERWORK, or jewel, and a **MAS**TERSTROKE is an extremely skillful action. ☞ *Chet's plan to get the city fathers cooperating turned out to be a masterstroke.*

MISTER (abbr. **M**R., pl. **M**ESSRS.) is a term of address for a man, but **MIS**TRESS (abbr. **M**RS., pl. **M**MES.) is not always a title of respect. The problem is that while mistress still applies to a woman who is the head of a household, institution, or other establishment, serving as a chief, supervisor, boss, principal, or matron, it can also refer to a lover, sweetheart, inamorata, concubine, or kept woman. **Ms.** (pl. **M**SES.) is a title of respect that bypasses the marital status of the recipient as **MIS**s and Mrs. do not.

A MAGISTRATE in this country is usually a justice of the peace, civil officer, or police judge. ☞ *The couple finally located a magistrate who could marry them.* But in Britain the term is not so limited; members of the executive government and even the king answer to the title of magistrate.

MAGISTERIAL means commanding, masterful, and majestic. ☞ *Jeeves, the valet or "gentleman's gentleman" in P. G. Wodehouse's humorous stories, plays his part with magisterial poise.* It also means imperious, arrogant, overbearing, and domineering. ☞ *If that snob speaks to me with that magisterial manner of his just one more time . . . I'll explode!*

Antonyms: *magisterial*—modest, meek, humble; *master*—subordinate, follower, incompetent, unfit, inept; *masterful*—amateurish, unable, bungling, clumsy, weak; *mastermind*—moron, simpleton, bungler, amateur.

MAGNUS, great, large: MAGN, MAJ

When King John of England was forced to sign the **MAGNA CARTA** on June 15, 1215, a great step forward was made in the cause of liberty. Today in democratic countries around the world the **MAJORITY** can call the shots. Although the English people refer to their monarch as His or Her **MAJESTY**, the **MAJOR** personage in their democratic government is the prime minister.

In earlier times a Venetian nobleman was called a **MAGNIFICO**, but today a person of such wealth and power is termed a **MAGNATE.** Our city governments are headed by **MAYORS,** and the person in charge of an enormous household, such as that of a monarch or other member of a royal family, is referred to as the **MAJOR DOMO.**

When we go to college, we major in a field or subject, such as English, math, history, political science, a foreign language, etc. In Speech 107 we learn to avoid talking in a **MAGNILOQUENT**, grandiose, and pompous manner.

Students who aim for the **MAXIMUM** graduating honor, summa cum laude, are sometimes disappointed if they hit only the second level of **MAGNITUDE** or importance, **MAGNA CUM LAUDE.** In reality, these **MAXIMA** academic rankings are both commendable. These are people who dream of someday creating their **MAGNUM OPUS**, a great work of art or writing.

There are times, too, when we decide that the words fine, nice, good, and excellent have lost their clout and find ourselves **MAGNIFYING**, overstating, exaggerating, and overdoing our compliments: "What a **MAGNIFICENT** coat!" "Your nail polish is simply **MAJESTIC**!" "What a

MAGNANIMOUS, noble, and selfless gesture, giving that poor soul all your spare change!"

A MAXIM, saying, adage, proverb, or axiom, is a general rule of truth. Benjamin Franklin's were serious and sober. "Early to bed and early to rise, makes a man healthy, wealthy, and wise," but more modern maxim makers minimize the moral meaning: James Thurber in the *New Yorker* (1939): "Early to rise and early to bed makes a male healthy and wealthy and dead" and Dorothy Parker in "News Item" (1937): "Men seldom make passes /At girls who wear glasses."

But not: *magnet* [Gk *magneta,* short for Magnes, the stone of Magnesia], thing or person that attracts; *magnolia* [after Pierre Magnol, F botanist], shrub and tree; *majlis* [Ar], Iranian house of parliament.
Combining forms: *-animous,* soul; *carta,* charter; *cum laude,* with praise; *domo,* house; *-ficent, -fico, -fy,* to make; *-loquent,* to talk; *opus,* work.
Antonyms: *magnanimous*—petty, mean, selfish; *magnificent*—humble, modest, ordinary; *majestic*—lowly, squalid, humble; *major*—minor, lesser, secondary; *majority*—minority, few, immaturity; *maximum*—minimum, iota, minimal, least.

MALLEUS, hammer: MALL

The **MALL**—that mercantile center where millions of modern Americans shop every day—owes its name to the ancestor of a popular lawn game that is today an intercollegiate sport.

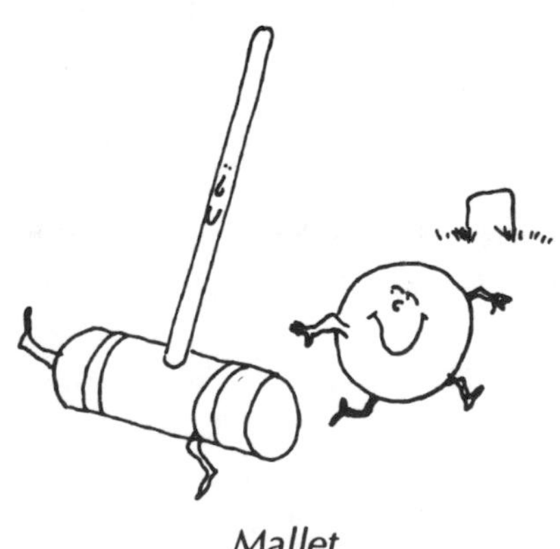
Mallet

In the seventeenth century, PALL MALL was introduced into London. In this game a round ball is struck with a mall (or **MALL**ET) through a high arch of iron. Its descendant is, obviously, our croquet.

Pall mall was first played in London alleys, one of which became so popular with the players that the street took on the name of the game. When young King Charles II and his courtiers discovered the pastime, he chose to move the playing field to a wide thoroughfare that ran through St. James Park.

When those two thoroughfares were no longer used for the game, both the Mall of St. James Park and Pall Mall became promenades, that is, public places for leisurely strolling and, in time, the displaying of goods for sale.

And that's the way it is today in the mall—shops, scores of not-so-leisurely walkers, and no one playing croquet.

Additional English words related to the root: malleable, maul.

MANDARE, to order: MAND, MEND

A comMAND is control, authority, power, or sovereignty. It is an injunction, fiat, order, or behest. ☞ *Who gave the command to lower the flag?* It also refers to comprehension, grasp, knowledge, or mastery. ☞ *Sue's the only one in town who has a really good command of French.* To command one must govern, rule, order, and require. ☞ *General George Patton commanded the 7th Army in World War II.* It also means to receive, inspire, motivate, and evoke. ☞ *Mark Twain commanded the admiration of readers everywhere.*

A comMANDment is an order, law, or decree. ☞ *The Ten Commandments of the Bible are also known as the Decalogue.* Dictionary definitions of command performance state that it is a play, ballet, opera, etc., that is presented at the request of a head of state. The phrase, however, has trickled down to other uses, particularly in regard to any social or business function that one is expected to attend. ☞ *You turned down the boss's dinner invite? Bad move, pal! Around here that's considered a command performance!*

To be a comMANDer one must also be a leader, chief, director, or boss; the president is the comMANDer in chief of the U.S. Army, Navy, and Air Force. ComMANDant is the title of the senior officer of the U.S. Marine Corps, the chief officer of a certain place or group, and the head of a military school. A comMANDo was a specially trained Allied military unit in World War II. To comMANDeer private property is to seize it for police or military use. ☞ *The officer commandeered a delivery truck to chase the getaway car.* Police and military units have comMANDing officers; a hockey team going into the third period ahead 6 to 0 has a commanding lead; a house high on a bluff overlooking the Mississippi Rivers offers a commanding view.

To comMEND is to praise, extol, acclaim, eulogize, and approve. ☞ *The reviewers commended both the actor's performance and the movie.* It also means to entrust, transfer, deliver, and hand over. ☞ *Upon his retirement Grandfather commended his two stores to Ed and his wife.* A comMENDable act is praiseworthy, laudable, and meritorious. ☞ *Generosity is a commendable trait.* ComMENDation is approval, praise, eulogy, or panegyric. ☞ *It was the scoutmaster's letter of commendation that got Sam into State.*

To counterMAND an order or command is to cancel, revoke, rescind, and nullify it. ☞ *The lieutenant countermanded the sergeant's order.*

A deMAND is an order, injunction, requisition, or ultimatum. ☞ *Mom's every demand was taken care of.* It is also a need, requirement, want, or market. ☞ *I doubt if there's a great demand for icemakers in Nome.* As a verb it means insist on, claim, require, and order. ☞ *Our new principal demands strict obedience to the rules.* It also means need, require, necessitate, and want. ☞ *It was a situation that demanded immediate action.* The adjective deMANDing means exacting, taxing, tough, and trying. ☞ *Brooks has applied to two of the most highly selective and demanding colleges.*

A MANDate is an order, command, writ, or authorization to act. ☞ *The candidate's clear majority has given her a mandate to push the reform program outlined in the party's manifesto.* It is also a protectorate or dependency. ☞ *This island is a mandate of the United States government.* An order or rule that is MANDatory is compulsory, obligatory, requisite, and binding. ☞ *The commission proposed that two years of Latin and Greek roots be mandatory in all high schools.*

In Shakespeare's *Macbeth* King Duncan says, "This castle (of Macbeth's) hath a pleasant seat; the air/Nimbly and sweetly recomMENDs itself unto our senses." Thus, when we recommend a book to a friend, we endorse, promote, praise, and sanction it. But when the police officer recommends that we use extreme caution on the wet road, he or she advises, counsels, proposes, and suggests. A recomMENDation is an endorsement, good word, or commendation. ☞ *It was Professor Bishop's recommendation that got me the scholarship.*

To reMAND is to send back; it is commonly used in sending a case back to a lower court and in sending an accused person or a prisoner back into custody. ☞ *The visiting judge ruled that the two prisoners who were awaiting trial be remanded to the state prison system.*

But not: *mendacious* [*mendax,* false], lying, dishonest.
Combining forms: *com-,* thoroughly; *counter-,* against; *de-,* down, away; *re-,* back, again.
Antonyms: *commend*—condemn, disparage, censure, discredit; *commendable*—inferior, blameworthy, culpable; *commendation*—blame, incrimination, disapproval;

demanding—easy, simple, leisurely; *mandatory*—optional, voluntary, discretionary; *recommendation*—criticism, objection, aspersion.

MANERE, to remain: MAN

The Old **MANSE,** a Unitarian parsonage in Concord, Massachusetts, was at different times the home of Ralph Waldo Emerson and Nathaniel Hawthorne; while living there the latter wrote his second collection of short stories under the title *Mosses from an Old Manse.* A manse is not necessarily very large and impressive, but a **MANSION** is, for this is the principal residence on a **MANOR,** the landed estate of a lord in England. A mansion and a **MANOR HOUSE** are the same, both employing **MENIALS,** those humble, servile, obsequious, or cringing domestic servants, sometimes still seen on black and white TV movies. A **MENAGE** is a household of any size; a **MENAGERIE** is a collection of animals, wild or unusual.

A thought or feeling that is **IMMANENT** is inherent, subjective, inborn, innate, and intrinsic, i.e., one that takes place only within the mind and often stubbornly remains there; in "Convergence of the Twain" (1914), novelist Thomas Hardy spoke of "the Immanent Will that stirs and urges everything."

PERMANENCE and **PERMANENCY** mean durability, stability, or longevity. ☞ *The lab is testing the new paint for permanence.* The person who erects a **PERMANENT** monument expects it to be everlasting, eternal, and infinite. One who seems to be **PERMANENTLY** at leisure appears to be so always, constantly, and incessantly. A **PERM** is a shortening of a permanent wave of the hair, and **PERMAPRESS** is the name given to a fabric that resists wrinkles. **PERMAFROST** can be found in the subsoil of the polar regions. **IMPERMANENT** objects are transient, fleeting, ephemeral, and temporary. ☞ *The recent flood showed how impermanent and feeble man's structures are.*

To **REMAIN** is to stay behind, survive, and persist. ☞ *I'm quite willing to remain here at home. We hope our country will remain at peace.* When one speaks of a human being's **REMAINS,** the reference is to the corpse, body, or cadaver. The remains left at the park after a picnic are scraps, debris, litter, or remnants. A **REMAINDER** is whatever is left, the **REMAINING** part or portion. ☞ *They spent the remainder of their days on the coast. After we subtract the rent and car payment, the remainder is negligible.* **REMAINDERS** are books that are sold at reduced prices after their sales have become unprofitable.

Combining forms: *-frost,* freezing; *im-,* in, not; *per-,* through; *re-,* back.
Antonyms: *immanent*—objective, extrinsic, alien; *remain*—leave, transfer, fail, disappear.

MANUS, hand, MAN

To illustrate how this root has evolved and taken on a multitude of different faces, consider the phrase **MANo a MANo.** Its literal meaning is "hand to hand," which in Italian means "little by little" and "as we go along." In the bullfighting rings of Spain it is the name of an event in which two rival matadors take turns fighting several bulls each. Some writers in America have used it to describe a head-on competition, while more than one political reporter has written, "The two candidates have been gearing up to go mano a mano." Head to head? Face to face? Hand to hand?

MANual labor is hand labor. One of the next steps up the labor ladder was the domestication of animals such as the horse, so it is not surprising that the original meaning of **MANage** was to control or handle a horse, and that **MANege** (the French word from which "manage" came) is the art of training and riding horses and the name of a school that teaches horsemanship. From that came **MANager, MANagement, MANageable,** and **unMANageable.**

Both **MANure** and **MANeuver** trace back to the Latin *manu operari,* "to work with the hand," as in cultivating the land for the raising of crops. Today's meanings of maneuver as a verb are operate, steer, pilot, guide, and manipulate. ☞ *This old bus is not very easy to maneuver in heavy traffic.* It also means to trick, scheme, plot, connive, and finesse. As a noun it is a military exercise, movement, campaign, or operation. It is also a trick, strategy, gambit, or ruse. ☞ *The junior partner's maneuver to gain control of the company fell short.*

When farmers cultivated the land in earlier times, they spread manure, the excrement of animals; today manure can mean any refuse or material that is composted or any natural or artificial fertilizer. To some people manure is an offensive word.

The **MANner** in which something is done is the way, method, or procedure. ☞ *Sarah holds her knife and fork in the English manner.* It is one's demeanor, bearing, or presence. ☞ *I thought his manner most suspicious.* It is also fashion, sort, type, or genre. ☞ *His poems are in the manner of Mother Goose.* A **MANnerism** is a trait, peculiarity, idiosyncrasy, quirk, or affectation. ☞ *That mannerism of his, pinching his earlobe,* *bugs me.* The adjective **MAN**NERED means affected, artificial, pompous, and phony. ☞*And that accent of hers! Completely mannered!* A **MAN**NERLY person is polite, well-bred, civil, and urbane. ☞*Emma's mannerly bearing serves her well as a role model.* ILL**MAN**NERED, UN**MAN**NERED, and UN**MAN**NERLY people are equally rude, discourteous, boorish, and uncouth.

President Abraham Lincoln earned the title of "The Great E**MAN**CIPATOR" for his support of the 13th Amendment to the Constitution of the United States, abolishing slavery forever as well as the Proclamation that he issued on January 1, 1862, which technically set free more than three million slaves. Amelia Jenks Bloomer, founder of *The Lily,* the first U.S. newspaper for and by women, ran this on its masthead: "The E**MAN**CIPATION of women from intemperance, injustice, prejudice, and bigotry." To E**MAN**CIPATE and **MAN**UMIT have the same meaning: to free, liberate, release, and unchain. **MAN**UMISSION and emancipation are also interchangeable; both order the removal of the **MAN**ACLES that have kept the oppressed in chains.

The word A**MAN**UENSIS originally meant "a servant of *hand*writing," hence, a secretary. ☞*Penny is my uncle's companion, amanuensis, and best friend.* In earlier times when all products were made by hand, **MAN**UFACTURED, fabricated, built, and constructed, the maker was a **MAN**UFACTURER, builder, producer, or fabricator. But tangible commodities are not the only things that are so made; one can also **MAN**UFACTURE, concoct, invent, and devise excuses, alibis, stories, histories, and prevarications.

The literal meaning of **MAN**IFEST is "grasped by the hand," and that grasp is obvious, clear, and apparent. ☞*It was manifest from the start that the judge did not believe our story.* As a verb it means to show, display, and reveal. ☞*My mother manifested her disapproval with that look of hers.* A **MAN**IFESTATION is an example, illustration, demonstration, or sign. ☞*The size of the crowd was a welcome manifestation of Mae's popularity.* A **MAN**IFESTO is a public proclamation, decree, or announcement; it is usually a statement of intentions, objectives, or goals issued by a government or organization.

The original meaning of MAINTAIN is "to hold in the hand," and when students manage to maintain their place on the honor roll or dean's list, that's what they do: keep up, keep a firm grip, continue, and uphold. MAINTENANCE is the upkeep, repair, or service of a property, as well as support, sustenance, or subsistence. ☞*Sal's father pays $300 a month for her maintenance.* It is also continuation, perpetuation, or prolongation. ☞*The maintenance of our friendly relationship with your country is of utmost importance.*

To **MAN**IPULATE is to handle, manage, use, and run. ☞ *Do you really know how to manipulate a bulldozer? The speaker knew exactly how to manipulate that crowd.* It is to rig, juggle, tamper with, and trick. ☞ *He's been manipulating the company accounts for years.* However, a **MAN**IPULATOR is not always engaged in illegal or underhanded activities. The same is true of **MAN**IPULATION; it can be skillful in a good cause or a dishonest one. ☞ *The candidate charged the press with manipulation of the news. The passengers owe their lives to the driver's expert manipulation of the bus.*

A MASTIFF is a breed of large and powerful dogs; the name most likely came from the dog's being accustomed to the hand (of man). The same combining form, *suescere,* "to become accustomed," gives us the word **MAN**SUETUDE, meaning mildness or gentleness. ☞ *Our late friend's greatness was in his unbounded mansuetude.* LEGERDEMAIN, which we know of as sleight of hand, is literally "light of hand," as in the sense of being light-fingered, skilled at picking pockets. A **MAN**ICURE is the care of the hands and fingernails; a **MAN**CIPLE is the purchasing officer of a monastery or college.

An additional English word related to the root: manuscript.

But not: *mandible* [*mandere,* to chew], the bone of the lower jaw; *manger* [*manducare,* to chew, eat], a feeder for fodder; *maniac* [Gk *mani,* madness], a violently insane person; *manifold* [AS *manifgeald,* many, fold] having many forms.

Combining forms: *a-,* from; *-cip,* to take; *-cure,* to care; *-date,* to give; *e-,* out; *-euver, -oeuvr,* to work; *fac-,* to make; *-fest,* hostile; *ill-,* not; *-miss,* to send; *-pul,* to fill; *-tain,* to hold; *un-,* not.

Antonyms: *emancipate*—enslave, oppress, dominate; *ill-mannered*—courteous, cultivated, refined; *maintain*—end, terminate, abandon, repudiate; *maintenance*—eradication, abolition, destruction; *manage*—follow, be under the care of, spoil, bungle; *manageable*—contrary, uncontrollable, unwieldy; *management*—labor, workers, employees, staff; *manager*—employee, worker; *manifest*—dubious, ambiguous, questionable, camouflage; *mannered*—unaffected, natural, down-to-earth, unsophisticated; *mannerly*—rude, discourteous, gauche, boorish; *manual*—sedentary, white-collar, office, mental, intellectual, automatic.

MAPPA, napkin, cloth

"I say, must you really catch the night rain? I mean, are you *that* short of water around here?"

"What? Night rain? No, no! I have to catch the night train."

Back some seven centuries ago when Geoffrey Chaucer was recording the tales of pilgrims going to Canterbury, the seat of the Christian church in England, it was that kind of oral confusion that was responsible for the changing of "a napron" into "an APRON." The same kind of change took place with the snake we know today as "an adder"; it was once "a nadder."

An early MAP of the world was once known as a *mappa mundi,* (the world), most likely because such maps were drawn on pieces of cloth.

NAPERY is the linen that covers our table, hence NAPKIN, a small piece of cloth. In England a napkin is a diaper, and in Scotland it's a handkerchief or neckerchief.

A MOP is a wadded-up piece of cloth or bundle of yarn used to wipe up a spill; to complete an action or operation today, we mop up. ☞ *What a tournament! The Tigers really mopped up on the Cats!* Long ago a mop was a rag doll; from that may have come the word MOPPET, a small child.

MATER, METER, mother: MAT, METRO

MATERNAL means motherly, kind, caring, and nurturing. **MAT**RIMONY refers to marriage, wedlock, or conjugal union. ☞ *"A lady's imagination is very rapid; it jumps from admiration to love, from love to matrimony in a moment," Jane Austen,* Pride and Prejudice. **MAT**RON is a mature and dignified married woman; a female prison or hospital overseer, supervisor; a dame or a dowager. **MAT**ERNITY refers to motherhood, delivery, or pertaining to pregnant women; and **MAT**RONLY is maturely dignified, sedate, and stately.

A **MAT**RIARCHY is a family, community, or society in which women have most of the authority. The acknowledged head is a **MAT**RIARCH, although the word is also used to designate any highly respected older woman.

An original meaning of **MAT**RIX is "the womb," stemming from an earlier Latin word for a female animal kept for breeding purposes. Today it refers to a mold, cast, die, stencil, or template, as well as the place or point from which something else develops.

A **MAT**RICULANT is someone who **MAT**RICULATES or enrolls in a college or university as a candidate for a degree, one to be obtained many semesters later. With sheepskin in hand, the graduate will be privileged to look back upon and sing about his or her **ALMA MATER.**

The mother city or parent state in a colony of ancient Greece was called a **METROPOLIS.** Because it was a principal place, hub, center, or seat of many activities, the citizens came to be regarded as **METROPOLITAN,** urbane, cosmopolitan, and sophisticated. In short, **METROPOLITES.** Today some of those live in a **METROPLEX** (like Dallas–Fort Worth), have at their convenience a high-speed railway called a **METROLINER** (Boston–New York–Washington, D.C.), watch ballgames in a **METRODOME** (Minneapolis–St. Paul), and speed between work and home on the underground **METRO** (Washington, D.C., Paris, Montreal).

But not: *mate* [G *gemate,* companion], a spouse; *material* [*materia,* matter], substance; *metronome* [Gk *metro,* measure], instrument used in musical practice.
Combining forms: *alma,* nourishing; *-arch,* ruler; *-dome,* roof shaped like an inverted bowl; *-liner,* plane, ship, or train operated by a transportation company; *-plex,* having parts; *-polis,* city, state.
Antonyms: *metropolitan*—suburban, rural, countrified, rustic.

MERX, goods, trade, traffic: MERC

In Sir Walter Scott's *Ivanhoe,* published in 1819, a character says, "**GRAMERCY** for thy caution." This useful word meaning "great thanks" has, unfortunately, become obsolete. Like the French **MERCI,** our **MERCY** once meant "thank you," and there is still a hint of it in the phrase "That's a mercy," meaning, something to be thankful for. But its prevailing meaning is compassion, kindness, charity, or clemency: In the *Old Testament* (Micah 6:8) the people are required "to do justly, and to love mercy, and to walk humbly with thy God." A secondary meaning is blessing, boon, godsend, or luck. ☞ *What a mercy you weren't killed!*

Something **MERCILESS** is cruel, heartless, ruthless, and callous. One of the Beatitudes of the "Sermon on the Mount" says, "Blessed are the **MERCIFUL,** for they shall obtain mercy," or, as it is in *The Living Bible,* "Happy are the kind and merciful, for they shall be shown mercy."

A **MERCENARY** person is greedy, avaricious, materialistic, and selfish. ☞ *Joe turned out to be a mercenary candidate, and the party withdrew* *its support.* The Hessians of the American Revolution were German **MERCENARIES** hired by the British.

A **MERCANTILE** nation is one engaged in trade, business, dealing, and **MERCHANDISING. MERCHANDISE** is the goods, wares, or commodities bought and sold by **MERCHANTS.** A **MERCHANTMAN** is a trading ship, one of those belonging to the fleet of a nation's **MERCHANT MARINE. MERCHANTABLE** goods are those that are salable or **MARKETABLE.** In one sense a **MARKETPLACE** is an open area where a market is held; in a larger sense it is the entire world of business, trade, and economics. A **MART** is a trading center, exposition, marketplace, or fair; when Chicago's Merchandise Mart was completed in 1930, it was the world's largest building devoted entirely to **COMMERCE,** business, exchange, trading, buying and selling, and **MERCANTILISM.**

A **COMMERCIAL** is an advertisement, promotion, or paid announcement. An **INFORMERCIAL** (also **INFOMERCIAL**) is a radio or television message that informs or instructs in an entertaining manner while advertising a product. ☞ *Our brewery has launched a series of infomercials concerning the wisdom of having a designated driver.*

MERCURY was the ancient Roman god of commerce, thievery, eloquence, and science; it is the name of the planet closest to the sun; and it is the name of a metallic element used in thermometers and sometimes spoken of metaphorically. ☞ *"He disappeared in the dead of winter: / The brooks were frozen, the airports almost deserted, / And snow disfigured the public statues; / The mercury sank in the mouth of the dying day," wrote W. H. Auden from "In Memory of W. B. Yeats" (1940).* A **MERCURIAL** person is fickle, capricious, impulsive, and unpredictable. ☞ *He's so mercurial you never know how he's going to vote on any issue.*

In London a **MERCER** is a dealer in fine fabrics; the shop is known as a **MERCERY.**

An additional English word related to the root: unmerciful.

But not: *mercerized* [after John *Mercer,* inventor] thread treated to make it stronger.

Combining forms: *com-,* together; *gra-,* grand, great.

Antonyms: *mercenary*—generous, high-minded, idealistic, voluntary; *merciful*—implacable, relentless, unfeeling; *merciless*—forgiving, lenient, kindhearted; *mercurial*—stable, fixed, steadfast; *mercy*—cruelty, vindictiveness, sternness, brutality.

MIKROS, small: MICRO

There are many more *micro* words in our everyday world than there are those with its contrasting form, *macro,* meaning large, long, and great. **MICRO**WAVE ovens for speedy cooking and **MICRO**PHONES for use with tape recorders or video cameras are standard equipment in many homes. In the science labs in schools there are **MICRO**SCOPES to study **MICRO**ORGANISMS such as **MICRO**BES along with the worlds in miniature called **MICRO**COSMS. The libraries often have collections of **MICRO**FILMS, geography students locate **MICRO**NESIA on maps and globes, and in auto mechanics they learn to use a **MICRO**METER.

MICROLOGY has two very different meanings. On the one hand it is the science dealing with the functions of microscopes in laboratories. But it also refers to the paying of undue attention to trivial matters.

> **Combining forms:** *-be,* life; *-cosm,* world; *-logy,* the study of; *-meter,* measuring device; *-nesia,* islands; *-organism,* animal or plant; *-phone,* sound; *-scope,* to watch.

MISCERE, to mix: MISC, MIX

A **MISC**ELLANY is a collection, and its synonyms fill ragbags, grabbags, and **MIX**ED bags of unusual and interesting companions. Some owe their beginnings to foods, often the stews and soups that the cook of the house can throw any edible into: chowchow, farrago, gallimaufry, salmagundi, smorgasbord, or hotchpotch, and its offspring, hodgepodge. Some stem from *miscere:* MEDLEY, MELANGE, and **MIX**TURE, while others derive from various sources: chrestomathy, crazy quilt, jumble, mishmash, motley, pastiche, potpourri, or patchwork. Washington Irving used one of the above in 1808 as part of the title of a collection of essays: *Salmagundi; or, The Whim-Whams and Opinions of Launcelot Langstaff, Esq. and Others* and many of H. L. Mencken's best writings are gathered in *A Mencken Chrestomathy.*

A thrift or second-hand shop is usually chockfull of **MISC**ELLANEOUS, varied, assorted, and sundry items.

The word PRO**MISC**UOUS is in itself a kind of mixed bag; it has both neutral and pejorative-negative-unpleasant-derogatory connotations. It means miscellaneous, random, INTER**MIX**ED, haphazard, and diverse. ☞ *Wait'll you see the promiscuous junk in their garage!* It also means uncritical, indiscriminate, careless, and slipshod. ☞ *Okay, so I have a very promiscuous love of rich, fatty foods.* The flip side means loose, lax, wanton, licentious, lascivious, and immoral. ☞ *I'm afraid that he'll never be able to live down his promiscuous past.* **PROMISCUITY** is profligacy, immorality, debauchery, or degeneracy. ☞ *After a lifetime of promiscuity, he now sought salvation.*

A marriage between persons of different races is sometimes called **MISCEGENATION**; in Latin America and the Philippines a person of racially-mixed parentage may be referred to as a **MESTIZO.**

A **MEDDLESOME** person is officious, pushy, and bothersome. A **MEDDLER** is a busybody, snoop, and pest, and one who meddles, interferes, intrudes, **INTERMEDDLES,** and butts in.

A **MIX** is a combination, blend, or amalgam; to mix is to join, **ADMIX, COMMIX,** combine, and unite. When Mark Antony paid his final tribute to Julius Caesar in Shakespeare's play, he said, "This was the noblest Roman of them all . . . his life was gentle, and the elements/So **MIX'D** in him that nature might stand up / And say to all the world, 'This was a man!' "

A **MIXOLOGIST** is a fancy name for a bartender; a **MIXUP** is confusion, muddle, or quandary; a **MIXED-UP** person is bewildered, distraught, and troubled. An **UNMIXED** substance is pure. ☞ *We hugged our rescuer with unmixed joy.* **MISCIBLE** ingredients can be mixed together; if they cannot be—such as oil and water—they are **IMMISCIBLE.**

A **MELEE** is a brawl, brouhaha, fracas, or confusing struggle. The small, hardy horse known as a **MUSTANG** got its name from being rounded up on the plains years ago with a mixed lot of other animals. **PELL-MELL** means disorderly, hastily, rashly, and slapdash. ☞ *Everyone took off pell-mell when we heard the fire alarm.* As a noun it means rumpus, commotion, or flurry. ☞ *Man, it was pure pell-mell when they finally opened the doors!*

But not: *miscue* [*mis-*, wrong + *cue,* pool stick], mistake.
Combining forms: *ad-*, to; *com-*, together; *-gen,* race; *im-*, not; *inter-*, together; *pro-*, thoroughly; *un-*, not.
Antonyms: *meddlesome*—aloof, standoffish, restrained; *miscellaneous*—homogeneous, specific, unmixed; *mix*—separate, isolate, segregate; *mixed-up*—lucid, clear-headed, composed; *mixup*—clarification, simplification, explanation, appeasement; *pell-mell*—calmly, methodically, serenely; *promiscuity*—propriety, virtue; *promiscuous*—discriminating, choosy, moral, chaste, pure.

MISEIN, to hate: MISA, MISO

A MISAnthrope, as Moliere's 1666 play of that name demonstrates, is a hater of humankind and the society it has produced. When Alceste, the hero, concludes that the accepted forms of what we call civilization are nothing but hypocrisy, he becomes MISAnthropic, gloomy, and disillusioned.

MISAndry is the hatred of men. ☞ *Our psychology teacher says Julia is a misandrist because of her mother's bitter experiences.* MISOgynism is the hatred of women. ☞ *Juddson's a misogynic writer whose women characters are hateful hypocrites. Our psychology teacher says he's a misogynist because of his early childhood.* A MISOgamist is not someone who is simply leery of or uncomfortable with the idea of marriage; he or she has a deep-seated hatred of it. ☞ *Rebecca's misogamic attitude is Dr. Phink's classic illustration of misogamy in his Abnormal Psych class.*

MISOcainea is an abnormal animus, adversion, abhorrence, and antagonism toward new ideas, and MISOneism is the hatred or intolerance of anything new or changed. ☞ *By the time Dudley was approaching his eighth decade, he was a true misoneist, clinging to the order of things as he had known it for so many years.* MISOlogy is the hatred, dislike, or distrust of argument, enlightenment, or reasoning. ☞ *There was no way that a misologist such as Lemworth was ever going to make it as a philosophy major.*

Combining forms: *-andry,* man; *-anthrope,* humankind; *-cainea,* new, recent; *-gamy,* marriage; *-gyny,* woman; *-logy,* reason; *-ne,* new.

MITTERE, to send: MISE, MISS, MIT, MITT

To adMIT is to let in, accept, include, and receive. ☞ *Only seniors were admitted to the party.* It is to acknowledge, concede, confess, and avow. ☞ *We all saw him cheat, but he never would admit it.* It also means to allow, grant, brook, tolerate, and let. ☞ *The new rules admit no seating after the play begins.*

AdMISSible evidence is that which is adMITTed, allowed, adMITTable, and tolerated. ☞ *No typing errors will be admissible in this contest! The judge ruled that the child's testimony was inadmissible.* AdMISSion is access, entry, or the right to enter. ☞ *Admission is free for children five and under.* It is a confession, declaration, or acknowledgement.

☞ *Thanks to her admission of guilt she was let off with a suspended sentence.*

A sign reading "No Admission" is usually intended to mean "No ADMITTANCE," in other words, "Keep Out!" If the intention is that there is no entry fee, the sign should say, "No Admission Charge." ADMITTEDLY is an adverb meaning by one's own admission. ☞ *Barnwell was admittedly the one who first entered the store.*

When people COMMIT to do something, they oblige, pledge, and resolve. ☞ *The school board committed itself to spend no further funds on the new athletic complex.* It means to do, perpetrate, enact, and carry out. One who breaks the law may be committed, imprisoned, incarcerated, and confined. As an adjective committed means pledged, bound, and sworn. ☞ *We now have enough committed delegates; only a half dozen remain uncommitted.* NONCOMMITTAL means indefinite, vague, undecided, and equivocal. A COMMITMENT is a pledge, guarantee, assurance, vow, or resolution. ☞ *You made a commitment, and we expect you to stand by it.*

In the heyday of communism there were many COMMISSARS, government officials whose job it was to lay down the law regarding party loyalty, and their department in the Soviet Union was known as the COMMISSARIAT until 1946 when the name was changed to ministry.

A COMMISSARY in the military is a store for equipment and provisions, while on the outside it is often known as a lunchroom. A COMMISSIONED officer in the U.S. military holds his or her rank by the authority of the president; a NONCOMMISSIONED officer or NONCOM is a sergeant or corporal.

A COMMISSION is a board, committee, council, delegation, or agency. ☞ *The county commissioner announced that the citizens' request has been granted.* Salespeople often operate on a commission, their earnings based on their productivity; it is a percentage, fee, or portion. ☞ *Guy has finally moved up into a higher commission level.* A machine that is out of commission is not in operating order. ☞ *I'll have this old bus in commission in no time at all.* As a verb it means to appoint, delegate, assign, authorize, or contract. ☞ *No architectural firm has yet been commissioned to draw up plans for the pavilion.*

A COMPROMISE is an agreement, accord, or settlement. To compromise is to agree, adjust, meet halfway, and make a deal. ☞ *Let's compromise and go fifty-fifty.* It is also to endanger, risk, jeopardize, and prejudice. ☞ *I'll resign rather than compromise with my principles.* UNCOMPROMISING means firm, rigid, unrelenting, and inflexible. ☞ *I feel that we finally have a candidate of uncompromising integrity.*

DEMIT is in limited use, meaning only to relinquish or resign a job, public office, or membership in an organization. ☞ *Two more members demitted from the club yesterday.* For living beings **DEMISE** means death, decease, end, or departure. ☞ *Morley's untimely demise was caused by overexertion.* For entities such as empires, powers, governments, or organizations it means collapse, ruin, or fall. ☞ *The causes of the demise of the Roman Empire were at work long before A.D. 476.*

To **DISMISS** is to discharge, fire, and oust. ☞ *Bid goodbye to Jane: she was dismissed this morning.* It is to send off, write off, and send packing. It is also to release, excuse, allow to leave, and disperse. ☞ *The children were dismissed early because of the storm reports.* **DISMISSAL** is cancellation, adjournment, or termination. ☞ *The judge and the attorneys agreed to the dismissal of the charges.* It is also expulsion, notice, firing, release, or laying off. ☞ *Frankie's dismissal came as a complete surprise to me.*

A factory that **EMITs** toxic gases into the atmosphere discharges, ejects, and vents. Such an **EMISSION** is a discharge, expulsion, or exhalation, but an **EMISSARY** is a horse of a different feather; he or she is a VIP sent out or away as an agent, ambassador, delegate, envoy, or deputy. ☞ *Emissaries from six countries are scheduled to meet in Cairo tomorrow.*

The literal meaning of *intermittere* is "to leave a space between, leave off, drop (for a while)." And so Shakespeare used it, ". . . pray to the gods to **INTERMIT** the plague," to "stop for a time, to suspend for a bit, to cease for a while." Occasionally those of us with hearts experience an **INTERMITTENT** pulse, one that skips a beat, and many automobiles have intermittent windshield wipers, ones that are discontinuous, alternating, and sporadic. An **INTERMISSION** is an interlude, interval, interim, hiatus, or break. ☞ *It's a long movie and there's no intermission.*

A **MISSION** is an assignment, charge, or undertaking that someone is sent on. Gene Roddenberry said this of his TV series *Star Trek:* "These are the voyages of the starship *Enterprise,* its five-year mission: . . . to boldly go where no man has gone before." A mission is an occupation, calling, or vocation. ☞ *Her mission in life is to preach the Gospel.* It is also a delegation, task force, group, or committee sent out on an assignment. ☞ *The United Nations mission has now completed its work.* A **MISSIONARY** is a person sent out on a mission as a **MISSIONER,** evangelist, propagandist, or proselytizer. ☞ *Binky has become a civil rights missionary.* As an adjective it suggests increased intensity, passion, ardor, and vehemence. ☞ *She has approached her new assignment with missionary spirit.*

The MASS of some religious services is thought to derive from the phrase *missa est,* "it is the dismissal" (at the end of the service); in the Roman Catholic Church the book of prayers used in celebrating the mass is called the **MISSAL**. A **MISSIVE** is a letter; a letter usually contains a MESSAGE, which, in turn, can be a moral, point, principle, theme, or serious idea.

MISSILES are projectiles, darts, grenades, bullets, lances, or any object that can be hurled, shot, or thrown. A **MISSILEER** is a **MISSILEMAN**, one who designs, constructs, or operates guided missiles and who is expert in **MISSILERY**, the science of building projectiles and rockets.

MESS as a noun refers to chaos and clutter. ☞ *Clean up this mess!* It means predicament and quandary. ☞ *What a mess we're in now!* And it means amount or quantity. ☞ *Let's pick a mess of beans and onions for the stew.* As a verb mess means ruin or botch. ☞ *Drugs messed up his life.* It means dirty or clutter up. ☞ *Now don't mess up the living room.* And it refers to meddle or tamper with. ☞ *Hey, quit messing with my bike!* A MESSY place or person is rumpled, untidy, tousled, bedraggled, and disheveled; a messy situation or predicament can be unpleasant, awkward, and embarrassing. ☞ *Hani's candidacy has created a messy political dilemma.*

Something that is **oMITTED** is left out, deleted, passed over, and forgotten. ☞ *We're always afraid that we might omit the name of one of the donors.* It also may mean to neglect, fail, ignore, and overlook. ☞ *I omitted to tell you that we have company coming for dinner tonight, Mother.* An **oMISSION** is an absence, elimination, or excision. ☞ *I assure you that the omission of your name was unintentional.* It may also mean oversight, shortcoming, failure, or negligence. ☞ *Many people believe that sins of omission are forgivable, venial, but that sins of commission, that is, those done on purpose, are not.*

License, authorization, franchise, sanction, passport, or visa are synonyms for the noun **perMIT**. ☞ *Our parking permit expired last month.* Allow, authorize, admit, grant, let, and OK are verb synonyms. ☞ *Common courtesy does not permit such actions.* **PerMISSIBLE** actions are legal, allowable, acceptable, and admissible. ☞ *I doubt that your evidence will be permissible in a court of law.* **PerMISSION** is consent, approval, or approbation. ☞ *All students on the honor roll have permission to go to the library this period.* A **perMISSIVE** person or rule is lenient, tolerant, **perMITTING**, and indulgent. ☞ *Aunt Selene may be permissive in some regards but not to that kind of offensive language.*

The **preMISE** (also **preMISS**) of a debate, argument, or discussion is its basis for reasoning, hypothesis, assumption, theorem, or theory. ☞ *Our attorney's premise is that we were completely innocent.* As a verb it means to assume, postulate, conjecture, and surmise. ☞ *The debate judges said that we shouldn't have premised our argument on such flimsy grounds.* **PREMISEs** refers to buildings, property, vicinity, land, or grounds.

To **proMISE** is to pledge, vow, guarantee, and vouch. ☞ *I promise never to promise you anything again.* It also means to indicate, hint at, and suggest. ☞ *A sunset like this one promises good weather for tomorrow.* Promise as a noun is assurance, bond, or commitment.

One who is said to "have promise" is believed to have talent, ability, potential, or good prospects. ☞ *Jeeves is said to be a musician with real promise.* A promising future is favorable, bright, and optimistic; a promising student is thought to be gifted, intelligent, endowed, and enterprising. A **proMISSory** note is a written pledge to pay a certain amount at a specified time.

To **reMIT** is to send, pay, and compensate. ☞ *Our check is in the mail; we have remitted the full amount.* It is to abate, lessen, and diminish. ☞ *On the fourth day the fever began to remit.* It is to pardon, forgive, and exonerate. ☞ *At long last we were able to remit his offensive behavior.* To be **reMISS** is to be careless, forgetful, negligent, and delinquent. ☞ *I was remiss in not telling you about the defective air conditioner.* **ReMISSion** is an abatement, alleviation, interruption, or **reMITTal.** ☞ *Helen's doctors assured her that her cancer is in remission.* It is also amnesty, reprieve, absolution, or pardon. ☞ *With the granting of remission of your contemptible actions, you are free to leave.*

Something **unreMITTing** is incessant, constant, relentless, and **unreMITTent.** ☞ *It was the unremitting sounds of gunfire that finally drove him off the deep end.* A **reMITTent** fever, storm, or noise is one that abates, decreases, or ceases from time to time.

To **subMIT** is to surrender, capitulate, yield, and comply. ☞ *The school board finally submitted to the teachers' demands.* It is to tender, offer, put forward, and propose. ☞ *Three plans have now been submitted for the new park.* It is also to contend, assert, suggest, and claim. ☞ *I submit that there are far too few minority students on campus.* A **subMISSive** person tends to be obedient, docile, compliant, passive, and obsequious. ☞ *While Denny was out there fighting for our rights, all of us submissive guys were hiding in our rooms.* **SubMISSion** is capitulation, surrender, compliance, or obedience. ☞ *The sailors were shocked by their captain's submission to the pirate's demands.* **ManuMISSion** is emancipation, and to **manuMIT** is to release from slavery or servitude, to free, and liberate. Submission is also contribution, **subMITTal,** presentation, entry, or **subMITTing.** ☞ *All submissions for this contest must be postmarked before January 1.*

To surMISE is to guess, imagine, conjecture, and theorize. ☞ *I surmised that Lynn would make Phi Beta Kappa.* As a noun it is a supposition, assumption, or presumption. ☞ *It's just a surmise, but I've got a feeling that Bartlett will win the case.*

To transMIT is to send, communicate, pass on, phone, fax, broadcast, and televise. **TransMISSion** is conveyance, conduction, transference, or explanation. ☞ *The double agents were apprehended just as they were arranging for the transmission of the secret papers.* It is also broadcasting, sending, communication, or telecasting. ☞ *The station will not resume transmission today.*

But not: *amiss* [AS *missan,* to fail], wrong; *commiserate* [*miser,* wretched], empathize with; *missay,* [ME *misseyen*], to slander, to speak incorrectly.
Combining forms: *ad-,* to; *com-,* together; *de-,* down; *dis-,* away; *e-,* out; *in-,* not; *inter-,* between; *manu-,* hand; *non-,* no; *o-,* to; *per-,* through; *pre-,* before; *pro-,* forth; *re-,* back; *sub-,* underneath; *sur-,* above; *trans-,* across; *un-,* not.
Antonyms: *admissible*—disallowed, unacceptable, intolerable; *admission*—denial, disavowal, withholding, silence; *admit*—exclude, keep out, prohibit, forbid; *commission*—omission, salary, let go; *commit*—omit, hold back, receive, accept; *compromise*—difference, dispute, argue, boost, enhance, establish, assure; *demise*—birth, commencement, origin; *dismiss*—hire, accept, admit, confine, restrict, hold; *emission*—injection, reception; *intermission*—continuance, prolongation; *intermittent*—incessant, perpetual, constant; *mess*—tidiness, orderliness, neatness; *messy*—trim, orderly, pleasant, comfortable; *noncommittal*—decisive, outspoken, positive, conclusive; *permissible*—forbidden, banned, illegal, unauthorized, illicit; *permission*—refusal, prohibition, ban; *permissive*—strait-laced, stern, rigid, domineering, forbidding; *remiss*—attentive, diligent, scrupulous, meticulous; *remission*—increase, continuation, intensification; *remit*—withhold, condemn, intensify, deteriorate; *submission*—triumph, victory, rebellion, mutiny, defiance; *submissive*—haughty, arrogant, aggressive, refractory; *submit*—resist, defy, hold fast; *uncompromising*—accommodating, flexible, yielding, pliable; *unremitting*—unsteady, irregular, spasmodic.

MORS, death: MORT

A **MORTal** is a human being, a creature subject to death. As an adjective the word has a wide variety of meanings. First, it refers to deadly, relentless, implacable, and irreconcilable. ☞ *Howell spent a large part of his life running from Tarkel, his mortal enemy.* Second, it means extreme, severe, grievous, enormous, and inordinate. ☞ *All the time that he was the general manager I was in mortal fear of losing my job.* And third, it means causing death or fatal. ☞ *It was not, as we had all feared, a mortal wound.*

MORTality refers to death, destruction, or extermination. ☞ *The mortality from the hurricane was devastating.* When one considers mortality in terms of mankind's impermanence, transience, or evanescence, one can, as philosopher George Santayana did, strike a lighter vein: "mortality has its compensations: one is that all evils are transitory, another that better times may come."

ImMORTality is deathlessness and eternity, combined with fame and glory. While no human being is **imMORTal**, we speak of certain qualities such as wisdom as being everlasting, and certain evils as being constant and perpetual. At the age of thirteen Joan of Arc, a French peasant girl, heard voices telling her to liberate her country from the English. Clad in white armor, she led a small army to victory, changing the trend of the Hundred Years' War. Charged with witchcraft and heresy, she was burned at the stake when she was nineteen. In the twentieth century she was beatified and canonized by two popes and **imMORTalized** by people around the world.

When a living plant or animal is **moribund**, it is dying. When one has been **MORTified**, horribly embarrassed and humiliated, one would sometimes just as soon be dead. It also means to discipline oneself. ☞ *He mortified himself by fasting for three days.* A wound that has mortified has putrified and become gangrenous; timely medical help may postpone one's visit with a **MORTician** at the neighborhood **MORTuary.**

To liquidate a debt by paying it off in installments is to **aMORTize** it. A **MORTgage** is the pledging of property as security for the repayment of money borrowed.

AnteMORTem means before death. ☞ *The dying man's antemortem confession prompted the district attorney's decision to reopen the murder case.* Most **postMORTems** are autopsies performed on a cadaver. They also can occur at the bridge table after a hand has been played, in the locker room after a 64 to 3 football loss, or on the way home from a party that turned unpleasant.

Memento mori is a Latin phrase meaning "remember that you must die"; a human skull, for example, is a memento mori, a reminder of our mortality.

But not: *morgue* [F after the name of a building in Paris used to house unidentified bodies in the nineteenth century], place where bodies are kept; *mortar board* [*mortarium,* bowl for mixing certain powdery materials and the mixture], the square cap worn by graduates who wear gowns; *remorse* [*mordere,* to bite], regret, sorrow.
Combining forms: *ante-,* before; *a-,* to; *-fy,* to make; *-gage,* a pledge; *im-,* not; *post-,* after.
Antonyms: *immortal*—ephemeral, temporary, transitory, fleeting; *moribund*—potent, viable, vital; *mortal*—imperishable, lasting, incorporeal, undying.

N

NASCI, to be born, NAT

CogNATe means related by birth and having the same ancestors. In the world of words, English and German are cognate languages; their parent is the Germanic branch of the Indo-European language family. The English "cold" and "milk" and the German *kalt* and *Milch* are, obviously, related in ancestry. French, Italian, and Spanish are also cognate languages, as is shown by these same two words: French, *froid, lait;* Italian *freddo, latte;* and Spanish *frio, leche.* There are also cognates within the English language; "time" and "tide," for example, are kin.

One's NATive land is the one in which he or she was born. Native means inherent, that is, belonging to a person by NATure or NATivity. Persons living in a country in which they were not born can gain the rights and privileges of a citizen through the process of NATuralization.

Tourists hire native guides, note the native dress, shop for native pottery, and listen to native expressions. Persons with native ability may also be described as having inborn, inNATe, NATural, and indigenous talent.

One's native tongue is, NATurally, the language one first speaks. ☞ *In spite of the fact that Margaret was born in Indonesia, her native tongue is English; although it may seem so, that is not unnatural, for her parents were in the diplomatic corps.*

A NATion is a group of people living under a unified government. One's NATionality is that of the country of which he or she is a citizen. Patriotism and NATionalism are synonyms, but one can be a patriot without the fervor that sometimes characterizes a NATionalist; the latter are not usually ardent interNATionalists. A nascent nation is one that is just emerging, developing, and maturing. ☞ *The Peace Corps workers were welcomed by the citizens of the nascent republic.*

When a person who wrote stories or poems, for example, during high school begins to write again after years of inactivity in such fields, he or she experiences a rebirth, renascence, and revival; it could also be termed a renascent interest in writing. Similarly, the period of about A.D. 1350 to 1650, between the Middle Ages and modern times, is known as the Renaissance because it was a great revival of learning, literature, and art in Europe.

The word **NATAL**, relating to birth, is commonly seen in PRE**NATAL** and POST**NATAL**, referring to the before and after care of a pregnant woman. A NEO**NATE** is a newborn child, and NEO**NATAL** pertains to such children.

NOEL is the yuletide season, a Christmas carol, and a male given name; it usually refers to the birth of Christ and in French means "Christmas."

NEE is an everyday newspaper word; "Mrs. Key, nee Lee" tells us that Mrs. Key was born Miss Lee.

PREGNANT has a number of meanings in addition to with child, having a baby, expecting, or in a family way, and the French *enceinte.* It also means creative, fruitful, productive, imaginative, or meaningful. ☞ *The committee has come up with a number of ideas that are pregnant with possibilities.*

Each year we could rightfully celebrate our natal day instead of our birthday, but it would involve getting rid of all those greeting cards stocked in stores, and few of us are **NAIVE** (born yesterday) enough to think that would ever happen. **NAIVETE** is a word meaning simplicity, inexperience, innocence, or foolishness.

Additional English words related to the root: naif, puny.
But not: *natant* [*natare,* to swim], swimming, floating; *natty* [perh. var. of *neat*], spiffy, neatly dressed.
Combining forms: *co-,* together; *in-,* in; *neo-,* new; *post-,* after; *pre-,* before; *pu-,* after; *re-,* again.
Antonyms: *cognate*—dissimilar, distant, unrelated; *innate*—acquired, learned, superimposed; *naive*—artful, worldly, calculating; *naivete*—urbanity, sophistication; *nascent*—dying, ceasing, ending; *native*—imported, alien, immigrant, foreigner; *natural*—studied, guarded, disingenuous, factitious; *pregnant*—trivial, dull, barren, sterile, arid.

NAUS, ship: NAU

People who have suffered through a siege of the stomach disturbance known as seasickness are not surprised when they learn that the literal meaning of **NAU**SEA is "ship sickness." And if they have suffered enough, they readily accept its alternate meaning: disgust, revulsion, contempt, disdain, or animosity. ☞ *The rabblerouser's ranting filled me with nausea.* To **NAU**SEATE is to sicken, repel, repulse, and offend. ☞ *The sight of the children searching the garbage for something to eat nauseated the tourists.*

To feel sick, whether from food or disgust, is to be **NAUSEATED** or **NAUSEOUS.** ☞ *We became nauseated during the interminable speech. The movie was so nauseous many of the audience left before the end.*

NAUTICAL pertains to ships and sailors and navigation. ☞ *Jack Tar always wears some nautical reminder of his navy days.* The pearly or chambered **NAUTILUS** is a mollusk consisting of 36 chambers or rooms. "Build thee more stately mansions, O my soul," wrote Oliver Wendell Holmes in his poem entitled "The Chambered Nautilus." The U.S. Navy's *Nautilus,* launched in 1955, was the first nuclear-powered submarine.

NOISE once meant sickness, too. Today it is a clamor, disturbance, racket, or uproar. ☞ *Living so close to the airport with all that noise would drive me crazy.* As a verb, it is to make public, circulate, and gossip. ☞ *Don't noise this about, but I think the boss is about to retire.* **NOISY** means loud, deafening, lively, and shrill. ☞ *The reading room at the library is way too noisy for me to concentrate.* When the NOISELESS typewriter was introduced, it was advertised as being silent, muted, soundless, and hushed.

But not: *naught* [AS *nauht*], nothing, zero.

NEKROS, corpse: NECRO

People who have an abnormal fear of death are afflicted with **NECROPHOBIA** or thanatophobia; if they have a fiendish attraction to corpses, the affliction is **NECROPHILIA.**

NECROMANCY is a state in which people believe they are communicating, can communicate, or have communicated with the dead. It is a kind of magic or sorcery practiced by a witch. The word **NECROPOLIS,** literally means "city of the dead." And **NECROLATRY** refers to worship of the dead.

NECROBIOSIS is the death of tissue or cells caused by disease or aging. **NECROSIS** is the death of living tissue in one's body. A **NECROPSY** is an autopsy, and a **NECROLOGY** is a list of persons who have died in a certain place or time; such registers are often kept in churches or monasteries, while newspapers and magazines frequently list the names of those who have expired during a recent period.

Combining forms: *-biosis,* mode of life; *-logy,* study of; *-mancy,* divination, prophesying; *-osis,* abnormal state; *-philia,* unnatural attraction; *-phobia,* fear; *-polis,* city.

NEPOS, grandson, nephew; NEPTIS, granddaughter, niece

Several centuries ago, NEPHEW, the common word that refers to the son of a sister or brother, was used by churchmen not only in regard to those genuine nephews upon whom they bestowed churchly favors, but for quite different purposes as well. Clergy who fathered illegitimate sons and daughters referred to them as their nephews and NIECES, thus hoping to avoid any suspicions that they had broken their vows of celibacy, chastity, or abstinence.

Out of this emerged the word NEPOTISM, one that has spawned such synonyms as favoritism, patronage, bias, or partisanship. It is the practice of showing favoritism to members of one's family when making political appointments or business promotions.

> **Antonyms:** *nepotism*—fairness, detachment, impartiality, evenhandedness.

NOCERE, to harm; NOXA, harm: NOC, NOX

Thanks to the negative prefix *in-,* not, we have as many positive and harmless words from this root as we do those with "harmful" meanings.

"There are few ways," said Dr. Samuel Johnson in Boswell's *The Life of Samuel Johnson* (1791), "in which a man can be more INNOCENTLY employed than in getting money"; that's harmlessly, guiltlessly, and blamelessly.

"Ralph wept for the end of INNOCENCE, the darkness in man's heart, and the fall through the air of the true, wise friend called Piggy," wrote William Golding at the end of his *Lord of the Flies.* That's harmlessness, naivete, guiltlessness, and simplicity.

INNOCENT means harmless, upright, impeccable, and ingenuous. INNOCUOUS refers to harmless, INNOXIOUS, safe, inoffensive, and bland.

Without the negative prefix the mood changes—from positive to negative.

"What we call progress is the exchange of one NUISANCE for another nuisance," said Havelock Ellis in *Impressions and Comments* (1914). That's bother, vexation, annoyance, irritation, or aggravation.

"Of all NOXIOUS animals," wrote British clergyman Francis Kilvert in his diary (1870), "the most noxious is a tourist. And of all tourists the most vulgar, ill-bred, offensive and loathsome is the British tourist." That's injurious, destructive, unwholesome, lethal, and deadly.

"I know no method to secure the repeal of bad or OBNOXIOUS laws so effective as their stringent execution," said President Ulysses S. Grant in his Inaugural Address in 1869. That's offensive, disgusting, repulsive, reprehensible, and abominable.

"Oh, these NOCUOUS mosquitoes!" cried the picnickers as they slapped the air. That's harmful, bothersome, and noxious.

But not: *inoculate* [*oculus,* eye], inject a needleful of serum as a disease preventative.
Combining forms: *in-,* not; *ob-,* toward.
Antonyms: *innocence*—guilt, corruption, cunning, guile, worldliness; *innocent*—guilty, culpable, reprehensible, worldly, sophisticated, offensive; *innocuous*—noxious, harmful, deleterious, pernicious; *nocuous*—harmless, benign, safe; *noxious*—wholesome, beneficial, salubrious; *nuisance*—delight, pleasure, happiness, joy; *obnoxious*—likable, engaging, congenial, welcome.

NOMEN, name: NOM

In ancient Rome the first name of a male citizen was called his PRAENOMEN (also PRENOMEN), as Gaius, in Gaius Julius Caesar. Julius, the second name, was called an AGNOMEN; it reflected the ancestral line to which he belonged. Today an agnomen is another word for a nickname, sobriquet, moniker, or diminutive. Caesar was his COGNOMEN; we call it a surname or family name.

Praenomen

A MISNOMER is an error, slip, malapropism, or mistake, especially in calling out someone's name. A NOM DE GUERRE is an assumed name, pseudonym, anonym, or alias. Its literal meaning is "war name," but it is often used when seeking to conceal other kinds of activity, such as painting, writing, traveling, etc. However, the term ordinarily reserved for writers is NOM DE PLUME, literally a "pen name." Among the more well-known are Lewis Carroll (Charles Lutwidge Dodgson), George Eliot (Mary Ann Evans), Saki (H. H. Munro), Mark Twain (Samuel Langhorne Clemens), and George Sand (Amandine Aurore Lucille Dupin, Baronne Dudevant).

NOMENCLATURE is a set or system of names, terms, vocabulary, or phraseology peculiar to an occupation, profession, science, or similar. ☞ *My new job is rather easy, but learning a whole new nomenclature hasn't been.* There are not many **NOMENCLATORS** around these days, but of those who are, if they are *people* their specialty is giving, **DENOMINATING**, or inventing names for things; if they are *books,* they contain lists or collections of words. But back in ancient Rome there was a good supply; they were slaves who accompanied political candidates on their rounds to whisper to them the names of the people they were soliciting votes from.

A **DENOMINATION** is a sect, religious group, church, affiliation, brotherhood, or clan. ☞ *Gramps goes to church, but he doesn't care what denomination he happens to end up in.* It is a grade or degree of value or size. ☞ *I warned him about flashing bills of such large denominations in that neighborhood.* It is also a designation, name, category, or class. ☞ *I have no idea what denomination that animal belongs to.*

In arithmetic, a **DENOMINATOR** is the number written below the line in a fraction, and a common denominator is a number into which each of the denominators in a set of fractions divides evenly. Outside of class it is something shared by all the members of a group.

IGNOMINY is disgrace, dishonor, shame, or infamy. ☞ *Thomas Paine went from being a hero of the American Revolution to spending the last years of his life in ignominy.* Something **IGNOMINIOUS** is dishonorable, disgraceful, humiliating, shameful, and wretched. ☞ *". . . the fear of an ignominious death [from execution], I believe, never deterred anyone from the commission of a crime," said Mary Wollstonecraft, eighteenth century feminist in letters written in 1796.*

NOMINAL is often used to mean minimal, slight, moderate, and reasonable. ☞ *There's but a nominal charge for a ticket and a box lunch.* It is also used to mean so-called, in name only, and titular. ☞ *Burr is the nominal head of the campaign, but we all know who will actually run it.*

To **NOMINATE** is to present, name, put forward, and recommend. On March 31, 1968, President Lyndon Baines Johnson announced to the country that, "I shall not seek, and I will not accept, the **NOMINATION** of my party for another term as your President." He was not **RENOMINATED** and was not, therefore, a **NOMINEE**.

NOUNS are, of course, the names of persons, places, and things. They come in various types such as common, proper, and substitute nouns, or **PRONOUNS**.

Genesis, the first book of the Bible, records that "There were giants in the earth in those days . . . mighty men . . . men of **RENOWN**," thus men of fame, repute, prominence, or status. Its adjective form is **RENOWNED,** which means celebrated, famous, eminent, well-known, notable, and distinguished. ☞ *Eudora Welty is one of our most renowned writers.*

> **But not:** *economical* [Gk *oikonomikos,* relating to household management], frugal.
> **Combining forms:** *a-,* additional; *co-,* together; *-cla,* to call; *de-,* down, fully; *guerre,* war; *i(g)-,* not; *mis-,* wrongly; *plume,* pen; *prae-,* before; *pre-,* before; *pro-,* in place of; *re-,* again.
> **Antonyms:** *ignominy*—credit, pride, glory, honor; *ignominious*—honorable, reputable, creditable; *nominal*—real, true, actual, large, exorbitant, substantial; *renown*—obscurity, unpopularity, infamy, disgrace; *renowned*—unknown, obscure, unrecognized, anonymous.

NOVUS, new: NOV

A **NOVEL** idea is new, original, **INNOVATIVE,** fresh, and unique. ☞ *What a novel place to wear an earring!* A novel in a library or bookstore is a work of prose fiction, usually of 30,000 to 100,000 words in length. In length a **NOVELETTE** is often classified as either a short novel or a long short story, but there are others who look upon one as a cheaply sensational romance. **NOVELIST** Ernest Hemingway's *The Old Man and the Sea,* a book of about 25,000 words, is often called a **NOVELLA.** What is obviously needed here is an **INNOVATOR** who will come up with a new set of game rules to clear up the confusion.

NOVELTY is newness, freshness, originality, or variation. ☞ *The novelty of the new sales campaign soon wore off.* It is also a toy, gimmick, knickknack, trinket, or ornament. ☞ *It's just a tourist trap; all they sell is novelties.* An **INNOVATION** is change, invention, modernization, or alteration. ☞ *According to a survey of the average weight registered on the country's bathroom scales, the innovation of TV remote controllers has broadened the bases of many couch potatoes.* To **RENOVATE** is to renew, repair, remodel, refurbish, and modernize. ☞ *We'll have to renovate this entire place before we can move in.*

A **NOVICE** is a beginner, trainee, neophyte, apprentice, or rookie. ☞ *Did you see that serve? Whoever she is, she's no novice.* **NOVITIATE** has several facets: it is the period of being a novice of a religious order; it is the name of the quarters novitiates live in; and it is the state or condition of being a beginner in any field. It is also a synonym of novice.

A star that suddenly becomes exceedingly bright and then fades away in months or years is called a **NOV**A—is it new. During the era of exploration and settlement of the so-called New World, nova became a part of numerous placenames such as Nova Scotia, Canada; Nova Iguacu, Brazil; and Nova Lisboa, Portugal. It is also the title of a long-running series of filmed documentaries on scientific subjects on public television.

NOUVEAU means newly or recently developed or changed. ☞ *I told you that the new casino would create at least one nouveau millionaire—the owner.* A person who has become newly rich is called a parvenu, upstart, social climber, or **NOUVEAU RICHE**, whereas someone who has just lost his shirt investing his life savings in a one-wheel skateboard is called a **NOUVEAU PAUVRE**, a newly poor person. One modern style of French cooking is called **NOUVELLE CUISINE**, meaning new cooking.

> **But not:** *novena* [*novem,* nine], a Roman Catholic prayer lasting nine consecutive days.
> **Combining forms:** *in-,* in; *re-,* again.
> **Antonyms:** *novel*—trite, old, timeworn, customary, typical; *novice*—veteran, master, expert, professional.

NOX, night: NOCT

NOCTURNAL pertains to night and is opposed to diurnal, which comes from *dies,* day. ☞ *It's the nocturnal animals that are appreciating our garden this year.* The calendars that were used in ancient Mexico are called **NOCT**IDIURNAL because they were based on a sequence of a day and a night.

A **NOCT**URNE is a piece of music written for and appropriate to evening or night, often dreamy or pensive. ☞ *That nocturne of Chopin's is my favorite.* A **NOCT**AMBULIST is a sleep-walker or somnambulist. A **NOCT**OGRAPH is a frame used to aid the blind in writing. **NOCT**ILUCENT clouds are those visible during summer nights.

The vernal EQUINOX (of spring) and the autumnal equinox (of fall), are the two times during the year when the day and the night are approximately the same length; they occur on or about March 21 and September 22. EQUI**NOCT**IAL is an adjective pertaining to an equinox or equinoxes: equinoctial rains, storms, moods, etc.

> **Combining forms:** *-ambulist,* one who walks; *-diurnal,* day; *equi-,* equal; *-graph,* write; *-lucent,* shine.

NUMERUS, number: NUMER

To NUMBER is to count, compute, figure, NUMERATE, ENUMERATE, and quantify. ☞ *I trust you numbered the pages in sequence this time.* It is to be included, comprised of, constitute, and contain. ☞ *Allyson never realized that she numbered among the country's best writers.* It also means restricted, limited, and counted. ☞ *Rudnuk finally realized that his days were numbered.*

As a noun it is a digit, integer, unit, figure, NUMERAL, amount, or total. ☞ *First off we must assign a number to each mailbox.* Number also refers to quantity, multitude, scores, or army. ☞ *An enormous number of mourners lined the avenues outside the church.* And number means edition, book, magazine, paper, chapter, division, or section. ☞ *And now for our last number for the evening. There's an interesting interview in the current number of that magazine.*

INNUMERABLE means countless, NUMBERLESS, incalculable, UNNUMBERED, and endless. ☞ *Count the stars? You kidding? They're innumerable.* NUMEROUS means many, plentiful, copious, and abundant. ☞ *There were numerous entrees on the menu.*

NUMBER-ONE is chief, head, NUMERO UNO, oneself, or first in rank. NUMERICAL pertains to numbers. ☞ *As a prank, the uniformed team members lined up in numerical order rather than by alphabet, size, or height.* NUMERATION is the act of counting, calculating, or reckoning. A SUPERNUMERARY is whatever exceeds the usual or the necessary number; hence an actor employed to play a walk-on is a supernumerary, an extra. As an adjective it means superfluous, excessive, unnecessary, and redundant. ☞ *The editor agreed that the brackets were supernumerary.*

A NUMERIST is a person who attaches great importance to numbers and to NUMEROLOGY, the belief that they affect the lives of human beings, in particular the numbers designating the year of one's birth.

INNUMERACY is called mathematical illiteracy. In this sense, an INNUMERATE is to numbers and mathematics what an illiterate is to letters, words, and reading.

Combining forms: *e-*, out; *in-*, not; *super-*, above.
Antonyms: *innumerable, numberless*—numbered, limited, finite, restricted; *numerous*—scant, few, sparse, meager; *supernumerary*—essential, necessary, important, required.

Q

OCULUS, eye: OC

Not only has this root given us a strange hodgepodge of words, but some of their paths have been rather extraordinary, too. Take the word for those branched horns on the male of the deer family—ANTLERS. The first three letters come from *ante-,* before + *ler,* from *ocular,* of the eye, thus the literal meaning is "before or in front of the eyes." In Middle English it was *auntelere.*

PINOCHLE is the name of a card game; the word most likely came to us through a mixed bag of French, Swiss-French, and Swiss-German words for eyeglasses.

The eye of a potato is the bud from which a new plant grows; when a tree shoot is grafted onto a root stock to grow a new tree, a bud of new growth is used. This is the path that led to our word **INOCULATE**, meaning to inject a serum containing a small amount of germs in order to make the recipient's body immune to those germs.

When someone tries to **INVEIGLE** us into doing something, we're being enticed, tricked, beguiled, and bamboozled. In Latin, it meant "eyeless," *ab-,* without + *oculis,* eye; hence, blinded, we were in danger of getting tricked.

Those holes in our shoes that the laces go through are grommets or **EYELETS**. The French word for eye is *oeil,* so their word for the little hole was *oeillet.* Someplace along the path after the word got into English it evolved into what we have today: *oeillet* to *eyelet.*

A **MONOCLE** is one of those single lenses that old-time British movie actors playing aristocratic roles sometimes wore, and **BINOCULARS** are for birdwatchers and sports fans with two eyes. An **OCULIST** is an eye doctor; **OCULAR** pertains to the eyes.

> **But not:** *occult* [*occulere,* to cover over], hidden, secret; *octet* [Gk *okta-,* eight], company of eight singers; *octuple,* a shell rowed by a crew of eight; *octuplets,* group of eight; *octuplicate,* to make eight copies of, to multiply by eight.
> **Combining forms:** *ant-,* before; *bi-,* two; *in-,* without; *mono-,* one.

ODIUM, hatred: NO

ODIOUS refers to hateful, abhorrent, loathsome, nauseating, and abominable.

In William Congreve's play *The Way of the World* (1700) Mirabell, a gentleman, explains part of his strategy to win the hand and love of Millamant, a sweet young lady, "I chiefly made it my own care to initiate her very infancy in the rudiments of virtue, and to impress upon her tender years a young **ODIUM** and aversion to the very sight of men." That's hatred, enmity, detestation, or abhorrence.

Ralph Waldo Emerson, a New England philosopher, wrote this poem, "Each and All" (1847), after a trip to Cape Cod:

> I wiped away the weed and foam,
> I fetched my sea-born treasures home;
> But the poor, unsightly, **NOISOME** things
> Had left their beauty on the shore,
> With the sun and the sand and the wild uproar.

Things noisome are unwholesome, unhealthful, smelly, rancid, and putrid, like the stench from a garbage dump.

ANNOY can be traced to the Latin phrase *in odio,* literally meaning "in hatred." To annoy may mean simply to bother, tease, and chafe someone, but it can also mean to provoke, harass, disturb, rile, and vex. And all that is bound to bring trouble. In Chapter 6 of Lewis Carroll's *Alice's Adventures in Wonderland,* Alice pays a visit to the Duchess, who is holding a baby in her arms and singing "a sort of lullaby" that goes like this: "Speak roughly to your little boy,/And beat him when he sneezes:/He only does it to annoy,/Because he knows it teases."

In *Pudd'nhead Wilson* Mark Twain wrote, "Few things are harder to put up with than the **ANNOYANCE** of a good example." And approximately two thousand years before that, Ovid, a Roman poet, declared in *Ex Ponto,* "It is **ANNOYING** to be honest to no purpose."

An additional English word related to the root: ennui.
But not: *annotated* [*nota,* a mark, note], supplied with explanations; *noise* [*nausea,* seasickness], sound.
Combining form: *an-,* in.
Antonyms: *annoying*—pleasant, agreeable, soothing; *odious*—agreeable, pleasing, attractive, likable; *odium*—honor, respect, regard, esteem.

OIKOS, house: ECO

In about 1870 Ernst Haeckel, a German biologist, coined the word *okologie,* which became oECOLOGY in English before the "o" was dropped. Its literal meaning is "study of houses," but in this case it may be more fitting to say, "the study of our house," meaning the planet Earth.

There have been many spin-offs from the word, such as **ECOCATASTROPHE** (disaster), **ECOCIDE** (oil spills and chemical dumping), **ECOFREAK** (overly zealous environmentalist), and **ECOHAZARD** (something considered dangerous to a habitat).

If charity, as it is said, begins at home, so does **ECONOMY**, etymologically, at any rate, for the Greek root *oikonomia* means "household management."

ECONOMIC and **ECONOMICAL** are adjectives, and their meanings overlap at times, but they are not always interchangeable. Both mean frugal, thrifty, and money-saving. ☞ *We always buy this brand for economic / economical reasons.* But most of us would be uncomfortable with "Economic shoppers love Chedley's bargains," and "Senator Villet criticized the administration's economical policy."

To **ECONOMIZE** is to skimp, scrimp, and conserve. The practice of economy is frugality, husbandry, prudence, and austerity. When **ECONOMISTS** speak of the nation's economy, they have in mind financial structure, monetary resources, productive power, or financial management.

Understandably, a number of words pertaining to affairs of the church come from *oikos.* A **DIOCESE** is a district of churches presided over by a **DIOCESAN** bishop. A **PARISH** is a part of a diocese that has its own church; it is also any local church and its field of activity, and in Louisiana it is a county. ☞ *Pointe a la Hache, Louisiana, is the seat of Plaquemines parish.* The **PARISHONERS** of the church are its congregants.

PAROCHIAL pertains to parishes and parish schools. It also means narrow, provincial, and insular. ☞ *With parochial views like those she'll never win an election in this town.* **PAROCHIALISM** is ignorance and extreme narrowness of interests and attitudes.

ECUMENICAL means universal and worldwide; the **ECUMENICAL MOVEMENT** is a largely Protestant attempt to achieve universal Christian unity, and an **ECUMENICAL MARRIAGE** is interdenominational or interreligious, that is, between two people of different religions.

Combining forms: *dio-,* completely; *-logy,* study of; *-nomy,* managing; *par-,* near.

Antonyms: *economic, economical*—extravagant, spendthrift, wasteful, lavish, ample, expansive, expensive, exorbitant, high-priced; *economize*—squander, waste, dissipate, misuse; *economy*—extravagance, wastefulness; *ecumenical*—local, regional, limited.

ONOMA, a name: ONYM

An **ANONYM** is a false or assumed name, an alias, a **PSEUDONYM,** pen name, or nom de plume. ☞ *Mark Twain was the anonym of Samuel Langhorne Clemens.* **ANONYMOUS** is an adjective meaning nameless, incognito, unnamed, unidentified, and **PSEUDONYMOUS.** ☞ *The writer of that editorial has received several anonymous threats.* **ANONYMITY** is the state of being unknown, unidentified, or anonymous. ☞ *The witness demanded anonymity.* An **ANTONYM** is a word opposite in meaning to another.

An **EPONYM** is usually a personal name from which a common or proper noun has evolved. A stetson is a hat; it comes from John Stetson, a hatter. Constantinople comes from the Roman emperor Constantine. In 1812 when U.S. politician Elbridge Gerry redrew a map of voting districts to favor his party, it turned out to resemble an outline of a salamander; hence the eponym, gerrymander. A **TOPONYM** is a placename such as Denver, Hudson Bay, or Mount McKinley; it is also the name of something derived from or associated with the placename: cashmere from Kashmir in India, jeans from Genoa, and muslin from Mosul in Iraq.

A **HETERONYM** is a word spelled the same as another but having different pronunciation and meaning: lead, to guide or lead, a metal; bow, a knot or bow, the front of a ship. A **HOMONYM** is a word that is identical in pronunciation and spelling from another but different in meaning: bank refers to a business, a slope, or a row of objects.

A **METONYMY** is a figure of speech in which a name is used in place of another of which it is a part. For example, the word stage is substituted for the word theater (Her whole life is the stage) or the word White House is used in place of the word president (Like it or not, that's the White House tax policy).

ONOMATOPOEIA is a figure of speech in which words are formed from natural sounds: cock-a-doodle-doo, ding-dong, Wham!, or Crunch!

A **PATRONYMIC** is a name derived from the name of a father or male ancestor. Thus Robinson is Robin's son, McDonald is the son of Donald, and O'Casey is a descendent of Casey.

A SYNONYM is a word that is the same or similar in meaning as another. *Its* synonyms are analogue and equivalent; those three words are, therefore, SYNONYMOUS. A SYNONYMY is a thesaurus, a list or book of synonyms, as well as a study of them.

Combining forms: *an-*, again, negative; *ant-*, opposite; *e-*, to; *heter-*, different, other; *hom-*, same; *met-*, change; *-opoeia,* to make; *patr-*, father; *pseudo-*, false; *syn-*, same; *top-*, place, region.
Antonyms: *anonymous*—well-known, attributed, famous, credited, signed.

ORDO, order: ORD

Samuel Taylor Coleridge in *Table Talk* (1835) offered definitions of prose and poetry for young poets when he said "prose = words in their best ORDER;—poetry = the *best* words in the best order." His meaning of the word order is the best arrangement, grouping, form, pattern, structure, or ORDERLINESS.

Order as a noun means command, decree, instruction, or rule. ☞ *They don't sound too bright to me, either, but those are the orders they left for us.* A second meaning is silence, harmony, tranquility, or discipline. ☞ *The job of the sergeant-at-arms is to maintain order.* A third meaning is class, division, rank, position, or classification. ☞ *Her talents are of the very highest order.* Order also refers to goods or items that have been purchased or sold. ☞ *Their initial order was large, but their reorder was enormous!* And finally, order means a society, organization, association, sect, or lodge. ☞ *Pat has decided to join a religious order.*

As a verb order means to command, dictate, rule, and direct. ☞ *The principal ordered the unruly boys to go to her office.* It is to ask for, request, call for, and purchase. It is also to arrange, organize, catalogue, and straighten out or up. ☞ *All my books are ordered by subject matter.*

DISORDER means disarray, chaos, confusion, DISORDERLINESS, or clutter. ☞ *Willie's room is in its usual state of complete disorder.* It is tumult, pandemonium, or turbulence. ☞ *It took three police squadrons to quell the disorder.* It is also an ailment, malady, or illness. ☞ *Dr. Lyle said it was a digestive disorder.* To disorder is to upset, mess up, disorganize, disarrange, or confuse. DISORDERED items are disorganized, jumbled, haphazard, and scrambled. ☞ *The store's disordered array of used books was at once charming and frustrating.* The mess and clutter of a DISORDERLY toolbox can be annoying, but disorderly conduct, a petty misdemeanor, can result in a fine or jail stay.

An **ORD**INARY person is average, normal, unexceptional, and unremarkable, whereas an EXTRA**ORD**INARY one is distinguished, unique, outstanding, and uncommon.

The adverb **ORD**INARILY means usually, mostly, generally, and customarily. ☞ *Ordinarily I'm at work long before nine.* EXTRA**ORD**INARILY therefore means unusually, uncommonly, incredibly, and unbelievably. ☞ *Mindy is an extraordinarily capable young woman.*

A person who has been **ORD**AINED a priest has been vested, elected, appointed, and consecrated; the ceremony at which this occurs is called the **ORD**INATION. An **ORD**O is a Roman Catholic booklet containing the Mass of each day in the year. When a high-ranking authority **ORD**AINS a plan or arrangement, it is decreed, ruled, pronounced, and ordered. ☞ *The rulers ordained that the land along the rivers belonged to the state.* An **ORD**INANCE is a rule, law, decree, statute, or act. ☞ *Possession of fireworks is illegal under the new ordinance.* **ORD**INAL numbers express degree or order in a series, such as first, tenth, and twentieth; cardinal numbers are one, ten, twenty, etc. **ORD**NANCE is military weapons; it is the branch of an army that obtains, stores, maintains, and issues its weapons, ammunition, vehicles, etc.

By itself **ORD**INATE is a word of limited usage: it is a description of a mathematical figure; it also means arranged in rows, as the spots on the wings of an insect.

CO**ORD**INATE refers to equal, parallel, analogous, or correlative. ☞ *Latitude and longitude are the coordinates that hurricane trackers pay close attention to.* As a verb it means to classify, arrange, organize, and order. ☞ *Let's coordinate our procedures before the meeting.* It also means synchronize, unify, and pull together. ☞ *The various municipal agencies need to coordinate their efforts if we're to succeed.* One's physical CO**ORD**INATION is the harmonious functioning of one's body parts. ☞ *She's certainly got the coordination necessary for tennis.* An UNCO**ORD**INATED person is clumsy, awkward, gawky, and maladroit. A CO**ORD**INATING conjunction is used in a sentence to connect two equal elements such as, Mary *and* Marty, and win *or* lose, as well as two equal clauses such as Vilma went to law school *and* Francisco went into politics. The CO**ORD**INATOR of an event is the one whose job it is to keep everything running smoothly.

IN**ORD**INATE refers to excessive, immoderate, and exorbitant, as well as irregular, disorderly, and deplorable. ☞ *Beth's inordinate appetite for* *sweets has become a real problem. We hope that these regulations will control the inordinate hunting of deer in the park.* INORDINATELY and extraordinarily are synonyms. ☞ *Was Zarko ambitious? I'll say! Inordinately so!*

SUBORDINATE means secondary, minor, marginal, and supplementary. ☞ *First on the agenda is the matter of finances; finding parking space is of subordinate concern.* As a noun it is an underling, assistant, aide, attendant, or retainer. ☞ *Suzi started at the top; she's never been a subordinate.* As a verb it means to make secondary, subservient, and dependent. ☞ *That man has always subordinated pleasure to work.* A SUBORDINATING conjunction in a sentence introduces a subordinate clause; the words because, when, if, while, and although are subordinating conjunctions when they introduce clauses such as, *because you were at work,* or *when the dam broke.* They are subordinating because something more must be added to complete the thought. A SUBORDER is the group next below in the ordering or classifying of plants and animals. ☞ *The suborder Cichoraceae includes dandelion and lettuce.* Sometimes suborder is applied to human activities. ☞ *Billie Beavy has joined the Kits, a suborder of the Beaver Lodge at our Youthful Citizens' Activity Center.* An INSUBORDINATE person is defiant, disobedient, refractory, and insolent. ☞ *What is the meaning of this check beside the word insubordinate on your report card?* INSUBORDINATION in the military is the equivalent of rebellion, mutiny, or insurgence. ☞ *The sailors were thrown in the brig for insubordination.*

But not: *ordeal* [AS *ordel,* judgment], severe experience; *primordial* [*primus* first + *ordiri,* to begin], original.
Combining forms: *co-,* together, with; *dis-,* apart; *extra-,* beyond; *in-,* not; *re-,* again; *sub-,* under; *un-,* not.
Antonyms: *coordinate*—unequal, disparate, disorganize, muddle; *disorder*—method, neatness, tidiness, vigor, vitality; *disorderly*—trim, tidy, organized, civil, restrained, peccable; *extraordinary*—average, usual, unremarkable; *inordinate*—moderate, reasonable, meager, scanty; *insubordinate*—obedient, deferential, law-abiding; *order*—plea, request, jumble, hodge-podge, chaos, plead, supplicate; *ordinarily*—infrequently, rarely, seldom; *ordinary*—distinguished, exceptional, novel, impressive; *subordinate*—first, superior, ruling, sovereign, commanding; *uncoordinated*—deft, expert, skilled, polished.

P

PAIS, child, PED

PEDiatrics is the medical branch that deals with children; it is also known as **PEDology.** A **PEDiatrician** is a physician who specializes in that field. **PEDodontics** is the branch of dentistry that deals with the care and treatment of children's teeth; a **PEDodontist** is the specialist to whom children go. **OrthoPEDics** is the surgical branch of medicine that deals with bone deformities, diseases, and injuries; **orthoPEDic** surgeons most frequently work with the young, particularly in the correction of crippling impairments or diseases.

EncycloPEDia is a word that did not get the correction it needed when it was young. In brief this is what happened: the intended meaning was based on the Greek *enkuklios paideia,* meaning a circular or well-rounded education. But somewhere along its journey the *paid* became *paed* and then *ped,* thus going around from the word circle, to the word child. **EncycloPEDic** refers to comprehensive, broad, and erudite.

In ancient Greece a *paidagog* (**PEDagogue**) was a child's tutor. An educational idea is **PEDagogic** or **PEDagogical.** ☞ *Miriam's revolutionary pedagogical scheme was to allow her children to read anything they wanted to.* **PEDagogics** is the art of teaching.

The meanings of the rest of the words that stem from *pais* tend to have a pejorative effect or force, i.e., a connotation that is disparaging, belittling, and derogatory. A **PEDant** used to be defined as a schoolmaster; today it's a somewhat negative word that describes one who makes a show of scholarship or learning. Its synonyms are egghead, highbrow, show-off, or dogmatist. A **PEDantic** answer to a question is generally considered to be pompous, overly meticulous, nitpicking, erudite, and pedagogical. Such is the stuff of **PEDantry,** an excessive display of learning.

Then there's **PEDerasty,** an abnormal man-boy relationship; a **PEDerast** is a **PEDophile,** a psychiatrist's word to describe an adult who is sexually attracted to young children; the attraction is called **PEDophilia.**

> **But not:** *peddling* [*ped,* a basket], trifling, piddling; *pedestrian* [*pes,* foot], dull; *pediculosis* [*pedis,* louse], infestation of lice.

Combining forms: *cyclo-*, circular, general; *en-*, in; *-erast*, love; *-gogue*, to lead; *-iatric*, medical; *-logy*, body of knowledge; *-odont*, having teeth; *ortho-*, correction of deformities; *-philia*, unnatural attraction.
Antonyms: *encyclopedic*—limited, confined, specialized; *pedantic*—comprehensive, general, vague.

PAR, equal, peer: PAR

When people come down with the flu, they sometimes complain that they are not feeling up to **PAR**. When they are playing a round of golf, they are delighted when they are shooting below par. Par is a measure, guideline, or standard that is used whether one is in a sick bed with 102 degrees of temperature and the blinds drawn or out on the links on a sunny day when cool breezes waft across the fairways. **ComPARisons** are being made: how does one feel with 98.6 degrees as **comPARed** with 102 degrees? How does one feel with 72 strokes compared with 92 or 86 or 102?

Something that is **comPARable** is similar, like, and analogous. ☞ *Oh, I think life in a town this size is quite comparable to that in a big city.* **ComPARative** means relative, approximate, similar, and near. ☞ *Janice may be a comparative newcomer in politics, but she has demonstrated that she's a comparatively quick learner.* In grammar the comparative forms of good, near, friendly, and thoughtful are better, nearer, more friendly, and more thoughtful.

Anything that is said to be **incomPARable** is matchless, unrivaled, unsurpassed, and **nonPAReil.** ☞ *Only the sight of such incomparable beauty could have inspired Wordsworth to write that poem.*

PARity is equality, correspondence, or similarity. ☞ *The Ministers of Finance met in Paris to seek parity in value of the currencies of the two countries.* **DisPARity** is difference, inequality, inconsistency, or incongruity.

To **disPARage** someone or something is to belittle, discredit, criticize, and put down. ☞ *Please, let's not disparage good manners. I'm afraid cousin Lem's remarks disparaged our whole family.*

Susan Glaspell's short story "A Jury of Her **Peers**" is about a group of Martha Hale's friends and neighbors, they being her equals, fellow citizens, or colleagues. Peer and **compeer** are synonyms, but the latter also means a close friend, comrade, or companion. ☞ *Only her compeers knew of her* *plans.* In Great Britain and Ireland a peer is a member of the nobility, or the PEERAGE, and, if a man, is a duke, marquis, earl, viscount, or baron.

When two people have a dispute over, say, where their property lines are, the PAIR may have to call upon an UMPIRE to settle the question. Umpire derives from the French *nompere* (*nom,* not + *per,* equal), the sense being that if the arbiter is not equal, then he or she must be neutral.

An AU PAIR is a person who is employed by a family to take care of the children and do housework in what is considered an equal exchange for board and room. ☞*The children have gone to shop with the au pair.*

People who bet at the horse races usually do so on the **PAR**IMUTUEL system, in which those holding winning tickets divide the total amount bet according to how much each wagered. Those who take their winnings plus the original bet and gamble it all on the next race **PAR**LAY their bet. One need not be at the racetrack to parlay something. ☞*The young couple parlayed their talents into a successful business partnership.*

But not: *disparate* [*parare,* to prepare], dissimilar; *parity* [*parere,* to bear], ability to give birth; *parley* [Gk *ballein,* to throw], conference.
Combining forms: *au,* at the; *com-,* together; *dis-,* apart; *in-,* not; *-mutuel,* mutual; *non-,* not; *um-,* not.
Antonyms: *comparable*—different, unlike, unequal, dissimilar; *disparage*—esteem, value, appreciate, cherish; *disparity*—accord, unity; *incomparable*—pedestrian, lackluster, second-rate, ordinary; *nonpareil*—average, mediocre, commonplace, usual; *parity*—difference, inquality, diversity.

PARERE, to give birth to, come in sight: PAR

As **PAR**ENTS we are fathers, mothers, progenitors, ancestors, or antecedents. But we are much more, too: as part of our **PAR**ENTAL status, we are prototypes, models, or exemplars. With **PAR**ENTHOOD come many challenges. ☞*Martin's father claims that Martin is a young man of very distinguished parentage.* The current in word for parenthood, rearing, or upbringing is **PAR**ENTING. ☞*The worst moments of parenting for me were having to lie to my children about the Easter bunny and the tooth fairy and Santa, and then having to tell them that I had lied.*

A BI**PAR**OUS birth is one in which two offspring are brought forth. ☞*Dolly and Molly R., Jack and Zack D., and Harry and Mary L. all have biparous parents.* In a UNI**PAR**OUS birth only one egg or offspring is produced, and a MULTI**PAR**OUS birth produces more than one or for a second time. FETI**PAR**OUS animals bear young before they are truly developed and thus often carry them in a pouch. ☞ *In science today we learned that kangaroos and opossums are fetiparous marsupials.*

Birds and most reptiles and fishes are OVI**PAR**OUS, that is, they produce eggs that hatch after being expelled. Most mammals are VIVI**PAR**OUS, bringing forth live young rather than eggs. A viper [*vivus,* alive] is a venomous snake that is so named because some of them give birth to live young, but when Philip Wylie wrote *Generation of Vipers,* he was referring not to snakes but to spiteful and evil human beings.

PARTURITION is the act or process of giving birth to a child. ANTE**PAR**TUM and prenatal, as well as POST**PAR**TUM and postnatal, are synonymous pairs, meaning before birth and after birth, respectively.

The catalog of songs, plays, skills, or tricks, and such that an actor or a theatrical troupe can perform is a REPERTOIRE. A REPERTORY theater or company is one that produces a season of several works year after year; such a theater "brings forth."

When Shakespeare's Macbeth says, "Thou canst not say I did it. Never shake thy gory locks at me," he is speaking to an AP**PAR**ITION, one that APPEARS to him to be the ghost of Banquo, the general he has recently had three murderers do away with. The ghost's APPEARANCE is but momentary; it soon DISAPPEARS as mysteriously as it had come. It is AP**PAR**ENT to those with him at the royal banquet that "his Highness is not well," but Macbeth AP**PAR**ENTLY recovers, saying, "I drink . . . to our dear friend Banquo, whom we miss," at which point the ghost REAPPEARS. The audience finds the scene quite TRANS**PAR**ENT, obvious, and overt, for it has been privileged to witness several scenes that those at the banquet can know nothing about.

When students become overwhelmed by the large number of characters in a novel, play, or short story, many teachers list the names and roles they play on the chalkboard or on a TRANS**PAR**ENCY to put on an overhead projector.

But not: *paranoia* [Gk *paranoia,* madness], a mental disorder characterized by delusions, etc.; *parentheses* [Gk *parenthesis,* a putting in beside], the marks () used to set off an explanatory or qualifying element.

Combining forms: *ante-,* before; *ap-,* toward; *bi-,* two; *dis-,* away; *feti-,* fetus; *multi-,* more than one; *ovi-,* an egg; *post-,* after; *pre-,* before; *re-,* again; *trans-,* across; *uni-,* one; *vivi-,* alive.

Antonyms: *apparent*—uncertain, doubtful, covered up, obscure; *appearance*—departure, passing, vanishing; *transparent*—covert, opaque, murky, wily, devious.

PASCHEIN, to suffer: PATH

PATHETIC means pitiful, distressing, sad, and deplorable. The word is also used in the somewhat lighter sense of feeble, meager, puny, crummy, and measly. ☞ *All I get for my masterpiece is a D+? That's pathetic!*

A PATHETIC FALLACY, a term coined by art critic John Ruskin in *Modern Painters* (1856), refers to the attributing of human traits and feelings to nature or inanimate objects: cruel sea, smiling clouds, laughing daffodils, ravenous flames, or wistful deer. Ruskin's definition of pathetic refers to the arousing of feeling: are the flames *truly* ravenous, greedy, and voracious? Or is that the author's emotions taking over?

PATHOS is the power or quality in actual life or in literature that arouses feelings of compassion, pity, or sorrow. ☞ *The book was so filled with pathos that I couldn't finish it.* The sometimes-companion word *bathos,* [Gk, depth] means insincere or false pathos, hence it is sentimentality, mawkishness, slush, mush, or schmaltz.

PATHOLOGY is the science or study of diseases, their origin, nature, and course. Its adjective form **PATH**OLOGICAL pertains to diseases and means diseased. When someone is described as a pathological liar, the reference is usually to a mentally disturbed condition. A **PATH**OGEN is a disease-producing agent, such as a virus or other microorganism.

"The death of democracy is not likely to be an assassination from ambush," Robert Maynard Hutchins wrote in *Great Books* in 1954, "It will be a slow extinction from A**PATH**Y, indifference, and undernourishment." From, in other words, unconcern, inattention, passiveness, or disinterest. An A**PATH**ETIC person is indifferent, unfeeling, uninterested, impassive, and lethargic. ☞ *After days of hoping that their distress signal would be seen, the group on the mountainside slowly became apathetic.*

ANTI**PATH**Y is dislike, aversion, antagonism, animus, or enmity. ☞ *I knew I would never be able to rid myself of my antipathy toward that racist organization.* ANTI**PATH**ETIC means opposed, averse, contrary, and hostile. ☞ *Every member was antipathetic to anyone who was different from their group.* A SOCIO**PATH** is one whose behavior is antisocial and who lacks a social conscience; a PSYCHO**PATH**IC person lacks the ability to love or establish meaningful personal relationships.

EMPATHY is the ability to identify oneself with another person so as to share his or her feelings; therefore one feels commiseration, compassion, and sympathy. ☞ *Having been down that road myself, I felt empathy for the youngster.* As an intransitive verb, meaning to pity, identify with, and imagine, it is usually followed by *with.* ☞ *Not until I became able to empathize with people of other backgrounds was I able to find myself.*

SYMPATHY is harmony, congeniality, rapport, and empathy. ☞ *"When a member of my family complains that he or she has bitten his tongue, bruised her finger, and so on," wrote psychoanalyst Sigmund Freud in* The Psychopathology of Everyday Life *(1901), "instead of the expected sympathy I put the question, 'Why did you do that?' "* SYMPATHETIC means pitying, tenderhearted, compassionate, and kind. ☞ *The sympathetic teacher was besieged by the troubled students.* It also means agreeable, approving, friendly, congenial, and amiable. ☞ *My mom isn't at all sympathetic to my idea of taking a semester off to work.*

To SYMPATHIZE is to agree, understand, support, and back. ☞ *Her family sympathized with Rebecca in her dispute with the phone company.* It also means to commiserate, identify with, and feel compassion for. ☞ *The setting of the following scene is the shore of an ocean; the characters are an English-speaking Walrus and a Carpenter; the two of them have conned a gathering of oysters into joining them as they walk along the beach; the conversation goes like this: " 'I weep for you,' the Walrus said: / 'I deeply sympathize,' / With sobs and tears he sorted out / Those of the largest size . . ." for, of course, his and the carpenter's lunch. From* Through the Looking-Glass, *by Lewis Carroll.*

The world TELEPATHY was invented in 1882 to describe the communication of thought between two persons without the use of words; it is often referred to as thought-transference and comes under the umbrella of ESP, extrasensory perception.

HOMEOPATHY is the treatment of disease by small doses of drugs that in a healthy person would produce symptoms similar to those of the disease; its opposite is ALLOPATHY, a method of treating a disease by using drugs or similar agents that produce effects that are different from those of the disease. An OSTEOPATH treats certain diseases and abnormalities by manipulating bones and muscles; he or she is a practitioner of OSTEOPATHY.

But not: *pathfinder* [AS *paeth*], an explorer.
Combining forms: *a-*, not; *allo-*, opposition; *anti-*, against; *em-*, within; *homeo-*, similar; *-ology*, study of; *path-*, *patho-*, *-path-*, *-pathic*, *-pathy*, feeling, suffering; *sym-*, together; *tele-*, distance.

Antonyms: *apathetic*—caring, concerned, sensitive, responsive, committed; *apathy*—attention, interest, enthusiasm, fervor; *antipathetic*—agreeable, amenable, inclined, disposed; *antipathy*—affinity, affection, attraction, sympathy, partiality; *empathy*—animosity, friction, discord, abhorrence, dissent; *pathetic*—funny, comical, ludicrous, entertaining; *pathos*—amusement, humor, fun; *sympathetic*—indifferent, unmoved, hard-hearted, unmerciful; *sympathize*—oppose, disagree, reject, disallow, misunderstand; *sympathy*—hostility, unconcern, strife, conflict.

PATER, father: PATRI, PATRO

"I am delighted that you **PATRO**NIZE my store," said the shopkeeper, "but I hate it when you patronize me."

The first use means to shop at, trade with, and buy from, and is a word with a neutral, evenhanded, and impartial connotation. The second use of the word, however, carries a load of unpleasant, pejorative baggage; it means to put down, talk down to, act in a superior way to, and treat haughtily. **PATRO**NIZING people are seldom winners of blue ribbons or gold medals for humility.

PATRONAGE is versatile, too. The shopkeeper welcomes his customers' patronage. Most charitable organizations owe their existence to the support, backing, and patronage of their donors or **PATRO**NS. In politics patronage is the granting of political appointments, contracts, or favors; a popular synonym is porkbarreling. **PATRI**OT is another that carries a double load. One who loves his or her country is a patriot; Stephen Decatur, an American naval hero, stated the case of **PATRI**OTISM when he said in reply to a toast in 1816, "Our country, right or wrong!" But, wrote Thomas Paine in *The Crises* (1776), a hero of the American Revolution, there is "the summer soldier and sunshine patriot who will shrink from the service of their country in a crisis." One who displays a conspicuous or boastful and aggressive kind of patriotism may be tagged with such labels as flag-waver, chauvinist, or jingoist.

A COM**PATRI**OT is a person of one's own country or a colleague. An EX**PATRI**ATE is one who has been banished from a country or one who initiates the move to another country. Many American writers chose to live as expatriates in Paris after World War I.

A PADRE is usually addressed or referred to as father. British cartoonists often show the country squire being addressed by his children as **PAT**ER, a snobbish term, as he leaves in his chauffeured Rolls Royce for the House of Lords, a place where only he and other **PATRI**CIANS are entitled to sit; a cynic once wondered how in the world they could find that many people who are noble, dignified, genteel, or aristocratic. Well, their **PATRI**MONY probably helped; a hefty inheritance from one's father tends to do that, especially if Pater was the **PATRI**ARCH of a very wealthy family. It may have helped, too, to inherit a highly respected **PATRO**NYMIC, i.e., father's good name.

PATERNAL advice is fatherly. ☞ *Coach said he wanted to give me some paternal counseling about my problems.* PATERNALISM is an attitude or practice in a business or government agency in which management treats the employees as a well-meaning father would his children; it is often resented. PATERNITY is fatherhood. ☞ *We never could establish the paternity of the puppies.*

The word PERPETRATE has negative connotations. ☞ *What demented soul perpetrated this crime? Who perpetrated this tasteless magazine?* A PERPETRATOR is an egregious transgressor, outlaw, or offender.

The **PAT**ERNOSTER is the Lord's Prayer; its literal meaning is "our father."

Combining forms: *-arch,* ruler; *com-,* together; *ex-,* out of; *noster,* our; *-nymic,* a name; *per-,* thoroughly.
Antonyms: *patriot*—subversive, traitor; *patriotism*—treason, subversion; *patronizing*—humble, tactful, discreet, respectful.

PAX, peace: PAC, PEACE

British Prime Minister Neville Chamberlain announced in London on October 1, 1938, that he and German Chancellor Adolf Hitler signed an agreement in Munich. "I believe it is **PEACE** in our time . . . peace with honor," the Prime Minister said upon his return from Germany. Opposition leaders immediately criticized the agreement, charging that Chamberlain had been duped by the German leader. "We must not try to APPEASE Hitler," Lord Huffingshire said. Obviously he did not want to give in, submit, conciliate, and accede to the demands of the German ruler.

On September 1, 1939, 1.25 million German troops swept across the Polish border at dawn. The **PAC**IFICATION-through-APPEASEMENT policy of Prime Minister Chamberlain had failed. Communiques from Berlin indicated that the troops were expected to bring order to Poland and help the Polish people. Outside observers likened it to a **PAX ROMANA,** the imposing of peace through force or an uneasy or hostile peace, literally, "a Roman peace." With that World War II began.

Winston Churchill, who took over from Chamberlain as prime minister in 1940, had written ten years earlier that he had "always been against the **PACIFISTS** during [a war], and against the Jingoes at its close." Pacifists are those who are opposed to war and violence of any kind; a jingo is a flag-waver or militarist. Albert Einstein, the formulator of the theory of relativity, had left Germany for America following the rise of Hitler; at the beginning of the war he said, "My **PACIFICISM** is not based on any intellectual theory but on a deep antipathy to every form of cruelty and hatred."

A quarter of a century later there was much talk of **PEACEFUL** coexistence, i.e., competition without war. Those opposed to the wars of the time were derided as **PEACE-NIKS.**

Students in honors English courses often read John Keats' poem stating that when he saw the ancient Greek sculptures known as the Elgin Marbles he felt ". . . like stout Cortez when with eagle eyes / He star'd at the **PACIFIC.**" Babies take to gumming plastic or rubber **PACIFIERS.** And baseball fans enjoy the advice given by the legendary baseball pitcher Satchel Paige in *How to Stay Young* (1953), "Avoid fried meats which angry up the blood. If your stomach disputes you, lie down and **PACIFY** it with cool thoughts. Keep the juices flowing by jangling around gently as you move."

History teaches that at times our Big Choice boils down to an either-or-situation. In 1813 United States Representative Henry Clay argued that the government had bùt two options regarding the Missouri Compromise of 1820. "**PEACEABLY** if we can, forcibly if we must." For his work he was given the nickname of the great **PACIFICATOR.**

A few hundred years before that, PAY meant "to pacify"; the sense was that one had to give whatever money was PAYABLE, due, and allowed in order to quiet one's creditor. But today, pay stretches beyond money; we realize that quitting the team or dropping out of school, doesn't pay, yield a return, or bear fruit; we pay, give, deliver, and extend our respects to a visiting dignitary; and we listen carefully when the judge tells an offender that he or she must pay, meaning to suffer the consequences, be punished, and answer for.

Combining forms: *ap-,* to; *fi-, -fic, -fy,* to make.

Antonyms: *appease*—exacerbate, antagonize, anger, irritate; *pacific*—troubled, turbulent, agitated, ruffled; *pacify*—arouse, perturb, inflame, provoke, madden; *pay*—owe, be in debt, charge, cost, withhold, suppress, retain; *peace*—hostilities, conflict, agitation, turmoil; *peaceful*—warlike, bellicose, hostile, violent.

PECCARE, to stumble, sin: PECCA

In the spring of 1843 British forces under the command of Sir Charles Napier defeated the armies of Sind (today a province of Pakistan) and annexed the area to what was then British India. It has been reported that Sir Charles sent a war dispatch back to the London magazine *Punch* consisting of four words: "**PECCAvi**—I have Sind." Although it broke the unspoken rule for puns, it was considered acceptable on the grounds that most people would not know that a peccavi is a confession of sin, with the literal meaning, "I have sinned"—which he had.

A **PECCAble** person is liable to sin; a **PECCAnt** is one who has apparently already done so, for he or she is guilty, wrong, and sinful; and a **PECCAtophobic** is one who lives in mortal fear of sinning.

Strictly speaking, to be **imPECCAble** is to be perfect, to be incapable of sinning or wrongdoing. Because there are not many qualifiers, the use of the word is usually limited to such matters as manners, reputation, or command of one's language. ☞*Ms. Brown's impeccable style is a pleasure to read.* A **PECCAdillo** is a very minor or slight sin, for instance, a white lie, a trifling slip, an indiscretion, or a faux pas. ☞*Surely I will be forgiven that! Just a teeny-weeny peccadillo, don't you know.*

But not: *peccary* [Sp *pecari*], a piglike, hoofed animal, a javelina.
Combining form: *im-*, not.
Antonyms: *impeccable*—imperfect, defective, compromised; *peccant*—saintly, moral, righteous, pure.

PECUS, cattle, property: PECU

Ages ago, long before the sporty, two-seater convertible and the chauffeur-driven stretch limo, evidence of a person's wealth was the number of cattle that he counted among his properties. A man's cattle—horses, sheep, swine as well as bulls, cows, steers—were his capital; interestingly, both cattle and capital derive from *caput,* head.

So it is not surprising that *pecus,* the Latin word for cattle and property gives us words related to money. **PECU**NIARY is synonymous with monetary, financial, fiscal, and economic. ☞ *Hap's depression was the result of his pecuniary difficulties.* One who is IM**PECU**NIOUS is penniless, indigent, destitute, broke, and financially embarrassed. ☞ *Hilda was an eager, impecunious young woman who didn't mind her condition at all.*

To **PECU**LATE is to steal and embezzle, usually from money entrusted to one's care or from public funds. **PECU**LATION and embezzlement are synonyms, as are **PECU**LATOR and embezzler.

PECULIAR once meant "special, privately owned, and belonging to oneself"; we see traces of that when we use the word to mean distinctive, personal, and individual. ☞ *Corn-pone is an expression peculiar to Southerners. Every pup in the litter had its own peculiar markings.* But it is perhaps more often that we use the word in the sense of odd, curious, eccentric, quaint, weird, and bizarre.

A **PECU**LIARITY is a trait, quality, or attribute. ☞ *One of the peculiarities of that pioneering automobile was its seven-speed gearbox.* It is also an eccentricity, idiosyncrasy, oddity, or quirk. ☞ *Don't be put off by his monocle. It's just one of his peculiarities.*

Combining form: *im-,* not.
Antonyms: *impecunious*—affluent, prosperous, opulent; *peculiar*—normal, ordinary, regular, conventional.

PELLERE, to drive: PEL, PUL

As a verb APPEAL means to plead, ask, and beg. ☞ *The devastated community appealed to Washington for emergency aid.* It also means to interest, attract, tempt, and fascinate. ☞ *Skydiving does not really appeal to me.* As a noun it is a plea, entreaty, or request. ☞ *The woman's appeal to the court was dismissed.* It is also a charm, fascination, or attraction. ☞ *Their new advertising gimmick proved to have little appeal.* Something that is APPEALING is charming, engaging, and enchanting. ☞ *It is an appealing movie, largely because of Ms. Burton's captivating performance.* It can also be pleading, imploring, and entreating. ☞ *The boys chose the ragged mutt with the appealing, frightened look.*

An AP**PEL**LANT is a person who appeals; in law, it is one who appeals to a higher court. An AP**PEL**LATE court is one that has the power to review and decide appeals. An **APPELLATION** is a name, title, or designation by which something is known. ☞ *The farmer called it a road, but I thought that a pretty odd appellation for a cow path.*

To **COMPEL** is to force, coerce, require, and necessitate. ☞ *Financial problems compelled him to drop out of school.* Synonyms of **COMPELLING** are convincing, driving, over-powering, and persuasive. ☞ *This is a compelling novel. We had compelling reasons for our absence. Miss Lange has a compelling personality.* **COMPULSION** is coercion, pressure, duress, or urgency. ☞ *Grover admits to having this irresistible compulsion to stop all the traffic on Main Street. I signed the ticket, but only under compulsion.* To be **COMPULSIVE** is to be obsessive, coercive, **COMPELLED**, and driven. ☞ *He's a compulsive workaholic who always seems near the breaking point.* **COMPULSORY** tasks, jobs, duties, or assignments are mandatory, required, and requisite. ☞ *I won't be able to take any electives until I get these compulsory courses out of the way.*

To **DISPEL** is to disperse, dismiss, and banish. ☞ *We did our best to dispel her suspicions. When the winds shifted, the clouds were dispelled.*

To **EXPEL** is to eject, oust, remove, and dismiss. ☞ *The club treasurer was expelled as soon as the shortage was discovered.* It is also to force out, discharge, and spew. ☞ *The volcanic eruption expelled massive amounts of fluid rock.* An **EXPULSION** is a discharge, ejection, ouster, and banishment. ☞ *The two school expulsions on her record ended her thoughts of applying at her father's alma mater.*

Synonyms of **IMPEL** are drive on or forward, push, prod, and incite. ☞ *Despite our friendship, I felt impelled to vote against him for secretary.* An **IMPELLER** in a well pump drives the water into the pipes. An **IMPULSE** is an urge, drive, or desire. ☞ *I couldn't resist the impulse to buy a rose for Emily.* As an adjective it means marked by or acting on impulse. ☞ *Lorna always stays with her shopping list, rejecting any impulse buying.* An **IMPULSIVE** person is impetuous, spontaneous, wild, capricious, and rash. ☞ *Jumping into the pool was an impulsive act, but I'd do it again.*

PROPEL means to push, drive, prompt, thrust, and catapult. ☞ *His failure to win a promotion propelled him to register for night courses.* **PROPELLANTS** are necessary parts of explosives, rockets, and aerosol containers. **PROPELLERS** are found on ships, certain aircraft, and electricity-producing wind plants. **PROPULSION** is momentum, drive, projection, force, thrust, or power. ☞ *I can't imagine the amount of propulsion needed to lift that space shuttle into orbit!*

To **REPEAL** means to nullify, cancel, and rescind. ☞ *The dress code rule was repealed at last month's meeting.* As a noun it means revocation, nullification, or annulment. ☞ *The repeal of the 18th Amendment occurred in 1933.* To **rePEL** is to drive back, **rePULse,** and rebuff. ☞ *The seniors once again repelled the attacking juniors in the annual snowball battle.* It also refers to disgust, nauseate, revolt, and offend. ☞ *I think I'll pass; those horror movies really repel me.* Something **rePELlant** is disgusting, offensive, **rePULsive,** obnoxious, and loathsome. ☞ *Several members of the board found the victim's story to be utterly repellant.*

Repulsion

RePULsion is disgust, revulsion, antipathy, or abhorrence. ☞ *You want to see repulsion? Bring in a snake.*

Peal, a shortened form of appeal, is the ringing of bells and the crash of thunder; as a verb it means to resound, reverberate, toll, and blast. ☞ *It was an odd moment, what with the bells and the thunder pealing at the same time.* To **PELt** is to strike, batter, pummel, and clobber. ☞ *The hail pelting the roof of our bunkhouse frightened the younger kids.* To **PULsate** is to throb, palpitate, tremble, beat, and vibrate. ☞ *I think all of us were pulsating with anticipation when we heard the train.* One's **PULse** beats, throbs, or thumps. ☞ *My pulse was pounding in my ears. The pulse of the drums grew louder and louder as we approached the village.* It is a mood, feeling, or disposition. ☞ *The pollsters hoped to capture the pulse of the public on the tax issue.*

To **push** is to drive, force, propel, thrust, and shove. ☞ *We could only watch as our hero pushed her way through the dense crowd.* It is to promote, advocate, and tout. ☞ *Good ol' Xavier; he never quits pushing that invention of his.* It is to urge, encourage, and stimulate. ☞ *We don't have to push Junior to do his homework anymore.* As a noun it means jolt, propulsion, impulse, or thrust. ☞ *Marian needs a gentle push once in a while.* It also means energy, drive, ambition, or vitality. ☞ *Talk about push! He's got a world of it!* A **pushover** is a sure thing, piece of cake, or cinch. ☞ *Hey, that test was a pushover!* It is also a chump, sucker, or dupe. ☞ *Of course Lee lost the bet; she's a pushover for any kind of wager.* A **pushy** person is aggressive, brazen, impertinent, **pushing,** and arrogant. ☞ *He's one of those pushy salesmen who you can never get away from.*

But not: *pelt* [*pellis,* a skin], an animal's skin.

Combining forms: *ap-,* to; *com-,* together; *dis-,* away; *ex-,* out; *im-,* on; *pro-,* forward; *re-,* back.
Antonyms: *appeal*—refusal, denial, repulse, alienate, bore; *appealing*—repugnant, unpleasant, distasteful; *compel*—deter, thwart, hinder, prevent; *compelling*—unconvincing, inconclusive, feeble; *compulsion*—free will, choice, option, election; *compulsive*—resistible, uncompelling, controllable; *compulsory*—optional, voluntary, free, discretionary, unnecessary, non-binding; *dispel*—gather, collect, accumulate; *expel*—ingest, inhale, admit, accept, engage, hire; *expulsion*—acceptance, inclusion, injection; *impel*—check, repulse, inhibit, rebuff, withhold, curb; *impulsive*—cautious, deliberate, premeditated, calculating, rehearsed, contrived; *pushy*—deferential, modest, humble; *repeal*—confirm, reestablish, validate; *repel*—attract, delight, please, encourage, fascinate, enchant; *repellant*—agreeable, congenial, charming, likable; *repulse*—yield, submit, accept, welcome; *repulsive*—tasteful, pleasant, attractive, warm, friendly, affable, sociable.

PENDERE, to weigh, hang, pay: PEN, PEND, PENS, POND

For many centuries the value of currency or money was determined by the weight and value of such precious metals as gold and silver. The names of three popular monetary units come from *pendere:* **POUND,** a currency in more than a dozen nations, **PESO,** a coin common to many countries of Latin America and the Philippines, and the Spanish **PESETA.** Today, of course, money is no longer weighed.

But we do weigh facts before we arrive at a decision; that is, when we **PONDER,** we weigh, deliberate, contemplate, and speculate. When we are **PENSIVE,** we are thoughtful, reflective, and engrossed, all this while we carefully weigh matters. To **PERPEND** is to weigh ideas as well as ponder, consider, and deliberate. The names of the brightly-colored flowering plant we call a **PANSY** came about when someone fancied that the blossom resembled the face of a thoughtful person.

When we have a **PREPONDERANCE** of citizens voting for a change of government, we have a majority, plurality, or predominance; the literal meaning of the word is "to outweigh." A **PREPONDERANT** idea or concept or feeling is one that is superior in weight, force, numbers, and influence, etc.; synonyms are paramount, ruling, and prevailing. ☞ *Friends and relatives of the accused were preponderant at the hearing.* To **prePONDerate** is to prevail, outweigh, and dominate. ☞ *The attorney for the accused felt sure that the evidence he had presented would preponderate at the trial.*

A **PONDerous** person or object is weighty, heavy, awkward, clumsy, and corpulent. ☞ *How the movers managed to maneuver that ponderous piece of furniture up the stairs was incredible.* A ponderous speech is dull, tedious, boring, pedestrian, and soporific. ☞ *Had we known Dr. Lack's talk would be so ponderous, we would have sat nearer the exit.*

When people **apPEND** a note to a letter, a glossary to a book, or a signature to a will, they add, attach, fasten, and tack on. An **apPENDage** is the note, the glossary, the signature; it is also a carport added on to a house as well as an extremity attached to a body. ☞ *At first we couldn't recognize the insect because it had lost one of its appendages.* An **apPENDix** is an appendage containing additional material and is found at the end of a book, text, document, or article; if you have two or more, they may answer to either **apPENDixes** or **apPENDices.**

ApPENDant pertains to something attached, and from it, via a winding evolutionary trail, we got our word **PENthouse.** Originally it was, as Dr. Samuel Johnson described it in his 1755 dictionary, "a shed hanging out aslope from the main wall" of a larger structure. When it later found a place on the top of a building, it was a simple shed with a simple mission: to cover either a stairway opening onto the roof or mechanical equipment in residence there. Today, the word has more chic and glamorous connotations.

The **vermiform appendix,** a small abdominal tube with no known function in humans, can become diseased; this condition is known as **apPENDicitis,** and an **apPENDectomy** is most likely in order.

To **comPENSate** is literally "to weigh together," hence, to offset, counterbalance, make amends, and even up. ☞ *Gertie's inspired acting compensated for the weak role she was given.* It also means repay, reimburse, and reward. ☞ *I hope this check will compensate you for your trouble.* **ComPENSation** is repayment, redress, or remuneration. ☞ *The court granted the couple $15,000 in compensation.* It is also pay, wages, earnings, or profit. ☞ *No one dreamed that our compensation would be less than minimum wage.* A **comPENSatory** payment is one that is made to atone or compensate for injury, loss, harm, or damages. ☞ *Cranworth's gift to the church was rumored to be a compensatory payment for his past sins.*

To **DEPEND** is literally "to hang down from"; this can be sensed in such synonyms as hinge on, rest on, and revolve around. ☞ *Whether we take the trip depends on how much money we can save up.* It also means to rely on, count on, trust in, and believe in. ☞ *Eva is a person we know we can depend on.* Something **DEPENDABLE** is reliable, trusted, true, and steady. ☞ *She may be old and rusty, but she's a dependable old jalopy.* Whereas, an **UNDEPENDABLE** automobile (or person) is unreliable, erratic, and unstable. ☞ *I wouldn't count on Doug's getting here on time; he's quite undependable.*

Both **DEPENDENCE** and **DEPENDENCY** mean need, reliance, trust, or confidence. ☞ *We had hoped to end our dependence upon the public transportation system.* The latter, however, is also used to designate a territory governed by another country. ☞ *This island is a dependency of France.* **INDEPENDENCE** is freedom, liberty, autonomy, or self-reliance. ☞ *"Independence?" wrote George Bernard Shaw in* Pygmalion, *"That's middle-class blasphemy. We are all dependent on one another."* **DEPENDENT** means relying on one another for aid, support, maintenance, comfort, help, etc.

An **INDEPENDENT** person is individualistic, self-reliant, self-assured, and competent, or, in a different vein, well-heeled and solvent. ☞ *Pat's quite independent for a six-year-old. Thanks to her inheritance, Fern is quite independent.* Independent countries are self-governing and autonomous, and independent businesses are separate and unattached.

DISPENSE means to distribute, parcel out, dole, or allocate. ☞ *The Peace Corps workers dispensed medical supplies to the stricken villagers.* Dispense with means to do without, eschew, give up, relinquish, and get rid of. ☞ *Let's dispense with the formalities and get to work on this project.*

DISPENSABLE items are superfluous, unnecessary, and extraneous. ☞ *When we moved to the country, we learned how dispensable so many of our possessions were; but at the same time, we discovered that other properties were indispensable to rural life.* **INDISPENSABLE** means requisite, basic, imperative, and fundamental.

A **DISPENSARY** (also **DISPENSATORY**) is a place where medicines are dispensed. Vending machines are **DISPENSERS** of small amounts of merchandise. The **DISPENSATION** of goods or materials is their distribution, allotment, or allocation. ☞ *The dispensation of food and dry clothing will begin immediately.* In certain religions it is the making of an exception, exemption, relaxation, or permission. ☞ *Catholic couples wishing to divorce must obtain a special dispensation from the Pope.*

To **EXPEND** funds is to pay out, disburse, and dispense. ☞ *The Women's Club expended $25,000 on the remodeling of their headquarters.* If it is time and energy that is expended, it is consumed, used up, exhausted, and depleted. **EXPENDABLE** substances are dispensable, disposable, and insignificant. ☞ *In wars even the lives of soldiers are expendable.* The **EXPENSE** of something is its cost, price, payment, fee, or charge. ☞ *This you can charge off to your expense account. I had no idea our trip would entail such expenses.* "At the expense of" means sacrifice, toll, detriment, and destruction. ☞ *Farnley continues to smoke at the expense of his health.* **EXPENDITURES** are expenses, costs, or outlay. ☞ *Keep written records of your expenditures.* We also speak of expenditures, i.e., spending, output, or use of energy, strength, effort, and time. **EXPENSIVE** articles and objects are precious, costly, and exorbitant. ☞ *Don't you think that's a bit expensive for us?* **INEXPENSIVE** means more economical, reasonable, and affordable.

An earlier, literal meaning of **IMPEND** was "to hang over," and today's meaning still carries the essence of it. ☞ *The lieutenant felt that danger impended.* The adjective **IMPENDING** has two meanings. The first is threatening, menacing, looming, and brewing. ☞ *The impending campaign was making Fay more and more nervous.* The second meaning refers to imminent, coming, approaching, and nearing. ☞ *Their impending marriage gladdened many hearts.*

A **PENDANT** (also **PENDENT**) is an ornament, such as a piece of jewelry or watch that hangs from a necklace or a chandelier that hangs from a ceiling. As an adjective it means hanging, dangling, and swinging, as do **PENDULANT** and **PENDULOUS. PENSILE** has a similar meaning, but it is most often used in referring to hanging bird's nests, such as those of the northern oriole. **PENDING** is a preposition in the sense of during, until, awaiting, and while. ☞ *Pending the committee's decision, let's drop the subject.* As an adjective it means unsettled, unresolved, and unfinished. ☞ *The pending negotiations should solve the matter at last.* The phrase "patent pending" stamped on an article means that a patent has been applied for but has not yet been granted; it is, instead, up in the air, on hold, or in abeyance.

Both **PENCHANT** and **PROPENSITY** mean tendency, inclination, proclivity, or fondness. ☞ *Zach bragged of his penchant / propensity for licorice, biking, and the Beatles.*

PENDULAR pertains to the action or movement of a **PENDULUM,** a swinging weight found on certain clocks and in science museums. "The swing of the pendulum" is a phrase sometimes used to describe changes in the fortunes of political parties. Hanging weights, known as a plumb line, are also used to determine right angles to the horizontal—**perPENDicularity**—as well as measuring the depth of water.

A **PENnant** is a flag that flies on ships and above the home playing field of the championship baseball teams in Canada and the United States; the word is a blend of *pendant* and *pennon* (see *penna,* feather).

A **PENSion** is the fixed amount paid at regular intervals to one who has retired from work to become a **PENSioner.** What Americans know as boardinghouses are called **PENSions** in France, Germany, and Spain and **PENSiones** in Italy; most often they are small hotels.

Poise is balance, equilibrium, **counterpoise, equipoise,** or **equiPONDerance;** it is to carry on or hold in balance. ☞ *The woman walked along gracefully with her water jug poised on her head.* One who is **poised** in manner has composure, self-assurance, and presence of mind, and is cool, unflappable, and self-confident. ☞ *Had Cat not been so poised, she would never have been chosen.*

A SWAT team that is poised to storm a house where a hostage is held is ready, prepared, and on the brink. It also means to hover, teeter, and be hanging. ☞ *The company is rumored to be poised on the edge of bankruptcy. Through binoculars we saw the man poised on the edge of the cliff.*

About twenty-five hundred years ago Confucius offered this advice: "**RecomPENSe** injury with justice, and recompense kindness with kindness"; i.e., repay, reward, and reimburse. As a noun it is wages, compensation, retribution, payment, or stipend. ☞ *Twenty dollars didn't seem fair recompense for a whole day's work in* that *garden.*

To **sPEND** money is to pay out, expend, and shell out; to spend one's energy, strength, or time is to use, deplete, squander, and waste.

A **sPENDthrift** is a wastrel, squanderer, and showoff. ☞ *When his parents discovered that Kelly was a spendthrift, they put her inheritance into a trust fund.* As an adjective it means wasteful, extravagant, improvident, and lavish. ☞ *The mayor's spendthrift budget is not going to solve our problems.* One who is **sPENt** is exhausted, tired, and fatigued. ☞ *After sitting in the waiting room all night, I felt completely spent.*

To **susPEND** is to hang, dangle, and fasten. ☞ *Let's suspend the hammock from these two trees.* It is to withhold, shelve, postpone, and defer. ☞ *We agreed to suspend judgment until we heard Ned's side of the argument.* It is also to bar, exclude, ban, and dismiss. ☞ *Because your dues are six months in arrears, your membership in the club has been suspended.* **SusPENSion** is disbarment, rejection, expulsion, or ejection.

☞ *Your suspension is effective immediately.* It is also moratorium, interruption, or discontinuation. ☞ *The suspension of hostilities was in answer to our prayers.* SusPENSe is insecurity, uncertainty, anticipation, or tension. ☞ *Barney always reads the last chapter first; he can't abide suspense.*

Suspicion is doubt, distrust, skepticism, or bad vibes. ☞ *If you'd seen this guy, you'd have been filled with suspicions too!* It is also a notion, inkling, trace, or hint. ☞ *If you have even a suspicion of doubt about his guilt, you must not find him guilty.* Suspicious behavior is doubtful, dubious, questionable, and ambiguous. ☞ *Ruggles' story seemed suspicious to us from the beginning.* It is also distrustful, mistrustful, and leery. ☞ *Officer Keene was suspicious of her alibi because of her police record.*

But not: *penance* [*poenitere,* repent], remorse; *pennon* [*penna,* feather], flag borne by medieval knights; *pent* [AS *penn,* pen], held in; *Pentecost* [Gk *pente,* five + *konta,* "ten times"], religious festival.

Combining forms: *ap-,* to; *com-,* together; *counter-,* parallel; *de-,* down; *dis-,* out; *equi-,* equal; *ex-,* out; *im-,* on; *in-,* not; *per-,* thoroughly; *pro-,* forward; *re-,* again; *sus-,* under; *un-,* not.

Antonyms: *append*—remove, omit, leave out; *appendage*—body, main part; *appendix*—front matter, introductory material, body of the text; *compensate*—emphasize, worsen, exaggerate; *dependable*—untrustworthy, questionable, unreliable; *dependence*—self-reliance, autonomy, control, self-sufficiency; *dependent*—mature, autonomous, self-reliant; *dispensable*—necessary, needed, essential, integral; *dispensation*—prohibition; *expend*—conserve, save, collect, receive, earn; *expendable*—indispensable, crucial, essential, necessary; *expense*—income, return, receipts, proceeds; *expensive*—moderate, affordable, cheap, economical, reasonable; *inexpensive*—costly, high-priced, exorbitant, dear; *pensive*—thoughtless, frivolous, carefree, heedless; *poise*—imbalance, instability, excitability, clumsiness; *spendthrift*—tightwad, cheapskate, penny pincher; *spent*—energetic, strong, peppy, dynamic; *suspend*—invest, confirm, reinstate, instate; *suspense*—resolution, certainty, certitude; *suspicion*—confidence, trust, belief, credulity; *suspicious*—open, reliable, respectable, gullible.

PENNA, feather: PEN

For about thirteen centuries Europeans who were sufficiently educated to be able to write used a quill, a large feather made from the wing or tail of a bird such as a goose. Thus the name **PEN,** from *penna.* The small **PEN**KNIVES that people carry were used to sharpen the quills. By the mid-nineteenth century pens made of metal had become popular; whether **PEN**MANSHIP generally improved is not known, but presumably the birds of planet Earth began to feel more at ease. The terms PEN NAME and nom de plume (the feather and the quill being the same) arc still used by writers who use pens only to sign their names.

Flags are intended to be noticed and attract attention, and if they move and flutter much like the wings of a bird, so much the better. That is why the names of some flags derive from *penna.* A **PEN**NON, usually tapered or triangular, was once proudly borne on the lance of a knight. A ship's flag, used for identification and signaling, is a **PEN**NANT, as is the long, tapering flag that is symbolic of a league championship in baseball. ☞ *What a day this is, folks! For the first time in the history of this ball club the league pennant proudly flies in the wind!*

Winning that pennant is like reaching the PINNACLE of a lofty peak. To bind or cut off the wings of a bird is to PINION them; it also means to shackle or restrain someone. ☞ *The guards quickly pinioned the prisoner's arms.*

When knights wore helmets, they liked to attach a colorful plume of feathers on them; it was called a PANACHE. And someone daring enough to wear feathers while fighting a battle was demonstrating that he was a person of great style and flair. The hero of Edmond Rostand's famous play *Cyrano de Bergerac,* is a man with an extremely large nose. As he is dying, lying on his back, his nose pointing heavenward, he declares that there is one thing that he can call his own, "Et c'est . . . mon panache" ("And that is . . . my panache"). Which was that nose of his. Today the word signifies style, verve, dash, spirit, or brio.

But not: *pen* [AS *penn*], an enclosure; *penchant* [*pendere,* to hang], a strong liking for something; *pentad* [Gk *pent-,* five], a period of five years.
Antonyms: *panache*—apathy, lethargy, indolence, languor; *pinnacle*—minimum, nadir, depths, zilch.

PES, foot: PED

To IMPEDE something is to slow it down; to EXPEDITE something is to speed it up. IMPEDIMENTA is cumbersome baggage or paraphernalia that slows us down at, for example, the airport; it is an IMPEDIMENT, hindrance, obstacle, or barrier to our progress. An EXPEDITIOUS move is prompt and speedy. ☞ *The crisis called for expeditious action.* EXPEDIENT means suitable, advantageous, and advisable. ☞ *Sonia thought it expedient to take notes at the meeting.* It also means selfish, self-serving, and conniving. ☞ *The city council's move to raise their own salaries was an expedient one.* As a noun an expedient is an advantage, resource, and benefit. ☞ *Advertising in the paper has been an expedient to our business.*

EXPEDITIONS are journeys, trips, or excursions, and in earlier times the many who were not sufficiently privileged to ride on four-legged animals marched on their own feet, and that certainly included the foot soldiers, the PEONS and PAWNS. And, no doubt, their cousins, the PIONEERS.

PEDALS and PEDOMETERS were nonexistent way back then, and perhaps PEDICURES were rare except for ladies of Cleopatra's standing. But at the foot of the mountains there were always the PIEDMONTS, PEDESTALS, the flat feet that supported statues at the amphitheaters, CENTIPEDES and MILLIPEDES that scurried about, and TRIVETS that had all three feet firmly planted on the tables.

There has always been respect for bloodlines, that is, our (and our neighbors') ancestry, lineage, or extraction. That our ancestors were sometimes hard put to come up with new words is illustrated by PEDIGREE. The word comes from the Middle French *pie de grue,* literally, "the foot of a crane," the lines the crane's toes made in the sand apparently seeming similar to those on a chart showing the descent of us BIPEDS. People who own livestock and dogs are often interested in the pedigree of their QUADRUPEDS, too.

CAP-A-PIE means "head-to-foot." A PIED-A-TERRE is a secondary or temporary residence; its literal meaning is "one foot on the ground." Prospective renters look for one that has been recently REVAMPED: new paint, wallpaper, carpeting, etc. A VAMP is the part of a shoe that covers the instep and the toes, and shoes often are in need of repair; today as a verb it means to patch up or together, mend, and repair.

IMPEACH traveled down this road, too; the word that means to accuse a public official of misconduct or even to remove him or her from office once meant "to fetter or put shackles on one's feet." PEDESTRIAN came the same way; while it has always named one who walks, it has also become an adjective meaning plodding, dull, commonplace, and insipid. ☞ *Dr.*

Thikrik's commencement speech was so pedestrian it reminded us of being caught at a red light that never changed.

An additional English word related to the root: sesquipedalian.
But not: *pedant* [Gk *paidos,* child], one who shows off learning; *peddler* [ME *ped,* basket], seller of small items.
Combining forms: *bi-,* two; *cap,* head; *centi-,* hundred; *-cure,* to care for; *ex-,* out; *-gree,* crane; *im-,* in; *-meter,* measure; *milli-,* thousand; *-mont,* mountain; *quadru-,* four; *re-,* again; *-stal,* standing piece; *-terre,* earth; *tri-,* three.
Antonyms: *expedient*—detrimental, impractical, altruistic, ethical; *expedite*—retard, hinder, block, obstruct; *expeditious*—dilatory, sluggish, inefficient, leisurely; *impede*—facilitate, abet, promote, aid; *impediment*—aid, assistance, encouragement; *pedestrian*—imaginative, exciting, significant, remarkable.

PIUS, devoted: PI

Many Renaissance artists sculpted statues of the **PIETA** showing the dead Christ lying in the lap of his mother, but the most famous is the marble masterpiece by Michelangelo (c. 1500) in St. Peter's Basilica. It is viewed each year by hundreds of thousands of devout and **PIOUS** pilgrims as well as secular, nonreligious, and **IMPIOUS** tourists. Some are there in hopes of **EXPIATING** their sins of **IMPIETY** and becoming renewed with godliness, reverence, and **PIETY.**

When a family is down-and-out, its condition is **PITEOUS, PITIFUL,** and **PITIABLE;** it is also heart-rending, distressing, and touching. Pitiful also means mean, contemptible, and despicable. ☞ *What a pitiful trick that was to play on your best friend!*

A **PITILESS** person is merciless, ruthless, and implacable, one without a **PITTANCE,** shred, or iota of common decency. **PITY** can be used as a verb. ☞ *Oh, how we pitied them as they watched all their possessions go up in smoke.* Pity is also a noun referring to sympathy or regret. ☞ *I don't want your pity.*

But not: *piebald* [*pie,* a magpie, a bird with black and white plumage], having patches of black and white or other colors (said of a horse); *pitted* [*puteus,* a well, pit], marked or scarred with pits.

Combining forms: *ex-*, out; *im-*, not.
Antonyms: *impious*—respectful, reverent; *piety*—infidelity, blasphemy, faithlessness; *piteous*—delightful, happy, joyful, pleasant; *pitiful*—fortunate, prosperous, laudable, admirable; *pittance*—abundance, excess; *pity*—apathy, disdain.

PLEBES, DEMOS, the people: PLEB, DEM, DEMO

The *plebs* of ancient Rome and the *demos* of ancient Greece were the common people, the populace, but some of the words that stem from these two roots have, over the centuries, followed divergent paths. For instance, whereas a **DEMagogue** in Athens was a popular leader of the people, today the word has a pejorative, negative, or derogatory connotation, and **DEMagoguery** is the attempt to arouse and play on the emotions, fears, and prejudices of the populace.

PLEBes are members of the freshman classes at Annapolis and West Point, and a **PLEBiscite** is a direct vote by the people of a country on a public question. But a person with **PLEBeian** ideas and tastes is said to be base, common, ordinary, uncultured, and unrefined.

However, not all the words from these roots are so highly charged. **EnDEMic** means indigenous, native, being natural to a people or place. ☞ *These plants are endemic to this region.* An **epiDEMic** refers to something that is prevalent, widespread, rampant, or pervasive. ☞ *The flu is reported to have reached epidemic proportions. An epidemic of break-ins has alarmed the citizens of our town.* A **panDEMic** outbreak is one that covers a much larger area, hence general, global, and universal. ☞ *Such an attack could create a pandemic fear of an atomic war.*

DEMOphobia is a mental disorder in which one has an abnormal fear of or aversion to crowds; it is similar to agoraphobia. **DEMOgraphy** is the science of the statistics of a population—births, deaths, marriages, gender, age, ethnic origin, occupations, diseases, and much more.

DEMOcrats believe in the political equality of everyone; their lifestyle and government of choice are **DEMOcratic**, they tend to agree with Winston Churchill's statement in a speech in 1947 that "No one pretends that **DEMOcracy** is perfect or all-wise. Indeed, it has been said that democracy is the worst form of Government except all those other forms that have been tried from time to time."

A political candidate who adjusts his or her language to fit the crowd that gathers outside the office doors or factory gates may be making an effort to be **DEMOtic**, that is popular, common, and of the people. ☞*Senator Hassel's failure to develop an acceptable demotic touch has hurt his campaign.* The word also pertains to the everyday, common, popular speech of the people. ☞*Ms. Ruth owes much of her popularity to her keen ear for the demotic rhythms and idioms of ordinary folk.*

But not: *demo* [*de-,* + *monstrare,* to show], a demonstrator, such as a car; *indemnify* [*in-,* not + *damnum,* harm], to protect against loss; *pandemonium* [the principal city in Hell in Milton's *Paradise Lost,* where all the demons were], bedlam, chaos, tumult.
Combining forms: *-agogue,* leader; *-cracy,* to rule; *en-,* in; *epi-,* among; *-graphy,* form of recording; *pan-,* all; *-phobia,* abnormal fear; *-scite,* to know.
Antonyms: *democratic*—autocratic, despotic, snobbish; *demotic*—exclusive, private, elitist; *endemic*—alien, foreign, naturalized; *epidemic*—contained, limited, isolated; *pandemic*—exclusive, local, sporadic; *plebeian*—elite, aristocratic, cultured, noble.

POLIS, city: POLI

POLItics is the science or art of **POLItical** government; it is the practice of conducting political affairs. Newspaper columnist Will Rogers had his own slant on the subject: "Politics has got so expensive that it takes lots of money to even get beat with. . . . The more you read about politics, the more you got to admit that each party is worse than the other. . . . If you ever injected truth into politics you would have no politics."

When Rogers wrote those words, he was not attacking the American **POLIty** or form of government. What he did was mock politics, **POLIticians** (or **POLIticos**), and those who engage in **POLIticking,** that is, promoting themselves or their **POLIcies** at every turn. He did it by making fun of them and holding them up to ridicule. But the world of politics wasn't his only target; he also aimed his pen at big business, communist **POLItburos,** and the military, as well as snobs, speechifiers, hero-worshippers, and all others who he felt took themselves too seriously.

He was neither **POLItic,** discreet, tactful, prudent, nor diplomatic, but only those who were his enemies could have called him **imPOLItic,** rude, ill-mannered, or tactless. His humor was his strong suit, and the American **body POLItic**—the people as a whole—loved it. Certainly no one ever accused Rogers of being **aPOLItical,** i.e., being neither involved nor interested in politics.

In ancient Greece a city-state was known as a **POLIs,** the most famous of which was Athens with its fortified **ACROPOLIs** and Parthenon. A large cemetery in those days was known as a **NECROPOLIs,** and a **METROPOLIs** was the mother city of a colony. Today the latter is any large, busy city with its surrounding **METROPOLITAN** area, which, in turn, may be but one of several that comprise a **MEGALOPOLIs.** Small wonder that it's almost impossible to **POLICE** the place adequately, from either the standpoint of patrolling, regulating, protecting, and safeguarding. ☞ *The captain doubted that he had sufficient personnel to police such a large event on short notice.* Police also refers to cleaning, straightening, and tidying. ☞ *The scouts were asked to police the area after the picnic.* Noun synonyms are authorities, patrol, force, troopers, or cops.

COSMOPOLITE and **COSMOPOLITAN** refer to a person who feels at home in many places, a citizen of the world, taking pride in being free of provincial prejudices and narrow thinking; synonyms are urbane, sophisticated, and broadminded. ☞ *As a cosmopolite, she felt that she would feel at home in San Francisco, a very cosmopolitan city.* Cosmopolite is also the name of a butterfly otherwise known as "painted lady."

> **But not:** *polish* [*polire,* to polish], to make smooth; *polite* [*polire*], courteous.
> **Combining forms:** *acro-,* height; *-buro,* bureau; *cosmo-,* world; *im-,* not; *mega-,* large; *metro-,* mother; *necro-,* dead.
> **Antonyms:** *cosmopolitan*—narrow, local, provincial, parochial; *impolitic*—prudent, diplomatic, shrewd, artful; *metropolitan*—rural, rustic, bucolic; *police*—neglect, disarray, mess, dilapidate; *politic*—rude, blundering, rash, careless.

PORCUS, hog, pig: POR

Had an errant arrow not hit England's King Harold II in the eye at the Battle of Hastings in 1066, felling him and shattering the morale of his troops and enabling the French-speaking William the Conqueror to lead his Norman army on to London where he was crowned king of England, our language would be far different today.

Not only would we be shopping for meaty pigchops and plump pig roasts, our politicians would be busying themselves trying to pass pigbarrel rather than **PORKBARREL** legislation. **PORKCHOPPERS,** those officials, lobbyists, legislators, and others who are primarily interested in personal gain from their positions of power, would be known as pigchoppers.

Hat manufacturers would be pushing for the return of the pigpie snapbrim, pigupines would roam the woods with their needle-sharp quills, boaters would delight at the sight of pigpoises breaking the surface of the sea, and the fashionable set would dine off pigelain plates. Such words as **PORkpie, PORcupine, PORpoise,** and **PORcelain** would never have been born.

The words of the Anglo-Saxons of early England were those of the field; in addition to *pigge* (pig), there were *cealf* (calf), *deor* (deer), *cu* (cow), *bole* (bull), *oxa* (ox), and *sceap* (sheep). It was the more civilized and sophisticated newcomers from across the Channel who brought words for the table. As pig turned into **PORk,** so calf became veal; deer became venison; cow, bull, and ox became beef; and sheep became mutton.

Resemblances have often played roles in the coinage of words. The connection between our **PORcine** friends and the name of the material used in the making of porcelain dinnerware and Dresden figurines is said to have come about because of the resemblance of the shape of a highly polished seashell called PORCELLANA in Italian to the curved back of a **PORca,** pig. The porcupine was a *porc d'espine* in Middle French, so called because it looked like a thorny pig, and the porpoise was a *porcopiscis* from its resemblance to what someone fancied a sea hog would look like.

But not: *porch* [*porticus,* portico], veranda.

PORTARE, to carry: PORT

A s**PORT** is a game, contest, physical activity, diversion, or recreation. It is also play, jesting, antics, and fun.

The word, the activity, and the idea have been with us for a long time. It was originally DIS**PORT,** a word that came with the Norman's from France and means to play, amuse, and divert oneself. ☞ *The children disported themselves in the shallow pool.*

Sport

To sport is to treat lightly and mockingly, to fool, tease, and pull one's leg. ☞ *"For what do we live, but to make sport for our neighbors, and laugh at them in our turn?," Jane Austen says in* Pride and Prejudice. It is to display, show off, exhibit, flaunt, and wear. ☞ *You mean he* still *sports those gaudy neckties and Italian shoes.*

Then there's **sPORTING**, meaning fair, **sPORTSMANLIKE**, even, or honorable. ☞ *Danny gave me a sporting chance in the game by playing with a ratty, old, half-strung tennis racket.* A **sPORTIVE** kitten is playful, jaunty, and frisky. A **sPORTY** person's dress is informal, casual, fashionable, and chic, if, sometimes, a bit on the showy side. **SPORTSMANSHIP** means fair play, honesty, evenhandedness, or integrity, as well as being a cheerful loser and modest winner. But a **SPOILSPORT** is a wet blanket, killjoy, complainer, sourpuss, or party pooper.

A second interesting feature of *portare* is that we can easily track how one word leads to another. For example, men who carry heavy baggage and other burdens have long been called **PORTERS**; their favorite drink at English pubs, a dark-brown bitter brew, thus became known as **PORTER'S ALE.** The choice cut of beef from between the prime ribs and the sirloin now known as a **PORTERHOUSE** steak supposedly got its name from houses or inns where porter and other alcoholic beverages were sold.

A third feature stems from **PORTMANTEAU**, a compound name of a bag or suitcase that owes its origin to the combining of two words, *port,* carry, and *mantle,* a coat or cloak. This process of blending two words together led Lewis Carroll, the author of *Through the Looking-Glass* and, of course, other wonderland adventures of Alice, to give the process its name. It was he who concocted the word chortle, a blend of the words chuckle and snort; slithy, a combining of the words lithe and slimy; and snark from the words snake and shark.

A **PORTFOLIO** is a flat, **PORTABLE** case that is roomy enough to hold large pieces of paper known as *folios;* a minister without a portfolio is a government official who is not appointed to any specific department.

COMPORTMENT and **DEPORTMENT** are similar in meaning; both denote conduct, demeanor, or behavior, although the latter is more commonly used on school report cards. In one sense **COMPORT** and **DEPORT** are twins; they both mean to conduct or behave oneself. ☞ *The hostage comported himself with dignity.* But they part their ways at times. Comport also means agree, correspond, conform, and concur. ☞ *Lynn's story does not comport with the facts.* Deport also means expel, banish, exile, and cast out. ☞ *Two members of her family were deported for illegal entry.* The latter process is called **DEPORTATION.**

IMPORT and **EXPORT** refer to international trade. ☞ *We import silk from Japan and export wheat to Russia. Our exportation of exportable goods varies from year to year.* As a verb import also means to convey, signify, and denote. ☞ *He was a barbarian in every sense that the word imports.* As a noun it means sense, connotation, suggestion, or implication. ☞ *It was not until morning that the import of the message hit me.* It means

imPORTance, weight, substance, or significance. ☞ *As soon as they walked into the room we knew they were people of considerable import.* As is apparent, the words import and importance are often interchangeable.

Synonyms of **imPORTant** are weighty, substantial, meaningful, and serious. ☞ *The President's speech is being billed as extremely important.* It also means preeminent, influential, prominent, and distinguished. ☞ *We regard her as one of our most important poets.* **UnimPORTant** matters are insignificant, immaterial, inconsequential, and petty.

Something **imPORTunate** is urgent, pressing, insistent, and persistent, sometimes annoyingly so, hence officious and troublesome. ☞ *The community's importunate requests finally got the attention of our representative in Washington. I found the children's importunate demands quite impossible.* To **imPORTune** is to press, harass, request, and demand, always with urgency. ☞ *The panhandlers' importuning compelled me to return to the hotel.*

The one **PORT** that derives from *portare* is a verb in military use meaning to carry a rifle with both hands in a slanting position across the body. To **PORTage** is to carry a canoe or other kind of boat over land from one body of water to another. **PORTly** was once a complimentary adjective meaning dignified, imposing, majestic, and stately; today it means fat, stout, corpulent, plump, and obese; its noun form, **PORTliness**, means tubbiness, rotundity, and fleshiness.

To **purPORT** is to imply, convey, claim, and allege. ☞ *Leslie purports to be the candidate of the working class.* As a noun it means significance, intention, or purpose. ☞ *Just what was the purport of your visit to Washington?* **PurPORTed** means rumored, supposed, and assumed. ☞ *We've long been suspicious of their purported connections.* **PurPORTedly** means supposedly, presumably, **rePORTedly**, and ostensibly. ☞ *Both doctors had, purportedly, studied under Dr. Freud in Vienna.*

To have a **rapPORT** with someone is to have empathy, harmony, affinity, or compatibility. ☞ *Abby established a close rapport with her students almost immediately.*

On June 2, 1897, the *New York Journal* quoted Mark Twain: "The **rePORT** of my death was an exaggeration," newspaper reports had said he was ill or dead, confusing him with Dr. Jim Clemens, his cousin, who *was* ill in London. Synonyms of report are account, story, statement, or article.

Nelson Rockefeller, in a speech to the Anti-Defamation League (1972) about the need for a free press, said, "I'm convinced that if **rePORTers** should ever lose the right to protect the confidentiality of their sources, then serious investigative REPORTING will simply dry up." Reporter synonyms are journalist, correspondent, columnist, broadcaster, or anchor; those of reporting are relating, narrating, describing, revealing, informing, announcing, publishing, and broadcasting. REPORTAGE is a written account of something witnessed; it is the technique of reporting the news.

The word SUPPORT refers to subsistence, maintenance, help, assistance, or consolation. Another kind of support is a prop, buttress, brace, or pedestal. A third kind is backing, patronage, advocacy, or promotion. ☞ *We thank you for your generous support.*

As a verb support means to prop up, hold up, sustain, and shore up. ☞ *I hope a two-by-four is strong enough to support this end.* It also means maintain, fund, sponsor, assist, and bankroll. ☞ *That project is one we should support.*

A SUPPORTABLE position on an issue is tolerable, acceptable, bearable, and sufferable. ☞ *I'm not wild about Pat's idea, but I do think it's a supportable one.* An INSUPPORTABLE situation is unendurable, insufferable, unbearable, and excruciating. ☞ *On the other hand, McSmitt's proposal is absolutely insupportable.* A SUPPORTER is a backer, defender, benefactor, or ally. ☞ *The candidate thanked her many supporters.* A person who is SUPPORTIVE is helpful, encouraging, and reassuring. ☞ *We owe so much to you who have been so supportive during these difficult days.*

The industrial world TRANSPORTS goods and materials, i.e., carries, moves, hauls, and carts. One's emotions are transported, too, i.e., lifted, captivated, enraptured, and charmed. ☞ *Visiting the recovering children in the hospital transported all of us.* A TRANSPORT or TRANSPORTER is a carrier of cargo, a vehicle or conveyance such as a ship, truck, train, plane, or bus. Transport is also strong emotion, rapture, elation, or bliss. TRANSPORTATION is delivery, conveyance, shipments, dispatch, or transit. ☞ *Transportation is the biggest item in our budget.*

But not: *port* [*portus,*], harbor; *port* [*Oporto,* a town in Portugal from which it is shipped], a wine; *porthole* [*porta,* gate], an opening on the side of a ship; *portrait* [*pro-,* forth + *trahere,* a likeness.

Combining forms: *com-,* together; *de-,* away; *dis-,* away; *ex-,* out; *-folio,* sheet of paper; *im-,* in; *in-,* not; *-manteau,* coat; *pur-,* forth; *rap-,* back; *re-,* back; *sup-,* near; *trans-,* across; *un-,* not.

Antonyms: *comport*—disagree, contrast, clash; *comportment, deportment*—misconduct, misbehavior, impertinence, rudeness; *deport*—welcome, admit, receive, accept; *importance*—pettiness, triviality, insignificance; *important*—slight, minor, negligible, inconsequential; *importunate*—irresolute, changeable, temporary; *insupportable*—bearable, tolerable; *portable*—stationary, anchored, fixed; *portliness*—thinness, slenderness; *portly*—lean, bony, slender; *rapport*—hostility, disagreement, alienation; *report*—keep secret, withhold, conceal; *support*—discourage, abandon, refute; *supportive*—detrimental, adverse, counterproductive.

PUNGERE, to point, stab: PUN, PUNC

It is interesting to note that among the more than two-dozen definitions of the verb POINT in *Merriam-Webster's New Third International Dictionary* is to **PUNC**TUATE, as in "He was pointing the text of his speech." Several centuries ago the insertion of points, dots, and straight and wiggly lines to indicate pauses in writing was referred to as pointing. As we often point at or point out an object to direct one's attention to it, so the word punctuate is commonly used to point out and give emphasis to. ☞ *The boy's tears punctuated his tragic story.* It also emphasizes interruptions. ☞ *The flashes of gunfire punctuated the darkness of the night.*

A POINTED remark is one that is directed at someone. ☞ *The principal's pointed remarks made Harry and Merry squirm.* A remark that is POINT-BLANK is plain and blunt. ☞ *Mrs. Ohm said point-blank that Tommy was never to enter her house again.* POINTERS are pieces of advice. ☞ *The editor gave us pointers on how to organize our themes.* POINTY-HEADED is a term disparaging someone whom the speaker thinks is stupid, idiotic, pretentious, and self-important.

A **PUNC**TILIOUS person is finicky, fussy, and meticulous, one who broods and frets about the fine points, the nuances, the **PUNC**TILIOS, or the niceties, whether they be of proper **PUNC**TUATION or elevator-exiting procedures.

Being **PUNC**TUAL is considered important, too. "**PUNC**TUALITY is the politeness of kings," said Louis XVIII of France. But then again, not to everyone: "Punctuality is the virtue of the bored," said the novelist Evelyn Waugh in "Irregular Notes 1960–1965."

PUNCHY is a word that means dazed, **PUNC**H-DRUNK, and befuddled. ☞ *I say, that chap over there. Acts punchy, don't you think?* It also refers to forceful, dynamic, and vigorously effective. ☞ *Punchy prose! Action-packed! Best-seller candidate! A great read!*

Tangy, spicy, peppery, savory, and piquant seasonings are **PUNGENT.** Odors can be pungent, too. ☞ *Auntie has long complained about the pungent reek of Uncle's cigars.* Pungent remarks may be caustic, acrimonious, cutting, and sarcastic. ☞ *The book editor laced into McHare's book with pungent criticism.*

POIGNANT remarks can also be stinging, sharp, and barbed. ☞ *The principal's poignant remarks about loyalty and honesty really got to me.* The more usual meaning of the word is moving, heartrending, touching, and sorrowful. ☞ *The book covers her most poignant years, her parents' death and those spent in the orphanage.*

COMPUNCTIONS are feelings of shame, guilt, regret, remorse, or anxiety. ☞ *The thief obviously had no compunctions about stealing the poor family's food.* If the culprit does feel guilt, then he or she can offer an apology and restoration to help **EXPUNGE,** eradicate, and obliterate the wrongdoing.

POUNCE, meaning to jump and leap also comes from *pungere,* as does **PUNCHEON,** the name of both a heavy timber and a stamping tool.

Then there's **PUN,** a play on words. Here's one of the most famous: About two hundred years ago when Thomas Hood, a British poet and humorist, fell ill, he sensed that an undertaker he was acquainted with was becoming uncomfortably interested in his health. Thinking that the man seemed anxious to earn a livelihood by seeing that Hood's ashes were stashed away in a vase or urn, he phrased it this way: "I fear he is too eager to urn a lively Hood." Small wonder that there was talk of nominating Hood for the "Pun Gent of the Year" award.

An additional English word related to the root: pivot.
But not: *punch* [perh. Hindi *panch,* from Sanskrit, *panca,* five (there were originally five ingredients: spirits, water, lemon juice, sugar, spice)], a sweetened drink; *pundit* [Skt *pandita,* learned, wise], learned person.
Combining forms: *-blank,* white center of a target; *com-,* greatly; *ex-,* out.
Antonyms: *pointed*—vague, aimless, inappropriate; *punchy*—alert, mild, tepid; *punctilious*—careless, casual, negligent; *punctual*—tardy, late, irregular; *punctuate*—minimize, understate; *pungent*—bland, tasteless, unstimulating, uninteresting, dull, vapid.

Q

QUAERERE, to seek: QUEST, QUIR, QUIS

A **QUEST**ion can be a problem, topic, argument, or theme. ☞ *Whether we want a new car is not the question; the question is, how are we going to manage without one?* It is doubt, difficulty, uncertainty, contention, or qualm. ☞ *I trust there isn't any question about my ability to handle the job.* To question is to interrogate, examine, query, in**QUIR**e, and sound out. ☞ *I'll question Leslie about her whereabouts.* It is to doubt, mistrust, dispute, and suspect. ☞ *A number of us question his credentials.* Something beyond question is without doubt; if it's in question, it's in doubt; if it's out of the question, it's impossible.

Supreme Court Chief Justice Earl Warren said in *Miranda v. Arizona,* "When an individual is taken into custody . . . he must be warned prior to any **QUEST**ioning that he has the right to remain silent. . . ." A questioning mind is one that is in**QUIR**ing, searching, curious, and probing. A **QUEST**ionable matter is dubious, debatable, moot, and suspect. ☞ *Hart's been involved in some pretty questionable business deals.* An un**QUEST**ionable statement is indisputable, certain, unimpeachable, irrefutable, and un**QUEST**ioned. ☞ *The couple's integrity and their principles are considered unquestionable.*

A **QUEST** is a search, pursuit, pilgrimage, investigation, enterprise, or adventure. ☞ *On the third day the captain admitted that our quest was hopeless.* As a verb quest is usually followed by the words after or for. ☞ *Only a few miners still quested for gold. Her life is spent questing after knowledge.*

Conquest

An in**QUEST** is a probe, investigation, in**QUIR**y (also en**QUIR**y), or hearing regarding or into the cause of a death. A con**QUEST** is a victory, dominion, or ascendancy. ☞ *Marion's research has led to the conquest of more than one disease.* A re**QUEST** is a desire, demand, petition, or entreaty. ☞ *Chuck put in a request to be transferred to the shipping department.* It is to ask for, seek, demand, and solicit. ☞ *Who requested the tea with four lumps of sugar?*

To ACQUIRE is to get, obtain, attain, procure, and reap. ☞ *Harley acquired a fortune before he was 20 and lost it all gambling in Monte Carlo.* The full name of the AIDS disease is ACQUIRED immune deficiency syndrome, meaning that those afflicted have lost the immunity that they had possessed or acquired.

An ACQUISITION is a purchase, ACQUIREMENT, gift, possession, or property. ☞ *The van Gogh is the museum's latest acquisition.* It is an attainment, obtainment, or achievement. ☞ *That man has devoted his life to the acquisition of money.* An ACQUISITIVE or ACQUISITORY person is grasping, greedy, avaricious, and materialistic. ☞ *Sorney always defended his materialism by saying he was a loyal, tax-paying member of an acquisitive society.*

One day in 1879 when W.A. Spooner, an English clergyman, announced the title of the hymn to be sung in New College Chapel at Oxford University, it came out, "Kinquering Congs their Titles Take." He meant, of course, "CONQUERING Kings"; today such mix-ups are called Spoonerisms. To CONQUER is to defeat, overcome, subdue, and quell. ☞ *Pete did what he had said he would: he conquered the normally fatal disease.* When William the Duke of Normandy defeated the English forces in 1066 he became known as William the CONQUEROR, i.e., victor, lord, or champion.

A DISQUISITION is a formal inquiry into or discussion of a subject; it is generally synonymous with dissertation, essay, thesis, treatise, paper, or monograph.

EXQUISITE means delicate, fine, elegant, well-crafted, and dainty. ☞ *They have a collection of the most exquisite porcelain figurines!* It also means superlative, superb, incomparable, flawless, and consummate. ☞ *This necklace is an example of exquisite workmanship.*

An INQUISITIVE person is prying, curious, meddling, and intrusive. ☞ *Must you be so inquisitive about my personal affairs?* It also has a more positive sense: interested, analytical, questioning, and probing. ☞ *If I had your naturally inquisitive nature, I'd major in science.* An INQUISITION is an investigation, usually one that is marked by prejudiced INQUISITORS together with a lack of regard for individual rights and the infliction of cruel punishments. The infamous Spanish inquisition ran from 1479 to 1834; during the term of Torquemada as Grand Inquisitor, some 2,000 alleged heretics were burned.

A PERQUISITE or PERK is a privilege, benefit, extra, bonus, or dividend. ☞ *One of the perquisites / perks of the job is my own shut-the-door office!*

A REQUISITE is a requirement, necessity, or obligation. ☞ *One of the requisites for this position is a degree in mechanical engineering.* As an adjective it means required, indispensable, and imperative. ☞ *Among her requisite talents is the ability to get along well with our other employees.* **PREREQUISITE** and requisite are generally interchangeable. A **REQUISITION** is a request or demand for services or supplies, usually on a written form. ☞ *Sorry, but I can't release those without the official requisition form—that's #A330-879—with the boss's okay on it.*

An additional English word related to the root: conquistador.

But not: *bequest* [ME *biqueste*], a gift, legacy; *esquire* [*scutum,* a shield], a title of respect; *quirk* [?], peculiarity; *quisling* [V. *Quisling,* Norwegian Nazi, WW II], a traitor; *sequester* [*sequi,* to follow], withdraw; *vanquish* [*uincere,* to conquer], to defeat.

Combining forms: *ac-,* to; *con-,* thoroughly; *dis-,* apart; *ex-,* out; *in-,* in; *per-,* thoroughly; *pre-,* before; *re-,* away; *un-,* not.

Antonyms: *acquire*—lose, discard, relinquish; *acquisitive*—abstemious, altruistic, generous; *conquer*—lose, fail, surrender, yield to, capitulate; *conqueror*—loser, defeated, victim, failure; *conquest*—surrender, loss, submission, failure; *exquisite*—gross, rough, coarse, vulgar, unrefined, ugly; *inquire*—reply, answer, respond; *inquisitive*—indifferent, apathetic, uninterested; *question*—reply, answer, trust, conviction, resolution; *questionable*—obvious, proven, seemly, legitimate, conventional; *requisite*—optional, elective, marginal, dispensable; *unquestionable*—uncertain, ambiguous, doubtful.

QUALIS, of what kind: QUAL

One of today's ongoing discussion topics is the **QUALITY** of life, i.e., the character, nature, or caliber of daily existence. Where is living most suitable to a certain individual, the inner city, a suburb, a small town, a megalopolis, an exurb, or a rural area?

There are those who say that in order to **QUALIFY**, be eligible, and prepared to debate the subject, one should have at least sampled several of the options. Others do not believe that such **QUALIFICATIONS**, requisites, conditions, provisos, or requirements are necessary, claiming that a person who has lived in only one place is perfectly **QUALIFIED**, suited, capable, and competent to voice an opinion.

However, qualified has another meaning: limited, restricted, conditional, and contingent. ☞ *Any opinion Archie expresses is bound to be a qualified one considering his limited experiences. Therefore, I feel that he is unfit, unqualified, and unprepared to join the debate.*

But the word **unQUALified** also has two entirely different meanings. One is *not* modified, restricted, limited, conditional, and circumscribed. ☞ *Latisha warrants our unqualified praise.* The second meaning is absolute and out-and-out. ☞ *You, sir, are an unqualified liar.*

In grammar a **QUALifier** is a modifier, such as an adjective or an adverb, or a word that expresses degree or intensity. One who survives the **QUALifying** heats, rounds, or tests in an academic or athletic competition becomes a qualifier. ☞ *Maria is one of the qualifiers for the finals; Andy, however, was disqualified.*

A **QUALitative** style, change, or list would be concerned with the quality of something, rather than how much something costs.

But not: *qualm* [?], pang of conscience, uneasiness.
Combining forms: *dis-,* not; *un-,* not.

QUANTUS, how many, how much: QUANT

It happened at a political debate shortly before a recent election. One of the incumbent's supporters claimed that his candidate's twenty-four years of elective and appointive federal service **QUANTified** him as one of the nation's most responsible leaders.

" '**QUANTify**,' yes," a woman in the audience said; " 'qualify,' no. There's an enormous distance between the two. It's the distance and the difference between **QUANTity** and quality, and that's the difference between numbers and merit." Quantity refers to volume, extent, mass, aggregate, amount, or magnitude.

QUANTitative pertains to the measurement of quantity. ☞ *The missionary said he hoped the shipment of foodstuffs would not have any quantitative limitations.*

A **QUANTifier** is a word or number that indicates the amount or size of something.

QUANTum (pl. **QUANTa**) refers to the amount of something. ☞ *Professor Sachs remarked on the tiny quantum of knowledge we have of the universe.* A quantum jump (or leap) is a term from physics that has made its way into other areas. ☞ *The CEO spoke of the quantum jump in the company's productivity.*

QUI, who; QUAM, how; QUOM, when

QUIBBLE means to argue over minor points, especially by using evasive, ambiguous arguments. ☞ *The oppositions' quibbling over a dozen irrelevant, minor points served only to delay the passage of the bill.*

QUORUM refers to the number of members of a group required to be present in order to transact business. ☞ *Irwin got to the meeting just in time to make it a quorum.*

QUASI means seeming, almost, and virtual. ☞ *Laverne is technically not a member of the organization; she's what we call a quasi member.* As a combining form, and usually hyphenated, it has the meaning of close-but-not-quite-there. Thus something that is quasi-scientific is not truly scientific, but it does *resemble* the real thing. Depending upon the intent of the user, it may take on the meaning of pseudo, bogus, and counterfeit. ☞ *Abraham Lincoln never did that; the book you got that story from is quasi-historical fiction.*

QUASAR, the name given to the starlike objects thought to be the most distant and luminous in the universe, is a blend of *quas(i)* and *(stell)ar,* hence, *nearly* a star.

QUONDAM refers to former, one-time, and erstwhile. ☞ *Both Cecilia and Albert are quondam general managers at Sylvester's; they left here years ago.*

Antonyms: *quasi*—real, genuine, true, authentic.

QUID, what, something

As Henry, Prince of Wales, and Sir John Falstaff, his boon companion, play with words in Shakespeare's *Henry IV, Part 1,* Falstaff says, "How, now, how, now, mad wag! what, in thy QUIPS and thy QUIDDITIES?" The quips are the witticisms, wisecracks, puns, jokes, or gags that they exchange; the quiddities are the trivial or quibbling distinctions they make as they argue.

The literal meaning of QUIDNUNC is "what now?" Hence it is gossip, idle talk, hearsay, or small talk. A quidnunc is a gossip, busybody, scandalmonger, magpie, or yenta.

A QUID PRO QUO ("something for something") is the substitution or return of one thing for another. ☞ *At Vic's school the quid pro quo is the exchange of the students' maintenance work for their education.*

In Spain an HIDALGO is a man of the lower nobility; in South America he is one who is highly esteemed or owns considerable property; in central Mexico it is the name of a state.

But not: *quid* [var. of *cud,* the portion of food that a cow, for one, returns from the first stomach to the mouth to chew again, AS *cwudu*], a portion of something to be chewed but not swallowed, as with tobacco; *quid* [?], British slang word for one pound sterling.

QUIES, quiet, rest: QUI

To ACQUIESCE is to yield, comply, submit, consent, and give in. ☞ *"If we . . . acquiesce in the face of discrimination, we accept the responsibility ourselves. . . . We should, therefore, protest openly everything . . . that smacks of discrimination or slander," Mary McLeod Bethune, civil-rights leader, in "Certain Unalienable Rights" (1944).* ACQUIESCENCE is agreeing or complying by being silent. ☞ *Look, when the head honcho demands something, she expects acquiescence.* An ACQUIESCENT child is obedient, compliant, submissive, and docile.

To ACQUIT a defendant is to free, exonerate, set free, and vindicate him or her. ☞ *They were acquitted of all charges.* It is also to conduct, behave, act, and deport oneself. ☞ *Selling acquitted himself well in the final game.* ACQUITTAL is the act of discharge, exoneration, or release.

A COY person is shy, diffident, bashful, timid, and modest, although sometimes the word is used in the sense of an annoying elusiveness or reluctance to reveal the truth. ☞ *It was obvious that the CEO was being coy about his plans.* Coy and QUIET originally were like Siamese twins, but they separated successfully; the word quiet came to mean still, calm, tranquil, peaceful, and undisturbed, as in the title of Erich Maria Remarque's novel of World War I, *All Quiet on the Western Front.* Among the word's other synonyms are unobtrusive, sober, inconspicuous, and conservative. As a noun it is silence, lull, QUIETUDE, QUIETNESS, QUIESCENCE, peace, or serenity. ☞ *The only place I can study is in the quiet of the library.* Irish playwright John Millington Synge claimed in *The Aran Islands* (1907) that "there is no language like the Irish for soothing and QUIETING." A QUIETUS is death and extinction, but it also has a more popular, lighter meaning, such as a finishing stroke, ending, concluding, or kibosh. ☞ *I did my best to give the quietus to the argument. Hey, let's put the quietus on that rumor right now!*

To QUIT is to cease, terminate, take off, and depart; as an adjective it means to be free, clear, and rid of. ☞ *Hector wasn't at peace until he was quit of his obligations.* A QUITTER is a dropout, slacker, defeatist, or loser.

QUITE means completely, totally, thoroughly, and entirely. ☞ *Markington was quite obnoxious at the club yesterday.* But there are times when one wishes to temper such extremes, perhaps having to a degree or considering in mind. ☞ *Yes, I do think that her last poem was quite good.*

The RIP one sees on a tombstone is an abbreviation of an anonymous Latin saying, **REQUIESCAT IN PACE.** A **REQUIEM** is a musical service or hymn for the repose of the dead.

To **REQUITE** is to repay, reward, compensate for, and recompense. ☞ *Maud's years of faithful service were requited with thanklessness and ingratitude.* It also means avenge, revenge, retaliate, and pay back. ☞ *We must requite the humiliation they have inflicted upon us.* Thus a **REQUITAL** can be, depending upon the circumstances, either remuneration, reward, retribution, or revenge.

> **But not:** *require* [*quaerere,* to seek], demand.
> **Combining forms:** *ac-,* to; *re-,* again.
> **Antonyms:** *acquiesce*—argue, rebel, disagree, contest; *acquit*—convict, condemn, doom, weigh down, misbehave; *coy*—bold, saucy, brazen, impudent, pert; *quiet*—restless, rough, tumultuous, roaring, disturbance; *quietness, quietude*—flurry, agitation, hubbub, resonance; *quit*—persist, continue, abide, stand fast; *quite*—barely, scarcely, somewhat, merely, fairly.

QUOT, how many

QUOTA is short for the Latin phrase *quota pars,* how great a part? In 1921 Congress passed the Quota Act, instituting limits on immigration to three percent of each nationality that lived in America in 1910. The act was repealed in 1965. The United States government has also long employed quotas on goods and services that are exported or imported. Synonyms are part, share, allotment, percentage, or portion. ☞ *The quota set by the University's Board of Regents for students of your race is 16%; we'll put your name on the waiting list. Each person in this club has a quota of two prospective members each month. If I don't sell a car to this couple, I won't make my quota this month.*

The quantity resulting from the division of one quantity by another is called the **QUOTIENT.** One's intelligence Quotient (IQ) is obtained by dividing an individual's mental age (as determined by the score on an intelligence test) by the chronological age and multiplying the result by one hundred. So with the Achievement Quotient (AC). However, the Triple DQ or Desire-Determination-Drive Quotient employed by those who find the IQ culturally biased does not use this mathematical formula.

Quotidian [*quot* + *dies,* day] reports are those that are made every day. A quotidian fever recurs daily. Because happenings or events that occur with regularity tend to become common, quotidian has also come to mean commonplace, ordinary, and as usual. ☞ *We expected to see another boring, quotidian flick, but it turned out to be super, a real sleeper.*

To **quote** a person is to repeat a statement he or she has made in writing or speaking. ☞ *Look, I'm quoting the truant officer verbatim, word for word, snarl for snarl!* What is quoted then becomes a **quotation**; they fill thousands of pages in the scores of books devoted to them. ☞ *Scudley was surprised to find that the Bible drama was so full of familiar quotations.*

Some remarks are **quoteworthy** and **quotable** and some are not. ☞ *Yes, I heard what the senator said, but it's not what my paper considers quotable stuff.* They may be irrelevant and uninteresting or, sometimes, inappropriate, unsuitable, and unprintable.

But not: *quoth* [AS *cwethan,* to say], said.
Combining forms: *-dian,* day; *-worthy,* deserving.

RADERE, to scrape: RAS

A **RASCAL** is an imp, tease, prankster, trickster, or mischief-maker. It also refers to a villain, miscreant, scoundrel, reprobate, or rogue, names reserved for a base, dishonest, or unprincipled person. In a story entitled "The Disappearance of Lady Frances Carfax" detective Sherlock Holmes says to his friend Dr. Watson, "We are dealing with . . . one of the most unscrupulous rascals that Australia has ever evolved." It's a safe bet that Holmes wasn't talking about a prankster or joker.

Mark Twain's Huckleberry Finn and Jim had a similar word for mean and dishonest people. One night on the raft when those two infamous con men, the duke and the dauphin, were asleep, Jim says . . . "Huck, dese kings o' ourn is reglar **RAPSCALLIONS**," to which Huck replies, "Well, that's what I'm a-saying; all kinds is mostly rapscallions, as fur as I can make out."

Both Sherlock and Huck knew **RASCALITY** when they came up against it—dishonesty, fraud, skulduggery, villainy, or wickedness.

An eruption on one's skin is called a **RASH**, but any repeated occurrence of something over a short period of time can qualify as a rash, too. ☞ *The police finally put an end to the recent rash of robberies.*

RASORIAL is an adjective pertaining to the scratching of the ground for food by a chicken or other fowl; the words scratch and scrape are much alike. The **RAIL**, a bird found in most parts of the world, has a narrow body and long toes; that may account for its being a scratcher, too.

To **ABRADE** is to rub and scrape. An **ABRASION** is a wearing away, chapping, rubbing, roughness, or scratch. ☞ *The nurse said I needed to keep a bandage on my abrasion.* Sandpaper is an **ABRASIVE**, and people with abrasive personalities rub others the wrong way.

Running water, wind, and glaciers **CORRODE** or wear down surfaces that they pass over. So does the **ERASER** on the end of a pencil and on the rail of a chalkboard. To **ERASE** is to obliterate, delete, eradicate, and efface. ☞ *The judge said he would erase the charges from their records if their community service was faithfully completed.*

To **RAZE** a building is to tear it down and demolish it. It also means to shave and scrape off.

An additional English word related to the root: razor.

But not: *rash* [ME *rasch*], headstrong.
Combining forms: *ab-*, off; *cor-*, together; *e-*, out.
Antonyms: *abrasive*—soothing, comforting, pleasant, mollifying; *raze*—build, erect, construct, set up.

RADIX, a root: RADI

In math a **RADI**x is a number taken as a base or root of a system of numbers, logarithms, or similar. In the kitchen a **RADI**SH is a red and/or white root that is crisp and pungent when fresh, and is sometimes used to give a bit of brightness to a dish at the table.

To DERACINATE is to pull up by the roots, hence to obliterate, extirpate, and exterminate, but when the word describes an action of human beings, it usually means to uproot, isolate, or alienate them physically or emotionally, as from their native customs or environment. ☞ *The tribe of Native-Americans was cruelly deracinated and forced to move westward.*

To E**RADI**CATE has similar senses, but it more often means wipe out, remove, destroy, and abolish. ☞ *"The savage in man is never quite eradicated," Henry David Thoreau,* Journal.

In a literal sense **RADI**CAL means "going to the root of things." A radical is an extremist, iconoclast, freethinker, revolutionary, or zealot. ☞ *Because his father was an outspoken and diehard conservative, young Karson opted to become a radical.* As an adjective it means extreme, revolutionary, militant, fanatic, and immoderate. ☞ *"It is well known that the most radical revolutionary will become a conservative on the day after the revolution," wrote Hannah Arendt, U.S. teacher, in the* New Yorker *(1970).* In another context it means fundamental, essential, complete, and profound. ☞ *Even though they are members of the same party, there are radical differences in their political philosophies.* It also means rash, inordinate, drastic, and exhaustive. ☞ *When Sylvia announced her resignation, we all felt it was a radical move that we would all regret.*

To RAMIFY is to divide and spread out into branches or subdivisions; thus a RAMIFICATION is a branch, consequence, implication, or development. ☞ *We supported the bill at first, but its unforeseen ramifications are giving us second thoughts.*

But not: *radiant* [*radius,* a ray], shining.
Combining forms: *die-*, apart; *e-*, out.
Antonyms: *eradicate*—originate, create, construct, erect, raise; *radical*—partial, superficial, trivial, inessential, conservative, traditional, reactionary.

REX, king: REG, ROY

A king is the chief male authority in a country that still supports a **ROYAL** family. He is a monarch or sovereign who gained his position by heredity and expects to hold it for life. Royal covers a sizeable piece of ground: the king and his family and their surrounding court and society, along with an even larger array of synonyms: kingly, queenly, princely, aristocratic, **REGAL**, noble, majestic, imperial, monarchical, sovereign, courtly, august, grand, resplendent, purple, etc.

Royalty

The size of the world's **ROYALTY**, that is, those people holding royal status or power, has dwindled sharply during the twentieth century. As he was being forced to abdicate in 1952, Farouk I, the last king of Egypt, predicted that "There will soon be only five kings left—kings of England, Diamonds, Hearts, Spades, and Clubs." Yet from time to time a **ROYALIST**, a supporter of a king or monarchy, pops up in the news to say that he's available to **REIGN** should a vacancy occur.

Many siblings remain with us. Authors, composers, and owners of mineral and oil rights, for example, receive **ROYALTIES**, their portion of the income from their works or properties. We speak of people receiving the royal or red carpet treatment while others secretly hope to stumble onto the royal road to success, dream of a royal flush when they play poker, and complain that Cousin Irene is once again being a royal nuisance.

Apartments and stores are sometimes given such upscale names as **CHATEAU ROYALE** and **PALAIS ROYALE.** Shoppers for kitchen and other household products are familiar with such kingly and queenly brand names as Regal and **REGINA.** Regina, meaning queen, is also a given name as is **REX,** meaning king for males.

REGALIA refers to the ceremonial insignia, emblems, or dress of a high office, order, or position, as well as fancy and dressy clothing. ☞ *Everyone will be wearing formal party regalia tonight.* To **REGALE** people is to entertain, amuse, delight, charm, and entrance them. ☞ *The juggler regaled the carnival crowd.* It also means to wine and dine. ☞ *The local brass regaled the visitors with a sumptuous banquet.*

A **VICEROY** is a king's deputy appointed to rule a province or another country, which is known as a **VICEROYALTY.** His wife is a **VICEREINE,** and the gossip columnists describe their dress and manner as being **VICEREGAL.**

REGNANT (reigning and ruling) usually follows the noun it modifies, as in a queen regnant, in much the same manner as the official title of a reigning queen: Elizabeth Regina. The children of the state of Arkansas are expected to learn that their state's motto is **REG**NAT POPULUS, "The people rule." The highest honor for a professor at such British universities as Cambridge and Oxford is to hold a **REG**IUS CHAIR, an appointment traditionally made by the ruling monarch; he or she is then known as a Regius Professor. **REG**ULUS is a first magnitude star in the constellation Leo.

Students of European history learn that an INTERREX was the person who stepped in when an INTER**REG**NUM occurred, i.e., the period between the end of one king's reign and the onset of the next one's; today in kingless countries it is sometimes used to refer to an interim period between the terms of elected officials.

REGICIDE refers to the killing of a king or to the person who commits the crime. The 58 men who signed the death warrant of Charles I of Great Britain and Ireland in 1649 were called the Regicides; most were imprisoned or executed.

> **But not:** *regular* [*regere,* to rule] usual; *roy* [Scots Gaelic word meaning "red"], a male given name.
> **Combining forms:** *inter-,* between; *vice-,* deputy.
> **Antonyms:** *regal*—common, low; *regale*—bore, tire, economize; *royal*—plebian, vulgar, coarse.

RIDERE, to laugh: RID, RIS

In the chapter entitled "The Mock Turtle's Story" in *Alice's Adventures in Wonderland,* Alice and the Mock Turtle are discussing their schooling. When Alice tells him that she learned French and music, the Mock Turtle says that his school offered those courses, too, but he couldn't afford the cost: "I only took the regular course. . . . Reeling and Writhing [and] the different branches of Arithmetic—Ambition, Distraction, Uglification, and DE**RIS**ION." As we know, all laughter is not the same; sometimes it is fun, but sometimes it is cruel. Mockery, scorn, heckling, sneering, and contempt are synonyms of derision. ☞ *The stuck-up, snooty student came up with the wrong answer and became the object of derision.*

To **RID**ICULE something or someone is also to poke fun in a contemptuous, nasty way.

To **DERIDE**, scoff at, sneer at, taunt, mimic, humiliate, disparage, all fit into the bin labeled **DERISIVE**, **DERISORY** words. It's somewhat comforting to know, however, that those whose laughter is mean-spirited often appear to be **RIDICULOUS** in the eyes of others. Even though the word ridiculous often conveys the connotation of meanness, it is just as likely to be on the laughable, ludicrous, nonsensical, and comical side of the coin. ☞ *That is the most ridiculous, absurd, wild, screwy, crazy movie I've ever been to; you've just got to see it!*

That's the side of the coin where **RISIBLE** can always be found, right along with humorous, farcical, amusing, facetious, and jocular. ☞ *Hey, he's no sourpuss; Joe's a risible person who enjoys a good laugh. The new sitcom on Monday nights is supposed to be risible, but I didn't see the humor.* **RISIBILITY** is the ability to laugh, to see the funny side of life. ☞ *Wait'll you hear what happened to good old Smith on his last fishing trip! I tell you, that'll tickle your risibilities!*

And last there's **RIANT**, a word that has wallowed in crossword puzzles for a long time but really deserves to be pulled out into the open. It means cheerful, laughing, smiling, and pleasantly mirthful.

> **But not:** *uprising* [AS *risan*], a revolt.
> **Combining form:** *de-*, completely.
> **Antonyms:** *derision*—approval, commendation, kudos; *derisive*—respectful, appreciative, admiring, deferential; *ridicule*—esteem, praise, encourage, hearten; *ridiculous*—sensible, sober, serious, logical; *risible*—grave, doleful, sad, somber.

RODERE, to gnaw: ROD, ROS

When the surface of the earth is worn away by **EROSION**, the **EROSIVE** agent is usually water, waves, or wind. When a material or substance is worn away by **CORROSION**, the **CORROSIVE** agent is usually a chemical action. And when a human being is crushed, embarrassed, humiliated, and mortified, the corrosive agent is usually a caustic, scathing, sarcastic, cutting, and cruel wit. ☞ *If you ask me, it was his corrosive wit that meant curtains for that marriage.*

CORRODE means to eat away or disintegrate. **ERODE** refers to waste, spoil, and wear away. ☞ *John's commitment to salvaging his nearly bankrupt company was eroding his family's life.*

RODENTS are mammals with four continually growing incisors; they're beavers, chipmunks, mice, rats, and squirrels—all expert gnawers. Yet no matter how gifted the gnawer, there always remains a tough, uneven, and erosive edge. A **RODENTICIDE** is a substance for killing rodents.

But not: *morose* [*morosus,* fretful], gloomy.
Combining forms: *-cide,* act of killing; *cor-,* completely; *e-,* off.
Antonyms: *corrosion, erosion*—upkeep, repair, maintenance, preservation; *corrosive*—courteous, soft-spoken, soothing, pleasant.

ROGARE, to ask: GAT, GATE

Etymologists, those detectives who specialize in tracking down the history of a word, are sometimes in disagreement. Consider, for example, the word **ROGUE.** Some of the word sleuths label it [Origin unknown], [Obscure origin], or simply [?]. Others propose [Perh L *rogare*], [perh. akin to *rogare,* to ask], while still another suggests that it came [from "roger," a beggar, which was based on Latin *rogare*].

The important consideration here is the definition which stretches out from rascal, scoundrel, or scalawag, and rotter to louse, stinker, or bum, plus a few unprintables. As an adjective it means wild, lawless, undisciplined, unruly, and incorrigible. ☞ *The rogue elephant destroyed most of the village.*

There may never be a clear-cut decision about its origin, but the word's spin-offs are interesting. **ROGUERY** is trickery, rascality, subterfuge, chicanery, or quackery. ☞ *Roger's my name, roguery's my game.* **ROGUISH** folks come in two categories: some are playful, mischievous, puckish, and picaresque. ☞ *Calm down now; that's just Pete's roguish nature at work.* But on the other hand they may be unscrupulous, unprincipled, villainous, crooked, and corrupt. ☞ *I can't recommend him; he's the same roguish schemer who sold all those worthless stocks.* A **ROGUES' GALLERY** is a collection of mug shots of criminals often on display at a police station or postoffice.

ABROGATE is familiar to lawyers and legislators; it means to annul, repeal, abolish, and cancel. ☞ *Rep. Jure argued that Congress must abrogate the new tax law.* An **ABROGATION** is, then, an annulment.

To **ARROGATE** is to assume, seize, usurp, or claim in the sense of doing so without having the right to do so. ☞ *The armed trio arrogated the right* *to arrest anyone they disagreed with.* **ARROGANCE** is conceit, pretension, egoism, scorn, or contempt. ☞*The arrogance of our leading family led to their downfall.* An **ARROGANT** person is haughty, conceited, disdainful, and imperious. ☞*You think the boss is arrogant? Wait'll you meet her daughter!*

To **DEROGATE** is to disparage, belittle, ridicule, criticize, and deprecate. ☞*The coach derogated every move the youngster made on the field.* **DEROGATORY** comments are slanderous, contemptuous, defamatory, and disparaging. ☞*The debate turned out to be a lesson in the use of insulting, derogatory remarks.*

To **INTERROGATE** is to question, probe, examine, and investigate. ☞*We thought the interrogator would never come to the end of his list of questions.* **INTERROGATIONS** come in different settings and styles; there are questionings, investigations, cross-examinations, or inquiries. An **INTERROGATIVE** or **INTERROGATORY** word or sentence is one that asks a question. An interrogative mark or point is a question mark. An **INTERROBANG** (also **INTERABANG**) started out as printer's slang for an exclamation point, but then it grew into a quirky combination of a question mark (?) and an exclamation mark (!) to be used at the end of sentences that express both query and emotion [? + ! = ‽] ☞*What was I supposed to do, for crying out loud, manufacture a fire extinguisher out of thin air*‽

Your **PREROGATIVE** is your privilege, license, authority, right, option, or choice. ☞*John Dryden put it like so in* The Hind and the Panther *(1687): "Reason to rule, mercy to forgive:/The first is law, the last prerogative."*

SUPEREROGATION is the act of performing more than one's duty, obligation, or need requires, thus something beyond the call of duty. ☞*Kate's taking in those homeless children ought to win her a supererogation award.* But be warned: it also means excess, superfluity, overabundance, profusion, or surplus. ☞*If Brander tells that tedious, boring story one more time, I'm going to present him with a supererogation award—a mouth gag.* **SUPEREROGATORY** means superfluous, unnecessary, and excessive.

A **SURROGATE** is a deputy, substitute, or successor. ☞*Janzen appointed his brother as his surrogate in the controversy.* To surrogate or **SUBROGATE** is to appoint someone to act in place of another. As an adjective it means substitute. ☞*When Calvin was in the service, his brother served as his children's surrogate father.* A surrogate mother is one who carries the fetus for another woman.

But not: *castigate* [*agere,* to act], criticize; *congregate* [*con-,* + *greg,* herd], assemble; *instigate* [*in-,* + *stig,* to goad], incite; *obligate* [*ob-,* + *ligare,* to bind], oblige.
Combining forms: *ab-,* away; *ar-,* to; *-bang,* printers' slang for an exclamation point; *de-,* away; *inter-,* between; *pre-,* before; *pro-,* before; *super-,* above; *sur-,* in place of.
Antonyms: *abrogate*—create, establish, ratify, enact, uphold, support; *arrogance*—modesty, humility, shyness, bashfulness, politeness; *arrogant*—modest, humble, shy, self-effacing, deferential, servile; *derogatory*—flattering, respectful, appreciative, congratulatory, favorable; *interrogate*—answer, respond, reply, rejoin; *supererogation*—shortage, need, dearth, deficiency; *supererogatory*—necessary, vital, required, indispensable, minimal; *surrogate*—first, original, primary, actual.

RUMPERE, to break: RUPT

An ab**RUPT** reply is curt, brusque, blunt, and snappish. ☞ *Forgive my abrupt answer to your question; my mind was elsewhere.* An abrupt break in the terrain is steep, sharp, precipitous, and sudden. ☞ *That path leads to an abrupt drop of a couple hundred feet.* An abrupt action is unexpected, unforeseen, hasty, and precipitate. ☞ *The rock group's abrupt departure angered the crowd.*

The money-changers of earlier times sat on benches in the courtyard of the temple; the word for bench was *banca,* and from it came "bank." When the money-changer ran short of ready cash, the result was *banca rotta,* "broken bench," which in time evolved into bank**RUPT** and bank**RUPT**cy. A bankrupt person is broke; he or she is insolvent, ruined, wiped out, failed, and a debtor. A person without principle is said to be morally bankrupt.

The verb cor**RUPT** means to degrade, deprave, pervert, subvert, and debauch. ☞ *"Power tends to corrupt and absolute power corrupts absolutely," Lord Acton, English historian.* Thus power affects those who are cor**RUPT**ible, leading one into cor**RUPT**ion, fraud, dishonesty, or wickedness. An incor**RUPT**ible person is trustworthy, conscientious, and blameworthy.

To dis**RUPT** is to break up, inter**RUPT**, upset, disturb, and unsettle. ☞ *The protesters' outbursts disrupted the meeting.* A dis**RUPT**ion is a break, INTERRUPTION, or disturbance; a DISRUPTIVE person is distracting, unruly, and troublemaking; and a disruptive event is unsettling, upsetting, and troublesome.

Geysers and volcanoes ERUPT, burst forth, eruct, and gush; so do skin rashes and angry people. ☞ *The sounds of angry words erupted from the crowd outside.* The ERUPTION of Mount Vesuvius in A.D. 79 killed thousands in Pompeii. Audiences viewing comedians can be guilty of eruptions of laughter.

To IRRUPT, on the other hand, is to break or burst in suddenly. ☞ *It was during that lonely period after my accident that Chauncey irrupted into my life.* Both the verb and noun forms, irrupt and IRRUPTION, are used to describe a sudden increase in animal population. ☞ *The irruption of rabbits in the area puzzled the ecologists.*

A ROUT is a retreat, stampede, panic, flight, exodus, or debacle. ☞ *The king's forces suffered a disastrous rout at the hands of the rebels.* To rout is to defeat, trounce, vanquish, and overpower. ☞ *The Bills routed the Oilers 42–6 en route to the Super Bowl.* A ROUTE is a way, path, trail, itinerary, or road. ☞ *What's the shortest route from here to Portland?* It is a beat, run, circuit, or round. ☞ *The new cop's beat is the toughest route in town. They had to get a paper route to make ends meet.* It is also a means, way, method, procedure, or process. ☞ *I guess the shortest route to a promotion around here is to keep your nose to the grindstone.* As a verb it is to direct, send, channel, and steer. ☞ *Because of the flood, traffic was routed to I-45.*

A ROUTINE is a custom, habit, formula, practice, or system. ☞ *Saturdays I get up quite late; it's a routine I try not to break.* As an adjective it means customary, conventional, regular, typical, and usual. ☞ *Dr. Jeff advises yearly routine medical checkups.* It also refers to boring, predictable, tedious, and ordinary. ☞ *It's the routine plot of old with a new set of characters.*

A RUPTURE is a break, split, fracture, or fissure. ☞ *The cause of the rupture of the water main is being investigated.* It also means break, breach, schism, friction, clash, or disagreement. ☞ *That argument caused a rupture that cost us the election.* When something ruptures, it breaks, snaps, cracks, and bursts. ☞ *Hey, much more air and that balloon's going to rupture.*

Men and women who have been honorably discharged from the United States armed forces are given official papers with a sketch of an eagle with outspread wings; during World War II a small lapel button accompanied it which was worn to let others know that they were not slackers or draft dodgers; for obscure reasons the symbol became fondly known as a RUPTURED DUCK.

In the workaday world a RUT is a dull routine, habit, grind, or dead end. ☛ *Their lives sank into a rut they couldn't find a way out of.* Physical ruts are trenches, ditches, gouges, or gutters.

Combining forms: *ab-,* off; *cor-,* wholly; *dis-,* apart; *e-,* out; *in-,* not; *inter-,* among; *ir-,* in.
Antonyms: *abrupt*—expected, anticipated, deliberate, gentle, gracious; *bankrupt*—solvent, successful, flourishing, prosperous; *corrupt*—pure, upright, moral, honorable, ethical; *corruptible*—honest, trustworthy, law-abiding, conscientious; *corruption*—honesty, integrity, purity, nobility; *incorruptible*—selfless, altruistic, trustworthy, impeccable, reliable.

S

SALIRE, to leap, spring forward: SAL, SULT/XULT

To INSULT is to leap upon someone using words instead of the sticks and stones that break your bones. Sometimes this is done with contempt, scorn, abuse, hurt, and rudeness. In one of the many letters he wrote to his son and godson, Lord Chesterfield, an English statesman, said, "An injury is much sooner forgotten than an insult."

But it seems doubtful that the following famous exchange was intended and received as contempt. Said Lady Nancy Astor to Sir Winston Churchill, "If you were my husband, I'd put poison in your coffee." Replied Sir Winston to Lady Astor, "If you were my wife, I'd drink it."

In a similar face-to-face encounter an actress told playwright Noel Coward that she had seen his latest comedy and hadn't laughed once, to which he quipped, "How strange. I saw you acting in a recent play and I laughed all the time."

But one wonders how many of these insults are launched not so much with the intention of offending someone as it is to show off one's wit, to up-stage another, or to amuse an audience.

In many quotation books, it is the legendary Irish wit Oscar Wilde who dominates the index to the extent that we wonder how one INSULTER could think up (or borrow) so many of them. Once while in the company of the artist James McNeill Whistler, Wilde, overhearing a witty retort, whispered, "I wish I'd said that." To which his companion responded, "You will, Oscar, you will." One of Wilde's most cutting and scornful insults was his remark about the death of Little Nell as Charles Dickens described it in *The Old Curiosity Shop:* "One must have a heart of stone to read the death of Little Nell without laughing."

Books and authors are always fair game. One of satirist Dorothy Parker's most INSULTING book reviews ended with, "This is not a novel to be tossed aside lightly. It should be thrown with great force." What she did was ASSAIL, ASSAULT, attack, and malign both book and author from a safe distance using the mighty power of the pen. But that beats all hollow the physical side of assail and assault, such as batter, bruise, molest, violate, invade, mug, and rape. The offenders are labeled ASSAILANTS and ASSAULTERS.

Fortunately, there are some things, qualities, and values that are UNASSAILABLE, i.e., certain, unquestionable, irrefutable, and invincible. ☞ *The commander of the outpost was sure that the fort was unassailable. Our debate team won on the strength of their unassailable logic. Despite a few nit-pickers, Lincoln's place in history is unassailable.*

In earlier times a circus rider who leaped from one horse to another was known as a **DESULTOR.** Today when we jump from one subject to another in an aimless, disorganized, random, or chaotic fashion, the word for it is **DESULTORY.** ☞ *How can anyone make sense of that desultory conversation? The mayor's desultory efforts to end the strike didn't help much.*

To **EXULT** is to rejoice, revel, delight, and celebrate. ☞ *The seniors exulted as the commencement ceremony came to an end.* **EXULTANT** people are delighted, jubilant, gleeful, and ecstatic. ☞ *Fan's family and friends were exultant to learn that she was safe.* **EXULTATION** is triumph, delight, elation, or celebration. ☞ *The reporter said that there was only one word that could accurately describe the feelings of the town: exultation.*

RESULTS are outcomes, conclusions, ends, or decisions. The results of an exciting new venture are the fruits, rewards, products, or effects. To result is to conclude, terminate, and wind up, and is usually followed by the words in or from. ☞ *All my hard work finally resulted in an A+!* It also means to follow, happen, and come to pass. ☞ *Well, that's what results from their spoiling that child!*

RESILIENCE is one's bounce, buoyancy, flexibility, or elasticity. ☞ *Winston Churchill's retort to Lady Astor demonstrated his resilience.* It is said in regard to one's determination or strength, too, as describing whatever it takes to recover from illness, depression, setbacks, or misfortune. ☞ *Don't worry about Dora; she's got a lot of resilience.* Rubber is RESILIENT; so is a person who is hardy, responsive, adaptable, irrepressible, and tenacious.

The word SALLY that derives from *salire* is a sudden rush of hemmed-in troops upon the enemy, hence a sortie, bursting forth, or counterattack. A sally is also a journey, trip, outing, expedition, or jaunt, usually off the main road. ☞ *We made a sudden sally over to Uncle Jim's bike shop.* And it is a witticism, quip, clever retort, joke, or pleasantry. ☞ *Our guest's sally amused everyone.* As a verb it means to rush out, attack, dash, and erupt. ☞ *The protestors sallied forth, but they were repulsed by the line of defenders.*

A SAULT is a waterfall or rapid in a river. ☞ *We visited Sault Ste. Marie, the rapids in the St. Marys River between Michigan and Ontario.* The first part of SOMERSAULT probably comes from *super,* meaning over, hence, leaping over, as in head over heels. When one suddenly does a complete reversal of opinion or a position, it is called a somersault. ☞ *Senator Smedley's support of this bill represents a complete somersault.*

SALIENCE means prominence, such as a physical projection or protuberance. ☞ *The salience of the church steeple sets our town off from the others.* Something **SAL**IENT is prominent, noticeable, striking, and impressive. ☞ *Let me point out the salient features of our new model. Beryl's most salient feature is her charming accent.* Salience also refers to emphasis, importance, stress, attention, or prominence.

A **SAL**ACIOUS remark is wanton, lewd, obscene, indecent, tasteless, and offensive. ☞ *Several members of the group said that the salacious poems disgusted them.*

A **SAL**IENTIAN is a tailless, jumping amphibian such as a frog or toad, and jumping spiders belong to the family **SAL**TICIDAE. The **SAL**MON is noted for its leaping ability as it swims upstream to spawn.

As might be expected, several words related to music and dancing derive from *salire:* **SAL**TANDO, the bouncing of the bow on the strings of a musical instrument; **SAL**TANT, meaning dancing, leaping, or jumping; **SAL**TARELLO, a lively Italian dance; and **SAL**TATION, a leaping, hopping, or dancing movement.

To SAUTÉ food is to fry it in a little fat; it may have been so named from the way small drops of fat appear to leap or jump around in the pan. **SAL**TIMBOCCA, an Italian dish often made into a roll of ham, veal, cheese, and sage, is so named because it jumps into one's mouth.

But not: *consult* [*consulere,* to take counsel], refer to; *salubrious* [*salus,* health], healthful; *sultry* [AS *sweltan,* to die], oppressively hot.

Combining forms: *as-,* to; *de-,* down; *ex-,* out; *in-,* on; *re-,* back; *un-,* not.

Antonyms: *assail, assault*—protect, defend, resistance, withdrawal; *desultory*—methodical, purposeful, steady, pointed; *exult*—feel sad, be downcast, gloomy, blue; *exultant*—disappointed, defeated, dejected, downcast, subdued; *exultation*—dejection, depression, disappointment; *insult*—praise, compliment, honor, please, homage; *insulting*—respectful, deferential, flattering, courteous; *salacious*—clean, modest, proper, puritanical, prudish; *salient*—low-lying, depressed, sunken, minor, insignificant, unimportant; *sally*—retreat, subside, retire, give way; *unassailable*—uncertain, dubious, doubtful, unfounded.

SALUS, health: SALU

To **SALU**TE someone is to greet, welcome, honor, and congratulate that person; it's a rather handy, all-purpose, almost any-occasion word. ☞ *It had been a long, tiring day, and when I finally got home about five minutes later than usual, I was saluted with, "Where in the world have you been?"*

In Rome one says "Sa LOO tay" (spelled salute) as a toast or to one who has just sneezed; in Spanish-speaking countries the word for such occasions is **SALU**D. These words are cognates, kindred, related, or of the same family, just as are our *sneeze,* the Anglo-Saxon *sneosan,* the Dutch *sniezen,* and the Danish and Swedish *nysa*. In Berlin, a *niesen* brings out a hearty "Gesundheit!," meaning "Health!" Hereabouts the response to a sneeze is often "Bless you!"

Salus explains why the **SALU**TATION of a letter comes at the beginning and why the **SALU**TATORY, the **SALU**TATORIAN's speech at a school's commencement exercises, is always the first one on the program. The other student speech, coming an hour or so later, is the "Farewell!" said by the valedictorian.

The goddess of health in ancient Rome was **SALU**S. To her we also owe **SALU**BRIOUS and **SALU**TARY, twins that mean beneficial, healthful, healthy, curative, and wholesome. ☞ *Wetherford found it necessary to move to a more salubrious/salutary climate.*

But not: *Saluki* [after *Saluq,* ancient city of Arabia], breed of dog similar to the greyhound.
Antonyms: *salubrious, salutary*—debilitating, deleterious, harmful, detrimental.

SALVUS, safe: SAL

On April 2, 1917, in a speech to Congress asking for a declaration of war, President Woodrow Wilson said, "The world must be made SAFE for democracy. Its peace must be planted upon the tested foundations of political liberty." Twenty years after the end of World War I historian James Harvey Robinson wrote in *The Human Comedy* (1937), "With supreme irony, the war to 'make the world safe for democracy' ended by leaving democracy more UNSAFE in the world than at any time [before]."

In October, 1944, toward the end of World War II, the Japanese Naval Command claimed that most of the U.S. Third Fleet had either been sunk or had retired; when Admiral William "Bull" Halsey, Jr., got the message, he issued the following radio dispatch: "Our ships have been **SAL**VAGED and are retiring at high speed toward the Japanese fleet." To **SAL**VAGE something is to recover, restore, retrieve, rescue, **SAL**VE, and rehabilitate it. Soon after that, no doubt, there were rounds of **SAL**VOS, successive bursts of artillery, volleys of fire given in salute, and outbursts of cheers and applause.

There are two senses of the word **SAL**VATION. The first sense refers to rescue, preservation, survival, salvage, or protection. ☞ *The Constitution, wrote Supreme Court associate justice Benjamin Cardozo in* Baldwin v. Seelig, *"was framed upon the theory . . . that in the long run prosperity and salvation are in union and not division."* And the second means grace, redemption, deliverance, election, or absolution. ☞ *Three things are necessary for the salvation of man: to know what he ought to believe; to know what he ought to desire; and to know what he ought to do," wrote Saint Thomas Aquinas in* Two Precepts of Charity *(1273).*

SAVIOR (also SAVIOUR) means rescuer, defender, champion, guardian, or emancipator. ☞ *"For it's Tommy this, an' Tommy that, an' 'Chuck him out, the brute!' / But it's 'Savior of 'is country' when the guns begin to shoot," Rudyard Kipling, "Tommy."* Savior also refers to Christ, Redeemer, the Son of God, Prince of Peace, or the Messiah. ☞ *Some say that ever 'gainst that season comes / Wherein our Savior's birth is celebrated, / The bird of dawning singeth all night long. . . ," Shakespeare,* Hamlet.

In her book *God Knows,* Minnie Louise Haskins wrote of stopping at heaven's gate and saying, "Give me a light that I may tread SAFELY into the unknown," to which the gatekeeper replied, "Go out into the darkness and put your hand into the Hand of God. That shall be to you better than light and SAFER than a known way," hence more secure, protected, guarded, and unendangered.

James Thurber remarked in "The Fairly Intelligent Fly" that "There is no SAFETY in numbers, or in anything else." That means no security, protection, SAFENESS, refuge, SAFEKEEPING, or surety. A SAFEGUARD is a precaution, protection, palladium, or amulet; it is to fortify, preserve, armor, shield, and conserve.

To SAVE is to rescue, help, deliver, and liberate. ☞ *They were able to save nothing of value in the fire.* It is also to put by, hoard, set aside, and reserve. ☞ *We need to save enough money to get Mac's car fixed.* In baseball it is both a verb and a noun, ☞ *Pitcher Rockwell chalked up his sixth save of the season; he saved the team from dropping into last place.* It is a preposition when it means but or except. ☞ *Everybody had a ride home save Mike.* As a conjunction occurring at the beginning of a clause, it has the same meaning. ☞ *I would have won, save I hurt my foot.*

The money we put aside for a rainy day we call **SAVINGS;** a saving person is frugal, thrifty, and prudent; and one's **SAVING GRACE** is one's redeeming feature. ☞ *Job's one saving grace was his patience.*

SAGE, an herb familiar to cooks, and **SALVIA,** a flowering plant, are members of the mint family. A **SALVER** is a tray or serving platter. ☞ *The butler brought the mail in on the shiny silver salver.*

But not: *salve* [AS *sealf*], an ointment.
Combining form: *un-,* not.
Antonyms: *safe*—hazardous, exposed, injured, hit, unreliable, insecure, risky, uncertain; *safeguard*—peril, hazard, jeopardize, expose, risk; *safekeeping*—negligence, laxity, slackness, indifference; *safety*—jeopardy, danger, peril; *salvage*—destroy, discard, waste, expend, scatter; *salvation*—damnation, judgment, malediction, doom; *save*—sacrifice, abandon, lose, spend, squander, dissipate; *savior*—bane, betrayer, nemesis, Judas, traitor.

SANGUIS, blood: SANG

If a book you are reading describes a man as being **SANGUINE** about the future of the human race, he is being cheerfully optimistic. If it is about children who live in the northern hemisphere and have sanguine complexions, they are youngsters with rosy, ruddy cheeks. If it is a book written a century or so ago, and the battle between warring factions has turned sanguine, that means the blood is flowing.

SANGUINARY is the generally preferred word for bloody and bloodthirsty. Thomas Paine urged in *The Rights of Man* that we "teach governments humanity. It is their sanguinary punishments which corrupt mankind." A soldier writes from the front about this bitter and sanguinary war that is waged under inconceivable conditions. A newspaper editorializes about the wave of sanguinary and murderous crime that is sweeping our community.

CONSANGUINEOUS refers to kinship, to being related by blood and ancestry. A person exhibiting **SANG-FROID** (in French, literally, "cold blood") is composed, imperturbable, coolheaded, poised, and unflappable, but *not* cold-blooded. ☞ *The robbers carried off the heist with complete and incredible sang-froid.* **SANGRIA,** a cold drink made of red wine, fruit juice, sugar, soda water, and fruit slices, is so called because of its bloodlike color.

But not: *sang,* past tense of *sing* [AS *singan*].
Combining forms: *con-,* together; *froid,* cold, frigid.
Antonyms: *sang-froid*—discomfiture, uneasiness, agitation, nervousness; *sanguine*—pessimistic, morose, somber, pale, wan.

SAPERE, to taste, to be wise: SAV

In the movie *Rain Man,* Dustin Hoffman plays the role of Raymond, an autistic IDIOT SAVANT, a psychiatric term describing a mentally defective person who has exceptional skill in a special field, such as music or math. In the movie a box of toothpicks is spilled onto the floor of a restaurant, and in what seems like a nano-second Raymond counts them, all 495.

A **SAV**ANT is a learned scholar, an extremely knowledgeable person, a pundit, or a guru.

A SAGE is a wise and learned philosopher or an intellectual who is sometimes referred to as an egghead. A SAPIENT person is scholarly, wise, discerning, and judicious, and radiates sound judgment and sagacity. One who is **SAV**VY is equipped with know-how, common sense, shrewdness, and practical, street-wise knowledge; he or she is canny, wily, clever, and sly. As a verb, savvy means to know and understand. An UN**SAV**VY person is, of course, a hopeless clod.

A person endowed with **SAV**OIR FAIRE is self-assured, tactful, poised, and diplomatic. An UN**SAV**ORY person is offensive and obnoxious, while unsavory food is bland, flat, and tasteless. When food is **SAV**ORY and SAPID, it's palatable, appetizing, and delicious. INSIPID food also is flavorless and bland; insipid books and movies are dull and boring; insipid people are namby-pamby blahs.

To **SAV**OR life (flowers, travel, friends, sunsets, books, etc.) is to relish, appreciate, and enjoy it. That only HOMO SAPIENS have that gift is illustrated by Robert Frost in his poem "Stopping by Woods on a Snowy Evening." While the narrator sees the woods as "lovely, dark and deep," his little horse "gives his harness bells a shake/to ask if there is some mistake."

But not: *savage* [*silvaticus,* of the woods], primitive man; *savior* [*salvare,* save], rescuer.
Combining forms: *faire,* to do; *homo,* man; *in-,* in; *un-,* not.
Antonyms: *insipid*—savory, delicious, exciting, provocative; *sapid*—bland, unpalatable; *savant*—dolt, ignoramous, lowbrow; *savoir faire*—awkwardness, clumsiness.

SCALA, ladder: SCAL

The verb ESCALADE, meaning to climb ladders to reach a higher level (☞ *To get to the fortified encampment, the warriors escaladed the series of cliffs by means of ladders*), is obviously the word that the inventors of the ESCALATOR had on their idea pads when they chose to adopt it as their trademark. And it is a most appropriate word, too, for the mechanism millions ride on every day is actually a continuously moving ladder.

There may be some who would argue that there is no "down" in SCALE, for its synonyms are climb, mount, rise, ascent, and go up, but all loyal readers of the society columns know that there are as many downs on the social escalator as there are ups. It is also a fact that many of the UPSCALE get a kick out of an occasional visit to a store that caters to the DOWNSCALE. The fact is that it took about forty years after ESCALATE was given birth before someone came up with DE-ESCALATE. ☞ *The president refused to say whether the order meant that he was de-escalating or escalating the war.*

LA SCALA, the name of one of the principal opera houses of the world, is properly Teatro Alla Scala, Italian for "Theater at the Stairway." It was built in Milan in 1776 by the Empress Maria Theresa of Austria. A stairway is a series of steps, and that is what a scale is, as, for example, the numbers on a thermometer.

Some corporation headquarters are organized so that the upper ECHELON executives' offices are on the top floors of their building. ☞ *Wilfred always intimated that his office was upper echelon, nineteenth floor or higher, but I never knew; I got off on the eighth.*

> **But not:** *scale* [ON *skal,* bowl], a weighing device; *scale* [OF *escale,* husk], skin outgrowth as on fish, etc.; *scaloppine* [OF *escalope, shell* (of a nut, snail, etc.)], pounded slices of veal breaded and sautéed, as scaloppine alla Marsalla.

SCANDERE, to climb, leap: SCEN, SCEND

When the Julius Caesar of Shakespeare's play returns to Rome after military triumphs, he is met by a worshipful populace. Yet among many Roman citizens there lurks the fear that he will now be proclaimed emperor. Brutus, Caesar's friend, is among them, and he speaks of how a man climbing "ambition's ladder" soon scorns "the base degrees/By which he did **ASCEND,**" i.e., climb, mount, rise, escalate, and scale.

Eighteen and a half centuries later, in 1814 in Paris, the Emperor Napoleon, in accord with the Act of Abdication and "faithful to his oath declares that he is ready to **DESCEND** from the throne, to quit France . . . for the good of his country," and to be exiled to the island of Elba, thus to go down, fall, plunge, and plummet.

An **ASCENT** is a climb, rise, advancement, **ASCENSION**, or scaling. ☞ *The fireman made a cautious ascent to the roof of the building.* A **DESCENT** is a fall, drop, dip, decline, or decrease. ☞ *Be careful on the path's sharp descent to the river.* Both words mean slope, incline, grade, pitch, or ramp, but one is up, the other down.

Descent, however, has additional senses such as ancestry, origin, lineage, pedigree, or parentage. ☞ *The troops are of African descent.* It also means a sudden raid, attack, assault, or incursion. ☞ *The troops barely escaped the descent of the invaders.*

ASCENDANCE and **ASCENDANCY** means dominance, rule, control, power, or command. ☞ *The group that split from the party hopes to gain ascendance / ascendancy in the state legislature.* **ASCENSION** in the Bible refers to the bodily ascent of Christ into heaven.

A **DESCENDANT** is an off-spring, child, progeny, heir, or heiress. ☞ *She's the woman who claims to be a descendant of Eugenie, the Empress of France. The game of croquet is said to be a descendant of pall-mall.*

To **CONDESCEND** is to patronize, deign, stoop, lower oneself, and humble oneself. ☞ *We knew he would never condescend to speak to a mere assistant manager.* A person with a **CONDESCENDING** manner is haughty, pretentious, snobbish, disdainful, and patronizing. ☞ *I can't stand her condescending attitude toward her employees.* **CONDESCENSION**, on the other hand, can be either commendable or contemptible, depending upon how it is used; it can demonstrate an eminent person's humility, graciousness, modesty, egalitarianism, or deference. ☞ *We admired the Nobel laureate's condescension toward the young students with whom she spoke.* But it can also reflect disdain, hauteur, or haughtiness, as well as a high and mighty patronizing attitude. ☞ *The movie star's condescension toward the fans was sickening.*

SCAN is another word with two faces. When Alexander Pope in *An Essay on Man* (1733–34), used it in these lines, "Know then thyself, presume not God to scan;/The proper study of mankind is man," the meaning is clear: study, scrutinize, examine, inspect, and probe. But there are times when we scan a chapter in a textbook because we don't have the time to really study it; it is then that we glance at, skim, browse, thumb through, read hastily, and look over. ☞ *I'm afraid I missed the fine points; I just had time to scan the lesson.* And then there's the scanning we do when we study poetry; SCANSION is the analysis of the metrical form or structure of the lines. ☞ *My poem is "I think I'd like to see / An elephant climb a tree in a mall in someplace like a big city." You mean it doesn't scan? How come?* SCANNERS are important mechanisms in such areas as radar, computers, medicine, radio, television, photography, fire fighting, and police work.

A SCANDENT plant climbs, and SCANSORIAL animals, such as lizards, squirrels, and woodpeckers, are capable of climbing.

To TRANSCEND is to exceed, go beyond, surpass, rise above, and outdo. ☞ *The story of Joe's big day is one that absolutely transcends belief.* It also means to overshadow, beat, outstrip, and eclipse. ☞ *Anne's latest novel transcends all of her other books.* Things that are TRANSCENDENT are peerless, incomparable, unique, and superb. ☞ *Medical researchers are examining Einstein's brain in hopes of finding out what made him a transcendent genius.* Transcendent and TRANSCENDENTAL are sometimes synonymous, but the latter also refers to TRANSCENDING experiences that are beyond the ordinary or common ones; that is, they are supernatural. Essayist Ralph Waldo Emerson in *Self Reliance* urged mankind to "Trust thyself . . . To believe your own thought, to believe that what is true for you is true for all men. . . ." This was at the heart of TRANSCENDENTALISM, a philosophy-religion for which he was the principal American spokesman in the mid-nineteenth century.

But not: *crescendo* [*crescere,* to grow], gradual increase in force.
Combining forms: *a-,* to; *con-,* together; *de-,* down; *trans-,* across.
Antonyms: *ascend*—alight, dismount, drop; *ascendancy*—subjugation, subservience, subordination; *condescend*—accept, respect, treat as equal; *condescending*—simple, unassuming, unpretentious; *condescension*—pride, arrogance, superiority, haughtiness; *descend*—rise, soar, climb, mount; *descendant*—parent, ancestor, progenitor, forefather; *descent*—upward climb, improvement, increase, regeneration; *transcendent*—ordinary, common, everyday, mediocre; *transcendental*—mundane, material, empirical, physical.

SCIRE, to know: SCI

One's **conSCIence** is the inner sense of knowing what is right and wrong; in a Fourth of July speech in 1852, Frederick Douglass, an escaped slave, said ". . . [It] is not light that is needed, but fire . . . the conscience of the nation must be roused." A **conSCIentious** person is one who heeds that inner voice. ☞ *We've always trusted our attorney; she's extremely conscientious.* Something that is **unconSCIonable** is unscrupulous, unprincipled, preposterous, immoral, and unethical. ☞ *Did you hear that in the same period that the company laid off 13,000 employees the brass split more than $50,000,000 among themselves? Now that's unconscionable!*

A **conSCIous** act is one that is deliberate and intentional. ☞ *It didn't seem to be a conscious insult; I took it as a slip of the tongue.* **ConSCIousness** is awareness, sensibility, cognizance, or perception. ☞ *Bill's every action is motivated by his class-consciousness.* One who is **self-conSCIous** often appears to be ill at ease, uncomfortable, embarrassed, and uptight. ☞ *When Hazel realized that she was the only woman in slacks rather than a dress, she became acutely self-conscious.*

SubconSCIous pertains to the mysterious down-deep mind, the one the psychoanalysts probe. ☞ *Way down deep in my brother's subconscious, he hates me. I'm serious!* An **unconSCIous** impulse or act is one that is not premeditated or planned out; it is unwitting, inadvertent, involuntary, and fortuitous. ☞ *Man, did you see that shot? Fifty feet out and never touched the rim! Unconscious!* One can be temporarily devoid of consciousness, as the result of an accident. ☞ *The paramedic examined the unconscious man.*

OmniSCIent people are all-knowing, all-seeing, and supreme, knowing everything and taking pride in their **omniSCIence,** their infinite and total knowledge, gifts that are usually suspected as being figments of their imaginations. Those who are **preSCIent** claim to have the gifts of foresight, clairvoyance, premonition, prophecy, or **preSCIence.** One who is **neSCIent** is ignorant, uninformed or, at least, agnostic; **neSCIence** is ignorance or lack of knowledge.

A **plebiSCIte** is a direct vote taken on a matter of public importance, such as a determination of autonomy or affiliation with another country. ☞ *A 1935 plebiscite in Saarland determined that the state would be reunited with Germany.*

A **SCIence** is a branch of knowledge dealing with facts arranged systematically and brought under general principles. ☞ *Biology is the science of life or living matter.* Over the ages the word's meanings have broadened considerably; now they include skill, art, craft, expertise, method, or discipline. ☞ *Starting my ancient jalopy by parking it on a hill or rise probably seems nutty, but I've got it down to a science now.*

Something that is **SCI**ENTIFIC is empirical, systematic, verifiable, tangible, and technical. ☞ *Of all the members of the department, only Dr. Schwann truly epitomized the scientific spirit.* An UN**SCI**ENTIFIC experiment or report or analysis does not conform to the principles of science.

SCIOLISM means superficial knowledge. Examples of **SCI**OLISTS are the phrenologists who read the shape of one's head and the palmists who study the lines on one's hand.

An additional English word related to the root: nice.
But not: *scintillating* [*scintilla,* spark], vivacious, witty; *sciosophy* [*skio,* shadow + *sophy,* wisdom], supposed knowledge.
Combining forms: *con-,* together; *ne-, ni-,* not; *omni-,* all; *pre-,* before; *sub-,* under; *un-,* not.
Antonyms: *conscientious*—unreliable, negligent, irresponsible, slovenly; *conscious*—asleep, unaware, dead, oblivious; *consciousness*—impassivity, insensibility, ignorance, unawareness; *omniscient*—fallible, ignorant, unknowing, limited; *prescience*—hindsight, retrospect, afterthought, postscript; *scientific*—spiritual, intuitive, ineffable, transcendental; *self-conscious*—confident, relaxed, spontaneous, secure, trustful.

SCRIBERE, to write: SCRI

In "Bartleby," Herman Melville's first published short story, the **SCRI**VENER who worked in the narrator-lawyer's office was a law-copyist whose amusing and startling reply to almost anything his employer asked him to do was, "I would prefer not to." In time professional copyists such as he lost out to the typewriter and other marvels that came into being a century ago. Today scriveners might be clerks, court reporters, or notaries public, or **SCRI**BES (journalists).

A **SCRI**BBLER is a hack or an inferior writer. A piece of **SCRI**P is temporary money or a certificate to be used when trading at the company store. The literal meaning of MANU**SCRI**PT is "written by hand," a definition that seems a bit strange today when almost no professional writers use pen or pencil. That's what the copyists did for many centuries, dipping Chinese brushes, Egyptian reeds, or quills fashioned from bird feathers into ink and writing on papyrus, parchment, and, eventually, paper. Monks preserved the learning of early eras when they wrote in **SCRIptoriums** in their monasteries, often copying **SCRIpture.** Others, later, sat at **eSCRItoires,** an elaborate writing desk or secretary. In 1883 Mark Twain donned his pioneer's hat when his *Life on the Mississippi* became the first typewritten manuscript to be submitted to a publisher.

A **SCRIpt** is the manuscript of a play or movie; it also refers to the characters and letters that are used in handwriting. A **superSCRIpt** is a letter or number written above the line; a **subSCRIpt** is written slightly below. A **postSCRIpt** is a message written after one has signed a letter, usually headed by P.S. To **inSCRIbe** is to autograph a book or picture, or to write, etch, or engrave. The result is an **inSCRIption.** To **tranSCRIbe** is to note, write down, copy, and record. A **tranSCRIpt** is a written copy, as of one's academic record. A **tranSCRIption** is a recording, as of a program or notes from dictation.

A **preSCRIpt** is a rule, law, or ordinance. **PreSCRIptive** grammar is concerned with the correct and incorrect rules, such as not ending sentences with a preposition and never splitting infinitives. **DeSCRIptive** grammar, on the other hand, is concerned with the observation and study of how the language actually works.

To **proSCRIbe** is to prohibit, forbid, and outlaw; hence a **proSCRIbed** area is one to which access is restricted because of possible danger or because it is private property. To **circumSCRIbe** an area or an activity is to enclose, limit, and draw a line around it. ☞ *His meager education circumscribed his dreams. Before we left on our trip, we circumscribed all the major cities in red on our map.*

To **aSCRIbe** is to credit and attribute. ☞ *I ascribe my good health to the exercises I do. That painting has been ascribed to several artists, I fear.* A **conSCRIpt** is someone who has been drafted through military **conSCRIption.** To **subSCRIbe** to an idea or proposal is to concur and agree with it; to subscribe to a cause is to contribute to it; to subscribe to a document is to sign it; and to subscribe to a magazine is to order and pay for a **subSCRIption.**

A physician orders or **preSCRIbes** medicine, usually with a **SCRIbble** on the **preSCRIption** form.

If we were to wait at the airport terminal for a person who a mutual friend has **deSCRIbed** by saying, "Well, frankly, the only **deSCRIption** that I can come up with is to say that he's **nondeSCRIpt,** as useless as that may be," we would be on the lookout for someone uninteresting, ordinary, usual, insipid, and dull. Had the mutual friend indicated that he was **indeSCRIbable,** we would not have been any closer to the truth, for it means beyond words, inexpressible, ineffable, and too extraordinary for description. ☞ *The sun setting on the mountain top was indescribable, but in a quite different way from the indescribable mess in Junior's room.*

But not: *scrimmage* [ME *scarmishe,* skirmish, minor battle], football practice session; *scrimp* [Scand], economize drastically.
Combining forms: *a-,* to; *circum-,* around; *con-,* with; *de-,* down; *in-,* not, on; *manu-,* by hand; *non-,* not; *-orium,* place for; *post-,* after; *pre-,* before; *pro-,* before; *sub-,* under; *super-,* above; *tran-,* over.
Antonyms: *descriptive*—abstract, general, vague; *proscribe*—approve, permit, encourage; *subscribe*—reject, dissent, be opposed.

SEDERE, to sit, settle: SED, SESS, SID

The literal or etymological meaning of **preSIDe** is "to sit before or in front of"; its kin are chair, head, moderate, direct, and administer. Hence a **preSIDent** is one who figuratively "sits in front of"; its synonyms bear this out: head of the nation, chief of state, first citizen, or highest executive officer. To **reSIDe** is to settle back, remain in place, occupy, and rest; hence a **reSIDent** is one who settles and remains in a particular place and is known as an inhabitant, settler, occupant, denizen, **reSIDer,** dweller, or local.

The **preSIDency** is the function, office, or term of office of a president. ☞ *Lifting the test ban was a prerogative of the presidency.* **PreSIDential** is an adjective pertaining to the office. ☞ *Get me somebody from central casting who has that presidential look.* The **preSIDium** is a government committee of the former Soviet Union, and a **preSIDio** is a military post or fort.

One's home, dwelling, domicile, quarters, flat, house, apartment, or abode is one's **reSIDence;** a person employed for a set length of time by a university is sometimes called poet-/artist-/sculptor-/author- in residence. The term of a physician who joins a hospital medical staff for advanced training is a **reSIDency. ReSIDential** neighborhoods are those composed of private homes.

ReSIDue is what's left over; it's the leavings, scraps, remains, dregs, **reSIDuum,** or refuse. ☞ *We always put the coffee grounds and the rest of the residue in our compost bucket for the garden. Traces of arsenic were found in the residue at the bottom of the victim's glass.* **ReSIDual** also means remainder and leftover; **reSIDuals,** however, are additional payments to a performer or writer for reruns of films, commercials, etc.

When governments **asSESS** taxes, they charge, fine, levy, impose, and exact; the process itself requires weighing, evaluating, rating, valuing, estimating, and appraising. ☞ *The clubhouse was assessed at $40,000; each club member was assessed $500 for the repairs.* A tax **asSESSor** was originally a judge's assistant, one who sat next to him.

An **asSIDuous** person is diligent, industrious, tireless, persevering, and dedicated; its early and literal meaning was "to sit down and apply oneself." ☞ *Henry's assiduous study habits paid off in the long run.* **Assizes** are court **SESSions** held in England where people sit down to settle matters at hand. From this came **size,** which originally meant to "settle or fix an amount"; it still does in the sense of dimensions, bulk, magnitude, or proportions; as a verb it means to gauge, measure, catalog, sort, calibrate, rank, and range. ☞ *Heinrick judges everything by size rather than quality. After sizing up the other team, the Hawks decided to forfeit the game.* **Sizable** objects are considerable, ample, substantial, and generous. ☞ *Our food drive collected a sizable amount of mostly the large-sized cans.*

In military terms a **siege** is the surrounding and isolating of a fortified position. ☞ *In the Civil War the Union army's siege of Vicksburg under Gen. U.S. Grant lasted 47 days.* In another sense it is an attack, stretch, spell, bout, or course. ☞ *That's quite a siege of the flu you've had.* To **besiege** means to attack, surround, encircle, and blockade. ☞ *Troy was besieged by the Greeks for a decade.* It also means to pester, inundate, assail, harass, and annoy. ☞ *The lottery winner was besieged by requests for money.* Besiege was the original meaning of **obSESS,** i.e., to sit down opposite or before the enemy. Today it means to haunt, preoccupy, dominate, torment, and bedevil. ☞ *The man's obsessed by the poverty of his childhood.* An **obSESSion** is a fantasy, preoccupation, delusion, fixed idea, phobia, monomania, or hang-up. ☞ *Leslie has one obsession: to be accepted by the country club set.* An **obSESSive** fear or idea or thought is haunting, unshakable, compulsive, irrational, and fanatical. ☞ *If you want to see an obsessive fear, get Shirley to ride with you when you drive over the mountains.*

PosSESS is a combination of two roots, *potis,* able and having power, and *sedere;* hence its literal meaning is "to sit down as the person in control." It now means to own, hold, have, maintain, and occupy. ☞ *Our family once possessed this whole area.* A person **posSESSed** by spirits is hexed, bewitched, cursed, and bedeviled, but one who is **self-possessed** is composed, poised, serene, calm, and collected. **PosSESSion** is ownership, custody, retention, title, or tenure; **posSESSions** are one's belongings, property, assets, or worldly goods. To **disposSESS** is to take away or back, eject, drive out, evict, and expel. ☞ *Now that we've got our rent current, they can't dispossess us.* To **repoSSESS** is to get back something owned. ☞ *The finance company will repossess our car if we fall further behind.* A **repo,** short for repossessed, is a commodity—usually a car or a house—that has been put up for resale.

SEDate beings are cool, quiet, demure, and unflappable. ☞ *Mark requested the oldest, most sedate horse they had at the riding academy.* A **SEDative** is a narcotic, tranquilizer, opiate, or barbiturate that causes **SEDation,** the calming of mental excitement.

SEDiment is the dregs, residue, sludge, or silt that sit on the bottom of a liquid. ☞ *Sedimentation from the stream is gradually filling in our small lake.* **SEDentary** jobs are those at which one sits, is seated, or is inert. ☞ *I sought a sedentary position for the term of my recovery.*

When flood waters **subSIDe,** they recede, sink, lower, and settle. ☞ *It was weeks before the water subsided.* It also means to abate, calm down, diminish, lessen, and ease. ☞ *My fright didn't subside until I was on terra firma again.* A **subSIDiary** is an auxiliary, addition, adjunct, or supplement. ☞ *Out here in the country, our electric generator is our most valued subsidiary.* The subsidiaries of large corporations are branches, divisions, or affiliates. ☞ *Our newest subsidiary is in Oakhurst.* As an adjective it means supplementary, additional, and extra. ☞ *What would we do without our subsidiary income from Grandpa's annuity.* It also means lesser, lower, junior, secondary, and inferior. ☞ *Ian said he'd quit rather than be reassigned to a subsidiary position.*

A **subSIDy** is funding, financing, aid, or support. ☞ *Many manufacturing plants received government subsidies during that period.* To give a subsidy is to **subSIDize,** fund, finance, underwrite, and support. ☞ *Sue and Sam wouldn't have finished school if Doc hadn't subsidized them.*

Participants at a séance are usually seated around a table as they seek to communicate with the spirits of the dead. The seat or central jurisdiction or office of a bishop is known as a **see,** in medieval times the head servant in charge of serving those seated at the tables was called a **sewer.** When people or things are supplanted, replaced, or succeeded by others, they are **superSEDed;** the literal meaning is "to sit above," in the sense that the new replaces the obsolete. ☞ *Regulation XL888R supersedes all previous rules.*

A **disSIDent** is one who sits apart, a protester, a nonconformist, an iconoclast, or a dissenter. ☞ *Only a few of the dissidents were allowed to leave the country.* **DisSIDence** is disagreement, dissension, discord, conflict, or rupture. ☞ *It was political dissidence that finally broke up the meeting.*

HOSTAGES might be said to be forced to sit until rescued or ransomed. An INSIDIOUS plan is treacherous, duplicitous, conniving, and Machiavellian. ☞ *A number of our fellow townsmen were taken in by the insidious plan.*

But not: *sedition* [*sed,* aside + *-itio,* a going], a treasonous act; *sedulous* [*sedulo,* sincerely], assiduous.
Combining forms: *as-,* at, near; *be-,* before; *dis-,* apart; *in-,* on; *ob-,* before; *pre-,* before, in front of; *re-,* back; *sub-,* under; *super-,* above.
Antonyms: *assiduous*—lazy, slothful, inactive, lethargic, cavalier; *dissident*—conformist, consenting, contented, satisfied; *insidious*—frank, overt, straightforward, candid, innocuous; *obsess*—purge, liberate, rid, exorcise; *resident*—traveler, gypsy, vagabond, stranger, alien; *sedate*—agitated, excitable, impassioned, demonstrative, flighty, frivolous; *sedative*—irritating, stimulating, agitating; *siege*—lull, pause, respite, remission; *subside*—ascend, rise, advance, climb, aggravate, stir up.

SEMEN, seed: SEMIN

SEMINARIANS are students who specialize in theology and religious history at a **SEMIN**ARY, a special school that prepares them for the ministry, priesthood, or rabbinate. Many of their advanced classes, as in many colleges and universities, are **SEMIN**ARS, usually small and informal gatherings or groups in which students and teachers exchange information and hold discussions.

SEMINAL ideas are creative, original, germinal, and productive, the seeds that tend to influence the development of future events. ☞ *One of the seminal ideas that came out of the French Revolution was the concept and ideal of social equality.*

SEMEN is the fluid from the male production organ that carries the sperm or seed. IN**SEMIN**ATION is the sowing or implanting of seed; artificial insemination is a common practice among raisers of livestock. Both **SEMIN**ATION and DIS**SEMIN**ATION pertain to the sowing of seeds, but the latter has a wider meaning, such as the broadcasting, dispersing, scattering, or spreading of ideas. ☞ *Henry David Thoreau's philosophy of civil disobedience has been disseminated throughout the world.*

Birds who feed mainly on seeds are said to be **SEMINivorous.**

Combining forms: *dis-*, apart; *in-*, in.
Antonyms: *disseminate*—contract, narrow, shrink; *seminal*—hackneyed, sterile, useless, worn-out.

SENEX, old; old man: SEN

That the average age of our **SENators** is considerably greater than that of our representatives in the House is hardly surprising considering the Latin root the word springs from. The **SENate** in ancient Rome was a council of elders; so is that of the United States. It is also called the upper or **SENior** legislative body, the word senior meaning older, even though the two branches were born at the same time. Those having **SENiority** in either chamber have served the longest and are usually the oldest.

Sir and **sire** are male terms of respect in English, as are **SENhor** in Portuguese, **SENor** in Spanish, **signor** and **signore** in Italian, and **monsieur** in French. The French **monseigneur** is a title of honor reserved for princes, bishops, etc.; its literal meaning is "my sir" or "my lord." **Monsignor** is a title conferred upon certain high-ranking prelates.

A person who is **SENescent** is growing old. A **SENile** person is weak and infirm, often mentally and physically; the condition is called **SENility.**

To sire is to father an offspring; a sire is the male parent of a quadruped. As a verb it means to beget and, as a kind of spin-off, to author. ☞ *Our tireless author has sired another novel.*

A feudal lord was called a **seigneur** or a **seignior.** One who assumed lordly airs in those days was called **sirly** (sir-like) meaning lordly (lord-like), which eventually came to mean arrogant, rude, and ill-mannered, and to be spelled **surly.** ☞ *Ms. Etta Kett, the columnist, says surly behavior is now reserved for certain waiters, parking lot attendants, and store employees at the exchange counter.*

Antonyms: *senior*—junior, apprentice, underling, newcomer; *surly*—amiable, civil, courteous, gracious.

SEQUI, to follow: SECU/XECU, SEQU, SUIT

The **conSEQUence** of an act is what follows: it is the result, outcome, development, aftermath, outgrowth, issue, or repercussion. ☞ *As a consequence of his police record, Sims was hard pressed to find a job.* **ConSEQUent** means following as an effect or result. ☞ *The mayor* *discussed the passage of the curfew ordinance consequent to the riotous protest march.* **CONSEQUENTLY** refers to therefore, hence, accordingly, or thus. **CONSEQUENTIAL** means important, eventful, memorable, and momentous. ☞*Our club's only consequential project was our holiday food drive.* It also means pompous and self-important. ☞*His success is due to his loud, consequential voice and manner.*

An **INCONSEQUENT** remark is one that does not follow from what has been said previously; it is, therefore, irrelevant, trivial, and pointless. Something **INCONSEQUENTIAL** is unimportant, insignificant, immaterial, or petty. ☞*Why worry about an incident as inconsequential as that?*

An **OBSEQUIOUS** person follows near, in other words is servile, subservient, fawning, cowering, kowtowing, and apple-polishing. ☞*Mr. Lord never hires anyone who's not an obsequious dweeb.* **OBSEQUIES** are funeral rites or a funeral ceremony; they follow shortly after one's death.

The original *Star Trek* made its debut on television in 1966; twenty-one years later it **SEQUEL**, *Star Trek: The Next Generation,* was born. **SUBSEQUENTLY**, in 1979, *Star Trek—The Motion Picture* came out and was followed by a **SEQUENCE** of four films, *Star Trek II, III, IV,* and *V.* We can see according to the numbers that these programs were scheduled to be shown **SEQUENTLY**, one following another. Viewers who missed any one of the parts did not see the series in its **SEQUENTIAL** order. A **PREQUEL**, incidentally, is a story that comes before, one that foreshadows the later work and depicts the same characters at a younger age; it is not an uncommon happening in filmland.

Most dictionaries do not list **SEQUITUR**, meaning a conclusion or consequence, but its cousin, the Latin phrase **NON SEQUITUR**, is in the smallest paperback lexicons; its literal meaning is "it does not follow," it refers to an illogical conclusion or an irrelevant, unconnected remark: There is no way Sue'll make the honor roll, *for she can't chew gum and fry eggs at the same time.*

It is probable that **SEQUESTER** derives from *sequi,* too. It means to seclude, isolate, quarantine, **SEQUESTRATE**, and segregate. ☞*The jury in the murder case will be sequestered for as long as it takes to deliver a verdict.*

CONSECUTIVE numbers follow one another in uninterrupted order: 1, 2, 3, 4, 5, etc.; 10, 20, 30, 40, 50, etc. They are successive, sequential, and continuous. ☞*We've had no rain now for twenty-one consecutive days.*

To **EXECUTE** is to follow out, accomplish, implement, and engineer. ☞*Coach Robyns' game plan was executed to perfection.* Execute refers to perform, render, play, enact, act, portray, and do. ☞*Brahms' piano* *concerto was executed with great skill.* It also means put to death, kill, dispatch, liquidate, and remove. ☞ *Thanks to the governor's stay, the convicted murderer was not executed.*

EXECUtion refers to an accomplishment, achievement, or fulfillment. ☞ *The execution of our plan must be done quickly.* It also means killing, capital punishment, or slaying. ☞ *The execution was delayed at the last moment because an executioner could not be located.*

An **eXECUtive** is usually the one who gives the orders. He or she is the administrator, manager, director, CEO, chief executive officer, head, or chairman of the board. ☞ *The new executive has had wide business experience.* As an adjective executive refers to managerial, governing, supervisory, administrative, and regulatory. ☞ *Alice was hired on the basis of her executive potential.*

A group, family, or race that is **perSECUted** is oppressed, victimized, punished, tyrannized, abused, and harassed. Felix Frankfurter, a Jewish Supreme Court justice wrote in *Flag Salute Cases,* "One who belongs to the most vilified and persecuted minority in history is not likely to be insensible to the freedoms guaranteed by our Constitution . . . But as judges we are neither Jew nor Gentile, neither Catholic nor agnostic." **PerSECUtion** is oppression, subjugation, torment, maltreatment, affliction, or cruelty. ☞ *"Power is not a means, it is an end . . . The object of persecution is persecution. The object of torture is torture. The object of power is power," George Orwell,* 1984.

To **proSECUte** is to take to court, indict, charge, arraign, accuse, and bring to trial. In the "Notice" that Mark Twain inserted between the table of contents and the opening words of *The Adventures of Huckleberry Finn* he warned, facetiously, "Persons attempting to find a motive in this narrative will be prosecuted; persons attempting to find a moral in it will be banished; persons attempting to find a plot in it will be shot." There are two other senses of prosecute that need mentioning: **pursue,** persist, persevere, and finish; and perform, carry on, exercise, conduct, handle, and manage. ☞ *I resigned because I wasn't sure I would be able to prosecute my responsibilities effectively.* **ProSECUtion** is the carrying on of legal proceedings against a person as well as the body of officials, including the **proSECUtor** (or **proSECUting** attorney) who do this.

To **sue** someone is to start a **lawSUIT,** take legal action, prefer charges, and litigate against. ☞ *No, I did not threaten to sue them.* A lawsuit is a case, action, proceeding, process, trial, or cause. ☞ *They declined to enter a lawsuit over the damages to their car.* A **SUIT** is a petition, plea, request, entreaty, or appeal. ☞ *Edith's parents rejected the several suits for her hand* *in marriage; she had quite a few suitors.* As a verb it means to accommodate, adjust, adapt, and fit. ☞ *Are you sure this building will suit our needs?* It also means to please, satisfy, be **SUITABLE,** have **SUITABILITY,** and conform to. ☞ *Help yourself to a few of my sketches that suit you.*

Something UN**SUIT**ABLE, such as a remark, is improper, in bad taste, unbecoming, and incongruous. ☞ *Your manner of dress is unsuitable for a courtroom appearance.* It also means worthless, UN**SUIT**ED, inadequate, and ineffectual. ☞ *This heavy motor oil is unsuitable for winter driving.* **SUIT**ED means appropriate, fitting, and proper. ☞ *His baseball cap didn't seem suited to the occasion.*

A PUR**SUIT** is a quest, hunt, PURSUANCE, seeking, or searching. ☞ *Among the unalienable rights that Thomas Jefferson mentioned in* The Declaration of Independence *are life, liberty, and the pursuit of happiness.* A pursuit is also one's occupation, vocation, profession, calling, business, job, or career. ☞ *Jock's new pursuit will probably be in the field of electronics.*

A **SUIT**E is a SET of furniture, two or more connected rooms, as in a hotel, and a series of dances or musical pieces, such as Ferde Grofe's "Grand Canyon Suite."

A SECT is a faction, cult, splinter group, denomination, religious subgroup, SUBSECT, or order. ☞ *The Amish sect was founded by the followers of Jakob Ammann in the 17th century.* A SECTARIAN is a member of a sect; as an adjective it means narrow-minded, bigoted, biased, provincial, and prejudiced. A NONSECTARIAN is broad-minded, nonpartisan, catholic, impartial, eclectic, and liberal.

To SEGUE is to make a smooth transition from one item or topic or theme to another. ☞ *Notice how the first musical theme segues into the second. The president's opening remarks segued neatly into his principal topic.* To ENSUE is to follow, result, succeed, and come after. ☞ *The story of what ensued after the body was discovered will have to wait until tomorrow.*

Anything INTRINSIC is essential, inherent, innate, fundamental, and indigenous. ☞ *The plot is interesting enough, but I can't see much intrinsic value in the book.* If it is EXTRINSIC, it is external, extraneous, irrelevant, unrelated, and superfluous. ☞ *What you're arguing seems extrinsic to me, completely and totally beside the point.*

But not: *section* [*secare,* to cut], part, portion.
Combining forms: *con-,* together; *en-,* on; *ex-,* outside, throughout; *in-,* inside, not; *non-,* not; *ob-,* near; *per-,* thoroughly; *pro-,* forward; *pur-,* forward; *sub-,* under, near; *un-,* not.

Antonyms: *consecutive*—random, haphazard, intermittent, simultaneous; *consequence*—source, cause, origin, paltriness, insignificance, obscurity; *executive*—subordinate, laborer, hired hand, underling; *non sequitur*—relevance, appropriateness, suitability; *obsequious*—arrogant, domineering, assertive, forceful, impudent; *persecution*—protection, indulgence, reward; *prosecute*—abandon, discontinue, withdraw; *sectarian*—nonpartisan, nonsectarian, broad-minded; *sequence*—discontinuity, disorder, permutation; *sequester*—invite, accept, participate, socialize; *suit*—disagree with, upset, displease, inconvenience, discommode; *suitable*—ill-advised, unbecoming, unseemly, inappropriate, unfit; *unsuitable*—fitting, eligible, satisfactory, qualified.

SIGNUM, a mark, seal, sign: SIGN

The meaning of **SIGN** in Latin is "a mark denoting something"; it was not until the 15th century that it came to mean in English "to write one's name." Today it is still a mark, token, glance, hint, or suggestion. ☞ *For the fourth week there wasn't a sign of rain in the sky. The shouts of the crowd were a sign that our team had won the race.* It is a symbol, emblem, stamp, brand, logo, or trademark. ☞ *Our sign is our guarantee of quality.* It is also a billboard, advertisement, placard, theme, or shingle. ☞ *The candidates' signs are plastered all over the town.*

To sign a paper is to affix one's **SIGNATURE,** autograph, inscription, name, and endorsement, or John Hancock, the latter being the first **SIGNER** or **SIGNATORY** of the Declaration of Independence. Walt Whitman said in his *Song of Myself,* "I find letters from God dropt in the street, and every one is sign'd by God's name."

A **SIGNAL** is a sign, cue, password, gesture, indicator, or notice. ☞ *I'll clap once as the signal to begin, twice to stop.* As an adjective it means remarkable, extraordinary, special, and unusual. ☞ *It was a signal example of how* not *to sing the national anthem.* As a verb it means to motion, communicate, beckon, gesture, and wave. ☞ *With a wink at the audience, comedian Danny Kaye signalled half the orchestra to rise and the other half to remain seated.* **SIGNALLY** means eminently, conspicuously, and especially. ☞ *It was a signally disrespectful comment to make, and those of us within hearing were embarrassed.*

To **SIGN**IFY is to signal, indicate, communicate, make known, and convey. ☞ *Fernando signified his agreement with a nod of his head.* It is to imply, suggest, mean, and represent. ☞ *In the final act of Shakespeare's play, Macbeth learns that his wife is dead; his famous soliloquy ends with, "Life's but . . . a tale / told by an idiot, full of sound and fury, / signifying nothing."* In dramas of that period a series of notes called a SENNET was played on a trumpet or cornet to signal the entrance or exit of a group of actors.

Matters of **SIGN**IFICANCE are matters of importance, consequence, relevance, **SIGN**IFICATION, or value. ☞ *We were never sure that Gerold understood the significance of Dr. Frank's diagnosis.* The literal meaning of **SIGN**IFICANT is "worthy of an IN**SIGN**IA, badge, emblem, mark, or sign"; hence, it means important, paramount, noteworthy, and remarkable. ☞ *The Daphnes have made a significant contribution to the university.* It also means suggestive, indicative, pregnant, and eloquent. ☞ *The moment Mother Teresa entered a significant hush fell over the crowd.* IN**SIGN**IFICANT concerns are trifling, paltry, trivial, and inconsequential. ☞ *Considering what happened to Albert, the game itself was insignificant.*

A SEAL is a mark, insignia, sign, **SIGN**ET, crest, emblem, or imprint used to indicate authority; as a symbol it is often attached to a legal document. A memorable character in James Thurber's *Fables for Our Time* is the circus seal who became such a great performer that "when he read in a book a reference to the Great Seal of the United States, he thought it meant him." A seal of approval printed on a product is an endorsement, guarantee, or certification of its quality. To seal an envelope is to secure it; the same meaning applies to the sealing off of an area by the police. To seal an agreement, with, say, a handshake is to settle, conclude, finalize, and validate. ☞ *The contract was not signed, sealed, and delivered until one minute before deadline.* When the walrus in Lewis Carroll's *Through the Looking-Glass* says, "The time has come . . . To talk of many things: / Of shoes—and ships—and sealing wax / . . . And whether pigs have wings," he is referring to the wax used as a SEALANT in earlier times to fasten and certify documents and such with a seal, sign, or signet impressed into the heated wax.

To AS**SIGN** is to DE**SIGN**ATE, allocate, earmark, and reserve. ☞ *Student parking spaces will be assigned Monday.* It is to appoint, nominate, delegate, and commission. ☞ *Two reporters were assigned to cover the governor's junket.* It is also to fix, specify, determine, stipulate, and attribute. ☞ *Our last order of business is to assign a day and time for our* *next meeting.* **AsSIGNments** are chores, duties, lessons, tasks, or exercises. ☞ *All assignments are due at the beginning of the period.* Some assignments, such as to a post or job, are appointments, nominations, or commissions. ☞ *Her last assignment was to the embassy in Bonn; Peg hopes that her reassignment will be to Rome.* A third meaning is distribution, allotment, or parceling out. ☞ *Job assignments will be posted on the bulletin board today.* An **asSIGNation** is a meeting of lovers, usually a secret one; synonyms are tryst, rendezvous, liaison, clandestine appointment, date, or affair.

To **conSIGN** is to hand over, entrust, deliver, and delegate. ☞ *Ed's oldest brother consigned his car and other belongings to him.* The **conSIGNment** of property is its transfer, delivery, entrusting, and handing over to another. ☞ *The consignment of the warehouse to its new owners will take place tomorrow.* Goods consigned or handed over to a shop by a person known as a **conSIGNee** are offered for sale on consignment and are owned by the **conSIGNor** until sold.

To **counterSIGN** a check or document is to add a second or additional signature. ☞ *Our records show that all checks from your company must be countersigned by Mrs. Haycroft.* In the military a countersign is a secret signal or sign such as a password.

A **deSIGN** is a plan, scheme, pattern, project, or conception. ☞ *The design for the new building has been approved.* It is a shape, form, style, motif, or configuration. ☞ *Does everyone approve the design of this new logo?* It refers to an aim, purpose, target, intention, or objective. ☞ *Her design has always been to end up in Hollywood.* It also means a plan, scheme, plot, intrigue, conspiracy, or connivance. ☞ *It was clear that he had designs on his partner's holdings.*

As a verb it means to plan, think of, draw up, contemplate, and visualize. ☞ *Their house was originally designed for two families.* It refers to invent, devise, delineate, form, and fashion. ☞ *Marlys has designed a new format for our sales brochure.* It also means to intend, set up, plot, and destine. ☞ *This school was designed to prepare worthy students for college.*

To **deSIGNate** is to indicate, signify, denote, **SIGNalize,** and dub. ☞ *The attorney suggested we designate our heirs in our will.* It is to appoint, nominate, select, choose, and assign. ☞ *Jules has not yet designated her successor as chair.* It also refers to identify, term, label, name, christen, and call. ☞ *The consensus is that we designate Toni Executive Sales Manager. I move that her designation be unanimously approved.*

DeSIGNer works two ways. On one hand it means a creator, inventor, architect, or deviser. ☞ *We owe our thanks to the three designers of this exciting new product.* On the other hand a designer is a schemer, plotter, conspirator, intriguer, or conniver. ☞ *We were not surprised to learn that McTague, ever the crafty designer, had worked her way into the O'Riches family.* As an adjective it denotes a product that carries the name of a fashion designer, such as designer jeans. A **deSIGNing** person is artful, foxy, scheming, cunning, tricky, contriving, and crooked. ☞ *You'd better watch out for that bunch; they're as designing as they come.* **UndeSIGNing** people are unoffending, innocent, open, guileless, and sincere. ☞ *Not trust Una? She's as undesigning as they come!*

An **enSIGN** is a banner, flag, pennant, standard, or streamer. It is a sign, symbol, or token such as the dove, an ensign of peace. The lowest commissioned officer in the U.S. Coast Guard and Navy is an ensign.

To **reSIGN** is to step down, quit, abdicate, and give notice. ☞ *The director said he would not resign; he would have to be fired.* It also means to yield, acquiesce, cope with, give in, and accede. ☞ *"I like trees because they seemed more resigned to the way they have to live than other things do," Willa Cather,* O Pioneers. To **re-sign** is to sign again, as, for instance, when renewing a contract. ☞ *Pug finally re-signed with the Vultures.* **ReSIGNation** has two meanings: notice, retirement, or quitting and patience, capitulation, passivity, or submission. ☞ *The saddest sight was the look of resignation on the faces of the refugees from the war-torn country.*

But not: *signora; signore* [*senex,* old], Italian titles of respect, married woman; man.

Combining forms: *as-,* to; *con-,* together; *counter-,* over against; *de-,* down; *en-,* upon; *in-,* not, upon; *re-,* back, again; *un-,* not.

Antonyms: *consign*—receive, keep, retain, withhold; *design*—chaos, anarchy, chance, purposelessness; *designing*—open, candid, honest, forthright, direct; *resign*—continue, pursue, go on, battle, contest, resist, oppose; *resignation*—involvement, attachment, retention, rebellion, protest; *seal*—leak, unplug, unfasten, loosen; *signal*—unremarkable, obscure, ordinary, commonplace, everyday; *significance*—triviality, irrelevance, inconsequence, frivolity; *significant*—inconsequential, ambiguous, meaningless, paltry, trivial, picayune.

SIMILIS, like; SIMUL, at the same time: SEMBL, SIMIL, SIMUL

The First Amendment to the Constitution of the United States stipulates that "Congress shall make no law . . . abridging the freedom of speech, or of the press; or the right of the people peaceably to ASSEMBLE"; that is, to convene, gather, flock, congregate, summon, meet, and rally. It means to piece, fit, set up, construct, and put together. ☞ *If I hadn't become confused by the instructions, I probably could have assembled this bicycle in half the time.* It also refers to compile, accumulate, bring together, and amass. ☞ *Now that you've finished your research, what you have to do is assemble all that information for your term paper. The foreman had to assemble a new crew.* To DISASSEMBLE is to dismantle, separate, break up, and take apart. ☞ *This product is much easier to disassemble than to assemble.*

GENERAL ASSEMBLY is the name of the lawmaking bodies of nineteen states. ASSEMBLY is the name of the lower house of five states, and its members are called ASSEMBLYMEN and ASSEMBLYWOMEN. In addition to being a group, meeting, gathering, or an elective body, an assembly is the process of setting up, putting together, and construction. In the military it is a signal, often by bugle, for troops to fall in.

An ASSEMBLAGE is the act of ASSEMBLING; it is the aggregate or collection of the gathered people or items; it is also a form of sculpture in which unrelated—and often discarded—objects are composed or gathered into a whole.

To ASSIMULATE is to absorb, incorporate, take in, and learn. ☞ *Craig assimilates so much in class that he seldom has to burn the midnight oil.* It also means to integrate, adopt, embrace, and mix. ☞ *The foreign exchange students quickly assimilated into our routines and ways.* ASSIMILATION is the process of taking in, as food into the body, nutrition into a plant, information into the mind, and people into a cultural group. DISSEMBLE and DISSIMULATE are SIMILAR in meaning: pretend, feign, disguise, conceal, and mask.

An ENSEMBLE is an assemblage, aggregate, collection, or set. ☞ *The exhibit was a strange ensemble of dissimilar objects.* It is one's clothes, apparel, garb, outfit, attire, or wardrobe. ☞ *I'll need a hat, gloves, and shoes to complete my ensemble.* It is also a band, orchestra, combo, group, chorus, troupe, or company. ☞ *The jazz ensemble was given a standing ovation.*

To reSEMBLe is to look like, take after, parallel, correspond approximately, and mirror. ☞ *In Shakespeare's play, Lady Macbeth comes out of the room where King Duncan is sleeping and says, "Had he not resembled / My father as he slept I had done 't."*

A reSEMBLance is a likeness, closeness, affinity, analogy, or congruence, usually regarding appearances. ☞ *There is a striking resemblance between those two.* **SIMILarity** has the same general meaning, but it often goes beyond appearance. ☞ *There is an unusual similarity in those two candidates' ideas and attitudes.* One's **SEMBLance** is one's outward appearance, guise, front, facade, veneer, bearing, or exterior. ☞ *Let's try to show at least a semblance of a happy family.* It is also a replica, copy, reproduction, likeness, or image. ☞ *The portrait was not a good semblance of her face.* A **SIMULacrum** is a slight, superficial, or unreal likeness or semblance. Stories, tales, or excuses that are veriSIMILar have the appearance of truth and are probable, likely, reasonable, and plausible. ☞ *Kent's story may have been pure fantasy, but it struck me as being a verisimilar excuse.*

VeriSIMILitude, then, is likelihood, probability, credibility, and veracity. ☞ *Your play has possibilities, but at this stage it seems to me to lack verisimilitude.* **SIMILitude** is parity, similarity, resemblance, or likeness. ☞ *The similitude between our candidate and Abraham Lincoln is a bit of a stretch.* **DisSIMILitude** and disSIMILarity are twins; they mean diversity, difference, contrast, disparity, or unlikeness. ☞ *At first blush, the two plans seemed almost identical, but we soon became aware of their dissimilarities / dissimilitudes.*

A **SIMILe** is a figure of speech using *as* or *like* in which two unlike things are compared: "I wandered lonely as a cloud," William Wordsworth and "O, my luve is like a red, red rose/That's newly sprung in June," Robert Burns.

A facSIMILe is an exact copy; it is also the name of the method of transmitting printed matter and graphics by electronic means using a FAX machine. Fax is a shortened and respelled form of facsimile; it is both a noun and a verb.

A **SIMULation** is a model, copy, facsimile, imitation, or dry run. ☞ *Attention! This emergency signal is a simulation; I repeat, this. . . .* To **SIMULate** is to put on, pretend, act out, mimic, and affect. ☞ *Pay no attention to him. He's been known to simulate tears to get noticed.* A **SIMULator** is a mechanism for creating or simulating certain conditions for training or experimentation. ☞ *Trainees spend hours in the flight* *simulator.* **SIMUL**ATED objects are artificial, synthetic, fabricated, manmade, counterfeit, and forged. ☞ *Of course it's a simulated beaver coat; I wouldn't wear the real thing.*

There are several kinds of **SIMUL**CASTS: programs broadcast **SIMUL**TANEOUSLY on both radio and television, on more than one channel or station, and in two or more languages. **SIMUL**TANEOUS translations are concurrent, synchronous, coexistent, and contemporaneous. ☞ *Visitors to the General Assembly of the United Nations can twist a dial on their headsets and hear what the speaker is saying in simultaneous translations of five different languages.*

Combining forms: *as-,* to; *dis-,* not; *en-,* in; *fac-,* to make; *re-,* again; *veri-,* true.
Antonyms: *assemble*—disperse, break up, dismiss, disconnect, separate; *assembly*—dispersal, separation, disbanding, disruption; *dissemble, dissimulate*—show, manifest, evidence, reveal; *dissimilar*—alike, corresponding, identical, equivalent, kindred; *resemblance*—dissimilarity, unlikeness, contrast, disparity; *similar*—unlike, alien, contrary, diverse, opposite; *similarity*—disparity, diversity, disagreement, incongruity; *simulated*—authentic, true, natural, bona fide; *simultaneous*—diachronous, distant, staggered; *verisimilar*—unlikely, improbable, inconceivable, unexpected; *verisimilitude*—improbability, unlikelihood, untenability.

SKHIZEIN, to split: SCHIZ

A SCHISM is a breach, break, or division, especially in a religious body, but it also occurs in political parties. A SCHISMATIC is a person who promotes such a break or who goes along with it.

A **SCHIZ**OPHRENIC or **SCHIZ**OID is a person with mental or personality problems that may be manifested in one or more of the following disorders: abnormal shyness, delusions, withdrawal, hallucinations, or multiple or split personalities; in each there is a sense of a split from the world or from reality. The words are also adjectives. Psychiatrists call the disorder **SCHIZ**OPHRENIA; in the past it has also been called dementia praecox; its literal meaning is "split mind."

Combining form: *-phrenia,* mind.
Antonyms: *schism*—union, fusion, agreement, compromise, harmony.

SKOPEIN, see, look at: SCOPE

Of the many **SCOPEs** we have available to us, a few play important roles in our lives, directly or indirectly. **FLUOROSCOPEs** can help locate hairline fractures; **MICROSCOPEs** are invaluable in medical laboratories; **SPECTROSCOPEs** are useful for producing and observing a spectrum of light or radiation; **RADARSCOPEs,** the viewing screen of radar equipment, are indispensable to the airline industry; and **TELESCOPEs** provide scientists with information that affects our daily lives.

PERISCOPEs are important to the crew of a submarine; **KALEIDOSCOPEs** provide hours of entertainment for children as well as ideas for designers; **HOROSCOPEs,** which are charts rather than instruments, are scanned daily by those who believe that our lives are influenced by heavenly bodies; and the **KINETOSCOPE,** an early motion-picture device invented by Thomas Edison, was instrumental in the development of our modern movie projectors.

To **TELESCOPE** an object is to compress or shorten the image of it; years ago there were two-part suitcases with that name that could expand as one part got more than full. To telescope a piece of writing is to summarize or epitomize it. A **TELESCOPED** word has been formed by contracting two words or squeezing together two or more words or phrases: Sitcom is a telescope of sit(uation) + com(edy); smog comes from sm(oke) + (f)og; and biodegradable comes from the telescoping of biologically degradable.

A **MICROSCOPIC** object is miniscule, infinitesimal, imperceptible, and minute.

The scope of an individual is his or her range, vision, reach, knowledge, or grasp. The scope of a piece of property is its area, span, or spread. A creative person who needs a wide scope should be given elbow room, freedom, and latitude. To scope something out is to look it over. ☞ *The speaker scoped out the audience as she waited at the head table for her cue.*

A **BISHOP** is an overseer, watching over the flock, scoping it out. **EPISCOPAL** comes from *skopein* by way of bishop, for an **EPISCOPATE** is the order or body of bishops that governs the church that **EPISCOPALIANS** belong to.

Combining forms: *bi-,* over; *eido-,* shape; *epi-,* upon; *fluoro-,* fluorescence; *horo-,* hour; *kal-,* beautiful; *kineto-,* moving; *micro-,* small; *peri-,* around; *radar-,* locating device; *spectro-,* spectrum; *tele-,* far off.
Antonyms: *microscopic*—macroscopic; *telescope*—extend, lengthen, amplify, flesh out.

SOLUS, alone: SOL

At some point during our grammar school days we learn that a few words have multiple personalities, that is, they can function as four different parts of speech: adjective, adverb, noun, and verb. Take the word last, for example. That's my last cent. I finished last. The shoemaker worked on a last. Will these flowers last? **SOLo** is another: There's a part here for solo clarinet. Sis never jogs solo. I love that piano solo. Sam will solo today at Brice Field.

SOLitude is seclusion, isolation, withdrawal, or loneliness. "Solitude is," wrote Nobel Prize winner Octavio Pax in *The Labyrinth of Solitude* (1990), "the profoundest fact of the human condition. Man is the only being who knows he is alone." A **SOLitudinarian** is a recluse, hermit, or ascetic; it is a word that both does and does not apply to Henry David Thoreau, the author of *Walden;* true, he found solitude, yet he often walked the railroad tracks into town.

DeSOLate is double-edged as both adjective and verb: deserted, uninhabited, isolated, barren, cheerless, and bleak. ☞ *That area is so desolate you swear you are at the end of the world.* It also means forlorn, pitiable, friendless, and bereft. ☞ *JoJo was desolate when Bud's unit was called up.* And as a verb it means ruin, ravage, destroy, and devastate. ☞ *The hurricane desolated the fishing village.* It also means depress, sadden, dishearten, and crush. ☞ *We were desolated when we got the news of the explosion.* **DeSOLation** is destruction, dreariness, loneliness, or misery. ☞ *And in the midst of all this desolation, the guy says to me, "Have a nice day!" Jeez!*

A **SOLfidian** is a person who believes that faith is the **SOLe** requirement necessary for salvation. **SOLipsism** is the theory that nothing is real or exists but the self; it is also what may lie beneath a case of egocentricity, egomania, or narcissism. A monologue is a **SOLiloquy,** a long speech in which one is or appears to be talking to oneself. ☞ *Dr. Garret's annual lecture on Shakespeare's soliloquies never draws much of an audience.* But no matter what manner of speech—sermon, oration, tirade, diatribe, or address—poor speakers often begin **SOLiloquizing** and the audience dozing.

A **SOLitaire** is a single large, sparkling diamond set in a ring, as well as the name of a card game for one player. Something **SOLitary** is alone, unattended, forsaken, unique, or singular. ☞ *Not one solitary soul from our department showed up at the ceremony. Hardened, unruly prisoners are often placed in solitary confinement.*

All this solitude and loneliness can make one **SULLEN,** glum, melancholy, morose, and depressed. The remarkable Dr. Samuel Johnson put it nicely in a letter to James Boswell, his biographer: "Are you sick, or are you sullen?" The symptoms have long been quite similar.

But not: *sole* [*solea,* sandal], European flatfish; *solecism* [Gk *soloi,* after a city in which a corrupt form of Greek was spoken], an ungrammatical usage; *solicitous* [*ciere,* to arouse], anxious, concerned.
Combining forms: *de-,* completely; *-fid,* faith; *-ips,* self; *-loquy,* talk.
Antonyms: *desolate*—inhabited, populated, cheerful, cultivate, encourage; *desolation*—happiness, comfort, contentment, pleasure; *sole*—shared, divided, joint; *solitary*—sociable, gregarious, several, multiple, popular, included, busy; *solitude*—conviviality, participation, sociability, gregariousness; *solo*—communal, group; *sullen*—animated, enthusiastic, vivacious, buoyant, merry.

SOLVERE, to loosen: SOLU, SOLV

An **ABSOLUTE** ruler is supreme, unlimited, arbitrary, and tyrannical; "Power," wrote Great Britain's Lord Acton in 1887, "tends to corrupt and absolute power corrupts **ABSOLUTELY,**" i.e., definitely, positively, and utterly. Absolute also means certain, definite, reliable, and unquestionable. ☞ *We have absolute proof that your gang was involved.* And it refers to perfect, total, complete, utter, and outright. ☞ *I suppose you know that you made an absolute fool of yourself last night.*

It has been said that a New Year's **RESOLUTION,** with its intention, purpose, or aim is similar to promises and pie-crusts; they, too, are made to be broken. "Great actions," wrote the poet Samuel Butler in *Hudibras* (1663), "are not always true sons / Of great and mighty resolutions." A resolution is also the outcome, end, denouement, **SOLUTION,** or result of a conflict or problem. ☞ *Worrying about the resolution of the contract dispute caused Marti considerable stress, but she remained firm, resolute, adamant, purposeful, and steadfast.*

One who is **IRRESOLUTE** is infirm, faint-hearted, wishy-washy, **UNRESOLVED,** and indecisive; he or she is short on **RESOLVE,** perseverance, tenacity, or determination. ☞ *"[The English people have] decided only to be undecided, resolved to be irresolute. . . ." Winston Churchill* *said in a 1936 speech, lamenting his country's seeming lack of will power to face the threats of the dictators of Germany and Italy before World War II.*

The disSOLUtion or disSOLVing of a partnership or union—however indisSOLUble it may have been or appeared to be—brings it to an end, termination, extinction, or divorce. Some substances, problems, and partnerships are, of course, more **SOLUble,** more easily **SOLVed** or **disSOLVed,** than others and thus may come to an end of resolution more quickly.

Someone who is without means of financial support is bankrupt, **inSOLVent,** and penniless. For one to become **SOLVent** again may be a problem that is **inSOLUble, unSOLVable,** and incapable of being **SOLVed.**

Persons who are **disSOLUte** are immoral, depraved, licentious, and debauched. ☞ *Their selfish, dissolute lives have cost them dearly.* Such poor souls may hope to find **abSOLUtion,** pardon, forgiveness, or indulgence, and to thus be **abSOLVed,** exonerated, and pardoned of their wrongdoings.

> **But not:** *solunar* [blend of *solar* and *lunar*], a listing of the rising and setting times of the sun and the moon, moon phases, eclipses, etc.
> **Combining forms:** *ab-,* from; *dis-,* apart; *in-,* not; *ir-,* not; *re-,* again.
> **Antonyms:** *absolute*—conditional, partial, conjectural; *absolutely*—reasonably, approximately, probably; *absolve*—accuse, blame, prosecute; *dissolute*—chaste, austere, puritanical; *insolvent*—sound, prosperous, flush; *irresolute*—steadfast, firm, fixed; *resolution*—uncertainty, indecision, inconstancy; *solvent*—risky, unreliable.

SONARE, to sound: SON, SOUND

In Italian, the word **SONnet** means "little song." In form this little song is a fourteen-line poem, usually on one idea, sentiment, or thought, sometimes in two groups, eight lines and six, sometimes in three stanzas of four lines (quatrains) and a final couplet. It was introduced to England early in the sixteenth century and has been a popular form ever since. Elizabeth Barrett Browning's *Sonnets from the Portuguese* contains a sequence of forty-four love poems, among them the much anthologized "How do I love thee? Let me count the ways."

Sounding

A **SONata** is a musical composition usually in three movements and frequently for the piano or another instrument with piano accompaniment. The public speaker who has a **SONorous** style has one that is flamboyant, grandiose, and impressive, and if the style is accompanied by a sonorous voice, it will be loud, full-toned, rich **SOUNDing**, and reverberating.

A voice or noise that **reSOUNDs**, fills the air, rings, and echoes. And it is said to tintinnabulate, too, having the **SOUND** of ringing bells. In addition to meaning echoing, plangent, and ringing, **reSOUNDing** is also used in an emphatic sense. ☞ *The Cats scored a resounding victory over their archrivals yesterday.* A **reSONant** voice is one that is thunderous, booming, tumultuous, and stentorian.

Sound bites are brief or attention-getting statements that candidates for political office make in hopes they will be repeated on the evening news broadcasts; they are first cousins of factoid, a fictitious statement presented as a fact and constantly (and irritatingly) repeated.

AsSONance is also called vowel rhyme; examples are: free as a breeze, high as a kite, and mad as a hatter. Alliteration, on the other hand, is the repetition of initial **conSONant** sounds, as in dead as a doornail, fit as a fiddle, and pretty as a picture. As an adjective, consonant means in accord and in agreement. ☞ *As an applicant for the position of headmistress, Jeanette hopes that her views are consonant with those of the trustees.* In addition to being a rhyming device, **conSONance** means harmony, agreement, or concord. ☞ *The school nurse felt that the child's recent behavior pattern was quite out of consonance with his usual comportment.*

Jarring, harsh, grating, and clashing sounds are **disSONant.** ☞ *The dissonant noises from the band room forced us to close the windows.* Theories or groups or individuals that are at variance with one another can also be dissonant. ☞ *Jorge hopes that the dissonant factions will soon settle their differences.* **DisSONance** is discord, strife, or contention. ☞ *In the early days of their marriage they seemed to be in unison on many matters, but before long the relationship dissolved into dissonance.*

SONics is the branch of science dealing with the applications of sound. The adjective **SONic** pertains to a speed of approximately 738 miles per hour at sea level. A **sonic boom** is a loud noise from a shock wave caused by an aircraft moving at **SUPERSONIC** speed, that is, a speed greater than that of sound. **TRANSONIC** speed is between 700 and 780 miles per hour.

But not: *son* [AS *sunu*], male child; *song* [AS *sang*], lyric; *sound* [AS *gesund*], healthy; *sound* [OF *sonder,* to plumb], to measure the depth of water; *sound* [AS *sund,* act of swimming], body of water.
Combining forms: *as-,* to; *con-,* together; *dis-,* away; *re-,* again; *super-,* over; *trans-,* through; *uni-,* one.
Antonyms: *consonance*—dissonance, disparity, conflict; *consonant*—opposed, contrary, discordant; *dissonant*—harmonious, tuneful, compatible, uniform; *resounding*—slight, faint; *sonorous*—weak, tinny, plain, unadorned.

SPARGO, to scatter, besprinkle: SPER

When political candidates hit the campaign trail these days, they often cast **ASPERSIONS** on their principal rivals, sprinkling them with slander, calumny, libel, or vilification. To **ASPERSE,** then, is to malign, slander, vilify, impugn, and denigrate. ☞ *Claiming that his reputation has been hopelessly aspersed, the incumbent dropped out of the race.*

But if an **ASPERSION** takes place in a church, it is a sprinkling of a much different nature: it is a baptism. In the Roman Catholic church the rite or ceremony is known as **ASPERGES,** the vessel that holds the holy water is an **ASPERSORIUM,** and the brush or perforated globe for sprinkling is an **ASPERGILLUM.**

To **INTERSPERSE** is to scatter or place here and there. ☞ *The speaker interspersed her talk with fascinating anecdotes. The book was interspersed with drawings.* To **DISPERSE** is to scatter, dissipate, break up, and spread. ☞ *The police dispersed the unruly crowd. The wind dispersed the smoke. The press conference dispersed information about the crisis. The dispersion of the troops to other areas lessened the risk of casualties.*

Things that are **SPARSE** are thin, scanty, spare, meager, and skimpy. **SPARSELY** means thinly and scantily. ☞ *It was a forlorn area, sparsely populated.*

But not: *asperity* [*asperitas,* rough], irritability; *vesper* [*vesper,* evening], the evening star, Venus.
Combining forms: *as-,* to; *dis-,* away; *inter-,* between; *-orium,* place for.

Antonyms: *asperse*—praise, extol, laud, eulogize; *aspersion*—compliment, commendation, plaudit; *disperse*—combine, assemble, converge, gather; *sparse*—dense, crowded, thick, plentiful.

SPONDERE, to pledge: SPOND, SPONS

The society pages of our newspapers often refer to marriage or wedding ceremonies as nuptials; ESPOUSALS and SPOUSALS are synonyms, but today they are considered a bit old-fashioned. SPOUSE remains with us, however, especially since more and more women have opted for public life. Not too long ago it was acceptable to write, "Congressmen and their wives are invited," but today that would have to be worded, "Representatives [or Congresspersons] and their spouses [or guests] are invited."

In earlier times ESPOUSE meant "to become married and to unite in marriage"; today its principal meaning is to champion, support, advocate, embrace, and boost a cause. ☞ *The committee voted to espouse the recycling program.*

When a letter to one's beloved is returned with a note of rejection, one DESPONDs, becomes depressed, DESPONDENT, dejected, and sinks into a state of DESPONDENCY. ☞ *Dearest: I'm so despondent I have lost heart and hope. Farewell!*

A SPONSOR is a patron, angel, supporter, backer, or financier. ☞ *If we're going to have a parade this year, we'll need to find a sponsor.* To sponsor is to promote, support, vouch for, and guarantee. ☞ *Rep. Whigdon has agreed to sponsor the recycling bill in the House.*

One who RESPONDs is one who answers, replies, retorts, and acknowledges. A RESPONDENT is one who replies; he or she is also the defendant in a law suit, especially a divorce case. As such, her or his RESPONSES may determine the outcome of the dispute, depending on how RESPONSIVE the jury is to the attorney's arguments.

RESPONSIBLE has numerous meanings. The first refers to a person who is reliable, dependable, conscientious, or mature. ☞ *Christine's our candidate for the job; she's a very responsible person.* Second, it means accountable, liable, and answerable. ☞ *You are responsible for any damages done by any of your group in this park.* Third, it refers to important, executive, administrative, and demanding. ☞ *Sol now holds a very responsible office.* And finally, it means guilty, culpable, at fault, and to blame. ☞ *No one leaves this room until we find out who's responsible for putting that mouse in my desk.* A RESPONSIBILITY is a trust, charge, task, obligation, or job. ☞*It is your responsibility to see that your son gets to school everyday.* It is guilt, blame, or liability. ☞*I accept full responsibility for what happened; it was on my watch.* It is also dependability, reliability, or trustworthiness. ☞*We mustn't let his mistake lead us to doubt his responsibility.* An IRRESPONSIBLE person is immature, careless, imprudent, unreliable, and undependable. ☞*Skipping your final exam was an irresponsible act.*

To CORRESPOND is to agree, concur, parallel, tally, and be similar. ☞*Binnerd's words do not always correspond to his actions. Their Parliament corresponds to our Congress; they are corresponding legislative bodies.* It is to write letters and carry on a CORRESPONDENCE with someone; correspondence is also similarity, agreement, resemblance, conformity, or analogy. ☞*Finding a correspondence between our Civil War and that two-bit police action is an absurdity.* A letter writer is a CORRESPONDENT; so is a person who reports the news from a distant place. ☞*A foreign correspondent's life isn't quite as glamorous as you might think.*

> **Combining forms:** *cor-*, together; *des-*, away; *ir-*, not; *re-*, back.
> **Antonyms:** *correspondence*—dissimilarity, incongruity, discordancy; *despondency*—elation, optimism, courage; *despondent*—cheerful, spirited, upbeat; *espouse*—reject, spurn, disown, repudiate; *irresponsible*—dependable, thoughtful, conscientious; *responsible*—unaccountable, fickle, irrational; *responsive*—inert, passive, aloof, unapproachable.

STINGUERE, to quench, pierce: STINCT, STINGU

The dodo, the great auk, and the passenger pigeon are EXTINCT, dead, defunct, and nonexistent birds. The dodo died because it was slow, flightless, and dumb; the last extant, or living, great auk was EXTINGUISHED, destroyed, and exterminated a century and a half ago; and the EXTINCTION, obliteration, extirpation, and death of the last of several billion passenger pigeons occurred in the Cincinnati Zoo in 1914.

It did not matter that they, like all creatures, had an INSTINCTIVE and innate will to live; the survival INSTINCT, impulse, or tendency was no match for the Dutch settlers in search of food on the dodo's island of

Mauritius, or for the men who clubbed the last great auk to death on an island near Iceland in 1844, or for the irresponsible shooting appetites of the pigeon hunters. Today many species are protected from such EXTINGUISHERS or exterminators, and the whooping crane has the DISTINCTION of being one of the few species that are on the comeback trail.

Many birds have well-defined, clear-cut, DISTINCT, and individual markings, voices, and songs. The crested head and bright red of the male cardinal is unique and DISTINCTIVE. It is easy to single out, recognize, and DISTINGUISH the mourning dove's slow, moaning *coo-ah-coo-coo* from the whippoorwill's haunting, nocturnal *whip-poor-weel,* as well as to note the differences between the roadrunner/chaparral and any other bird on the run, for this stilt-legged, two-foot-long cuckoo has been clocked at fifteen miles per hour.

To the untrained eye, some birds are unclear, INDISTINGUISHABLE, and indiscernible from certain others. The principal markings of many sparrows, for example, are INDISTINCT, but such a renowned ornithologist as the notable and DISTINGUISHED Roger Tory Peterson could tell one from another at a glance.

> **But not:** *tincture* [*tingere,* to dye], a solution, as tincture of iodine.
> **Combining forms:** *di-,* apart; *ex-,* completely; *in-,* in, not.
> **Antonyms:** *distinct*—obscure, vague, merged; *distinctive*—common, ordinary, conventional; *distinguished*—mediocre, ordinary, commonplace; *extinct*—thriving, flourishing, extant; *indistinct*—clear, defined, evident; *instinctive*—learned, acquired, premeditated.

STRUERE, to construct: STRU, STRUCT

To CONSTRUCT is to build, erect, devise, fabricate, and shape. ☞ *"Since wars begin in the minds of men, it is in the minds of men that the defenses of peace must be constructed," from the constitution of UNESCO.* A construct is an idea, image, or theory. ☞ *To Lou, time and space is a four-dimensional construct.*

A CONSTRUCTION is a building, erection, invention, or creation. It is the process of building or erecting. ☞ *The construction of the bridge took a year.* However, when King Duncan used the word in Shakespeare's *Macbeth,* it meant makeup, composition, form, or meaning. ☞ *"There's no art / To find the mind's construction in the face. . . ."*

Something that is **conSTRUCTive** is affirmative, helpful, positive, practical, and beneficial. ☞*I don't mind criticism if it's constructive.*

When we **conSTRUe** something, we interpret, explain, analyze, or explicate it. In his first inaugural address President Abraham Lincoln said, "I take official oath today with no . . . purpose to construe the Constitution or laws by any hypercritical rules." To **misconSTRUe** is to misunderstand, misinterpret, or mistake.

To **destroy** is to obliterate, eradicate, decimate, and annihilate. A **destroyer** is a fast warship smaller than a cruiser.

At the opening of each episode of an old TV series called *Mission Impossible,* government agents would receive a tape-recorded message outlining their assignment. It always ended with the warning, "This tape will **self-deSTRUCT** in five seconds," at which time it would automatically destroy itself, expire, or terminate. In a tongue-in-cheek poem about whether the world would eventually be destroyed by "Fire or Ice" (1923), Robert Frost wrote, "I think I know enough of hate / To say that for **deSTRUCTion** ice / Is also great / And would suffice." Destruction is havoc, ruin, extermination, wreckage, or obliteration. Nathaniel Lee, a seventeenth-century English playwright, had a character in *Theodosius* (1680) say, "Man, false man, smiling, **deSTRUCTive** man," i.e., harmful, injurious, detrimental, and ruinous. "The Constitution, in all its provisions," Salmon P. Chase, U.S. Supreme Court Chief Justice, wrote in *Texas v. White* in 1968, "looks to an **indeSTRUCTible** Union composed of indestructible states," i.e., enduring, permanent, imperishable, everlasting, and infrangible.

To **inSTRUCT** is to enlighten, teach, inform, and school; the French playwright Moliere offered this sound advice in *The School for Husbands,* "I maintain, in truth, / That with a smile we should instruct our youth." **InSTRUCTion** is teaching, indoctrination, enlightenment, or edification. In his book *Operating Manual for Spaceship Earth* (1969), R. Buckmeister Fuller, architect, designer, and engineer, claimed our trouble with Earth "is that no instruction book came with it." A properly **inSTRUCTive** manual would be informative, explanatory, edifying, and perceptive.

English author Samuel Butler once said in a speech at the Somerville Club (1895), "Life is like playing a violin solo in public and learning the **inSTRUment** as one goes on." Instruments are also agencies, means, intermediaries, or expediters. ☞*Police and firefighters are necessary instruments in every community.* Anything that is **inSTRUmental** is useful, essential, crucial, and utiliarian. ☞*"The head is not more native to the heart, / The hand more instrumental to the brain, / Than is the throne of Denmark to thy father,"* Hamlet, *Shakespeare.*

A "No Parking—Do Not **OBSTRUCT** Traffic" sign means do not hinder, impede, stall, and thwart it. Obstruct also means to hide, obscure, and close off, as, for example, a view. ☞ *The woman's hat obstructed my view of the stage.* An **OBSTRUCTION** is an obstacle, barricade, hindrance, blockage, or impediment. ☞ *"Throughout the greater part of his rule George III was a kind of 'consecrated obstruction,' " Walter Bagehot,* The Monarchy (1867). An **OBSTRUCTIONIST** is a person who impedes, delays, or thwarts an action. ☞ *You, sir, are an obstructionist senator who is trying to kill this amendment with your delaying tactics.*

In *My Early Life,* Sir Winston Churchill wrote of how he escaped learning Latin and Greek because he was not clever enough to qualify for such courses, thus "I was taught English [and] got into my bones the essential **STRUCTURE** of the ordinary English sentence—which is a noble thing." As Churchill used the word it means organization, arrangement, or composition. A structure is also a building or edifice, and as a verb it means to put together, organize, assemble, and design. ☞ *This course has been structured to appeal to everyone who is interested in good writing.*

STRUCTURAL pertains to the physical makeup of something such as a plant, an animal body, or a building; the structural details of a house, for instance, are the floor joists, wall studs, rafters, etc. The footing or foundation of a building is its **SUBSTRUCTURE**, and the part above it is the **SUPERSTRUCTURE.** The **INFRASTRUCTURE** of a country is its basic underlying framework, notably its communication and transportation systems, power plants, and schools. ☞ *The candidate promised that the rebuilding of the country's infrastructure would be high on her agenda.*

But not: *abstruse* [*ab-,* away + *trudere,* to push], difficult to understand, recondite; *nostrum* [*noster,* ours, sold by the maker], quick-fix scheme, quack medicine; *rostrum* [*rostrum,* beak, a ship's bow, from using the bows of captured enemy ships as decorations on the speakers' platform at the Forum in ancient Rome], raised platforms for speakers.

Combining forms: *con-,* together; *de-,* down; *in-,* in, not; *infra-,* below; *mis-,* wrong; *ob-,* before; *sub-,* below; *super-,* above.

Antonyms: *construct*—destroy, dismantle, tear down; *constructive*—useless, unhelpful, adverse, negative; *destroy*—create, construct, preserve, conserve, institute; *destruction*—renewal, creation, recovery; *destructive*—beneficial, positive, good, helpful; *indestructible*—delicate, brittle, flimsy; *instructive*—baffling, befuddling, ambiguous, unfathomable;

instrumental—negligible, inconsequential, useless, ineffectual; *obstruct*—clear, open, aid, benefit, facilitate, expedite, spur; *obstruction*—assistance, freeing, encouragement, aid.

T

TACERE, to be silent: TACIT

Sir William Osler (1849–1919), a renowned physician and professor of medicine once offered this advice to medical students: "Things cannot always go your way. Learn to accept in silence the minor aggravations [and] cultivate the gift of **TACIT**URNITY." That's reserve, restraint, soundlessness, or diffidence; that's being silent even in the midst of conversation, even being able to accept small annoyances silently, **TACIT**URNLY.

In a speech at Johns Hopkins University in 1905 Sir Osler, however, did not observe that same silence, RETICENCE, reserve, or restraint that he had urged upon his students; instead he spoke of "the uselessness of men above sixty years of age," suggesting that if we all stopped work at that age the result would be of "incalculable benefit." What an outcry followed! One newspaper headline screamed, "Osler Recommends Chloroform at Sixty." To Oslerize, became a byword. And yet when he died in 1919 he was still a professor of medicine at Oxford University in England—and seventy years old!

RETICENT and **TACIT**URN people are diffident, retiring, uncommunicative, and secretive. ☞ *That man in the corner's so reticent/taciturn he must be a secret agent.* Something that is **TACIT** is implied, understood, unspoken, and undeclared. ☞ *Everyone on our block is in tacit agreement that we watch out for any suspicious strangers. When the chair looked at me tacitly, I knew she approved of my plan.*

But not: *Tacitus,* Publius Cornelius, Roman historian, A.D. 55–120.
Combining form: *re-,* again.
Antonyms: *reticent*—bold, aggressive, outspoken, frank, open; *tacit*—explicit, spoken, spelled out; *taciturn*—talkative, loquacious, verbose, outgoing.

TARDUS, slow: TARD

The withholding of sunlight from a plant will RE**TARD** or slow its growth. The economic and social progress of a country will be RE**TARD**ED or delayed by continuing uprisings. Malnutrition and a turbulent home life will retard or hinder the academic progress of a child, often resulting in the **reTARDation** of a year or more in the child's schooling.

A **reTARDate** or **reTARDee** is a person whose educational or mental development is abnormally slow or has ceased. A retarded person is handicapped or disabled in such ways.

Fire-reTARDant materials are mandatory in the construction of public buildings and recommended for all others.

The ten o'clock scholar who comes at noon is **TARDy,** dilatory, dawdling, late, or unpunctual. ☞ *I've been tardy in thanking those who helped us survive during our recent difficulties.* Glaciers and income-tax refunds move **TARDily,** sluggishly, reluctantly, and listlessly, and constant **TARDiness** or lateness is a demerit on one's record.

> **Combining form:** *re-,* again.
> **Antonyms:** *retard*—hasten, move ahead, speed; *retardation*—acceleration, advancement; *tardy*—quick, speedy, punctual, prompt.

TEKHNE, art, craft, skill: TECHN

TECHNique is skill, method, style, know-how, and modus operandi, an important asset whether one is fishing, drawing house plans, painting, etc. ☞ *Yes, she does have a gift, but I think she now needs to concentrate on her technique.* A **TECHNician** is a specialist, expert, or craftsman trained or skilled in the technique of an art or craft. Informally such a person is known as a **techie** or **tekkie.** ☞ *I finally got the hang of the computer, but not until I got a couple of techies to help me.*

TECHNical matters tend to be detailed, complex, specialized, and intricate; technical details are peculiar to a particular art, science, trade, profession, and endeavor. ☞ *I really didn't know how to explain it to the kids; it's such a technical matter. It's difficult enough to explain it to adults, there are so many technicalities involved.* Technical or vocational schools are those that train and instruct students in the mechanical arts and applied sciences. They are sometimes known as **polyTECHNic** schools. A **TECHNicality** is a technical point, detail, or expression. ☞ *My paper was the best in the class; had I got it in on time I would have won the blue ribbon; I lost on a mere technicality.*

TECHNology is the scientific study of certain arts and sciences such as engineering and how they can be applied, as in industry. **TECHNocracy** is a political theory and movement that surfaced in 1932 to have government controlled by engineering experts and **TECHNologists.**

Combining forms: *-cracy,* rule, government; *-logy,* body of knowledge; *-poly,* many.

TEMNEIN, to cut: TOM, TOMY

An aTOM is very small; in size it is an iota, speck, jot, mite, or scintilla—and you just can't get any smaller than those. When one squeezes the bulb on an aTOMizer, the contents are reduced to a fine, atom-sized spray. When certain materials are blown apart by an explosion such as an aTOMic bomb, they are aTOMized, i.e., cut into atoms, particles, or fragments.

When a person is said to be an epiTOMe of a certain quality, it means that he or she is the essence or embodiment of that particular quality or characteristic. ☞ *Lori is the epitome of honesty; I am the epitome of laziness.* It is also a summary, digest, abridgement, or synopsis. ☞ *Please, not a rehash of the entire ugly scene; an epitome will suffice quite nicely.* To epiTOMize is to summarize, condense, or cut a report, story, tale, etc. It is also to represent, typify, personify, and symbolize. ☞ *Sal epitomizes the wholesomeness of that entire group of fine young people.*

A dichoTOMY is something that has been divided, split, or cut into two parts. ☞ *Because of the recent dichotomy of our party, we can say goodby to any thoughts of winning this election.* Its adjective form means divided, cut, and split. ☞ *The dichotomous state of affairs that tore our town apart seems to be over at last.*

The anaTOMY of an animal or plant is its structure, hence a skeleton and, informally, the human body. In the 1600s William Harvey, the English physician who discovered the circulation of the blood, wrote in *De Motu Cordis et Sanguinis,* "I profess both to learn and teach anatomy, not from books but from dissections." That was long before the 1901 publication of (Henry) *Gray's Anatomy,* an exhaustive study of the human body, a TOMe of nearly 1,300 pages and more than 800 drawings. Anatomy also means any thorough analysis or examination. ☞ *The committee was commissioned to draw up an anatomy of the community's structure.* An enTOMologist, a person knowledgeable in the branch of zoology dealing with insects, has to be familiar with the anatomy of such creatures.

The names of many surgical operations calling for the removal of a body part end in *-tomy:* appendecTOMY (appendix), gastrecTOMY (stomach), hysterecTOMY (uterus), mastecTOMY (breast), mastoidecTOMY (mastoid), tonsillecTOMY (tonsils), and vasecTOMY (vas deferens).

But not: *pantomime* [Gk *pantomimos*], dumb show; *ptomaine* [Gk *ptoma,* corpse], poison sometimes caused by food bacteria.
Combining forms: *a-,* not; *ana-,* up; *dicho-,* in two; *en-,* in; *epi-,* upon; *-logy,* the study of.
Antonyms: *tome*—pamphlet, booklet, brochure, tract.

TEMPERARE, to regulate: TEMPER

To lose one's **TEMPER,** composure, self-control, or cool can lead to unpleasantness. ☞ *The boss sure lost her temper this morning; I mean, she had a temper tantrum like no storm that I've ever seen.* It refers to one's frame of mind, humor, mood, or disposition. ☞ *The disgruntled employee was in no temper to listen to reason.* It is also fury, rage, anger, or passion. ☞ *Believe me, he'll stalk out of the room in a burst of temper if you mention that fellow's name.* If a steel blade or axe head loses its temper, it loses some of its hardness, toughness, or strength. ☞ *Ah, ah, ah! Don't sharpen that good knife on your electric grindstone; it will get so hot, it will lose its temper.* To temper is to modify, mitigate, soften, and tone down. ☞ *That's one of Judge Barr's strong points: he always tries to temper justice with mercy.* An EVEN-**TEMPER**ED person is usually easy to get along with, while an ILL-**TEMPER**ED person is impatient, irritable, and irascible.

A person's **TEMPER**AMENT is his or her disposition, nature, personality, or spirit. ☞ *It seemed to the board that Dr. Stoke's temperament was not a really good match for the job.* A **TEMPER**AMENTAL person tends to be high-strung, excitable, volatile, mercurial, and histrionic. ☞ *Val said it was okay for* her *to be temperamental for she is, after all, an artist.*

A **TEMPER**ATE climate is mild, balmy, clement, and moderate. A temperate response to an antagonistic remark is controlled, stable, calm, and unexcited. A person of temperate habits will be controlled, restrained, prudent, and sensible. One who is IN**TEMPER**ATE is undisciplined, unrestrained, unbridled, and excessive. ☞ *I'm sure your intemperate language shocked her.*

TEMPERANCE is self-restraint, self-control, or moderation. ☞ *The assembly speaker listed the cardinal virtues as fortitude, justice, prudence, and temperance.* To many the word means teetotaling, abstinence, sobriety, or prohibition, as regards the use of alcohol. ☞ *The Women's Christian*

Temperance Union was founded in 1874 in opposition to the consumption of alcohol. InTEMPERance in this regard is thought to be synonymous with alcoholism, drunkenness, or dipsomania.

DisTEMPER is a virus that often affects dogs. In another field it is a technique of decorative painting; TEMPERa is a painting technique that employs an emulsion in which pigment is mixed with egg yolk, etc. Tempura is a Japanese dish in which vegetables and seafood are dipped in batter and deep-fried.

TEMPERature is a measure of coldness or heat. ☞ *The patient insisted that he had no temperature, but we knew he wouldn't be alive if that were true.* To tamper with something is to meddle, fiddle, monkey around with, and interfere. ☞ *Will you quit tampering with the antenna? Now we haven't got a picture at all!*

Combining forms: *dis-*, away; *in-*, not.
Antonyms: *intemperate*—moderate, reasonable, restrained, pleasant; *temper*—weaken, aggravate, stir, increase; *temperamental*—easy-going, unexcitable, unflappable, dependable, reliable; *temperate*—inordinate, irrational, hotheaded, frenzied, inclement, harsh, severe, passionate.

TEMPUS, time: TEMP

An antihero in literature is a protagonist who lacks the qualities—such as vision, spirit, courage, or purpose—that make for a truly heroic figure. Willy Loman is such a character in Arthur Miller's play *Death of a Salesman.* Willy had been but a baby when his father abandoned the family, and Willy has long regretted that he never had had a chance to talk with him. So one day when his older brother Ben suddenly appears (in Willy's mind), he begs him to tell him about the father he never knew because, as he puts it, "I still feel—kind of TEMPorary about myself," meaning *not* fixed, *not* settled, *not* lasting, and *not* durable.

A municipal official who, in the mayor's absence, takes over his or her duties TEMPorarily is known as mayor pro tem (short for *pro tempore,* "for the time being"). ☞ *Council member E.W. Blandings was chosen mayor pro tem during this morning's session.* A secretary or bookkeeper, for instance, who wishes to be employed only from time to time is known as a TEMP. ☞ *We'll have to hire a few temps during the back-to-school sale.*

Earthly life is **TEMPoral** rather than eternal, the length of that stay perhaps being determined to some extent by the **TEMPo,** pace, or beat of our lifestyle. If our sojourn here is **TEMPestuous,** violent, raging, **TEMPest-tossed,** and stormy, it may well be brief indeed.

When we are in a bind, we may **TEMPorize,** stall, hedge, and attempt to draw matters out in order to gain time, but such a move is often a dicey ploy at best. ☞ *The pressure on Walz was enormous, and his only chance to salvage his business was to temporize with the opposition until a buyer or a merger appeared on the horizon.*

ExTEMPoraneous means impromptu, unrehearsed, spontaneous, and off the cuff. ☞ *When our scheduled speaker failed to arrive, George came up with an extemporaneous talk on ecology.* To speak **exTEMPoraneously** is to do so without notes or advance preparation; to **exTEMPorize** is to play a musical instrument, compose a song, or act a part or speak on the spur of the moment. ☞ *We were dumbfounded when Artie extemporized a sidesplitting impression of Sen. Snork delivering a campaign speech in a maternity ward.* **ExTEMPore** is an adjective meaning impromptu and spontaneous. ☞ *Shirley's extempore speech was perfect.* As an adverb, it means on the spur of the moment and offhand. ☞ *After the debate it was agreed that questions could be asked extempore from the floor.*

ConTEMPorary furniture is modern, trendy, and current; it is sometimes shortened to **conTEMPo.** It also means coexistent, concurrent, and living at the same time. Abraham Lincoln, Walt Whitman, and Robert E. Lee were **conTEMPoraries.** Events that occur and people who live during the same time period are **conTEMPoraneous.** ☞ *The assassinations of Sen. Robert F. Kennedy and Dr. Martin Luther King, Jr. were contemporaneous tragedies.*

An additional English word related to the root: tense.
But not: *temperate* [*temperare,* to exercise restraint], moderate; *temple* [*templum,* sanctuary], house of worship; *tempt* [*tendere,* to stretch], to entice.
Combining forms: *con-,* together; *ex-,* out; *pro-,* for.
Antonyms: *contemporary*—out-of-date, old-fashioned, historical, past; *extemporaneous*—prepared, planned, memorized, rehearsed; *tempestuous*—unruffled, tranquil, relaxed, smooth, serene; *temporal*—lasting, durable, religious, spiritual; *temporary*—fixed, tenured, settled; *temporize*—act, confront, expedite.

TERERE, to rub, wear away: TRI, TRIT

AtTRITion is the act of wearing away as by friction, abrasion, erosion, scraping, or grinding. ☞ *The canyon was formed by thousands of years of attrition.* It is a wearing down or weakening, resulting in a reduction in numbers, size, or strength. ☞ *The debaters hammered away at their opposite number and eventually wore them down by sheer attrition. With so many families moving to the suburbs, attrition will take its toll at our school.* Other synonyms are decrease, loss, decimation, or attenuation. ☞ *The negotiators demanded that the jobs be eliminated by attrition, specifying that it be accomplished through enforced early retirement.*

ConTRITion is remorse, penitence, sorrow, regret, or self-reproach. ☞ *The minister asked if her class thought Judas felt contrition for his betrayal of Jesus.* A **conTRITe** person is apologetic, sorry, remorseful, conscience-stricken, and chastened. ☞ *"A broken and contrite heart, O God, you will not ignore," Psalm 51:17.*

DeTRIment is harm, injury, loss, disadvantage, or liability. ☞ *Karl has all the ability called for, but his lack of a degree has been a detriment to his career.* **DeTRImental** means bad, prejudicial, injurious, harmful, unfortunate, and disadvantageous. ☞ *I have no information that would be detrimental to either brother. Smoking was detrimental to his health.* Technically, **deTRITus** is the particles of rock that have been worn or broken away by water or the action of a glacier, but its meaning today includes debris, trash, rubbish, junk, or waste. ☞ *The critic wrote that she was putting Cal's latest book on her detritus shelf.*

A **TRIbulation** is trouble, hardship, suffering, affliction, agony, or adversity. ☞ *"Older men declare war," President Herbert Hoover said in a 1944 speech, "but it is . . . youth who must inherit the tribulation [and] the sorrow . . . that are the aftermath of war."*

The literal meaning of **TRITe** is "worn by use"; that sense has held firm, for today it means stale, overused, stereotyped, hackneyed, clichéd, and pedestrian. ☞ *Not even the acting of those two great performers could save the play from its trite plot.*

To **TRITurate** is to reduce something to fine particles or powder by rubbing or grinding; it is to pulverize.

> **But not:** *tribune* [*tribus,* tribe], an administrative officer in ancient Rome; *triskaidekaphobia* [Gk *triskaideka,* thirteen + phobia], fear concerning the number 13; *tritagonist* [Gk *tri-,* three + *agoniste,* actor], third member of a three-party acting group in ancient Greece.

Combining forms: *at-*, at; *con-*, together; *de-*, down.
Antonyms: *attrition*—increase, expansion, reinforcement, fortification; *contrite*—unrepentent, callous, proud, unapologetic; *contrition*—satisfaction, guiltlessness, pride; *detriment*—improvement, enhancement, advantage, benefit, gain; *detrimental*—advantageous, helpful, favorable, beneficial; *tribulation*—happiness, joy, ease, pleasure; *trite*—original, fresh, innovative, unusual, novel, imaginative.

TERRA, earth, land: TERR, TERRA

Terra is part of several Latin phrases that we use today. **TERRA COTTA,** literally "baked earth," is a hard, brownish-red, fired clay used to create decorations, often on pottery. **TERRA FIRMA** is firm or solid earth. When Venice, Italy, a **TERRA**QUEOUS (land and water) city of 118 islands, was an empire in the 15th century, its rulers referred to their mainland possessions as terra firma. ☞ *After two weeks on a boat, I was glad to set foot on terra firma once again.* **TERRA INCOGNITA** is unknown land, uncharted areas, or an unexamined subject. ☞ *There are several technologies that are—and, I'm afraid, will always be—terra incognita to me.*

TERRITORY is land, **TERR**AIN, acreage, tract, district, locale, expanse, area, or vicinity. ☞ *Many animals stake out their own territory which they then protect. The mountainous territory was too rugged for our vehicle.* It is also a bailiwick, domain, sphere, province, or realm. ☞ *Key West is part of Florida's territory. At the funeral of the salesman Willy Loman in Arthur Miller's* Death of a Salesman *his friend Charley says, "Nobody dast blame this man. A salesman is got to dream. It comes with the territory."* In a 1938 speech, Nazi dictator Adolf Hitler used the adjective form of the word shortly before annexing part of Czechoslovakia and less than a year before invading Poland: "Before us stands the last problem that must be solved . . . It is the last **TERR**ITORIAL claim which I have to make in Europe." History, of course, refutes that.

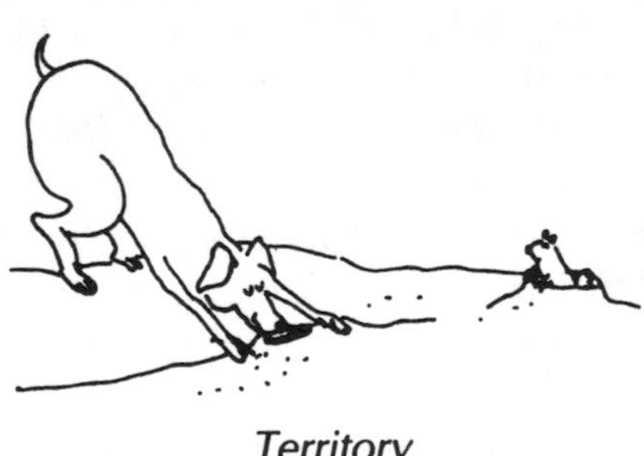

Territory

A **TERRA**CE was originally a platform made from a pile of earth, often as the site of a small garden; today it is frequently a series of such levels, one or more parts of which may be connected to a house and used as a living area, as a deck, porch, or patio. ☞ *Eventually we plan to terrace this part of our lot.* A **TERRAzzo** is a kind of flooring made of colored bits of marble or other kinds of rock embedded in concrete and polished.

There are two varieties of **TERRAriums.** The most common is a glass container for growing and displaying plants. The other is a vivarium for land creatures, as distinguished from an aquarium for aquatic animals and plants.

The **MediTERRAnean** Sea is surrounded by Africa, Asia, and Europe; hence, it is inland and midland. Things that exist or operate underground or beneath the surface of the earth are **subTERRAnean, subTERRAneous,** and **subTERRestrial;** they are buried, underground, hidden, and secret. ☞ *"Not in Utopia,—subterranean fields,— / Or some secreted island . . . / But in this very world . . ./We find our happiness, or not at all!"* The Prelude, *William Wordsworth.* The word has also branched out to mean hidden, covert, clandestine, and stealthy. ☞ *The government has a world-wide subterranean network of secret agents.*

The adjective **TERRestrial** pertains to the earth as distinct from the other planets and to the land as distinct from water; it means ground, land, earthbound, and riparian. ☞ *Polar bears can swim, but they are terrestrial animals.* It also means earthly, worldly, mundane, and **TERRene.** ☞ *Space travel is a waste; we should be concentrating on terrestrial problems.* As a noun a terrestrial is an earthling, tellurian, mortal, or human. The small, glassy objects found in Australia and known as tektite are believed to have actually come about from the impact of **extraTERRestrial** meteorites.

A **TERReplein** is the top surface of a rampart where guns are mounted. A **tureen** is a deep dish usually used for serving gravy or soup. The **parTERRe** of a theater is a section of the ground floor; it is also a flower garden arranged in a design. The breed of small dogs known as **TERRiers** were once known as "dogs of the earth" because they were used to drive animals out of their burrows or holes.

The literal meaning of **inter** is "put into the earth"; it means bury, entomb, inurn, and sepulcher. ☞ *Their dog was interred at Petland.* **Interment** is burial or the act or ceremony of interring. To **disinter** is to dig up, as from a grave, to exhume.

The trade name **TERRAmycin** is an antibiotic that owes its name to the fact that it is isolated from a soil mold.

But not: *terrapin* [Algonquian, *torope*], small turtle; *terrible* [*terrere,* to frighten], awful; *terry cloth* [?], cotton material.
Combining forms: *-aqueous,* water; *cotta,* baked, cooked; *dis-,* away; *extra-,* beyond; *in-,* in; *incognita,* unknown;

medi-, middle; *-mycin*, fungus; *par-*, on; *-plein*, level; *sub-*, under.
Antonyms: *terrestrial*—spiritual, unearthly, metaphysical, unworldly.

THEOS, a god: THE

The English Puritans who sailed to the New World from 1620 to 1640 in search of religious freedom established a **THEocracy.** They called it a Holy Commonwealth, for it was governed by God or by priests who claimed divine rights that were little different from those that English monarchs had long laid claim to for themselves. The settlers were **THEocrats** and there was no separation between church and state.

Their **THEology** was based on the Christian Bible, and what *they* said *it* said was the law. Thus it was that **THEologians,** men versed in the Word of God via the teachings of John Calvin of Switzerland, were those who decided: what was right, what was not, who the witches were in the community, and when a happening was or was not the result of the magic of **THEurgy,** a miracle resulting from supernatural assistance or intervention.

THEism is the belief in a personal God as creator and ruler of the universe. Add the prefix *a-* and **aTHEism** results, the disbelief in a supreme being; "I am an **aTHEist** still," said Spanish film director Luis Bunuel in *Le Monde* (1959), "thank God."

PanTHEism is the belief that God is everything and everything is God. **MonoTHEism** is the belief in only one God, whereas **polyTHEists** believe in more than one god or in many gods. The Greek word *pantheion* means a temple dedicated to all the gods; that was the purpose of the **PanTHEon** at Rome. It was begun in 27 B.C., destroyed, and then completely rebuilt by emperor Hadrian in about A.D. 118–119; today it is a Christian church. Modern pantheons are buildings in which a country's heroes are buried or honored, but sometimes the word refers to a figurative group. ☞ *Mark Twain deserves a prominent place in the pantheon of American literature.*

A **THEophany** is a divine manifestation or appearance of God or a god to human beings. **THEomania** is a delusional mental illness in which a person believes that he or she is God or has been especially chosen by God to found a religious order.

An **apoTHEosis** is the elevation or deification of a person to the position or status of a god. ☞ *The speaker ridiculed what he called the apotheosis of the rock star.* It also is used as a synonym of epitome, quintessence, or ultimate. ☞ *Helen is the apotheosis of womanhood.* To APOTHEOSIZE is to deify, sanctify, idolize, and worship. ☞ *Our visitor said that Americans apotheosize their sports heroes.*

The literal meaning of ENTHUSIASM is "to be inspired by a god." Philosopher Ralph Waldo Emerson said in *Essays: First Series* that "Nothing great was ever achieved without enthusiasm," a word that brings with it ebullience, exuberance, ardor, or zeal. Consider how the lack of it affected Nick Carraway, the narrator of F. Scott Fitzgerald's *The Great Gatsby.* On the day he turned thirty, he saw the future darkly, envisioning how "the promise of a decade of loneliness, . . . a thinning briefcase of enthusiasm [and] thinning hair" would translate into ten years of wasted life.

To be ENTHUSIASTIC is to be eager, avid, fervent, passionate, and spirited. ☞ *The applause for the next comedian was somewhat less than enthusiastic.* An ENTHUSIAST is a fan, aficionado, booster, zealot, adherent, or disciple. ☞ *Talk about soccer enthusiasts! That family never misses a game!*

Proud parents of new babies often search for names that are in, becoming, or even blessed. Perhaps that was why **THEODOSIUS** (later, "the Great") was inflicted on the baby who would become the Roman Emperor from A.D. 372–392 and, a century or so later, **THEODORIC** ("the Great") on the infant who would grow up to be the king of the Ostrogoths. For less ambitious contemporary couples there are a number of options: **DOROTHEA, THEO,** and **THEDORA** all stem from "gift of God," while **THEODORE** and **TIMOTHY** mean "God-honoring."

> **But not:** *theory* [Gk *theorein,* to look at], plan.
> **Combining forms:** *a-,* without; *apo-,* change; *-cracy,* rule; *-crat,* ruler; *doron-, -doron,* gift; *en-,* in; *-logy,* study of; *-mania,* excessive enthusiasm; *mono-,* one; *pan-,* all; *-phany,* to show; *poly-,* many; *timo-,* honor.
> **Antonyms:** *apotheosize*—profane, defile, desecrate, blaspheme; *atheism*—faith, belief, religion; *atheist*—religionist, believer, God-fearing person; *enthusiasm*—indifference, apathy, coolness, half-heartedness; *enthusiastic*—lukewarm, apathetic, dispassionate, disinterested, nonchalant.

TITHENAI, to put, place: THES

A **THESAURUS** (pl. **THESAURI, THESAURUSES**) is a TREASURE, storehouse, arsenal, or repository. ☞ *It is hoped that this book will be regarded* *as a thesaurus of linguistic treasures.* It is also a synonym dictionary or lexicon. ☞ *He checked in his thesaurus for a synonym of the word idea.*

To treasure is to cherish, hold dear, value, love, adore, revere, and appreciate. The describing of a thesaurus as a "treasure" comes in part from the fact that the two words are doublets; that is, they derive from the same root but followed different paths on their way to our language.

Peter Mark Roget was the author of the first important thesaurus, begun when he was 70 years old and published three years later, in 1852. Like "Webster's" (I looked it up in *Webster's*—meaning *any* dictionary), "Roget's" has become an informal term to *any* book of synonyms and, often, antonyms (I can't work this crossword without my *Roget's*).

A **THES**is (pl. **THES**es) is a subject, argument, idea, premise, essay, or **THEME.** ☞ *Your paper is well written, but I think that illustrating your thesis with several specific examples would improve it.* It is also a long paper, written as a requirement for a degree, a bachelor's in some colleges and almost always in graduate schools for advanced degrees: master's thesis, doctoral thesis. Other words for long papers are treatise, dissertation, monograph, disquisition, research, essay, or investigation.

The anti**THES**is of something is its opposite, reverse, negation, or antipode. ☞ *Your statement is the antithesis of everything I believe in.* Notice how thesis (central point) and antithesis (opposite point) work in these two statements: "For many are called, but few are chosen," Matthew 22:14 and "To err is human, to forgive divine," Alexander Pope. ANTITHETIC and ANTITHETICAL are adjectives meaning opposite, directly opposed, and contrasted. ☞ *The two countries' antithetic forms of government doomed their plans for forming a union.*

And then there's the syn**THES**is, a blend, mixture, fusion, combination, or amalgamation. ☞ *If we could ever get all these factions to form a synthesis, we'd have a perfect proposal.* To syn**THES**ize is to concoct, mix, fuse, blend, merge, and coalesce. ☞ *In her new book Dr. Crane attempts to synthesize the teachings of these two religions.* A syn**THES**izer is an electronic device used to combine, modify, or create the sounds of musical instruments. A SYNTHETIC product is artificial, man-made, ersatz, manufactured, and synthesized; thus we have synthetic detergents, gems, furs, fibers, and vitamins, to name but a few.

Sometimes synthetic is used in a derogatory or pejorative sense, meaning fake, phony, counterfeit, or bogus. ☞ *I could find no words of comfort that would not have sounded synthetic. My joke brought a laugh, but it was obviously forced and synthetic.*

An **HYPOTHESIS** is an assumption, conjecture, theory, proposal, postulate, or premise. If something is **HYPOTHETICAL**, it is assumed, speculative, conjectural, theoretical, or postulated. ☞ *Our paramedical training course consisted of writing analyses of hypothetical occurrences and incidents.* To **HYPOTHESIZE** is to theorize, speculate, guess, suppose, and presume. ☞ *After a half hour, we hypothesized that the commencement address would go on forever.*

PARENTHESES are "put in beside" the word or words that one desires to set off from the others in a sentence. To insert such material between the marks is to **PARENTHESIZE**; when speakers parenthesize, they put in, insert, add, or throw in an additional statement, often as an ad lib, something thought of and said on the spur of the moment. Such additional words are called **PARENTHETIC** or **PARENTHETICAL**, and are often casual, irrelevant, and superfluous, but they may also be significant bits of information that come to the speaker spontaneously and are deemed important enough to be mentioned. Commas, dashes, and brackets may also be used to set off such material when writing.

A **PROSTHESIS** is a device that supplements or substitutes for a defective or missing part of a body. ☞ *It took me many months after the accident to learn to walk using my prosthesis.* **PROSTHETICS** is the branch of surgery or dentistry that works with the manufacture and fitting of replacement parts.

Anything that is an **ANATHEMA** is an abomination, pariah, enemy, or persona non grata. ☞ *Please, sir! Do not mention that villain, for his very name is an anathema in this house!* An anathema is also a curse, malediction, ban, denunciation, or vituperation. ☞ *Many people in the congregation squirmed as they heard the anathemas shouted out by their pastor.*

An **EPITHET** is a nickname, appellation, sobriquet, or label. ☞ *"The Unready" was the epithet of Ethelred, the 14th King of England; that his predecessor was Edward the Martyr may explain Ethelred's plight.* But it is also an abusive word, expletive, obscenity, or curse. ☞ *When his new car sputtered to a stop three blocks from the dealer's, Rocky launched a string of screaming epithets that could be heard for a country mile.*

An **APOTHECARY** is a pharmacist or druggist as well as a pharmacy or drugstore. In Shakespeare's *Romeo and Juliet,* it is an apothecary who says to Romeo as he hands him the poison that he will drink now that he thinks Juliet is dead, "Put this in any liquid thing you will, / And drink it off; and, if you had the strength / of twenty men, it would dispatch you straight."

An additional English word related to the root: boutique.
But not: *anesthesia* [Gk *anaisthesia,* want of feeling], pain-deadener; *thespian* [after Thespis, a 6th century B.C. Greek poet], an actor or actress.
Combining forms: *ana-,* up; *anti-,* against; *apo-,* away; *en-,* in; *epi-,* besides; *hypo-,* under; *par-,* beside; *pros-,* to.
Antonyms: *anathema*—beloved, welcomed, favor, approbation; *hypothetical*—literal, factual, real, demonstrable, substantiated, verified; *synthesize*—analyze, separate, disintegrate; *synthetic*—natural, original, genuine, organic; *treasure*—scorn, disregard, spurn, forsake, abandon.

TOPOS, a place: TOP

In 1516 Sir Thomas More, an English statesman, published a book which he called ***UTOPIA,*** a word he coined from the Greek, *ou-,* not + *topos.* His Utopia, or "No-place land," was an imaginary island where all the ills of life on earth were nonexistent; today the word means any ideal or perfect community. A u**TOP**ian is an idealist, dreamer, visionary, or romantic. As an adjective it means impractical, idealistic, quixotic, and unrealistic, and is often used in a belittling or negative sense. ☞ *I truly believe that my distinguished colleague's plan is nothing but a Utopian daydream.*

Of course, not all visions of the future are ideal. In 1872 Samuel Butler's *Erewhon,* (reverse the "w" and "h" and read it backwards) satirized certain attitudes and customs of the English people. His book is a vision of an antiu**TOP**ia or dys**TOP**ia. So is George Orwell's book *1984,* a nightmare tale of Big Brother, Thought Police, and Doublethink: "War is Peace, Freedom is Slavery, Ignorance is Strength."

The **TOP**ography of a place or area is a description of its physical features, often shown on a map that is constructed by a **TOP**ographer so that one can visualize or even feel with one's fingers the mountains, rivers, and lakes.

TOPonymy is the study of **TOP**onyms or placenames, the names given to towns, cities, villages and their origin: Lincoln (famous person), Nebraska; Warm Springs (physical attribute), Georgia; Chicago (Native American), Illinois; St. Paul (Biblical personality), Minnesota.

Topiary

TOPiary is the art of trimming shrubs or trees into unusual shapes. Latin turned the Greek root into *topia,* referring to a place or field where there is ornamental gardening.

The Greek philosopher Aristotle gave us the word **TOPic**; his book entitled *Ta Topika* means "things pertaining to the commonplace." Today a topic is a subject, theme, text, thesis, or question to be discussed as well as the motif, argument, subject matter, point, or issue of a speech or paper. ☞ *I don't think that's a suitable topic for a dinner-table conversation. My topic this afternoon will be "The Role of the River in* Huckleberry Finn." A topic sentence is one that expresses the central, essential idea of a paragraph, usually at or near the beginning.

TOPical matters are commonplace, local, current, contemporary, up-to-date, and particular. ☞ *The Literary Society reviews only topical selections.* In medicine, a topical anesthesia or anesthetic is localized—in a special place—rather than a general one that affects the entire body.

> **But not:** *topaz* [*topazus*], a gem.
> **Combining forms:** *anti-,* against; *dys-,* bad, ill.
> **Antonyms:** *antiutopia, dystopia*—Eden, Elysian fields, nirvana, bliss, paradise, Shangri-la; *topical*—traditional, historical, comprehensive; *utopia*—hell, hell on earth, Hades, inferno, purgatory, the abyss; *utopian*—horrible, atrocious, savage, diabolical, grim, brutal.

TORQUERE, to twist: TOR, TORT

Ages ago when *homo erectus* wanted to see what the bear was up to that was messing around outside the cave, he needed a **TORch.** What to do? No problem: gather a handful of long, dry grass stems, twist them together, hold one end to the home fire, and voila! Bear, begone! Today we carry a torch for someone who does not return our love, athletes carry the Olympic torch every four years, and the British carry a torch that we know as a flashlight.

ConTORTionists get all twisted up on purpose, often in **conTORTed,** bent, knotted, and warped positions or poses that to those of us less agile, lithe, and nimble seem like pure **TORTure.** And sometimes people **conTORT** their faces when they scowl or sneer.

Fingers can become **disTORTed** from arthritis, and facts can become distorted when we twist them to suit ourselves. ☞ *The officer said that my version of how the accident happened was distorted. The distortion of the TV picture was caused by the nearby electrical storm.*

An **exTORTionist** attempts to twist or **exTORT** money or information from someone by using threats or violence. **ExTORTion** and blackmail are kin. Something **exTORTionate** is exorbitant, prohibitive, unconscionable, and excessive. ☞ *The price of medicine these days is extortionate.*

When one is **TORmented** or **TORTured,** distressed, abused, and mistreated by force, pain, or memories, it is like being twisted, emotionally or physically. A **TORTuous** road twists and winds and turns and meanders; so does a tortuous, ambiguous, devious, and deceptive answer to a question or explanation of one's actions. ☞ *The judge chewed out the witness for his tortuous responses to his question.*

TORsion is the act of twisting, and **TORque** is the force that produces or tends to produce rotation or torsion. A torque wrench produces torsion or rotation. ☞ *The mechanic said if I didn't use a torque wrench, I'd snap those bolts in two.*

TORToises and turtles owe their names to their twisted feet, and the **nasturtium** is named for its pungent taste and odor; its literal meaning is "to twist the nose."

Several bread names are said to come from *torquere;* the twist factor probably stemming from the process of making **TORTes, TORTellini,** or **TORTillas.** But there is no doubt about **reTORT,** a quick, sharp, or witty comeback, nor its namesake, the bent tube found in the chem lab.

A **TORT** is a wrongful act for which a civil suit can be brought. A **truss** is a girder, brace, or support, and as a verb it means to bind and tie. A **tart** is both a small open pie with a sweet filling and a fallen woman, sometimes referred to as a harlot, strumpet, wench, or hooker.

But not: *torpedo* [*torpere,* to be numb], an explosive; *torrent* [*torrere,* to burn], violent stream or downpour of rain; *torso* [Gk *thyrsos,* stem], the trunk of the body.
Combining forms: *con-,* together; *dis-,* apart; *ex-,* out; *nas-,* nose; *re-,* back.
Antonyms: *contort*—align, straighten, unbend; *tortuous*—direct, reliable, straightforward, simple.

TORRERE, to parch: TOAST, TORR

Besides the slice of bread that got stuck in the **TOASTer** and burned and the piece that slipped off the plate and fell to the floor, jelly-side down, there is the **TOAST** that is pledged with a drink in honor of someone. Its meaning comes from the piece of spiced toast that on festive occasions in days of yore was dropped into a glass of wine or a tankard of beer.

The person at the decorative head table who introduces the after-meal speakers (among them, no doubt, the TOAST OF THE TOWN) is called a **TOASTmaster, TOASTmistress,** or, today, **TOASTperson.** Those less sure of themselves brush up for the event by making notes from a book entitled *Toasts for All Occasions.*

TOASTing forks are essential tools for toasting wieners and marshmallows over an open fire; slender willow twigs with a sharpened end make excellent ones. On such outings, one must be careful not to **TORRefy** the food, for scorched wieners are apt to have a bitter taste. Sometimes the weather is uncooperative and a **TORRential** rain puts a damper on both the fire and the outdoor spirit—and, worse, turns the babbling brook that one drove over earlier into an impassable **TORRent.**

Heat-seeking people who live in regions resembling the Arctic Circle might consider moving to the **TORRid** zone, the global band between the tropics of Cancer and Capricorn, where it is hot year-round. A torrid person or situation is apt to be passionate, amorous, ardent, and intense. ☞ *And they called that a torrid love scene?*

Antonyms: *torrent*—drizzle, mist, shower, sprinkle; *torrid*—cool, chilly, indifferent, apathetic.

TROPOS, a turn: TROP

The winners of the final tennis matches of the U.S. Open receive **TROPhies;** historically, that means that they have forced the enemy to turn round and run away. A trophy was originally a "monument to the enemy's defeat."

The area we call the **TROPics** lies between the tropic of Cancer (a parallel of latitude that lies 23½ degrees north of the equator) and the tropic of Capricorn (which occupies an identical position south of it) and is known as the Torrid Zone. A **TROPical** climate is usually hot and humid, and tropical animals, fish, plants, storms, and skies are, of course, native to that region.

A HELIOTROPE is any plant, such as a sunflower, that turns toward the sun; in biology this leaning or turning toward is called a **TROPISM.** In rhetoric, the art of speaking or writing, a **TROPE** was once known as a turn of phrase, i.e., a different and unusual way of saying something; it is what today's textbooks call a metaphor. In the 17th century Samuel Butler wrote of a man who "could not open his mouth, but out there flew a trope." In today's language, that means a figure of speech: alliteration, hyperbole, metaphor, oxymoron, pun, simile, etc.

ENTROPY refers to the prevailing trend of the universe to turn toward death and disorder; another definition of it is a thermodynamic measure.

> **Additional English words related to the root:** contrive, retrieve, troubador, trove.
> **But not:** *apostrophe* [Gk *apostrephein,* to turn away], punctuation mark, figure of speech; *atrophy* [Gk *trephein,* to nourish], decay; *catastrophe* [Gk *katastrephein,* to overturn], disaster.
> **Combining forms:** *con-,* together; *en-,* within; *helio-,* sun.

TUPOS, a blow, impression: TYPE

When we classify objects we see around us, we do so by **TYPEs,** i.e., kinds, categories, breeds, orders, species, or divisions.

When we hear someone say, "He's not the type of man I feel should be representing us in Congress," the meaning is model, standard, example, **ARCHETYPE, PROTOTYPE,** specimen, paradigm, or epitome.

A third kind of type is the one that has printed the letters that form the words on this page; it comes in various fonts, designs, **TYPEFACES,** styles, or patterns. ☞ *Our printer suggested Bodini type for the invitations.*

Writers may send their manuscripts to a TYPIST to be TYPED or, if already typed on a **TYPEWRITER, RETYPED.** The **TYPESCRIPT** may then go to a printer to be **TYPESET,** always with the hope that there will be few **TYPOGRAPHICAL** errors or **TYPOS.**

Actors dread the thought of becoming **TYPECAST** (once a villain, always a villain). This is also known as **STEREOTYPING,** i.e., pigeonholing, categorizing, classifying, and designating. ☞ *As she feared, she'd been stereotyped as a dumb blonde.* A **STEREOTYPE** is a hackneyed, trite, threadbare, shopworn, over-simplified, and platitudinous description. ☞ *The belief that women are best suited to the tasks of cleaning and cooking is an old-fashioned and sexist stereotype.*

Things that are TYPICAL are standard, normal, PROTOTYPAL, model, ordinary, and representative. ☞ *As a typical teen, Jo would have spent her days moving through the usual schoolgirl routine.* ATYPICAL means uncommon, nontypical, and unusual.

To TYPIFY something is to represent, exemplify, embody, signify, and characterize. ☞ *Kasnor's views typify those of one born with a silver spoon in his mouth.*

Logo and LOGOTYPE are the same. ☞ *We can leave our name off our company logo / logotype and 62% of the public will recognize it as ours.* A STENOTYPE is a keyboard instrument that produces shorthand and is often used by court reporters. A TINTYPE is an earlier-era photograph printed on tin.

A set of kettledrums in a band or orchestra is called a TIMPANI (also TYMPANI), and the drummer is a TYMPANIST. A TYMPANUM is, among other things, a drum. A TIMBREL is a tambourine or similar kind of sound apparatus, and TIMBRE is the characteristic quality of the sound produced by a musical instrument or a singer's voice.

Combining forms: *a-,* not; *arche-,* original, first; *logo-,* word; *proto-,* first, earliest form of; *steno-,* narrow, little; *stereo-,* solid.
Antonyms: *archetype, prototype*—copy, imitation, facsimile, duplicate; *atypical*—standard, normal, usual, common, familiar; *typical*—odd, irregular, unique, singular, unconventional, weird, uncharacteristic.

ULTRA, beyond: ULT

So you're in the market for a new car. You begin to flip through the pages of an upscale magazine and an advertisement in the center spread announcing the "daring new SK999 all-wheel drive **U*T*M*O*S*T**" jumps out at you. It is the **ULTimate** in luxury, beyond anything else ever engineered in the automotive world! And get this: *ALL FOR A REASONABLE $333 PER MONTH!* How about that!

And then you read the fine print at the bottom of the page, and what you discover there about the total price amidst the cloudy clauses strikes you as an **outrage,** offense, insult, or affront. In fact, you are so **outraged,** angered, provoked, and shocked that you consider writing a letter to the manufacturer and the dealer and the magazine to tell them and the rest of the world what an **outrageous,** shameless, flagrant, and immoral deception the advertisement is.

In time, as your emotions cool, you resume your search for the right car. Since the Utmost is unthinkable, you check out the other two makes on your list. First there's the **PenULTimate XKZ-54,** not quite the ultimate, but very close; better price, but not better enough. And then, at last, you get a good look at the **AntepenULTimate JG-142,** the one before the next to the last on your list.

Meanwhile, let's consider how words so different in meaning and appearance could possibly be members of the same family. According to Eric Partridge in his *Origins, A Short Etymological Dictionary of Modern English,* it came about like this: the Latin *ultra* turned into *ultre* when it moved into Old French; then over the years it passed through a series of evolutionary steps: first *outre* and then *ultrage,* followed by *oultrage,* and later *outrage.*

Two words other than outrage took part in that progression. **Outre** means bizarre, eccentric, freakish, odd, kooky, or peculiar. **ULTra** means beyond the usual, excessive, and extreme. It is most often used as a prefix attached to almost any base; thus we have extremes, such as ultracold–ultrahot, ultralarge–ultrasmall, and ultraconservative–ultraliberal.

A person who has an **ULTerior** motive is hiding something. ☞ *When Suzzi hung on to Buddy Bigbucks all evening, you knew she had an ulterior motive.*

An **ULTIMATUM** is a final, no-nonsense demand or proposal. ☞ *Only when Mugsy issued an ultimatum—Get lost or else!—did Putzi back off.*

Combining forms: *ante-*, before; *pen-*, almost.
Antonyms: *outraged*—calmed, soothed, pacified; *outrageous*—fair, just, reasonable, moderate; *outre*—ordinary, typical, familiar; *ulterior*—obvious, open, manifest; *ultimate*—least, minimum, first, beginning.

UMBRA, shadow: UMBRA

UMBRAGE means offense, resentment, pique, displeasure, antipathy, or bitterness. ☞ *I was insulted, and I felt umbrage.*

A person who is **UMBRAGEOUS** is inclined to take offense, tending to be belligerent and resentful. ☞ *Because we had been warned that Sam was sometimes umbrageous, we were wary of his hair-trigger temper.*

Umbrageous also means shady. ☞ *A majestic leafy oak, shaped much like an umbrella, can create an umbrageous setting for one to rest and cool off in.*

Umbrageous

An **UMBRA** is shade or shadow; it can also be, hence, a phantom or ghost. But it is in the field of astronomy that we most often see umbras and **PENUMBRAS**; they have to do with the shadows of sunspots and planets and lunar eclipses.

To **ADUMBRATE** is to foreshadow, hint, portend, and herald. ☞ *As I look back on it now, I can see that the problems at the office adumbrated his eventual breakdown.*

An **UMBLE** is a characteristic of certain flowering plants, and **UMBER** is a kind of natural earth used as a pigment, as in **RAW UMBER** and **BURNT UMBER**.

Additional English words related to the root: somber, sombrero.
Combining forms: *ad-*, toward; *pen-*, almost.
Antonyms: *umbrage*—cordiality, sympathy, good will, harmony.

UNDA, wave: UND

To **ABOUND** is to teem, flourish, **SUPERABOUND**, and thrive. ☞ *Malnutrition abounds among the people of that Third World country.*

To REDOUND is to result in, lead to, eventuate, cause, and affect. ☞ *What we as individuals do for our brothers will redound to the good of the community.*

An ABUNDANCE is profusion, sufficiency, plethora, surplus, or glut. ☞ *There isn't the abundance of drinking water now that there used to be.* The adjective ABUNDANT means ample, overflowing, teeming, profuse, and sufficient.

An INUNDATION is a flood, overflow, or deluge. ☞ *The lottery winner was swamped by an inundation of requests for help.* To INUNDATE is to flood, engulf, drench, overwhelm, and deluge. ☞ *The water that rose over the banks of the river inundated the farmers' fields.*

Something REDUNDANT is superfluous, unnecessary, extra, and wasteful. Redundant writing is repetitious, verbose, tautological, and reiterative. ☞ *It's a short, concise book, and never redundant.* A REDUNDANCY is a wordiness, pleonasm, verbiage, or circumlocution. ☞ *After that speech, Sen. Snort is a sure bet to win this decade's Redundancy Award.* Redundant phrases are common in everyday speech: the final end, past history, 4 P.M. this afternoon, repeat again, and close proximity, among others.

To SURROUND is to encircle, encompass, envelop, and circumscribe. ☞ *Brenda is the woman who's surrounded by flowers.* One's SURROUNDINGS are the environment, milieu, setting, atmosphere, or neighborhood. ☞ *Webb didn't take the job; he said the surroundings just didn't feel right to him.* It is also an adjective meaning neighboring, nearby, adjoining, and bordering. ☞ *The surrounding countryside is a pageant of colors in the fall.*

An UNDULATION is a wave-like motion. ☞ *At evening, casual flocks of pigeons make / Ambiguous undulations as they sink / Downward to darkness, on extended wings," wrote poet Wallace Stevens in "Sunday Morning" (1923).* To UNDULATE is to move in a wave-like motion. ☞ *The sound of a siren undulates in the distance, and overhead a flag undulates in the breeze.*

But not: *rebound* [*bombos,* a humming sound], bounce back.
Combining forms: *ab-,* away; *in-,* upon, over; *re-,* again, back; *sur-,* over, above.
Antonyms: *abundance*—scarcity, inadequacy, paucity, want, need; *abundant*—sparse, scarce, lacking, wanting; *redundancy*—shortage, sparseness, brevity, compactness; *redundant*—necessary, essential, indispensable, concise, terse.

UNGUERE, to anoint

Bible passages refer to precious and very precious OINTMENTS. In Ecclesiastes it is argued that "A good name is better than precious ointment." The baths of ancient Rome often contained a room called an UNCTUARIUM, where ointments or UNGUENTS or other oily liquids were applied. In the early 17th century Francis Bacon wrote in *Essays* that "the odors of ointments are more durable than those of flowers." They were used mainly for cosmetic purposes, beautifying the body as well as being soothing to the skin and pleasing to the nose. Today many ointments are employed medicinally, to help in the healing of burns, rashes, and scars. They are also called salves, balms, lotions, liniments, or emollients.

The *Random House Dictionary* describes an ointment as "a soft, UNCTUOUS preparation, often medicated, for application to the skin." Ointments and unguents are oily and greasy; so are certain edibles. ☞ *Their doctor told them to avoid unctuous foods.* People with unctuous personalities are thought to be excessively smooth, suave, sycophantic, smarmy, obsequious, and fawning. ☞ *The salesman was so unctuous, I quickly moved on to another booth.*

UNCTION is the act of ANOINTING, which is the rubbing, smearing, or sprinkling of an oily liquid as a part of a religious rite that consecrates, blesses, hallows, ordains, and sanctifies. In Shakespeare's *Macbeth* when Macduff reveals that King Duncan has been murdered, he cries out, "Confusion now hath made his masterpiece! / Most sacrilegious murder hath broke ope / The Lord's ANOINTED temple, and stole thence / The life o' the building." An anointed temple is holy, sacred, divine, consecrated, and blessed.

An additional English word related to the root: preen.
Combining form: *-arium,* a place for.
Antonyms: *unctuous*—blunt, frank, candid, sincere, independent, straightforward.

UTI, to use: USE, UTI

A few moments before Alice fell down the rabbit-hole and found herself in Wonderland, she said to herself, "What is the **USE** of a book without pictures or conversations?" *Her* "use," of course, meant worth, purpose, object, or point. It also means service, work, assistance, or enjoyment. ☞ *We got a lot of use out of that old jalopy.* As a verb it means to employ, operate, handle, and UTIlize. ☞ *Are you sure you know how to use a chain saw?* And it means to consume, expend, deplete, waste, and squander. ☞ *Owen used all his money to buy a watch that doesn't work.* It also means to exploit, manipulate, misuse, take advantage of, and handle. ☞ *We were outraged when Jack used Aunt Gayle's bonus to his own advantage.*

To get USEd to someone or something means to get accustomed to, hardened to, familiar with, and tolerant of. Usual refers to customary, expected, normal, typical, or habitual. The word used also indicates a former fact or state. ☞ *Sue used to be an extremely shy person. We used to go to the lake every summer.*

Used as an adjective means secondhand, worn, castoff, hand-me-down, threadbare, and shopworn. Today's used cars are sometimes advertised as previously owned, preUTIlized, hardly broken-in, and practically unUSEd. Some buyers have been heard to complain that their cars acted as if they had been ill-USEd and overUSEd, could no longer be reUSEd, and were now in a state of disUSE.

USEful books contain information that is helpful, beneficial, usable (also USEable), advantageous, UTIle, fruitful, UTIlitarian, and conducive. A USEless product or bit of advice is worthless, unusable (also unUSEable), futile, impractical, feckless, inept, and vain.

Use and usage are often interchangeable. ☞ *Even rough usage / use won't damage that furniture.* Synonyms are treatment, handling, care, operation, and manipulation.

But not when the word usage means custom, manner, habit, or vogue. ☞ *It's usage that governs who precedes whom at formal functions.* Nor in English class where (and when) usage or diction is the topic *du jour* and mention is made about which words and expressions are currently considered most preferable, acceptable, and effective among educated speakers. Is it snuck or sneaked? Dove or dived? Different from or different than?

Usually means customarily, mostly, for the most part, and as per usual. ☞ *We usually jog right after work.* Unusual means odd, atypical, abnormal, and uncommon. ☞ *"Excessive bail shall not be required nor excessive fines imposed, nor cruel and unusual punishment inflicted," Eighth Amendment to the Constitution.*

To usurp is to seize illegally (for one's own use), appropriate, wrest, arrogate, preempt, and infringe upon. ☞ *He's one of those who were in on the plan to usurp the authority of the committee chair.* The literal meaning of usury is "the use of money lent"; it is the practice of lending money at illegal and usually enormous rates of interest.

The public **UTI**LITIES we live with furnish our homes with electricity, gas, telephone; public transportation systems are similar in nature. **UTI**LITY means USEFULNESS, practicality, function, or advantage. ☞ *This neighborhood offers us the utility of a nearby school, church, medical clinic, and shopping strip.* As an adjective it means alternate, substitute, extra, auxiliary, and secondary. ☞ *Felix signed on with the Sox as their utility infielder.* A UTENSIL is an implement, tool, instrument, receptacle, or container, one having a useful purpose.

To AB**USE** is to harm, MIS**USE**, mistreat, hurt, and injure. ☞ *You abuse your new bike when you leave it out in the rain.* It is to speak insultingly, scold, berate, castigate, and denigrate. ☞ *It's a story about an old shrew who abused every person who wandered into the village.* Thus abuse is insults, criticism, cursing, invective, or vilification. ☞ *We refused to take any more of the man's abuse.* It is addiction or dependency. ☞ *They both need treatment for drug abuse.* ABUSIVE actions are hurtful, injurious, destructive, cruel, and improper. ☞ *We finally called the authorities regarding the man's abusive treatment of the stray dog.* Abusive language is defamatory, scurrilous, maligning, derogatory, and offensive. ☞ *Marshals finally removed the hecklers because of their abusive language.* ABUSAGE is a much milder word; it has to do with the improper use of words or ungrammatical language.

To DISAB**USE** is to correct, enlighten, set straight, and open the eyes of. ☞ *Hey, someone's got to disabuse Lana of even thinking about dating that guy.*

A PERUSAL is a close reading, scrutiny, examination, survey, or review. ☞ *The committee found nothing obscene in its perusal of the books in question.* To PER**USE** a text or similar is to read, study, scrutinize, or examine thoroughly and carefully. ☞ *Each member of the committee has perused each book.*

But not: *amuse* [*a-*, to + *muser,* to idle], entertain; *ruse* [F *ruser,* to repulse], trick.

Combining forms: *ab-,* away; *dis-,* apart, not; *ill-,* badly; *mis-,* wrongly; *over-,* too much; *per-,* before, thoroughly; *re-,* again; *-rp,* seize; *un-,* not.

Antonyms: *abuse*—care for, respect, praise, compliment, flatter, acclaim, extol; *abusive*—complimentary, courteous, respectful, supportive; *disabuse*—deceive, trick, mislead, fool; *unusual*—common, familiar, normal, routine, unremarkable, traditional, conventional; *use*—conserve, drawback, obstacle, detriment; *used*—brand-new, fresh, original, virgin; *useful*—

inapplicable, vain, worthless, unprofitable; *useless*—workable, fruitful, worthwhile, practical; *usual*—uncommon, exceptional, singular, sparse, unorthodox, novel, unique; *usurp*—relinquish, yield, surrender, renounce; *utilitarian*—visionary, impractical, utopian, worthless; *utility*—futility, uselessness, original, basic, essential.

V

VACARE, to be empty: VAC, VOID

Toward the end of a long day on the road, weary **VAC**ATIONING travelers often begin to look for **VAC**ANCY signs on the fronts of motels. On holiday weekends their search for a **VAC**ANT room might be in VAIN. When they do have a choice, they might be well advised to A**VOID** motels whose signs flash **VAC**UITY, a VANITY word sometimes used to impress unsuspecting travelers.

A vacuity is also an empty, **VAC**UOUS remark, a platitude, cliché, banality, or truism, the A**VOID**ANCE of which often requires turning a deaf ear. "Have a nice day," "How ya doin'?," and "Hot enough for you?" are empty phrases that seem almost UNA**VOID**ABLE in daily life.

A **VAC**UUM is an unfilled or unoccupied space; Bishop Desmond Tutu of South Africa once explained in *The Christian Science Monitor* (1984) that he had become "a leader by default, only because nature does not allow a vacuum." Because he stepped into the **VOID** and furthered the cause of peace, he was awarded the Nobel Prize in 1984.

We **VAC**ATE the apartment when we move, and we E**VAC**UATE the area when we hear flood warnings, becoming E**VAC**UEES.

To VAUNT is to boast about, flaunt, show off, and gasconade. ☞ *How long will Frankston continue to vaunt his promotion?* VAUNTED is an adjective meaning boasted about and praised to the skies. A vain person is conceited, stuffed with VAIN-GLORY, vanity, egotism, and narcissism. A VAINGLORIOUS person is boastful, egotistical, haughty, and narcissistic.

As adjectives, DE**VOID** and void are usually interchangeable. The latter, however, is also a noun. ☞ *When Ma left, Pa felt a great void in his life.* NULL AND VOID means not valid or without force or effect. ☞ *The judge voided their licenses; they were then null and void.*

But not: *vaccine* [*vacca,* cow], inoculation virus; *vacillate* [*vacillare,* to sway to and fro], to waver.
Combining forms: *a-,* out; *de-,* from; *e-,* out; *un-,* not.
Antonyms: *avoid*—meet, face, confront, approach, solicit; *devoid*—full, fraught, replete; *vacancy*—profusion, fullness, plenitude; *vacant*—occupied, alert, intelligent, full; *vacuity*—fullness, content; *vacuous*—bright, attentive, knowledgeable;

vacuum—substance, matter; *vain*—humble, modest, practical, productive; *vanity*—humility, modesty, diffidence, self-effacement; *vaunt*—disparage, detract, repress, suppress; *void*—complete, occupied, valid, uphold, fill, ingest.

VARIUS, bent, changeable, crooked, diverse, manifold, speckled: VARI

As is obvious, this Latin root has **VARI**OUS meanings. But whether that results in a great **VARI**ETY of words is open to question. Back in the Middle Ages, in the lands and times dominated by dukes and duchesses and kings and queens, spotted animal fur was the trim of choice on the elaborate ceremonial robes of the royals. The fur came from ermines or weasels and was called MINIVER, literally, "small fur." The pattern of spots on such animals usually **VARI**ES from one to another. That's just the way they develop their coats, i.e., **VARI**ABLE, unpredictable, inconstant, and VARYING.

VARICOLORED or **VARI**EGATED houseplants are the ones that are higher priced because their leaves have streaks or specks of white or yellow on them. They are **VARI**ANTS, deviations from the normal, UNVARYING, usual, and ordinary all-green leaves.

A **VARI**ATION is a change, modification, departure, innovation, or metamorphosis. ☞ *The poor chap needs a bit of variation from the dull routine of his life.* **VARI**ANCE is used to express the degree of difference. ☞ *In this experiment we found a daily variance of ten degrees centigrade.* It also refers to an official permit to do something usually forbidden. ☞ *We got a variance from city hall to put up a larger sign.* To be AT VARIANCE is to be in disagreement. ☞ *Everything we did was at variance with the rules.*

Additional English words related to the root: invariable, prevaricate.
But not: *varicose* [*varix,* swollen vein], swollen, as a vein.
Combining forms: *-gate,* to do; *mini-,* small; *ver,* fur, from *varius,* speckled, partly colored.
Antonyms: *variable*—fixed, predictable, immutable, rigid; *variance*—similarity, correspondence, accord, unison, agreement; *variation*—uniformity, permanence, sameness; *variegated*—monotone, monochromatic; *variety*—homogeneity, uniformity, conformity; *various*—identical, alike, same.

VERBUM, word: VERB

Sam Goldwyn, the legendary Hollywood producer, is reported to have once said, "A **VERBAL** contract isn't worth the paper it is written on." Since verbal means oral, spoken, expressed, stated, and articulated, it definitely is *not* written, which may well have been Mr. Goldwyn's point.

To **VERBALIZE** is to say something in words. ☞ *I've got a picture in my mind of what I want this invention to look like, but I just can't verbalize it.* Both **VERBIAGE** and **VERBOSITY** mean wordiness, long-windedness, blather, or garrulity. ☞ *Poor Dr. Sanger. He never realized that he was suffering from a case of acute verbiage / verbosity.*

Someone who is **VERBOSE** is long-winded, loquacious, vociferous, garrulous, and effusive. ☞ *It probably was an amusing story, but the mayor was so verbose that most of us lost the point.* To **VERBIGERATE** is to babble, jabber, and repeat meaningless words and phrases endlessly. ☞ *The deposed dictator pathetically verbigerated ideas that had lost their meaning years before.* A **VERBALIST** is skilled in the use of words, but often at the expense of ideas and reality.

VERBATIM means word for word, literal, and in precisely the same words. ☞ *Ed's lunchtime routine is to give us a verbatim report of everything his kids said at breakfast.* But if a word for word account puts you to sleep, consider the French phrase *verbatim et literatim,* meaning "word for word *and* letter for letter."

A **VERB** denotes being or action. A **PRO-VERB** is a word that can substitute for a verb; its function is similar to that of a pronoun. In the following sentence, the word do acts as a pro-verb: Our neighbors never mow their lawn, but we do. An **ADVERB** is a word that modifies a verb, an adjective, another adverb, or a clause. It also expresses some relation of time, manner, place, or degree.

A **PROVERB** is a short, popular saying, sometimes expressing wisdom. It is also called an adage, maxim, axiom, aphorism, apothegm, or epigram. Dorothy Parker's "Men seldom make passes / At girls who wear glasses" is considered a modern (1920s) proverb, although the invention of the contact lens diminished some of its punch. The book of Proverbs of the Bible contains wisdom that still packs a wallop, to wit: "Where there is no vision, the people perish."

PROVERBIAL is the word of choice when referring to something that has *been* the subject of a proverb, such as, "Too many cooks spoil the broth." ☞ *The officials were like the proverbial cooks: because there were too many of them milling around, they spoiled the pageant.*

Proverbial also refers to something that has become common or legendary. ☞ *The boss lost his proverbial temper once again.*

Combining forms: *ad-*, to; *-gerate,* to carry on; *pro-*, before.
Antonyms: *verbalize*—suppress, inhibit, contain, repress; *verbatim*—inexact, imprecise, garbled, distorted; *verbiage, verbosity*—terseness, precision, concision, laconism; *verbose*—concise, laconic, terse, succinct, pithy, curt, reticent, brusque.

VERERI, to fear, feel awe: REVERE

To **REVERE** someone or something is to honor, respect, idolize, adore, and worship. ☞ *Joseph reveres his parents. We learned to revere the wisdom of our Founding Fathers and the Constitution they created.*

REVEREnce is devotion, adoration, veneration, deep respect, adulation, or obeisance. ☞ *The Native American, wrote Interior Secretary Stewart Udall in* The Quiet Crisis *(1963), had "a reverence for the life-giving earth" coupled with the understanding that "the land was alive to his loving touch, and he, its son, was brother to all creatures."* The word is sometimes used as a verb. ☞ *The land has been reverenced throughout their history.*

REVEREnd means worthy of being revered; it is a title prefixed to the name of a member of the clergy: the Reverend Lynn Plante, the Very Reverend H.R. Blodget, the Right Reverend Jan Miller, or the Right Reverend Monsignor Thom Bennett.

REVEREnt means worshipful, pious, **REVEREntial,** humble, respectful, and obeisant. ☞ *The family gave a reverent contribution to the church.* **REVEREntly** means piously, religiously, devoutly, respectfully, and adoringly. ☞ *"[Matrimony] is not by any to be entered into unadvisedly or lightly; but reverently, discreetly, advisedly, soberly, and in the fear of God,"* The Book of Common Prayer *(1928).*

IrREVEREnce is disrespect, disregard, skepticism, or impudence. ☞ *The children treated their elders with complete irreverence.* Irreverence is also impiety, blasphemy, profaneness, ungodliness, or sacrilege. ☞ *The priest chastised the man for his irreverence.* **IrREVEREnt** means contemptuous, mocking, sneering, and derisive.

But not: *reverie,* [*rabere,* to rage], daydream.
Combining forms: *ir-*, not; *re-*, again.
Antonyms: *irreverence*—veneration, piety, homage, deference; *irreverent*—awed, reverential, submissive,

idolatrous; *revere*—scorn, disdain, despise, dishonor; *reverend*—contemptible, base, unworthy, infamous; *reverence*—disrespect, contempt, scorn, mockery, hatred; *reverent*—scornful, blasphemous, disdainful, impious.

VERUS, true: VER

As he pointed at the accused sitting across from him in Judge Smith's courtroom, Will Brown **aVERred,** swore, attested, contended, and avowed, "I saw that **VERy** man enter the building on the evening of June 30. I know of a number of people who can **VERify,** corroborate, substantiate, and confirm my being there at that hour."

"Not only that," he said as he pulled a paper from his pocket, "I have this photograph of the scene that I took with my own camera. I now offer this as further **VERification,** validation, proof, and evidence.

At that moment the judge banged his gavel loudly. "I believe the witness is completely **VERacious,** honest, candid, and truthful. I find the other guy guilty!"

The courtroom erupted into a **VERitable,** real, genuine, and demonstrable circus of joy!

The judge had no doubt of Will Brown's **VERacity,** honesty, candor, and sincerity.

Additional English words related to the root: verdict, verity, verisimilitude.
But not: *asseverate* [*severus,* grave, serious], declare earnestly; *aversion* [*a-,* away + *vertere,* to turn], strong feeling of dislike; *vermin* [*vermis,* worm], obnoxious pests.
Combining forms: *a-,* to; *-fication,* a making; *-fy,* to make; *-similitude,* a likeness.
Antonyms: *veracious*—deceitful, lying, dishonest, mendacious; *veracity*—duplicity, mendacity, deceitfulness, lying; *veritable*—counterfeit, fake, fraudulent; *verity*—inaccuracy, lie, error, fiction, falsehood.

VESTIS, garment: VEST

Today's **VEST** is commonly a close-fitting, sleeveless, waist-length item of clothing, but three hundred years ago in England the vests men wore were similar to the long cassocks or **VESTments** worn by some members of the clergy. These are customarily kept in a room called a **VESTry,** which in the Episcopal church is also the name of a committee elected by the congregation. At one time **VEST**ure was clothing and garments, but now it is anything else that covers; in law it is whatever covers or grows on the land except trees. James Baldwin said in his *Notes of a Native Son,* "The making of an American begins at that point where he himself . . . adopts the vesture of his adopted land"; his vesture is the style, the language, or the nature of that land.

When we in**VEST** money in a business venture, we hope that it will prove to be a profitable in**VEST**ment. When we become involved in a charitable undertaking, we invest our time and energy in it. ☞ *I've got too big an investment in this amusement park to let it fall through now.* When we are installed in an office or position, we are in**VEST**ed with certain powers and responsibilities. ☞ *The president is invested with the power of veto by the Constitution.* To disin**VEST** is to reduce or do away with capital investment, as in an industry or an area which then becomes a disin**VEST**ment.

The ceremony of being installed in an office or of receiving a distinguished honor is called an in**VEST**iture, and it is often a formal and elaborate affair. A di**VEST**iture, however, is not so joyous an occasion, for to di**VEST** people of their property or rights is to strip them away. ☞ *The court ordered them divested of all their stock holdings.*

A **VEST**ed interest is one in which a person has a personal stake. ☞ *Would Craig like to see the biology textbooks changed? You better believe he would. With all the stock he owns in Bio-Sci Publishers, Inc., he has a vested interest.*

A trans**VEST**ite is one who wears the clothing of the opposite sex. Newspaper columnist Jimmy Breslin alluded to some transvestites he mingled with one night when he wrote, "Precious was one of a large number of people on the street, many of whom appeared to be women; some, like Precious, actually were."

A tra**VEST**y is sometimes a joke, farce, parody, or caricature. But it can also convey a sense of shame, mockery, perversion, or disgrace. ☞ *The poor migrant workers' treatment by the district attorney was a travesty of justice.*

To re**VEST** or rein**VEST** is to reinstate or put one back in office. ☞ *The king was revested after the civil war ended.* To revet is to put a new face of stone or concrete or other material on the bank or embankment of a canal, dike, or river, etc.; the word's literal meaning is "to reclothe."

But not: *investigate* [*vestigium,* footprint], look into; *vestibule* [*vestibulum*], entrance hall; *vestige* [*vestigium*], trace.

Combining forms: *di-,* from; *dis-,* do the opposite; *in-,* in; *tra-,* over; *trans-,* over.
Antonyms: *divest*—confer, empower, sanction; *invest*—withdraw, deny, withhold; *vest*—unfrock, expose, uncover, lay bare; *vested*—contingent, occasional, provisional.

VETUS, old, long-standing: VET

VETERINARY medicine is the branch that treats animals, small and large, but ordinarily those of the domesticated variety. **VET**ERINARIANS, however, do often specialize, those in metropolitan areas generally treating cats and dogs and other household pets, while those in or around smaller towns taking in large farm animals as well.

To **VET** is to examine and treat, as a medical doctor or a veterinarian, while others who vet, verify and check something for accuracy, authenticity, or validity. ☞ *The sports editor vetted the young reporter's story. We suggested that our attorney vet the deed just to make sure.* A vet may be a veterinarian or a **VET**ERAN.

An IN**VET**ERATE liar is a pathological, habitual, confirmed, and hopeless prevaricator. Something that goes on and on and on, such as a disease or habit or feeling can be called inveterate, too, but chronic works just as well.

Combining forms: *in-,* in, with the sense of "very."
Antonyms: *inveterate*—sporadic, occasional, transitory, rare; *veteran*—novice, neophyte, beginner, inexperienced.

VIA, way, road: VIA, VIO, VIUM

When we travel from one place to another **VIA** a third place, we are going "by way of." ☞ *They flew from Chicago to Copenhagen via the North Pole.*

But in an Italian city most of the streets are called Via or **VIA**LE. ☞ *In Rome we walked down Viale Manzoni to where it intersects Via Marulana.* Perhaps the world's most famous road is the VIA APPIA (the Appian Way) built in 312 B.C. from Rome to Brindisi, a distance of some 350 miles. The road that Jesus took to Calvary is known as the VIA DOLOROSA (from *dolorous,* sorrowful; Sorrowful Road).

A VIA MEDIA is a mean between two extremes, a middle course. ☞ *The mediation board was determined to find the via media between the company and the union.*

Scholars in the Middle Ages felt that there was a fourfold way to knowledge: arithmetic, astronomy, geometry, and music [QUADRI**VIUM**, four ways], and a threefold way to eloquence, fluency, and oratory: grammar, logic, and rhetoric [**TRIVIUM,** three ways].

The Latin *trivium* also meant "crossroads, an intersection or junction of three roads," a convenient place for people to meet to discuss the latest news and to catch up on the current gossip and neighborhood **TRIVIA.** **OBVIOUSLY,** much of the chitchat was **TRIVIAL,** petty, and piddling, the trifles and **TRIVIALITIES** that we sometimes call small change, small potatoes, and small talk.

PERVIOUS soil is absorbent, permeable, and porous; **IMPERVIOUS** material is sealed, impenetrable, and waterproof. A person who seems impervious to aging or criticism is immune to, unaffected by, and protected against. ☞ *No one seemed impervious to the family's anguish as the tragic story unfolded before their eyes.*

To **DEVIATE** is to wander, differ, digress, and defect. ☞ *By the time she had finished her first college semester, Vi had deviated completely from her parents' lifestyle.* **DEVIANT** social behavior is that which departs from the accepted norm. ☞ *The dean told the freshman that their deviant conduct would not be tolerated, and he charged them with being deviants and deviates.* A **DEVIATION** is a departure from a standard. ☞ *Deviations from the rules will be dealt with severely.* **DEVIOUS** methods are dishonest, deceitful, sly, and foxy, whether in business, politics, law, or evangelism. A person who has had **PREVIOUS** encounters with the likes of con men will be in the best position to **OBVIATE,** ward off, discourage, and prevent an **OBVIOUS,** unmistakable, apparent, evident, and patent scam.

To **CONVEY** a message is to tell, relate, and communicate. ☞ *Kindly convey my best wishes to your family.* To convey a package is to transport, carry, and move. ☞ *The oil is conveyed here by pipeline.* To convey a title to a piece of property is to grant, bequeath, and transfer. ☞ *I hereby convey to you my golf shoes, socks, and tees.* The **CONVEYOR** is the person or instrument that does the conveying, the **CONVEYANCE** is the method of communication or transportation.

If it is merchandise, an **INVOICE** may be attached. If it is the transfer of an army unit to another post, the vehicles may form a long **CONVOY.** If it is to be shipped by freighter to an **ENVOY** at an overseas embassy, it should be readied for a long **VOYAGE.** If it is to go by rail, it will travel across a number of **VIADUCTS.**

But not: *viable* [*vita,* life], practicable.
Combining forms: *con-,* together; *de-,* from; *-duct,* to lead; *en-,* on; *im-,* not; *in-,* on; *ob-,* before; *per-,* through; *pre-,* before; *tri-,* three.

Antonyms: *deviate*—follow, conform, comply, continue; *devious*—forthright, truthful, reliable, open, frank; *impervious*—vulnerable, susceptible, exposed; *obviate*—necessitate, compel, make essential, cause, permit; *obvious*—obscure, ambiguous, abstruse, concealed, unapparent; *previous*—later, following, subsequent, opportune, timely; *trivia*—basics, essentials, fundamentals, substance; *trivial*—momentous, vital, crucial, important, unusual, exceptional.

VICIS, change, instead of: VIC

In the Church of England **VICARS** are persons serving as parish priests in place of the rector; in essence, they are deputies or substitutes. In a larger sense, all Christian clergy serve as God's vicars on earth, as, in the Roman Catholic church, the pope is referred to as the vicar of Christ. A vicar lives at a **VICARAGE**, a residence that in other churches might be called a parsonage, manse, rectory, or presbytery.

The **VICISSITUDES** of life are the changes, the ups and downs, or the variations in one's fortune. ☞ *Despite the extraordinary vicissitudes of their married lives, the two stayed in love and together for more than fifty years.*

When Emily Dickinson, the nineteenth-century poet who spent most of her life secluded in her home, wrote, "I never saw a Moor— / I never saw the Sea— / Yet know I how the Heather looks / And what a Billow be," she demonstrated what a **VICARIOUS** experience is: she knew of the moor, the sea, the heather, and the billow through the eyes and other senses of people who had known them firsthand. When we read a story or watch a play or movie, we are participating in the experiences of one or more of the characters **VICARIOUSLY**.

The term **VICE VERSA** means in the opposite order, the other way around, or in reverse order from the stated. ☞ *I would like my soup before my salad, if you please, and not vice versa.* The combining form *vice-* also means instead of, deputy, or substitute; thus we have vice-admirals, vice-chairpersons, vice-presidents, and, elsewhere, viceroys.

But not: *vice* [*vitium,* a fault], evil, sin; *vicennial* [*vicen,* twenty], occurring once every twenty years; *vicinity* [*vicinus,* near], neighborhood; *vicious* [*vitium*], malicious.
Combining form: *versa,* turn.
Antonyms: *vicarious*—direct, firsthand, personal, own, proper; *vicissitudes*—stability, constancy.

VIGILARE, to watch: VEIL, VIG

In 1791 an Irish judge in Dublin named John Curran said, "The condition upon which God hath given liberty to man is eternal **VIG**ILANCE," meaning heed, caution, prudence, or attention. Like the sentry at the gate, those who prize liberty must be **VIG**ILANT, watchful, alert, wary, circumspect, and attentive.

But that assumes one works within the law. **VIG**ILANTES take the law into their own hands, often in avenging a wrong, and what is known as vigilante justice is sometimes violent and without warning. Vigilante committees terrorized blacks and abolitionists in the South before and during the Civil War, as well as establishing their own kind of justice in the rough and tumble era during the westward expansion. In many respects the iniquities were reminiscent of what happened—legally—during the reign of terror in Salem, Massachusetts, in and before 1692, in which more than 150 people, mostly women, were charged with witchcraft; twenty were executed.

SUR**VEIL**LANCE is a form of vigilance, sometimes carried out by tailing, tracking, or trailing. ☞ *The suspects were kept under surveillance on an around-the-clock schedule.* SUR**VEIL**LANT guards are expected to keep close watch and maintain their **VIG**IL, a watch or period of watchful attention.

Vigil candles are kept burning in churches in front of icons and shrines, and in some churches vigils are services on the eve of a festival. The vigil flame over the grave of former president John Fitzgerald Kennedy in Arlington National Cemetery is never allowed to go out.

RE**VEIL**LE is the military signal to awaken, to assemble; once awake, the personnel are expected to remain vigilant.

> **But not:** *veil* [*velum,* a salt], cover.
> **Combining forms:** *re-,* again; *sur-,* over.
> **Antonyms:** *vigilance*—negligence, carelessness, laxity, inattention; *vigilant*—remiss, unwary, trusting, heedless.

VILLA, farmhouse: VILLA

Yesteryear's **VILLA** was a farmstead, a country house; by the time Rome fell in A.D. 476 the word meant "village." Modern American cities bear the name today; Florida's Jacksonville is, literally, (Andrew) Jackson's town; Kentucky's Louisville was named for King Louis XVI of France.

The serfs of the age of feudalism in medieval Europe were known as **VILLEINS**, some of whom were free, some of whom were bound in service to a lord; those left occupied a middle ground, neither free nor slave. Whatever their station, as members of the lower classes, the villeins, being persons of uncouth mind and manners, were looked down upon by people of means.

Yet in time there came from the peasants of the villages the creation of a rustic part song called a **VILLANELLA** and sung without accompaniment, as well as a short poem of fixed form given the name **VILLANELLE.**

Over the centuries spellings and the attitudes changed, and the simple villeins of the past were undeservedly and unwittingly transformed into **VILLAINS** and **VILLAINESSES.** Had this alteration been a deliberately **VILLAINOUS,** fiendish, criminal, or cruel act, one might have accused the perpetrators of **VILLAINY,** evil, infamy, or wickedness, but etymological changes are neither intentional nor controllable; they are, instead, the results of an evolutionary process.

And so as the villas multiplied, they consolidated into **VILLAGES,** most of which eventually qualified for Zip Code numbers. The "Village Blacksmith" (1839) may no longer toil under Henry Wadsworth Longfellow's "spreading chestnut tree" and Marshall McLuhan's "global village" from *The Gutenberg Galaxy* (1962) may not yet have truly materialized, but one aspect still hangs on: the community's inhabitants still take pride in calling themselves **VILLAGERS.**

Antonyms: *villainous*—heroic, saintly, moral, humane; *villainy*—virtue, benefit, good deed.

VIR, man: VIR

Even a brief study of the Latin root *vir* throws considerable light on our social history. For starters let's put the spotlight on **VIRTUE:** Alexander Pope wrote in *An Essay on Man,* "Know then this truth, enough for man to know,/'virtue alone is happiness below.' " Benjamin Franklin followed that up with this advice in *On Early Marriages:* "Be in general **VIRTUOUS,** and you will be happy." What is of interest here is that our word for this most esteemed quality stems from *man,* almost as though it can be possessed by him alone.

Next, we find that virtue's blood brother is **VIRILITY,** that much sought-after property that includes machismo, force, vigor, or browniness. For to be **VIRILE** is to be macho, muscular, masculine, mighty, and manly.

A **VIR**TUOSO is a male artist, genius, prodigy, whiz, wizard, or master, particularly in the performing arts. A female is a **VIR**TUOSA.

VIRTUOSITY means polish, artistry, accomplishment, expertise, or bravura. It is a **VIR**TUAL star that any and all can reach for; synonyms are practical, understood, effective. And consider a TRIUM**VIR**, a person who joins with two others in an office, commission, management team, or CEO TRIUM**VIR**ATE.

VIRILISM refers to a female disorder that results in, among other undesirable masculine features, a deep voice. And a **VIR**AGO is a woman like Washington Irving's Dame Van Winkle, Rip's "termagant wife," a loud-voiced, ill-tempered, scolding shrew to whom Rip was "an obedient henpecked husband."

> **But not:** *virgin* [*virgo,* a maiden], pure, chaste, pristine, untarnished maiden; *viridity* [*viridis,* green], greenness; *virulent* [*virus,* slime, poison], noxious, lethal.
> **Combining form:** *trium-,* three.
> **Antonyms:** *virile*—spineless, weak, impotent, effeminate; *virtual*—direct, express, explicit, definite; *virtue*—sin, curse, weakness, evil, vice, promiscuity; *virtuosity*—mediocrity, ineptness, amateurishness, dullness; *virtuoso*—tyro, beginner, neophyte, novice; *virtuous*—immoral, wicked, corrupt, sinful, venal.

VIVERE, to live: VIT, VIV

CON**VIV**IAL people are lively, **VIV**ACIOUS, gregarious, jolly, and affable. ☞ *It was a good tour group because everyone was convivial.* CON**VIV**IALITY refers to liveliness, sociability, **VIV**ACIOUSNESS, affability, and cordiality.

Vivacious

To RE**VIV**E someone or something is to bring it back to life, to reanimate, RE**VIT**ALIZE, restore, RE**VIV**IFY, and reawaken. ☞ *The cold water revived us. Our conversation revived my interest in Robert Frost's poetry. The theater group is reviving some of the old slapstick comedies for the festival.*

A RE**VIV**AL is a renewal, RE**VIT**ALIZATION, renaissance, rebirth, awakening, or rediscovery. ☞ *The revival tent* *will be on the fairgrounds. The President called for a revival of our spirit of brotherhood. The market's revival surprised the economists.*

To SURVIVE literally means "to live beyond." In his Inaugural Address in 1961, President John F. Kennedy said, "Let the word go forth . . . that we shall pay any price, bear any burden, meet any hardship, support any friend, oppose any foe to assure the survival and the success of liberty." A SURVIVALIST is a person who makes preparations to survive (live beyond) a coming catastrophe such as an atomic holocaust.

A VIABLE seed is one that is capable of living; some seeds that have been sealed in permafrost have remained viable for 10,000 years. A viable plan is one that is workable, practical, sensible, and feasible. ☞ *I like the plan, but I have these nagging doubts about whether it's really viable.*

VIANDS are foods: a century ago poet Eugene Field wrote in "The Bottle and the Bird," "When I demanded of my friend what viands he preferred,/ He quoth; 'A large cold bottle, and a small hot bird!' " Today it usually refers to choice dishes fit for a gourmet. VICTUALS (also VITTLES, which is the way it is pronounced) are foods and provisions. ☞ *"The German dictator," Great Britain's Winston Churchill said in a 1938 speech, referring to Adolf Hitler and his designs upon Europe, "instead of snatching his victuals from the table, has been content to have them served to him country by country."*

A VIPER is a snake, so called because long ago it was thought to be VIVIPAROUS, that is, giving birth to live young rather than laying eggs. It didn't and doesn't, but it is still VIPEROUS or venomous. Human beings who are false, spiteful, mean, and treacherous are still called vipers, and catty, nasty gossips are still said to have VIPERINE tongues.

When one applies for a job, a brief biographical sketch or resume may prove helpful; common names for one of these are VITA, VITAE, and CURRICULUM VITAE, literally "course of life." A person who is VITAL is lively, dynamic, vibrant, vigorous, vivacious and spirited. ☞ *When the Jordan family moved here, our community gained several vital citizens.* It also means important, critical, crucial, serious, and essential. ☞ *This health care bill is one of the most vital issues Congress has faced in this decade.* Our vital signs are our blood pressure, pulse rate, body temperature, and whatever else the doctor can check or probe. Our VITALS are those bodily organs that are essential to life, such as the brain, heart, liver, lungs, or stomach. Millions of people take millions of VITAMINS everyday.

VITALITY is vigor, exuberance, energy, or strength. ☞ *Now there's a person who exudes vim, vigor, and vitality.* To VITALIZE something is to energize, enliven, invigorate, and quicken.

AQUAVIT (also **AKVAVIT**), a drink of the Scandinavian countries, means "water of life," as does **AQUA VITAE.**

VIVA! is an exclamation or shout meaning "Life!" or "Long life!" In European countries a viva or **VIVA VOCE** (the living voice) is the name of the oral part of a university examination. A **BON VIVANT** is a person who savors the luxuries of life; literally, it is "good living."

Vivacious and convivial people are noted for their elan, **VIVACITY,** spirit, and animation. **VIVID** colors are intense, bright, rich, and florid, and, sometimes, garish, loud, and showy. ☞ *You can't miss Brenda; she'll be the one in the dreadfully vivid dress.* A vivid image is sharp, distinct, graphic, and clear. ☞ *I have a vivid mental picture of our first meeting there on the Spanish steps in Rome.* A vivid imagination may be creative, inventive, fruitful, and prolific. ☞ *Stephen's vivid fantasies are second only to Edgar Allan Poe's.* To **VIVIFY** is to enliven, animate, inspire, and exhilarate, as well as to make more bright, clear, and sharp. ☞ *Marti says that sometimes her dreams vivify scenes that would be dull and dreary if they were to really occur.*

VIVISECTION is the dissection of the living body of an animal for medical research; Charles Darwin, the English naturalist, felt that the practice "is justifiable for real investigations on physiology; but not for mere . . . curiosity." Other scientists hold to the idea that animals should be either free to roam or, if the subjects of research, be kept in **VIVARIUMS,** enclosures where conditions simulate their natural environments.

But not: *vitiate* [*vibum,* blemish, debase, invalidate]; *vitriolic* [*vitrum,* glass], caustic, scathing.
Combining forms: *con-,* together; *-parous,* giving birth to; *re-,* again, back; *-section,* cutting; *sur-,* beyond.
Antonyms: *convivial*—unsociable, reticent, taciturn, serious, solemn; *conviviality*—sobriety, reticence, dourness, taciturnity; *viable*—unworkable, impracticable, ineffectual, futile; *vital*—lifeless, inanimate, unimportant, superficial, lethargic, listless; *vitality*—inertia, apathy, weakness, torpor, lifelessness; *vitalize*—check, discourage, dampen, destroy, kill; *vivacious*—listless, lifeless, boring, melancholy, spiritless, sad; *vivid*—pale, hazy, dull, colorless, vague, indistinct, nondescript.

VOCARE, to call: VOX; voice: VOC, VOK

It is a sunny but chilly April day in New England, and Robert Frost the poet is chopping firewood when two "hulking tramps" not long out of the lumber camps come by. They want to do for pay what the poet is doing out of love, blending his job—what had to be done—with his hobby—what he really enjoyed doing. As he says in "Two Tramps in Mud Time," "My object in living is to unite / My aVOCation and my VOCation / As my two eyes make one in sight."

When he turns down the men's offer, he may well proVOKe, anger, irritate, and nettle them; they may think that he "had no right to play / With what was [their] work for gain." But it is not, it seems, sufficient proVOCation, cause, or stimulus to eVOKe, arouse, or induce anger.

They are not, after all, proVOCateurs, i.e., agitators or troublemakers. Nor does their brief exchange of words become VOCiferous, clamorous, noisy, blatant, or obstreperous, with one side or the other VOCiferating, shouting, crying, bawling, and yelling at the tops of their lungs.

ProVOCative means stimulating, challenging, and interesting. It also means sensual, alluring, tantalizing, and seductive. ☞ *I feel the movie's too provocative for young kids.* EVOCative refers to call forth, elicit, and summon.

To conVOKe is to call together, as an assembly or conVOCation. To inVOKe is to beg, appeal, and pray for something. ☞ *The condemned man invoked God's mercy.* It also means to call forth. ☞ *The widow of the great magician Houdini tried in vain to invoke his spirit.* An inVOCation is a prayer.

To reVOKe a driver's license is to cancel, annul, void, and invalidate it. If such a reVOCation is for only a short period, it is possible that it would be simply annoying and bothersome. But if the directive or order is declared irreVOCable, unalterable, immutable, and unchanged, it may well be calamitous or disastrous. If the decision is to be appealed, one must consider engaging a competent adVOCate from a reliable law firm to plead, argue, or fight for his or her innocence. A devil's advocate is one who champions a cause or a point of view for the sake of argument or to make others think about it. ☞ *Hey! Back off! I was just playing the devil's advocate to show you what you're likely to be up against!*

In times of stress one hopes, of course, to be avouched or vouched for by vouchers, meaning character witnesses or solid citizens who do not equiVOCate but, instead, swear in unequiVOCal language to one's honesty and integrity. It also helps to have vox populi on one's side, i.e., the voice of the people or popular opinion.

Additional English words related to the root: vocabulary, vocal.
Combining forms: *a-*, away; *ad-*, to; *con-*, together; *e-*, out; *equi-*, equal; *-fer*, to carry; *in-*, on; *ir-*, not; *pro-*, forth; *re-*, back; *un-*, not.
Antonyms: *advocate*—oppose, counter; *equivocal*—precise, explicit, clear; *irrevocable*—changeable, variable; *provocative*—dull, unstimulating, uninteresting; *provoke*—calm, ease, please; *unequivocal*—ambiguous, enigmatic, noncommital; *vocation*—distraction, diversion, leisure pursuit; *vociferous*—quiet, reticent, still, silent.

VORARE, to devour: VOR

One may DEVOUR books by the dozens, delighting in them, soaking them up, feasting on them, and thoroughly enjoying and appreciating them; one can also drink in and devour the beauty of the sunrise on a spring morning. If you're really hungry, you may devour your food by wolfing it down, stuffing it in, gobbling it up, or attacking it as if it might try to escape.

A **VOR**ACIOUS eater might be greedy, hoggish, and piggish. A voracious business competitor might be avaricious, grasping, and covetous. A voracious lover might be intemperate, uncontrolled, and unappeasable. But a voracious reader of historical novels or romances or collector of old bottles or seashells will not be likely to offend or harm anyone. Some folks even have a voracious love of life.

CARNI**VOR**OUS animals are meat-eating. Bears, cats, dogs, seals, and weasels make up the order of CARNI**VOR**ES. HERBI**VOR**OUS animals, such as deer and cattle, are plant-eating; INSECTI**VOR**OUS ones, such as moles, are insect-eating and ignore the poison some gardeners place in their runs; PISCI**VOR**OUS creatures are fish-eating. OMNI**VOR**OUS beings have broad appetites; they eat both animals and plants and will read just about any kind of book they can get their hands on.

But not: *vortex* [*vertere*, to turn], a whirlpool.
Combining forms: *carni-*, meat; *de-*, down; *herbi-*, plants; *omni-*, all; *pisci-*, fish.
Antonyms: *voracious*—fussy, delicate, satisfied, moderate, undemanding, temperate.

VOVERE, to vow, pledge, wish: VOT, VOW

When we **VOTE**, whether for dogcatcher, president, or other **VOTABLE** issues, as we pull the lever on the **VOTING** machine or mark our ballot with pen or pencil, we are expressing our wishes and exercising our rights. Amendments to our Constitution state that "the right of citizens of the United States to vote shall not be denied or abridged . . . on account of race, color, or previous condition of servitude" (Fifteenth Amendment).

Recent legislation such as the **MOTOR-VOTER** legislation has reduced the numbers of **VOTELESS** citizens. When **VOTE-GETTERS** "appeal to 'Every intelligent **VOTER**,' " wrote newspaper columnist Franklin P. Adams in *Nods and Becks* (1944), "they mean everybody who is going to vote for them."

A **VOTARY** is a fan, admirer, enthusiast, or **DEVOTEE**. ☞ *Renata is a votary of rock 'n' roll.* It is also a person, such as a monk or nun, who is bound by religious **VOWS**, promises, pledges, or oaths. ☞ *They made their wedding vows before a justice of the peace.* To vow is to promise, swear, declare, and contract. ☞ *Mapes vowed he would never buy another lottery ticket.* Something that is **VOTIVE** is dedicated, given, and offered, often in fulfillment of a vow. ☞ *There were many votive offerings for the victims of the tragedy.*

A **DEVOUT** person is religious, reverent, dedicated, and holy. ☞ *Only the truly devout braved the storm to attend the services.* It also means serious, earnest, and sincere. ☞ *We send you our devout best wishes.* In his famous soliloquy "To be, or not to be," Shakespeare's Hamlet says that to die is "a consummation / **DEVOUTLY** to be wished."

DEVOTE is a verb meaning dedicate, concentrate, and give oneself up to. ☞ *Those two have devoted their lives to helping the less fortunate.* A **DEVOTED** person is steadfast, committed, dedicated, and loyal. ☞ *She is a truly devoted public servant.* **DEVOTION** is love, fondness, **DEVOTEDNESS**, or allegiance. ☞ *Their devotion to each other is genuine.* The word was used sarcastically by Washington Irving, the author of *Rip Van Winkle:* "The almighty dollar, that great object of universal devotion." It is also piety, consecration, devoutness, reverence, or godliness. ☞ *It was their devotion that led them into the ministry.* **DEVOTIONS** and **DEVOTIONALS** are religious observances or services.

But not: *vowel* [*vocalis,* vocal], speech sound.
Combining form: *de-,* fully.
Antonyms: *devoted*—detached, unconcerned, indifferent, disloyal; *devotion*—disinterest, irreverence, unfaithfulness, impiety; *devout*—impious, sacrilegious, insincere, passive, indifferent.

VULGARE, to make common, publish: VULG

VULGus means the common people or the masses. When St. Jerome translated the Bible into Latin near the end of the 4th century, it became known as the **VULG**ate because it made the book available to the common people. **VULG**ar Latin is popular or vernacular Latin (as distinguished from literary Latin); it is from this that came the Romance languages, among them French, Italian, Portuguese, Romanian, and Spanish. Thus vulgar meant ordinary, plebeian, popular, and general; it was not a put-down or sneer as it is today.

But the meaning of the words common and popular of that era eventually took on other connotations, generally moving in the direction of coarse, low, vulgar, cheap, shoddy, boorish, and uncouth. The word also has the meaning of obscene, offensive, risque, scurrilous, and filthy. ☞ *Herschel's comedy routine is too close to vulgar to make it with this audience.*

A **VULG**arity was once the ordinary sort or class of something; today it has two meanings. The first one is coarseness, crudeness, or lack of refinement. ☞ *If you knew what her background is, you might be able to understand her vulgarity.* The second meaning is dirt, smut, filth, ribaldry, obscenity, or pornography. ☞ *The comedian's vulgarity was really sickening.* A **VULG**arism is crude behavior or coarse speech. To **VULG**arize is to lower, coarsen, demean, disgrace, or debase. A **VULG**arian is someone who is crude, obnoxious, or offensive; it is often used as an exaggeration. ☞ *My sister's five "precious little dears" turned out to be one short of a half-dozen vulgarians.*

To di**VULG**e something is literally to "make known to the common people." It means to reveal, disclose, publish, or give away. ☞ *I don't recall the governor divulging any such information. Had there been such a divulgence, I would have known of it.*

Combining form: *di-*, abroad.
Antonyms: *divulge*—conceal, keep secret, secrete, dissemble; *vulgar*—elegant, refined, privileged, educated, standard, clean, acceptable.

X

XENOS, foreign, strange: XENO

A **XENOphobe** is a person who distrusts, fears, and hates foreign cultures, customs, and people, right along with anything that has another country's label on it. **XENOphobia** is that distrust and, therefore, it is also a fanatical nationalism.

A **XENOphile** is one who is attracted to whatever a xenophobe is repelled by. **XENOphilia** is the attraction to things foreign. **XENOmania** is an abnormal, irrational, or extreme attraction to everything foreign, usually at the expense of and distaste for all things domestic. People so afflicted are sometimes accused of being snobs and elitists.

XENOn is a chemical element discovered in 1898 by Sir William Ramsay; he gave the gas its "strange" name.

> **Combining forms:** *-mania,* enthusiasm that is often extreme and not long lasting; *-philia,* a strong and often unnatural attraction; *-phobia,* a fear, dread, or aversion.

Z

ZELOS, ardor: JEAL, ZEAL

Jealousy

A person who is **JEAL**OUS is possessive, suspicious, and obsessed with. **JEAL**OUSY is suspicion, resentment, hostility, intolerance, or distrust. ☞ *"Jealously is all the fun you think they had," Erica Jong, novelist, from* How to Save Your Own Life *(1977).*

ZEAL is enthusiasm, gusto, fervor, verve, passion, fanaticism, vehemence, and devotion. A **ZEAL**OT is a fanatic, enthusiast, devotee, or extremist. ☞ *"For forms of government let fools contest; / Whatever is best administered is best; / For modes of faith let graceless zealots fight; / His can't be wrong whose life is in the right," from an* Essay on Man *by Alexander Pope, poet.*

Someone who is **ZEAL**OUS is enthusiastic, fervent, devoted, and monomaniacal.

> **Antonyms:** *jealous*—trusting, open, indifferent, uncaring; *jealousy*—trust, confidence, assurance, openness; *zeal*—apathy, detachment, nonchalance, languor, torpor; *zealot*—cynic, unbeliever, detractor; *zealous*—bored, lazy, dispassionate, lackadaisical.

ZOION, animal: ZOO

In 1829 the **ZOO**LOGICAL Society of London opened up an exhibit of wild animals; they called it the Zoological Gardens. In time that got pared down to The Zoological and, finally, to just **ZOO.** Since then it has taken on other meanings, such as a place or activity marked by chaos. ☞ *Hey, that class turned into a zoo once the teacher left.*

ZOOLOGY is the branch of biology dealing with animals, and a **ZOO**LOGIST is one who specializes in animal studies.

ZOONOSIS is a disease such as malaria or rabies that can be transmitted from animals to human beings. **ZOOGRAPHY** is the biological description of animals, and **ZOOTOMY** is the dissection of animals in medical or other research.

ZOOLATRY is the worship of animals, and **ZOOMORPHISM** is the giving of animal characteristics and qualities to a god or gods. **ZOOPHILIA** is an abnormal fondness for animals; **ZOOPHOBIA** is an abnormal fear of them.

> **But not:** *zoom* [imit.], sound, rapid movement; *zoot suit* [based on rhyming sound], man's suit popular c. 1940–50.
> **Combining forms:** *-graphy,* writing; *-latry,* worship; *-logy,* study of; *-morphism,* having the shape or form of; *-philia,* love; *-phobia,* fear.

List of Latin and Greek Words

aedes
aevum
ager
agere, *act*
agere, *gate*
agere, *gen*
agere, *gi, gu*
agora [Gk]
akademia [Gk]
akros [Gk]
albus
alere
allos [Gk]
amare
amicus
amplus
angelos [Gk]
animus
annus
anthos [Gk]
antiquus
aristos [Gk]
arkhein [Gk]
astron [Gk]
athlon [Gk]
ballein [Gk]
bassus
battuere
bellum
bene
bibere
biblion [Gk]
bombos [Gk]
caballus
cadere
calere
calvi
canere
capere, *cap*
capere, *capt*
capere, *cas, chas*
capere, *ceit, ceiv*
capere, *cept*
capere, *cip, cup*
carus
censere
chronos [Gk]
civis
clamere
claudere
colare
coquere
credere
dare
decem
deka [Gk]
demos [Gk]
derma [Gk]
dexter
dicare
dicere
didonai [Gk]
discere
docere
dokein [Gk]
dolere
dominus
donare
dromein [Gk]
dunamis [Gk]
duo
durare
ego
eidos [Gk]
eikon [Gk]
ergon [Gk]
errare
esse
eus [Gk]
facere, *fac, face*
facere, *fact*
facere, *feas, feat*
facere, *fect*
facere, *feit, fit*
facere, *fic, fice*
fallere
felix
femina
fendere
ferre
fervere
fidere
figere
fluere
forma
fortis
fortuna
gamos [Gk]
genus
gignoskein [Gk]
glossa [Gk]
gnoscere
gradi
granum
gratus
gravis
gregare
gustus
helios [Gk]
hepta [Gk]
heres
hodos [Gk]
horrere
hostis
insula
ire
jacere
jugum
jungere
jurare
juvenis
kaiein [Gk]
kamara [Gk]
kosmos [Gk]
krinein [Gk]
kyklos [Gk]
labor
latus
laudare
legare
legein [Gk]
levare
lex
liber
lingua
liquere
lithos [Gk]
littera
locare
logos [Gk]
longus
loqui
lucere
lumen
luna
magister
magnus
malleus
malus
mandare
manere
manus
mappa
mater
merx
meter [Gk]
mikros [Gk]
miscere
misein [Gk]
mittere
mors
nasci
naus [Gk]
nekros [Gk]
nepos
neptis
nocere
nomen
novus
nox
noxa
numerus
oculus
odium
oikos [Gk]
onoma [Gk]
ordo
pais [Gk]
par
parere
paschein [Gk]
pater [L, Gk]
pax
peccare
pecus
pellere
pendere
penna
pes
pius
plebes
polis [Gk]
porcus
portare
pungere
quaerere
qualis
quam
quantus
qui
quid
quies
quom
quot
radere
radix
rex
ridere
rodere
rogare
rumpere
salire
salus
salvus
sanguis
sapere
scala
scandere
scire
scribere
sedere
selene [Gk]
semen
senex
sequi
signum
similis
simul
skhizein [Gk]
skopein [Gk]
sol
solus
solvere
sonare
spargo
spondere
stinguere
struere
tacere
tardus
tekhne [Gk]
temnein [Gk]
temperare
tempus
terere
terra
theos [Gk]
tithenai [Gk]
topos [Gk]
torquere
torrere
tropos [Gk]
tupos [Gk]
ultra
umbra
unda
unguere
uti
vacare
varius
verbum
vereri
verus
vestis
vetus
via
vicis
vigilare
villa
vir
vivere
vocare
vorare
vovere
vulgare
xenos [Gk]
zelos [Gk]
zoion [Gk]

List of English Words

abase	*bassus*
abasement	*bassus*
abate	*battuere*
abatement	*battuere*
abattoir	*battuere*
abdicate	*dicar*
abdication	*dicare*
aberrant	*errare*
aberration	*errare*
abhor	*horrere*
abhorrent	*horrere*
abject	*jacere*
abjure	*jurare*
ablate	*latus*
abound	*unda*
abrade	*radere*
abrasion	*radere*
abrasive	*radere*
abrogate	*rogare*
abrogation	*rogare*
abrupt	*rumpere*
absence	*esse*
absent	*esse*
absentee	*esse*
absenteeism	*esse*
absentia	*esse*
absolute	*solvere*
absolution	*solvere*
absolve	*solvere*
abundance	*unda*
abundant	*unda*
abusage	*uti*
abuse	*uti*
abusive	*uti*
academe	*akademia*
academese	*akademia*
academic	*akademia*
academician	*akademia*
academy	*akademia*
accent	*canere*
accentuate	*canere*
accept	*capere*
acceptable	*capere*
acceptance	*capere*
accident	*cadere*
accidental	*cadere*
acclaim	*clamere*
acclamation	*clamere*
accredit	*credere*
accreditation	*credere*
acquaint	*gnoscere*
acquaintance	*gnoscere*
acquiesce	*quies*
acquiescence	*quies*
acquiescent	*quies*
acquire	*quaerere*
acquirement	*quaerere*
acquisition	*quaerere*
acquisitive	*quaerere*
acquisitory	*quaerere*
acquit	*quies*
acquittal	*quies*
acrobat	*akros*
acrobatic	*akros*
acromegaly	*akros*
acronym	*akros*
acrophobia	*akros*
acropolis	*akros*
acropolis	*polis*
acrostic	*akros*
act	*agere*
action	*agere*
activate	*agere*
active	*agere*
activism	*agere*
activist	*agere*
actor	*agere*
actress	*agere*
actual	*agere*
actuality	*agere*
actuary	*agere*
actuate	*agere*
add	*dare*
addenda	*dare*
addendum	*dare*
addict	*dicare*
addiction	*dicare*
addictive	*dicare*
addition	*dare*
additive	*dare*
adjacent	*jacere*
adjective	*jacere*
adjoin	*jungere*
adjudge	*dicare*
adjudicate	*dicare*
adjudication	*dicare*
adjudicator	*dicare*
adjunct	*jungere*
adjust	*jurare*
adjustment	*jurare*
admissible	*mittere*
admission	*mittere*
admit	*mittere*
admittable	*mittere*
admittance	*mittere*
admix	*miscere*
adolescence	*alere*
adulthood	*alere*
adumbrate	*umbra*
adverb	*verbum*
advocate	*vocare*
aedile	*aedes*
aerie	*ager*
aerodrome	*dromein*
affect	*facere*
affectation	*facere*
affection	*facere*
affectionate	*facere*
affiance	*fidere*
affidavit	*fidere*
affix	*figere*
affluence	*fluere*
affluent	*fluere*
afionado	*facere*
agency	*agere*
agenda	*agere*
agendum	*agere*
agent	*agere*
aggravate	*gravis*
aggregate	*gregare*
aggregation	*gregare*
aggression	*gradi*
aggressive	*gradi*
aggressor	*gradi*
aggrieve	*gravis*
agile	*agere*
agility	*agere*
agitate	*agere*
agitation	*agere*
agitator	*agere*
agnomen	*nomen*
agnostic	*gignoskein*
agnosticism	*gignoskein*
agora	*agora*
agoraphobia	*agora*
agrarian	*ager*
agree	*gratus*
agreeable	*gratus*
agreement	*gratus*
agriculture	*ager*
air	*ager*
airdrome	*dromein*
akvavit	*vivere*
alb	*albus*
albatross	*albus*
albedo	*albus*
albinism	*albus*
albino	*albus*
albion	*albus*
album	*albus*
albumen	*albus*
alexia	*legein*
aliment	*alere*
alimentary	*alere*
alimentation	*alere*
alimony	*alere*
allegation	*legare*
allege	*legare*

alleged	*legare*
allegorical	*allos*
allegory	*allos*
allergen	*allos*
allergen	*ergon*
allergic	*allos*
allergic	*ergon*
allergist	*allos*
allergist	*ergon*
allergy	*allos*
allergy	*ergon*
alleviate	*levare*
alliteration	*littera*
allocate	*locare*
allocation	*locare*
allogamy	*gamos*
allopathy	*paschein*
alum	*alere*
alumna	*alere*
alumnus	*alere*
amanuensis	*manus*
amateur	*amare*
amatory	*amare*
ambiance	*ire*
ambidextrous	*dexter*
ambience	*ire*
ambient	*ire*
ambiguity	*agere*
ambiguous	*agere*
ambition	*ire*
ambitious	*ire*
ambitiousness	*ire*
ami	*amicus*
amiable	*amicus*
amicable	*amicus*
amicus	*amicus*
amie	*amicus*
amiga	*amicus*
amigo	*amicus*
amity	*amicus*
amoretto	*amare*
amorous	*amare*
amortize	*mors*
amour	*amare*
ample	*amplus*
amplification	*amplus*
amplifier	*amplus*
amplify	*amplus*
amplitude	*amplus*
anabolic	*ballein*
anachronism	*chronos*
anachronistic	*chronos*
analog	*legein*
analogous	*logos*
analogue	*legein*
anarchy	*arkhein*
anathema	*tithenai*
anatomy	*temnein*
android	*eidos*

anecdotage	*didonai*
anecdotal	*didonai*
anecdote	*didonai*
angel	*angelos*
angeleno	*angelos*
angelic	*angelos*
anima	*animus*
animacule	*animus*
animadversion	*animus*
animadvert	*animus*
animal	*animus*
animalism	*animus*
animalistic	*animus*
animalize	*animus*
animate	*animus*
animation	*animus*
animator	*animus*
animism	*animus*
animosity	*animus*
animus	*animus*
annal	*annus*
annalist	*annus*
anniversary	*annus*
annoy	*odium*
annoyance	*odium*
annual	*annus*
annuity	*annus*
anoint	*unguere*
anonym	*onoma*
anonymity	*onoma*
anonymous	*onoma*
antebellum	*bellum*
antemortem	*mors*
antepartum	*parere*
antepenultimate	*ultra*
anther	*anthos*
anthesis	*anthos*
anthologist	*anthos*
anthologize	*anthos*
anthologizer	*anthos*
anthology	*anthos*
anthology	*logos*
antic	*antiquus*
anticipate	*capere*
anticipation	*capere*
antidote	*didonai*
antipathetic	*paschein*
antipathy	*paschein*
antiquarian	*antiquus*
antiquary	*antiquus*
antiquate	*antiquus*
antique	*antiquus*
antiquer	*antiquus*
antiquity	*antiquus*
antithesis	*tithenai*
antithetic	*tithenai*
antiutopia	*topos*
antler	*oculus*
antonym	*onoma*

apathetic	*paschein*
apathy	*paschein*
apolitical	*polis*
apologetic	*logos*
apologia	*logos*
apologize	*logos*
apothecary	*tithenai*
apotheosis	*theos*
apotheosize	*theos*
apparent	*parere*
apparition	*parere*
appeal	*pellere*
appear	*parere*
appearance	*parere*
appease	*pax*
appeasement	*pax*
appellant	*pellere*
appellate	*pellere*
appellation	*pellere*
append	*pendere*
appendage	*pendere*
appendant	*pendere*
appendectomy	*pendere*
appendectomy	*temnein*
appendicitis	*pendere*
appendix	*pendere*
apperception	*capere*
apricot	*coquere*
apron	*mappa*
aquavit	*vivere*
aquifer	*ferre*
arch	*arkhein*
archaeology	*arkhein*
archaic	*arkhein*
archangel	*angelos*
archangel	*arkhein*
archbishop	*arkhein*
archconservative	*arkhein*
archdeacon	*arkhein*
archdiocese	*arkhein*
archducal	*arkhein*
archduchess	*arkhein*
archduchy	*arkhein*
archduke	*arkhein*
archdukedom	*arkhein*
archenemy	*arkhein*
archeology	*arkhein*
archeology	*logos*
archetype	*arkhein*
archetype	*tupos*
archfiend	*arkhein*
archipelago	*arkhein*
architect	*arkhein*
archive	*arkhein*
archivist	*arkhein*
archpriest	*arkhein*
archrival	*arkhein*
aristocracy	*aristos*
aristocrat	*aristos*

aristocratic	*aristos*
arrant	*ire*
arrogance	*rogare*
arrogant	*rogare*
arrogate	*rogare*
artifice	*facere*
artificial	*facere*
ascend	*scandere*
ascendance	*scandere*
ascendancy	*scandere*
ascension	*scandere*
ascent	*scandere*
ascribe	*scribere*
asperge	*spargo*
aspergillum	*spargo*
asperse	*spargo*
aspersion	*spargo*
aspersorium	*spargo*
assail	*salire*
assailant	*salire*
assault	*salire*
assaulter	*salire*
assemblage	*similis*
assemble	*similis*
assembly	*similis*
assess	*sedere*
assessor	*sedere*
assiduous	*sedere*
assign	*signum*
assignation	*signum*
assignment	*signum*
assimilation	*similis*
assimulate	*simul at similis*
assize	*sedere*
assonance	*sonare*
aster	*astron*
asterisk	*astron*
asterism	*astron*
asteroid	*astron*
asteroid	*eidos*
asteroidean	*astron*
astral	*astron*
astro	*astron*
astrodome	*astron*
astrology	*astron*
astrology	*logos*
astronaut	*astron*
astronautic	*astron*
astronomer	*astron*
astronomical	*astron*
astronomy	*astron*
astroturf	*astron*
atheism	*theos*
atheist	*theos*
athlete	*athlon*
athletic	*athlon*
atom	*temnein*
atomic	*temnein*
atomizer	*temnein*
attrition	*terere*
atypical	*tupos*
au pair	*par*
aubade	*albus*
auburn	*albus*
autarchy	*arkhein*
autogamy	*gamos*
avenge	*dicare*
avengeful	*dicare*
aver	*verus*
avocation	*vocare*
avoid	*vacare*
avoidance	*vacare*
avouch	*vocare*
ballistic	*ballein*
bankrupt	*rumpere*
bankruptcy	*rumpere*
bas-relief	*bassus*
base	*bassus*
bass	*bassus*
basset	*bassus*
basso	*bassus*
bassoon	*bassus*
bate	*battuere*
battalion	*battuere*
batter	*battuere*
batterie	*battuere*
battery	*battuere*
battledore	*battuere*
battlement	*battuere*
battleship	*battuere*
beatific	*facere*
becalm	*kaiein*
bedaub	*albus*
beer	*bibere*
belabor	*labor*
bellatrix	*bellum*
bellicose	*bellum*
bellicoseness	*bellum*
bellicosity	*bellum*
belligerence	*bellum*
belligerency	*bellum*
belligerent	*bellum*
bellona	*bellum*
benedick	*dicare*
benedict	*dicare*
benediction	*bene*
benediction	*dicare*
benefaction	*bene*
benefactor	*bene*
benefactor	*facere*
benefic	*bene*
beneficence	*facere*
beneficial	*facere*
beneficiary	*facere*
beneficient	*bene*
benefit	*facere*
benevolence	*bene*
benevolent	*bene*
benign	*bene*
benison	*bene*
benison	*dicare*
besiege	*sedere*
betray	*dare*
beverage	*bibere*
bevy	*bibere*
biannual	*annus*
bib	*bibere*
bible	*biblion*
biblicism	*biblion*
biblicist	*biblion*
biblioclast	*biblion*
bibliography	*biblion*
biblioklept	*biblion*
bibliolatry	*biblion*
bibliomania	*biblion*
bibliophage	*biblion*
bibliophile	*biblion*
bibliophobe	*biblion*
bibliotaph	*biblion*
biblist	*biblion*
bibulous	*bibere*
bicameral	*kamara*
bicentennial	*annus*
bicycle	*kyklos*
biennial	*annus*
bigamist	*gamos*
bigamy	*gamos*
bike	*kyklos*
biker	*kyklos*
bikeway	*kyklos*
bilingual	*lingua*
binocular	*oculus*
biodegradable	*gradi*
biodynamic	*dunamis*
biology	*logos*
biparous	*parere*
biped	*pes*
biscuit	*coquere*
bishop	*skopein*
bomb	*bombos*
bombard	*bombos*
bombardier	*bombos*
bombardment	*bombos*
bomber	*bombos*
bombinate	*bombos*
bombshell	*bombos*
bombsight	*bombos*
bon vivant	*vivere*
bouillabaisse	*bassus*
bound	*bombos*
bound	*unda*
cabaret	*kamara*
cable	*capere*
cadaver	*cadere*
cadaverous	*cadere*
cadence	*cadere*

English word	Root
cadenza	*cadere*
caducity	*cadere*
caducous	*cadere*
caitliff	*capere*
caldron	*calere*
calenture	*calere*
calm	*kaiein*
calmative	*kaiein*
caloric	*calere*
calorie	*calere*
calumnious	*calvi*
calumny	*calvi*
camarada	*kamara*
camarade	*kamara*
camaraderie	*kamara*
camcorder	*kamara*
camera	*kamara*
camera obscura	*kamara*
cameral	*kamara*
cant	*canere*
cantabile	*canere*
cantata	*canere*
canticle	*canere*
canto	*canere*
cantor	*canere*
cap-a-pie	*pes*
capability	*capere*
capable	*capere*
capacitate	*capere*
capacitator	*capere*
capacity	*capere*
capstan	*capere*
capsule	*capere*
caption	*capere*
captious	*capere*
captivate	*capere*
captive	*capere*
captivity	*capere*
captor	*capere*
capture	*capere*
cardiology	*logos*
caress	*carus*
carnival	*levare*
carnivore	*vorare*
carnivorous	*vorare*
cascade	*cadere*
case	*cadere*
case	*capere*
casement	*capere*
cash	*capere*
cashier	*capere*
cask	*capere*
casket	*capere*
cassette	*capere*
castigate	*agere*
casual	*cadere*
casualty	*cadere*
casuistry	*cadere*
casus belli	*bellum*
catalog	*legein*
catalogue	*legein*
categorical	*agora*
categorize	*agora*
category	*agora*
caudle	*calere*
cauldron	*calere*
caustic	*kaiein*
cauterize	*kaiein*
cavalcade	*caballus*
cavalier	*caballus*
cavalry	*caballus*
censor	*censere*
censorious	*censere*
censure	*censere*
census	*censere*
centennial	*annus*
centipede	*pes*
certificate	*facere*
chafe	*calere*
chaff	*calere*
challenge	*calvi*
challenger	*calvi*
chamber	*kamara*
chamberlain	*kamara*
chambermaid	*kamara*
chance	*cadere*
chancy	*cadere*
chant	*canere*
chanter	*canere*
chanteur	*canere*
chanteuse	*canere*
chantey	*canere*
chanticleer	*canere*
chantry	*canere*
chanty	*canere*
charitable	*carus*
charity	*carus*
charm	*canere*
chase	*capere*
chassis	*capere*
cheat	*cadere*
cherish	*carus*
chowder	*calere*
chronic	*chronos*
chronicle	*chronos*
chronicler	*chronos*
chronogram	*chronos*
chronological	*chronos*
chronology	*chronos*
chronometer	*chronos*
chrony	*chronos*
chute	*cadere*
circuit	*ire*
circuitous	*ire*
circumference	*ferre*
circumjacent	*jacere*
circumlocution	*loqui*
circumscribe	*scribere*
citify	*civis*
citizen	*civis*
citizenship	*civis*
city	*civis*
civic	*civis*
civil	*civis*
civility	*civis*
civilization	*civis*
civilize	*civis*
claim	*clamere*
claimant	*clamere*
clamant	*clamere*
clamor	*clamere*
clamorous	*clamere*
clause	*claudere*
claustrophobe	*claudere*
cloister	*claudere*
closet	*claudere*
closure	*claudere*
cloture	*claudere*
coagulant	*agere*
coagulate	*agere*
coagulum	*agere*
coalesce	*alere*
coalition	*alere*
coeval	*aevum*
cogency	*agere*
cogent	*agere*
cogitate	*agere*
cogitation	*agere*
cognate	*nasci*
cognitive	*gnoscere*
cognizance	*gnoscere*
cognizant	*gnoscere*
cognomen	*nomen*
cognoscente	*gnoscere*
cognoscenti	*gnoscere*
coincide	*cadere*
coincidence	*cadere*
colander	*colare*
collaborate	*labor*
collaboration	*labor*
collaborator	*labor*
collate	*latus*
collateral	*latus*
collation	*latus*
colleague	*legare*
college	*legare*
collegial	*legare*
collegian	*legare*
collegiate	*legare*
collocate	*locare*
colloquial	*loqui*
colloquium	*loqui*
colloquy	*loqui*
combat	*battuere*
combatant	*battuere*
combative	*battuere*
comes	*ire*

comfit	*facere*
comfort	*fortis*
comfortable	*fortis*
comforter	*fortis*
comfrey	*fervere*
comitia	*ire*
command	*mandare*
commandant	*mandare*
commandeer	*mandare*
commander	*mandare*
commandment	*mandare*
commando	*mandare*
commence	*ire*
commencement	*ire*
commend	*mandare*
commendable	*mandare*
commendation	*mandare*
commerce	*merx*
commercial	*merx*
commissar	*mittere*
commissariat	*mittere*
commissary	*mittere*
commission	*mittere*
commissioner	*mittere*
commit	*mittere*
committment	*mittere*
commix	*miscere*
comparable	*par*
comparative	*par*
compare	*par*
comparison	*par*
compatriot	*pater*
compeer	*par*
compel	*pellere*
compensate	*pendere*
compensation	*pendere*
compensatory	*pendere*
comport	*portare*
comportment	*portare*
compromise	*mittere*
compulsion	*pellere*
compulsive	*pellere*
compulsory	*pellere*
compunction	*pungere*
comrade	*kamara*
conceit	*capere*
conceivable	*capere*
conceive	*capere*
concept	*capere*
conception	*capere*
conceptual	*capere*
conceptualize	*capere*
conclude	*claudere*
conclusion	*claudere*
conclusive	*claudere*
concoct	*coquere*
concoction	*coquere*
concomitant	*ire*
condescend	*scandere*
condescension	*scandere*
condition	*dicare*
conditional	*dicare*
condole	*dolere*
condolence	*dolere*
condolent	*dolere*
condominium	*dominus*
condonable	*donare*
condone	*donare*
confection	*facere*
confectioner	*facere*
confectionery	*facere*
confer	*ferre*
conferee	*ferre*
conference	*ferre*
confidant	*fidere*
confide	*fidere*
confidence	*fidere*
confluence	*fluere*
conformable	*forma*
conformance	*forma*
conformation	*forma*
conformist	*forma*
conformity	*forma*
congratulate	*gratus*
congratulation	*gratus*
congregant	*gregare*
congregate	*gregare*
congregation	*gregare*
congregationalist	*gregare*
congress	*gradi*
congressional	*gradi*
coniferous	*ferre*
conjecture	*jacere*
conjoin	*jungere*
conjuctive	*jungere*
conjugal	*jungere*
conjugate	*jugum*
conjugation	*jugum*
conjunct	*jungere*
conjunction	*jungere*
conjuration	*jurare*
conjure	*jurare*
conjurer	*jurare*
conquer	*quaerere*
conqueror	*quaerere*
conquest	*quaerere*
consanguineous	*sanguis*
conscience	*scire*
conscientious	*scire*
conscious	*scire*
consciousness	*scire*
conscript	*scribere*
conscription	*scribere*
consecutive	*sequi*
consequence	*sequi*
consequent	*sequi*
consequential	*sequi*
consign	*signum*
consignee	*signum*
consignment	*signum*
consignor	*signum*
consonance	*sonare*
consonant	*sonare*
construct	*struere*
construction	*struere*
constructive	*struere*
construe	*struere*
contempo	*tempus*
contemporaneous	*tempus*
contemporary	*tempus*
contort	*torquere*
contortionist	*torquere*
contracept	*capere*
contraception	*capere*
contraceptive	*capere*
contradict	*dicare*
contradiction	*dicare*
contradictory	*dicare*
contrite	*terere*
contrition	*terere*
convey	*via*
conveyance	*via*
conveyor	*via*
convivial	*vivere*
conviviality	*vivere*
convocation	*vocare*
convoke	*vocare*
convoy	*via*
cook	*coquere*
cookery	*coquere*
coordinate	*ordo*
coordination	*ordo*
coordinator	*ordo*
corrade	*radere*
correlate	*latus*
correlation	*latus*
correlative	*latus*
correspond	*spondere*
correspondence	*spondere*
correspondent	*spondere*
corrode	*rodere*
corrosion	*rodere*
corrosive	*rodere*
corrupt	*rumpere*
corruptible	*rumpere*
corruption	*rumpere*
cosmetic	*kosmos*
cosmetician	*kosmos*
cosmetology	*kosmos*
cosmic	*kosmos*
cosmodrome	*kosmos*
cosmogony	*kosmos*
cosmography	*kosmos*
cosmology	*kosmos*
cosmonaut	*kosmos*
cosmopolis	*kosmos*
cosmopolitan	*kosmos*

cosmopolitan	*polis*
cosmopolite	*kosmos*
cosmopolite	*polis*
coulee	*colare*
counteract	*agere*
counterfeit	*facere*
counterfeiter	*facere*
countermand	*mandare*
counterpoise	*pendere*
countersign	*signum*
coy	*quies*
credence	*credere*
credential	*credere*
credenza	*credere*
credible	*credere*
credit	*credere*
creditable	*credere*
creditor	*credere*
credo	*credere*
credulity	*credere*
credulous	*credere*
creed	*credere*
crisis	*krinein*
criteria	*krinein*
criterion	*krinein*
critic	*krinein*
critical	*krinein*
criticism	*krinein*
criticize	*krinein*
critique	*krinein*
cronyism	*chronos*
crucifix	*figere*
crucifixion	*figere*
crucify	*figere*
cryptogam	*gamos*
cuisine	*coquere*
culinary	*coquere*
cullender	*colare*
cum laude	*laudare*
cumrade	*kamara*
curriculum vitae	*vivere*
cyclable	*kyklos*
cyclamen	*kyklos*
cycle	*kyklos*
cyclery	*kyklos*
cyclic	*kyklos*
cyclical	*kyklos*
cyclist	*kyklos*
cyclocross	*kyklos*
cycloid	*kyklos*
cyclometer	*kyklos*
cyclone	*kyklos*
cyclonic	*kyklos*
cyclopean	*kyklos*
cyclopedia	*kyklos*
cyclops	*kyklos*
cyclorama	*kyklos*
dam	*dominus*
dama	*dominus*
dame	*dominus*
damsel	*dominus*
danger	*dominus*
daredevil	*ballein*
data	*dare*
date	*dare*
dateless	*dare*
dateline	*dare*
dative	*dare*
datum	*dare*
daub	*albus*
de-escalate	*scala*
deactivate	*agere*
dean	*decem*
debase	*bassus*
debatable	*battuere*
debate	*battuere*
decade	*decem*
decadence	*cadere*
decadent	*cadere*
decalogue	*decem*
decalogue	*legein*
decathlete	*athlon*
decathlete	*decem*
decathlon	*athlon*
decathlon	*decem*
decay	*cadere*
deceit	*capere*
deceitful	*capere*
deceive	*capere*
december	*decem*
decemvir	*decem*
decennial	*decem*
decennium	*decem*
deception	*capere*
deceptive	*capere*
deciduous	*cadere*
decimate	*decem*
declaim	*clamere*
declamation	*clamere*
declamatory	*clamere*
deconstruct	*struere*
deconstruction	*struere*
decuple	*decem*
dedicate	*dicare*
dedication	*dicare*
deface	*facere*
default	*fallere*
defeasance	*facere*
defeat	*facere*
defect	*facere*
defection	*facere*
defective	*facere*
defector	*facere*
defend	*fendere*
defendant	*fendere*
defense	*fendere*
defenseless	*fendere*
defensible	*fendere*
defer	*ferre*
deference	*ferre*
deferment	*ferre*
defiance	*fidere*
defiant	*fidere*
deficiency	*facere*
deficient	*facere*
deficit	*facere*
deforce	*fortis*
deform	*forma*
deformation	*forma*
deformity	*forma*
defy	*fidere*
degeneracy	*genus*
degenerate	*genus*
degradable	*gradi*
degradation	*gradi*
degrade	*gradi*
degree	*gradi*
deject	*jacere*
delegate	*legare*
delegation	*legare*
deliquescence	*liquere*
deliver	*liber*
deliverable	*liber*
deliverance	*liber*
delivery	*liber*
demagogue	*demos*
demagoguery	*demos*
demand	*mandare*
demilune	*luna*
demise	*mittere*
demit	*mittere*
democracy	*demos*
democrat	*demos*
democratic	*demos*
demography	*demos*
demophobia	*demos*
demotic	*demos*
denominate	*nomen*
denomination	*nomen*
denominator	*nomen*
depend	*pendere*
dependable	*pendere*
dependence	*pendere*
dependency	*pendere*
dependent	*pendere*
deport	*portare*
deportation	*portare*
deportment	*portare*
deracinate	*radix*
deride	*ridere*
derision	*ridere*
derisive	*ridere*
derisory	*ridere*
dermatitis	*derma*
dermatologist	*derma*
dermatology	*derma*
dermatology	*logos*

dermatosis	*derma*
dermis	*derma*
derogate	*rogare*
derogatory	*rogare*
descant	*canere*
descend	*scandere*
descendant	*scandere*
descent	*scandere*
description	*scribere*
descriptive	*scribere*
desegregation	*gregare*
design	*signum*
designate	*signum*
designation	*signum*
designer	*signum*
desolate	*solus*
desolation	*solus*
despond	*spondere*
despondency	*spondere*
despondent	*spondere*
destroy	*struere*
destroyer	*struere*
destruction	*struere*
destructive	*struere*
desultor	*salire*
desultory	*salire*
detriment	*terere*
detrimental	*terere*
detritus	*terere*
deuce	*duo*
deuterogamy	*gamos*
deviant	*via*
deviate	*via*
deviation	*via*
devil	*ballein*
devilkin	*ballein*
devilment	*ballein*
devilry	*ballein*
deviltry	*ballein*
devious	*via*
devoid	*vacare*
devote	*vovere*
devotedness	*vovere*
devotee	*vovere*
devotion	*vovere*
devotional	*vovere*
devour	*vorare*
devout	*vovere*
dexter	*dexter*
dexterity	*dexter*
dexterous	*dexter*
dextroglucose	*dexter*
dextrose	*dexter*
dextrosinistral	*dexter*
dextrous	*dexter*
diabolic	*ballein*
diabolical	*ballein*
diabolism	*ballein*
diabolo	*ballein*
diagnose	*gignoskein*
diagnosis	*gignoskein*
diagnostic	*gignoskein*
diagnosticate	*gignoskein*
diagnostician	*gignoskein*
dialect	*legein*
dialectic	*legein*
dialog	*legein*
dialogue	*legein*
dice	*dare*
dichotomous	*temnein*
dichotomy	*temnein*
dicker	*decem*
dictate	*dicare*
dictator	*dicare*
dictatorial	*dicare*
diction	*dicare*
dictionary	*dicare*
dictum	*dicare*
die	*dare*
differ	*ferre*
difference	*ferre*
different	*ferre*
differential	*ferre*
differentiate	*ferre*
difficult	*facere*
difficulty	*facere*
diffidence	*fidere*
diffident	*fidere*
digamy	*gamos*
digress	*gradi*
digression	*gradi*
digressive	*gradi*
dilate	*latus*
dilatory	*latus*
diocesan	*oikos*
diocese	*oikos*
disabuse	*uti*
disaffect	*facere*
disagree	*gratus*
disagreeable	*gratus*
disagreement	*gratus*
disappear	*parere*
disassemble	*similis*
disaster	*astron*
disastrous	*astron*
disciple	*discere*
disciplinarian	*discere*
disciplinary	*discere*
discipline	*discere*
disclaim	*clamere*
disclaimer	*clamere*
disclose	*claudere*
disclosure	*claudere*
discomfit	*facere*
discomfiture	*facere*
discomfort	*fortis*
discredit	*credere*
discreditable	*credere*
disenchant	*canere*
disfeature	*facere*
disgrace	*gratus*
disgraceful	*gratus*
disgust	*gustus*
disincentive	*capere*
disinform	*forma*
disinformation	*forma*
disinherit	*heres*
disinter	*terra*
disinterest	*esse*
disinvest	*vestis*
disinvestment	*vestis*
disjoin	*jungere*
disjoint	*jungere*
disjunct	*jungere*
disjunction	*jungere*
dislocate	*locare*
disloyal	*lex*
dismiss	*mittere*
dismissal	*mittere*
disorder	*ordo*
disorderliness	*ordo*
disparage	*par*
disparity	*par*
dispel	*pellere*
dispensable	*pendere*
dispensary	*pendere*
dispensation	*pendere*
dispensatory	*pendere*
dispense	*pendere*
dispenser	*pendere*
disperse	*disprgo*
disperse	*spargo*
dispersion	*spargo*
disport	*portare*
dispossess	*sedere*
disquisition	*quaerere*
disrupt	*rumpere*
disruption	*rumpere*
disruptive	*rumpere*
dissemble	*similis*
disseminate	*semen*
dissemination	*semen*
dissidence	*sedere*
dissident	*sedere*
dissimilarity	*similis*
dissimilitude	*similis*
dissimulate	*simul at similis*
dissoluble	*solvere*
dissolute	*solvere*
dissolution	*solvere*
dissolve	*solvere*
dissonance	*sonare*
dissonant	*sonare*
distemper	*temperare*
distinct	*stinguere*
distinction	*stinguere*

distinctive	*stinguere*
distinguish	*stinguere*
distort	*torquere*
distortion	*torquere*
disuse	*uti*
ditto	*dicare*
ditty	*dicare*
divagate	*agere*
divest	*vestis*
divestiture	*vestis*
divulge	*vulgare*
divulgence	*vulgare*
dix	*decem*
dixie	*decem*
docent	*docere*
docile	*docere*
doctor	*docere*
doctoral	*docere*
doctorate	*docere*
doctrinaire	*docere*
doctrinal	*docere*
doctrine	*docere*
docudrama	*docere*
document	*docere*
documentary	*docere*
documentation	*docere*
docutainment	*docere*
dogma	*dokein*
dogmatic	*dokein*
dogmatism	*dokein*
doleful	*dolere*
dolor	*dolere*
doloroso	*dolere*
dolorous	*dolere*
domain	*dominus*
dominant	*dominus*
dominate	*dominus*
domine	*dominus*
domineer	*dominus*
domingo	*dominus*
dominic	*dominus*
dominica	*dominus*
dominick	*dominus*
dominion	*dominus*
dominique	*dominus*
domino	*dominus*
don	*dominus*
dona	*dominus*
donable	*donare*
donatee	*donare*
donation	*donare*
donator	*donare*
donee	*donare*
donna	*dominus*
donor	*donare*
dorothea	*theos*
dosage	*didonai*
dose	*didonai*
double	*duo*
doublet	*duo*
doubt	*duo*
doubter	*duo*
doubtful	*duo*
doubtless	*duo*
downscale	*scala*
doxology	*dokein*
doxy	*dokein*
doyen	*decem*
doyenne	*decem*
dozen	*decem*
dromedary	*dromein*
dromos	*dromein*
dual	*duo*
dualism	*duo*
duality	*duo*
dubbeltje	*duo*
dubiety	*duo*
dubious	*duo*
dubloon	*duo*
duel	*bellum*
duel	*duo*
duelist	*bellum*
duelist	*duo*
duenna	*dominus*
duet	*duo*
dungeon	*dominus*
duple	*duo*
duplex	*duo*
duplicate	*duo*
duplicator	*duo*
duplicitious	*duo*
duplicity	*duo*
durability	*durare*
durable	*durare*
duration	*durare*
duress	*durare*
during	*durare*
dynamic	*dunamis*
dynamism	*dunamis*
dynamite	*dunamis*
dynamize	*dunamis*
dynamo	*dunamis*
dynamoelectric	*dunamis*
dynast	*dunamis*
dynasty	*dunamis*
dyslexia	*legein*
dyslexic	*legein*
dystopia	*topos*
ease	*jacere*
easement	*jacere*
easy	*jacere*
echelon	*scala*
eclectic	*legein*
ecocatastrophe	*oikos*
ecocide	*oikos*
ecofreak	*oikos*
ecohazard	*oikos*
ecology	*logos*
economic	*oikos*
economical	*oikos*
economist	*oikos*
economize	*oikos*
economy	*oikos*
ecumenical	*oikos*
edict	*dicare*
edification	*aedes*
edification	*facere*
edifice	*aedes*
edifice	*facere*
edify	*aedes*
edile	*aedes*
edit	*dare*
edition	*dare*
editor	*dare*
editorial	*dare*
editorialize	*dare*
efface	*facere*
effaceable	*facere*
effect	*facere*
effective	*facere*
effectual	*facere*
effectuate	*facere*
effeminate	*femina*
effervescence	*fervere*
effervescent	*fervere*
efficacious	*facere*
efficiency	*facere*
efficient	*facere*
effluent	*fluere*
effluvia	*fluere*
effort	*fortis*
effortless	*fortis*
ego	*ego*
egocentric	*ego*
egocentricity	*ego*
egocentrism	*ego*
egoism	*ego*
egoist	*ego*
egoistic	*ego*
egoistical	*ego*
egomania	*ego*
egomaniac	*ego*
egotism	*ego*
egotist	*ego*
egotistic	*ego*
egregious	*gregare*
egress	*gradi*
egression	*gradi*
eidetic	*eidos*
eidolon	*eidos*
eject	*jacere*
ejecta	*jacere*
ejection	*jacere*
elaborate	*labor*
elate	*latus*
elation	*latus*
elevate	*levare*

elevation	*levare*
elevator	*levare*
elocution	*loqui*
elongate	*longus*
eloquence	*loqui*
eloquent	*loqui*
elucidate	*lucere*
elucubrate	*lucere*
emancipate	*capere*
emancipate	*manus*
emancipation	*capere*
emancipation	*manus*
emancipator	*capere*
emancipator	*manus*
emblem	*ballein*
emblematic	*ballein*
emblemize	*ballein*
embolism	*ballein*
embolus	*ballein*
embrue	*bibere*
emissary	*mittere*
emission	*mittere*
emit	*mittere*
empathize	*paschein*
empathy	*paschein*
enact	*agere*
enactment	*agere*
enamor	*amare*
encapsulate	*capere*
encase	*capere*
enchant	*canere*
enchanter	*canere*
enchantment	*canere*
enchantress	*canere*
enchase	*capere*
enclose	*claudere*
enclosure	*claudere*
encyclical	*kyklos*
encyclopaedia	*kyklos*
encyclopedia	*kyklos*
encyclopedia	*pais*
encyclopedic	*kyklos*
encyclopedic	*pais*
endanger	*dominus*
endemic	*demos*
endurable	*durare*
endurance	*durare*
endure	*durare*
enduro	*durare*
enemy	*amicus*
energetic	*ergon*
energize	*ergon*
energizer	*ergon*
energy	*ergon*
enforce	*fortis*
enforceable	*fortis*
enforcement	*fortis*
enforcer	*fortis*
engender	*genus*
enjoin	*jungere*
enjoinder	*jungere*
enquiry	*quaerere*
ensemble	*similis*
ensign	*signum*
ensue	*sequi*
enthusiasm	*theos*
enthusiast	*theos*
enthusiastic	*theos*
entity	*esse*
entomologist	*temnein*
entropy	*tropos*
enumerate	*numerus*
envoy	*via*
epidemic	*demos*
epidermis	*derma*
epilog	*legein*
epilogue	*legein*
episcopal	*skopein*
episcopalian	*skopein*
episcopate	*skopein*
episode	*hodos*
episodic	*hodos*
epithet	*tithenai*
epitome	*temnein*
epitomize	*temnein*
eponym	*onoma*
equanimity	*animus*
equinoctal	*nox*
equinox	*nox*
equipoise	*pendere*
equiponderance	*pendere*
equivocate	*vocare*
eradicate	*radix*
erase	*radere*
eraser	*radere*
erg	*ergon*
ergomania	*ergon*
ergophobe	*ergon*
ergophobia	*ergon*
erode	*rodere*
erosion	*rodere*
erosive	*rodere*
err	*errare*
errant	*ire*
errata	*errare*
erratic	*errare*
erratum	*errare*
erroneous	*errare*
error	*errare*
erupt	*rumpere*
eruption	*rumpere*
escalade	*scala*
escalate	*scala*
escalator	*scala*
escheat	*cadere*
escritory	*scribere*
espousal	*spondere*
espouse	*spondere*
essence	*esse*
essential	*esse*
etymology	*logos*
eucharist	*eus*
eugene	*eus*
eugenic	*eus*
eulogize	*eus*
eulogize	*logos*
eulogy	*eus*
eunice	*eus*
euphemism	*eus*
euphonia	*eus*
euphonious	*eus*
euphonium	*eus*
euphony	*eus*
euphoria	*eus*
euphuistic	*eus*
euthanasia	*eus*
euthenic	*eus*
evacuate	*vacare*
evacuee	*vacare*
evangel	*angelos*
evangelical	*angelos*
evangelist	*angelos*
evangelize	*angelos*
evangelizer	*angelos*
evocative	*vocare*
evoke	*vocare*
ex posto facto	*facere*
exact	*agere*
exactitude	*agere*
exactness	*agere*
exanimate	*animus*
except	*capere*
exception	*capere*
exceptional	*capere*
excisable	*censere*
excise	*censere*
exclaim	*clamere*
exclamation	*clamere*
exclamatory	*clamere*
exclude	*claudere*
exclusion	*claudere*
exclusive	*claudere*
execute	*sequi*
execution	*sequi*
executioner	*sequi*
executive	*sequi*
exigent	*agere*
exiguous	*agere*
exit	*ire*
exodus	*hodos*
expatriate	*pater*
expedient	*pes*
expedite	*pes*
expedition	*pes*
expeditious	*pes*
expel	*pellere*
expend	*pendere*

expendable	*pendere*
expenditure	*pendere*
expense	*pendere*
expensive	*pendere*
expiate	*pius*
export	*portare*
exportable	*portare*
exportation	*portare*
expulsion	*pellere*
expunge	*pungere*
expurgate	*agere*
exquisite	*quaerere*
extemporaneous	*tempus*
extempore	*tempus*
extemporize	*tempus*
extinct	*stinguere*
extinction	*stinguere*
extinguish	*stinguere*
extinguisher	*stinguere*
extort	*torquere*
extortion	*torquere*
extortionate	*torquere*
extortionist	*torquere*
extraordinary	*ordo*
extraterrestrial	*terra*
extrinsic	*sequi*
exult	*salire*
exultant	*salire*
exultation	*salire*
eyelet	*oculus*
facade	*facere*
face	*facere*
facet	*facere*
facial	*facere*
facile	*facere*
facilitate	*facere*
facility	*facere*
facsimile	*facere*
facsimile	*similis*
fact	*facere*
faction	*facere*
factionalism	*facere*
factious	*facere*
factitious	*facere*
factoid	*facere*
factor	*facere*
factory	*facere*
factotum	*facere*
factual	*facere*
faculty	*facere*
fail	*fallere*
failure	*fallere*
faith	*fidere*
faithful	*fidere*
faithless	*fidere*
faithlessness	*fidere*
fallacious	*fallere*
fallacy	*fallere*
fallible	*fallere*

false	*fallere*
falsehood	*fallere*
falsetto	*fallere*
falsification	*fallere*
falsify	*fallere*
falsity	*fallere*
fault	*fallere*
faultless	*fallere*
faulty	*fallere*
faux	*fallere*
faux pas	*fallere*
fealty	*fidere*
feasance	*facere*
feasible	*facere*
feature	*facere*
felication	*felix*
felice	*felix*
felicia	*felix*
felicific	*facere*
felicific	*felix*
felicita	*felix*
felicitate	*felix*
felicitous	*felix*
felicity	*felix*
felix	*felix*
feminine	*femina*
femininism	*femina*
femininity	*femina*
feminist	*femina*
femme fatale	*femina*
fence	*fendere*
fencer	*fendere*
fend	*fendere*
fender	*fendere*
ferment	*fervere*
fermentation	*fervere*
fertile	*ferre*
fertility	*ferre*
fervency	*fervere*
fervent	*fervere*
fervid	*fervere*
fervor	*fervere*
fetiparous	*parere*
fiance	*fidere*
fiancee	*fidere*
fidelity	*fidere*
fiduciary	*fidere*
fire-retardant	*tardus*
fix	*figere*
fixation	*figere*
fixative	*figere*
fixture	*figere*
flu	*fluere*
fluorescent	*fluere*
fluoridation	*fluere*
fluoride	*fluere*
fluoroscope	*fluere*
fluoroscope	*skopein*
flush	*fluere*

force	*fortis*
forceful	*fortis*
forcible	*fortis*
foreclose	*claudere*
forfeit	*facere*
forfeiture	*facere*
form	*forma*
formal	*forma*
formalist	*forma*
formality	*forma*
formalize	*forma*
format	*forma*
formation	*forma*
formative	*forma*
formless	*forma*
formula	*forma*
formulate	*forma*
fort	*fortis*
forte	*fortis*
fortepiano	*fortis*
fortification	*fortis*
fortify	*fortis*
fortissimo	*fortis*
fortitude	*fortis*
fortress	*fortis*
fortuitous	*fortuna*
fortuity	*fortuna*
fortuna	*fortuna*
fortunate	*fortuna*
fortune	*fortuna*
fumigate	*agere*
fustigate	*agere*
garner	*granum*
garnet	*granum*
gastrectomy	*temnein*
gender	*genus*
genealogy	*logos*
general	*genus*
generality	*genus*
generalization	*genus*
generalize	*genus*
generate	*genus*
generation	*genus*
generator	*genus*
generic	*genus*
generosity	*genus*
generous	*genus*
genre	*genus*
genus	*genus*
girasol	*sol at helios*
gloss	*glossa*
glossal	*glossa*
glossary	*glossa*
glossolalia	*glossa*
glottis	*glossa*
gnosis	*gignoskein*
gnostic	*gignoskein*
gnosticism	*gignoskein*

grace *gratus*
graceful *gratus*
gracefulness *gratus*
graceless *gratus*
gracious *gratus*
gradation *gradi*
grade *gradi*
gradient *gradi*
gradual *gradi*
gradualism *gradi*
graduate *gradi*
grain *granum*
grainy *granum*
gramercy *merx*
granary *granum*
grandiloquence *loqui*
grange *granum*
granger *granum*
granite *granum*
granola *granum*
grant *credere*
grantsmanship *credere*
granular *granum*
granulate *granum*
granule *granum*
grateful *gratus*
gratefulness *gratus*
gratification *gratus*
gratify *gratus*
gratis *gratus*
gratitude *gratus*
gratuitous *gratus*
gratuity *gratus*
grave *gravis*
gravitate *gravis*
gravitation *gravis*
gravity *gravis*
gravy *granum*
gregarious *gregare*
grenade *granum*
grenadier *granum*
grenadine *granum*
gressorial *gradi*
grief *gravis*
grievance *gravis*
grieve *gravis*
grievous *gravis*
gustable *gustus*
gustation *gustus*
gustatory *gustus*
gustful *gustus*
gusto *gustus*
hagiology *logos*
heir *heres*
heiress *heres*
heliocentric *helios*
heliograph *helios*
heliotherapy *helios*
heliotrope *helios*
heliotrope *tropos*
helium *helios*
hematology *logos*
heptad *hepta*
heptagon *hepta*
heptahedron *hepta*
heptameter *hepta*
heptarchy *hepta*
heptateuch *hepta*
heptathlon *athlon*
heptathlon *hepta*
herbivorous *vorare*
hereditary *heres*
heredity *heres*
heritable *heres*
heritage *heres*
heterodox *dokein*
heteronym *onoma*
hidalgo *quid*
hierarch *arkhein*
hierarchy *arkhein*
hippodrome *dromein*
holocaust *kaiein*
homeopathy *paschein*
homo sapien *sapere*
homologous *logos*
homonym *onoma*
honorific *facere*
horoscope *skopein*
horrendous *horrere*
horrible *horrere*
horrid *horrere*
horrific *horrere*
horrify *horrere*
horror *horrere*
host *hostis*
hostage *sedere*
hostile *hostis*
hostility *hostis*
hyperbola *ballein*
hyperbole *ballein*
hyperbolic *ballein*
hypocrisy *krinein*
hypocrite *krinein*
hypocritical *krinein*
hypothesis *tithenai*
hypothesize *tithenai*
hypothetical *tithenai*
hysterectomy *temnein*
ichthyology *logos*
icon *eikon*
iconic *eikon*
iconoclasm *eikon*
iconoclast *eikon*
iconoclastic *eikon*
iconography *eikon*
iconolatry *eikon*
iconology *eikon*
idee fix *figere*
idol *eidos*
idolater *eidos*
idolatrous *eidos*
idolatry *eidos*
idolize *eidos*
idyll *eidos*
idyllic *eidos*
ignoble *gnoscere*
ignominious *nomen*
ignominy *nomen*
ignoramus *gnoscere*
ignorance *gnoscere*
ignorant *gnoscere*
ignore *gnoscere*
ikon *eikon*
illegal *lex*
illegitimate *lex*
illiberal *liber*
illiberalism *liber*
illiquid *liquere*
illiteracy *littera*
illiterate *littera*
illogical *logos*
illuminati *lucere*
illumination *lucere*
imbibe *bibere*
imbrue *bibere*
immanent *manere*
immiscible *miscere*
immortal *mors*
immortality *mors*
immortalize *mors*
impeach *pes*
impeccable *peccare*
impecunious *pecus*
impede *pes*
impediment *pes*
impedimenta *pes*
impel *pellere*
impeller *pellere*
impend *pendere*
imperceptible *capere*
imperfect *facere*
imperfectible *facere*
imperfection *facere*
imperishable *ire*
impermanent *manere*
impervious *via*
impiety *pius*
impious *pius*
impolitic *polis*
import *portare*
importance *portare*
important *portare*
importunate *portare*
importune *portare*
impulse *pellere*
impulsive *pellere*
inactivate *agere*

inadmissable	*mittere*
inamorata	*amare*
inamorato	*amare*
inanimate	*animus*
incantation	*canere*
incapable	*capere*
incapacitate	*capere*
incentive	*canere*
inception	*capere*
incidence	*cadere*
incident	*cadere*
incidental	*cadere*
incipient	*capere*
incivility	*civis*
inclose	*claudere*
include	*claudere*
inclusive	*claudere*
incogitant	*gnoscere*
incognito	*gnoscere*
incognizant	*gnoscere*
incomparable	*par*
inconceivable	*capere*
inconsequent	*sequi*
inconsequential	*sequi*
incorruptible	*rumpere*
incredible	*credere*
incredulous	*credere*
indefensible	*fendere*
independence	*pendere*
independent	*pendere*
indescribable	*scribere*
indestructible	*struere*
index	*dicare*
indicate	*dicare*
indication	*dicare*
indicative	*dicare*
indicator	*dicare*
indicatory	*dicare*
indict	*dicare*
indictable	*dicare*
indictment	*dicare*
indifferent	*ferre*
indispensable	*pendere*
indistinct	*stinguere*
indistinguishable	*stinguere*
indite	*dicare*
indocile	*docere*
indoctrinate	*docere*
indolence	*dolere*
indolent	*dolere*
indubitable	*duo*
indurate	*durare*
ineffaceable	*facere*
ineffective	*facere*
ineffectual	*facere*
inexact	*agere*
inexactitude	*agere*
inexpensive	*pendere*
infallible	*fallere*
infect	*facere*
infection	*facere*
infectious	*facere*
infelicitous	*felix*
infelicity	*felix*
infer	*ferre*
inference	*ferre*
infidel	*fidere*
infidelity	*fidere*
infix	*figere*
influence	*fluere*
influenza	*fluere*
infomercial	*forma*
infomercial	*merx*
inform	*forma*
informal	*forma*
informality	*forma*
informant	*forma*
information	*forma*
informative	*forma*
informer	*forma*
informercial	*forma*
informercial	*merx*
infrastructure	*struere*
ingrain	*granum*
ingrate	*gratus*
ingratiate	*gratus*
ingratitude	*gratus*
ingredient	*gradi*
ingress	*gradi*
ingression	*gradi*
inherit	*heres*
inheritable	*heres*
inheritance	*heres*
inheritress	*heres*
inheritrix	*heres*
inimical	*amicus*
initial	*ire*
initialism	*ire*
initiate	*ire*
initiation	*ire*
initiative	*ire*
initiatory	*ire*
injudicious	*dicare*
injunction	*jungere*
injure	*jurare*
injurious	*jurare*
injury	*jurare*
injustice	*jurare*
innate	*nasci*
innocence	*nocere*
innocent	*nocere*
innocuous	*nocere*
innovation	*novus*
innovative	*novus*
innovator	*novus*
innoxious	*noxa at nocere*
innumerable	*numerus*
innumeracy	*numerus*
innumerate	*numerus*
inoculate	*oculus*
inoffensive	*fendere*
inordinate	*ordo*
inquest	*quaerere*
inquire	*quaerere*
inquiry	*quaerere*
inquisition	*quaerere*
inquisitive	*quaerere*
inquisitor	*quaerere*
inscribe	*scribere*
inscription	*scribere*
insectivorous	*vorare*
insemination	*semen*
insidious	*sedere*
insignia	*signum*
insignificant	*signum*
insipid	*sapere*
insolate	*sol at helios*
insolation	*sol at helios*
insoluble	*solvere*
insolvent	*solvere*
instinct	*stinguere*
instinctive	*stinguere*
instruct	*struere*
instruction	*struere*
instructive	*struere*
instrument	*struere*
instrumental	*struere*
insubordinate	*ordo*
insubordination	*ordo*
insufferable	*ferre*
insufficiency	*facere*
insufficient	*facere*
insular	*insula*
insulate	*insula*
insulation	*insula*
insulin	*insula*
insult	*salire*
insulter	*salire*
insupportable	*portare*
intemperance	*temperare*
intemperate	*temperare*
inter	*terra*
interabang	*rogare*
intercept	*capere*
interception	*capere*
interceptor	*capere*
intercollegiate	*legare*
interdict	*dicare*
interdiction	*dicare*
interest	*esse*
interface	*facere*
interjacent	*jacere*
interject	*jacere*
interjection	*jacere*

interlocutor	*loqui*
interlunar	*luna*
intermeddle	*miscere*
interment	*terra*
intermission	*mittere*
intermit	*mittere*
intermittent	*mittere*
internationalist	*nasci*
interregnum	*rex*
interrex	*rex*
interrobang	*rogare*
interrogate	*rogare*
interrogation	*rogare*
interrogative	*rogare*
interrogator	*rogare*
interrogatory	*rogare*
interrupt	*rumpere*
interruption	*rumpere*
intersperse	*spargo*
intracollegiate	*legare*
intransigent	*agere*
intransitive	*ire*
intrinsic	*sequi*
introit	*ire*
inundate	*unda*
inundation	*unda*
inveigle	*oculus*
invest	*vestis*
investiture	*vestis*
investment	*vestis*
inveterate	*vetus*
invocation	*vocare*
invoice	*via*
invoke	*vocare*
irreclaimable	*clamere*
irrelevance	*levare*
irrelevancy	*levare*
irrelevant	*levare*
irresolute	*solvere*
irresponsible	*spondere*
irreverence	*vereri*
irreverent	*vereri*
irrevocable	*vocare*
irrupt	*rumpere*
irruption	*rumpere*
isle	*insula*
islet	*insula*
isogloss	*glossa*
isolate	*insula*
isolation	*insula*
isolationism	*insula*
isolatos	*insula*
issue	*ire*
itineracy	*ire*
itinerant	*ire*
itinerarium	*ire*
itinerary	*ire*
itinerate	*ire*
jealous	*zelos*
jealousy	*zelos*
jess	*jacere*
jet	*jacere*
jetsam	*jacere*
jettison	*jacere*
jetty	*jacere*
join	*jungere*
joiner	*jungere*
joint	*jungere*
joist	*jacere*
judge	*dicare*
judgment	*dicare*
judicator	*dicare*
judicial	*dicare*
judiciary	*dicare*
judicious	*dicare*
jugular	*jugum*
junction	*jungere*
juncture	*jungere*
junior	*juvenis*
junta	*jungere*
junto	*jungere*
juridical	*dicare*
juridical	*jurare*
jurisdiction	*dicare*
jurisdiction	*jurare*
jurisprudence	*jurare*
jurist	*jurare*
juror	*jurare*
jury	*jurare*
just	*jurare*
justice	*jurare*
justifiable	*jurare*
justification	*jurare*
justify	*jurare*
juvenal	*juvenis*
juvenescence	*juvenis*
juvenescent	*juvenis*
juvenile	*juvenis*
juvenilia	*juvenis*
kaleidoscope	*eidos*
kaleidoscope	*skopein*
kaleidoscopic	*eidos*
kamerad	*kamara*
kiln	*coquere*
kinetoscope	*skopein*
kitchen	*coquere*
knight-errantry	*errare*
knights-errant	*errare*
knights-errant	*ire*
la scala	*scala*
labor	*labor*
laboratory	*labor*
laborer	*labor*
laborious	*labor*
language	*lingua*
lateral	*latus*
latitude	*latus*
latitudinarian	*latus*
latitudinous	*latus*
laud	*laudare*
laudable	*laudare*
laudation	*laudare*
laudatory	*laudare*
lawsuit	*sequi*
leaven	*levare*
legacy	*legare*
legal	*lex*
legate	*legare*
legation	*legare*
legerdemain	*levare*
legerdemain	*manus*
legerity	*levare*
legislative	*lex*
legislator	*latus*
legislator	*lex*
legislature	*lex*
legit	*lex*
legitimate	*lex*
letter	*littera*
letterhead	*littera*
levant	*levare*
levantine	*levare*
levee	*levare*
lever	*levare*
leverage	*levare*
levigate	*agere*
levigate	*levare*
levitate	*levare*
levitation	*levare*
levity	*levare*
levy	*levare*
lexical	*legein*
lexicographer	*legein*
lexicography	*legein*
lexicology	*logos*
lexicon	*legein*
liberal	*liber*
liberalize	*liber*
liberate	*liber*
libertarian	*liber*
libertine	*liber*
liberty	*liber*
lingua	*lingua*
linguine	*lingua*
linguini	*lingua*
linguist	*lingua*
linguistics	*lingua*
liquescent	*liquere*
liqueur	*liquere*
liquid	*liquere*
liquid-crystal	*liquere*
liquidate	*liquere*
liquidation	*liquere*
liquidity	*liquere*
liquify	*liquere*
liquor	*liquere*
literacy	*littera*

literal	*littera*
literary	*littera*
literate	*littera*
literati	*littera*
lithium	*lithos*
lithograph	*lithos*
lithographer	*lithos*
lithography	*lithos*
lithology	*lithos*
lithophyte	*lithos*
lithosphere	*lithos*
litigant	*agere*
litigate	*agere*
litigation	*agere*
liturgy	*ergon*
livery	*liber*
local	*locare*
localism	*locare*
localize	*locare*
locate	*locare*
locomotion	*locare*
locus	*locare*
locution	*loqui*
logic	*logos*
logical	*logos*
logician	*logos*
logistics	*logos*
logo	*logos*
logodaedalist	*logos*
logodaedaly	*logos*
logogram	*logos*
logogriph	*logos*
logomachy	*logos*
logotype	*logos*
logotype	*tupos*
longanimity	*longus*
longevity	*aevum*
longevity	*longus*
longitude	*longus*
longitudinal	*longus*
longueur	*longus*
loquacious	*loqui*
loyal	*lex*
loyalty	*lex*
lucent	*lucere*
lucid	*lucere*
lucubrate	*lucere*
lucubration	*lucere*
luminosity	*lucere*
luminous	*lucere*
lunacy	*luna*
lunar	*luna*
lunarian	*luna*
lunate	*luna*
lunatic	*luna*
lunation	*luna*
lune	*luna*
lunge	*longus*
macrocosm	*kosmos*

madam	*dominus*
madame	*dominus*
mademoiselle	*dominus*
madonna	*dominus*
magisterial	*master*
magistrate	*master*
magna carta	*magnus*
magna cum laude	*laudare*
magna cum laude	*magnus*
magnanimity	*animus*
magnanimous	*animus*
magnanimous	*magnus*
magnate	*magnus*
magnificence	*facere*
magnificent	*facere*
magnificent	*magnus*
magnifico	*magnus*
magnify	*magnus*
magniloquent	*magnus*
magnitude	*magnus*
magnun opus	*magnus*
maintain	*manus*
maintenance	*manus*
majestic	*magnus*
majesty	*magnus*
major	*magnus*
major domo	*magnus*
majority	*magnus*
malaise	*jacere*
malediction	*dicare*
malediction	*malus*
malefaction	*malus*
malefactor	*facere*
malefactor	*malus*
malefic	*malus*
maleficent	*malus*
malevolence	*malus*
malevolent	*malus*
malfeasance	*facere*
malformation	*forma*
malign	*malus*
malignancy	*malus*
malignant	*malus*
malison	*dicare*
malison	*malus*
mall	*malleus*
mallet	*malleus*
manacle	*manus*
manage	*manus*
manageable	*manus*
management	*manus*
manager	*manus*
manciple	*capere*
manciple	*manus*
mandate	*mandare*
mandatory	*mandare*
manege	*manus*
maneuver	*manus*
manicure	*manus*

manifest	*manus*
manifestation	*manus*
manifesto	*manus*
manipulate	*manus*
manipulation	*manus*
manipulator	*manus*
manner	*manus*
mannerism	*manus*
manor	*manere*
manse	*manere*
mansion	*manere*
mansuetude	*manus*
manual	*manus*
manufacture	*facere*
manufacture	*manus*
manufacturer	*manus*
manumission	*manus*
manumission	*mittere*
manumit	*manus*
manumit	*mittere*
manure	*manus*
manuscript	*scribere*
map	*mappa*
marketable	*merx*
marketplace	*merx*
mart	*merx*
mass	*mittere*
mastectomy	*temnein*
master	*master*
masterful	*master*
mastermind	*master*
masterpiece	*master*
masterstroke	*master*
masterwork	*master*
mastiff	*manus*
mastoidectomy	*temnein*
mater	*mater*
maternal	*mater*
maternity	*mater*
matriarch	*arkhein*
matriarch	*mater*
matriarchy	*mater*
matriculant	*mater*
matriculate	*mater*
matrimony	*mater*
matrix	*mater*
matron	*mater*
maxim	*magnus*
maxima	*magnus*
maximum	*magnus*
mayor	*magnus*
meddler	*miscere*
meddlesome	*miscere*
mediaeval	*aevum*
medieval	*aevum*
mediterranean	*terra*
medley	*miscere*
megalith	*lithos*
megalopolis	*polis*

Word	Root
melange	*miscere*
melee	*miscere*
mellifluous	*fluere*
memento mori	*mors*
menage	*manere*
menagerie	*manere*
menial	*manere*
mercantile	*merx*
mercantilism	*merx*
mercenary	*merx*
mercer	*merx*
mercery	*merx*
merchandise	*merx*
merchant	*merx*
merchantman	*merx*
merci	*merx*
merciful	*merx*
merciless	*merx*
mercurial	*merx*
mercury	*merx*
mercy	*merx*
mesolithic	*lithos*
mess	*mittere*
message	*mittere*
messy	*mittere*
mestizo	*miscere*
metabolism	*ballein*
metallurgy	*ergon*
meteorology	*logos*
method	*hodos*
methodic	*hodos*
methodical	*hodos*
methodist	*hodos*
methodology	*hodos*
metonymy	*onoma*
metro	*mater*
metrodome	*mater*
metroliner	*mater*
metroplex	*mater*
metropolis	*mater*
metropolis	*polis*
metropolitan	*mater*
metropolitan	*polis*
metropolite	*mater*
microbe	*mikros*
microcosm	*kosmos*
microcosm	*mikros*
microfilm	*mikros*
micrology	*mikros*
micrometer	*mikros*
micronesia	*mikros*
microorganism	*mikros*
microphone	*mikros*
microscope	*mikros*
microscope	*skopein*
microscopic	*skopein*
microwave	*mikros*
millennium	*annus*
millipede	*pes*
miniver	*varius*
misandry	*misein*
misanthrope	*misein*
misanthropic	*misein*
miscegenation	*genus*
miscegenation	*miscere*
miscellaneous	*miscere*
miscellany	*miscere*
miscible	*miscere*
misconstrue	*struere*
miscreant	*credere*
misfeasance	*facere*
misfortune	*fortuna*
misinform	*forma*
misinformation	*forma*
misnomer	*nomen*
misocainea	*misein*
misogamic	*misein*
misogamist	*misein*
misogamy	*misein*
misogynic	*misein*
misogynism	*misein*
misogynist	*misein*
misologist	*misein*
misology	*misein*
misoneism	*misein*
misoneist	*misein*
miss	*master*
missal	*mittere*
missile	*mittere*
missileer	*mittere*
missileman	*mittere*
missilery	*mittere*
mission	*mittere*
missionary	*mittere*
missioner	*mittere*
missive	*mittere*
mister	*master*
mistress	*master*
misuse	*uti*
mitigate	*agere*
mix	*miscere*
mixologist	*miscere*
mixture	*miscere*
monarch	*arkhein*
monarchy	*arkhein*
monocle	*oculus*
monogamous	*gamos*
monogamy	*gamos*
monolith	*lithos*
monolog	*legein*
monologue	*legein*
monotheism	*theos*
monseigneur	*senex*
monsieur	*senex*
monsignor	*senex*
mop	*mappa*
moppet	*mappa*
moribund	*mors*
mortal	*mors*
mortality	*mors*
mortgage	*mors*
mortician	*mors*
mortify	*mors*
mortuary	*mors*
motorbike	*kyklos*
motorcycle	*kyklos*
multilingual	*lingua*
multiparous	*parere*
municipal	*capere*
municipality	*capere*
municipium	*capere*
munificence	*facere*
munificent	*facere*
mustang	*miscere*
mythology	*logos*
naive	*nasci*
naivete	*nasci*
napery	*mappa*
napkin	*mappa*
nascent	*nasci*
nasturtium	*torquere*
natal	*nasci*
nation	*nasci*
nationalism	*nasci*
nationalist	*nasci*
nationality	*nasci*
native	*nasci*
nativity	*nasci*
natural	*nasci*
naturalization	*nasci*
nature	*nasci*
nausea	*naus*
nauseate	*naus*
nauseous	*naus*
nautical	*naus*
nautilus	*naus*
navigable	*agere*
navigate	*agere*
navigation	*agere*
necrobiosis	*nekros*
necrolatry	*nekros*
necrology	*nekros*
necromancy	*nekros*
necrophilia	*nekros*
necrophobia	*nekros*
necropolis	*nekros*
necropolis	*polis*
necropsy	*nekros*
necrosis	*nekros*
nee	*nasci*
neolithic	*lithos*
neology	*logos*
neonatal	*nasci*
neonate	*nasci*
nephew	*nepos*
nepotism	*nepos*
nescience	*scire*

nescient	*scire*
niece	*nepos*
noble	*gnoscere*
noctambulist	*nox*
noctidiurnal	*nox*
noctilucent	*nox*
noctograph	*nox*
nocturnal	*nox*
nocturne	*nox*
nocuous	*nocere*
noel	*nasci*
noise	*naus*
noiseless	*naus*
noisome	*odium*
noisy	*naus*
nom de plume	*nomen*
nomenclator	*nomen*
nomenclature	*nomen*
nominal	*nomen*
nominate	*nomen*
nomination	*nomen*
nominee	*nomen*
non sequitur	*sequi*
nonchalant	*calere*
nonpareil	*par*
notice	*gnoscere*
noticeable	*gnoscere*
notify	*gnoscere*
notion	*gnoscere*
notoriety	*gnoscere*
notorious	*gnoscere*
noun	*nomen*
nouveau	*novus*
nouveau riche	*novus*
nouvelle cuisine	*novus*
nova	*novus*
novel	*novus*
novelette	*novus*
novelist	*novus*
novella	*novus*
novelty	*novus*
novice	*novus*
novitiate	*novus*
noxious	*noxa at nocere*
nuisance	*nocere*
number	*numerus*
numberless	*numerus*
numeral	*numerus*
numerate	*numerus*
numeration	*numerus*
numerical	*numerus*
numerist	*numerus*
numerology	*logos*
numerology	*numerus*
numerous	*numerus*
obdurate	*durare*
obit	*ire*
obiter dictum	*dicare*
obituary	*ire*
object	*jacere*
objectionable	*jacere*
objective	*jacere*
objectivity	*jacere*
objurate	*agere*
objurgate	*agere*
objurgate	*jurare*
oblate	*latus*
oblation	*latus*
obliterate	*littera*
oblong	*longus*
obloquy	*loqui*
obnoxious	*noxa at nocere*
obsequious	*sequi*
obsequy	*sequi*
obsess	*sedere*
obsession	*sedere*
obsessive	*sedere*
obstruct	*struere*
obstruction	*struere*
obstructionist	*struere*
obviate	*via*
obvious	*via*
occasion	*cadere*
occasional	*cadere*
occident	*cadere*
occlude	*claudere*
occlusion	*claudere*
occupancy	*capere*
occupant	*capere*
occupation	*capere*
occupational	*capere*
occupy	*capere*
ocular	*oculus*
oculist	*oculus*
odious	*odium*
odium	*odium*
oecology	*oikos*
offend	*fendere*
offender	*fendere*
offense	*fendere*
offensive	*fendere*
offer	*ferre*
offertory	*ferre*
office	*facere*
officer	*facere*
official	*facere*
officious	*facere*
ointment	*unguere*
oligarchy	*arkhein*
omission	*mittere*
omit	*mittere*
omniscience	*scire*
omniscient	*scire*
omnivorous	*vorare*
onomatopoeia	*onoma*
ophthalmology	*logos*
ordain	*ordo*
order	*ordo*
orderliness	*ordo*
ordinal	*ordo*
ordinance	*ordo*
ordinary	*ordo*
ordinate	*ordo*
ordination	*ordo*
ordnance	*ordo*
ordo	*ordo*
ordure	*horrere*
orifice	*facere*
orthodox	*dokein*
orthodoxy	*dokein*
orthopedic	*pais*
osteopath	*paschein*
osteopathy	*paschein*
outrage	*ultra*
outrageous	*ultra*
outre	*ultra*
overdose	*didonai*
overuse	*uti*
oviparous	*parere*
pachyderm	*derma*
pachydermatous	*derma*
pacific	*facere*
pacific	*pax*
pacification	*pax*
pacificator	*pax*
pacificism	*pax*
pacifier	*pax*
pacifist	*pax*
pacify	*pax*
padre	*pater*
pair	*par*
palaver	*ballein*
paleolithic	*lithos*
paleontology	*logos*
palindrome	*dromein*
palindromic	*dromein*
pall mall	*malleus*
panache	*penna*
pandemic	*demos*
panegyric	*agora*
pantheism	*theos*
pantheon	*theos*
par	*par*
parable	*ballein*
parabola	*ballein*
parabolic	*ballein*
parachute	*cadere*
paradox	*dokein*
paralegal	*lex*
parallel	*allos*
paramour	*amare*
parasol	*sol at helios*
pardon	*donare*
pardonable	*donare*

pardoner	*donare*
parent	*parere*
parentage	*parere*
parental	*parere*
parenthesis	*tithenai*
parenthesize	*tithenai*
parenthetic	*tithenai*
parenthetical	*tithenai*
parenthood	*parere*
parimutuel	*par*
parish	*oikos*
parishoner	*oikos*
parity	*par*
parlance	*ballein*
parlay	*par*
parley	*ballein*
parliament	*ballein*
parliamentarian	*ballein*
parlor	*ballein*
parochial	*oikos*
parochialism	*oikos*
parterre	*terra*
participant	*capere*
participate	*capere*
participation	*capere*
participator	*capere*
participial	*capere*
participle	*capere*
parturition	*parere*
pater	*pater*
paternal	*pater*
paternalism	*pater*
paternity	*pater*
paternoster	*pater*
pathetic	*paschein*
pathogen	*paschein*
pathological	*paschein*
pathology	*paschein*
pathos	*paschein*
patriarch	*arkhein*
patriarch	*pater*
patrician	*pater*
patrimony	*pater*
patriot	*pater*
patriotism	*pater*
patron	*pater*
patronage	*pater*
patronize	*pater*
patronymic	*onoma*
patronymic	*pater*
pawn	*pes*
pax romana	*pax*
payable	*pax*
peace	*pax*
peaceable	*pax*
peaceful	*pax*
peal	*pellere*
peccable	*peccare*
peccadillo	*peccare*

peccant	*peccare*
peccatophobic	*peccare*
peccavi	*peccare*
peculate	*pecus*
peculation	*pecus*
peculator	*pecus*
peculiar	*pecus*
peculiarity	*pecus*
pecuniary	*pecus*
pedagogic	*pais*
pedagogical	*pais*
pedagogue	*pais*
pedal	*pes*
pedant	*pais*
pedantic	*pais*
pedantry	*pais*
pederast	*pais*
pederasty	*pais*
pedestal	*pes*
pedestrian	*pes*
pediatric	*pais*
pediatrician	*pais*
pedicure	*pes*
pedigree	*pes*
pedodontic	*pais*
pedodontist	*pais*
pedology	*pais*
pedometer	*pes*
pedophile	*pais*
pedophilia	*pais*
peer	*par*
peerage	*par*
pell-mell	*miscere*
pelt	*pellere*
pen	*penna*
penchant	*pendere*
pend	*pendere*
pendant	*pendere*
pendent	*pendere*
pendulant	*pendere*
pendular	*pendere*
pendulous	*pendere*
pendulum	*pendere*
peninsula	*insula*
penknive	*penna*
penmanship	*penna*
pennant	*pendere*
pennant	*penna*
pennon	*penna*
pensile	*pendere*
pension	*pendere*
pensioner	*pendere*
pensive	*pendere*
pentathlon	*athlon*
penthouse	*pendere*
penultimate	*ultra*
penumbra	*umbra*
peon	*pes*
perceivable	*capere*

perceive	*capere*
perceptible	*capere*
perception	*capere*
perceptive	*capere*
perceptiveness	*capere*
percipient	*capere*
percolate	*colare*
percolation	*colare*
percolator	*colare*
perdition	*dare*
perdurable	*durare*
perdure	*durare*
peregrinate	*ager*
peregrine	*ager*
perennial	*annus*
perfect	*facere*
perfection	*facere*
perfectionist	*facere*
perfecto	*facere*
perfervid	*fervere*
perfidious	*fidere*
perfidy	*fidere*
period	*hodos*
periodic	*hodos*
periscope	*skopein*
perish	*ire*
perishable	*ire*
perjure	*jurare*
perjury	*jurare*
perk	*colare*
permafrost	*manere*
permanance	*manere*
permanancy	*manere*
permanent	*manere*
permapress	*manere*
permissible	*mittere*
permission	*mittere*
permissive	*mittere*
permit	*mittere*
perpend	*pendere*
perpendicularity	*pendere*
perpetrate	*pater*
perpetrator	*pater*
perquisite	*quaerere*
persecute	*sequi*
persecution	*sequi*
perusal	*uti*
peruse	*uti*
pervious	*via*
peseta	*pendere*
peso	*pendere*
phraseology	*logos*
physiognomy	*gignoskein*
pianoforte	*fortis*
pied-a-terre	*pes*
piedmont	*pes*
pieta	*pius*
piety	*pius*
pilgrim	*ager*

pilgrimage *ager*
pinion *penna*
pinnacle *penna*
pinochle *oculus*
pioneer *pes*
pious *pius*
piscivorous *vorare*
piteous *pius*
pitiable *pius*
pitiful *pius*
pitiless *pius*
pittance *pius*
pity *pius*
planetoid *eidos*
plebe *plebes*
plebeian *plebes*
plebiscite *plebes*
plebiscite *scire*
pluperfect *facere*
poignant *pungere*
point *pungere*
pointer *pungere*
poise *pendere*
police *polis*
policy *polis*
polis *polis*
politburo *polis*
politic *polis*
political *polis*
politician *polis*
politico *polis*
politics *polis*
polity *polis*
polygamous *gamos*
polygamy *gamos*
polyglot *glossa*
polytechnic *tekhne*
polytheist *theos*
pomegranate *granum*
ponder *pendere*
ponderous *pendere*
pontifical *facere*
pontificate *facere*
porca *porcus*
porcelain *porcus*
porcellana *porcus*
porcine *porcus*
porcupine *porcus*
pork *porcus*
porkbarrel *porcus*
porkchopper *porcus*
porkpie *porcus*
porpoise *porcus*
port *portare*
portable *portare*
portage *portare*
portcullis *colare*
porter *portare*
portfolio *portare*
portliness *portare*
portly *portare*
portmanteau *portare*
possess *sedere*
possession *sedere*
postbellum *bellum*
postmortems *mors*
postnatal *nasci*
postpartum *parere*
postscript *scribere*
pounce *pungere*
pound *pendere*
praenomen *nomen*
precept *capere*
preceptor *capere*
preceptorial *capere*
preclude *claudere*
precocious *coquere*
precognition *gnoscere*
precognitive *gnoscere*
predicament *dicare*
predicate *dicare*
predict *dicare*
prediction *dicare*
predictive *dicare*
predictor *dicare*
predominant *dominus*
predominate *dominus*
prefect *facere*
prefecture *facere*
prefer *ferre*
prefix *figere*
pregnant *nasci*
prejudge *dicare*
prejudice *dicare*
prejudicial *dicare*
prelate *latus*
premise *mittere*
premiss *mittere*
prenatal *nasci*
prenomen *nomen*
preoccupation *capere*
preoccupy *capere*
preponderance *pendere*
preponderant *pendere*
preponderate *pendere*
prequel *sequi*
prerequisite *quaerere*
prerogative *rogare*
prescience *scire*
prescient *scire*
prescribe *scribere*
prescript *scribere*
prescription *scribere*
prescriptive *scribere*
presence *esse*
present *esse*
presentable *esse*
presentation *esse*
presentee *esse*
presenter *esse*
preside *sedere*
presidency *sedere*
president *sedere*
presidential *sedere*
presidio *sedere*
presidium *sedere*
preutilize *uti*
previous *via*
primaeval *aevum*
primeval *aevum*
prince *capere*
princess *capere*
principal *capere*
principality *capere*
principle *capere*
privilege *lex*
pro forma *forma*
pro tem *tempus*
problem *ballein*
problematic *ballein*
proclaim *clamere*
proclamation *clamere*
prodrome *dromein*
proficiency *facere*
proficient *facere*
profit *facere*
profitable *facere*
profiteer *facere*
prognonsis *gignoskein*
prognostic *gignoskein*
prognosticate *gignoskein*
prognosticator *gignoskein*
progress *gradi*
progression *gradi*
progressive *gradi*
project *jacere*
projectile *jacere*
projection *jacere*
projector *jacere*
prolegomenon *legein*
proliferate *ferre*
prolific *facere*
prolix *liquere*
prolixity *liquere*
prolog *legein*
prologue *legein*
prolong *longus*
prolongate *longus*
promiscuity *miscere*
promiscuous *miscere*
promise *mittere*
promissory *mittere*
pronoun *nomen*
propel *pellere*
propellant *pellere*
propeller *pellere*
propensity *pendere*

propulsion	*pellere*
proscribe	*scribere*
prosecute	*sequi*
prosecution	*sequi*
prosecutor	*sequi*
prosthesis	*tithenai*
prosthetic	*tithenai*
prototypal	*tupos*
prototype	*tupos*
proverb	*verbum*
proverbial	*verbum*
provocateur	*vocare*
provocation	*vocare*
provocative	*vocare*
provoke	*vocare*
pseudoacademic	*akademia*
pseudonym	*onoma*
pseudonymous	*onoma*
psychopathic	*paschein*
pulsate	*pellere*
pulse	*pellere*
pun	*pungere*
punch-drunk	*pungere*
puncheon	*pungere*
punchy	*pungere*
punctilios	*pungere*
punctilious	*pungere*
punctual	*pungere*
punctuality	*pungere*
punctuate	*pungere*
punctuation	*pungere*
pungent	*pungere*
purchase	*capere*
purloin	*longus*
purport	*portare*
purported	*portare*
pursuance	*sequi*
pursue	*sequi*
pursuit	*sequi*
push	*pellere*
pushover	*pellere*
pushy	*pellere*
pusillanimous	*animus*
quadrivium	*via*
quadruped	*peds*
quaint	*gnoscere*
qualification	*qualis*
qualifier	*qualis*
qualify	*qualis*
qualitative	*qualis*
quality	*qualis*
quanta	*quantus*
quantifier	*quantus*
quantify	*quantus*
quantitative	*quantus*
quantity	*quantus*
quantum	*quantus*
quasar	*quam at qui*
quasi	*quam at qui*
query	*quaerere*
quest	*quaerere*
question	*quaerere*
questionable	*quaerere*
quibble	*qui*
quid pro quo	*quid*
quiddity	*quid*
quidnunc	*quid*
quiescence	*quies*
quiet	*quies*
quietness	*quies*
quietude	*quies*
quietus	*quies*
quincentennial	*annus*
quintessence	*esse*
quintessential	*esse*
quip	*quid*
quit	*quies*
quite	*quies*
quitter	*quies*
quondam	*quom at qui*
quorum	*qui*
quota	*quot*
quotable	*quot*
quotation	*quot*
quote	*quot*
quoteworthy	*quot*
quotidian	*quot*
quotient	*quot*
rabbet	*battuere*
radarscope	*skopein*
radical	*radix*
radiology	*logos*
radish	*radix*
radix	*radix*
ragout	*gustus*
rail	*radere*
ramification	*radix*
ramify	*radix*
rapport	*portare*
rapscallion	*radere*
rascal	*radere*
rascality	*radere*
rash	*radere*
rasorial	*radere*
raze	*radere*
react	*agere*
reaction	*agere*
reactionary	*agere*
reactivate	*agere*
reactor	*agere*
readjust	*jurare*
readjustment	*jurare*
reappear	*parere*
rebate	*battuere*
rebel	*bellum*
rebellion	*bellum*
rebellious	*bellum*
rebound	*bombos*
recant	*canere*
recapture	*capere*
receipt	*capere*
receivable	*capere*
receive	*capere*
receiver	*capere*
receivership	*capere*
recension	*censere*
receptacle	*capere*
reception	*capere*
receptionist	*capere*
receptive	*capere*
recidivate	*cadere*
recidivism	*cadere*
recidivist	*cadere*
recipe	*capere*
recipient	*capere*
reclaim	*clamere*
reclamation	*clamere*
reclame	*clamere*
recluse	*claudere*
reclusion	*claudere*
reclusive	*claudere*
recognition	*gnoscere*
recognizance	*gnoscere*
recognize	*gnoscere*
recommend	*mandare*
recommendation	*mandare*
recompense	*pendere*
reconnaissance	*gnoscere*
reconnoiter	*gnoscere*
recook	*coquere*
recreant	*credere*
recyclable	*kyklos*
recycle	*kyklos*
redact	*agere*
redactor	*agere*
redouble	*duo*
redoubtable	*duo*
redound	*unda*
redundancy	*unda*
redundant	*unda*
reenact	*agere*
reenactment	*agere*
reenforce	*fortis*
refection	*facere*
refectory	*facere*
refer	*ferre*
referee	*ferre*
reference	*ferre*
referendum	*ferre*
referent	*ferre*
referral	*ferre*
reform	*forma*
reformation	*forma*
reformatory	*forma*

reformer	*forma*
reformist	*forma*
regal	*rex*
regale	*rex*
regalia	*rex*
regenerate	*genus*
regeneration	*genus*
regicide	*rex*
regina	*rex*
regnant	*rex*
regress	*gradi*
regression	*gradi*
regressive	*gradi*
regulus	*rex*
reign	*rex*
reinforce	*fortis*
reinforcement	*fortis*
reinvest	*vestis*
reject	*jacere*
rejection	*jacere*
rejoin	*jungere*
rejoinder	*jungere*
rejuvenate	*juvenis*
rejuvenation	*juvenis*
relate	*latus*
relation	*latus*
relationship	*latus*
relative	*latus*
relativity	*latus*
relevance	*levare*
relevancy	*levare*
relevant	*levare*
relief	*levare*
relieve	*levare*
remain	*manere*
remainder	*manere*
remand	*mandare*
remiss	*mittere*
remission	*mittere*
remit	*mittere*
remittal	*mittere*
remittent	*mittere*
renaissance	*nasci*
renascence	*nasci*
renascent	*nasci*
render	*dare*
rendezvous	*dare*
renovate	*novus*
renown	*nomen*
rent	*dare*
rental	*dare*
renter	*dare*
reorder	*ordo*
repeal	*pellere*
repel	*pellere*
repellant	*pellere*
repertoire	*parere*
repertory	*parere*
report	*portare*
reportage	*portare*
reporter	*portare*
repossess	*sedere*
represent	*esse*
representation	*esse*
representational	*esse*
representative	*esse*
repulse	*pellere*
repulsion	*pellere*
repulsive	*pellere*
request	*quaerere*
requiem	*quies*
requiescat in pace	*quies*
requisite	*quaerere*
requisition	*quaerere*
requital	*quies*
requite	*quies*
resemblance	*similis*
resemble	*similis*
reside	*sedere*
residence	*sedere*
residency	*sedere*
resident	*sedere*
residential	*sedere*
resider	*sedere*
residual	*sedere*
residue	*sedere*
residuum	*sedere*
resign	*signum*
resignation	*signum*
resilience	*salire*
resilient	*salire*
resolute	*solvere*
resolution	*solvere*
resolve	*solvere*
resonant	*sonare*
resound	*sonare*
respond	*spondere*
respondent	*spondere*
responsibility	*spondere*
responsible	*spondere*
responsive	*spondere*
result	*salire*
retard	*tardus*
retardate	*tardus*
retardation	*tardus*
retardee	*tardus*
reticence	*tacere*
reticent	*tacere*
retort	*torquere*
retroactive	*agere*
retrogress	*gradi*
reuse	*uti*
revamp	*pes*
reveilie	*vigilare*
revel	*bellum*
revelry	*bellum*
revenge	*dicare*
revengeful	*dicare*
revere	*vereri*
reverence	*vereri*
reverend	*vereri*
reverent	*vereri*
reverential	*vereri*
revest	*vestis*
revet	*vestis*
revitalization	*vivere*
revival	*vivere*
revive	*vivere*
revivify	*vivere*
revocation	*vocare*
revoke	*vocare*
rex	*rex*
ricotta	*coquere*
ridicule	*ridere*
ridiculous	*ridere*
risibility	*ridere*
risible	*ridere*
rodent	*rodere*
rodenticide	*rodere*
rogue	*rogare*
roguery	*rogare*
rout	*rumpere*
route	*rumpere*
routine	*rumpere*
royal	*rex*
royalist	*rex*
royalty	*rex*
rupture	*rumpere*
rut	*rumpere*
sacrifice	*facere*
sacrificial	*facere*
safe	*salvus*
safeguard	*salvus*
safekeep	*salvus*
safeness	*salvus*
safer	*salvus*
safety	*salvus*
sage	*salvus*
sage	*sapere*
salacious	*salire*
salience	*salire*
salient	*salire*
salientian	*salire*
sally	*salire*
salmon	*salire*
saltando	*salire*
saltant	*salire*
saltarello	*salire*
saltation	*salire*
salticidae	*salire*
saltimbocca	*salire*
salubrious	*salus*
salud	*salus*
salus	*salus*
salutary	*salus*
salutation	*salus*
salutatorian	*salus*

salutatory	*salus*
salute	*salus*
salvation	*salvus*
salve	*salvus*
salver	*salvus*
salvia	*salvus*
salvos	*salvus*
sang-froid	*sanguis*
sangria	*sanguis*
sanguinary	*sanguis*
sanguine	*sanguis*
sapid	*sapere*
sapient	*sapere*
satisfactory	*facere*
sault	*salire*
sauté	*salire*
savant	*sapere*
save	*salvus*
savior	*salvus*
saviour	*salvus*
savoir faire	*sapere*
savor	*sapere*
savory	*sapere*
savvy	*sapere*
scald	*calere*
scale	*scala*
scan	*scandere*
scandent	*scandere*
scanner	*scandere*
scansion	*scandere*
scansorial	*scandere*
schism	*skhizein*
schismatic	*skhizein*
schizoid	*skhizein*
schizophrenia	*skhizein*
schizophrenic	*skhizein*
science	*scire*
scientific	*scire*
sciolism	*scire*
sciolist	*scire*
scope	*skopein*
scribble	*scribere*
scribbler	*scribere*
scribe	*scribere*
scrip	*scribere*
script	*scribere*
scriptorium	*scribere*
scripture	*scribere*
scrivener	*scribere*
seal	*signum*
sealant	*signum*
seance	*sedere*
seclude	*claudere*
seclusion	*claudere*
seclusive	*claudere*
sect	*sequi*
sectarian	*sequi*
sedate	*sedere*
sedation	*sedere*
sedative	*sedere*
sedentary	*sedere*
sediment	*sedere*
sedition	*ire*
seditious	*ire*
see	*sedere*
segregate	*gregare*
segregation	*gregare*
seigneur	*senex*
seignoir	*senex*
seismology	*logos*
selenography	*selene at luna*
selenology	*selene at luna*
semblance	*similis*
semen	*semen*
semiannual	*annus*
semicentennial	*annus*
seminal	*semen*
seminar	*semen*
seminarian	*semen*
seminary	*semen*
semination	*semen*
seminivorous	*semen*
senate	*senex*
senator	*senex*
senescent	*senex*
senhor	*senex*
senile	*senex*
senility	*senex*
senior	*senex*
seniority	*senex*
sennet	*signum*
senor	*senex*
seque	*sequi*
sequel	*sequi*
sequence	*sequi*
sequential	*sequi*
sequently	*sequi*
sequester	*sequi*
sequestrate	*sequi*
sequitur	*sequi*
sesquicentennial	*annus*
session	*sedere*
set	*sequi*
sewer	*sedere*
siege	*sedere*
sign	*signum*
signal	*signum*
signalize	*signum*
signatory	*signum*
signature	*signum*
signer	*signum*
signet	*signum*
significance	*facere*
significance	*signum*
significant	*facere*
significant	*signum*
signify	*signum*
signor	*senex*
signore	*senex*
similar	*similis*
similarity	*similis*
simile	*similis*
similitude	*similis*
simulacrum	*simul at similis*
simulate	*simul at similis*
simulation	*simul at similis*
simulator	*simul at similis*
simulcast	*simul at similis*
simultaneous	*simul at similis*
sir	*senex*
sire	*senex*
sirly	*senex*
sizable	*sedere*
size	*sedere*
sociopath	*paschein*
soffit	*figere*
solar	*sol at helios*
solarium	*sol at helios*
solarize	*sol at helios*
sole	*solus*
solfidian	*solus*
soliloquy	*loqui*
soliloquy	*solus*
solipsism	*solus*
solitaire	*solus*
solitary	*solus*
solitude	*solus*
solitudinarian	*solus*
solo	*solus*
solstice	*sol at helios*
soluble	*solvere*
solution	*solvere*
solve	*solvere*
solved	*solvere*
solvent	*solvere*
somersault	*salire*
somniloquy	*loqui*
sonata	*sonare*
sonic	*sonare*
sonnet	*sonare*
sonorous	*sonare*
soporific	*facere*
sound	*sonare*
sparse	*spargo*
specific	*facere*

Word	Root
specification	*facere*
spectroscope	*skopein*
spend	*pendere*
spendthrift	*pendere*
spent	*pendere*
spoilsport	*portare*
sponsor	*spondere*
sport	*portare*
sportive	*portare*
sportsmanlike	*portare*
sportsmanship	*portare*
sporty	*portare*
spousal	*spondere*
spouse	*spondere*
stenotype	*tupos*
stereotype	*tupos*
structural	*struere*
structure	*struere*
subconscious	*scire*
subito	*ire*
subjacent	*jacere*
subject	*jacere*
subjective	*jacere*
subjoin	*jungere*
subjoinder	*jungere*
subjugate	*jugum*
subjugation	*jugum*
subjunctive	*jungere*
sublunary	*luna*
submission	*mittere*
submissive	*mittere*
submit	*mittere*
submittal	*mittere*
suborder	*ordo*
subordinate	*ordo*
subrogate	*rogare*
subscribe	*scribere*
subscript	*scribere*
subscription	*scribere*
subsect	*sequi*
subsequently	*sequi*
subside	*sedere*
subsidiary	*sedere*
subsidize	*sedere*
subsidy	*sedere*
substructure	*struere*
subterranean	*terra*
subterraneous	*terra*
subterrestrial	*terra*
sudden	*ire*
sue	*sequi*
suffer	*ferre*
sufferable	*ferre*
sufferance	*ferre*
suffice	*facere*
sufficient	*facere*
suffix	*figere*
suit	*sequi*
suitability	*sequi*
suitable	*sequi*
suite	*sequi*
suitor	*sequi*
sullen	*solus*
summa cum laude	*laudare*
superabound	*unda*
supererogation	*rogare*
supererogatory	*rogare*
superficial	*facere*
superfluity	*fluere*
superfluous	*fluere*
superjacent	*jacere*
superlative	*latus*
supernumerary	*numerus*
superscript	*scribere*
supersede	*sedere*
supersonic	*sonare*
superstructure	*struere*
support	*portare*
supportable	*portare*
supporter	*portare*
supportive	*portare*
surface	*facere*
surfeit	*facere*
surgeon	*ergon*
surgery	*ergon*
surgical	*ergon*
surly	*senex*
surmise	*mittere*
surrender	*dare*
surrogate	*rogare*
surround	*unda*
surveillance	*vigilare*
surveillant	*vigilare*
survivalist	*vivere*
survive	*vivere*
susceptibility	*capere*
susceptible	*capere*
suspend	*pendere*
suspense	*pendere*
suspension	*pendere*
suspicion	*pendere*
suspicious	*pendere*
syllogism	*logos*
symbol	*ballein*
symbolic	*ballein*
symbolism	*ballein*
symbolist	*ballein*
symbolize	*ballein*
sympathetic	*paschein*
sympathize	*paschein*
sympathy	*paschein*
sync	*chronos*
synch	*chronos*
synchronize	*chronos*
synchronous	*chronos*
syndrome	*dromein*
synod	*hodos*
synonym	*onoma*
synonymous	*onoma*
synonymy	*onoma*
synthesis	*tithenai*
synthesize	*tithenai*
synthesizer	*tithenai*
synthetic	*tithenai*
tacit	*tacere*
taciturn	*tacere*
taciturnity	*tacere*
tamper	*temperare*
tardiness	*tardus*
tardy	*tardus*
tart	*torquere*
tautology	*logos*
technical	*tekhne*
technicality	*tekhne*
technician	*tekhne*
technique	*tekhne*
technocracy	*tekhne*
technologist	*tekhne*
technology	*logos*
technology	*tekhne*
telepathy	*paschein*
telescope	*skopein*
televangelist	*angelos*
temp	*tempus*
temper	*temperare*
tempera	*temperare*
temperament	*temperare*
temperamental	*temperare*
temperance	*temperare*
temperate	*temperare*
temperature	*temperare*
tempest	*tempus*
tempestuous	*tempus*
tempo	*tempus*
temporal	*tempus*
temporary	*tempus*
temporize	*tempus*
tempura	*temperare*
terra cotta	*terra*
terra firma	*terra*
terra incognita	*terra*
terrace	*terra*
terrain	*terra*
terramycin	*terra*
terraqueous	*terra*
terrarium	*terra*
terrazzo	*terra*
terrene	*terra*
terreplein	*terra*
terrestrial	*terra*
terrier	*terra*
territorial	*terra*
territory	*terra*
thedora	*theos*
theism	*theos*
theo	*theos*
theocracy	*theos*

theocrat	*theos*
theodore	*theos*
theodoric	*theos*
theodosius	*theos*
theologian	*theos*
theology	*theos*
theomania	*theos*
theophany	*theos*
thesaurus	*tithenai*
thesis	*tithenai*
theurgy	*theos*
timbre	*tupos*
timbrel	*tupos*
timothy	*theos*
timpani	*tupos*
tintype	*tupos*
toast	*torrere*
toaster	*torrere*
toastmaster	*torrere*
toastmistress	*torrere*
toastperson	*torrere*
tome	*temnein*
tonsillectomy	*temnein*
topiary	*topos*
topic	*topos*
topical	*topos*
topographer	*topos*
topography	*topos*
toponym	*onoma*
toponym	*topos*
toponymy	*topos*
torch	*torquere*
torment	*torquere*
torque	*torquere*
torrefy	*torrere*
torrential	*torrere*
torrid	*torrere*
torsion	*torquere*
tort	*torquere*
tortellini	*torquere*
tortilla	*torquere*
tortoise	*torquere*
tortuous	*torquere*
torture	*torquere*
tradition	*dare*
traditional	*dare*
traditionalism	*dare*
traditionalist	*dare*
traditor	*dare*
traitor	*dare*
traitorous	*dare*
trajectory	*jacere*
trance	*ire*
transact	*agere*
transaction	*agere*
transcend	*scandere*
transcendent	*scandere*
transcendental	*scandere*
transcendentalism	*scandere*
transcribe	*scribere*
transcript	*scribere*
transcription	*scribere*
transfer	*ferre*
transfix	*figere*
transform	*forma*
transformation	*forma*
transformer	*forma*
transgress	*gradi*
transgression	*gradi*
transient	*ire*
transit	*ire*
transition	*ire*
transitive	*ire*
transitory	*ire*
translate	*latus*
translation	*latus*
transmission	*mittere*
transmit	*mittere*
transonic	*sonare*
transparency	*parere*
transparent	*parere*
transport	*portare*
transportation	*portare*
transporter	*portare*
transvestite	*vestis*
travelog	*legein*
travelogue	*legein*
travesty	*vestis*
treason	*dare*
treasonable	*dare*
treasonous	*dare*
treasure	*tithenai*
triathlon	*athlon*
tribulation	*terere*
tricycle	*kyklos*
trilingual	*lingua*
trite	*terere*
triturate	*terere*
triumvir	*vir*
triumvirate	*vir*
trivet	*pes*
trivia	*via*
trivial	*via*
triviality	*via*
trivium	*via*
trope	*tropos*
trophy	*tropos*
tropical	*tropos*
tropics	*tropos*
tropism	*tropos*
truss	*torquere*
tureen	*terra*
tympani	*tupos*
typanist	*tupos*
type	*tupos*
typecast	*tupos*
typeface	*tupos*
typescript	*tupos*
typeset	*tupos*
typewriter	*tupos*
typical	*tupos*
typify	*tupos*
typist	*tupos*
typo	*tupos*
typographical	*tupos*
ulterior	*ultra*
ultimate	*ultra*
ultimatum	*ultra*
ultra	*ultra*
umber	*umbra*
umble	*umbra*
umbra	*umbra*
umbrage	*umbra*
umbrageous	*umbra*
umpire	*par*
unanimity	*animus*
unanimous	*animus*
unction	*unguere*
unctuarium	*unguere*
unctuous	*unguere*
undulate	*unda*
undulation	*unda*
unicameral	*kamara*
unicycle	*kyklos*
uniform	*forma*
uniformity	*forma*
uniparous	*parere*
unusual	*uti*
upscale	*scala*
usage	*uti*
use	*uti*
useable	*uti*
useful	*uti*
usefulness	*uti*
useless	*uti*
usual	*uti*
usurp	*uti*
usury	*uti*
utensil	*uti*
utile	*uti*
utilitarian	*uti*
utility	*uti*
utilize	*uti*
utmost	*ultra*
utopia	*topos*
utopian	*topos*
vacancy	*vacare*
vacant	*vacare*
vacate	*vacare*
vacation	*vacare*
vacuity	*vacare*
vacuous	*vacare*
vacuum	*vacare*
vain	*vacare*
vainglorious	*vacare*
vainglory	*vacare*
valediction	*dicare*

English word	Root
valedictorian	*dicare*
valedictory	*dicare*
vamp	*pes*
vanity	*vacare*
variable	*varius*
variance	*varius*
variant	*varius*
variation	*varius*
varicolor	*varius*
variegate	*agere*
variegate	*varius*
variety	*varius*
various	*varius*
vary	*varius*
vasectomy	*temnein*
vaunt	*vacare*
vend	*dare*
vendee	*dare*
vendible	*dare*
vendor	*dare*
vendue	*dare*
vengeance	*dicare*
vengeful	*dicare*
ventriloquist	*loqui*
veracious	*verus*
veracity	*verus*
verb	*verbum*
verbal	*verbum*
verbalist	*verbum*
verbalize	*verbum*
verbatim	*verbum*
verbiage	*verbum*
verbigerate	*verbum*
verbose	*verbum*
verbosity	*verbum*
verification	*verus*
verify	*verus*
verisimilar	*similis*
verisimilitude	*similis*
veritable	*verus*
very	*verus*
vest	*vestis*
vestment	*vestis*
vestry	*vestis*
vesture	*vestis*
vet	*vetus*
veteran	*vetus*
veterinarian	*vetus*
veterinary	*vetus*
via	*via*
viable	*vivere*
viaduct	*via*
viaie	*via*
viand	*vivere*
vicar	*vicis*
vicarage	*vicis*
vicarious	*vicis*
vice versa	*vicis*
viceregal	*rex*
vicereine	*rex*
viceroy	*rex*
viceroyalty	*rex*
victual	*vivere*
vigil	*vigilare*
vigilance	*vigilare*
vigilant	*vigilare*
vigilante	*vigilare*
villa	*villa*
village	*villa*
villager	*villa*
villain	*villa*
villainous	*villa*
villainy	*villa*
villanella	*villa*
villanelle	*villa*
villein	*villa*
vindicable	*dicare*
vindicate	*dicare*
vindication	*dicare*
vindictive	*dicare*
vindictiveness	*dicare*
viper	*vivere*
viperine	*vivere*
viperous	*vivere*
virago	*vir*
virile	*vir*
virilism	*vir*
virility	*vir*
virtual	*vir*
virtue	*vir*
virtuosa	*vir*
virtuosity	*vir*
virtuoso	*vir*
virtuous	*vir*
visissitude	*vicis*
vita	*vivere*
vitae	*vivere*
vital	*vivere*
vitality	*vivere*
vitalize	*vivere*
vitamin	*vivere*
vittle	*vivere*
viva	*vivere*
vivacious	*vivere*
vivaciousness	*vivere*
vivacity	*vivere*
vivarium	*vivere*
vivid	*vivere*
vivify	*vivere*
viviparous	*parere*
viviparous	*vivere*
vivisection	*vivere*
vocation	*vocare*
vociferate	*ferre*
vociferate	*vocare*
vociferous	*ferre*
vociferous	*vocare*
void	*vacare*
voracious	*vorare*
votable	*vovere*
votary	*vovere*
vote	*vovere*
voteless	*vovere*
voter	*vovere*
votive	*vovere*
vouch	*vocare*
voucher	*vocare*
vow	*vovere*
vox populi	*vocare*
voyage	*via*
vulgar	*vulgare*
vulgarian	*vulgare*
vulgarism	*vulgare*
vulgarity	*vulgare*
vulgarize	*vulgare*
vulgate	*vulgare*
vulgus	*vulgare*
xenomania	*xenos*
xenon	*xenos*
xenophile	*xenos*
xenophilia	*xenos*
xenophobe	*xenos*
xenophobia	*xenos*
zeal	*zelos*
zealot	*zelos*
zealous	*zelos*
zoo	*zoion*
zoography	*zoion*
zoolatry	*zoion*
zoological	*zoion*
zoologist	*zoion*
zoology	*logos*
zoology	*zoion*
zoomorphism	*zoion*
zoonosis	*zoion*
zoophilia	*zoion*
zoophobia	*zoion*
zootomy	*zoion*